THE PULSE OF WISDOM

The Philosophies of
India, China, and Japan

Michael C. Brannigan

La Roche College

Wadsworth Publishing Company

I⃝TP™ *An International Thomson Publishing Company*

Belmont • Albany • Bonn • Boston • Cincinnati • Detroit • London • Madrid • Melbourne
Mexico City • New York • Paris • San Francisco • Singapore • Tokyo • Toronto • Washington

Philosophy Editor: Tammy Goldfeld
Editorial Assistant: Kelly Zavislak
Production: Ruth Cottrell
Print Buyer: Barbara Britton
Art: Sherry Monarko

Permissions Editor: Robert Kauser
Copy Editor: Alan Titche
Cover: Cassandra Chu
Compositor: Bookends Typesetting
Printer: Malloy Lithographing, Inc.

For more information, contact Wadsworth Publishing Company.

Wadsworth Publishing Company
10 Davis Drive
Belmont, CA 94002
USA

International Thomson Editores
Campos Eliseos 385, Piso 7
Col. Polanco
11560 México D. F. México

International Thomson Publishing Europe
Berkshire House 168–173
High Holborn
London WC1V 7AA
England

International Thomson Publishing GmbH
Königswinterer Strasse 418
53227 Bonn
Germany

Thomas Nelson Australia
102 Dodds Street
South Melbourne, 3205
Victoria, Australia

International Thomson Publishing Asia
221 Henderson Road
#05–10 Henderson Building
Singapore 0315

Nelson Canada
1120 Birchmount Road
Scarborough, Ontario
Canada M1K 5G4

International Thomson Publishing Japan
Hirakawacho Kyowa Building, 3F
2-2-1 Hirakawacho
Chiyoda-ku, Tokyo 102
Japan

Library of Congress Cataloging-in-Publication Data

Brannigan, Michael C.
    The pulse of wisdom : the philosophies of India, China, and Japan
/ Michael C. Brannigan.
        p. cm.
    Includes bibliographical references and index.
    ISBN 0-534-24384-3
    1. Philosophy, Oriental. 2. Asia—Religion.
B5005.B73 1994
181—dc20   94-28443

To my wife, Brooke, my benediction and support

Contents

Preface   xiii

Introduction
Philosophical Thinking in India, China, and Japan   1

India   1
  Finding Our True Nature   1
  Questioning Transforms the Questioner   2
  Philosophy as a Religious Activity   2
  Wisdom as Knowledge and Compassion   3
China   4
  Harmony: Intuition and Reason   4
  How To Be Truly Human: Moral Cultivation   5
  Harmony: Self and Other   5
  Sagehood   6
Japan   6
  Language and Philosophical Thinking   6
Notes   8

CHAPTER ONE   Historical Survey   9
INDIAN PHILOSOPHIES   9
Hindu Philosophies   10
  The Vedic Age (c. 1500–700 B.C.E.)   10
  The Epic Age (c. 800 B.C.E.–200 C.E.)   12

The Age of Sutras (400 B.C.E.–500 C.E.) 14
The Age of Commentaries or Scholastic Age (400–1700 C.E.) 16
The Renaissance and Modern Thought (1800–Present) 17
Indian Buddhism 19
Early Buddhism 20
Sectarian Buddhism 22
Mahayana Buddhism 24
The Fate of Indian Buddhism 27

CHINESE PHILOSOPHIES 27
Ancient Period of Chinese Philosophy 27
Confucian School 28
Taoist School 29
Mohist School 30
School of Names 30
Yin-Yang School 31
Legalist School 31
Middle Period (221 B.C.E.–960 C.E.) 32
Rise of Confucianism 32
Neo-Taoism 33
Chinese Buddhism 33
Neo-Confucianism (960–1912) 36
School of Principle (Ch'eng-Chu School) 37
School of Mind (Lu-Wang School) 38
Empirical School 38
Modern Period 39

JAPANESE PHILOSOPHIES 40
Period of Antiquity: Nara and Heian Schools 40
Early Japanese Buddhism 40
Early Confucianism 42
Medieval Buddhism 43
Jodoshu, or Pure Land School 43
Hokke School of Nichiren 43
Zen School 44
Tokugawa Confucianism 46
Neo-Confucian Schools 46
Rangaku and Nationalism 49
Modern Period 49
Kyoto School of Philosophy 51
Watsuji Tetsuro (1889–1960) 51
Study Questions 51
Notes 53

CHAPTER TWO   Reality   57

INDIAN PHILOSOPHIES   57
Hindu Perspectives on Reality   57
  Vedas   58
  Upanishads   58
  Bhagavad Gita   *59*
  Orthodox Schools   60
Buddhist Perspectives on Reality   65
  The Four Noble Truths and the Three Marks of Existence   67
  Early Buddhist Schools (Theravada)   68
  Mahayana School   68

CHINESE PHILOSOPHIES   71
Basic Themes Concerning Reality   71
  Reality as Transformation   71
  Yu *and* Wu   *72*
  Li *and* Ch'i   *72*
  Harmony   73
Ancient Chinese Views of Reality   73
  Taoism   73
  Hui Shih's Paradoxes   74
  Yin-Yang School   75
Confucianism and Reality   75
  Tung Chung-shu and Correspondence   75
  Wang Ch'ung and Spontaneity   76
  Tao as Wu: *Neo-Taoism and Reality   77*
Chinese Buddhism and Reality   77
  Seng Chao: Yu and Wu Co-Exist   77
  Chi-tsang's Double Truth Theory   78
  Hsuan-tsang: Consciousness Only   78
  T'ien-t'ai School   79
  Fa-tsang and the Hua Yen School: The Golden Lion   80
  Ch'an School   81
Neo-Confucianism and Reality   81
  School of Principle: Ch'eng Yi and Chu Hsi   82
  School of Mind: Lu Hsiang-shan and Wang Yang-ming   83
  Empirical School: Tai Chen   83

JAPANESE PHILOSOPHIES   84
Early Buddhism and Reality   84
  Sanron School: Sunya   84
  Kegon School: Dependent Origination   84

Tendai School: The One Is the Many 85
Shingon School: The World is Vairocana 85
Medieval Buddhism and Reality 85
Jodo School: Tariki 85
Zen Buddhism and Dogen 86
Tokugawa Confucianism and Reality 87
Chu Hsi School of Principle (Shushi) 87
Ito Jinsai: Ancient Learning (Kogakuha) 88
Kyoto School and Reality 89
Nishida Kitaro: Pure Experience and Nothingness 89
Tanabe Hajime: Logic of Species 90
Nishitani Keiji: Nihility and Sunyata 91
Study Questions 92
Notes 94
Readings 97
• *Nasadiya* (Creation Hymn), from *Rig Veda* 98
• Sankara, Introduction to Commentary on the *Vedanta Sutras of Badarayana* 98
• Nagarjuna, "An Examination of Relational Condition," from *Madhyamika Karika* 102
• Lao Tzu, *Tao Te Ching* 104
• Wang Ch'ung, "The Nature of Things" (*Wu-shih*), from *Lun-Heng* 107
• Seng Chao, "On *Sūnyatā*," from *Chao Lun* 110
• Chu Hsi, "Principle (Li) and Material Force (Ch'i)," from *Complete Works of Chu Hsi* 113
• Fung Yu-Lan, From *Hsin li-hsueh* (*The New Rational Philosophy*) 116
• Dogen, "One Bright Jewel," from *Shōbōgenzō* 121
• Nishida Kitaro, "The Fundamental Mode of True Reality" 125
• Nishitani Keiji, "The Standpoint of *Sūnyatā*" 129

CHAPTER THREE   Self   133

INDIAN PHILOSOPHIES 133
Hindu Perspectives 133
Upanishads: Tat Tvam Asi 133
Orthodox Schools 134
Aurobindo and Divine Descent 138
Buddhist Perspectives 138
Basic Themes 139
Mahayana 140

CHINESE PHILOSOPHIES   143
Chuang Tzu: "Forget the Self"   143
Confucius and Tung Chung-shu   144
Neo-Confucianists   145
   Chu Hsi School   145
   Wang Yang-ming School: Intuitive Knowledge of Self   146
Buddhists   147
   Hsuan-tsang and Consciousness Only   147
   Ch'an Buddhism   147

JAPANESE PHILOSOPHIES   148
Shushi, Chu Hsi Neo-Confucianism   148
Japanese Buddhism   149
   Zen   149
   Dogen: Zazen and No-Self   149
Kyoto School   150
   Nishida Kitaro   150
   Tanabe Hajime: Self Through Metanoesis   152
Watsuji Tetsuro: Self and Climate   153
Study Questions   154
Notes   156
Readings   158
• From the *Chandogya Upanishad*   158
• Ishvarakrishna, from the *Sâmkhya Kârikâ*   161
• Swami Vivekananda, Commentary on Patanjali's *Yoga Aphorisms*   166
• Sri Aurobindo, "The Eternal and the Individual"   171
• "There Is No Ego," from the *Milindapanha* and the *Visuddhi-Magga*   174
• Nagarjuna, "Examination of Self Nature," from *Madhyamika Karika*   178
• Vasubandhu, *Trimsika-Karika (Thirty Verses)*   180
• Wang Yang-ming, From *Instructions for Practical Life*   183
• Wang Yang-ming, From a Letter to Shu Kuo-yung   185
• Hsuan-tsang, "The Nonexistence of the Self," from *The Treatise on the Establishment of the Doctrine of Consciousness Only*   187
• Dogen, "The Issue at Hand" ("Genjokōan"), from *Shōbōgenzō*   190
• Watsuji Tetsuro, The Phenomena of Climate   193

CHAPTER FOUR   Knowledge   197

INDIAN PHILOSOPHIES   197
Hindu Perspectives   197
   Nyaya School   198
   New Logic (Navya Nyaya School)   202
   Yoga School: Restraining Citta   203

Vedanta Schools   203
Radhakrishnan's Synthesis of Vedanta Schools   205
Buddhist Perspectives   206
Buddhist Sources of Knowledge   206
Early Buddhism (Theravada)   207
Mahayana Schools   208
Buddhist Logic   209
Esoteric Buddhism   211

CHINESE PHILOSOPHIES   212
Chuang Tzu   212
Confucianists   212
Confucius and Mencius   212
Hsun Tzu: Correspondence of Names   213
School of Names (Logicians)   214
Ch'an Buddhism: No-Mind   215
Wang Yang-ming: Intuitive Knowledge   216
Chang Tung-sun: Culture and Knowledge   217

JAPANESE PHILOSOPHIES   217
Japanese Buddhism   217
Tendai School: Higher Knowledge as Samadhi   217
Zen Buddhism   218
Dogen   220
Nishida Kitaro   220
Acting Intuition   220
Basho   221
Pure Experience   222
Nishida and Aristotle   222
Double Aperture   222
Study Questions   223
Notes   225
Readings   227
- Gautama, From the *Nyayasutra,* with commentary by Vatsyayana   227
- Gangesa, "A Discourse on Absence," from *Tattvacintamani*   228
- Raghunatha, "A Discourse on the Significance of Negative Particles," from *Nañ-vāda*   231
- Radhakrishnan, Ways of Knowing   232
- Dharmakirti, From *Nyaya-bindu (A Short Treatise of Logic),* with commentary by Dharmottara   236
- Wang Ch'ung, "The Real Nature of Knowledge," from *Lun-Heng*   240
- Chang Tung-sun, "A Chinese Philosopher's Theory of Knowledge"   243
- Nishida Kitaro, "Intellectual Intuition"   248

CHAPTER FIVE   Ethics   253

INDIAN PHILOSOPHIES   253
Hindu Perspectives on Ethics   253
  Basic Themes in Hindu Ethics   254
  Bhagavad Gita: The Meaning of Dharma   *258*
  Mimamsa School: Metaphysical Status of Dharma   *260*
  Advaita Vedanta and Ethics   260
  Gandhi: Ahimsa and Satyagraha   *261*
Buddhist Perspectives on Ethics   261
  The Four Noble Truths   261
  The Middle Way   262
  Sangha   263
  Karma   263
  Virtues   263
  Dependent Origination   264
  Bodhisattva: *Compassion   264*
  Buddhist Critique of Castes   265

CHINESE PHILOSOPHIES   266
Ancient Schools and Ethics   266
  Confucianists   267
  Tao Te Ching   *269*
  Mohists and Legalists   270
Chinese Buddhism and Fa-tsang   271
Neo-Confucianism and Ethics   271
  The Ch'eng Brothers, Chu Hsi, and the School of Principle   271
  Wang Yang-ming and the School of Mind   272
  Empirical School   273

JAPANESE PHILOSOPHIES   274
Japanese Buddhism   274
  Karma   274
  Nichiren: Hokke School and the Lotus Sutra   *275*
  Dogen and the Shikan Taza School   275
Japanese Neo-Confucianism   275
  *Chu Hsi School (*Shushi)   *275*
  Ogyu Sorai and Kogakuha   277
Bushido   277
  Preparing to Die: Two Kinds of Death   277
  Giri   278
  Pure Heart   278
Nishida Kitaro and the Unifying Power of Consciousness   277
Watsuji Tetsuro and *Aidagara*   **280**

Study Questions 281
Notes 283
Readings 285
- The Buddha, "The Fire Sermon," from the *Maha-Vagga* 285
- The Buddha, "The Eightfold Path," from the *Digha-Nikaya* 286
- From *The Dhammapada* 288
- Hsun Tzu, "That the Nature Is Evil" 293
- Mo Tzu, "Universal Love" 301
- Chu Hsi, "Moral Cultivation," from *The Complete Works of Chu Hsi* 304
- Wang Yang-ming, Letter to Ku Tung-ch'iao 308
- Kaibara Ekken, "The Art of the Mind-and-Heart," from *Yamato Zokkun* 312
- Watsuji Tetsuro, From *Fudo (Climate and Culture)* 314

CHAPTER SIX   Death   317

INDIAN PHILOSOPHIES 318
Hindu Perspectives on Death 318
  Upanishads 319
  Bhagavad Gita 321
  Advaita Vedanta 322
Buddhist Perspectives on Death 324
  Major Themes in the Buddhist View of Death 325
  Early Buddhist View of Death: A Review 329
  Nagarjuna: Death as Sunya 329

CHINESE PHILOSOPHIES 330
Taoism 330
  Tao Te Ching 330
  Chuang Tzu's View of Death 331
  Religious Taoism: Seeking Longevity 331
Confucianism 332
  Confucius on Death 332
  Wang Ch'ung: Melting the Ice 332
Mo Tzu on Death 333
Chinese Buddhism 333
  Seng Chao on Time and Change 333
  Ch'an Buddhism 334
Social Immortality 335

JAPANESE PHILOSOPHIES 338
Basic Japanese Themes Concerning Death 339
  Transience 339
  Continuity Through Ancestors 339

Dying Properly   339
Bushido   340
Japanese Buddhism and Death   341
Jodo: Tariki   *341*
Zen Buddhism   342
Dogen: Life Is Death Is Sunya   *342*
Some Japanese Customs Concerning Death   344
Study Questions   345
Notes   346
Readings   349
• From the *Katha Upanishad*   349
• "Questions Which Tend Not to Edification," from the *Majjhima-Nikaya*   353
• "No Continuous Personal Identity," from the *Milindapanha* and the *Visuddhi-Magga*   357
• Wang Ch'ung, "Simplicity of Funerals," from *Lun Heng*   359
• Seng Chao, "On Time," from *Chao Lun*   364
• Dogen, "*Shoji*" ("Birth and Death"), from *Shōbōgenzō*   368

Glossary   369

Bibliography   383

Index   393

Preface

I remember well the time my mother was invited to speak to our sixth-grade class about her native Japan, where I was also born. She brought with her a small, exquisitely hand-carved Japanese house that owned a special spot in our living room. What was especially delightful about this wooden replica was that the parts were removable. Once its roof was detached we were able to explore its interior. We counted the number of tatami evenly spaced on the floors. We could move the sliding screens, or *shoji,* confidently constructed of rice paper, along with the interior screens, called *fusuma.* There was a special part of the house known as the *tokonoma,* an alcove where inhabitants could display flower arrangements or hand scrolls according to inner moods and outer seasons. We even examined the tiny wooden sandals, or *geta,* placed outside the entrance to keep the interior free of outside corruption.

I sensed a wonderful feeling of discovery among my classmates as some of the mystery behind this odd-looking dwelling was unraveled. Yet, for me, the more precious lesson had to do with the idea that we never really begin to know a house until we live in it for a time. We need to study a house from the inside, and cultivating this view-from-within is a crucial first step in understanding.

There is clearly a need for an introductory text in Asian philosophy that provides this view-from-within, and such a text needs to be accessible and comprehensive. This is particularly important these days, when global economies point to a singular fact: What used to be called the Far East is no longer far away. Yet, as long as we do not seek to understand the ways of thinking of our Asian neighbors, they will remain strangers to us. This book is designed to help readers cross that difficult conceptual bridge and acquire a more complete and intimate view of the philosophies of India,

China, and Japan. It is the result of teaching courses in Eastern philosophies for nearly fifteen years and stems from my personal background and affinity with Asian culture.

Features of This Text

Accessibility

Written in a clear, lucid style, this text combines readability and scholarship. Profound and complex teachings are presented in a fluent, comprehensible manner. The text is designed to be a careful introduction to the philosophies of India, China, and Japan, making its content accessible to students and general readers alike. There are no prerequisites other than an open mind and heart, and a willingness to see life through different eyes.

At the same time, the text is challenging. Those who are already somewhat familiar with these teachings therefore also stand to gain. The text remains faithful to these ideas in that it neither sacrifices substance nor unfairly simplifies Asian schools of thought.

Comprehensiveness

The comprehensiveness of the text lies in the manner in which it integrates regional, thematic, and historical approaches. In this way it introduces readers to the most formative philosophical teachings in Asian thought.

Each chapter is organized according to three distinct sections: India, China, and Japan. This fundamental framework provides readers with a comprehensive overview of the most important teachings, schools, and figures from these three areas. Even the selected readings represent these three regions.

The text is especially innovative in its thematic approach. After an introductory historical survey, each chapter explores the following crucial themes:

Chapter Two: Reality
Chapter Three: Self
Chapter Four: Knowledge
Chapter Five: Ethics
Chapter Six: Death

The text presents Indian, Chinese, and Japanese perspectives on each of the themes. All five themes explore the most important questions in Asian philosophy: Who am I? and What is the good life?

This thematic treatment retains both integrity and scholarship while avoiding a monolithic view of Eastern philosophy. It provides that view-from-within so that readers gain a sense of the many rooms and houses in Asian thought.

The opening chapter is an excellent historical survey of Asian philosophy and is valuable in itself. Moreover, the text sustains this historical sense because subsequent chapters are developed chronologically for each region. Each section ends with the more current streams of thought.

Selected Readings

The readings are carefully chosen and represent a balanced presentation of the most prominent and influential thinkers in India, China, and Japan. They are judiciously selected to initiate readers into Asian philosophy and to acquaint them with primary sources and their unique styles. Selections are arranged chronologically according to region.

An exciting feature is the inclusion of works by outstanding contemporary thinkers who are not so well known in the West, such as Chang Tung-sun and Watsuji Tetsuro. (Chinese and Japanese names are generally given in the traditional manner—family names first, followed by the personal name.)

Other Features

Study Questions   Located at the end of each chapter, they are useful for class discussions and help readers focus on the most significant ideas in the chapters. They are also valuable for exam review and as exam questions as well.

Glossary   The extensive glossary is written in simplified form. It is a valuable aid that covers the most important terms, texts, schools, and thinkers.

Extensive Bibliography   The bibliography is divided into secondary and primary sources for areas of study designated as General Studies and Indian, Chinese, and Japanese Philosophies. It is a comprehensive and instructive guide for further research.

Acknowledgments

Writing a book is not just an intellectual labor; it exacts a toll on one's time and heart. Those who occupy places in that heart leave their own silent, indelible imprint upon the result.

Let me first thank my friends and former colleagues at Mercy College who have always inspired me by setting high standards in both research and in the classroom: Joe Gannon, Ann Grow, Mary Kilgannon, Jeffrey Blustein, Charles Ephraim, and Frances Mahoney. I especially want to thank my Zen-companion and scholar-firefighter, Frank McCluskey.

Joe and Sally Cunneen continue to motivate me in a most special way through their own example and friendship. I am also indebted to Professors Gilbert Pollet and Frank De Graeve, distinguished scholars at the Universiteit te Leuven.

I am grateful to my colleagues at La Roche College who have been particularly supportive: to Bill Donohue and Ed Brett, for inspiring me with their passion for scholarship, and to Don Orr, George Matthews, and members of the Division of Humanities, especially Rev. Patrick O'Brien,

Sr. Rita Yeasted, Carol Moltz, and Michelle Maher, for their encouragement. Cole Puvogel and his library staff were very helpful in obtaining some primary sources and rare editions.

I am grateful to Ruth Lide and Ingrid Psuty for their splendid secretarial assistance with parts of the manuscript. And I am deeply grateful to Sherry Monarko for her rendition of the Oxherding Pictures.

The editorial staff at Wadsworth have been extremely supportive, and I wish to express my deepest thanks to each of them. Dave McKaughan introduced me to Wadsworth, and Ken King believed in the project from the start. Tammy Goldfeld has been exceptionally supportive and has advised me in a most valuable way. She is also blessed with consummate patience. Kristina Pappas has been tremendously helpful, especially with those fine points of detail.

The following reviewers have provided me with constructive suggestions and valuable comments: Bruce Bubacz, University of Missouri, Kansas City; Donald C. Lee, University of New Mexico; John Longeway, University of Wisconsin, Parkside; Robert Mellert, Brookdale Community College; Tom Morrow, Richland Community College; Robert Neilsen, D'Youville College; and Robert T. Sweet, Clark State Community College. For their expertise, careful reading, and sound measure of the text, I am very grateful.

Writing this text took time away from friends and family. I thank all of them for putting up with my silence. I am especially grateful to my mother and father for their immutable support, and to Carl and Del for their steady encouragement. My wife, Brooke, has been most patient throughout all of this, having had to deal with my moods and erratic state of being. For her gentle guidance through sometimes-hostile computer territories, and for her enduring confidence in me, I am forever grateful.

Introduction

Philosophical Thinking in India, China, and Japan

India

The people of India are no strangers to suffering, and philosophical activity is born of suffering. In this past year alone, floods have left millions of her inhabitants homeless and a devastating earthquake has claimed the lives of over 30,000 people. As seen throughout her history, a sense of pathos continues to fill India's landscape. And in this setting, ultimate questions are inevitably raised. Given the inherent condition of suffering, does existence have a purpose, and if so, what is it? More specifically, what is the meaning and purpose of my life? Who am I? Is freedom from suffering possible? If so, how? What is the ideal of life? How can I attain it? An awareness of the tragic sense of life stimulates such questions.

These questions have produced two of the world's most prominent philosophical traditions: Hindu and Buddhist. In both systems, philosophical activity originates from an elementary dissatisfaction with the human condition. Both traditions address issues of meaning, purpose, and salvation. Within the context of this inquiry into liberation from suffering, we find three characteristic traits in Indian philosophy:

- It aims to discover our true nature.
- It is transformative.
- It is religious.

Finding Our True Nature

Philosophy in India is essentially concerned with self-deliverance. This quest for deliverance is intimately bound up with the discovery of our true nature. For example, the aim in Hindu thought is to achieve enlightenment, or *moksha.*

And the experience of enlightenment comes about only with the realization of our true identity. For the Buddhist, liberation is called nirvana. Nirvana occurs when we realize our true nature. Therefore, in Indian philosophy, salvation and self-discovery are intimately linked with each other.

The whole of Indian thought, whether Hindu or Buddhist, centers around the task of self-discovery. This can properly occur only when our total personality is involved. Self-awakening transcends the confining boundaries of a pure intellectual pursuit and demands a complete engagement. There are many references in Hindu and Buddhist thought that warn us against relying too heavily upon the intellect for self-realization. Hindu and Buddhist theories of knowledge unceasingly emphasize the inherent limits to our ordinary ways of knowing.

Questioning Transforms the Questioner

This leads us to our second assertion: Indian philosophy is essentially transformative. It naturally transforms us because we are engaged in this radical questioning concerning our liberation and self-discovery. These questions are radical because they intimately and ultimately involve who we are in essence.

In this respect, the goal and the process are not separate, and self-transformation occurs in the act of questioning. This is why philosophical activity exercises more than just the intellect. Philosophy is not simply a way of thinking, but, more importantly, a way of being. It involves not just a search for truth, but a *life* of truth. At the same time, because it originates from a basic dissatisfaction with the human condition, it inspires a way of life that is profoundly concerned with deliverance. It is precisely this salvific intent of philosophy that makes it so deeply religious.

Philosophy as a Religious Activity

From all of this we see that philosophy in India bears a strongly religious character. By this we mean religion in its more fundamental senses:

- distinguishing the sacred from the profane
- pointing to a higher and deeper reality behind appearances
- showing a way to personal salvation

Philosophy and religion in India share these major elements. First, they partake of the same goal of salvation. They each seek both a genuine liberation from the transitory and freedom from suffering. Second, this salvific intent involves a deep excursion into one's innermost being. True freedom can only be accompanied by an authentic quest for self. Third, within this quest, the individual undergoes various degrees of transformation.

An example of the religious nature of Indian philosophy lies in the teachings of the philosopher Sankara. Although multitudes were drawn to his teachings, he specified a number of guidelines for those desiring to study under him:

1. They must be able to distinguish the abiding from the fleeting.
2. They must have a degree of detachment from this world (and any other world), knowing that all worlds are transitory.
3. They must have already cultivated such virtues as poise, truthfulness, and so on.
4. They must have a strong desire for liberation from the wheel of life.[1]

All of this has nothing to do with unquestioning allegiance to a set of creeds. Instead, it portrays a liberating profile of the philosophical-religious quest, a quest that is most intimate.

In Western cultures, religion and philosophy have developed into separate disciplines, as evidenced in colleges and universities, where they exist as separate departments. Even though many Indian thinkers acknowledge this distinction, they also maintain that, in essence, they are interdependent.

The religious character of Indian philosophy does not preclude its own philosophical rigor. Indeed, some Hindu schools of philosophy, such as Nyaya, combine logical subtlety and conceptual analyses. Yet, their investigations are conducted in light of achieving the inseparable goals of insight and liberation. Despite its many intricacies and varieties, Indian philosophy possesses a unique unitive aspect. All the different schools of thought are bound together in the common search for deliverance in and through insight into one's true identity. Indian philosophy pursues this quest through a radical questioning that transforms the questioner in the very process of examining the question.

Wisdom as Knowledge and Compassion

To conclude, let us examine the meaning of *darshana*, the closest equivalent to "philosophy" in Sanskrit. *Darshana* means a type of "seeing" or "viewing." It refers to both the activity of having a point of view and the outlook itself. In any case, *darshana* does not mean an absolute or totally comprehensive way of knowing.

What is interesting to note within our present context is that this "point of view" that we assume is not simply an intellectual, academic exercise. It exacts our full involvement in the act of perceiving. *Darshana*, "seeing," is more than an intellectualization, which in itself is only one type of seeing. Philosophical activity demands seeing with the heart as well as with the mind. This harmony of mind and heart constitutes the pulse of wisdom.

This kind of seeing incorporates two key terms: *prajna* and *karuna*. *Prajna* refers to the intellectual basis of wisdom. In this respect, it can mean knowledge. *Karuna*, on the other hand, means "love" or "compassion." True intelligence is wisdom and comprises a synthesis of knowledge and compassion. True wisdom is the harmony of mind and heart. This is beautifully portrayed in the Buddhist ideal of the *bodhisattva*. The *bodhisattva* represents one who has attained "awakening," or "enlightenment" and dedicates his or her life to sharing this wisdom with others. This ideal epitomizes the union of *prajna* and *karuna*.

China

Within the intellectual climate of China, three major streams of thought have nurtured the historical, cultural, and social life of its peoples: Taoism, Confucianism, and Buddhism. However, as with India, an assessment of Chinese philosophical activity remains limited if we confine ourselves within our own Western perspectives. To begin with, consider the Chinese language and its worldview.

In Chinese, characters replace the alphabet used by most other languages. These characters are ideographic representations within an experiential context. Therefore, the language lacks grammatical precision.

As for worldview, events are essentially viewed by the Chinese as interconnected phenomena. Each person and every activity is influenced by the harmonious working together of Heaven and Earth. Heaven and Earth are not diametrically separate realities. Material existence is infused with a profound spirituality. There is no natural versus supernatural, no spiritual opposed to physical, no divine in contrast to human. Rather, a principle of harmony, a confluence of apparent contrasts, characterizes existence. There is this balance between the two primordial and enduring forces of yin and yang. This vision of harmony provides a setting with which to examine the nature of philosophical activity.

In order to grasp the nature of Chinese philosophy, we need to understand it within this context of language and worldview. In this fashion, we discover that philosophy, religion, culture, and politics all interact. For instance, not only were many Chinese philosophers scholars and teachers, but they were actively involved socially and politically. The total cultural and intellectual milieu of Chinese thought reveals an intimate rapport between philosophy and its actualization in society.

Harmony: Intuition and Reason

All this leads us to one of the most vital aspects of Chinese philosophical activity: its attempt to achieve a harmonious balance between reason and intuition. We are not claiming that intuition is stressed in China at the expense of rationality or logic. Chinese philosophy does exhibit various degrees of analytic sophistication. The key idea in Chinese philosophical thought, however, is harmony—harmony between reason and feeling, between rationality and intuition.

For example, let us look at the relationship between Taoism and Confucianism. They have often been viewed as opposing schools of thought. Indeed, they differ with respect to emphases and styles of teaching. Taoism, the earlier of the two, emphasizes our rapport with nature and highlights our intuitive faculties. On the other hand, Confucianism stresses our relationship within the social fabric. It seeks to sustain communal harmony, and it heralds reason.

Despite these differences, they generally represent two complementary aspects within human nature. Complementarity, in this sense, allows for disagreement and even conflict. Although there are points upon which Taoism and Confucianism are at odds, they emphasize different paths to the essential goal of harmony. Taken as a whole, they produce a more unified picture. Taoism reflects our most personal and intuitive aspect, assuming our essential oneness with nature. Taoism thereby appeals to the deepest forces within us. It addresses this question: How can we live in harmony with ourselves and with nature? On the other hand, Confucianism represents our more social and reasonable character and addresses the reality of our collective existence. It asks the question, How can we properly live in harmony with others?

The fundamental point is this: Their complementarity reflects the needed balance between a more personally creative and a socially ordered life-style. The Chinese sage incorporates both in a creative symmetry. Chinese philosophy, therefore, does not exaggerate the importance of reason and intellect; nor does it overemphasize the level of feelings or intuition. As a whole, Chinese thought, as manifested in Taoism and Confucianism, seeks a synthesis of both intuition and reason, and its goal is harmony.

How to Be Truly Human: Moral Cultivation

The Chinese quest for harmony encompasses the need for self-cultivation. Self-cultivation and moral development, or the "rectification of the heart," work together. This is most apparent in Confucian thought, whose goal is attaining full humanness, called *jen. Jen* is considered the highest virtue, the essence of moral cultivation. For the Confucian, the person is involved in the cardinal task of learning how to be truly human.

What does this mean in Confucian terms? As indicated above, the attainment of full humanness comes about only when we achieve an interior balance. Learning to become human calls for a harmony of the two dimensions of self and other. On the other hand, for Taoists, being fully human requires an inner harmony and oneness with nature. Thus Taoists and Confucians define what it means to be human in different ways. Nevertheless, for both, harmony is essential. Let us look further at some Confucian ideas.

Harmony: Self and Other

Confucians view the self as the center of a nexus of connections of family, friends, society, and state. These connections, viewed as a series of concentric circles, define the self. And, particularly because the self is at the center of these relationships, the evolving of that same self in turn affects those various relations. In other words, the individual self and the social self interact in a way in which each defines the other.

This inherent reciprocity of self and other is illustrated by the Confucian teaching of the Five Cardinal Relationships. These associations are the concentric circles that define the self of the person (as well as the self of the community). They concern the ties between the following people:

- son and father
- government official and ruler
- younger brother and elder brother

- friends and friends
- wife and husband

Self-cultivation is necessarily a communal affair.

Sagehood

In Chinese philosophy, our various goals—harmony, inner peace, learning to be fully human, moral cultivation, external harmony—are all closely linked. All are steps in the process of achieving "sagehood." The Chinese believe that we bear the potential for sagehood. It is primarily a matter of developing a seed that has always been within us. Generally, the Chinese have a wonderfully optimistic view of human nature. All of us, no matter what our status, have the capacities to become sages.

Japan

Tokyo and Kyoto symbolize two contrasting images in modern Japan. A highly advanced technology has overtaken Tokyo, one of the world's business capitals. Meanwhile, Kyoto sustains the presence of tradition with its temples and other monuments of Japan's past. Japan remains a conspicuous example of a meeting between the forces of modernization and the spirit of tradition.

In view of this, how does this affect Japanese thought and philosophy? In order to address this question, we must have a clear understanding of what we mean by Japanese "philosophy." This incurs a special difficulty in trying to comprehend what may well be one of the most puzzling of cultures. Yet our attempt at understanding is certainly timely in light of our trade relations with Japan.

Japanese thought has often been viewed as being essentially unphilosophical in both nature and expression. Some scholars have felt that, with few exceptions, Japanese thought has lacked any strict philosophical foundations. Is this true? This text shows that there is, in fact, a strong philosophical tradition in Japanese thinking. Yet Japanese philosophy, as well as religion, is understood in a unique way. As with India and China, Japanese "philosophy" cannot be viewed solely according to Western philosophical categories.

Language and Philosophical Thinking

The Japanese written language possesses some features that appear to make it less conducive to logical and abstract thought: It is immediate, emotive, and relational. These three traits typify Japanese philosophical activity and provide a foundation for establishing the way of thinking for the Japanese. Because these qualities make abstract, analytic expression and thought all the more difficult, philosophical activity in general is approached in a different way. Let us look at each aspect.

Immediacy   When we claim that the Japanese language possesses immediacy, we refer to its ability to encapsulate a particular experience with a minimum of rationalization about that same experience. The idea is to express a specific situation or event in its unanalyzed, immediate form. A recent film by the renown director Akira Kurasawa, entitled *Ran,* depicts this tendency through its protagonist, the aging king Hidetora. Betrayed by one of his sons and trapped within a castle, his entire entourage is destroyed. He miraculously survives the devastation and roams the countryside for some days, encountering visions and voices. Upon being discovered by his loyal retainers, his immediate response is *"samui." Samui* literally means "cold," and it encapsulates the entirety of his experience with the least amount of reflection and analysis. Here, a single word becomes a lens through which to view a particular experience. Too much reflection and analysis dilutes the meaning of the experience.

It is this trait of immediacy that partly accounts for a diminished emphasis on formal logical analysis in Japan as a substructure for philosophic expression. This seems strange in light of Japan's highly developed interest in mathematics. And this is especially remarkable given their sophistication in computer technology. After all, both mathematics and computers share a logical foundation. This compels us to hold that although a formal system of logic has not developed as such in Japan, it still has its own "logical" way of thinking.

Much of Japanese philosophy stresses the importance of immediacy and direct experience. This means the simple, direct encounter with reality. "To the things themselves" is a common Japanese expression. To illustrate, Zen Buddhism, though imported from China (Ch'an Buddhism), is uniquely Japanese and stresses the primacy of the immediate, prereflective, "pure" experience. The main reason for its appeal to Japanese is probably its emphasis on the primacy of the experience. When Zen first came to Japan, it found favor with both monks and samurai. The samurai especially found it to be a unique method for mental discipline. Often confronted with life-and-death situations, the samurai could learn to practice their swordsmanship without interference from the thinking mind. Zen instructs us to go straight to the experience itself.

Emotiveness Another peculiarity of the Japanese language is that its expressions are often primarily emotive in character. The vocabulary is richly laden with expressions of sensitivity. Rational analysis is secondary to capturing the emotions that naturally flow in and through a given experience.

The Japanese language originated from the Chinese, and it was systematized after the third century. Terms such as *risei* ("reason") were not part of the original language structure. The same holds true for *gainen,* which means "concept." These terms were absent from the original system because the original vocabulary tended to emphasize feelings and emotions. The original characters were less conducive for indicating abstract, philosophical concepts.

To illustrate, here are the Japanese *kanji* (Chinese characters) for "love" and "hate." They demonstrate this emotive orientation inherent in the language. "Love" is represented by combining the characters for "woman," [女], and "child," [子]. The result is [好]. On the other hand, "hate" is represented as the "increasing," [曽], of one's "heart" or "state of mind," [忄]. It is written as [憎].

Relationality Probably the most unique characteristic of the Japanese language lies in its expression of relationships. Ideas, feelings, and objects are depicted in light of their connections with other ideas, feelings, and objects. This perfectly accords with the Japanese view of reality in which all things act and interact in relationship with each other.

For example, the use of certain pronouns in speech depends on their specific context, within which the Japanese have time-honored rules of propriety. Respect for one's superiors—whether they are parents, grandparents, teachers, the company boss, and so on—expresses itself in the forms of speech elicited through the use of certain pronouns. It is important to remember that for the Japanese there is no clear conception of the individual as *individual*. After the introduction of Western logic, the term *kobutsu* ("individual") was coined. Nevertheless, the individual is still defined within the web of human relationships.

This is often depicted in regular sentence structures in which the subject of the sentence is often omitted, for an emphasis on the subject could convey the idea of an independent, objective individual being. The subject is often omitted to indicate further that there is no sharp delineation between the subject and the predicate, between the actor and the act. This will become clearer when we more closely examine Japanese Buddhist philosophy.

This expression of relationality is clearly illustrated through many of its *kanji*. The character [月] sometimes takes on the meaning of "flesh" or "part of the body." By doubling this same character, "companion" comes about, [朋月]. Here we have a literal notion of the idea of relationality. The character for "elder brother" takes a bit more imagination. If we place the "mouth," [口] over the pair of "human legs," [儿], then we have the symbol for the sibling in the family who traditionally has the last say, [兄]. The Chinese depicted the "woman" as pregnant with her arms outstretched, as in comforting. The Japanese adopted this more simplistically as [母]. A good example of relationship lies in the character for "peace," which is represented by a "woman," [女], under a "roof" of a house, [宀]. Thus "peace," [安], occurs with the comforting, nurturing mother within the home.

In all this we see the strong link between linguistic expression and thought. And this carries itself into philosophical activity. It is clear that the structure of the Japanese language is such that it inhibits the expression of logical, abstract thinking. Yet, from the start, we need to use caution in applying a Western philosophical frame of reference to assess non-Western patterns of thought. It is quite the case that the Japanese do think philosophically in their own fashion. And their philosophy is typified by its concern for immediacy, sensitivity, and relationship. As we will see, the intellectual and cultural history of the Japanese conveys a unique philosophical tradition centering around these traits.

Notes

1. This is mentioned in Troy Wilson Organ, *Western Approaches to Eastern Philosophy* (Athens, Ohio: Ohio University Press, 1975), 21.

1

Historical Survey

Indian Philosophies

The long-standing philosophical heritage of the people of India begins with the Aryans, who penetrated the country between 2000 and 1500 B.C.E. The two major Indian philosophical systems are Hindu and Buddhist. Other systems have played an active role, but these are the most dominant. At the same time, these two contain a complex variety of divisions and subdivisions. Of the two, Hindu philosophy has exerted the more powerful impression throughout the country's history.[1]

Reconstructing a history of Indian philosophy within a purely chronological framework poses insurmountable difficulties for two reasons. First, in its early phases there is little certainty as to the authorship and dating of the literature. Those who were responsible for the transmission of the sacred teachings were more interested in conveying and explaining truths considered to be eternal in transcending historical limitations. Second, the various schools of thought actually emerged at almost the same time.

Indian thought unfolds in two primary directions: Hindu and non-Hindu. Hindu philosophy is distinct from non-Hindu ways of thought in that it accepts the authority of the sacred teachings of the collection of works called the Veda, the earliest recorded teachings. Schools that believe in the final authority of the Veda are considered to be orthodox. These orthodox schools, properly deemed "Hindu," are called Nyaya, Vaisheshika, Samkhya, Yoga, Mimamsa, and Vedanta. On the other hand, non-Hindus reject the Veda as the ultimate source of authority. These schools, which dispute the authority of the Veda, are viewed as heterodox. The more important heterodox schools are Buddhism, Jainism, and Carvaka.

9

Hindu Philosophies

Indian philosophy has generally been divided into the following periods:[2]

- Vedic Age, from about 1500 to 700 B.C.E.
- Epic Age, from around 800 B.C.E. to 200 C.E.
- Age of Sutras, from around 400 B.C.E. to 500 C.E.
- Age of Commentaries, from about 400 C.E. to 1700 C.E.
- Renaissance and Contemporary Thought, from 1800 to the present.

The Vedic Age (c. 1500–700 B.C.E.)

The origins of Indian philosophy occur after the Indus Valley was overrun by the Aryans between 1700 and 1500 B.C.E. It is reasonable to believe that the philosophies that developed after the invasions primarily manifest the Aryan influence, although there are probably traces of the indigenous Dravidian beliefs. *Dravidian* actually refers to the language of the indigenous culture consisting mostly of farmers who journeyed from the central regions of Asia and settled in the Indus Valley. This Indus Valley culture eventually became more urbanized. In any case, some beliefs of the Dravidians probably endured even after the Aryan conquest.

After 1500, sacred teachings were orally transmitted and eventually formed a collection of works known as the Veda. The Veda consists of four groups: *Rig Veda, Sama Veda, Yajur Veda,* and *Atharva Veda.* All four are known compositely as the Samhita, which means "collection." Each one of these in turn contains four parts: hymns, ritual works, forest writings, and Upanishads.

An important distinction to bear in mind is that between two types of literature: *sruti* and *smrti.* The entire Vedic corpus constitutes works that are considered to be *sruti,* or that which is "directly heard." The Veda is considered to be inherently sacred because it is believed that its teachings have been directly revealed to seers, who then committed these teachings to memory in order to pass them down orally to future generations. On the other hand, the literature in later ages—epics, histories, *shastras,* sutras, and so on—reflect works which are *smrti,* that which is "remembered." *Smrti* emphasize the written teachings, and they are still viewed as somewhat sacred, though not as important as *sruti.*

Rig Veda   The *Rig Veda* is the oldest collection in the Veda, probably composed over a period of six centuries between 1500 and 900 B.C.E. Furthermore, it is more philosophically relevant than the other Vedas because it contains the seeds of philosophical speculation, as found in the famous Nasadiya Hymn, or Hymn of Creation, composed no later than 900 B.C.E.

The *Rig Veda* consists of over 1,000 hymns in verse form that were intoned during sacrifices. The hymns of the *Rig Veda* were also used for occasions celebrating rites of passage, such as marriage and death. The hymns were arranged in ten sections, or cycles, called *mandalas.*

Who were these gods to whom sacrifices were made, and what gods played major roles in the *Rig Veda*? The most popular god was Indra, god of rain, thunder, and war. He led the Aryans in their victory over the indigenous Dravidians and eventually ruled over the entire sky. As ruler of the sky, he is life-giving, bestowing light as well as darkness. Other gods were Rudra, Varuna, Surya, and Soma. One of the more important is Varuna, who gives order to the cosmos. The universe remains under his watchful guidance according to principle of *rita*. Literally meaning "the course of things," it is the fundamental universal principle of order and harmony.[3]

Upanishads The Upanishads refer to those writings that conclude the Vedic literature. Because they appear at the end of the Veda, they are sometimes referred to as Vedanta, "at the end of the Veda." Not only do the Upanishads embody the substance of Vedic thought, but they also provide the cornerstone for most of Indian thought in general.

The Upanishads are generally considered to be written between 800 and 300 B.C.E., when more peoples settled into villages. In addition, the hierarchy of classes became more rigid then. This was also a time of growing critical reflection, and the teachings of the Vedas were exposed to further analysis.

The word *upanishad* literally means "sitting down near" (*upa ni sad*). This conveys a sense of receiving instruction that is somewhat secret and disclosed through special transmission by the teacher. Even though scholars have numbered at least 108 Upanishads, it is also generally agreed that eleven of them constitute the principal or earliest Upanishads. These principal Upanishads are therefore the most authoritative sources for later commentators. The principal Upanishads are the Brihadaranyaka, Chandogya, Taittiriya, Aitareya, Katha, Isa, Kena, Svetasvatara, Prasna, Mundaka, and Mandukya.[4]

The Upanishads possess a certain cohesiveness in theme in their effort to explain the nature of reality. The overriding theme surrounds the nature of *atman* and *Brahman*.

Atman is given many meanings throughout the Upanishads. Basically, it refers to our true nature. It is therefore divine, eternal, and unchanging. At this point in our study, we can describe it as our individual soul, or genuine self. The etymology of *atman* is revealing. Literally, it means "breath," and because breath is that without which we cannot live, it came to mean our essence, or spirit.

Brahman is regarded as the Absolute Reality, the universal soul. The term *Brahman* is derived from a word meaning "to grow." This signifies that *Brahman* is that which is ever-growing and always-nurturing.

The most profound teaching in the Upanishads is the identity of *atman* and *Brahman*. This is revealed in the famous phrase "*tat tvam asi*," or "that you are." The Upanishads claim that our way of perceiving this reality of *atman* and *Brahman* is usually shrouded in ignorance, or *avidya*.

Our fundamental condition in this state of *avidya* is one of *maya*, or what was later to be described as a state of illusion. Because of our basic condition of *maya*, we are unenlightened concerning reality and therefore experience *avidya,* or ignorance. It is this condition of *maya* that impedes us from realizing our true nature, *atman,* and that therefore compels us to remain on a nearly unending cycle of birth, death, and rebirth, which is called *samsara.*

While on this cycle (or wheel) of *samsara,* we go through countless transmigrations (reincarnations) of the soul, or self, *atman.* The soul is continually reborn into a succession of various psycho-physical forms such as human, animal, or insect. As long as we are ignorant of our true identity, we are stuck on this cycle of birth, death, and rebirth. This occurs until we finally achieve that ultimate state of self-realization, referred to by Hindus as *moksha.* (As we will see later, Buddhists refer to these transmigrations as "rebirths," and deliverance from rebirth is what Buddhists call nirvana. Although Buddhists believe in some type of rebirth, they do not believe in the rebirth of an independent soul.)

Therefore, our ultimate goal is to attain realization of our genuine self. Our true self is *atman,* and, as seen in the formula *tat tvam asi, atman* is identical to *Brahman.* This state of realization is called *moksha.*

The Epic Age (c. 800 B.C.E.–200 C.E.)

This period witnessed the composition of some of India's most beautifully written texts, such as the *Mahabharata* and *Ramayana.* Important discourses, called *shastras,* on social, legal, and ethical regulations were also written. This was also a time of creative ferment, with challenges to the Vedic and Brahmanic authority from materialism, Buddhism, and Jainism.

Epics   The *Mahabharata* ranks as one of the greatest achievements in world literature. It represents a portrayal of the Indian legacy and continues to influence the literature, history, and art of India.

The centerpiece of the *Mahabharata* involves the unfolding of a long and bitter conflict between two clans of the same family of the Bharata: the Pandavas and the Kauravas. It is a story of heroism, treachery, moral conflicts, human greatness, and human failings. The friction between the Pandavas and the Kauravas results in a fourteen-year exile of the Pandavas. After their exile, circumstances eventually lead to a devastating war in which the Pandavas were victorious, but at the cost of tens of thousands of lives.

One of the most enduring portions in the *Mahabharata* is the *Bhagavad Gita.* This may be the most influential work in Indian thought. The date often assigned to the *Gita* is around the fifth century B.C.E. The action takes place just before battle between the Pandavas and the Kauravas. Arjuna undergoes a moral conflict, to which his charioteer Krishna responds. Krishna is also a god in disguise, or what is called an avatar. He is the avatar of the deity Vishnu (one of the aspects of *Brahman*). The main themes in the poem center around the nature of *dharma* and ethical action. The Hindu concept of *dharma* refers to duties, observances, and laws that are appropriate to one's social class. Arjuna's conflict lies in whether he ought to perform his *dharma.*

The *Ramayana* has three leading characters: the just king Rama, his devoted wife Sita, and Rama's steadfast brother Laksmana. Sita is abducted by the evil king of Lanka (what is now Sri Lanka), Ravana. With the aid of an army of monkeys led by the general Hanumat, Rama is able to rescue his wife after destroying the treacherous king and his legion. Sita must then successfully undergo trials to prove that she has maintained her purity and faithfulness during her captivity. In the final book she reveals herself to be the daughter of the earth goddess. So also is Rama himself disclosed as an avatar of Vishnu, just as Krishna was in the *Bhagavad Gita*.

Dharma Shastras   The *Dharma Shastras* are part of a general collection called the Kalpa Sutras. The most important for our purposes is the *Manu Shastra*, or the Code of Manu. This has had a decisive impact upon India's legal system. The primary concern of these *shastras* was the maintenance of the social order by emphasizing the need for both material and physical well-being and ethical conduct. These were composed between 700 and 100 B.C.E.[5]

Another important work is the *Artha Shastra,* composed by Kautilya. It points out the need for material welfare in sustaining a healthy social order. It also suggests a strict, realistic political philosophy in that there is a need for a strong centralized government to maintain the social order. A healthy economy goes hand-in-hand with a stable political order.

Vatsyayana is the alleged author of the *Kama Shastra* (also know as the *Kama Sutra*), a text that candidly discusses the value of sensual pleasures.

Heterodox Challenges: Materialists, Buddhists, and Jainists   Carvaka is the proverbial founder of the materialist school, named the Carvakan. This school is sometimes assigned the name Lokayata, or naturalism. It flourished around the sixth century B.C.E. The uppermost teaching is the sole reality of matter. Therefore, material enhancement is all-important. Furthermore, in contrast to most other schools, survival after bodily death is rejected. The materialists do not accept the idea of a spiritual and eternal entity or force.

The life and teachings of Siddhartha Gautama became the cornerstone for Buddhism, a major religious-philosophical force enkindling much of East Asia. His dates of birth and death have been disputed, but it is fair to assign him to the sixth century B.C.E.

Eventually there came about two major schools of Buddhism, each with a set of subdivisions or distinct systems. The faction that broke away from the original Theravada school, or "Way of the Elders," referred to themselves as the Mahayana, or "Greater Vehicle," school. The traditional, more conservative Theravada school was called Hinayana, or "Lesser Vehicle." After exerting a powerful influence in Indian thought for centuries, Buddhism gradually disappeared from its country of origin by the fifteenth century. However, it successfully permeated China, Tibet, Japan, and other Asian countries. Theravada (Hinayana) Buddhism has become a pervasive force throughout Southeast Asia (Ceylon, Burma, Thailand, Cambodia, and so on). In contrast, Mahayana Buddhism has infiltrated Northeast Asia and has had a far-reaching influence in China, Korea, and Japan. More will be discussed of Buddhism's history and development in the next section.

Jainism is alleged to be founded by Vardhamana, whose traditional dates are 599–527 B.C.E. Vardhamana is often assigned the title *Mahavira,* or "Great Hero."

A distinct aspect of the Jainist teachings lies in an absolute respect for life. Their idea of *ahimsa,* or nonviolence, is based on the metaphysical idea that all souls are equally deserving of protection. This outlook finds its modern expression in Mahatma Gandhi.

In the first century, Jainists were divided into two sects: the Svetambara ("White-clad"), and Digambara ("Sky-clad"). The differences had to do with the degree to which they practiced asceticism. For example, the Digambara monks practiced nudity as an expression of detachment. During the medieval centuries, Jainists had a large following. Today there are probably over a million Jains in India, situated chiefly in the south and west.

Epic Age Summarized   Relative to earlier periods, the Epic age reveals particular patterns of philosophical articulation unfolding within Indian intellectual history. The Vedic age demonstrates a rather rudimentary level of discussion that became somewhat more advanced with the Upanishads. For instance, we see seeds of philosophical speculation concerning the nature of reality in the famous Nasadiya Hymn, included at the end of Chapter 2. And with the Upanishads, a basic measure of philosophical activity is expressed in specific questions about the nature of reality and the self. There is the apparent need for evidence to support the earlier beliefs in the *Rig Veda.*

In the Epic age, the degree of philosophical sophistication is still basic, and we have a popularization of the accepted premises established more rationally in the Upanishads. In this same period, however, a more critical level emerges when orthodox beliefs begin to be challenged and refuted. At the same time, these refutations also begin to assume a more cohesive and systematic form.

Due to these heterodox challenges, Hindu defenders are compelled to provide, in turn, a more systematic defense of Vedic, Brahmanic teachings. The more theistic efforts expressed in the *Bhagavad Gita* and the later Upanishads were not enough to counter the increasingly critical tide. The precritical stage during the Epic age led to the more critical levels of philosophical activity in the next phase, the age of Sutras.

The Age of Sutras (400 B.C.E.–500 C.E.)

This age is more properly philosophical. We now witness the appearance of *darshana,* meaning "point of view," as more strictly philosophy. Two major intellectual streams began to permeate India. The orthodox teachings defended Vedic authority and are known as *astika.* The heterodox teachings of materialism, Buddhism, and Jainism refuted Vedic authority and became more structured. They are referred to as *nastika.*

This is called the age of Sutras because the systematization of the Vedic ideas occurs through the composition of sutras—short sayings that could be more easily transmitted because they were easier to memorize. Various

Table 1.1 Six Orthodox Hindu Schools

School	Founder	Text
Nyaya	Gautama	Nyaya Sutras (c. 3rd century B.C.E.–2nd century C.E.)
Vaisheshika	Kanada	Vaisheshika Sutras (c. 3rd century B.C.E.–c. 100 C.E.)
Samkhya	Kapila (c. 7th century B.C.E.)	Samkhyapravacana Sutra
	Isvarakrsna	Samkhya Karika (c. 3rd century C.E.)
Yoga	Patanjali	Yoga Sutra (c. 2nd century B.C.E.)
Mimamsa	Jaimini	Purva-Mimamsa Sutra (c. 400 B.C.E.)
Vedanta	Badarayana	Brahma Sutra (4th–2nd century B.C.E.)

sutras were composed based on diverse renditions of specific Vedic teachings. These major sutras led to the formation of the six major philosophical schools of Hinduism: Nyaya school, Vaisheshika school, Samkhya school, Yoga school, Mimamsa school, and Vedanta school (see Table 1.1).

Not only do these sutras provide a framework for a more systematized (and certainly more philosophical) exposition of Hindu thought, but they are the bases for subsequent commentaries and more polemical works. Of the six systems, the Nyaya, Mimamsa, and Vedanta are still popular. The Vedanta, however, has been much more significant throughout Indian intellectual history.

Nyaya School As debates became more customary in philosophical discourse, rules of logic needed to be devised and applied. Nyaya is a school that emphasizes rules for proper reasoning. Its exposition of logical reasoning is fundamental, and it provides a common ground for all other schools in Hinduism.

Nyaya dates back to the fourth century B.C.E. *Nyaya* literally means "argument." A modern version of the school was established later in the fourteenth century by Gangesa (c. 1325 C.E.). His modern school of logic, New Logic, was even more rigorous and penetrating in its investigation of logical terms and concepts such as *absence*. (See the selection at the end of Chapter 4.)

Vaisheshika School The Vaisheshika system primarily attempts to examine the nature of the universe. Its discussion is therefore cosmological, and it argues that physical reality consists of invisible, indestructible atoms. This way of explaining the physical world is used to support the Upanishadic thesis that *atman* is *Brahman*. As with all of these schools, the authority of the Veda is upheld. The school probably originated before the Nyaya school because Nyaya assumes some of its teachings. Scholars think that Vaisheshika arose around the six century B.C.E., and therefore contemporary with both the Buddha and Vardhamana.

Samkhya School   The Samkhya system is essentially concerned with the evolution of the objective world by focusing on the distinction between *purusha,* or self, and *prakriti,* the material force or condition for material existence. The Samkhya school has been called "the most significant system of philosophy that India has produced."[6]

Yoga School   The Yoga school accepts the fundamental metaphysical position of Samkhya. The emphasis in the Yoga school is on yoga as a disciplined method to attain liberation. *Yoga* means a "yoking," as a joining together. In this case, it means a joining together of mind and body—that is, the intellectual, volitional, and physical faculties of the person.

Mimamsa School   After the appearance of Buddhism and Jainism, there came about an elaborate interpretation of ideas in the Vedas and Upanishads, leading to two texts: the Purva-Mimamsa and the Uttara-Mimamsa.

The Purva-Mimamsa discusses the first two parts of the Veda. It is concerned with the interpretation of sacrifice and ritual. Mimamsa is therefore an examination of the practical aspects of *dharma.* For our purposes, we will refer to it as Mimamsa, for the Uttara-Mimamsa became more commonly known as the Vedanta because it focuses on the last two parts of the Veda, especially the Upanishads.

Vedanta School   Of all these schools, the Vedanta is still the most influential and far-reaching. As stated above, the original name given to this system is Uttara-Mimamsa. *Vedanta* literally means "the end of the Veda." It is generally referred to as Vedanta because it is primarily an interpretation of the principal teachings of the Upanishads. It also deals with ideas from the *Bhagavad Gita.*

Its major text is traditionally assigned to Badarayana and is called by various names: the *Vedanta Sutra,* the *Saririka Sutra,* and the *Brahma Sutra.* The basis for this school therefore lies in the three texts: the Upanishads, *Bhagavad Gita,* and *Vedanta Sutra.*

The most critical concern in the Vedanta system is to examine more closely the nature of ultimate reality, or *Brahman.* In the process, the relationship among *Brahman, atman,* and the world is explored at length.

The Age of Commentaries or Scholastic Age (400–1700 C.E.)

During this period, scholars wrote interpretations and observations on various sutras. It is a phase of more penetrating philosophical analyses, and the six systems underwent further development that remains remarkably consistent.

Celebrated commentators include Kumarila, Sridhara, Sankara, Vascapati, Udayana, Bhaskara, Ramanuja, Madhva, Nimbarka, and Raghunatha. Of these, the most definitive commentaries were those of Sankara, Ramanuja, and Madhva. Their schools and dates are as follows:

Sankara: *Advaita* (nondualism), ninth century
Ramanuja: *Visistadvaita* (qualified nondualism), eleventh century
Madhva: *Dvaita* (dualism), thirteenth century

Together, these three schools make up the Vedanta system, and their interpretations of the Upanishads constitute a far-reaching and vital impact on
Indian thought.

Sankara (788–820 C.E.)   Sankara is perhaps the most celebrated champion of
the Vedanta school. Sankara was obviously influenced by the uncompromising monism of his predecessor, Gaudapada. Gaudapada literally believed that
the only reality was *Brahman*. However, Sankara does not adopt Gaudapada's
extreme literal position. Sankara's system is known as Advaita Vedanta. *Advaita* literally means "nondual." This means that all reality is *Brahman*. Reality
does not consist of irreducibly distinct substances. In Sankara's interpretation, *tat tvam asi* refers to a strict identity of soul and *Brahman*. Moreover, the
world is not totally an illusion, nor is it separate from *Brahman*. Only the
Brahman is real, and the world is a manifestation of *Brahman*. All reality is one.
    Sankara's works continue to be some of the most penetrating texts in
Indian intellectual history. They combine philosophical rigor with mystical
insight. His teachings embrace analysis and poetry, and his vision continues
to appeal to Hindus.

Ramanuja (c. 1017–1137 C.E.)   Whereas Sankara taught a strict nondualism,
Ramanuja advocated a more qualified nondualism in his interpretation of the
Upanishads. Whereas Sankara tells us that *atman* is strictly identical to *Brahman*
and that the world is not apart from *Brahman*, Ramanuja contends that all
three—soul, world, and *Brahman*—are distinct from each other, though not
radically different. His works strive to harmonize the Upanishads, the *Brahma
Sutra*, and the *Bhagavad Gita* with teachings of the Vaisnava faith, of which
he was a firm adherent. In this way, his teaching represents a blend of monism
and personal theism. He views *Brahman* more as Ishvara, a personal God.
And both soul and world belong to *Brahman* but remain distinct.

Madhva (1197–1276 C.E.)   Madhva is known for his critical acumen, often
displayed in his attacks on Sankara's teachings of nondualism. Like Ramanuja,
he was affiliated with the Vaisnavite sect; that is, he believed that the supreme
god was Vishnu. His ideas reflect an extreme opposition to the nondualism
of Sankara and are known as *dvaita*, or dualism. Madhva contends that soul,
world, and *Brahman* are radically distinct. Therefore, we see in the Vedanta
schools three unique interpretations of the message of *tat tvam asi* in terms
of the nature of the relationship between soul, world, and God.

Renaissance and Modern Thought (1800–Present)

A variety of factors created the background for the Indian Renaissance and
subsequent modern thought: increasing *bhakti* movements (*bhakti* emphasizes
the importance of devotionalism through various forms)[7]; the influence of
Islam and Christianity; the rule of the British; increasing modernization,
especially in science; and a growing sense of Indian nationalism. Leading per-
sonalities are worth examining.

Some Renaissance Figures   Ram Mohan Roy (1772–1833) led a reform movement in 1828 known as the Brahmo Samaj ("Divine Society"), which advocated social reform and worked within a Hindu framework. He placed great emphasis on the Upanishads as the grounding element in the Hindu tradition.

Dayananda Sarasvati (1824–83) founded another social reform movement called Arya Samaj ("Noble Society," or "Aryan Society") in 1875. Whereas Roy insisted on the primacy of the Upanishads, Sarasvati appealed to the early Vedic hymns as the sole authority.

Gadadhar Chatterji (1834–86) later became known as Ramakrishna. His interests turned to Tantra and Vedanta, and his form of *bhakti* was tempered by his involvement with these schools, as well as by his involvement with both Christian and Islamic positions. He discovered that meditative experiences along each path were similar, and he therefore believed in their harmony.

Narendranath Datta (1863–1902) was one of these followers, and he later became known as Swami Vivekananda. Vivekananda developed his own unique philosophical interpretation of Ramakrishna's ideas. Vivekananda essentially taught that there is a fundamental unity among all religions in that they all seek an indefinable Absolute. Vivekananda stressed that our own divine natures link us together in our striving for this Absolute.

Some Modern Thinkers   Rabindranath Tagore (1861–1941) is one of the most celebrated of Indian writers. A poet more than a philosopher, he won the Nobel Prize for literature in 1913. His works reflect a deep humanism and intercultural venture while remaining anchored in the spiritual message of Advaita Vedanta. While upholding Sankara's nondualism his work managed to emphasize the intrinsic value of human experience.

For Bhagavan Das (1869–1957), the three attributes of Prakriti, or the supreme spirit, are luminosity, activity, and immobility. These three play a role in shaping human personality and the disposition that enables one to belong to one of the traditional classes or castes: *Brahmana* (priestly class), *Kshatriya* (warrior or protector class), *Vaishya* (merchant class), or *Shudra* (laboring class). All of this is underscored by his metaphysics, in which he distinguishes between that which is spirit and nonspirit.[8]

Mohandas Karamchand Gandhi (1869–1948) was not strictly a philosopher, although his life and teachings have had a profound ethical and social content. His own teachings were influenced by thinkers such as Tolstoi, Ruskin, and Thoreau, as well as by classic works, particularly the *Bhagavad Gita* and the New Testament. Blending all these elements together and focusing on the Jainist belief in *ahimsa* (noninjury), Gandhi's teachings center around the idea of *satyagraha* ("force of truth").

Gandhi was a major force in India's drive for independence from British rule, finally granted in 1947. Although he was untiring in his attempts to alleviate the growing tensions between the Muslims and the Hindus in India, these conflicts became more embittered. Gandhi's idealism probably seemed dangerous to the cause of Indian nationalism, and in 1948 Gandhi was assassinated by a Hindu nationalist.

Sri Aurobindo Ghose (1872–1950) presented an interesting account of the descending and ascending process of the Divine in existence. Influenced heavily by the Vedas and the schools of both Saiva and Sakta, Ghose started his active career as an outspoken opponent of British rule and an ardent defender of Indian nationalism. He was eventually arrested by the British, released, and escaped to Pondicherry, a French possession. There he immersed himself in ascetic practice and the study of yoga. His most far-reaching work is *The Life Divine,* which explains the evolution of spirit into matter and of matter into spirit. Such a process discloses that the true nature of matter is essentially spirit; otherwise, mind or spirit could not evolve from matter.

Sarvepalli Radhakrishnan (1888–1975) is perhaps the most significant and respected of modern Hindu philosophers. Raju adds that "He is recognized also as one of the greatest thinkers of this century."[9] He is not only known as a philosopher, but as a statesman as well. He was President of India from 1962 to 1967.

Radhakrishnan is especially responsible for asserting the importance of comparative studies in philosophy. Comparative philosophy is now a vital and respected field in colleges and universities, and much of the interest is due to the efforts of Radhakrishnan.

Indian Philosophy Today   Current philosophical thought in India contains a number of constant elements:

- The philosophy of Vedanta continues to prevail, although in varying forms.
- The influence of Western philosophy shows itself in the strong interest in Western philosophical schools such as the Oxford schools of neo-Kantianism and neo-Hegelianism. (Neo-Kantianism attempts to revive and reinterpret central tenets in the philosophy of Immanuel Kant in order to make philosophy more scientific. Neo-Hegelianism sought to restore the synthesis of Hegel. Other Western schools of thought are imported, such as logical positivism and phenomenology. Logical positivism, originating with the Vienna Circle, arose in reaction to the assertions of idealism and metaphysics. It essentially challenges the validity of metaphysical questions. Husserl is the champion of phenomenology, which criticizes prevailing scientific attitudes as well as reductionism.)
- Comparative philosophy continues to be a burgeoning school of thought.[10]

Indian Buddhism

Because the roots of Buddhist teachings lie in the Hindu tradition, Buddhism is a heterodox system posing challenges to the traditional authority of the Vedas. The complex history of Indian Buddhism can be divided into three periods: early Buddhism, sectarian Buddhism, and Mahayana Buddhism.

Early Buddhism

The Upanishadic formula that *atman* is identical to *Brahman* surely attracted many followers. The idea of the oneness of the individual soul and the universal soul is profound. However, for others it may have been unnecessarily abstract and impersonal. The Buddha challenges the validity of these kinds of metaphysical statements. His message offers a more practical response of liberation from the reality of suffering.

The core of early Buddhist teachings center around what are known as the Three Jewels of Buddhism: the Buddha, *Dharma,* and the Sangha. The life of the Buddha embodies his teachings and continues to be a constant source of inspiration. His teachings are called *Dharma,* and they remain authoritative, even though they have been subject to various interpretations. And the power of the Buddhist order continues to make itself felt throughout much of Asia. The Sangha, the early community of Buddhist monks and nuns, is responsible for transmitting and recording the Buddha's teachings.

First Jewel: The Life of the Buddha (c. 536–476 B.C.E.)   A paramount problem exists when recounting the Buddha's life: It is often quite difficult to distinguish historical fact from legend. He was born in Lumbini as Siddhartha Gautama. It is said that his father, Suddhodana, was ruler of the Sakya clan near the Himalayas. (This region is today Nepal.) His mother, Maya, supposedly died while Siddhartha was an infant. He was then raised by Maya's sister, Mahapajapati.

Despite his father's desire to protect his son from the harsh realities of life outside his palace, Siddhartha managed to venture beyond the palace walls with his chariot driver. During the course of these journeys he witnessed the realities of old age, sickness, suffering, and death, and these experiences made an indelible impression on him.

He is reported to have married Yasodhara when he was sixteen, and when he was twenty-nine they had a son, named Rahula, which literally means "chain." His education included serious study of the Vedas, yet his penetrating mind was not satisfied with its teachings. Nor was he content in his life as a householder. Siddhartha decided to leave his home and family in pursuit of some resolution to the questions that plagued him, especially that of human suffering.

After leaving his family he went to the valley of the Ganges River and studied forms of meditation under some teachers. These techniques of meditation did not enable him to experience the insight he sought, so he then joined a band of wandering ascetics and practiced severe forms of asceticism for six years. As a result of fasting and practicing other forms of severe austerities, Siddhartha was virtually emaciated—and still no closer to his enlightenment.

Outside of the town of Bodh Gaya, he remained under a tree, known later as the *bodhi* tree, or the "tree of enlightenment," and after a long mental struggle he experienced insight and enlightenment. His "awakening" entailed a total transformation of his consciousness as he obtained insight into the fundamental truths of human existence.

Filled with a need to share these insights with others, he embarked upon a teaching venture lasting nearly forty-five years. During his famous first sermon, at Sarnath, he described his famous Four Noble Truths and the Middle Way. These ideas, which remain the bedrock of Buddhist teachings, will be discussed in more detail later.

The Buddha's teachings offered a practical and positive approach to the problem of suffering, and his following increased. His more liberal attitude with respect to enlightenment—that all are capable of attaining it—and his message of hope with respect to human suffering must have appealed to numerous peoples.

During his last days, the Buddha, which literally means the "Awakened One," continued to counsel and refused to appoint a successor to take his place. Instead, he instructed his followers to rely on his teachings, or *dharma,* as well as to maintain the discipline, or *vinaya,* that he enacted:

> Therefore, Ananda, be islands unto yourselves, a refuge unto yourselves; take the teachings as island, the teaching as refuge, have no other refuge![11]

The Buddha's followers claim that with his death, he reached parinirvana, that state of ultimate enlightenment in which he would no longer be reborn. To this day, four holy sites in the life of Buddha are places of pilgrimage: Lumbini, his place of birth; Buddhagaya, his place of enlightenment; Deer Park at Sarnath, the place of his first sermon; and Kusinagara, his place of death.

Second Jewel: The Buddha's Dharma The *Dharma* of the Buddha comprises his teachings. The term *dharma* is often used to refer to a specific truth. The root of the term is *dhr,* meaning "to keep," so the idea is that of a teaching that will always hold true and needs to be realized.

The most significant teachings of the Buddha, adhered to by all Buddhist schools, are called the Four Noble Truths:

1. All existence is filled with suffering.
2. Suffering is ultimately caused by craving.
3. We can be liberated from suffering.
4. Liberation requires following the Eight-fold Path.

The Buddha's Middle Way is another important teaching. It essentially means that the path to liberation from suffering must avoid the extremes of either excess or defect. Enlightenment can only result from harmony; it cannot be the result of bodily castigation or sensuality.

Another teaching of the Buddha is that all reality is constantly changing, even elements of our personality. For this reason, we cannot in truth necessarily maintain the existence of a permanent self. Not only do all things change, but all things change because all things are essentially interdependent with each other. This is called the concept of dependent (or codependent) origination, termed *pratityasamutpada.* Dependent origination means that all things that exist and cease to exist are mutually determined by other things that exist and cease to exist.

The idea of no-self especially differentiates Buddhist thought from Hindu. Whereas Hindus believe in an eternal *atman,* or soul, most Buddhists claim that the notion of an individual soul is merely an illusion. Realizing this illusion therefore constitutes an essential ingredient in attaining enlightenment, or nirvana.

Here is another crucial teaching of the Buddha: In Indian thought, the general goal was to achieve personal insight, or enlightenment. For Hindus, the term for this was *moksha*—the realization of *atman* as *Brahman.* Buddhists also emphasize the need for enlightenment but view and describe it differently, using the term *nirvana,* which literally means "extinguishing." In this sense it means the extinction of the false idea of some eternal, personal self. In other words, Buddhists do not believe in *atman.* Nirvana also means the extinction of the craving that keeps one chained to the wheel of *samsara* and that therefore brings about rebirth.

Buddhists do believe in a continual succession of rebirths. Rebirth occurs because we remain ignorant of our Buddha-nature and persist in believing in an independent self. What is reborn is not *atman* because, for Buddhists, there is no *atman.* Nevertheless, some stream of consciousness along with its *karma* is reborn. This is often a puzzling idea in Buddhism, and it will be further examined in Chapter 6.

Third Jewel: Sangha, the Buddhist Order   Groups of followers began to devote themselves to a wholehearted commitment to the Buddha's teachings. Many of these followers became monks and nuns. This community of mendicants was called the Sangha. Monks and nuns who belonged to the early Buddhist orders lived a strict and simple life-style.

The earliest Sangha was not a settled community. Rather, the earliest mendicants were itinerants, known as *bhikkus,* "beggars." Eventually, however, communities formed and established more fixed dwellings, especially during the rainy season (June through September).

Tradition tells us that about three months after the death of the Buddha, a certain monk, Mahakasyapa, called for a meeting of monks—the First Council (c. 543 B.C.E.)—in order to establish some consensus about the core of his teachings. Here we have the initiation of the Buddhist canon, or official works. Through a long process these ideas were eventually collected together and called *pitaka,* "baskets." Texts were composed on dried palm leaves and stored in baskets.

Sectarian Buddhism

Councils and Schisms   Subsequent Buddhist councils were assembled in order to deal with interpretation of certain ideas. At least three major councils confronted issues of controversy.

Some monks at Vaisali were alleged to have violated rules (*vinaya*) of the order. Many monks, sympathetic to the monks of Vaisali, banded together (the Second Council, c. 443 B.C.E.) and later split away from the mainstream Sangha. This instigated the first major split among Buddhists, referred to as the Great Schism, and formed two schools: Mahasanghika ("the great assembly"), who sided with the Vaisali monks, and Sthaviravada (also called Theravada, or "teaching of the Elders"), who held to a more strict inter-pretation of the *vinaya.*[12]

Differences of interpretation became so acute that there was a need to solidify the core of the Buddha's teachings. Records tells us that Asoka (268–232 B.C.E.), who fostered the spread of Buddhism, invited Moggaliputta Tissa to Pataliputra to preside over the Third Council. Moggaliputta defended the Theravadin position, and his work, called *Katthavattu,* attempts to refute what were considered to be heretical views.[13]

Asoka played a major role in promoting Buddhist teachings, and his Rock Edicts (inscriptions, carved on stone, describing Buddhist teachings) were an important factor in the successful spread of Buddhist missionary efforts.

It is said that Asoka's son, Mahinda, introduced Buddhism into Sri Lanka, where the Buddhist canon was finally compiled. Sri Lanka was the first country outside of India to become Buddhist. To this day, Sri Lanka (formerly Ceylon) continues to be a stronghold of Theravadin thought.

A result of the Third Council was the inclusion of the *Abhidharma* literature as an essential part of the Buddhist canon, or official writings. The *Abhidharma* teachings were analyses of the metaphysical and psychological doctrines put forth by Buddhists. The canon, now complete, is called the *Tripitaka* and consists of (1) Basket of Rules (*Vinaya-pitaka*), (2) Basket of Say-ings (*Sutra-pitaka*), and (3) Basket of Doctrine (*Abhidharma-pitaka*).[14]

By 300 years after the Buddha died, there were twenty Buddhist schools. Of these schools, four were most influential: Mahasanghika, Theravada, Sar-vastivada, and Sammatiya.

The Fourth Buddhist Council (c. 100 C.E.) was supposedly assembled by Emperor Kaniska. This meeting was probably attended mainly by Thera-vadins, even though they consisted of many different subschools, all claim-ing allegiance to the *Dharma.* This sectarianism eventually gave way to the formation of Mahayana, as the major break with the traditionalist schools.

Teachings of Some Early Schools   The Buddha was often asked about the reality of the world: Is it ultimately real, or illusory? The School of the Elders, or Sthaviravadins, tended to interpret their teacher's general silence on the matter as neither affirming nor denying the reality of the world.

The name for the Sarvastivadin school indicates its essential position: *Sarva* ("everything") and *vasti* ("exists"). Its followers contend that all reality consists of elementary constituents, *dharmas,* which, though momentary, do exist and in combined forms make up both material objects and mental events such as thoughts and desires. These *dharmas* are the component energies of all that exists, even consciousness and even the sense of a subsistent self, which does not really exist as subsistent or self-contained. The significant idea in this school is the objective reality of the external world. The most important

Table 1.2   Major Buddhist Schools

Main School	Subschool	Text
Theravada (Hinayana), or Teaching of Elders (4th–2nd century B.C.E.)	Sthaviravadin (Theravada) Sarvastivadin Sautrantika Sammitiya Mahasanghika	Pali Canon Tripitaka (Three Baskets)
Mahayana (Greater Vehicle)	Madhyamika (Nagarjuna, c. 150 C.E.)	Prajnaparamita Sutra Saddharmapundarika Sutra
	Yogacara (Asanga, c. 310–390, Vasubandhu, c. 320–400)	Lankavatara Sutra Avatamsaka Sutra Sandhinirmocana Sutra
	Logic (Dignaga, 480–540) Esoteric (Tantrayana) (2nd century C.E.)	Pramanasamuccaya

text describing this school is Vasubandhu's Abhidharmakosa. The Sarvastivadin school was later divided into two further schools: the Sautrantika and the Vaibhashika.

The Sautrantika school does admit the existence of constituent elements posited by Sarvastivadins. However, they underscore the essentially dynamic nature of *dharmas,* so that direct perception is not possible. Everything is in constant flux, so that what is perceived is not the moment itself, but an image of that moment left over, or a trace. There is only, at best, indirect perception.

The Sammitiya school is quite distinct among Buddhist schools for the following reason: Whereas Buddhists are generally disinclined to posit an eternal, subsistent entity called soul or self, the Sammitiya school does accept the existence of a personal entity, called *pudgala.*

The early schools and their texts are listed in Table 1.2.

Mahayana Buddhism

The seeds of Mahayana Buddhism originated early in the Second and Third Buddhist Councils. At that time, for instance, the Mahasanghika school proposed a view of the Buddha that transcended that of an ordinary human. In addition, the Sammitiya school posited an enduring entity called *pudgala,* or "person," in direct contrast to the traditional view of *anatman.* In addition, the Sarvastivadin school posed the idea of the three bodies of the Buddha:

- The historical body of the Buddha, born as a human, called *nirmanakaya*
- The transcendent body of the Buddha, called the *sambhogakaya*
- The mystical body of the Buddha, essentially indescribable, called the *dharmakaya.*

A growing number of Buddhists began to disassociate themselves from the mainstream of Buddhists, even though they claimed that their interpretations were in line with the intent and spirit of their founder. In time, they referred to themselves as Mahayana, and assigned the rather derogatory name Hinayana to all schools associated with the conservative Theravada and Sarvastivada systems. *Mahayana* means "Great Vehicle," whereas *Hinayana* means "Lesser (more inferior) Vehicle." By "vehicle" we mean the *Dharma,* the teachings of the Buddha. These teachings are likened to a ferryboat that takes one from the shore of ignorance to the shore of enlightenment. Mahayana Buddhism later spread to the north and became the dominant Buddhist school in China, Korea, and Japan.

Mahayana Sutras   Mahayana sutras were written in Sanskrit. The major texts (see Table 1.2) are the *Prajnaparamita Sutras,* called "Perfection of Wisdom," compiled between 100 B.C.E. and 600 C.E. One legend tells us that because these teachings were beyond the grasp of ordinary understanding, they were kept in the Nether region in the palace of Serpents, who symbolized wisdom. The teachings were then resurrected from this region by the great philosopher Nagarjuna.[15]

The teachings include the Diamond Sutra and the Heart Sutra. In the Diamond Sutra we have a discussion of the essence of the Buddha that transcends the historical and is known as the *"dharma body,"* which can be known only through wisdom, or *prajna.* The Heart Sutra speaks of the idea of *sunya,* "emptiness," which constitutes the novel foundation for Mahayana beliefs. This is especially emphasized in the Mahayana school of Madhyamika.

The *Saddharmapundarika Sutra,* better known as the Lotus Sutra, is an early work. This text provides a discussion of the nature of the Buddha in reference to the state of Buddhahood. These are just a few of the sutras.

Mahayana Teachings   Perhaps the most important innovation that Mahayana introduces is its notion of the *bodhisattva.* In early Buddhist beliefs, a *bodhisattva* was considered to be a human being who seeks to attain liberation. The Mahayana interpretation expands this idea further.

First of all, the *bodhisattva* acquires a more idealized image with the teaching that the Buddha's previous lives, before his historical birth, were lived as a *bodhisattva* working for the salvation of other humans. His past lives set the stage for him to finally achieve enlightenment. As we can see here, Buddhists do believe in a series of rebirths, with each succeeding rebirth dependent on actions and thought in previous lives. However, as we will see in Chapter 6, Buddhists reject the belief in the transmigration of an independent soul, or *atman.* In any case, this doctrine of the *bodhisattva* emerges more fully in the *Saddharmapundarika Sutra.*

An important teaching is that of *sunyata* (*sunya* literally means "empty"), which will be described in more detail in other chapters. Essentially it refers to the belief that all things are without permanence. This is particularly the case with what we take to be our "self." All things are empty or void.

Tathagata, another teaching, comes from the term *tathata,* which literally means "suchness." Mahayanists refer to the Buddha as Tathagata, one who realized the "suchness" of things. *Tathata* is somewhat coterminous with the idea of *sunyata.*

Mahayana Schools   The formation of distinct schools within Mahayana reflects different emphases on these essential teachings. Here we touch on the more prominent schools. (See Table 1.2 for schools and texts.)

The founder of the Madhyamika school is Nagarjuna, one of the most original of Buddhist philosophers. His most important teaching centers around the idea of *sunyata.* His school is called Madhyamika because it literally means "the school of the Middle." And he clearly pursues, in line with the Buddha's Middle Way, a path between the ontological extremes of positing existence and positing nonexistence in reference to *sunyata,* reality. Furthermore, he steers the middle path in avoiding the epistemological, or logical, extremes of either affirmation or negation, again with respect to *sunyata*; that is, we can neither affirm or deny that reality exists or does not exist.[16]

Tradition has it that two brothers, Asanga and Vasubandhu, founded the Yogacara, or Vijnanavada school. Both of them were, at first, immersed in the Theravadin tradition. Vasubandhu authored the important *Abhidharmakosa.* He was converted to the Mahayanist position by Asanga, and he consequently became one of its most ardent defenders. This school is also referred to as Vijnanavada because its central concern is consciousness (*vijnana*). (In Buddhism, the concepts of mind, thought, and consciousness are often used interchangeably.)[17]

The Logic school arose when the scholastic drive to engage in dialectic discussion and analysis evoked the need for an examination of the principles of logical inquiry. There was increasing interest in the art of debating. This was particularly urgent in order to attain some modicum of success in arguing with Hindu scholars. The real pioneer in systematic exposition of Buddhist logic and epistemology is Dignaga.

Esoteric forms of Buddhism resulted from the gradually increasing emphasis on devotionalism. The most significant manifestation of these new expressive forms was in Tantric Buddhism. There were essentially four forms of Tantric Buddhism: Vajrayana, Sahaja (Sahajiya), Kalacakra, and Mantra (Mantrayana).

In Vajrayana, *vajra* means "diamond" or "thunderbolt." It symbolizes the inherent Buddha-nature in all sentient beings. The deity that portrays our Buddhahood is Vajrasattva. *Mandalas,* literally meaning "circles," were often used as aids in meditation, depicting a sort of map of this spiritual order or realm occupied by *bodhisattvas* and buddhas.

The *sahaja* is the term for the inherent *bodhicitta,* which refers to the "heart of wisdom" or Buddha-nature within each sentient creature. This school describes ways to achieve the union with wisdom through *upaya,* or skillful means. For the Vajrayana, adherents were usually attached to universities. In contrast, devotees of the Sahaja were free from institutions, often living an itinerant life-style. The school was therefore more iconoclastic in its activity and perhaps better exemplifies the Tantric tradition, which is essentially a direct challenge to the prevailing monastic tradition.

The Kalacakra school probably started around the tenth century. *Kalacakra* means "Wheel of Time" and reflects the pattern of heavenly movement. It also refers to the character of the heavenly Buddha. The main text of this school is the Kalacakra Tantra, and human beings are described in more astrological processes.

The Mantra school teaches that all things are interrelated. Therefore, things can be made to occur by influencing other things and events. This can come about through the use of mantras, or sacred syllables. The use of mantras by the student or adept (*sadhaka*) can bring about an inner awakening to the adept's oneness with Buddha nature.

The Fate of Indian Buddhism

One of the ironies in Asian history is the fate of Indian Buddhism: Its influence diminished in the country of its origin. However, it gained strength elsewhere as it acculturated itself to surrounding countries and became a permanent fixture and profound influence on the unfolding of China and Japan.

The reasons for Buddhism's decline in India are several and include the following:

- Hinduism experienced a gradual revival, especially through its popular *bhakti* movements.
- Sankara's teachings became widespread, and even though Vedanta thought has often been linked by scholars to Buddhism, Sankara himself often spoke out openly against Buddhist ideas.
- Royal support of Buddhism lessened.
- Buddhism's increasing devotional emphases made it more difficult for adherents to discern its distinction from Hindu practices.
- Buddhism was still, in the eyes of many Hindus, a monastic-centered system and therefore was disconnected from public affairs.

▬▬▬ Chinese Philosophies ▬▬▬

Chinese philosophy unfolds in four major phases:[18]

- Ancient Period (before 221 B.C.E.)
- Middle Period (221 B.C.E.–960 C.E.)
- Neo-Confucianism (960–1912)
- Modern Period (1912 to the present).

Ancient Period of Chinese Philosophy

This period is also known as the time of the Hundred Schools, when many different philosophical positions were being expounded. The height of the period occurred during the political and social conflict of the Warring States

(403 B.C.E.–221 B.C.E.), when the great philosophers laid the foundation for the remainder of over 2,000 years of Chinese thought and culture.

The most important teachings during this period came from the following schools: Confucian, Taoist, Mohist, Names, Yin-Yang, and Legalist. We next discuss each school and its leaders in turn.

Confucian School

Confucius (551–479 B.C.E.)[19]   Originally called K'ung Fu Tzu, or Master K'ung, this great teacher is known in the West as Confucius. Confucius's teachings express a radical turn from the traditional preoccupation with spirits. His teachings embody the centrality of the human.

Interested in matters of politics, he supposedly became quite successful as a public figure and advisor to the government in Lu. At age 56 he supposedly retired from his government position and spent the next thirteen years traveling and teaching. At 68 he then returned to his home in Lu and proceeded to teach until his death in 479 B.C.E.

Confucius is, without a doubt, one of the most illustrious teachers in human history. He was especially concerned that his students develop as humans in the most moral sense. A strong humanism highlights all aspects of his teaching, from education to politics. His teachings are summed up in the words of his student Tsang:

> The doctrine of our master is to be true to the principles of our nature and the benevolent exercise of them to others—this and nothing more.[20]

Here is his idea of "unity"—or better, of harmony, as represented in the Doctrine of the Golden Mean. Confucius tells us that "To go beyond is as wrong as to fall short."[21] This Doctrine of the Golden Mean emphasizes the crucial need for living a life of balance and moderation. This entails avoiding the extremes of both excess and defect. Only this can bring about inner harmony, and only by virtue of inner peace can we live in harmony with others.

He made his teachings available to all classes. Opening the doors of learning to people of all classes was to have a profound effect on the remainder of Chinese culture and history. Many of his conversations were subsequently recorded by his students in the classic work called the Analects.

Mencius (c. 372–c. 298 B.C.E.)   Mencius is one of the most important adherents of Confucius's teachings. He elaborates on many of Confucius's ideas and, in his creative way, provides more of a psychological and metaphysical basis. His famous work is *The Book of Mencius,* written in dialogue fashion with conversations. In it he discusses central ideas, such as human nature, virtue, and benevolence, or *jen.*

Confucius teaches that one must live a life of virtue and develop moral character. Mencius explains that this is especially necessary because by doing so we are acting according to our nature; that is, we are naturally good. And we possess an intuitive sense of what is right and wrong, without having been taught. Mencius favors a government whose primary interest is directed to the well-being of the people. He defended the idea of a king who was first and foremost a sage.

Hsün Tzu (c. 313–c. 238 B.C.E.)   Hsün Tzu's profession as an official was rather short-lived. He often attacked the corruption he found to be rampant within government. He was also critical of the prevailing climate of superstition, even among scholars. He is especially known for his work *The Hsün Tzu,* covering a variety of topics such as human nature, education, and logic.

In contrast to Mencius, who considered human nature to be basically good, Hsün Tzu believed that we tend to be evil by nature. Despite our evil natures, we also have the potential to be sages, according to Hsün Tzu. Although we carry the seeds of corruption, we also possess an intelligence that distinguishes us from other creatures. This raises us to a level whereby we can learn to both know and practice good.

Hsün Tzu speaks of ceremonials and rules of right conduct, or *li,* as avenues to achieve some social order. Most importantly, each individual must practice virtue so that it becomes habitual.

Taoist School

Whereas the teachings of Confucius are essentially oriented toward the social order, Taoism advocates a return to the simplicity of nature to achieve an interior harmony. (Both Confucianism and Taoism point to the need for harmony, though they each find it in different paths.) The two most prominent thinkers in early Taoism are Lao Tzu and Chuang Tzu.

Lao Tzu (c. sixth century B.C.E.)   According to the Shih-chi, Lao Tzu's real name was Li Erh, and he was library curator in the capitol of Chou. It is believed that he was later assigned the name "Lao Tzu," meaning "elderly (*lao*) philosopher (*tzu*)." The work attributed to him, *Tao Te Ching* ("Classic of the Way and Its Virtue," also called *Lao Tzu*), was probably subsequently compiled over a period of time by a number of scholars. It stresses simplicity and nature. Its most important teachings concern *Tao, te,* and *wu-wei.*

Tao literally means "way." It is the principle for all things and the source of things coming into existence and of things ceasing to exist. Tao cannot be defined or named.

Te means "power," and it is the power of Tao. It is the spontaneous expression of the force of Tao manifest throughout nature. *Te* can also mean "virtue."

Wu-wei literally means "nonacting" and refers to allowing the natural course of things to unfold. It is a yielding, a noncontrived way of acting, or a letting-be to Tao.

Chuang Tzu (c. 369–286 B.C.E.)   Due to his reputation, King Wei of Ch'u once approached Chuang Tzu through messengers, inviting him to be the next prime minister. Chuang Tzu declined the invitation, asserting that he could never become embroiled in the defilements of political office. The text traditionally attributed to Chuang Tzu is called *Chuang-tzu*. As in the case of the *Tao Tê Ching*, the text was compiled much later by students and commentators.

Chuang Tzu broadens the meaning of Tao by including the characteristic of constant transformation to reality. Both being and nonbeing act according to the principle of transformation, or perpetual flux, or change.

In Chuang Tzu, there is no ground in actuality for discrimination. "This" and "that" are essentially the same. Tao is therefore also the principle of unity in which apparent opposites are reconciled. Furthermore, *te* as spontaneity means (just as in Lao Tzu) living according to Nature, avoiding artificiality, and minimizing that which is superficial.

Mohist School

It appears that at some point, Mo Tzu (c. 479–381 B.C.E.) was a city clerk. Moreover, some commentators felt that he was part of a militant group known as the *hsieh,* a group hired for protection.[22] The capital text of the Mohist school is a book to which Mo Tzu contributed, which his students called the *Mo-tzu.*

Mohist thought has a strong utilitarian emphasis; that is, the essential criteria is accordance with what brings about the greatest benefit for most of the people. For example, he proposes that order can only occur through universal harmony or love, and he interprets "universal" quite literally. This means regarding others as one regards oneself—seeing all equally without rank, without discrimination, without partiality.

Despite this equality, just as a governing hierarchy exists in which the supreme God and the will of Heaven dictates universal love and sanctions its exercise, so is it the case with the State. In the same fashion, the true ruler on earth exercises strict control over his people.

School of Names

This school, also called the School of Dialecticians and the School of Logic, emphasizes debate and epistemological analysis. The debate is often centered on the relationship between a thing and what it is called—between an actual object, experience, or person, and its designation. Two of the most prominent figures in this school are Hui Shih and Kung-sun Lung.

Only a few of Hui Shih's (c. 370–310 B.C.E.) many writings have survived, namely his "Ten Paradoxes," alluded to in Chapter 33 of *Chuang-tzu.* Here, his main ideas are relativity, change, and emphasis on particulars more than on universals.

As for Kung-sun Lung (c. 380 B.C.E.), very little is known of his life, except that he was born in the state of Chao and that he gained popularity as a foremost dialectician. He was particularly eager to investigate the nature of the relationship between things and names, between what are called particulars and universals. His work is called *Kung-sun Lung Tzu.* His theory of universals is best illustrated in his well-known essay called "The Discourse on the White Horse."

Yin-Yang School

The roots of the Yin-Yang school extend deep into Chinese history and play a crucial role throughout the course of Chinese intellectual development.

In the early history of China, the practice of divination was quite common. Not only was divination popular, but there was an enduring interest in astrology and numerology. The classic text, *I Ching,* was originally used for divination. The *I Ching* attempts to represent, in a composite way, the changes that occur throughout the universe. In fact, the later appendices to the *I Ching* were so important that during the Burning of the Books (213 B.C.E.) the Ch'in dynasty would not allow these to be burned.

The two universal forces are yin and yang. The *yin* is the passive principle, represented by the female; the *yang* is the active, male principle. *Yin* literally refers to darkness, whereas *yang* means light, or sunshine. Yin came to represent not just darkness, but passivity, softness, femininity, coldness, and so on. At the same time, yang came to mean not only light, but hardness, activity, masculinity, heat, and so forth. These two forces interact to bring forth all phenomena.

In this school, the five elements, or *Wu Hsing,* are seen as dynamic forces interacting with each other. These five elements—water, fire, wood, metal, and earth—also considered forces, serve to reinforce the belief in the interaction between humanity and nature.[23]

Legalist School

The Period of the Warring States witnessed the collapse of the feudal system. With its breakdown, class separations became blurred, and a need for a new order arose. During this time the Legalist school came to prominence. Its teachings provided a theoretical basis for a centralized government and for the eventual nearly absolute authority of the ruler, who ruled by delegating his authority and by strictly controlling the people through the "two handles" of reward and punishment. However, the purpose of the Legalist teachings was not to repress subjects, but to establish order and harmony so that the people would benefit.

According to Confucianism, genuine authority lies in the past, in tradition. In contrast, instead of appealing to past tradition the Legalists put forth the radical proposition that genuine authority must be adapted to the circumstances in the present.

Han Fei Tzu (c. 280?–233 B.C.E.) studied under Hsün Tzu and led a reform movement that had far-reaching political consequences, especially in the state of Ch'in. His most representative text is *Han-fei-tzu.* He supposedly died in prison, forced to commit suicide (probably the result of antagonism on the part of a Ch'in official).

For Han Fei Tzu, there is no proper place for private standards of right and wrong. Standards are determined by the dictates of law, which in turn is determined by the rule of those in authority. Furthermore, those in authority do not receive their dictates from the mandate of Heaven; the law originates with the human ruler. This order is necessary because human nature is intrinsically evil.

The Ch'in dynasty assumed such strict control that it was able to unify all of China. It also tried to disparage heterodox ideas. Many private teachings and writings contrary to official state policy were ordered burned. This was the infamous Burning of the Books in 213 B.C.E.

Throughout this period, Confucius's teachings occupied a most prominent place in Chinese society. In fact, official appointments in the government were contingent on the passing of state examinations, which required knowledge of the Confucian classics. This examination system began early in the Han dynasty and remained in effect for nearly two millenia until it was revoked in 1905.

Middle Period (221 B.C.E.–960 C.E.)

The major highlights of the Middle Period include the following:

- Confucianism becomes the official state philosophy, and it assimilates elements and ideas from the Yin-Yang school.
- Taoism witnesses a resurgence in interest.
- Buddhism is introduced into China and gradually competes in popularity with Confucianism.

From the Middle Period on, even until the present, three dominant schools of thought have prevailed in China: Confucianism, Taoism, and Chinese Buddhism. We next examine each school in turn.

Rise of Confucianism

The Confucian school gained momentum at the beginning of the Han dynasty (206 B.C.E.–220 C.E.) and was influenced by other schools, especially by Yin-Yang teachings. An important philosopher who represents this syncretic aspect within Confucianism is Tung Chung-shu (176–104 B.C.E.).

Tung is a representative of the New Text school. During the Han dynasty a conflict arose between the Old Text school and the New Text school. The Old Text school held that Confucian thought should be based on the older, more archaic versions of the Confucian classics, whereas the New Text school contended that Confucian teachings should be grounded on newer versions written during the Han rule. Tung supposedly initiated the idea of government officials taking their examinations based on knowledge of the classics. This was a radical step. Not only did it curb the practice of favoritism, but it promulgated the spread of Confucian teachings. Most importantly, it contributed to the unification of Chinese thought.

Tung applied yin-yang ideas and the Five Elements to Confucian teachings, asserting a metaphysical correspondence between the will of Heaven and human affairs. This is his theory of correspondence. In addition,

Tung's teachings sanctioned imperial rule because it reflected the will of Heaven. His most important commentary is called *Copious Dew in Spring and Autumn.*

In opposition to the ideas and interpretations put forth by the New Text school, a group of scholars resorted to older versions of the classics. This group was founded on the "old learning." Perhaps the most prolific representative of this Old Text school is Wang Ch'ung (27–c. 100 C.E.). He was known for approaching his subject in a critical, scientific spirit. His important work is *Lun Heng (Critical Essays).*

As did others of the Old Text school, Wang Ch'ung severely criticized superstitions and emphasis on divinations. The confluence of extreme yin-yang and Five Elements theories with Confucianism (as we find in Tung Chung-shu) was, for him, quite dangerous.

Neo-Taoism

After the Han dynasty there was a concerted effort to revive Taoist teachings that involved specific revisions of some of the teachings. For instance, one revision revived the meaning of Tao so that the metaphysical principles of the new Taoism are posed on a higher level than in original Taoism. By raising the status of considerations of being and nonbeing to a more metaphysical status, Neo-Taoism paved the way for greater acceptance of Buddhist teachings.

In his brief life, Wang Pi (226–249) became a brilliant exponent of the Neo-Taoist school. He defines Tao in a much more metaphysical way. It is not simply the namelessness of things, as in the *Lao-tzu.* Tao, the source from which all being is manifested, is referred to more in terms of *wu,* or non-being. The ultimate source of being is nonbeing. Wang Pi's most important texts are commentaries on the *I Ching* and *Lao-tzu.*

Kuo Hsiang (d. 312) also describes Tao as *wu* and is more elaborate in his discussion than Wang Pi. He also speaks of the perfect person as one who does not retreat from the world of affairs. His major text is the *Commentary on Chuang-tzu (Chuang-tzu Chu).*

Chinese Buddhism

It is rather remarkable that Buddhism took root in China and became a major intellectual force. The hurdles were numerous. Next to the sheer complexity of Buddhist schools and the problems in translation, the Chinese worldview was essentially more practical and secular in nature. There were some clear differences between the worldviews of Confucianism and Buddhism. Within the Confucian perspective, the individual self is defined with respect to a collective web, stressing relationality and prescribed duties to family and to society. The Buddhist ideas of no-self, individual liberation, and monastic withdrawal probably seemed quite alien to the Chinese temperament. The Buddhist worldview was other-worldly and transcendentally oriented, as we can see in ideas such as nirvana. Confucian teachings centered on a strict secularity and immanence.

Despite this, Buddhism did take root and grow in Chinese soil, but only after an extremely complex process of modification and assimilation. A number of factors contributed to this process. First, during this time of political fracture (311–589 C.E.), the influence of Confucianism also waned. Confucianism was especially supported by the upper classes. The common people expressed interest in other approaches, including Buddhism. Especially during these times of political upheaval, many of the lower classes may have felt some comfort in the saving doctrines of Mahayana Buddhism. Second, during disunity a burgeoning Buddhist clergy acquired more patronage. Nevertheless, even though Buddhism is one of the three major systems in China, it still remains subordinate in influence to Confucianism.

Two great missionaries are responsible for bringing Buddhism into China from India. Bodhidharma (460–534) introduced the teachings of Ch'an Buddhism around 520, during the reign of Emperor Wu (502–549). Kumarajiva (c. 343–413) introduced the Madhyamika teachings into China. Because of his vast knowledge and reputation, he was held captive and later brought to the Ch'in dynasty capital, Ch'ang-an, in the early 400s. The remainder of his life was spent there translating Sanskrit texts. Two of his students, Seng-chao and Tao-sheng, continued the spread of Buddhism.

Although Seng-chao (384–414) came from a poor family, he was able to gain a thorough knowledge of the classics, and he especially favored the ideas of Lao Tzu and Chuang Tzu. His work is called *Chao Lun (Book of Chao).* His most important ideas concern time, change, and *sunya,* or emptiness.

An important idea of Tao-sheng (c. 360–434) is that a good act comes about from being in a state of both *wu-wei* and *wu-hsin*. *Wu-wei* refers to non-action, or spontaneous activity. *Wu-hsin* literally means "no mind." Acting morally requires acting without attachment to the act or to the results of the act.

It was under the Sui and T'ang dynasties (589–906) that Chinese Buddhism experienced its Golden Age. During this time, famous pilgrims such as Hsüan-tsang (596–664) journeyed to India and returned with acute observations and translations of Buddhist texts.

In the latter half of the T'ang dynasty, political and economic unrest grew, and Buddhism began to lose its prestigious foothold. This time also saw the revival of Confucianism.

The various expressions of Chinese Buddhism are represented in the following schools:

1. Three Treatises (San-lun) school
2. Consciousness Only school
3. T'ien-T'ai school
4. Hua-yen school
5. Ch'an school (see Table 1.3)

The eminent scholar who best represents the Three Treatises school and systematized its ideas was Chi-tsang. He was quite gifted and became

Table 1.3   Chinese Buddhist Schools

School	Prominent Figure	Text
Three Treatises (San-lun) or Middle Doctrine	Chi-tsang (549–623)	Commentaries on three Indian Treatises: Madhyamika Sastra, Dvadasamikaya Sastra; both by Nagarjuna Sata Sastra, by Aryadeva
Consciousness Only or Mere Ideation	Hsüan-tsang (596–664)	Completion of the Doctrine of Mere Ideation
T'ien-T'ai (Fa-hua) or Lotus School	Chih-k'ai (538–597)	Mahayana method of Cessation and Contemplation - school based on Lotus Sutra, or Saddharmapundarika Sutra
Hua-yen or Wreath School	Fa-tsang (643–712)	Essay on the Gold Lion - school based on Avatamsaka Sutra
Ch'an	Bodhidharma (fl. 460–534)	—

a Buddhist monk early in his life. The fundamental thesis of the Consciousness Only school is that the nature of our consciousness is such that we tend to cling to two illusions: ego (*atman, wo*) and objective, external things (*dharmas, fa*). In reality, both lack self-nature. After a few centuries the influence of these two schools lessened, perhaps because of the highly metaphysical character of these schools.

The T'ien-T'ai school ranks as one of the most important. Its major text is the Lotus Sutra, or *Saddharmapundarika Sutra*. First of all, there is "single, absolute mind," which is Bhutatathata. In Chinese this is *Chen-ju,* meaning "genuine suchness." This absolute mind has no beginning nor end and is eternal. This school gives a more positive status to phenomenal reality. In a qualified way, things do exist because they are natural manifestations of Tathagata-garbha. In the tension between *wu* and *yu*, this school seems to emphasize *yu* more than *wu*.

The founder of the Hua-yen school was Fa-tsang. One of the most important of his ideas is his notion that the realm of things is illusion or emptiness.

The most extreme expression of Buddhism is demonstrated in the Ch'an school. Its name etymologically stems from the Sanskrit term *dhyana*, literally meaning "meditation." The school stressed the Indian practice of sitting meditation in the hopes of freeing the mind of attachment to objects, or *dharmas.*

The school was introduced to China through Bodhidharma, who initiated a succession of patriarchs carrying on the meditation tradition.[24] Hung-jen was the fifth patriarch, and the question over his successor led to a split between the northern and southern schools. Before he died, Hung-jen decided to appoint as leader the monk who could best express the meaning of Ch'an in verse. The favored monk, Shen-hsiu (c. 600–706), wrote this poem:

> The body is like the *Bodhi* tree [enlightenment],
> The mind is like a clear mirror standing.
> Take care to wipe it all the time,
> Allow no grain of dust to cling.

Another monk, a young man named Hui-neng (638–713), composed this verse:

> The *Bodhi* is not like a tree,
> The clear mirror is nowhere standing.
> Fundamentally not one thing exists;
> Where, then, is a grain of dust to cling?[25]

These two poems inspired the later division of Ch'an into two branches. The northern branch was headed by Shen-hsiu, and the southern branch was led by Hui-neng. During the eighth and ninth centuries, Ch'an reached its zenith and posed one of the greatest threats to the traditional predominance of Confucian thought.

Among the principal teachings of Ch'an are the following ideas:

- Genuine realization is instantaneous. Hui-neng stressed this sudden awakening all the more because awakening is a total experience and does not occur gradually.
- Spiritual practice refers to the notion of working toward liberation. But in Ch'an, it means this: exerting an effort through noneffort, or cultivating through "noncultivation."
- Ch'an is not a retreat from the world. In fact, it synthesizes transcendence and immanence in its own unique manner. The sage, therefore, is not essentially different from the ordinary person.
- The extreme conceptual structures in early Buddhism are discarded by Ch'an as essentially useless. Scriptures and words are useless as the path to enlightenment. The far-reaching discovery of Ch'an is that enlightenment and ordinary experience are not incompatible.

Neo-Confucianism (960–1912)

The proliferation of Buddhist teachings evoked strong opposition from Confucianists. The Buddhist emphasis on the Void and no-self was considered too abstract and divorced from real human concerns. Its emphasis on transcending the wheel of life and death appeared to be escapist.

Confucianists looked to the original teachings in the classics and sought to reinterpret them in the light of current needs. The resulting Neo-Confucianism dominated the period, and it continues to be a major force

Table 1.4 Neo-Confucian Schools

School	Prominent Figure		Text
School of Principle (Li-Hsüeh)	Ch'eng Yi (1033–1108)		Commentaries on the *I Ching* and Spring and Autumn Annals
Sung dynasty (960–1297)	Chu Hsi (1130–1200)		
School of Mind (Hsin-hsüeh)	Lu Hsiang-shan (1139–1193)		—
Ming period (1368–1644)	Wang Yang-ming (1472–1529)		Questions of the Great Learning Record of Instructions
Empirical school (T'u-hsüeh)	Tai Chen	(1723–1777)	—
Ch'ing dynasty	K'ang Yu-wei	(1858–1927)	—
(1644–1911)	T'an Ssu-t'ung	(1865–1898)	—
	Liao P'ing	(1852–1932)	—

in Chinese thought (and in Japanese thought as well). It evolved in three distinct phases (see Table 1.4): the School of Principle, or Rational school; the School of Mind, or Idealist school; and the Empirical school.[26]

School of Principle (Ch'eng-Chu School)

Two brothers, Ch'eng Yi and Ch'eng Hao, were responsible for setting the tone for this major school. Through them, Neo-Confucianism became more organized. A number of Ch'eng Hao's ideas differed from those of his younger brother. It seems as if he paved the way for the later School of Mind.

The School of Principle is called the Ch'eng-Chu after its two most prominent representatives: Ch'eng Yi and the great systematizer Chu Hsi. The teachings of this school center around the Great Ultimate, *li*, and *ch'i*.

The Great Ultimate is *T'ai-chi*. It possesses manifoldness and plurality, the realities being asserted through the Heavenly principle, or *li*. *Li* does not operate on its own. Its agent is *ch'i*, in turn influenced by the yin-yang forces and the Five Elements, manifesting matter. There is a harmonious pattern between *li* and matter in which *li* is still the prior principle. Principle can exist outside of its manifested object. (For Ch'eng Hao, it can only exist within its object.) Later, Chu Hsi developed this distinction even further.

Chu Hsi (1130–1200) is, without a doubt, the most important Neo-Confucianist. He may be the greatest systematizer and synthesizer in Chinese philosophy. Having thoroughly studied both Buddhism and Taoism, he turned to Confucianism in mid-life. He held a number of government posts while continuing to teach and write. After his death, he was given the honorary title of Duke. Let us briefly review his leading ideas.

For Chu Hsi, the Great Ultimate, *T'ai-chi*, is the summation of all principles. It is the totality of *li*. It manifests itself in all phenomena, due to principle, *li*. The objective world is the actualization of *li*. But this actualization demands material force, or *ch'i*. *Ch'i* is responsible for actualizing *li* into the resulting objective manifestations. In any case, *T'ai chi* is both *li* and *ch'i*, principle and material force.

Each distinct object therefore possesses *T'ai-chi*. Not only does each object contain its own principle, but contains within itself *T'ai-chi*, or the completeness of all *li*. Furthermore, the Supreme Ultimate in each object is not manifest as such; it remains concealed.

Keep in mind that Chu Hsi admits that even though each particular object contains the Supreme Ultimate and that its principle is thereby equal to all other principles, he also admits the differences with respect to *ch'i* and physical manifestation.

What does this say about human nature? Principle is in itself good because it reflects *T'ai-chi*, which is good. Human nature is intrinsically good because it is principle. However, the actualization must come about through *ch'i*, which is imperfect.

School of Mind (Lu-Wang School)

Lu Hsiang-shan(1139–1193) was both Chu Hsi's friend and major opponent. He prepared the way for a systematic opposition to the Rationalist supremacy and brought about the Idealist school known as the School of Mind. He was critical of the School of Principle because it exaggerated the difference between *li* and mind, overstressing the significance of *li* at the price of mind, and because Chu Hsi's emphasis on the investigation of things was, for Lu, directionless and futile.

For Lu, mind is identical to principle. Because there is no difference between mind and *li*, then mind is also good, because principle is good. Lu does not make a sharp contrast between mind and nature, and thus did not distinguish between nature and feelings, as did Chu Hsi.[27]

Wang Yang-ming (1472–1529) was originally called Wang Shou-jen. His work is the culmination of the School of Mind (Idealist school). Along with Chu Hsi, he is probably the most significant philosopher until modern times. His systematization of the School of Mind became extremely influential for the next two centuries.

His most important idea is his theory of the "extension of knowledge." By knowledge, Wang means intuitive knowledge. Intuitive knowledge is completed by activity consistent with that knowledge. In this respect, he strongly upholds the unity of knowledge and action.

Empirical School

This school is also known as the Return to the Han Learning.[28] Members of this school believed that the teachings of neo-Confucianists during the Sung and Ming dynasties became overly speculative and impractical, polluted by Taoist and Buddhist ideas. They proposed a return to the original Confucian ideas, which were less abstract and more anchored in concrete, everyday concerns. They especially advocated those teachings espoused by Confucius and Mencius. This meant a revival of interest in the four great texts: *Analects, Mencius, Doctrine of the Mean,* and *Great Learning.*

Tai Chen is the most renown representative of this empirical (that is, more down-to-earth and practical) response. He attempted to restore the practical teachings of Confucius and Mencius. In so doing, he tried to reestablish a harmony between principle and material force.

K'ang Yu-wei proposed the radical thesis that Confucius was actually attempting a political reform. K'ang advocated a constitutional monarchy and was able to influence the emperor to enact reform measures. This was the famous, though unsuccessful, "Hundred Days of Reform" (June 11–September 20, 1898).

Because of his active role in the Hundred Days of Reform, T'an Ssu-t'ung was one of the "six martyrs" executed in 1898. In his own unique way he synthesized ideas from modern physics and chemistry and expounded on the idea of love and the role it plays in bringing about what he believed to be the coming third age of the Great Unity.

Liao P'ing proposed that both the original texts and New Text versions all reflect ideas from Confucius. He felt that Confucius's teachings transcended the borders of China and represented a world philosophy.

Modern Period

Three highlights mark the modern period in China. First, after the formation of the Chinese Republic in 1912, John Dewey and Bertrand Russell came in 1919 and 1920 to deliver special lectures at the University of Peking. Not only was this the first time Western philosophers had come to China, but it signaled a new interest in logic. Of all the Western philosophical imports in the early twentieth century (Nietzsche, Descartes, Bergson, Schopenhauer, James, Dewey, Marx, and so on), James and Dewey rank among the most prominent.

Second, Marxism found fertile ground in the Chinese temperament and eventually became the official doctrine. It stresses a more scientific, practical, world-affirming posture. A major proponent of dialectical materialism in China is Mao Tse-tung (1894–1976). Yet he is known more for his political stature, and his writings possess little philosophical value. Marxism had a minor bearing on contemporary Chinese thought; its success can be partly explained by its accommodation to Confucian teachings, such as filiality.

Third, Confucian thought was again revived, along with openness to Western teaching. Here are some examples.

Fung Yu-lan (1895–1990) taught at the universities of Pennsylvania and Hawaii after having been educated at Peking and Columbia universities. He went from being an ardent defender of traditional Confucianism to finally becoming a defender of Marxist-Maoist thought.[29]

Fung reflects more the Rationalist school in Neo-Confucianism. He deals with the primary metaphysical notions of *li, ch'i, Tao,* and Great Unity. He composed the classic *History of Chinese Philosophy,* and he is also known for forming his own combination of Neo-Confucianism and Western philosophical forms.

Hsiung Shih-li (1885–1968) taught philosophy at Peking University. His ideas are influenced by the *I Ching* and the Consciousness Only school, and he is regarded as one of the most original of contemporary thinkers.

Chang Tung-sun (1886–1962) is one of the most influential of contemporary philosophers. Perhaps the most important issue for him concerned the problem of knowledge. He was especially interested in the relationship between knowledge and culture.

To this day, China still wears its Confucian mantle, reinforcing the same Confucian virtues that have sustained Chinese culture over these millennia. China continues to cherish the virtues of filiality and to uphold the centrality of the family. It remains to be seen whether and to what extent Western influence, especially through technology, will affect the future of Chinese philosophy.

━━━ Japanese Philosophies ━━━

The history of Japanese philosophy can be divided into four periods:

- Period of Antiquity
- Medieval Buddhism
- Tokugawa Confucianism
- Modern Period

Period of Antiquity: Nara and Heian Schools

Early Japanese Buddhism

The indigenous belief system in Japan is known as Shinto, or *Kami-no-michi,* the Way of the Gods. It is a complex conglomeration of myths, beliefs in nature divinities, and varieties of rituals. As popular as the native Shinto beliefs were, however, they lacked a philosophical foundation.

Buddhism provided the Japanese with a more philosophical base, and its influence became so far-reaching that it has, without doubt, affected almost every aspect of Japanese life.

According to the first chronicle of Japan, the *Nihonshoki,* Buddhism first arrived in Japan from Paekche in Korea in the sixth century C.E. Buddhism was first considered to be a useful instrument to prevent illness and drought. For the Japanese, Buddhism also enhanced the central roles of loyalty and family.[30] Furthermore, it was not long before there was intense aristocratic patronage for Buddhism. In this regard, Prince Shotoku (574–622) played a significant role in its expansion. Due to his efforts, many great temples in the vicinity of the capital were constructed. The most famous temple of the period was Todaiji, completed in 749, containing a giant statue of Vairocana Buddha, the Supreme Buddha.

This period was marked by a dominance of two groups of schools: Nara schools and Heian schools.

Nara Schools (701–794) Differences in interpretation eventually led to the formation of six schools, located at the capitol, Nara. These six schools were the Sanron, Jojitsu, Hosso, Kusha, Ritsu, and Kegon.

Sanron means "three treatises," and this school is in effect the first philosophical school in Japan. This school of the Three Treatises was established in 625 by a Korean monk, Ekkan. These three treatises, the cornerstone of the Madhyamika tradition, are Nagarjuna's *Madhyamika Karika* and *Dvadasad-vara*, and Aryadeva's *Satrasastra*. Another important text from this school is Ansho's (763–814) *Churon-shoki,* a commentary on Nagarjuna's *Madhyamika-sastra.* The central teaching in the school centers around the idea of *sunyata,* or emptiness. All things are *sunya;* that is, without substantiality. No thing exists on its own.

Jojitsu was more of an exegetical school that later merged with Sanron. It utilizes ideas of *sunyata.* The school is based on the *Sattyasiddhi Sastra* (*Jojitsu-ron*), written by Harivarman (250–350).[31]

The Hosso school is founded upon the *Yuishiki* doctrine, "only consciousness," and continues the Yogacara tradition. This was introduced to Japan by Dosho around 650. The main teaching is that all reality is purely consciousness. Dosho's successors include some well-known Japanese patriarchs such as Gyogi (670–749), who is responsible for the spreading popularization of Buddhism.

The Kusha school assigns a qualified reality to *dharma,* the "ultimate elements of existence." This school is based on Vasubandhu's treatise, *Abhidharma-kosha-sastra.*

The Ritsu school arose partly in opposition to these metaphysical teachings and in reaction to the growing laxity of Buddhist monks. It is essentially based on the *vinaya* tradition, or code of monastic discipline. *Ritsu* means "discipline."

The Kegon school's central message is the "Net of *Brahma,*" or the myriad representations or manifestations of the universal Buddha, called Roshana. The Kegon school is founded on the teachings of the *Avatamsaka Sutra* (Jap. Kegon Sutra). The Kegon Sutra was to be the official work upon which the great Todaiji temple, Daikegonji, was built.[32] This was another step in further supporting the divine descent of the emperor. Today, three Nara schools still exist: Hosso, Ritsu, and Kegon.

Heian Schools (794–1185) For a number of reasons, the capital was moved to Heian. Buddhism became more interiorized, acquiring more Japanese features through two influential Buddhist schools: Tendai and Shingon.

The Tendai school was founded by Saicho (767–822), later called Dengyo Daishi (Master Dengyo). Saicho was commissioned by Emperor Kamu to travel to China and to return with the best type of Buddhism. In Japan, his monastery was situated on Mount Hiei, the center of the "new Tendai Lotus sect." Just as the T'ien-t'ai school in China was a reaction against other schools, the Tendai school in Japan grew in opposition to the metaphysical and overly abstract emphases of some of the Nara schools.

The main text of the Tendai school (as with T'ien-t'ai) is the *Saddharma-pundarika Sutra,* or the Lotus Sutra (in Japanese, *Hokke-kyo*). This work teaches that all are capable of becoming Buddhas.

The Shingon school was founded by Kukai (774–835), later known as Kobo Daishi, or Master Kobo. In the Chinese capital of Ch'ang-an he studied Esoteric Buddhism, or Tantric or Mantrayana Buddhism, known in China as Chen Yen. Shingon devotees are convinced that Kukai did not really die, but instead entered meditation waiting for the descent of Maitreya Buddha (the future Buddha).[33]

Shingon means "true word" and is derived from the Sanskrit term *mantra* and the Chinese term *chen-yen.* For the court and ordinary people, much of Shingon's appeal was its emphasis on spells and magical formula and mantras. Shingon had an immense effect on the arts. The central teaching in Shingon is that the entire universe is composed of the body of the supreme Buddha, Vairocana.

During this time there was a sense of historical crisis, a result of the change from a centralized bureaucracy to a feudalistic, fragmented political order. The theory of *mappo* (Latter Day of the Holy Law) illustrates this. According to this theory, Buddhism would experience a decline in three stages, and the last stage had already started. This instilled faith in the saving power of the Buddha Amida, and the sincere invocation and repetition of the formula "*Namu Amida Butsu*" would eventually ensure a place in Amida's paradise, known as the Pure Land.

Another popular belief, though less so than Amida, was belief in Maitreya's Paradise, a place where all would be welcome, depending on one's attitude of genuine remorse.

Early Confucianism

When the Chinese written language was introduced to Japan (c. 404), Confucian ideas also accompanied the passage.[34]

Whereas Buddhism provided the Japanese with a metaphysical scheme having practical application to ordinary life, Confucian ideas also provided notions of and justification for a more orderly universe. Its rich social ethics were especially attractive to the Japanese.

In centers of learning, Confucian thought became the most prominent discipline. Required texts included the *Analects, Book of Rites,* the *Odes, Spring and Autumn Annals,* the *Great Learning, I Ching, Mencius,* and *Doctrine of the Mean.*

Confucian ideas have had a far-reaching effect on early Japanese life in many ways. For example, for the Chinese the emperor possessed the "mandate" of Heaven, of *T'ien.* In other words, it was the will, or decree, of Heaven that the emperor establish order on earth, just as there is order in the heavens. Here we see a mutual relation between Heaven and human affairs that somehow fits in with the Japanese notion of divine ancestry.[35] Further, the Confucian emphasis on filial piety enhanced the indigenous Japanese belief in the critical importance of family and clan.[36]

The durability of Confucian thought in early Japan displays itself later during the Middle Ages, when it began to occupy a seat closer to center stage. During the Tokugawa period, Buddhism was almost completely displaced by Confucian thought.

Medieval Buddhism

After a long and bitter struggle for power, a whole new warrior class was eventually established, with headquarters at Kamakura. These times were generally marked by disorder, and there was a need for religious teachings to offer comfort.

Three new schools of Buddhism obtained such a strong foothold in the Japanese consciousness that they continue to be a major influence today. These schools are the Pure Land school (*Jodo*), the Lotus school (*Hokke*), and Zen Buddhism.

Jodoshu, or Pure Land School

Although the seeds of this school were planted earlier, it grew to be on its own through the teachings of Hōnen Shōnin.[37]

Hōnen Shōnin (1133–1212) is also known as Genku. After studying Tendai Buddhism, he believed that its teachings did not offer enough for ordinary people. His quest led him to the insight that through simple faith in the Amida Buddha—expressed in calling out the Buddha's name, *nembutsu*—rebirth into the Pure Land called *Jodo* could occur for the true believer. Thereupon Hōnen founded his school, called Jodoshu (Pure Land school), in 1175.

For Hōnen, one attains salvation either through self-exerted efforts, *jiriki* (self-power), or through total reliance upon another, *tariki* (other-power). Hōnen favored *tariki*. He taught that complete trust in the saving power of Amida will guarantee the believer an honored place in the Pure Land after death. It was left to his most influential disciple, Shinran, to carry Hōnen's idea to its extreme.

While exiled in the northern part of Japan, Shinran (1173–1262) founded the Jodo Shinshu, or True Sect of Jodo, one of a number of separate schools within Jodo. He singled out and underscored the idea of Amida's all-powerful compassion and mercy. In fact, Amida's mercy is such that the redemption of all human beings has already taken place. This meant that all persons were already saved. Shinran also taught that no real distinctions exist between monk and layperson, between teacher and student. Jodo teachings continue to act as a powerful influence in Japanese thought.

Hokke School of Nichiren

Nichiren (1222–1282) remains one of the most intriguing and influential figures in Japanese history. At age twelve he began to learn Chinese and to seriously study Tendai and Shingon ideas. Nichiren acquired a special interest in the Lotus Sutra, which he later claimed as the culmination of Buddha's teachings.

His task was to reform Tendai Buddhism. His new-found faith in the Lotus Sutra, and his insistence that only through it can one be saved, earned him some spirited animosity.[38] Nichiren spent his remaining years in retirement in a mountain retreat, still teaching and writing. For Nichiren, the degeneracy of the times was a symptom of the perversion in learning because the Jodo and Zen sects held sway over many followers.

Today there are still millions of adherents of the *Hokke,* or Lotus, school. They still proselytize in the same military spirit imbedded in the character of its founder.[39]

Zen School

The term *Zen,* meaning "meditation," is derived from the Chinese term *ch'an,* which comes from the Sanskrit *dhyana*—that is, meditation. In Chinese Ch'an, two main divisions came about: the Lin-chi and the Ts'ao-tung sects. The Lin-chi sect emphasized the immediacy of enlightenment through *koans,* or riddles. The Ts'ao-tung sect, on the other hand, emphasized the central role of quietly sitting in meditation as the method for achieving insight.

This division was later transplanted into Japan with the two schools, Rinzai and Soto: The Rinzai school represented the Lin-chi's emphasis on instant awakening through *koans.* Eisai was its founder. The Soto school underscored the importance of sitting meditation, or *zazen,* as a way of gradually achieving this enlightenment. Dogen was its founder. Actually, Zen monks and practitioners often utilize methods from each school. By the time Ch'an entered Japan, it incorporated features of Taoism. As it developed further, it acquired its own Japanese flavor.

It was Zen's stark simplicity that won its many adherents. It also instilled a practical code of ethics with real social significance. In a sense, Zen Buddhism in Japan came about as a result of a dialogue among Buddhism, Taoism, and Confucianism. It was certainly this practical ethics that curried favor with the samurai. Not only did it demand the utmost in self-discipline, but it taught a resolute indifference and courage in the face of death, with which the samurai constantly flirted.

Zen Buddhism has become genuinely representative of the Japanese temperament. It is difficult to find even one sphere of life and culture in Japan that has not been permeated profoundly by Zen teachings. Martial art forms such as archery, karate, kendo, and judo certainly use Zen ideas. Gardening and the tea ceremony (*cha-no-yu*), as well as calligraphy and poetry, exhibit Zen influence.[40]

The principal teaching behind Zen involves the following:

- Transmitting knowledge outside of scriptures
- Not relying on written material
- Pointing directly to one's Mind
- Attaining Buddhahood by seeing into one's Nature[41]

Here we see the special emphasis placed on the faculty of intuition in Zen—that is, a more immediate, preconceptualized form of knowing. There is no reliance on sacred writings or sutras. Furthermore, the experience is direct and truly intimate. Zen is intensely experiential. Furthermore, there is no need to depend on some external savior or force. The seeds of realization lie within one's own nature.

Eisai (1141–1214) is responsible for transplanting Ch'an teachings into Japan. He is often referred to as the father of Japanese Zen. In 1187 he transmitted the Lin-chi school of Ch'an to the Japanese. This was called the Rinzai school. Eisai believed that Zen was consistent with the true teachings of Tendai.[42]

During the Kamakura period, the Rinzai Zen of Eisai flourished due to official patronage. Zen grafted itself on many aspects of culture in China, such as the famous Sung dynasty paintings. Chinese influences in turn became deeply rooted in Japan while Japan finally began to achieve more identity on its own. The Rinzai influence on Japanese art is profound, perhaps more profound than as an intellectual force.

Dogen (1200–1253) is one of Japan's most original and brilliant thinkers. He is even revered as a *bodhisattva* by Buddhists. Upon the deaths of both parents when he was still young, Dogen realized the precocious nature of human existence and the transiency of all things.

As a young monk, his most plaguing question—one that was to carry him throughout his career—concerned the nature of the relationship between the truth of our intrinsic Buddha-nature and the need for spiritual cultivation through meditation and such. In other words, if we are already Buddhas, then why is practice so important?

In China, both Dogen and his beloved teacher Myozen came under the instruction of Ju-ching (1163–1268), who made a most lasting impression on the young monk Dogen. Ju-ching was known for his strict ascetic approach to Zen, and during meditation Ju-ching admonished a student, "In Zen, body and mind are cast off. Why do you sleep?" Dogen overheard this, and it is said that he immediately attained enlightenment.[43] Ju-ching himself transmitted the seal of succession to Dogen.

Dogen's most famous work is his classic treatise, *Shobogenzo (Treasury of Knowledge Regarding the True Dharma)*. It is a monument to the study of *zazen*, which is sitting meditation.[44]

The century before the reunification of Japan during the Tokugawa period (1603–1867) is known as *Sengoku,* "Warring States." This was the time of almost nonstop warfare among various factions for territorial control. This constant and bitter struggle forged the rise of new regional authorities called *daimyos,* or military leaders.

Then came a phase in Japanese history that is certainly one of the most colorful and is the subject of much legend and literature. Due to the strength and persistence of three brilliant military leaders, Japan was transformed from a fragmented nation filled with pockets of contentious *daimyo* rulers to a unified state. These three leaders were Oda Nobunaga (1534–1582), Toyotomi Hideyoshi (1536–1598), and Tokugawa Ieyasu (1542–1616). It was Ieyasu who was able to complete the work of Nobunaga and Hideyoshi and establish hegemony over the *daimyo* and initiate stability and unity lasting over two and a half centuries.

Tokugawa Confucianism

This period began with the absolute rule of the Shogun Tokugawa Ieyasu. It is marked by a number of outstanding features: a policy of national seclusion (*sakoku*), the suppression of Christianity, a change in the life-style and interests of the samurai, a strong class consciousness, the rise of the merchant class, and, most important, the increasing interest in and prestige allotted to Neo-Confucianism. The period witnessed three major streams of Neo-Confucianism:

- Chu Hsi (*Shushi-gakuha*)
- Wang Yang-ming (*Yomei-gakuha*)
- Ancient Learning (*Kogakuha*) (see Table 1.5)

Confucian teachings eventually provoked a vigorous reaction from a school called *Kokugaku*, or the School of National Learning, which helped forge a Japanese national consciousness and spirit.[45] Next we examine the three major streams of Neo-Confucianism.

Neo-Confucian Schools

Chu Hsi School (Shushi-gakuha)   The Chu Hsi school emphasized the following works: *Analects, Book of Mencius, Great Learning,* and *Doctrine of the Mean.*
　　To review, the Supreme Ultimate plays the key role in Chu Hsi's philosophy. From the Supreme Ultimate emanates the two universal forces, yin and yang, which then bring about the Five Elements, and through these elements express themselves, causing everything in the universe to exist and to develop. Humanity and nature are expressions of this Supreme Ultimate.
　　Scholarship and serious study also play a pivotal role in Chu Hsi's thought. It is through an intense investigation of things that an understanding of the principles of Heaven can come about. Despite competition from other schools, the Chu Hsi school maintained its hegemony due to the political patronage it received. Here are some of its representatives.
　　From early on, Fujiwara Seika (1561–1619) was introduced to Zen thought. However, he consequently became immersed in Chinese studies. Due to his prestige and his own influence and connections, he provided a "spiritual dimension" for the ruling class.[46] What was most important for him was the inner, personal assimilation of the truths expressed in the classics.
　　Hayashi Razan (1583–1657) came from a *ronin* (wandering, or masterless, samurai) family and studied under Fujiwara Seika. Because of his wide learning in Chinese studies, he came under the long employ of the *bakufu*, or official government, during the rule of the first three shoguns. Razan later founded a school called Hayashi College.
　　Yamazaki Ansai (1618–1682) was the son of a *ronin* who became an acupuncturist. Neo-Confucianism attracted him more firmly as he left the

Table 1.5 Japanese Neo-Confucian Schools

School	Prominent Figure		Text
Chu Hsi (Shushi)	Fujiwara Seika	(1561–1619)	—
	Hayashi Razan	(1583–1657)	—
	Yamazaki Ansai	(1618–1682)	—
	Kaibara Ekken	(1630–1714)	Yamato Zokkun Record of Grave Doubts
Wang Yang-ming (Yomei-gakuha)	Nakae Toju	(1608–1648)	—
	Kumazawa Banzan	(1619–1691)	—
	Oshio Heihachiro	(1794–1837)	—
Ancient Learning (Kogakuha)	Yamago Soko	(1622–1685)	The Essence of Confucianism
	Ito Jinsai	(1627–1705)	
	Ogyu Sorai	(1666–1728)	Bendo (Defining the Way) Bemmei (Definitions of Terms)

Rinzai Buddhist order when he was twenty-eight. His identity with Chu Hsi was strong. Eventually his interest turned more seriously to Shinto. In fact, he perceived a strong affinity between Shinto and Confucianism.

One of the most influential representatives of the Chu Hsi Neo-Confucian school was Kaibara Ekken (1630–1714).[47] Ekken's ancestors were Shinto priests, and he came from a samurai background. His wife was Buddhist, but he favored Confucian teachings. His brother Sonzai was profoundly influential in Ekken's life. Both Sonzai and his father were educated in medicine, and their interest was shared with Ekken. Due to encouragement from Sonzai, he turned his interest to Confucianism.

Ekken's interests were remarkably broad, including astronomy, the study of plants, medicine, and agriculture. He has been called the "Aristotle of Japan."[48] What is especially important about Ekken is his constant desire to make Neo-Confucianist teachings accessible and understandable to ordinary people.

Wang Yang-ming School (Yomei-gakuha) Wang Yang-ming's ideas were a radical turn from the orthodox teachings, for they emphasized the key role of intuition rather than intellection. This school stressed action over analysis as the determinant of valid knowledge. In addition, by endorsing self-scrutiny, his teachings enhanced a spirit of autonomy especially atypical in the Tokugawa period of strong conformity and deference to authority. The leading proponents of this school were Nakae Toju, Kumazawa Banzan, and Oshio Heihachiro.

Nakae Toju (1608–1648) is traditionally considered the founder of the *Yomei-gakuha* in Japan. His most important ideas centered around the intuitive character of each person, which can be reached thrugh both introspection and action. Furthermore, filial peity, or *ko,* is the most important virtue and the foundation for all existence. This emphasis on filial piety was universalized, extending to all classes, including women, and this was a powerful alluring aspect of Nakae's teachings.

Kumazawa Banzan (1619–1691) is perhaps the most famous student of Nakae Toju. He and his father were *ronin*. Banzan was most concerned about the plight of the poor peasants, and he used *Yomei* teachings in order to reform the fief he ministered close to Osaka.

Oshio Heihachiro (1794–1837) was a renowned scholar who showed special interests in both philosophy and the martial arts.[49] As police inspector at Osaka, he effectively mounted a campaign against the endemic corruption that existed among public officials. For example, he insisted that the 1837 famine in Osaka was not an "act of Heaven" (*tensai*) but an "act of government" (*seisai*) and an abuse of funds. He conducted a short-lived open revolt against the authorities, who swiftly suppressed the uprising. His remaining followers were apprehended and executed. Although Oshio managed to escape in dramatic fashion, upon his return to Osaka in disguise he and his son were discovered at the home of a towel-merchant, where they killed themselves in a burning shed.[50]

School of Ancient Learning (Kogakuha)   The School of Ancient Learning reacted against the Neo-Confucian dissemination. Its proponents felt that there needed to be a genuine return to the ancient teachings of the sages, both Confucius and Mencius. Among its leading representatives were Yamago Soko, Ito Jinsai, and Ogyu Sorai.

Not only was Yamago Soko (1622–1685) a leading advocate of *kogakuha*, but he is known as one of the proponents of *Bushido* ("Way of the Warrior"), a foundation for military ethics. As a young boy he became educated in Chu Hsi thought in the Hayashi College. An avid pursuit of his was the military arts, and he taught it in unique fashion, even advocating the use of firearms.

Due to his critique of Shushi and to his support of the use of firearms as well as other novelties in the martial arts, he was banished from the capital, Edo. During his sequester he taught several samurai in the surrounding area. Forty-seven of them would consequently achieve distinction for future generations of Japanese because of their revenge upon a nobleman who dishonored their lord. They afterwards committed suicide. Their story, *The Forty-seven Ronin,* has become a classic in Japanese literature and history.

Instructed early in Chu Hsi thought, Ito Jinsai (1627–1705) especially revered the teachings of Confucius and Mencius. Jinsai was opposed to the moral rigorism of the Chu Hsi School, which judged everything in terms of principle. In addition, for Jinsai it is the positive consequences of actions that are the real indicators of what is right, more so than the intentions.

Having been educated in the Chinese classics, at one point in his early career Ogyu Sorai (1666–1728) actually defended Chu Hsi's ideas against the critique of Ito Jinsai. He urged that the teachings of antiquity needed to be restored. He also emphasized the political significance of Confucian antiquity.[51]

In Chu Hsi's opinion, personal morality and public values were compatible. According to Sorai, the two were distinct, and motives (*kokoro*) clash here with what is in the public interest, which should always take precedence.

Rangaku and Nationalism

The Tokugawa period saw an increasing interest in Western studies and rationalism. This was known as *Rangaku*, or Dutch studies. Through the Dutch, the Japanese familiarized themselves more with Western sciences such as medicine. Several people were prominent in Rangaku.

Miura Baien (1723–1789) was especially interested in Western dialectics and sciences. Ando Shoeki (c. 17th–18th century), who studied medicine at Nagasaki, was quite critical of aspects of Shinto and Buddhism. Ishida Baigan (1685–1744) formulated a system of ethics combining approaches from various schools.

Kokugaku was the "national learning school," an effort to find support of a distinct national identity and preeminence in the early literature and native documents. In asserting that the shogun also serves the emperor, the school provided a direct challenge to the shogun's prevailing hegemony. Thus, a national consciousness is born and is signified in a concrete political tone.

Kamo Mabuchi (1697–1769) was responsible for instituting a school of "ancient learning" to resuscitate traditional ideas before the influx of both Buddhist and Confucian teachings in Japan. Motoori Norinaga (1730–1801) wrote commentaries on the *Kojiki,* the oldest recorded chronicles in Japanese history. He essentially provided a theoretical basis for a revival of Shinto.[52]

Modern Period

Japan's modern period starts with the Meiji Restoration in 1868, when Japan opened its doors to Western trade, signaling a radical break from the feudal tradition that had long held a tight grip on Japanese society and consciousness.

One of the prominent aspects of Japanese philosophy today is its inheritance of Western ideas and methodologies. This is an assimilation of various trends and eventually an adaptation of ideas germane to the characteristic features of Japanese thinking, though it should be clear by now (as with India and China) that there is no monolithic net we can cast over the Japanese.

The philosophical scene in the past few decades has been quite complex and has included a variety of trends imported from Western philosophy. Several striking new features have appeared in Japanese philosophy since World War II: (1) After World War II, Marxism became a dominant intellectual force. Marxists were among those few who registered protests against the strong tide of ultranationalism before the war. Marxism gained in strength for a variety of reasons, including its stance as a voice against the imperialist reign that has dominated Japan for some years. (2) Analytical philosophy, with special emphases on logical positivism and philosophy of language, became more popular. (3) The philosophy of science has enjoyed growing

Table 1.6   Modern Japanese Philosophers

Prominent Figure and Field		Prominent Figure and Field	
Nishi Amane (1829–1897)	*Tetsugaku*	Abe Jiro (1883–1959)	Personalism
Kato Hiroyuki (1836–1916)	German philosophy	Tomonaga Sanjuro (1871–1951)	Self and culture
Nakae Tokusuke	French philosophy	Amano Teiyu (1884–1978)	Universal ethic
Nishimura Shigeki (1828–1902)	Japanese morality	Hatano Seiichi (1877–1950)	Philosophy of religion
Inoue Enryo (1859–1919)	Tendai, Kegon, Hegel	Kawakami Hajime (1879–1946)	Marxism and Religion
Inoue Tetsujiro (1855–1944)	Nationalism	Miki Kiyoshi (1897–1945)	Marxist humanism
Onishi Hajime (1864–1900)	Critical thinking	Oshima Yasumasa (1917–)	Ethics
Watsuji Tetsuro (1889–1960)	Ethics	Nishida Kitaro (1870–1945) Tanabe Hajime (1885–1962) Nishitani Keiji (1900–1990)	Kyoto School

interest. (4) Special fields of study became more prominent, such as ancient Greek philosophy and comparative philosophy; Nakamura Hajime is a noteworthy philosopher of comparative studies. (5) There has been increasing interest in the individual, as demonstrated in the personalism that has grown in some circles.

Next we briefly consider some modern philosophers who represent a variety of fields (see Table 1.6). Nishi Amane (1829–1897) is also called the "father of modern philosophy in Japan."[53] In fact, the term for philosophy, *tetsugaku* ("science of questing wisdom"), originates with Nishi. Kato Hiroyuki (1836–1916) is responsible for advancing German philosophy as a major impetus at Tokyo University, of which he was president in 1881 and 1900. Inoue Enryo (1859–1919) believes that the Buddhist sects of Tendai and Kegon have an affinity with certain Hegelian ideas.

Onishi Hajime (1864–1900) underscored the importance of critical thinking, which he applied especially to the growing preoccupation with Western ideas and an increasing nationalism. Hatano Seiichi's (1877–1950) interests lay especially in a philosophy of religion, influenced especially by Plotinus and Kant. Kawakami Hajime (1879–1946) strove to resolve the conflict between religious principles and Marxist science. Miki Kiyoshi (1897–1945) represented the independent spirit of many Marxists during a time of increasing nationalism. Miki criticized the Japanese militarists, and his brand of Marxism is grounded on a strong Marxist humanism. He was imprisoned twice for his ideas, and he finally died in prison.

Kyoto School of Philosophy

Nishida Kitaro (1870–1945) is regarded as the most important modern philosopher in Japan. His followers spread his ideas and established the Kyoto school. He was one of the true original and creative thinkers in Japan. He is certainly unique in his effort to interpret Asian philosophical ideas such as intuition in a Western philosophical format and style. We will discuss him in further depth in some subsequent chapters. Nishida's premier philosophical work is *Zen No Kenkyu (A Study of the Good),* written in 1911. It consists of three leading ideas (reality, ethics, religion), all based on his notion of "pure experience."

Tanabe Hajime (1885–1962) is the second great representative of the Kyoto school. His interest in science is evident in his earlier works. He was quite impressed by Neo-Kantianism, Husserl, and Nishida. He is especially known for his "logic of species," also called "logic of mediation," through which he attempts to provide a more concrete, historical ground in his thought.

Nishitani Keiji (1900–1990) is the third leading representative of the Kyoto school. He further examined the Buddhist idea of emptiness to find positive merit in it as a teaching of "creative nothingness."[54]

Watsuji Tetsuro (1889–1960)

Watsuji stands as one of the most important modern philosophers in the field of ethics. His ethics is based on a philosophical anthropology that stresses the strong Japanese notion of relationality. Watsuji demonstrated a strong interest in early Greek philosophy, Nietzsche, and Kierkegaard. He was also interested in intellectual and cultural history, especially that of Japan.

An intriguing work is his *Fudo (Climate: A Philosophical Study),* written in 1928–29 (published in 1935). In it he discusses the importance of relationality with our environment and climate and gives this relationship a unique philosophical meaning. His system of ethics developed from his lectures at Kyoto University. His major premise is that ethics is related to the science of humanity and to humanity's natural relational intercourse.

Study Questions

India

1. What are the essential differences between orthodox and heterodox Indian schools, and between Hindu and non-Hindu systems?
2. What is the difference between texts that are inspired by *sruti* and those by *smrti?* Give examples.
3. What are the main teachings in the principal Upanishads?
4. Summarize the major plots in the great Indian epics.
5. Describe the heterodox schools and their major ideas.
6. Discuss the development of philosophical speculation from the Vedas through the Upanishads.

7. Describe the main emphases in each of the six orthodox Indian schools of philosophy.
8. What major texts form the basis of the Vedanta school?
9. Discuss the three most important commentators on Vedanta and their respective positions.
10. Describe some modern Indian thinkers and prominent features in modern Indian philosophy.
11. Discuss the Three Jewels of Buddhism.
12. Describe events in the splitting up of Buddhism into two major systems.
13. What are some of the more important teachings in the early Buddhist schools?
14. Discuss the prominent schools, representatives, and leading ideas in Mahayana Buddhism.
15. Describe major reasons for Buddhism's decline in India.

China

16. Name the most important early Confucians and describe some of their teachings.
17. Contrast emphases in the Taoist and Confucian teachings and give examples.
18. Discuss the meanings of *Tao, te,* and *wu-wei.*
19. Explain the meaning of Mo Tzu's utilitarianism in view of his teaching of universal love.
20. How do Han Fei Tzu and the Legalist school view the source of law, in contrast to Confucianists?
21. What are some highlights during the Chinese Middle Period?
22. What is the essential difference between the New Text and the Old Text schools in Confucianism? Name their representatives.
23. How did the Neo-Taoist view of Tao possibly enable more acceptance of Buddhist ideas?
24. Describe differences between Confucian and Buddhist teachings.
25. What are some reasons for the acceptance of Buddhist teachings in China?
26. Describe the major Chinese Buddhist schools and their teachings, especially T'ien-t'ai and Ch'an.
27. Why did Buddhist teachings arouse opposition from Confucians, and how did Neo-Confucians respond?
28. Elaborate upon Chu Hsi's teachings concerning *T'ai-chi, li,* and *ch'i.*
29. Contrast the leading ideas in the School of Principle and the School of Mind through teachings of their representatives.
30. What was the nature of the critique of Neo-Confucian rationalists by the Empirical school?
31. What are some features of modern Chinese philosophy?

Japan

32. What are some highlights in the development of early Buddhism in Japan?

33. Discuss the Tendai and Shingon Buddhist schools: their representatives, texts, and ideas.
34. What was the appeal of both Buddhism and Confucianism for the Japanese?
35. Give examples of the influence of Confucianism on the Japanese.
36. Describe leading ideas and figures in the following major Japanese Buddhist schools: Jodo, Hokke, and Zen.
37. Discuss the development of Zen Buddhism in Japan: its split into two schools, its main ideas, and the reasons for its appeal to the Japanese.
38. Describe the three schools of Neo-Confucian thought in Japan and the reaction by Kokugaku.
39. List the most important Confucian texts in the Japanese Chu-Hsi, or Shushi, school. Describe some of its representatives and their ideas.
40. Contrast the ideas of Shushi and O-Yomei. Illustrate through their representatives.
41. What was the purpose of the Kogakuha school, and what texts were emphasized?
42. Explain the connection between Rangaku (Dutch studies) and Westernization.
43. How did Kokugaku contribute to building a national identity and consciousness?
44. What are the more prevailing features in modern and contemporary Japanese philosophy? Identify some philosophers and their ideas.
45. Describe the major ideas and leading figures in the Kyoto school.
46. Describe the main ideas of Watsuji Tetsuro.

Notes

1. The term *Hindu* comes from the name of the river Sindhu, which later became known as the Indus River. See P. T. Raju, *Structural Depths of Indian Thought* (Albany: State University of New York Press, 1985), 1. In fact, up until the fifteenth century, Indians did not refer to themselves as "Hindus," but as followers of the Noble Way, or *"Arya Dharma."* This Way encompassed different emphases, depending on whether the teachings were more specifically Buddhist, Jain, or traditionally Brahmanic. See Raju, 147.
2. This chronology is the consensus of most scholars. See John Koller, *Oriental Philosophies,* 2nd ed. (New York: Charles Scribner's Sons, 1985), 14ff.
3. S. Radhakrishnan, *Indian Philosophy* (London: George Allen & Unwin Ltd., 1923), Vol. 1, 77–78.
4. This order of Upanishads is Raju's. See Raju, 25.
5. The Code of Manu was highly regarded by the British as a meaningful text for gaining further understanding of the Hindu legal code because it provided a basis for later legal works. See A. L. Basham, *The Origins and Development of Classical Hinduism,* ed. and annot. by Kenneth G. Zysk (Boston: Beacon Press, 1989), 102.
6. Cited in Radhakrishnan, Vol. 2, 249.
7. An example of this *bhakti* revival is the extreme devotionalism of Chaitanya in the sixteenth century. There were no caste distinctions among his *bhakti* followers. One disciple, Swami Prabhupada, established the International Society for Krishna Consciousness (ISKCON), better known in the West as Hare Krishna.
8. Raju treats this more fully, 550–52.
9. Raju, 542.

10. The philosopher and commentator Surendrenath Dasgupta (1885–1952) often opposed a comparative approach, feeling that it could lead to misconstrued similarities.

11. Diganikaya 16, in H. Wolfgang Schumann, *Buddhism: An Outline of its Teachings and Schools,* trans. Georg Feuerstein (Wheaton, Illinois: Theosophical Publishing House, 1974), 31.

12. See Akira Hirakawa, *A History of Indian Buddhism: From Śākyamuni to Early Mahāyāna,* trans. and ed. Paul Groner, Asian Studies at Hawaii (Honolulu: University of Hawaii Press, 1990), 80ff, for a more complete discussion and description of alleged violations.

13. David J. Kalupahana, *A History of Buddhist Philosophy: Continuities and Discontinuities* (Honolulu: University of Hawaii Press, 1992), 126.

14. Two sources—the Pali canon, preserved in Sri Lanka, of the Theravada school, and the Sanskrit fragments, translated into Chinese—are the primary sources for the Buddhist canon as we now know it. The Buddhist teachings also consisted of commentaries on the canon. The most famous of these is written in Buddhaghosa's *Visuddhimagga,* or Path of Purification.

15. Edward Conze, *Buddhism: Its Essence and Development,* preface by Arthur Waley, 1951 (New York: Harper Torchbooks, Harper & Row, 1975), 29.

16. In China, the counterpart of the Madhyamika school is the San loen t'sung. The Japanese counterpart, called Sanron, later had an influence on the development of what was called either Ch'an or Zen Buddhism, respectively, in China and Japan.

17. Yogacara was brought to China in the sixth century and has maintained its hold there. Also, the seventh century witnessed Yogacara's entrance into Japan as the Hosso school.

18. Based on Wing-tsit Chan's outline in "Chinese Philosophy," *Encyclopedia of Philosophy,* Vol. 2, 87–95.

19. Much of what we know—not only about Confucius, but of the others within the Confucian school, such as Mencius—is found in the *Historical Records,* or *Shih Chi.*

20. Analects IV, 15, in Confucius, *Confucius: Confucian Analects, The Great Learning, and The Doctrine of the Mean,* Oxford, at the Clarendon Press, 1893, trans. James Legge (New York: Dover Publications, 1971), 170.

21. Analects XI, 15, 3, in Legge, 242.

22. The *hsieh* were somewhat like knights who, for a fee, would provide military protection. The *hsieh* professed an ethical code of conduct, and this code may have had a later bearing on Mo Tzu's philosophy.

23. An important text, composed later during the Middle period, is the *Huai-nan-tzu.* It describes the early beginnings, discussing the interchange and union of yin and yang in terms of the descent of heaven and the ascent of earth. See Fung Yu-lan, *A History of Chinese Philosophy,* trans. Derk Bodde (Princeton, New Jersey: Princeton University Press, 1952, 1953), Vol. 1, 395.

24. These patriarchs were Hui-k'o (487–593), Seng-ts'an (d. 606), Tao-hsin (580–636), and Hung-jen (606–675).

25. Heinrich Dumoulin, S. J., *A History of Zen Buddhism,* trans. Paul Peachey (Boston: Beacon Press, 1969), 81–82.

26. Some of the more important precursors of Neo-Confucianism are: Han Yü (768–824), Li Ao (d. c. 844), Chou Tun-yi (1017–1073), Shao Yung (1011–1077), and Ch'ang Tsai (1020–1077).

27. Lu Shiang-shan's ideas were elaborated on by his student Yang Chien (1140–1226). Yang Chien discusses Lu's concept of the mind as universe in his work called *The Self and The Book of Changes.* He states all things are within the mind.

28. The more significant contribution of Han Learning lies in areas of textual criticism, such as philology and epigraphy.

29. Fung was an advisor to Mao's wife, Chiang Ch'ing, part of the infamous "Gang of Four," all of whom met public disgrace after Mao's death in 1976. See Koller, 338.

30. When Buddhist images were first created, they were dedications to parents, symbols of gratitude by children. See G. B. Sansom, *Japan: A Short Cultural History* (Stanford,

California: Stanford University Press, 1978), 118. Consequently, the connection between ancestor respect and the funeral became prominent. Japanese Buddhism became later known as funerary Buddhism due to its association with the dead.

31. Nakamura Hajime, *A History of the Development of Japanese Thought from A.D. 592 to 1868,* 2nd ed. (Tokyo: Kokusai Bunka Shinkokai, 1969), 39.

32. Imagine the erection of the imposing figure of the Great Buddha in the Great Hall, having over one million pounds of metal. The emperor would then face the image, looking north, as an audience would face its sovereign. See Sansom, *Short Cultural History,* 128ff.

33. Kukai wrote a philosophical novel called *Indications to the Three Teachings,* regarded as one of the earliest novels in Japanese literature. In this novel, there is a dialogue among the three teachings of Confucianism, Taoism, and Buddhism. One of Kukai's most important works is his well-known *Jujushin-ron (Treatises on the Ten Stages of Spiritual Development).*

34. The straightforward polysyllabic composition of Japanese differed radically from the more subtle and complex monosyllabic Chinese, with its variance in tonalities and far more comprehensive vocabulary. It was especially its script that appealed to Japanese. Yet the task of translating Chinese terms into Japanese was most difficult. For more, see Sansom, *Short Cultural History,* 110–11.

35. The two are still distinct because the Japanese emperor's authority does not rely on virtue, as it does in China.

36. The emphasis on the teachings of antiquity stressed in Confucian thought probably inspired the Japanese to preserve their indigenous traditions all the more. Shinto beliefs were somehow selectively amalgamated with ideas from Confucianism and Buddhism. An interesting example of this occurred in 732, when a series of calamities plagued Japan and the emperor confessed that he was responsible. He bid the people to recite Buddhist sutras and prayers at various Shinto temples. See George Sansom, *A History of Japan to 1334* (Stanford, California: Stanford University Press, 1958), 75–76.

37. This school claims that it originates from the second century sutras *Sukhavativyuha* and *Amitayurdhyana* in India. *Sukhavati* means "land of bliss" and refers to this Pure Land or paradise called Jodo.

38. Between 1256 and 1261 all sorts of natural disasters and misfortunes befell Japan, including typhoons, floods, earthquakes, plagues and epidemics, famine, and floods. Nichiren was convinced—and he tried to persuade others, especially officials—that these were the results of the failure to adhere to the teachings in the Lotus Sutra. See Philip B. Yampolsky, ed., *Selected Writings of Nichiren,* trans. by Burton Watson and others (New York: Columbia University Press, 1990), 11–12.

39. Some of today's religious movements in Japan, such as Rissho Koseikai, Reiyukai, and Soka Gakkai, have been influenced by the spirit of Nichiren's Hokke School.

40. Soseki (1275–1351), one of the most brilliant monks during the Muromachi period, is especially known for his famous gardens. The most famous Zen garden is at the Ryoanji temple in Kyoto. See Dumoulin, 188–94, for further discussion of Japanese gardens.

41. Cited in Abbot Zenkei Shibayama, *A Flower Does Not Talk: Zen Essays,* trans. Sumiko Kudo (Rutland, Vermont: Charles E. Tuttle Company, 1970), 19–20.

42. Some histories connect Eisai with the development of the tea ceremony (*cha-no-yu*). The introduction of tea was also credited to Kukai, or Kobo Daishi, leader of Shingon.

43. Dumoulin, 156.

44. A present-day philosopher, Masao Abe, gives a superb critical analysis of Dogen in his *A Study of Dogen: His Philosophy and Religion,* ed. Steven Heine (Albany: State University of New York Press, 1992). His work also compares Dogen with both Heidegger and Shinran.

45. The nature of the association between the governing Bakufu and Neo-Confucianism is a debated issue. Current scholarship indicates that the Tokugawa regime did not intend to justify its own rule through an ideological edifice that uses Neo-Confucian teachings. For an excellent analysis, see Herman Ooms, *Tokugawa Ideology: Early*

Constructs, 1570–1680 (Princeton, New Jersey: Princeton University Press, 1989). Nevertheless, Neo-Confucian thought did appeal to a majority of scholars, whose teachings reached many corners of Tokugawa society.

46. See Ooms, 120–21.
47. More is known of Kaibara due to recent studies, especially the splendid introduction to his thought and translation of *Yamato Zokkun* by Mary Evelyn Tucker in *Moral and Spiritual Cultivation in Japanese Neo-Confucianism: The Life and Thought of Kaibara Ekken, 1630–1714,* trans. by Tucker, SUNY Series in Philosophy (Albany: State University of New York Press, 1989). Portions of his biography are adapted from Tucker, 31ff.
48. Ekken was called this by Philip Franz von Siebold (1796–1866), a German physician who visited Japan. Cited in Tucker, 41.
49. The modern-day writer Yukio Mishima wrote an article on Yomei and Oshio Heihachiro just before his own suicide after a failed attempt to take over the military headquarters in Tokyo. He claimed that a genuine representative of the Japanese spirit is Oshio Heihachiro. See Ivan Morris, *The Nobility of Failure: Tragic Heroes in the History of Japan* (New York: Meridian, New American Library, 1975), 180.
50. Months later, the court officially declared them guilty of insurrection, and their corpses were crucified as a public display and warning against further revolts. The court also forbade any memorial indicating his grave in order to prevent homage by devotees. See Morris, 210–12 for this dramatic account.
51. An interesting illustration of his ethics centers around the vendetta of the famous forty-seven ronin, who stood trial for having avenged their lord's dishonor by killing the perpetrator. Confucian scholars offered varying opinions, ranging from calling for their acquittal to their execution. From the personal viewpoint of the samurai, and in light of their motives, Confucian teachings seem to uphold their act. From the view of law, however, the means of vindication were illegal. Ogyu believed in upholding public interests through the law and recommended that they be allowed to commit *seppuku,* which was the final verdict. See discussion and story in Masao Maruyama, *Studies in the Intellectual History of Tokugawa Japan,* trans. Mikiso Hane (Princeton, New Jersey: Princeton University Press, 1989), 71–75.
52. Along these lines, a limb of Neo-Confucianism produced a school known as the Mito school, a group of historians who sought to provide evidence for primary authority to be subsumed by the emperor instead of the shogun.
53. Gino K. Piovesana, S. J., "Contemporary Japanese Philosophy," in *Asian Philosophy Today,* ed. Dale Riepe (New York: Gordon and Breach, Science Publishers, 1981), 223. The philosophers subsequently described in the text are described in this work.
54. Piovesana, 269.

2

Reality

It was the time when the autumn floods come down. A hundred streams swelled the River, that spread and spread till from shore to shore, nay from island to island so great was the distance that one could not tell horse from bull. The god of the River felt extremely pleased with himself. It seemed to him that all lovely things under heaven had submitted to his power. He wandered downstream, going further and further to the east, till at last he came to the sea. He gazed eastwards, confidently expecting to see the further shore. He could discern no end to the waters. Then the god of the River began to turn his head, peering this way and that; but still he could see no shore. At last, addressing the ocean, he said with a deep sigh: "There is a proverb which says,

> None like me
> Proves none so blind as he.

I fear it applies very well to myself . . . as I realize only too well when I gaze at your limitless immensity. Had I not this day enrolled myself as your disciple, I might have made myself the laughing-stock of all who take the Wider View." (Chuang Tzu)[1]

Indian Philosophies

Hindu Perspectives on Reality

The principal question this chapter addresses is: What is real? This question is deceptively simple, yet it is the most profound question of all. It gives birth to further elemental questions: What is ultimately real? Are there degrees of reality? What is the distinction between reality and appearance? Generally, these are questions of metaphysics. Metaphysics deals with the nature of being, beings, and the relation to a possible all-encompassing Being. Addressing these questions demands that we step outside of our regular vantage point, beyond our conventional horizons in order to look at the bigger picture, the "wider view."

Vedas

The search for reality was not cloaked in strict philosophical terms in the earliest writings of the Indians, the Vedas. The early Vedas consisted primarily of hymns, sacrificial litanies, and matters of ritual for various gods. These gods were embodied in natural forces such as the sky and the sun. Therefore, the earliest beliefs about ultimate realities were both polytheistic and animistic in character. For example, Agni, the god of fire, is also considered life-giving, one without whose power humanity would exist in perpetual darkness.

This polytheism gradually changed with time and further reflection. It perhaps seemed to make better sense that, of all the different gods, one deity should exist as the highest while still preserving a plurality of deities. This belief system is called henotheism.[2] Yet, it would be incorrect to claim that no philosophical disposition exists in the Vedas. One of the most important hymns in the *Rig Veda* is the so-called *Nasadiya Hymn,* which ponders the question of the source of the world. It asks whether this source is being (*sat*) or nonbeing (*asat*). This short hymn is included among the readings at the end of this chapter.

Upanishads

The question of reality becomes more prominent in the Upanishads. In these works, we find a number of vital ideas that have had a far-reaching influence throughout Indian philosophy. The most important ideas are expressed by the terms *atman, Brahman,* and *tat tvam asi. Atman* refers to our individual, eternal soul, our true Self. *Brahman* is the soul of the universe, the source of all reality. It is the Absolute Principle, the condition for existence, or the universal soul. The term *Brahman* comes from the root verb *brh,* which literally means "to grow." *Brahman* therefore conveys the sense of that which is ever-growing and dynamic and therefore without limits. This is unlike a static, abstract notion of the universal essence.

The most significant and far-reaching claim made in the Upanishads is that of the oneness of both *atman* and *Brahman.* This is disclosed through the famous phrase *tat tvam asi,* or "that you are." "That" refers to the universal principle, *Brahman,* and "you" refers to our essence, or *atman.* This teaching of the identity of self and ultimate reality remains the distinguishing feature in orthodox Indian thought, or what later came to be called "Hindu."

What a radical notion! My own true essence is identical with the Absolute! We read this in the opening chapter of the *Brihadaranyaka Upanishad:*

> This [self] was indeed *Brahman* in the beginning. It knew itself only as "I am *Brahman.*" Therefore it became all. And whoever among the

gods had this enlightenment, also became That [*Brahman*]. It is the same with the seers (rishis), the same with men. The seer Vamadeva, having realized this [self] as That, came to know: "I was Manu and the sun." And to this day, whoever in a like manner knows the self as "I am *Brahman*," becomes all this [universe]. Even the gods cannot prevent his becoming this, for he has become their Self.[3]

Bhagavad Gita

Before we look at the *Bhagavad Gita's* teachings concerning reality, we need some context. *Bhagavad Gita* literally means "Sung by the Lord," the "Lord" referring to the god Krishna, who is in disguised form as the main character Arjuna's charioteer. Its context is dramatic, taking place within the more global epic setting of the *Mahabharata*.

The *Mahabharata* is the story of the long and harsh conflict between two clans who are cousins: the Kauravas, sons of the blind Dhrtarastra, and the Pandavas, sons of Pandu. Pandu assumed kingship in place of the rightful candidate, his brother Dhrtarastra, because Dhrtarastra was blind. An enduring enmity existed between the cousins until a bitter war virtually destroyed both sides.

The *Bhagavad Gita* takes place on the eve of the war. Arjuna, one of the Pandavas, is about to lead his clansmen into battle. Now that he faces the impending battle, he is all the more aware of the terrible destruction and loss of life that will result for many of both clans. He becomes despondent, and he contemplates aborting the plan and thereby retreating from his duty. His charioteer is Krishna, and the entire poem is Krishna's address to Arjuna concerning the ultimate truths of reality, death, action, and duty (*dharma*).

In this context, how does the *Gita* address the meaning of reality? The essential message of Krishna is that all is Being and *Brahman* is Being. Because all is Being, and Being is permanent, then there is truly no annihilation, no final death.

In the *Gita, Brahman* is viewed as personal. Yet this personal *Brahman* is not limited by the world or by its events. It goes beyond the world. In this way, Krishna both announces and manifests the radical transcendence of *Brahman*. *Brahman* is all-encompassing. *Brahman* is Being.

From the human perspective of Arjuna, who is clouded by illusion (*maya*) and ignorance (*avidya*), things are separate from each other, especially life and death. He is still ignorant of the nature of reality.

Arjuna's depression is heightened because he confuses his true self with his ordinary ego, or *guna*. Krishna's message reminds Arjuna that the eyes and mind with which he perceives and conceives are empirically real, but not substantially real. Due to the tremendous power of *maya,* the true self, or *atman,* is ignored. From the perspective of this *atman,* all things exist in *Brahman.* As Krishna proclaims,

The dweller in the body of every one, O Bharata (Arjuna), is eternal and can never be slain. Therefore thou shouldst not grieve for any creature.[4]

To illustrate, let us look at that crucial point in the *Gita* when Krishna reveals his true nature as God. There are three aspects of God's nature that persistently manifest themselves in the triune depiction of God, or *Brahman:* Brahma, Vishnu, and Shiva.

- Brahma is the underlying creative principle of reality.
- Vishnu represents that aspect of this principle that proceeds to nourish and sustain existence. That Krishna is actually Vishnu in disguise comes across quite clearly in the character of Krishna, a person of loyal devotion and love.
- Shiva represents the destructive aspects of the divine principle. But this does not mean devastation in the absolute sense, for the destruction that occurs is also a creative force; that is, destroying the old clears a path for the new to emerge. The destructive energy of Shiva is therefore transformative. Shiva is often depicted in imagery as Lord of the Dance. Shiva dances within a circle of fire, the fire symbolizing destruction and purification. Shiva's power represents the unending dance of existence as the constant transformation of creation and destruction. At the same time, Shiva signals with her hand in assuring humanity not to fear this dance. With respect to Arjuna, the power of Shiva means that death will inevitably occur. This is part of the natural rhythm of God. Yet, from death, new life results.

The *Bhagavad Gita* combines the essence of teachings from the Vedas and Upanishads. It reaffirms the notion that salvation from life's sorrow can be achieved only when one fully realizes the truth that all reality is Being and remains so. This teaching about reality and Being forms the basis for the *Gita*'s philosophy of *dharma,* duty, or human action. This subject will be addressed in more detail in Chapter 5 on Ethics.

Orthodox Schools

Before we look more closely at the Vedanta teachings concerning reality, let us first briefly review some of the other orthodox schools.[5]

Vaisheshika (Nyaya-Vaisheshika)   Because of the similarities in their metaphysics as well as their theories of knowledge, Nyaya and Vaisheshika are usually classed together as Nyaya-Vaisheshika. The Nyaya school, however, actually adopted the original metaphysics of Vaisheshika. Let us look briefly at their views of reality.

The term *Vaisheshika* contains *visesa,* which literally means "particularity." In turn, the main concern of the Vaisheshika school is with the nature of reality, particularly the nature of the universe, or cosmology. In Vaisheshika, all material objects are reducible to undetectable entities called atoms, of which there were four kinds: earth, air, fire, and water.

In all, nine substances together constitute the universe. Four of these are the atoms. The other five substances are mind, soul, ether, time, and space.

All things are a product of combinations of these substances. What is most important is that, because atoms are indestructible in nature, there is no real annihilation in the literal sense. Individual atoms simply recombine through the universal force of *dharma* to form new things.[6]

The atomist theory of Vaisheshika has a decisive impact in that its theory of atoms restores the status of substance. As we will see, the notion of substance, the existence of an independent entity, was called into question by Buddhists.

Samkhya (Samkhya-Yoga)   The Samkhya school's views of reality are quite similar to those of the Yoga school. For this reason, they too are classed together. (However, the Samkhya teachings refute a God, whereas Yoga believes in God.)

For both, reality embraces both *purusha,* which refers to Soul or Spirit, and *prakriti,* which refers to Nature. According to Samkhya, the world is a result of the infusion of *purusha* into *prakriti.* When this happens, the three states of *prakriti* are activated. These three states, known as *gunas,* are transparency (*sattva*), activity (*rajas*), and inactivity (*tamas*).

In this process of activation, the *prakriti* assumes what is called *buddhi,* or a sort of cosmic intelligence.[7] This intelligence is an actualization of what is latent. This suggests that, for both schools, the effect already exists, although in a dormant state, in the cause. This is the theory of existent effect, known as *satkarya-vada.* (The opposite theory, that of nonexistent effect, is termed *asatkarya-vada.* This latter position is defended by the Nyaya-Vaisheshika schools, which hold that the effect does not preexist in the cause.)

From *buddhi,* individual intellect and egos evolve. From these, individual minds evolve, and from these we have sense organs, and so on, resulting finally in the bringing about of material things.

In this process of evolution from *purusha,* the mind confuses its genuine self with its ego. And in doing so, it attaches itself to objects of its experience. Liberation can occur only when one is able to discriminate between *purusha* and *prakriti* and realize true reality.

Vedanta

Sankara's Nondualism (Advaita Vedanta)   The Vedanta system is essentially rooted in the interpretation of three works: the Upanishads, *Brahma Sutra,* and *Bhagavad Gita.* Of the three, Sankara relies more on the early Upanishads and the Brahma Sutras. Without a doubt, Advaita Vedanta is one of the most influential of all Indian philosophical schools. A selection from Sankara is included at the end of this chapter.

As we recall, Badarayana composed the *Brahma Sutra,* also called the *Vedanta Sutra,* which is the leading text in all Vedanta schools. Here, Badarayana strongly sustains the identity between *atman* and *Brahman.* He also presents the monistic view that all reality is one substance, that all is *Brahman.*

Badarayana's teachings were further developed by Gaudapada, who allegedly taught Govinda, the teacher of Sankara. Guadapada interpreted

Badarayana's monism quite literally; that is, he reasserted that the only reality is *Brahman*. In addition, he claims that the external world as we know it is unequivocally an illusion. The world is not created, because in essence it does not exist. He compares the world to the mirage of a circle of fire created by twirling a burning stick. The world, therefore, is only an appearance.

Sankara does not go to the extreme of Gaudapada in describing the world as illusion. He admits of the existence of the world. He establishes that the world as *ordinarily perceived* is still illusion. He uses the analogy of the rope that is mistaken for a snake. The snake represents our ordinary view of the world; what is actually present is the rope. In the same fashion, what actually exists is *Brahman*. This is a crucial idea in Sankara.

But how do we know what is real? The essential criterion for reality is that it cannot be contradicted by any new insight, discovery, or experience. Consider the following example: If at first we believe that the round object in a pond is a turtle, and then upon further inspection discover that it is a stone, the so-called "turtle" has been displaced by the new judgment that the object is a stone. In the same fashion, Sankara discloses that those objects that we think are essentially real are not genuinely real because only *Brahman* is real. Until we reach this realization, we remain in a state of ignorance, or *avidya*.

If *Brahman* is what is real, what more can we say about *Brahman*? The nature of *Brahman* is not clear in the Upanishads; the texts present a variety of positions. Vedanta grapples with this question and asks whether *Brahman* is more an impersonal force or a personal god.

For Sankara, ultimate reality is *Brahman*. *Brahman* can be viewed in two ways: as *nirguna*, without characteristics, or as *saguna*, with characteristics. Sankara stresses that *Brahman* is *nirguna*. As *nirguna*, *Brahman* remains ineffable, indescribable. Here, *Brahman* is a pure condition of being without the imposition of conceptual categories. This is what the sage Yajnavalkya had in mind when he asserted that *Brahman* can best be characterized as *Neti, neti* ("Not this, not this"):

> Now, therefore, the description of *Brahman:* "Not this, not this"; for there is no other and more appropriate description than this "Not this." Now the designation of *Brahman:* "The truth of truth." The vital breath is truth, and It (*Brahman*) is the Truth of that.[8]

Now *Brahman* cannot be defined in human terms because *Brahman* is indescribable or ineffable. Yet, as humans we have a need to make *Brahman* intelligible to us, and therefore we rely on specific impressions or concepts to evoke certain images. Therefore, Indian thought has also portrayed *Brahman* as *saguna*. *Brahman* as *saguna* is *Brahman* with specific qualities. *Brahman* as *saguna* is often described as Ishvara (Lord). As we mentioned with respect to the *Bhagavad Gita*, Ishvara is further rendered in a triune sense as creator, sustainer, and destroyer, or as Brahma, Vishnu, and Shiva.

Brahman as *saguna* can more easily be the object of devotion, or *bhakti*. Therefore, there is a strong tradition of *bhakti* devotion in Indian history. In any case, *nirguna* and *saguna* are complementary ways of depicting *Brahman* as the all-pervading reality.

Indeed, Sankara does assign qualities to *Brahman,* even though he teaches that *Brahman* is essentially indescribable. He claims that *Brahman* is pure consciousness; it is also portrayed within a trinitarian framework: being-consciousness-bliss (*sat-cit-ananda*). *Sat* means "being," *cit* means "consciousness," and *ananda* refers to "bliss." *Brahman* is thus the absolute consciousness from which, through the power of *maya,* varied finite consciousnesses result.

These finite consciousnesses are termed *jivas,* separate selves or souls. Yet this separateness is merely an illusion. In reality, these selves and *Brahman* are one and the same. *Jiva* is therefore *atman* as it is embodied in some psycho-physical form. Sankara depicts the relationship between *jiva* and *atman* as that between space within a jar and space itself.

In reality, one's self is *atman* and, in line with the Upanishadic teaching, identical to the *Brahman.* Yet, it is the power of *maya* that obstructs us in our realization of this truth. Once *avidya,* or ignorance, is overcome, the jars are seen for what they are. The space within the jars represents *atman.* As long as *atman* is enclosed within the jar, it is known as *jiva.* The jar represents body or form. *Jiva* is therefore *atman* embodied in a psycho-physical form, and the space within the jar is the same as the all-surrounding space, which represents *Brahman.* This explains that *atman* is *Brahman.* This shattering of ignorance is also referred to as *moksha,* or enlightenment as to one's true nature and reality.

Just what is the nature of the relationship between *Brahman* and the world? The world is an effect of *Brahman.* Sankara holds an interesting position: That which is an effect must already exist in some latent fashion in the cause. Therefore, the effect, in a way, exists before it comes about as effect. Being can only result from being. This means that if the world is an effect of *Brahman,* then there is no essential difference between the world and *Brahman.* In this way, the Advaita teaching is nondualist.

The Advaita school maintains the belief that *Brahman* causes the world due to *lila,* the play of *Brahman,* without any concern for consequences, without any attachment to purpose—in other words, not as some separate Creator. Ishvara, or *Brahman,* creates because it is by its nature spontaneously self-expressive.[9]

The real cause of the world is *Brahman.* Yet *Brahman* still stays the same, as real. This means that the effect, the world itself, remains "only an apparent manifestation of its cause."[10] This is the blisteringly radical thesis that Sankara attempts to formulate—namely, that the *Brahman* only appears to cause the world. Yet this is only an appearance. This is essential in the Advaita school; only the *Brahman* is real. Any appearance to the contrary arises out of *maya* and *avidya.*

What are *maya* and *avidya?* In early Vedic teachings, *maya* referred to a magical power of the gods who could easily trick humans. According to the Advaitin analysis, *maya* is the creative power of *Brahman.* This divine energy is so pervasive that, on account of *maya,* we are tricked into thinking that what we see is all there is. Because of *maya,* we confuse what is real and what appears to be real.

Maya and *avidya* are often used together. *Avidya* means ignorance, and it can be expressed, for example, through faulty predication. In other words, it is the common tendency to impose on an object a characteristic that does not belong to that object. It is a case of mistaken attribution. To ascribe the skill of carpentry upon a philosopher who has never cut wood would be a mistaken attribution. The classic example is mistaking the rope for a snake. A more serious example is to conceive of our ordinary, everyday selves as being our true selves. This results in grave consequences and thrusts us back onto the wheel of birth, death, and rebirth known as *samsara*. *Avidya* constantly obstructs us in attaining what, for the Indian, is the highest quest: to know one's true self and reality. Sankara seeks to demonstrate and explain the key idea: *tat tvam asi, atman* is *Brahman.*[11]

The most important point is this: Only *Brahman* is real. Yet this does not mean that the world is absolutely nonreal. To an extent, it does have a tempered-reality, or what Deutsch calls a "practical reality."[12]

Now, we can ask ourselves, if the world itself is a tempered reality, the only reality being *Brahman,* then where do we stand? Am I an illusion? No. Remember the key discovery in the Upanishads: *tat tvam asi;* that is, *atman* is identical to *Brahman.* We will discuss this further in Chapter 3. For now, understand that the Advaita school held to the same proposition that *atman* is *Brahman.* Therefore, if only *Brahman* is real, and if my true nature is identical to *Brahman,* then there is no fundamental difference between my genuine, divine self and what is real.

Ramanuja's Qualified Nondualism   Ramanuja's characterization of the nature of reality is unique in at least two ways: He personalizes the nature of *Brahman,* and he restores a more positive attribute to the world and individual souls. In a sense, matter and souls represent the body of God. In this way, they therefore also qualify the absolute Reality, God.

Let us be clearer. Ramanuja affirms that all of reality can be reduced to three fundamental entities: Ishvara, God; world, or matter; and souls, *jivas.* The world and the individual souls are the manifestation, the body, of God. (Note that God is the term used by Ramanuja, whereas *Brahman* is used in Sankara's Advaita.) In any case, these three remain distinct from each other, but not separate. In other words, all reality is encompassed by Ishvara, but souls are still distinct from Ishvara.

Just as the body depends on the soul for its existence, the souls and the world depend on *Brahman* for their existence. Yet even though the soul cannot exist independently of God, it is distinct. God exists within the soul, but is distinct from it. God remains the principle of all things. God's existence does not depend on anything else, even though all else depends on God for existence. And whatever occurs on the earthly plane affects souls and matter, but not God. In all this, what Ramanuja especially emphasizes is that these three entities are distinct from each other. There is no identity among the three.

Ramanuja is not at all denying that the ultimate reality is God, who is therefore one. He is, however, assigning a status to souls and to the world by claiming that they constitute the body of God. Souls and the world are modes of God, distinct from God (though not radically distinct, as Madhva claims). Therefore, as the body of God, they qualify God.

Ramanuja contends that a substance can only be known through its attributes. All attributes point to the substance they qualify. In this way, the world is an attribute of God. God is pure substance. Applying Ramanuja's premise, *Brahman,* or God, can only be known through the world. Therefore, the world acts as a qualifier.

For Ramanuja, salvation will not result from knowledge, but from devotion, or love, *bhakti.* Love occupies a higher level than intellect or knowledge in Ramanuja's system.

Madhva's Dualism Madhva's teachings concerning reality can be viewed within the context of what he considers to be five fundamental distinctions:

- between God and the soul
- between God and matter
- between the soul and matter
- between one soul and another soul
- between one part of matter and another part

Madhva's metaphysical position is one of strict dualism, and it counters the nondualism of Sankara. Madhva's position is therefore referred to as *dvaita* (dualist). Madhva's dualism is illustrated in his teaching concerning the personal God, whom he characterizes as Vishnu. Vishnu is regarded by him as totally transcendent and distinct from the plurality of souls and matter. Not only is this in sharp opposition to Sankara, but it also differs from the position of Ramanuja, who insisted that God exists within the realm of souls and matter.

In proposing the five fundamental distinctions, what he essentially claims is that each object is uniquely itself and no other. This being the case, he argues, all things are different. Therefore, difference does not in itself mean totally separate from, in a manner of independence. When he posits that God is different from matter, he is not saying that the world exists independently of God. Nor does difference mean separation in terms of strict transcendence. What he does assert is that there is only one self-subsistent reality, and that is God. All else is dependent on God.

Buddhist Perspectives on Reality

A story relates how the sage Malunkyaputta was not at all satisfied by the Buddha's silence on profound metaphysical questions as he thought the following to himself:

> These theories which The Blessed One has left unelucidated, has set aside and rejected—that the world is eternal, that the world is not eternal, that the world is finite, that the world is infinite, that the soul

and body are identical, that the soul is one thing and the body another, that the saint exists after death, that the saint does not exist after death, that the saint both exists and does not exist after death, that the saint neither exists nor does not exist after death—these The Blessed One does not elucidate to me. And the fact that The Blessed One does not elucidate them to me does not please me nor suit me.[13]

Malunkyaputta then approached the "Blessed One," the Buddha, with his concern. The Buddha responded by comparing the sage's interest to a situation in which a person is shot by a poisoned arrow, yet persists in knowing about the nature of the arrow, rather than having the arrow removed:

It is as if, Malunkyaputta, a man had been wounded by an arrow thickly smeared with poison, and his friends and companions, his relatives and kinfolk, were to procure for him a physician or surgeon; and the sick man were to say, "I will not have this arrow taken out until I have learnt whether the man who wounded me belonged to the warrior caste, or to the *Brahman* caste, or to the agricultural caste, or to the menial caste."

Or again he were to say, "I will not have this arrow taken out until I have learnt the name of the man who wounded me, and to what clan he belongs."

Or again he were to say, "I will not have this arrow taken out until I have learnt whether the man who wounded me was tall, or short, or of the middle height." . . .

Or again he were to say, "I will not have this arrow taken out until I have learnt whether the arrow which wounded me was an ordinary arrow, or a claw-headed arrow, or a vekanda, or an iron arrow, or a calf-tooth arrow, or a karavirapatta." That man would die, Malunkyaputta, without ever having learnt this.[14]

We can see from this that the Buddha confronted a different question— the universal truth of suffering—and he proposed a resolution to this question in light of empirically determined, rational explanations. With respect to metaphysical questions concerning ultimate reality, he remained reluctant to give any definite response.

The history of Buddhism is a variety of interpretations of the Buddha's silence. "Silence" is perhaps not the correct word here because the Buddha did make statements about reality. However, what we can gather from the texts is that he deliberately avoided making such definitive statements.

Therefore, a point of contention among Buddhists and Buddhist scholars is the degree to which the Buddha's original message contains a specified metaphysics. If we accept the prevailing opinion that earlier Buddhism per se contains little metaphysics, then it appears that the formulation of metaphysics did eventually develop as doctrine became the subject of further analyses and interpretation among the different schools.

It would be incorrect to assume that all Buddhists share the same metaphysical substructure. Just as we find in orthodox Indian philosophies, Buddhist thought reveals a complex picture of various positions concerning the nature of reality, ranging from realism to idealism.

The Four Noble Truths
and the Three Marks of Existence

There are some beliefs that are accepted by all schools and subdivisions of Buddhists, such as the Four Noble Truths. In response to the question concerning the nature of reality, the Four Noble Truths give us a movingly humane account, far removed from abstract philosophical speculation. Briefly, the Four Noble Truths are:

- All existence is filled with suffering (*dukkha*).
- Suffering ultimately comes from desire, or clinging (*trsna*).
- We can be liberated from suffering.
- We can be liberated by following the Eightfold Path.

The Buddha treats the question in the manner of a physician. First, the illness is pointed out and described: All life is suffering. Suffering is universal; it occurs in various forms and leaves no one exempt. Suffering manifests itself through poverty, illness, war, exploitation, death, and so on. Even the experience of pleasure is eventually accompanied by pain. This first truth points to the reality of suffering and misery on physical, moral, and existential levels.

Second, the Buddha points to the cause of the illness: Suffering is essentially derived from within us, from our tendency to cling and desire. All things have their cause, and the same can be said for suffering. No matter what level of suffering we address, whether it be the physical suffering of disease or the misery of human insensitivities and immoralities toward other humans, the pain we personally experience ultimately originates within. That is, it comes from our craving for permanence, such as the desire for immortality or the need to cling to unending pleasure. Many afflictions are beyond our control—for instance, a tidal wave that devastates an entire village within seconds. How we eventually deal with such misfortunes is in our control. And it is our craving for permanence that is the cause of further suffering, which can genuinely incapacitate us.

Third, the Buddha's prognosis is positive: We can be healed from suffering. This is an extremely significant truth, for it turns the Buddha's teaching into one that is now optimistic. If the cause of suffering lies within us (as craving), then we are also capable of freeing ourselves from misery and pain, because what lies within us can be within our control. Hence, we can liberate ourselves.

Fourth, the Buddha gives more specifics about our prognosis and the course of treatment: We can be freed from suffering only by following the Eightfold Path. This Eightfold Path may be called the Buddhist commandments. The eight ways consist of right views, right thought, right speech, right conduct, right livelihood, right effort, right mindfulness, and right concentration. *Right views* entails knowing these four truths as well as being aware of the goal of enlightenment. *Right thought* means maintaining a sincerity of heart and mind. *Right speech, conduct,* and *livelihood* indicate the need to acquire a life-style that is consistent with the proper goal. In this way, one's speech, behavior, and occupation needs to be congruous with the spiritual aim of enlightenment. *Right effort* means being vigilant so that one is not distracted from the pursuit of this goal. *Right mindfulness* means maintaining mental control, so that the mind is not sidetracked from following the proper path. *Right concentration* refers to proper meditation, which is an important avenue to enlightenment and signifies the harmony of mind and body.

Another belief in common among all Buddhists is their teaching concerning the three "signs of existence." Buddhists point to three fundamental features of reality, called the three marks of reality:

- suffering (*dukkha*)
- no-permanence (*anicca*)
- no-self (*anatta* or *anatman*)

Early Buddhist Schools (Theravada)

Sarvastivadin School   The name of this school provides a direct clue to its essential teaching concerning reality: *Sarva* means "everything," and *vasti* means "exists." Everything exists. This means that material things and mental events are not illusions and is in contrast to the nihilist position that claims that nothing exists. For this reason, Sarvastivadins are also called realists. Furthermore, all reality consists of constituent elements called *dharmas.* Seventy-five of these *dharmas* are the real component energies of all that exists. They combine in various ways to make up material objects. These *dharmas* also combine to form consciousness and mental events such as thoughts. These mental events produce the sense of an independent self. However—and this is a crucial point—this "self" does not really exist as subsistent or independent.

If this is so, how can continuity occur? Each *dharma* was considered to be somewhat fixed in time, for only a particular moment in time and space. Therefore, each *dharma* was not in itself always moving. According to the Sarvastivadin school, this contributes to the apparent continuity we perceive. Because each *dharma* is temporarily fixed, we can experience direct perception of an object.

Sautrantika School   The Sautrantika school accepts the existence of the constituent elements posited by the Sarvastivadins. However, they underscore the essentially dynamic nature of *dharmas,* so that direct perception of things is not possible, as it is with the Sarvastivadins. *Dharmas* do not hold their ground for even a moment. Everything, to the slightest degree, is in constant flux. This leads to at least two important conclusions: (1) What we do perceive are not things themselves but, at best, traces of these things. This means that all we can experience comes from indirect perception. (2) Nothing is actually "real" in an objective sense. Nothing is permanent.

Mahayana School

Sunyata   In response to the question of reality, Mahayanists point to the notion of *sunyata. Sunya* is synonymous with "empty." Literally, it means "relating to the swollen" because its root meaning (*svi*) is "to swell." The idea is that what looks swollen from the outside is actually hollow, or empty, on the inside.

Consider this illustration: To all outward appearances, there is reason to postulate an independent entity called self, or "I." Yet based on the empirical analysis of Buddhists, we discover that this entity may appear to exist, but in reality there are no adequate grounds to support its existence. Therefore, this leads to the Buddhist belief in no-self. Not only self, but all things are without substantial reality. All things are *sunya*.

Not only are things without substantial reality, but even our ideas, concepts, and ways of describing reality are *sunya*, empty, and therefore hollow. This includes Buddhist teachings. So, here we have a radical self-critique of any doctrines. Buddhist teachings are merely a vehicle (called *yana*) to appreciate this nonsubstantiality, or *sunyata*, of all reality. Buddhist teachings are like a canoe that brings one to the opposite shore: Once one arrives at the opposite shore, the canoe can be set aside. It is merely a means to an end.

Madhyamika Teaching of Nagarjuna   Nagarjuna is indisputably one of the most influential of Indian Buddhist philosophers.[15] His major work is entitled *Madhyamika Karika,* which means "Fundamentals of the Middle Way." It tells us of the centrality of the Buddhist Middle Way for Nagarjuna. A portion from the *Madhyamika Karika* is included at the end of this chapter.

The Middle Way (*Madhyamika*) properly avoids extremes. The notion that all reality is simply material is one extreme; the opposite belief—that there is no material reality, and that all is spiritual—is another extreme. The belief that all things exist eternally is one extreme; the opposing view—that nothing exists at all—is the other extreme. This latter view has been called the nihilist view.

With all extremes, that which is posited is viewed as a static entity. In other words, there is an objectification of "reality." Even "nonexistence" is objectified as an extreme. This objectification occurs because a point of view is assumed. And one becomes easily attached to this point of view, whatever it is. Thus, the attachment is not to the object itself, but to an idea of that object. It is quite alarming when the idea assumes more reality than the actuality, as we find in the following scenario:

ADMIRING FRIEND: "My, that's a beautiful baby you have there!"
MOTHER: "Oh, that's nothing—you should see his photograph!"[16]

The Middle Way avoids these extremes by neither affirming nor negating them. For Nagarjuna, either affirmation or negation still assumes an extreme position. The Middle Way avoids the extremes by embracing them. By embracing them, this middle way points to the truth of *sunya.*

Let us look more closely at all this. The first chapter of the *Madhyamika Karika* points out that assuming the positions of either affirmation or negation of reality is wrong. This first chapter lays the groundwork for the entire text. In his unique dialectic fashion, Nagarjuna examines the four possibilities of causation, the process of cause and effect. These four possibilities are:

1. Things cause themselves.
2. Things are caused by other things.
3. Things both cause themselves and are caused by other things.
4. Things are neither caused by themselves nor by other things.

In his examination, Nagarjuna repudiates all four positions. Why? Because they assume either an affirmative stance or a negative stance with regard to causation. According to Nagarjuna, to hold to any specific possibility assumes a static notion of being. It is precisely this static idea of being that he rejects. He concludes that all things are relative to all things, and so are dependent on all things and thus empty of self-nature. In other words, he reinterprets the idea of causation to mean that everything is essentially empty, or *sunya,* as illustrated by his famous "Eight Noes":

no birth	no unity
no death	no multiplicity
no destruction	no coming in
no permanence	no going out

Nagarjuna constructs an intriguing and challenging dialectical argument that subverts the very notion of causality. For Nagarjuna, causality is essentially *sunya,* or empty. In the opening verse we read:

At nowhere and at no time can entities ever exist by originating out of themselves, from others, from both (self-other), or from the lack of causes.[17]

It is difficult to condense his analysis. Essentially, it rests upon this premise: Whatever is real can only be real because it is caused by itself; in other words, it is self-derived:

As entities without self-nature have no real status of existence, the statement, "from the existence of that this becomes," is not possible."[18]

Buddhists believe that all things are becoming. If this is so, then what causes something to become? Nagarjuna argues that that which comes about can be caused neither by that which is real nor by that which is not real. Therefore, that which becomes can be neither the effect nor the cause of anything else, so that there is no causal relation whatsoever.

This defies our conventional understanding because we inherently situate things, people, and experiences within some relational framework. Nagarjuna asks us to see things as they are, apart from the conceptual framework we impose. To be able to do this is, no doubt, daunting. Conceptualization consists of issuing some sort of relationality, whether it be size, shape, distance, color, sequence, or so on. Thus *sunya* means empty of relation; it is that which is by itself. And all things are *sunya.*

Another radical idea of Nagarjuna is his thesis that nirvana and *samsara* are not in essence different from each other. *Samsara* refers to the circle, or "wheel," of continual birth-death-rebirth. He justifies this position on the premise that they also are *sunya*. According to one scholar, this idea "remains the most celebrated, outrageous and curious conclusion yet reached by a Buddhist philosopher."[19] In reality, this nondifference between nirvana and *samsara* indicates all the more the limits of conceptualization. The important issue is achieving liberation, including the liberation from concepts and ideas. Such liberation is part of the necessary path to becoming a *bodhisattva*.

Nagarjuna's Middle Way has certainly received its share of criticism. He has sometimes been accused of teaching a nihilism. Much of the difficulty is based on how one interprets the idea of *sunya*, which is the pivotal idea in Nagarjuna's teachings.

Vijnanavadin School   How did the Vijnanavadin school view reality? As the name indicates, reality is *vijnana*, meaning "consciousness." This is the central idea around which the school's teachings revolve.

Vasubandhu and his brother Asangha are the major representatives of this school. Vasubandhu's most important works are the *Vimsatika* and *Trimsika*. In these works he proposes that all things are essentially a projection of our mental states. Therefore, there is only Mind. That which is real is the Mind or pure Consciousness. Furthermore, the nature of this Mind can be realized, and once it is, true awakening occurs.

Asangha maintains the existence of different levels of consciousness, and that the ground of consciousness is a "store-consciousness," or *alaya-vijnana*. This concept is given its name because it is, in a sense, the storehouse of consciousness that contains the seeds that will produce all individual experiences. This storehouse is an eternal and unchanging force that dwells in and permeates all beings.

━━ Chinese Philosophies ━━

Throughout the history of Chinese philosophy, questions concerning the nature of reality were pursued primarily to support a system of ethics and practical philosophy. Questions of metaphysics are in themselves of less concern, and their significance lies in their practical merit. The foremost interests for the Chinese have been and continue to be: What is the good life? What is the nature of our relationship with each other? How can we live with each other to bring about the good life?

Basic Themes Concerning Reality

Reality as Transformation

A vital teaching running throughout Chinese thought is that the nature of reality is linked with the phenomenon of change. We see this even in the Chinese term for man, *hsing*. Part of the ideograph for this term contains *sheng,* which means "production." Reality is ultimately seen in terms of process or change.

The classic text that discusses this idea is the *I Ching.* It asserts that the Great Ultimate, or *T'ai-chi,* is the ultimate principle of all principles. It has no spatial or temporal limits. Its nature is such that it spontaneously produces the cosmic powers of yin and yang. From these two universal forces, all things come to be and all things come to pass. All things are the natural, spontaneous self-expression of *T'ai-chi,* the Great Ultimate.

Confucianists hold the view that due to change, things evolve; that is, all things move forward. The constant activity of yin and yang results in the progress of each new moment. Because change brings about progress, change is therefore welcomed.

Yu *and* Wu

Chinese perspectives on the nature and meaning of reality can be shown by considering the terms for "being" and "nonbeing." The Chinese term for "being" is *yu; wu* represents "nonbeing."[20]

Yu does not refer simply to existence. It does not mean only "being" or "that which is." It denotes the idea of "being present," so that it conveys the sense of presence. The difference is essential. My being at the bedside of a hospital patient is distinct from my presence with that patient. The idea of presence signals a more dynamic quality to my being, *yu,* whereas something's simple existence seems rather static.[21]

The meaning of *wu* has an interesting history. Taoism first assigned *wu* to be the origin of being. *Wu* meant not having a name, or being nameless. Subsequently, the meaning of *wu* attained a more metaphysical quality as nonbeing. *Wu* became the defining feature of Tao. *Wu,* meaning "nonbeing," basically embraces the belief that all things came into being due to their own inner force, not due to some external energy.

Li *and* Ch'i

Another predominant concern in Chinese views on reality deals with the relationship between *li* and *ch'i:*

- *Li* generally refers to the underlying principle behind all phenomena. *Li* is the reason or law of phenomena; it is universal, permanent, eternal, and "self-caused."
- *Ch'i* is the principle behind matter. It is therefore the concrete manifestation of *li.* It refers to material energy or force, sometimes referred to as Ether.

One of the major points of controversy among the various Neo-Confucian schools is the status of *li* in relation to *ch'i.* Does it precede *ch'i,* or does it depend on it for its existence?

Harmony

Another feature in the Chinese description of reality is the assumption of some metaphysical sense of order and harmony. For Taoists, harmony spontaneously issues from nature. The Taoist teachings of yin and yang enhance this idea of harmony. The forces of yin and yang co-penetrate. It is their relationship that counts, and not separate aspects of it. A similar relationship might occur in a team triathlon, in which one person swims, another cycles, and a third runs. Each individual contributes his or her strength for the well-being of the team.

For Confucianists, emphasis is placed on the necessity for social harmony. For instance, the importance Confucius attached to ritual is due to its philosophical merit as enhancing both personal and social order, which in turn reflects the universal, cosmic harmony.

Ancient Chinese Views of Reality

Taoism

Lao Tzu's View of Tao and Te   The two most important teachings concerning reality in Lao Tzu are Tao and *te. Tao,* which literally means "way" or "road," is the first principle of the beginning of all things. It is the source of things coming into existence and of things ceasing to exist.

One of the most prominent characteristics of Tao is its ineffable quality. We find this expressed in the opening lines of the *Tao Te Ching,* the classic text for Taoists:

Tao that can be spoken of,
Is not the Everlasting Tao.
Name that can be named,
Is not the Everlasting name.

Nameless, the origin of heaven and earth;
Named, the mother of ten thousand things.
Alternate,
Non-being, to name the origin
of heaven and earth;
Being, to name the mother of ten thousand things.[22]

Additional passages from the *Tao Te Ching* are included at the end of this chapter.

Te is the principle of spontaneity, the natural expression of Tao, and the actualization of Tao in specific things. Because Tao is embodied in all things, all things naturally express this power.

Chuang Tzu's View of Tao and Transformation   Chuang Tzu agreed with Lao Tzu concerning the basic meaning of both Tao and *te.* For him, Tao is the first principle, the condition for all being and nonbeing. It is the law of nature, the way. Yet Chuang Tzu also broadened the meaning of Tao to include the dimension of transformation.

> The life of man passes by like a galloping horse, changing at every turn, at every hour.[23]

This image of time and nature acting together in harmony is an essential theme running throughout Chuang Tzu's thought. All things change: Light becomes dark, young becomes old; old is reborn as young; spring turns into summer, autumn, winter, and back to spring in ceaseless transformation. This is the lesson taught to us by Nature. Amidst this incessant change, Tao is the principle of unity, and it therefore acts as a welcome complement to the reality of change. Everything changes, yet everything is one. An illustration of this is in Chuang Tzu's famous dream of the butterfly:

> Once Chuang Chou [Chuang Tzu] dreamt he was a butterfly, a butterfly flitting and fluttering around, happy with himself and doing as he pleased. He didn't know he was Chuang Chou. Suddenly he woke up and there he was, solid and unmistakable Chuang Chou. But he didn't know if he was Chuang Chou who had dreamt he was a butterfly, or a butterfly dreaming he was Chuang Chou.[24]

Chuang Tzu has an especially interesting perspective on reality. He tells us that all things are in essence equal to each other. According to him, all things may appear to be different, and we conventionally make distinctions. However, in actuality, all things are equal. For instance, this being so, how can we establish a standard for beauty?

> Men claim that Mao-ch'iang and Lady Li were beautiful, but if fish saw them they would dive to the bottom of the stream, if birds saw them they would fly away, and if deer saw them they would break into a run. Of these four, which knows how to fix the standard of beauty for the world?[25]

Hui Shih's Paradoxes

In the dialecticians' discussions of the relationship between names and their objects, issues about the nature of reality were often the subject of debate. Hui Shih is known for the Ten Paradoxes, in which he addresses questions concerning infinity, relativity, time, change, transformation, similarity, difference, spatial relativity, temporal relativity, unity and separation, and universal love. Let's consider three paradoxes dealing with size, space, and time.[26]

The first Paradox states:

> The greatest has nothing beyond itself, and is called the great unit; the smallest has nothing within itself, and is called the little unit.

Here we have a description of the notion of infinity by contrasting that which in theory would be the greatest with that which in theory would be smallest.

That is, greatness and smallness are relative (as we saw in the opening story of the Autumn Flood).

Another interesting paradox is the sixth, which reads:

The south has no limit and has a limit.

In discussing limits and limitlessness, Hui Shih intends to point out the relativity of space. In other words, limits exist only with respect to a point of reference. The point of reference of a dove is different from the point of reference of a tiger. In turn, both are different from the point of reference of a human being.

This is supported further by the seventh paradox:

I go to the state of Yüeh today, and arrive there yesterday.

Whereas the sixth paradox points to the relativity of space, the seventh points to the relativity of time.

Yin-Yang School

The Yin-Yang school's teachings concerning reality can be illustrated by the twofold universal forces of yin and yang, both emanating from the Supreme Ultimate, *Ta'i-ch'i.*

Yin is the passive principle, represented by the female; yang is the active, male principle. All phenomena are the manifestations of these two forces in constant interaction with each other. For example, in the *I Ching* there are eight major trigrams (three-part symbols). The trigram for Heaven is *Ch'ien,* known as father, and represents yang. The trigram for Earth is called *K'un,* known as mother, and represents yin.

The union of Heaven and Earth results in the other six trigrams: thunder, wood or wind, water or moon, fire and sun, mountain, and marsh. Starting with this most basic relationship between Heaven and Earth, yang and yin, all things in the universe are a result of their union. The Chinese believe that all things in existence are a product of the interplay between these two universal principles. Taoists later believed that these two principles reflect the all-encompassing principle of Tao.

Confucianism and Reality

Tung Chung-shu and Correspondence

In Tung Chung-shu's perspectives on reality, one of his more engaging ideas is his theory of the cosmological correspondence between Heaven and humanity. He assimilated the ideas of yin and yang and *wu hsing,* or Five Elements, into Confucian teachings.[27]

Tung's theory of a cosmological correspondence is shown in a number of ways. First, his idea of Heaven, or *T'ien,* comes quite close to resembling Nature. He regarded this force of Nature as divine. And yin and yang are the two universal forces reflected throughout Nature in various ways.

He then applied the forces of Heaven (Nature) to human affairs; that is, human actions and the mandate, or decree, of Heaven are mutually effective. This means that how people behave affects how Nature behaves. Deviant occurrences in Nature are therefore interpreted as the result of immoral human behavior. If we do not act appropriately, it affects Nature, and Heaven responds in the form of what Tung calls "visitations" and "prodigies."

Wang Ch'ung and Spontaneity

In 524 B.C.E., historical records describe an immense fire that broke out in four different states. The prevailing belief was that a comet witnessed in the previous year acted as an omen from Heaven portending this event. It was believed that the fire and its devastation were ultimately due to widespread immorality among humans. Wang Ch'ung strongly disagreed. For him, the fire was the result of Destiny, or Fate, and not the will of Heaven as a punishment to humans.

Wang Ch'ung insisted on a strict empirical approach to all issues, including questions concerning the nature of reality. He was therefore highly critical of the belief in a strict correspondence between the ways of Heaven and human affairs.

Wang Ch'ung adhered more to the humanist teachings in traditional Confucianism and Taoism. In doing so he revived the idea that the way of Heaven works spontaneously. This is especially the case because *wu-wei* is the principle of Tao. *Wu-wei* literally means "nonaction"; more specifically, it refers to action that is nondeliberate, or activity that is natural and spontaneous. (The spontaneity in Tao is expressed in the selection at the end of the chapter.) We read in his *Lun-Heng:*

> Reasoning on Taoist principles we find that Heaven emits its fluid everywhere. Among the many things of this world grain dispels hunger, and silk and hemp protect from the cold. For that reason man eats grain, and wears silk and hemp. That Heaven does not produce grain, silk, and hemp purposely, in order to feed and clothe mankind, follows from the fact that by calamitous changes it does not intend to reprove man. Things are produced spontaneously, and man wears and eats them; the fluid changes spontaneously, and man is frightened by it, for the usual theory is disheartening. Where would be spontaneity, if the heavenly signs were intentional, and where inaction?
>
> Why must we assume that Heaven acts spontaneously? Because it has neither mouth nor eyes. Activity is connected with the mouth and the eyes. . . .
>
> How do we know that Heaven possesses neither mouth nor eyes? From Earth. The body of the Earth is formed of earth, and earth has neither mouth nor eyes. Heaven and Earth are like husband and wife. Since the body of the Earth is not provided with a mouth or eyes, we know that Heaven has no mouth or eyes neither.[28]

For Wang Ch'ung, spontaneity belongs to the nature of Tao. Therefore, it is a pervading feature of reality. He was a strong critic of determinism;

he strongly felt that events occur due to chance and luck and are not the result of some preordained pattern.

Tao as *Wu:* Neo-Taoism and Reality

Wang Pi assigned a much more metaphysical status to the meaning of Tao. For him, Tao did not merely mean the namelessness of things, as in the *Lao-tzu.* He claimed that the primary characteristic of Tao is *wu,* or nonbeing, and *wu* is the condition or source from which being is manifested. All things in being constitute the manifestation of its source, nonbeing.

This idea of Wang Pi's was further elaborated on by Kuo-Hsiang. He also described Tao in terms of a metaphysical rendition of *wu* as nonbeing. He provided a clearer and more explicit exposition of Tao as *wu,* describing Tao literally as a state of nonbeing. And here is where he differs from Wang Pi.

For Kuo-Hsiang, Tao as *wu* cannot truly be the cause of being because the cause of being must be being. Being can only come from being. Rather, Tao as *wu* is the condition that underlies the cause. *Wu,* in Kuo Hsiang's exegesis, does not bear the responsibility for original causality. Things become what they are due to their own inner principles, and this occurs spontaneously.

Therefore, Kuo Hsiang made more of a distinction between *wu* and *yu.* *Yu* is the realm of being. In this realm, *T'ien* represents Heaven and Earth, which is considered the totality of being. (He seems to emphasize the significance of *yu,* whereas Wang Pi stressed *wu.*)

Chinese Buddhism and Reality

Seng Chao: Yu *and* Wu Co-Exist

One of the most prolific of Chinese Buddhists was Seng Chao. In his major work, *Chao Lun,* he reexamined the nature of the relationship between *yu* and *wu.* As we have so far seen, this is a celebrated question among Chinese philosophers.

Seng Chao proposed that what we normally consider to be *yu,* or being, cannot be entirely *yu* because it originates from causes. He proposed that, in actuality, *yu* is such that it must also contain aspects of *wu.* Conversely, *wu* is such that it must also possess features of *yu.* As we read in the *Chao Lun:*

> Whatever there is and what is not is one in essence. Impalpable and darkly concealed, surely this is not a matter for which an ordinary intellect can compass.[29]

He concluded that all things must therefore both exist and not exist at the same time. If this is the case, then there is no strict dichotomy between *wu* and *yu:*

> What do you propose? That things are not? Then negativism would not be heretical. That things are? Then positivism would be orthodox.

(Actually) because things are not simply nothing, negativism is a heresy; because things are not simply something, positivism is not orthodox. Then it is evident that these two negations describe Highest Truth (*paramartha satya*).[30]

(A selection from *Chao Lun* is included at the end of this chapter.)

Chi-tsang's Double Truth Theory

Chi-tsang, who represents the Three Treatises school, continued to investigate this relationship between *yu* and *wu*, and he recognized that extreme positions must be resolved somehow. He did this within the context of his theory of the double truth. He posited two categories of truths: (1) "mundane" or "common," and (2) "absolute" or "sage." His analysis takes place within three separate levels:

> Level 1: Here, common truth affirms *yu*, or being, whereas sage truth affirms *wu*, or negation.
>
> Level 2: Common truth affirms that existence must be either *yu* or *wu*. Common truth therefore perceives *yu* and *wu* as incompatible opposites. Sage truth, on the other hand, combines both *yu* and *wu*. In this way, sage truth denies any opposition between *yu* and *wu*.
>
> Level 3: Common truth accepts both the affirmation and the denial of *wu* and *yu*. This perspective, however, still remains within the realm of distinction. Sage truth on this highest level is that one can neither affirm nor deny *wu* and *yu*. (Here we see similarities with Nagarjuna.)

This theory represents Chi-tsang's effort to resolve extreme positions in order to establish a middle doctrine. (This school has also been called the School of Nonbeing.)

Hsuan-tsang: Consciousness Only

Hsuan-tsang addressed the nature of reality in terms of consciousness. All things only exist as objects of consciousness. In other words, apart from consciousness, nothing exists. He did not deny the existence of objects, for they do exist, but only as objects of our perception or consciousness.

According to Hsuan-tsang, the real nature of all things is called *Chenju* (*Bhutatathata*), which means real or genuine "thusness." We are, as in a dream, ordinarily not aware of this:

> Until we have awakened from the dream, we are incapable of realizing (that it is a dream). It is only after we have awakened that we catch up in our understanding. The same is true of our knowledge regarding the material world of our waking. Until we have truly awakened, we cannot ourselves know it. It is only when we reach the genuine awakening that we can catch up in our understanding. Before this

genuine awakening is achieved, we perpetually remain as in a dream. It is because of the failure to comprehend that the material world is Mere Ideation, that the Buddha speaks of the long night of trans-migration.[31]

Hsuan-tsang put forth the idea that phenomena are only a manifesta-tion of consciousness. This is why his school is called Mere Ideation. Yet it appears that the theories of Hsuan-tsang countered the appeal to common sense characteristic of Chinese thinking. This was different from an em-pirically based understanding of reality.

T'ien-t'ai School

Along with the Consciousness Only school, T'ien-t'ai teaches *Bhutatathata,* or single absolute mind. However, T'ien-t'ai considers this absolute to be un-changing or immutable. It is not influenced by its mutual relationship with its manifestations, which is the case in Mere Ideation.

In other words, nothing we perceive exists in and of itself. Everything exists only because of mind, because of universal consciousness; everything is a manifestation of mind. This means that our conventional view is based on an illusion. The contemporary philosopher Fung Yu-lan uses the exam-ple of the magician who is able to form a rabbit from a handkerchief; those with the conventional attitude are tricked into thinking there actually is a rabbit. For all Buddhists, as long as we mistake the illusion for reality, we are eternally stuck on the cycle of *samsara.*

This absolute mind is characterized by a duality because it possesses within its original nature, or *hsing,* both a pure aspect and an impure aspect. This means that the absolute mind will also manifest itself in pure or impure expressions. However, because the natures (pure and impure) are intrinsically integrated within the absolute, so also are the manifestations of these natures integrated. Therefore, mountains and rivers are integrated and equal. In essence, an ordinary being is the same as a Buddha, even though ordinary beings are unenlightened whereas Buddhas are enlightened.

Thus the T'ien-t'ai school attributes a positive status to phenomena because they are manifestations of the original mind, though not real in themselves. Phenomena are uplifted from the level of total nonbeing. Prob-lems occur when we cling to the notion of the manifestation as actually real, existing independently of the absolute mind. There is no self-subsistent ex-istence to phenomena, but there is a relative existence to phenomena.

What does all this have to do with the nature of the relationship be-tween *yu* and *wu?* We know that this is a classic question in Chinese thought. In the tension between *wu* and *yu,* this school seems to emphasize *yu* more than *wu.* This is apparent in that the school gives a more positive status to phenomenal reality. In a qualified way, things do exist because they are natural manifestations of *Tathagata-garbha.* We see that Hsuan-tsang empha-sizes nonexistence, or *wu,* at the expense of being, or *yu.* The T'ien-t'ai teachings counter this emphasis on *wu;* instead, they bestow a higher rank to *yu,* or being.

Fa-tsang and the Hua-Yen School: The Golden Lion

Imagine a circular hall of mirrors. In the center of the hall is a burning torch placed beside the image of the Buddha. Each mirror reflects this torch and the image. Not only does each mirror reflect this torch and the image, but also the image as it is captured in the other mirrors. Furthermore, each mirror reflects the countless reflections found in all the other mirrors. And so on. It is said that Fa-tsang used this imagery to illustrate the true meaning of the manifestation of reality.

Fa-tsang's teachings are in opposition to those of Hsuan-tsang. He agreed with Hsuan-tsang that that which is perceived, phenomena, is essentially a projection of the absolute, permanent mind. Therefore, in itself it does not exist. But here is where he diverged from Hsuan-tsang.

The existence of perceived phenomena is a tempered one. Fa-tsang clarified this by drawing a distinction between two realms: the realm of principle—the underlying, noumenal world—and the realm of phenomena—that which is visible and perceived.

Phenomena possess a degree of reality. Their reality is hypothetical because they are manifestations of what is absolutely real, the absolute mind. Nevertheless, Fa-tsang did credit phenomena with some degree of reality, in contrast to Hsuan-tsang.

Fa-tsang sought to illustrate all this in his famous Essay on the Gold Lion. In it he attempted to clarify for the Empress Wu the ten major axioms in the *Avatamsaka Sutra*. (There is no need to go into detail here regarding each axiom.) Let us summarize his findings.

The object of his analysis is a gold lion in front of the Empress Wu's palace. Here Fa-tsang applies his two distinct realms. The "realm of principle" is embodied in the gold metal of which the lion is made; the "realm of things" signifies the actual form or figure of the lion. Fa-tsang intends to demonstrate the mutual penetration of all things resulting in complete harmony. All phenomena include all other phenomena.

So far, this is no different from what the T'ien-t'ai school asserts. The difference, however, is this: Fa-tsang went even further to claim that all things not only include each other, but also signify all other things; that is, they mutually *define* each other. According to Fa-tsang, this mutually defining quality of all phenomena is consistent with the fact that all phenomena are empty of self-subsistence. Reality, therefore, can be perceived on a number of different planes:

- From the perspective of oneness, all things reveal the absolute, unchanging mind in its entirety. The eyes of the lion reflect the whole lion.
- From the perspective of plurality, the eyes of the lion are distinct from all other parts of the lion. Its eyes are not the same as its mouth, and so on.
- From another perspective, the eyes of the lion are seen within the context of the lion's whole body, and its eyes therefore

depend on the other parts for their own actuality. Thus, whereas the eyes may be distinct from the mouth of the lion, they are not truly separate because one embraces the other. That is, the meaning of each is completed by incorporating the meaning of the other. This perspective is universal embracement.

The eyes and mouth are not independent in an absolute sense; the eyes define the mouth, and vice versa. Remember, the relationship is not simply one of mutual penetration; it is also one of mutual definition. So also, even though the eyes of the one lion may be distinct from the eyes of another lion, they embrace each other in the manifestation of lion.

Just as Fa-tsang used the example of the hall of mirrors to illustrate the complex ideas of mutual interpenetration and implication in Hua-yen, he alludes to the famous metaphor of the Net of Indra. In Hindu thought, Indra is the ruler of Heaven whose net contained a brilliant jewel at each loop in the net. Each jewel therefore reflected all other jewels and their countless reflections of all the other jewels.[32]

What we witness in Fa-tsang is a synthesis between *wu* and *yu*. Fa-tsang cautions us against falling into the trap of two extremes: (1) nothing exists versus everything exists, and (2) absolute nonbeing versus absolute being. He intends to integrate *wu* and *yu* in a synthesis that transcends our ordinary discrimination. (This may explain why the influence of the Hua-yen school surpassed that of Mere Ideation.)

All this points to the idea that oneness is many and many is oneness. Fa-tsang integrated unity and plurality. It is this synthesis that perhaps appealed the most to the Chinese.

Ch'an School

The engaging discovery of Ch'an is that ultimate reality and everyday reality are not incompatible. This means that enlightenment and ordinary experience are not antitheses. The true sage does not leave the world of ordinariness; the sage chops wood, carries water, cooks, washes, and plants seeds. The difference is one of awakening. The sage is no longer attached to the ideas, concepts, or feelings surrounding his actions. In this way, the sage can truly act and be totally present.

With Ch'an we have a practicality of great appeal to the Chinese. The sage is one who is immersed fully in affairs yet is free of them. The sage is completely present in his or her actions and recognizes the compatibility of human existence, practical affairs, nature, and *wu*. In Ch'an, the transcendent and immanent are synthesized.

Neo-Confucianism and Reality

In Neo-Confucian thought, the discussion of the nature of reality centers around the relationship between *li* and *ch'i*. This is distinct from the Buddhist discussion concerning *yu* and *wu*.

School of Principle: Ch'eng Yi and Chu Hsi

According to Ch'eng Yi, ultimate reality, or Great Ultimate, is *T'ai-chi*. Furthermore, it contains a potential plurality of expression due to the heavenly principle of *li*. Yet *li* does not operate on its own, but through its agent, *ch'i*, called material force (also referred to as Ether). *Ch'i* in turn is influenced by the yin-yang energies and the Five Elements, and matter is produced.

What is important in this whole schema is that material force is the manifestation of *li*. Thus, there is a harmony of *li* and matter. Nevertheless, *li* still remains the prior principle. For Ch'eng Yi, this priority of *li* is important, and the School of Principle generates a distinction between *li* and *ch'i*.[33]

Ch'eng Yi distinguished between "what is above shapes" and "what is within shapes." "Shapes" refers to material phenomena. For Ch'eng Yi, *li*, or principle, is "what is above shapes." So too, for Ch'eng Yi, Tao is also that which is above shapes.[34]

Chu Hsi provided a culmination of these ideas. (Selections from Chu Hsi are at the end of this chapter. The relationship between *li* and *ch'i*, along with Chu Hsi's interpretation, is discussed by the contemporary philosopher Fung Yu-lan in another selection, also at the end of this chapter.) *T'ai-chi* is the totality of all principles, and is the highest principle. It contains *li*. *Li* and *ch'i* can be described in light of the distinction between that which exists "above shapes" and that which exists "within shapes": *Li* exists "above shapes," whereas *ch'i* is the material force residing "within shapes." *Li* is that of which *T'ai-chi* is composed. *Ch'i* is the material force, or Ether, and is responsible for the diversity of phenomenal reality.

Even though *li* naturally expresses itself through *ch'i*, *li* is logically prior with respect to *ch'i*. In other words, the principle of the moon exists prior to the phenomenon of the moon itself. But the nature of *li* is such that the moon is necessarily actualized. The moon has its own principle, and this principle naturally manifests itself as a moon. This all comes about due to *ch'i* combining with the energies of yin and yang and the Five Elements to produce matter.

From what we have seen so far, there is no duality between *li* and *ch'i*. Instead, *li* and *ch'i* are never separate, though logically distinct. In fact, *li* and *ch'i* are codependent. They, along with the universal forces of yin and yang, cooperate in bringing about phenomenal reality. In all this, *ch'i* is the source of the differences among things, whereas *li* is the source of their unity.

Chu Hsi's analysis extends further and makes the following striking claim: Not only does each object have within itself its own *li*, but each object also possesses the totality of all *li*s, the *T'ai-chi*.

We can summarize Chu Hsi's syntheses on a number of levels:

1. *Li* and *ch'i* are both necessary and codependent, even though Chu Hsi admits to the conceptual priority of *li*.
2. As diverse as objective reality is, its diversity stems from *ch'i*. Yet, its oneness is due to *li*.

3. Not only is every speck of dust and each object a reflection of *li*, but it also reflects *T'ai-chi*, the Great Ultimate. Although this Supreme Ultimate remains concealed in each object, it is still present.

School of Mind:
Lu Hsiang-shan and Wang Yang-ming

Both Lu Hsiang-shan and Wang Yang-ming strongly opposed what they believed was Chu Hsi's assertion of a difference between *li* and mind. How is it that Chu Hsi assumed a distinction between *li* and mind? Chu assumed this dichotomy when he emphasized that one must investigate things in order to discover their principle, and Lu and Wang felt that this presupposes a strict distinction between the mind (which does the investigating) and principle.

For Lu, mind is not simply a function of principle. Mind is principle. Mind is *li*. This is the case because mind is one with the universe, and all mind is the same. Because mind is universe and the universe is an expression of Tao, then mind is an expression of Tao.[35]

In the same way, Wang argued that mind and principle are essentially the same. However, let us first be clear about what Wang means by the "mind." Wang is not positing merely an individual mind, but a universal mind; that is, a mind that is united with all other minds.[36]

The most crucial point here is that, for Wang, there is no real distinction between that which exists "above shapes" and that which exists "within shapes." Furthermore, because mind is principle, then to understand principle one must understand mind. This is different from Chu Hsi, who advised that one must study external things in order to know principle.

Perhaps the most important feature in Wang Yang-ming's thought deals less with his view of reality and more with his theory of the "extension of knowledge." This is his unity of knowledge and action, even though it finds its basis in his teaching that mind and principle are one.

Empirical School: Tai Chen

The empirical response to the positions we have considered seeks to restore a primal unity between *li* and *ch'i*. Material force, or *ch'i*, is no longer subordinate to *li*; it has equal if not more significance. Tai Chen especially reasserted this harmony between principle and material force, which is best expressed through the concrete application of principle in daily affairs.

Tai Chen taught that the production and reproduction of all things occur due to *li*, which is not transcendent to *ch'i* but is actually immanent in *ch'i*. In positing this, he situated philosophy on empiricism in two ways. First, *li* is not transcendent to *ch'i*, but is actually immanent in *ch'i*. Second, he underscores the lack of any essential distinction between *li* and *ch'i* by pointing out that they *both* constitute the Tao. (Both rationalists and idealists contend that Tao is purely principle.)[37]

Japanese Philosophies

Addressing questions concerning the nature of reality is especially difficult when we survey Japanese thought. The general tendency throughout Japanese thought and culture has been to particularize the more universal questions concerning reality. Only when questions of reality are grounded upon the concrete do they make sense. This is why, when we discuss Japanese philosophy, we see relatively little in the form of systematic treatises. For the Japanese, philosophy is necessarily an engagement with everyday, concrete realities.

Early Buddhism and Reality

Various philosophical schools in Japan adopted the teachings of their counterparts in China. For instance, we find this reflected in the early Buddhist schools.

Sanron School: Sunya

The Sanron school is also called the Three Treatises school. The most important of the three treatises upon which the school is based is Nagarjuna's *Madhyamika Karika.* Therefore, the concept of *sunyata,* emptiness, or Void, is the key teaching concerning reality. As we noted earlier, *sunya* literally means "swollen" and indicates an emptiness within that which outwardly appears to be full. Sanron embraces this idea. Its fundamental teaching is therefore in line with Madhyamika in that all things are, in essence, devoid of self-subsistence. Because no thing is self-subsistent or exists independently, each thing is related to all other things.

Kegon School: Dependent Origination

The Kegon teachings have their source in the *Avatamsaka Sutra,* also called the *Kegon Sutra.* One of the main emphases of the Kegon school is the Buddhist teaching of dependent origination. The school emphasizes the interrelationship that exists among all things, particularly within the realm of human existence. The idea that the universe is contained, for example, in one single leaf is an important aspect in the relation between unity and plurality, between one and many. This relation exists both spatially and temporally.

Ri is the Japanese equivalent of the Chinese *li* and refers to principle. *Ji* refers to the manifold world of our experience. Although Kegon teaches that *ri* is distinct from *ji,* it goes on to claim that *ri* exists within *ji.* Principle, therefore, is immanent in the world. Here is an effort to integrate unity and plurality. This means that, for the Kegon school, each particular thing harbors within itself the totality of all things, which is principle. Within the temporal dimension, each particular moment in time possesses eternity.[38]

Tendai School: The One Is the Many

The principal text of the Tendai school is the *Saddharmapundarika Sutra,* popularly known as the *Lotus Sutra.* (The Japanese name for this is *Hokke-kyo.*) It provides an elaborate metaphysical synthesis in which ultimate reality and its individual manifestations are identical. All things are interrelated and one in an elaborate metaphysical network. The one and its manifestations are identical: "One thought is the three-thousand spheres [that is, the whole universe], and the three-thousand spheres are but one thought."[39]

Shingon School: The World Is Vairocana

Shingon was a most prominent and influential school during Heian Buddhism. The whole idea in Shingon is that all things, all phenomena, are the manifestation of the supreme Buddha. The supreme Buddha is called Vairocana, also known as Mahavairocana.

More specifically, Shingon teachings center around the notion of *dharma-kaya,* which refers to that which is without origin and without end. Another term for *dharma-kaya* is the Buddha Vairocana. Vairocana Buddha is immanent in this world; as a result, the world assumes an intrinsically divine character. The world is the Buddha, and the Buddha is the world.

Medieval Buddhism and Reality

Jodo School: Tariki

The Jodo school, also known as the Pure Land school, posits the absolute Buddha as Amida (known as Amitabha in Indian Vajrayana). What is most important is that this ultimate reality of the Buddha can be attained through faith in the saving power of Amida, the Buddha of Unending Light. Enlightenment cannot occur by one's self (*jiriki*). The Jodo school illustrates *tariki,* or "other-effort." Therefore, in contrast to the Shingon school, its teachings are specifically for ordinary people.

Because many people tend to view the Absolute as transcendent, they therefore need a way to bridge that gap between the human and the divine. The chasm is bridged through faith and prayer. This faith is not a matter of chanting prayers mechanically; it demands keeping Amida, the Buddha, with the proper attitude in mind and heart, as the popular litany, "*Namu Amida Butsu*" is repeated. In this way, we gain entry into the Pure Land paradise after we die. We do not remain there, however. Our birth in the Pure Land paradise is such that it entails returning to this world to work for the salvation of all others.

Amida embodies infinite compassion. A belief in the Buddha as infinite compassion has profound implications. It illustrates all the more the intimate nexus among all things in existence. By relying on the infinite compassion of Amida, we realize our oneness with all of reality, and especially with all living creatures.

Zen Buddhism and Dogen

Just as we find in Ch'an Buddhism, Zen Buddhists teach that ultimate reality is here and now; that is, "the mind is identical with the Buddha." Our ordinary minds and the Buddha-mind are the same. The aim in Zen is to eventually realize this awakening to our original Buddha-nature.

In contrast to the Jodo school, Zen emphasizes *jiriki* over *tariki*. Self-effort, or self-power, is involved, rather than reliance on the power of another. In Zen there is no discrimination between what is considered self and nonself. The goal is to realize our oneness with all reality. Although reality lies within us, we ordinarily seek the truth outside of ourselves. For Zen Buddhists, this is like "seeking the horse while riding the horse."[40]

Dogen's Question   Dogen, a classic representative of this Zen teaching, maintains that the Buddha-nature permeates all things. Due to this, there is already a "primal" enlightenment. Because of our original nature, we are already, in a sense, enlightened; otherwise, the practice of spiritual cultivation would not be possible. This practice of cultivation is through *zazen*, sitting meditation.

Now, a fundamental question was a burning source of concern for Dogen: How can we reconcile the truth of our original nature with the need to be enlightened? If we are Buddhas by nature, then why do we need to practice *zazen*? Or, put it another way: How compatible is our original awakening (in Japanese, this is called *hongaku*) with our acquired awakening (called *shikaku*)?

Dogen resolved this question with one of the most original ideas in Japanese intellectual history, a unique metaphysical posture: the identity of attainment and practice. But before we examine his resolution of his initial question, we must first get grounded in the major ideas that will support his resolution, for in these matters his views on reality are especially pertinent.

First of all, the general Mahayana teachings point out that all sentient beings possess Buddha-nature. Dogen went further and claimed that all being is Buddha-nature—that is, all being is sentient and nonsentient. Now this is a vital teaching in Dogen. Furthermore, the idea of "being" needs to be properly understood. When he claimed that all being is Buddha-nature, the idea of "being" goes beyond that which is simply existent. Dogen sought to transcend the ordinary distinction between existent and nonexistent entities. In other words, "being" includes the nonexistent realm as well.[41] It encompasses the broadest possible sense of existence, embracing being and nonbeing so that there is no essential opposition. In this way, he seeks to transcend subject/object, birth/death, and sentient/nonsentient distinctions.

Dogen never tired of emphasizing the oneness of being, and his essay, "One Bright Jewel" (included at the end of this chapter), clearly depicts this. This same essay points out to us that this oneness of all being does not mean the submersion of individuality in the whole.

Dogen's Resolution: The Wind Is the Fan   We can see from these ideas that Dogen's view of reality is nondual and dynamic. Everything constantly undergoes change. This led him to posit the oneness of being with time: At the same time, each moment in itself is absolute. This means that each moment contains all of existence in itself, just as each cell, particle, or grain of dust contains the Buddha. The absolute is contained in the particular.

When we apply this to the practice of *zazen,* we see that each moment of *zazen* is itself a full awakening. The Zen Buddhist scholar Heinrich Dumoulin stated it quite succinctly:

> To the one who practices, the Buddha innate in original enlightenment comes into being at every moment of time. To experience one's fleeting life without illusion and in accordance with the truth of the Buddha is to actualize the present in the present. This and nothing else is Zen.[42]

The resolution to Dogen's question about the reconciliation of original enlightenment and practice is found in his *"Genjokoan,"* or "The Issue At Hand." One passage reads:

> Zen Master Hotetsu of Mt. Mayoku was using a fan. A monk asked him about this: "The nature of wind is eternal and all-pervasive— why then do you use a fan?" The master said, "You only know the nature of wind is eternal, but do not yet know the principle of its omnipresence." The monk asked, "What is the principle of its omnipresence?" The master just fanned. The monk bowed.[43]

If we view the question in conventional terms, then dualism still exists— in this case between the wind and the fan, as well as between the fan and the master. Resolution comes about when it is realized that the activities of fanning and the wind are essentially one and the same. David Loy expressed it clearly when he said that "practice is the natural way in which one's 'original enlightenment' manifests itself."[44]

Tokugawa Confucianism and Reality

Just as we find with the early Buddhist schools, the Japanese adopted many of the teachings of the Confucianists. They were particularly attracted to the Neo-Confucian teachings of Chu Hsi concerning the nature of reality.

Chu Hsi School of Principle (Shushi)

For the Japanese Confucians, Chu Hsi's thought, known in Japanese as *Shushi,* is extremely important because it points to the synthetic relationship between the way of Heaven and the way of man. The way of Heaven is called *tendo,* and the way of man is called *jindo.* The creative power of Heaven is what gives birth to and sustains all things, including all of nature and all of humanity. Chi Hsi asserts a metaphysical kinship within all existence.

The natural processes we continually witness (the four seasons, life and death, and so on) are manifestations of the principle of Heaven, or *li. Li* is also manifested in human relationships, as in the Five Confucian relationships of duties and affection. *Li* sustains, therefore, an ethical order as well as the natural order. It is this symbiosis of metaphysics with morality that has special appeal to the Japanese.

The relation between *li* and *ch'i* is significant. Chu Hsi is interpreted as claiming that *li* is the causative force that brings about all things in the universe. *Li* exists along with *ch'i* in all things. Their distinction lies in this: *Li* is the metaphysical principle that permeates all things, whereas *ch'i* is the physical Ether that determines the form of all existing things. Insofar as *li* exists in each thing, all things are the same. Yet, each thing differs from all else due to its *ch'i*. This is similar to what we find in the Chinese school.

For Chu Hsi, investigating things led to knowledge of their principle. For the Japanese, Chu Hsi's teachings reveal that through a study of the natural sciences, one can perceive the universal principles at work. The study of the particular gives rise to an understanding of the universal principle. This study of nature is especially prominent in the work of Kaibara Ekken.

Despite his admiration for Chu Hsi, Kaibara had some doubts about some of his ideas. He was opposed to the dualism that he felt Chu Hsi posited between *li* and *ch'i*. For Chu Hsi, *li* is the foundational force and principle which transcended *ch'i*. *Li* is thus prior to and superior to *ch'i*. Instead, Kaibara contended that *li* is a principle that is immanent with *ch'i* itself. In doing so, he uplifts the significance of *ch'i*. He goes on to claim that *T'ai-chi*, or the Supreme Ultimate, is actually "primal material force." The Supreme Ultimate is a primal material energy that gives way to concrete physical expressions in the universe of that energy.

Kaibara criticized any attempt to suggest an idea of "emptiness" as the origin of existence. For Kaibara, existence can only come from existence. What is decisive in all this is that Kaibara wished to propose a life-affirming teaching that did not separate *li* and *ch'i*.

Ito Jinsai: *Ancient Learning* (Kogakuha)

The Ancient Learning scholar, Ito Jinsai, reaffirms Kaibara's emphasis on the primal material force. For Ito, the condition for all things rests upon a primal material energy called *ichi genki*, which literally means "eternal," without beginning or end. He holds that *ri*, or principle, is inherent in *ki* (this is the Chinese *ch'i*), which is material force. For Ito, it is *ki*, through yin and yang, that brings about the universe. In this way, Ito opposes the idea that principle exists prior to *ki*, or Ether. Ito transforms principle into a strictly physical force.

This being the case, what accounts for the ultimate origin of yin and yang and the Five Elements? Ito was not willing to assign an "emptiness" or nothingness to this ultimate principle. (He wanted to avoid this Buddhist tendency.) He claimed that there is nothing we can really know about this ultimate origin, what he calls the Will of Heaven. He avoids asserting an emptiness as origin by personalizing the Will of Heaven with titles such as "ruling prince" and "sovereign authority." The Will of Heaven is the ultimate causal factor in a changing world.

Kyoto School and Reality

Nishida Kitaro: Pure Experience and Nothingness

Nishida is truly one of the most important figures in Japanese philosophy. This "father" of the Kyoto school is profoundly influential in contemporary Japanese thought. It is therefore something of an injustice, as it is with other thinkers, to simply isolate one aspect—in this case, his view of reality—from his other views. Portions from his *An Inquiry into the Good* are included at the end of this chapter.

Reality As Pure Experience   Nishida's view is reminiscent of Zen Buddhism; he promotes Zen teachings using philosophical categories. Now Zen points directly to reality—what exists in its immediacy. Nishida viewed reality in much the same way; he directly pointed to pure experience as ultimate reality. Reality is that which underlies all our so-called "experience." (We say "so-called" because it is not experience in its purity; rather, our experience is conventionally mediated. In other words, it is filtered through our ideas of that experience.) We conventionally live in our ideas or images of the real, rather than in the real.

   Reality is the pure experience, which is the basis for conceptualization. Once conceptualization through reflection occurs, the experience becomes indirect. Reality remains the same, unaffected by reflection. Reflection, however, gives birth to apparent modes of reality that are not in themselves truly real. When Nishida declares that reality is "pure experience," this means that reality is necessarily prereflective, preconceptual, without any judgment, and totally within the present moment.[46]

Reality As Absolute Nothingness   All this is further sustained by his teaching concerning the primacy of "nothingness" over being. "Absolute nothingness" is another phrase he ascribes to this pure experience. It is crucial to be aware that this "nothingness" is not the same as nihilism. Rather, absolute nothingness transcends the opposition between being and nonbeing by embracing them.

   The term *transcend* can be misleading; it can give the impression of something *beyond* the realm of experience. The term *immanent* is also to be avoided because it may lead to the impression of being immersed in our world of experience. Each of these terms implies the other. They each set up a dichotomy between being and nonbeing. Therefore, for Nishida, the preferred designation is absolute nothingness.

Intellectual Intuition   A basic claim throughout Nishida is that we are able to directly experience this reality, pure experience, and absolute nothingness. The aim of his epistemology is to address more fully how this is possible. Nishida stressed an "intellectual intuition" that is able to acknowledge this reality. It is more of an immediate grasp of reality that is utterly transformative, so much so that, according to Nishida, the experience is essentially religious.

Our conventional, or ordinary, perception of things is that we mistake what we conceive to be real with what is real. Yet what we conceive as being real is inspired by the force of our intellect, and this drives us farther from the reality. Robert Carter's metaphor of perchings and flight is very appropriate:

> For Nishida, to be aware of pure experience is not to deny conception and the various systematizations resulting from thinking, but to ground them all in the original undifferentiated flow of pure flight. They are all perchings, and the only real error we make is to focus so fully on the perchings—the stable, fixed, resting places—that we forget altogether how to fly.[47]

This ultimate reality points to the essential unity of all being. The awareness of this is, for Nishida, religious consciousness. Nishida considered religion to be the fullest experiential integration of both world and self. This meant that God was equivalent to Nishida's Absolute Nothingness. At the same time, God is also Absolute Being.

Yet, for Nishida, ultimate reality is not God, if by "God" we mean a separate self-subsistent reality. Neither is God an idea. God is this pure experience, without abstraction:

> And just as color appears to the eye as color, and sound to the ear as sound, so too God appears to the religious self as an event of one's own soul. It is not a matter of God being conceivable or not conceivable in merely intellectual terms. What can be conceived or not conceived is not God.[48]

Tanabe Hajime: Logic of Species

For Tanabe, Nishida's general position is overly abstruse, even mystical, and without any real anchor in concrete social realities and history. Instead, Tanabe speaks of his "logic of species," which refers to the undercurrent of our social existence. In order to understand what Tanabe means by "species," we must recognize that this social existence acts as a primordial ground for our own individualized existence. Species comes about due to a fundamental will and desire to live. Species also works to sustain this will and desire. A social milieu manifests this will to live, and specific symbols of the group represent this will. For example, we have the sacred symbol of Japan's emperor.[49]

Therefore, by species, Tanabe meant, in a very elementary way, the state or nation. For Tanabe, nation plays a mediating role between mankind and the individual. Thus his logic is often called the "logic of mediation." Put another way, the individual is in tension between a dependency on species and individual free choice. He resolved this tension through a dialectic that embraces both positions.

By placing such emphasis on species, Tanabe stressed the role of the collective entity as opposed to the individual. In order for us to understand this better, we need to examine Tanabe's starting point: his view of nothingness. His view of reality in terms of absolute nothingness embraces aspects of Zen, Jodo (Pure Land), and Christianity. As we said, both Nishida and Tanabe posited an absolute nothingness as a rudimentary part of their understanding of reality. Given the stream of Asian philosophy that we've so far encountered, the idea of nothingness seems to be a starting point that finds few parallels in the West.

For Tanabe, Nishida's view of absolute nothingness manages to evade the historicity of experience. Historical factors need to be considered. Tanabe went on to claim that absolute nothingness is not the ground for genuine self-awareness. It is the ground for some external power acting upon the self. What Tanabe proposed is that absolute nothingness is revealed by way of the total mediating power of the Other.

In order to reach this state, one must express an attitude of repentance required because of the strong and overpowering pull of irrationality to which the individual naturally succumbs. According to Tanabe, the individual, realizing his or her fundamental condition of weakness, needs to undergo a metaphysical metanoesis, or conversion.

Nishitani Keiji: Nihility and Sunyata

Nishitani Keiji completes the famous triad often associated with the Kyoto school. Nishitani dealt with the nature of reality in terms of the question of meaninglessness. The problems surrounding the meaning of existence have always been the challenge of philosophy. In his classic work, *Religion and Nothingness,* part of which is found at the end of this chapter, he began with an examination of the question of meaning. He explained that this question is intimately associated with a religious quest. (Here, he deftly demonstrated the close link between religion and philosophy.)

In our contemporary climate, Nishitani argues that the question of meaning is all the more pressing. There is less faith in the traditional responses. For Nishitani, the idea that existence is ultimately without meaning is called nihilism. Nihilism is directly relevant to questions about reality, for it basically asserts that there is no ultimate reality.

The extreme responses to meaninglessness can assume two positions:

- Complete surrender to meaninglessness. In this case, one admits that nothing is meaningful.
- Surrender to some external "anchor," whether it be a person, God, book, or idea. For Nishitani, both of these responses are incomplete and inauthentic.

Sunyata and Nihility Nishitani, influenced very much by existentialists such as Nietzsche and Sartre, provided his own unique response to the question of meaning. At the center of his response is the Buddhist teaching of *sunyata,* emptiness. For him, *sunyata* is the way to overcome nihilism.

This entails a response to meaninglessness, involving what he terms "nihility." Nihility is a despair so radical that it can lead to transformation. Yet, in order for nihility to be transformative, it needs a necessary feature; that is, the only proper response to nihility, for Nishitani, lies in the idea of *sunyata,* emptiness. In fact, it is emptiness that is all the more reaffirmed precisely due to the three marks of Buddhism: suffering, impermanence, and no-self.

For Nishitani, *sunyata* is reality. Transformation from nihility can occur only through the realization of the truth of *sunyata.*[50] For Nishitani, nihility, although given a negative connotation, remains a necessary step to realizing *sunyata.* Also, by realizing *sunyata,* we can obtain a sound grasp on nihility.

The Field of Sunyata   Let us be clearer about Nishitani's *sunyata.* The term certainly inhabits a sizeable place in Buddhist writings. For Nishitani, *sunyata,* or emptiness, constitutes the ground for all that is—the world, events, experiences, and so on. In his text he often speaks of *sunyata* in terms of a place, or "field" (similar to Nishida). For Nishitani, *sunyata* is that ontological field from which all else derives. It is the field that grounds the interconnectedness of all things with each other. In order to avoid reification and anthropomorphic refinements concerning *sunyata,* Nishitani referred to *sunyata* as a "force." This force acts as a "sustainer" that informs, infuses, and holds everything together.[51]

This does not mean that individual things are submerged within some sort of mystical whole. *Sunyata* is such that it sustains individuality. The relationship between the whole and its individual parts is what Nishitani called "circuminsessional interpenetration." In this way, plurality is integrated with unity, yet plurality holds on to its unique particularity.[52]

Study Questions

India

1. Discuss the philosophical significance of the *Nasadiya Hymn.*
2. Describe the main ideas in the Upanishads.
3. How does Krishna's message about being, *atman,* and *Brahman* in the *Bhagavad Gita* have a bearing on the question of reality?
4. What are the three aspects of the nature of *Brahman?*
5. Discuss the atomist theory in Vaisheshika.
6. Describe the evolution of material things from *purusa,* and the relationship between *purusa* and *prakriti* in Samkhya.
7. Describe the three gunas of *prakriti* according to Samkhya.
8. Contrast the theories of *satkarya-vada* and *asatkarya-vada.*
9. How does Sankara's view of the world as illusion compare with that of Badarayana's?
10. Discuss the meaning of *Brahman* as both *nirguna* and *saguna* in Sankara.
11. What is the connection between *jiva* and *atman* in Advaita Vedanta?
12. What is the relation between *Brahman* and the world in Sankara's view?
13. Examine the meaning and role behind both *avidya* and *maya* in Vedanta thought.

14. In Ramanuja's view, what is the relationship among the three basic realities, and how does this bear upon his qualified nondualism?
15. In what way do Madhva's five distinctions relate to his dualism?
16. Despite their differences, what do the three schools of Vedanta have in common?
17. What do we mean by the Buddha's "silence" with respect to metaphysical questions?
18. Describe the Buddhist Four Noble Truths and the Three Marks of Existence.
19. Contrast the role of *dharmas* in both Sarvastivada and Sautrantika schools.
20. Discuss the meaning of *sunyata* in Mahayana Buddhism.
21. How does Nagarjuna's Middle Way, or *Madhyamika,* teaching apply to views of reality?
22. According to what rationale did Nagarjuna reject all four typical theories of causation? What is the relation between cause and *sunya*?
23. Discuss the Vijnanavada view of reality.

China

24. Discuss essential themes in Chinese philosophy concerning reality.
25. Explain the meanings of Tao and *te* in Lao Tzu. How did Chuang Tzu broaden the notion of Tao?
26. Explain Hui Shih's views of reality through some of his paradoxes.
27. Describe reality in terms of the interplay of yin and yang as, for example, in the *I Ching.*
28. Contrast the two theories of Tung Chung-shu and Wang Ch'ung: correspondence and spontaneity.
29. Explain how Tao is given a more metaphysical status in Neo-Taoist thinkers such as Wang Pi and Kuo Hsiang.
30. What is the nature of the relationship between *yu* and *wu* for Seng Chao?
31. How did Chi-tsang view the relation between *yu* and *wu* in terms of his double truth theory?
32. What did Hsuan-tsang mean when he claimed that all phenomena are merely manifestations of consciousness?
33. What is the distinction between the T'ien-t'ai school and that of Consciousness Only, and how does it bear upon the relation between *yu* and *wu*?
34. Explain how Fa-tsang sought to assign a qualified reality to phenomena; illustrate through his Hall of Mirrors and Golden Lion.
35. How does Fa-tsang's synthesis of *yu* and *wu* differ from the teaching of their relation in the T'ien-t'ai school?
36. Describe the compatibility of ultimacy and ordinariness in Ch'an Buddhism.
37. Discuss how Ch'eng Yi and Chu Hsi described the relation between *li* and *ch'i,* and the role of *T'ai-chi.*
38. Explain the synthesis of Chu Hsi.

39. What is the primary objection of the school of Mind to that of Principle, and on what basis is it founded?
40. In view of their understanding of "mind," how did Lu Hsiang-shan and Wang Yang-ming view the relation between *li* and mind?
41. How did Tai Chen restore significance to *ch'i* in terms of its relation to *li*?

Japan

42. How does the relation between *ri* and *ji* in the Kegon school manifest the meaning behind dependent origination?
43. Describe the teachings of both Tendai and Shingon concerning reality.
44. Explain the significance of *tariki* in Jodo.
45. How does Zen stress *jiriki* over *tariki*? Illustrate through Dogen's teachings.
46. How did Dogen resolve his question concerning the reconciliation of our original natures and practice? Illustrate this through his *Genjokoan*.
47. In what way did Dogen extend the Mahayana teaching further concerning beings and Buddha-nature?
48. Explain the relation between *li* and *ch'i* in the Japanese Confucian school of Shushi.
49. How did Kaibara Ekken describe the role of *li* while raising the status of *ch'i*? How is this supported by Ito Jinsai?
50. In what way is reality viewed as "pure experience" for Nishida Kitaro?
51. How is reality Absolute Nothingness for Nishida? What is the role of intellectual intuition?
52. Describe Tanabe's "logic of species" along with his view of "nothingness." How does this differ from Nishida?
53. What is the meaning of nihility according to Nishitani Keiji, and what fundamental problems does it seek to address?
54. In Nishitani's view, explain how *sunyata* overcomes nihilism.

Notes

1. From Chuang Tzu, "The Autumn Flood," in Arthur Waley, *Three Ways of Thought in Ancient China* (London: George Allen & Unwin Ltd., 1939), 55–56.
2. P. T. Raju, *Structural Depths of Indian Thought* (Albany: State University of New York Press, 1985), 10–11.
3. *Brihadaranyaka Upanishad* I.iv.10, in Swami Nikhilananda, trans., *The Upanishads*, abridged ed. (New York: Harper Torchbook, Harper & Row, 1964), 191–192.
4. S. Radhakrishnan, trans. and notes, *The Bhagavadgītā* (London: George Allen & Unwin Ltd., 1971) II.30, 111.
5. Remember that the Jains are considered heterodox. Their view of reality appears to be a metaphysical posture that holds that there are many substances, each qualified by their attributes. Yet, they do believe that *atman* is eternal, and that the individual needs to realize *atman* through vigilant and disciplined purification of the many defilements, especially physical, that act to obstruct genuine realization.
6. Amidst all this lies a strikingly controversial idea: The Vaisheshika school proposes that a personal God fashions the world from these nine elements; however, these nine substances in themselves were *not* created by God.

7. P. T. Raju, "Metaphysical Theories in Indian Philosophy," in *The Indian Mind: Essentials of Indian Philosophy and Culture,* ed. Charles A. Moore (Honolulu: East-West Center Press, University of Hawaii Press, 1967), 49.
8. *Brihadaranyaka Upanishad* II, 3, 6, in Nikhilananda, 200.
9. Eliot Deutsch, *Advaita Vedanta: A Philosophical Reconstruction* (Honolulu: University of Hawaii Press, 1990), 39. Some of the following discussion is adapted from this excellent introduction to Sankara.
10. Deutsch, 28.
11. It is important to keep in mind that Sankara is not positing an absolute idealism— the belief that all reality consists in the mind, or consciousness. Such an interpretation erroneously exaggerates the aspect of *Brahman* as absolute consciousness. In other words, Sankara does not contend that objects of our perception do not exist. In fact, it is due to our perception of objects that they do exist—as objects of our perception.
12. Deutsch, 32.
13. From "Questions Which Tend Not to Edification," from the Majjhima-Nikaya, in Henry Clarke Warren, trans., *Buddhism in Translations: Passages Selected from the Buddhist Sacred Books and Translated from the Original Pali into English,* student's edition, 1896 (Cambridge, Massachusetts: Harvard University Press, 1953), 117.
14. Majijhima-Nikaya, in Warren, 120–21.
15. Whether Nagarjuna was a Mahayanist is disputed. Most scholars propose his strong affiliation with the Mahayana school. Some have questioned this; see David J. Kalupahana's excellent study, *Nagarjuna: The Philosophy of the Middle Way,* SUNY Series in Buddhist Studies (Albany: State University of New York Press, 1986).
16. Daniel J. Boorstin, *The Image: A Guide to Pseudo-Events in America* (New York: Atheneum, 1972), 7.
17. Kenneth K. Inada, trans. and introductory essay, *Nāgārjuna: A Translation of his Mūlamadhyamakakārikā with an Introductory Essay* (Tokyo: The Hokuseido Press, 1970), Chap. 1, verse 1, 39.
18. Inada, Chap. 1, verse 10, 41.
19. A. L. Herman, *An Introduction to Buddhist Thought: A Philosophic History of Indian Buddhism* (Lanham, Md.: University Press of America, 1983), 315.
20. For a good discussion of these terms, see A. C. Graham, "Relation of Chinese Thought to Chinese Languages," Appendix 2, in *Disputers of the Tao* (La Salle, Ill.: Open Court Press, 1989), pp. 408–12.
21. In this way, David Hall and Roger Ames describe "being" within an *ars contextualis.* Things do not exist as separate fragments, but are present within an established context of interrelationship with other things. See the discussion of this in David L. Hall and Roger T. Ames, "Understanding Order: The Chinese Perspective," in Robert C. Solomon and Kathleen M. Higgins, ed., *From Africa to Zen: An Invitation to World Philosophy* (Lanham, MD.: Rowman & Littlefield Publishers, Inc., 1993), 6–7.
22. Ellen M. Chen, trans. and commentary, *The Tao Te Ching: A New Translation with Commentary* (New York: Paragon House, 1989) 1.1.2a, 51.
23. Herbert A. Giles, trans., *Chuang Tzu: Mystic, Moralist, and Social Reformer,* 2nd ed., rev. (London: Bernard Quaritch, Limited, 1926), 209.
24. Burton Watson, trans., *Chuang Tzu: Basic Writings* (New York: Columbia University Press, 1964), 45.
25. Watson, trans., *Chuang Tzu: Basic Writings,* 41.
26. These paradoxes are discussed in Fung Yu-lan, *A History of Chinese Philosophy,* trans. Derk Bodde (Princeton, N.J.: Princeton University Press, 1952), Vol. 1, 197–199.
27. His own rendition of the yin and yang forces is slightly different from that of the official Yin-Yang school. Whereas the official school places both yin and yang on an equal level, he raises yang to a higher status.
28. Alfred Forke, trans. and annotated, *Lun-Hêng: Philosophical Essays of Wang Ch'ung, Part 1,* 1907 (New York: Paragon Book Gallery, 1962), 92–93.

29. Walter Liebenthal, trans., intro., notes, and appendices, *Chao Lun: The Treatises of Seng-chao,* 2nd rev. ed. (Hong Kong: Hong Kong University Press, 1968), II.1.1., 55.
30. Liebenthal, *Chao Lun* II.11.3, 60.
31. Cited in Fung Yu-lan, *A History of Chinese Philosophy,* trans. Derk Bodde (Princeton: Princeton University Press, 1952, 1953), Vol. 2. 2, 325.
32. See the discussion in Wing-Tsit Chan, trans. and compiler, *A Source Book in Chinese Philosophy* (Princeton: Princeton University Press, 1963), 412, note 16.
33. On this point, Ch'eng Yi's brother Ch'eng Hao disagreed, arguing that *li* is actually contained within the specific material force, so that it is not external to the material object.
34. See Fung, *History of Chinese Philosophy,* Vol. 2, 511–12.
35. Lu's student, Yang Chien, carried this further. If all things are within the mind, then no things are external to self. Yang Chien illustrated this through Mencius's famous example of the child by a well. When we see a child by a well, ready to fall into it, we act immediately to save the child. According to Yang Chien, we cannot help but attempt to save the child because the child is actually "one with the self." See the discussion in Fung, *History of Chinese Philosophy,* Vol. 2, 582.
36. See Wing-tsit Chan, "The Story of Chinese Philosophy," in Charles A. Moore, ed., *The Chinese Mind: Essentials of Chinese Philosophy and Culture* (Honolulu: University of Hawaii Press, 1967), 62.
37. See the discussion in Fung, *History of Chinese Philosophy,* Vol. 2, 652–57.
38. Hanayama Shinshō, "Buddhism of the One Great Vehicle (Mahayana)," in Charles A. Moore, ed., *The Japanese Mind: Essentials of Japanese Philosophy and Culture* (Honolulu: University of Hawaii Press, 1987), 37–38. A significant idea in Kegon is "self-origination of the *dharma-datu*," or *hokkai engi.* See Hanayama, 47, note 14. This refers to the unfolding of the world through its own power, and not by some external power.
39. Hajime Nakamura, *A History of the Development of Japanese Thought from A.D. 592 to 1868.* 2nd ed. (Tokyo: Kokusai Bunka Shinkokai, 1969), 41.
40. Hanayama provides a good synopsis of the history and main ideas of these Mahayana schools in "Buddhism of the One Great Vehicle," in Moore, *The Japanese Mind,* 33–51.
41. See Masao Abe, *A Study of Dogen: His Philosophy and Religion,* ed. Steven Heine (Albany: State University of New York Press, 1992), 36.
42. Heinrich Dumoulin, S. J., *A History of Zen Buddhism,* trans. Paul Peachey (Boston: Beacon Press, 1969), 170.
43. Thomas Cleary, trans., *Shōbōgenzō: Zen Essays by Dōgen* (Honolulu: University of Hawaii Press, 1986), 35.
44. David Loy, *Nonduality: A Study in Comparative Philosophy* (New Haven, Conn.: Yale University Press, 1988), 248. Loy's is an excellent study of the meaning of nonduality.
45. Mary Evelyn Tucker, *Moral and Spiritual Cultivation in Japanese Neo-Confucianism: The Life and Thought of Kaibara Ekken, 1630–1740,* SUNY Series in Philosophy (Albany: State University of New York Press, 1989), 66–72.
46. David Dilworth, "The Initial Formations of 'Pure Experience,'" in Nishida Kitarō and William James', *Monumenta Nipponica* XXIV, no. 1–2.
47. Robert E. Carter, *The Nothingness Beyond God: An Introduction to the Philosophy of Nishida Kitaro* (New York: Paragon House, 1989), 13.
48. Kitaro Nishida, "Logic of the Place of Nothingness and the Religious Worldview," in *Last Writings: Nothingness and the Religious Worldview,* trans. David Dilworth (Honolulu: University of Hawaii Press, 1987), 48.
49. We can now see why Tanabe's teaching was misinterpreted as reinforcing nationalism. His intent was basically to examine the idea of a collective or national spirit, quite distinct from nationalism.
50. See Stephen H. Phillips, "Nishitani's Buddhist Response to 'Nihilism,'" *Journal of the American Academy of Religion* LV, no. 1: 77ff.
51. Phillips, 93.
52. Phillips, 88.

Nasadiya (Creation Hymn), from *Rig Veda*

There was neither non-existence nor existence then; there was neither the realm of space nor the sky which is beyond. What stirred? Where? In whose protection? Was there water, bottomlessly deep?

There was neither death nor immortality then. There was no distinguishing sign of night nor of day. That one breathed, windless, by its own impulse. Other than that there was nothing beyond.

Darkness was hidden by darkness in the beginning; with no distinguishing sign, all this was water. The life force that was covered with emptiness, that one arose through the power of heat.

Desire came upon that one in the beginning; that was the first seed of mind. Poets seeking in their heart with wisdom found the bond of existence in non-existence.

Their cord was extended across. Was there below? Was there above? There were seed-placers; there were powers. There was impulse beneath; there was giving-forth above.

Who really knows? Who will here proclaim it? Whence was it produced? Whence is this creation? The gods came afterwards, with the creation of this universe. Who then knows whence it has arisen?

Whence this creation has arisen—perhaps it formed itself, or perhaps it did not—the one who looks down on it, in the highest heaven, only he knows—or perhaps he does not know.

Reprinted from Wendy Doniger O'Flaherty, trans., *The Rig Veda: An Anthology*. London: Penquin Books, 1981, p. 25; reprinted with permission of the publisher. © 1981 by Wendy Doniger O'Flaherty.

Introduction to Commentary on the
Vedanta Sutras of Badarayana

Sankara

It is a matter not requiring any proof that the object and the subject[1] whose respective spheres are the notion of the "Thou" (the Non-Ego[2]) and the "Ego," and which are opposed to each other as much as darkness and light are, cannot be identified. All the less can their respective attributes be identified. Hence it follows that it is wrong to superimpose[3] upon the subject—whose Self is intelligence, and which has for its sphere the notion of the Ego—the object whose sphere is the notion of the Non-Ego, and the attributes of the object, and vice versa to superimpose the subject and the attributes of the subject on the object. In spite of this it is on the part of man a natural[4] procedure—which has its cause in wrong knowledge—not to distinguish the two entities (object and subject) and their respective attributes, although they are absolutely distinct, but to superimpose upon each the characteristic nature and the attributes of the other, and thus, coupling the Real and the Unreal[5], to make use of expressions such as "That am I," "That is mine"[6]—But what have we to understand by the term "superimposition?"—The apparent presentation, in the form of remembrance, to consciousness of something previously observed, in some other thing.

Some indeed define the term "superimposition" as the superimposition of the attributes of one thing on another thing.[7] Others, again, define superimposition as the error founded on the non-apprehension of the difference of that which is superimposed from that on which it is superimposed.[8] Others,[9] again, define it as the fictitious assumption of attributes contrary to the nature of that thing on which something else is superimposed. But all these definitions agree in so far as they represent superimposition as the apparent presentation of the attributes of one thing in another thing. And therewith agrees also the popular view which is exemplified by expressions such as the following: "Mother-of-pearl appears like silver," "The moon although one only appears as if she were double." But how is it possible that on the interior Self which itself is not an object there should be superimposed objects and their attributes? For every one superimposes an object only on such other objects as are placed before him (i.e. in contact with his sense-organs), and you have said before that the interior Self which is entirely disconnected from the idea of the Thou (the Non-Ego) is never an object. It is not, we reply, non-object in the absolute sense. For it is the object of the notion of the Ego,[10]

Reprinted from George Thibault, trans., *The Vedanta Sutras of Badarayana*, Part I. New York: Dover (Sacred Books of the East, 1890), 1962, pp. 3–9.

and the interior Self is well known to exist on account of its immediate (intuitive) presentation.[11] Nor is it an exceptionless rule that objects can be superimposed only on such other objects as are before us, i.e. in contact with our sense-organs; for non-discerning men superimpose on the ether, which is not the object of sensuous perception, dark-blue colour.

Hence it follows that the assumption of the Non-Self being superimposed on the interior Self is not unreasonable.

This superimposition thus defined, learned men consider to be Nescience (avidyâ), and the ascertainment of the true nature of that which is (the Self) by means of the discrimination of that (which is superimposed on the Self), they call knowledge (vidyâ). There being such knowledge (neither the Self nor the Non-Self) are affected in the least by any blemish or (good) quality produced by their mutual superimposition. The mutual superimposition of the Self and the Non-Self, which is termed Nescience, is the presupposition on which there base all the practical distinctions—those made in ordinary life as well as those laid down by the Veda—between means of knowledge, objects of knowledge (and knowing persons), and all scriptural texts, whether they are concerned with injunctions and prohibitions (of meritorious and non-meritorious actions), or with final release.—But how can the means of right knowledge such as perception, inference, &c., and scriptural texts have for their object that which is dependent on Nescience.—Because, we reply, the means of right knowledge cannot operate unless there be a knowing personality, and because the existence of the latter depends on the erroneous notion that the body, the senses, and so on, are identical with, or belong to, the Self of the knowing person. For without the employment of the senses, perception and the other means of right knowledge cannot operate. And without a basis (i.e. the body) the senses cannot act. Nor does anybody act by means of a body on which the nature of the Self is not superimposed. Nor can, in the absence of all that, the Self which, in its own nature is free from all contact, become a knowing agent. And if there is no knowing agent, the means of right knowledge cannot operate (as said above). Hence perception and the other means of right knowledge, and the Vedic texts have for their object that which is dependent on Nescience. (That human cognitional activity has for its presupposition the superimposition described above), follows also from the non-difference in that respect of men from animals. Animals, when sounds or other sensible qualities affect their sense of hearing or other senses, recede or advance according as the idea derived from the sensation is a comforting or disquieting one. A cow, for instance, when she sees a man approaching with a raised stick in his hand, thinks that he wants to beat her, and therefore moves away; while she walks up to a man who advances with some fresh grass in his hand. Thus men also—who possess a higher intelligence—run away when they see strong fierce-looking fellows drawing near with shouts and brandishing swords; while they confidently approach persons of contrary appearance and behaviour. We thus see that men and animals follow the same course of procedure with reference to the means and objects of knowledge. Now it is well known that the procedure of animals bases on the non-distinction (of Self and Non-Self); we therefore conclude that, as they present the same appearances, men also—although distinguished by superior intelligence—proceed with regard to perception and so on, in the same way as animals do; as long, that is to say, as the mutual superimposition of Self and Non-Self lasts. With reference again to that kind of activity which is founded on the Veda (sacrifices and the like), it is true indeed that the reflecting man who is qualified to enter on it, does so not without knowing that the Self has a relation to another world; yet that qualification does not depend on the knowledge, derivable from the Vedânta-texts, of the true nature of the Self as free from all wants, raised above the distinctions of the Brâhmana and Kshattriya-classes and so on, transcending transmigratory existence. For such knowledge is useless and even contradictory to the claim (on the part of sacrificers, &c. to perform certain actions and enjoy their fruits). And before such knowledge of the Self has arisen, the Vedic texts continue in their operation, to have for their object that which is dependent on Nescience. For such texts as the following, "A Brâmana is to sacrifice," are operative only on the supposition that on the Self are superimposed particular conditions such as caste, stage of life, age, outward circumstances, and so on. That by superimposition we have to understand the notion of something in some other thing we have already explained. (The superimposition of the Non-Self will be understood more definitely from the following examples.) Extra-personal attributes are superimposed on the Self, if a man considers himself sound and entire, or the contrary, as long as his wife, children, and so on are sound and entire or not. Attributes of the body are superimposed on the Self, if a man thinks of himself (his Self) as stout, lean, fair, as standing, walking, or jumping. Attributes of the sense-organs, if he thinks "I am mute, or deaf, or one-eyed, or blind." Attributes of the internal organ when he considers himself subject to desire, intention, doubt, determination, and so on. Thus the producer of the notion of the Ego (i.e. the internal organ) is superimposed on the interior Self, which, in reality, is the witness of all the modifications of the internal organ, and vice versa the interior Self, which is the witness of everything, is superimposed on the internal organ, the senses, and so on. In this way there goes on this natural beginning—and endless superimposition, which appears in the form of wrong conception, is the cause of individual souls appearing as agents and enjoyers (of the results of their actions), and is observed by every one.

With a view to freeing one's self from that wrong notion which is the cause of all evil and attaining thereby the knowledge of the absolute unity of the Self the study of the Vedânta-texts is begun. That all the Vedânta-texts have the mentioned purport we shall show in this so-called Sârîraka-mîmâmsâ.

Notes

1. The subject is the universal Self whose nature is intelligence; the object comprises whatever is of a non-intelligent nature, viz. bodies with their sense-organs, internal organs, and the objects of the senses, i.e. the external material world.

2. The object is said to have for its sphere the notion of the "thou," not the notion of the "this" or "that," in order better to mark its absolute opposition to the subject or Ego. Language allows of the co-ordination of the pronouns of the first and the third person ("It is I," "I am he who," &c.; ete vayam, ime vayam âsmahe), but not of the co-ordination of the pronouns of the first and second person.

3. Adhyâsa, literally "superimposition" in the sense of (mistaken) ascription or imputation, to something, of an essential nature or attributes not belonging to it. See later on.

4. Natural, i.e. original, beginningless; for the modes of speech and action which characterise transmigratory existence have existed, with the latter, from all eternity.

5. I.e. the intelligent Self which is the only reality and the non-real objects, viz. body and so on, which are the product of wrong knowledge.

6. "The body, &c. is my Self"; "sickness, death, children, wealth, &c., belong to my Self."

7. The so-called anyathâkhyâtivâdins maintain that in the act of adhyâsa the attributes of one thing, silver for instance, are superimposed on a different thing existing in a different place, mother-of-pearl for instance (if we take for our example of adhyâsa the case of some man mistaking a piece of mother-of-pearl before him for a piece of silver). The âmakhyâtivâdins maintain that in adhyâsa the modification, in the form of silver, of the internal organ is superimposed on the external thing mother-of-pearl and thus itself appears external. Both views fall under the above definition.

8. This is the definition of the akhyâtivâdins.

9. Some anyathâkhyâtivâdins and the Mâdhyamikas according to Ânanda Giri.

10. The pratyagâtman is in reality non-object, for it is svayamprakâsa, self-luminous, i.e. the subjective factor in all cognition. But it becomes the object of the idea of the Ego in so far as it is limited, conditioned by its adjuncts which are the product of Nescience, viz. the internal organ, the senses and the subtle and gross bodies, i.e. in so far as it is *ĝîva*, individual or personal soul.

11. Translated according to the Bhâmatî. We deny, the objector says, the possibility of adhyâsa in the case of the Self, not on the ground that it is not an object because self-luminous (for that it may be an object although it is self-luminous you have shown), but on the ground that it is not an object because it is not manifested either by itself or by anything else.—It is known or manifest, the Vedântin replies, on account of its immediate presentation (aparokshatvât), i.e. on account of the intuitional knowledge we have of it.

"An Examination of Relational Condition," from *Madhyamika Karika*

Nagarjuna

I pay homage to the Fully Awakened One,
   the supreme teacher who has taught
   the doctrine of relational origination,
   the blissful cessation of all phenomenal thought constructions.
(Therein, every event is "marked" by):
   non-origination, non-extinction,
   non-destruction, non-permanence,
   non-identity, non-differentiation
   non-coming (into being), non-going (out of being).

Verse 1

At nowhere and at no time can entities ever exist by originating out of themselves, from others, from both (self-other), or from the lack of causes.

Verse 2

There are four and only four relational conditions; namely primary causal, appropriating or objectively extending, sequential or contiguous, and dominantly extending conditions. There is no fifth.

Verse 3

In these relational conditions the self-nature of the entities cannot exist. From the non-existence of self-nature, other-nature too cannot exist.

Verse 4

The functional force does not inhere relational conditions, nor does it not inhere them. The relational conditions, vice versa, do not inhere the functional force, nor do they not inhere it.

Reprinted from Kenneth Inada, trans., *Nagarjuna: A Translation of His Mulamadhyamikakarika.* Tokyo: Hokuseido Press, 1970, pp. 39–42; copyright 1970 Hokuseido Press; reprinted with permission.

Verse 5

Only as entities are uniquely related and originated can they be described in terms of relational conditions. For, how can non-relational conditions be asserted of entities which have not come into being?

Verse 6

Relational condition does not validly belong to either being or non-being. If it belongs to being, for what use is it? And if to non-being, for whose use is it?

Verse 7

When a factor of experience does not evolve from being, non-being, nor from both being and non-being, how can there be an effectuating cause? Thus (such) a cause is not permissible.

Verse 8

It is said that a true factor of experience does not have an appropriating or objectively extending relational condition. If it does not exist, then again, wherein is this type of relational condition?

Verse 9

It is not possible to have extinction where factors of experience have not yet arisen. In an extinguished state, for what use is a relational condition? Thus the sequential or contiguous relational condition is not applicable.

Verse 10

As entities without self-nature have no real status of existence, the statement, "from the existence of that this becomes," is not possible.

Verse 11

The effect (i.e., arisen entity) does not exist separated from relational condition nor together in relational condition. If it does not exist in either situation, how could it arise out of relational conditions?

Verse 12

Now then, if non-entity arises from these relational conditions, why is it not possible that the effect (i.e., arisen entity) cannot arise from non-relational conditions?

Verse 13

The effect (i.e., arisen entity) has the relational condition but the relational conditions have no self-possessing (natures). How can an effect, arising from no self-possessing (natures), have the relational condition?

Verse 14

Consequently, the effect (i.e., arisen entity) is neither with relational nor without non-relational condition. Since the effect has no existing status, wherein are the relational and non-relational conditions?

Tao Te Ching

Lao Tzu

1. Tao that can be spoken of,
Is not the Everlasting Tao.
Name that can be named,
Is not the Everlasting name.

2a. Nameless, the origin of heaven and earth;
Named, the mother of ten thousand things.
Alternate,

2b. Non-being, to name the origin
of heaven and earth;
Being, to name the mother of ten thousand things.

3a. Therefore, always without desire,
In order to observe the hidden mystery;
Always with desire,

Excerpted from Ellen M. Chen, trans., *The Tao Te Ching: A New Translation with Commentary*. New York: Paragon, 1989, pp. 51, 60–61, 82–83, 88–89, 153–54, 175. Copyright 1989 by Paragon House Publishers; reprinted with permission.

In order to observe the manifestations.
Alternate,

3b. Therefore, by the Everlasting Non-Being,
We desire to observe its hidden mystery;
By the Everlasting Being,
We desire to observe the manifestations.

4. These two issue from the same origin,
Though named differently.
Both are called the dark.
Dark and even darker,
The door to all hidden mysteries.

4

1. Tao is a whirling emptiness,
Yet in use is inexhaustible.
Fathomless,
It seems to be the ancestor of ten thousand beings.

2. It blunts the sharp,
Unties the entangled,
Harmonizes the bright,
Mixes the dust.
Dark,
It seems perhaps to exist.

3. I do not know whose child it is,
It is an image of what precedes God.

11

1. Thirty spokes share one hub to make a wheel.
Through its non-being (*wu*),
There is (*yu*) the use of the carriage.
Mold clay into a vessel.
Through its non-being (*wu*),
There is (*yu*) the use of the vessel.
Cut out doors and windows to make a house.
Through its non-being (*wu*),
There is (*yu*) the use of the house.

2. Therefore in the being of a thing,
There lies the benefit.
In the non-being of a thing,
there lies its use.

14

1. What is looked at but not seen,
Is named the extremely dim.

What is listened to but not heard,
Is named the extremely faint.
What is grabbed but not caught,
Is named the extremely small.
These three cannot be comprehended,
Thus they blend into one.

2. As to the one, its coming up is not light,
Its going down is not darkness.
Unceasing, unnameable,
Again it reverts to nothing.
Therefore it is called the formless form,
The image of nothing.
Therefore it is said to be illusive and evasive.

3. Come toward it one does not see its head,
Follow behind it one does not see its rear.
Holding on to the Tao of old,
So as to steer in the world of now.
To be able to know the beginning of old,
It is to know the thread of Tao.

41

1. When a superior person hears Tao,
He diligently practices it.
When a middling person hears Tao,
He hears it, he doesn't hear it.

When the inferior person hears Tao, he roars.
If Tao were not laughed at,
It would not be Tao.

2. Therefore, established sayings have it this way:
"The illuminating Tao appears dark,
The advancing Tao appears retreating,
The level Tao appears knotty.

High *te* appears like a valley,
Great whiteness appears spotted,
Expansive *te* appears insufficient,
Well-established *te* appears weak,
The genuine in substance appears hollow.

Great square has no corners,
Great vessel is late in completion,
Great voice has hardly any sound,
Great image is formless,
Tao is hidden and without name."

3. Yet it is Tao alone,
That is good in lending help and fulfilling all.

51

1. Tao gives birth,
Te rears,
Things shape,
Circumstances complete.

2. Therefore the ten thousand things,
None do not respect Tao and treasure *te.*
Tao is respected,
Te is treasured,
Not by decree,
But by spontaneity.

3. Therefore Tao gives birth,
Te keeps, grows, nurtures, matures, ripens, covers and buries.

4. To give birth without possession,
To act without holding on to,
To grow without lording over,
This is called the dark *te.*

"The Nature of Things"
(*Wu-shih*), from *Lun-Heng*

Wang Ch'ung

The literati declare that Heaven and Earth produce man on purpose. This assertion is preposterous, for, when Heaven and Earth mix up their fluids, man is born as a matter of course unintentionally. In just the same manner a child is produced spontaneously, when the essences of husband and wife are harmoniously blended. At the time of such an intercourse, the couple does not intend to beget a child. Their passionate love being roused, they unite, and out of this union a child is born. From the fact that husband and wife do not purposely beget a child one may infer that Heaven and Earth do not produce man on purpose either.

However, man is produced by Heaven and Earth just as fish in a pond, or lice on man. They grow in response to a peculiar force, each species

Reprinted from 1907 edition of Alfred Forke, trans., *Philosophical Essays of Wang Chung,* Part I. New York: Paragon, 1962, pp. 103–106.

reproducing itself. This holds good for all the things which come into being between Heaven and Earth.

It is said in books that Heaven and Earth do not create man on purpose, but that man is produced unintentionally, as a matter of course. If anybody holds this view, how can he admit that Heaven and Earth are the furnace, all things created, the copper, the *Yin* and the *Yang,* the fire, and all the transformations, the working? If the potter and the founder use fire in order to melt the copper, and to burn their ware, their doings are dictated by a certain purpose. Now, they own that Heaven and Earth create man without a purpose, that, under given circumstances, he grows spontaneously. Can it be said of the potter and founder, that they too make their ware purposeless, and that it grows naturally, and of its own accord? . . .

Since Heaven and Earth cannot create man on purpose, the creation of all the other things and beings cannot be intentional either. The fluids of Heaven and Earth mixing, things grow naturally and spontaneously.

Tilling, weeding the ground, and sowing are designed acts, but whether the seed grows up, and ripens, or not, depends on chance, and spontaneous action. How do we know? If Heaven had produced its creatures on purpose, it ought to have taught them to love each other, and not to prey upon and destroy one another. One might object that such is the nature of the Five Elements, that when Heaven creates all things, it imbues them with the fluids of the Five Elements, and that these fight together, and destroy one another. But then Heaven ought to have filled its creatures with the fluid of one element only, and taught them mutual love, not permitting the fluids of the five elements to resort to strife and mutual destruction.

People will rejoin, that wishing to use things, one must cause them to fight and destroy each other, because thereby only can they be made into what they are intended to be. Therefore they say, Heaven uses the fluids of the Five Elements in producing all things, and man uses all these things in performing his many works. If one thing does not subdue the other, they cannot be employed together, and, without mutual struggle and annihilation, they cannot be made use of. If the metal does not hurt the wood, the wood cannot be used, and if the fire does not melt the metal, the metal cannot be made into a tool. Thus the injury done by one thing to the other turns out to be a benefit after all. If all the living creatures overpower, bite, and devour one another, it is the fluids of the Five Elements also that compel them to do so.

Ergo we are to understand that all created things must injure one another, if they are to be useful. Now tigers, wolves, serpents, snakes, wasps, and scorpions attack and hurt man. Did then Heaven design man to be made use of by those animals?

Furthermore, because the human body harbours the fluids of the Five Elements, man practises the Five Virtues, which are the outcome of the Five Elements. As long as he has the Five Organs in his bosom, those fluids are in order. If, according to this view, animals prey upon and destroy one another, because of their being endued with the fluids of the Five Elements, the human body with the Five Organs in its breast ought to be a victim of internecine strife, and the heart of a man living a righteous life be lacerated by discord. But what proves us that there is really an antagonism of the Five Elements, and that therefore animals oppress each other?

The sign *Yin* corresponds to wood, its proper animal is the tiger. *Hsü* corresponds to earth, its animal is the dog. *Ch'ou* and *Wei* correspond to earth likewise, *Ch'ou* having as animal the ox, and *Wei* having the sheep. Wood overcomes earth, therefore the dog, the ox, and the sheep are overpowered by the tiger. *Hai* goes with water, its animal being the boar. *Sse* goes with fire, and has the serpent as animal. *Tse* means also water, its animal being the rat. *Wu* also corresponds to fire, its animal is the horse. Water overcomes fire, therefore the boar devours the serpent. Fire is quenched by water, therefore, when the horse eats the excrements of rats, its belly swells up.

However, going more thoroughly into the question, we are confronted with the fact that not unfrequently it does not appear that animals overpower one another, which they ought, after this theory. *Wu* is connected with the horse, *Tse* with the rat, *Yu* with the cock, and *Mao* with the hare. Water is stronger than fire, why does the rat not drive away the horse? Metal is stronger than wood, why does the cock not eat the hare? *Hai* means the boar, *Wei* the sheep, and *Ch'ou* the ox. Earth overcomes water, wherefore do the ox and the sheep not kill the boar. *Sse* corresponds to the serpent, *Shên* to the monkey. Fire destroys metal, how is it that the serpent does not eat the monkey? The monkey is afraid of the rat, and the dog bites the monkey. The rat goes with water, and the monkey with metal. Water not being stronger than metal, why does the monkey fear the rat? *Hsü* is allied to earth, *Shên* to the monkey. Earth not forcing metal, for what reason is the monkey frightened by the dog?

The East is represented by wood, its constellation is the Blue Dragon, the West by metal, its constellation is the White Tiger. The South corresponds to fire, and has as constellation the Scarlet Bird, the North is connected with water, its constellation is the Black Tortoise. Heaven by emitting the essence of these four stars produces the bodies of these four animals on earth. Of all the animals they are the first, and they are imbued with the fluids of the Five Elements in the highest degree. Now, when the dragon and the tiger meet, they do not fight, and the scarlet bird and the tortoise do each other no harm. Starting from these four famous animals, and from those belonging to the twelve honorary characters, we find that all the other animals endued with the Five Elements, can much less be prompted to strife and discord by their natural organisation.

As all created things struggle and fight together, the animals subdue one another. When they try to tear their enemies to pieces, and devour them, all depends on the sharpness of their teeth, the strength of their muscles and sinews, the agility of their movements, and their courage.

If with men on earth the power is not equally divided, or their strength equally balanced, they vanquish and subjugate one another as a matter of course, using their strength to subdue, and their swords to despatch their foes. Man strikes with his sword just as the beasts butt, bite, and scratch with their horns, teeth, and claws. A strong arm, pointed horns, a truculent courage, and long teeth win the victory. Pusillanimity, short claws, cowardice, and blunted spurs bring about defeat.

Men are audacious or faint-hearted. That is the reason why they win or lose their battles. The victors are therefore not necessarily endowed with the fluid of metal, or the vanquished with the essence of wood.

"On *Sūnyatā*," from *Chao Lun*

Seng Chao

I.1

A perfect void where nothing grows (and decays) such is, perchance, the transcendent realm as it shows in the dark mirror of Prajñā. Into it all that exists (and non-exists) is resolved. Who, not having the mental power of the Sage with which to penetrate to full understanding, can attain that power of vision in which "existence" and "non-existence" lose their meaning? (Only) the Perfect Being may let his mind go beyond the borders of finality, unhemmed by these borders, may send his eyes and ears beyond the limits of seeing and hearing (to regions) where eyes and ears cannot reach. Is it not just that perfect "voidness," in which all things are equal, which prevents the Cosmic Soul from being troubled by individual sorrows?

Therefore:

When the Sage uses his true understanding to follow the natural course, there is no obstacle which he does not transcend; because he views the transformation (of the universe) as all of one breath, he passes through, adapting himself to whatever he encounters.

He transcends all the obstacles, hence he can reduce the turbid and the mixed to a state of clarity. He passes through whatever he encounters, so he sees oneness behind each particular experience.

This being so, although the various forms are different, they are not so in themselves; not being distinct in themselves, it follows that the (multitude of apparent) forms is not truly form; as that (multitude of) forms is not such, it is not form, although it (seems to be) form.

Reprinted from Walter Liebenthal, trans., *Chao Lun: The Treatises of Seng Chao*, 2nd rev. ed. Hong Kong University Press, 1968, pp. 54–55, 57, 59–60, 62–63; copyright 1968 by Hong Kong University Press; reprinted with permission.

Thus all things and He spring from the same root. Whatever there is and what is not is one in essence. Impalpable and darkly concealed, surely this is not a matter which an ordinary intellect can compass. . . .

II.1

The *Mahāyāna śāstra* says: "Dharma neither have the characteristics of existence nor those of non-existence." The *Chung-lun* says: "Dharma are neither existent nor non-existent." (These double negations define) *paramārtha satya.*

These double negations, do they imply that the thousand things must be blotted out, that the senses must be prevented from seeing and hearing, that a state must be created which is soundless, substanceless, void like a gap in a mountain range, in order to produce the true state? Be assured that things represent no obstruction whenever one passes through them knowing that they are identical (with what is not a thing). (Understanding that) they are not true (when seen from one angle) but true (when seen from the other angle) (he will know that) essentially they are without sides. Thus,

Being without sides, things, though in-existent, exist (as phenomena);

Representing no obstructions, things, though (appearing to) exist, in-exist (in truth).

In-existent (in truth), though they (appear to) exist, they are called different from (merely) existent things.

(Appearing to) exist, though they in-exist (in truth), they are called different from the in-existent.

Now, things which do not (merely) in-exist, are not truly existent things. If they are not truly existent things, what else does there exist apt to be designated "thing"? . . .

II.2

Surely, there is a reason why things are called in-existent, and also a reason why they are called not non-existent. For, in the first instance, though existent they in-exist; in the second instance, though in-existent they are not non-existent. For their "non-existence," as negated in the second clause, does not imply "spontaneous non-existence" (as of what could never exist) and their "existence," as negated in the first clause, does not imply "spontaneous existence" (as of what must always exist).

Now, if "existence" does not imply "existence as of the universe which is" and "non-existence" does not imply "non-existence as of the universe before it came into being" then these two terms though different as terms refer to the same item.

Therefore (in the *Vimalakīrti sūtra* the young (*kulaputra Ratnakūta*) says with a sigh (of admiration): "(The Buddha) has said: the dharma neither are nor are not, they (simply) arise from causes and conditions."

The (Great) *Bodhisattva-keyura sūtra* says: "When the Bodhisattva turns the Wheel-of-the-Law, there is neither turning nor no turning." This means that (the Buddhas) turn the Wheel where there is nothing to be turned. That then is the subtle meaning of all the sūtras.

What do you propose? That things are not? Then negativism would not be heretical. That things are? Then positivism would be orthodox. (Actually) because things are not simply nothing, negativism is a heresy; because things are not simply something, positivism is not orthodox. Then it is evident that these two negations describe Highest Truth (*paramārtha satya*). . . .

II.4

. . . If one searches for a thing using its name as a guide (he will discover that) where the name is found the thing is not found also. If one searches for a name using the thing (it names) as a guide (he will discover that) what the thing achieves the name does not also achieve. If the thing is not found where the name is found it is the wrong thing; if the name does not achieve what the thing achieves it is the wrong name. Thus, names do not correspond with facts and facts do not correspond with names. Now, if names and facts do not correspond with each other, how are the ten thousand things to be found (with the help of ordinary language)?

Therefore the *Chung-kuan* says: "Things are not this or that. But some one (in the position of this) makes this a this and that a that, while (in the position of that) he makes this a that and that a this."

This and that do not denote only one kind of thing, but ignorant people believe that (these words) have a definite significance. It follows that this and that at first do not exist, while ignorant people believe that (even) at first they may not non-exist. Once one has recognized the non-existence of this and that, what else could there be whose existence he would be willing to assert?

So we know: things are not real, they are just symbols.

That is why the *Ch'eng-chu* maintains that names are artificially applied to things, and *Yüan-lin* uses the similes of the finger and the horse. So, profound doctrines may be found anywhere.

The Sage rides the thousand (waves) of becoming yet remains unchanged; he falls into a thousand errors but emerges from all of them. Why? Because he knows that *śūnyatā* is the very nature of phenomenal life and does not misunderstand this term as meaning absence of existence.

Therefore a sūtra says: "Marvellous, World-honoured One! Unchanging Reality (*bhūtakoti*) is the realm where all dharma are assigned their places." Not outside of Reality are they placed. Where they are placed (in the world) that indeed is Reality. This being so, is Tao far away? This life of ours is Reality. Is the Sage far away? Recognize him as in truth he is, and you are the (cosmic) Spirit.

"Principle (*Li*) and Material Force (*Ch'i*)," from *Complete Works of Chu Hsi*

Chu Hsi

In the universe there has never been any material force without principle or principle without material force.

Question: Which exists first, principle or material force?

Answer: Principle has never been separated from material force. However, principle "exists before physical form [and is therefore without it]" whereas material force "exists after physical form [and is therefore with it]." Hence when spoken of as being before or after physical form, is there not the difference of priority and posteriority? Principle has no physical form, but material force is coarse and contains impurities.

Fundamentally principle and material force cannot be spoken of as prior or posterior. But if we must trace their origin, we are obliged to say that principle is prior. However, principle is not a separate entity. It exists right in material force. Without material force, principle would have nothing to adhere to. As material force, there are the five Agents (or Elements) of Metal, Wood, Water, and Fire. As principle, there are humanity, righteousness, propriety, and wisdom.

> *Comment.* Much discussion has taken place on the question whether Chu Hsi is a dualist. No one can doubt that principle is a universal, that there is a distinction between what exists before physical form and is therefore without it and what exists after form and is therefore with it, and that principle and material are different in many respects. As already suggested, Ch'eng Hao tended more to the monistic view while Ch'eng I tended more to the dualistic view, but it was also noted that whatever dualism there was, was superficial. What Chu Hsi did was to harmonize the two trends of the Ch'eng brothers. In his system, principle has not only a logical priority. It actually exists before physical form and is without it because it is the principle of being. But it is not something outside of material force that imparts a principle of being into it. This is the reason why he said that principle has never been separate from material force. Thus principle is both immanent and transcendent. In other words, he is neither a monist nor a dualist, or he is both a monist and a dualist. Perhaps one may say that with respect to ultimate reality, he is a monist but with respect

to phenomena he is a dualist. But since principle and material force are never separate, they do not exist independently of each other, much less in opposition. The fact is that any contrast of monism and dualism does not apply to his philosophy.

Question about the relation between principle and material force.

Answer: I-ch'uan (Ch'eng I) expressed it very well when he said that principle is one but its manifestations are many. When heaven, earth, and the myriad things are spoken of together, there is only one principle. As applied to man, however, there is in each individual a particular principle.

Question: What are the evidences that principle is in material force?

Answer: For example, there is order in the complicated interfusion of the yin and the yang and of the Five Agents. Principle is there. If material force does not consolidate and integrate, principle would have nothing to attach itself to.

Question: May we say that before heaven and earth existed there was first of all principle?

Answer: Before heaven and earth existed, there was after all only principle. As there is this principle, therefore there are heaven and earth. If there were no principle, there would also be no heaven and earth, no man, no things, and in fact, no containing or sustaining (of things by heaven and earth) to speak of. As there is principle, there is therefore material force to operate everywhere and nourish and develop all things.

Question: Is it principle that nourishes and develops all things?

Answer: As there is this principle, therefore there is this material force operating, nourishing, and developing. Principle itself has neither physical form nor body.

K'o-chi asked: When the creative process disposes of things, is it the end once a thing is gone, or is there a principle by which a thing that is gone may return?

Answer: It is the end once a thing is gone. How can there be material force that has disintegrated and yet integrates once more?

Question: "The Lord on High has conferred even on the inferior people a moral sense." "When Heaven is about to confer a great responsibility on any man. . ." "Heaven, to protect the common people, made for them rulers." "Heaven, in the production of things, is sure to be bountiful to them, according to their natural capacity." "On the good-doer, the Lord on High sends down all blessings, and on the evil-doer, He sends down all miseries." "When Heaven is about to send calamities to the world, it will always first produce abnormal people as a measure of their magnitude." In passages like these, does it mean that Heaven has no personal consciousness and the passages are merely deductions from principle?

Answer: These passages have the same meaning. It is simply that principle operates this way.

Principle attaches to material force and thus operates.

Throughout the universe there are both principle and material force. Principle refers to the Way, which exists before physical form [and is without it] and is the course from which all things are produced. Material force refers to material objects, which exists after physical form [and is with it]; it is the instrument by which things are produced. Therefore in the production of man and things, they must be endowed with principle before they have their nature, and they must be endowed with material force before they have physical form.

> *Comment.* Needham correctly understands Neo-Confucian philosophy, especially as developed by Chu Hsi, as essentially organic. As he aptly summarizes it: "The Neo-Confucians arrive at essentially an organic view of the universe. Composed of matter-energy [material force] and ordered by the universal principle of organization [principle], it was a universe which, though neither created nor governed by any personal deity, was entirely real, and possessed the property of manifesting the highest human values (love, righteousness, sacrifice, etc.) when beings of an integrative level sufficiently high to allow of their appearance, had come into existence." Surely the Neo-Confucian conception of the universe is that of a single organism. All things exist in relations, and all relations follow a definite pattern according to which things are organized on various levels. That the universe is a set of relations goes far back to the *Book of Changes,* for Change itself is but relation. Tao as the principle of being is basically a principle of relationship. Impressed with this relational character of Chinese philosophy, Needham saw a striking similarity between Chinese organism and that of Whitehead. He also has made a most illuminating study of Chu Hsi's influence on Leibniz and the philosophy of organism. We must remember, however, that in Chu Hsi's philosophy, the world is more than just an organism, for principle is metaphysical. Moreover, while the many similarities between Neo-Confucianism and Whitehead's organism as pointed out by Needham are surprising, there is absent in Neo-Confucianism Whitehead's God, who, as the principle of concretion, is ultimate irrationality.

What are called principle and material force are certainly two different entities. But considered from the standpoint of things, the two entities are merged one with the other and cannot be separated with each in a different place. However, this does not destroy the fact that the two entities are each an entity in itself. When considered from the standpoint of principle, before things existed, their principles of being had already existed. Only their principles existed, however, but not yet the things themselves. Whenever one studies these aspects, one should clearly recognize and distinguish them, and consider both principle and material force from the beginning to the end, and then one will be free from error.

There is principle before there can be material force. But it is only when there is material force that principle finds a place to settle. This is the process by which all things are produced, whether large as heaven and earth or small as ants. Why should we worry that in the creative process of Heaven and Earth, endowment may be wanting? Fundamentally, principle cannot be interpreted in the senses of existence or nonexistence. Before Heaven and Earth came into being, it already was as it is.

Considering the fact that all things come from one source, we see that their principle is the same but their material force different. Looking at their various substances, we see that their material force is similar but their principle utterly different. The difference in material force is due to the inequality of its purity or impurity, whereas the difference in principle is due to its completeness or partiality. If you will please examine thoroughly, there should be no further doubt.

The nature of man and things is nothing but principle and cannot be spoken of in terms of integration and disintegration. That which integrates to produce life and disintegrates to produce death is only material force. What we called the spirit, the heavenly and earthly aspects of the soul (*hun-p'o*), and consciousness are all effects of material force. Therefore when material force is integrated, there are these effects. When it is disintegrated, there are no more. As to principle, fundamentally it does not exist or cease to exist because of such integration or disintegration. As there is a certain principle, there is the material force corresponding to it, and as this material force integrates in a particular instance, its principle is also endowed in that instance.

From *Hsin li-hsueh* (*The New Rational Philosophy*)

Fung Yu-lan

1. The World and Principle

What makes a thing square is the square. As explained before, the square can be real but not actual. If in fact there are no actual square things, the square is then not actual. But if in fact there are actual square things, they must have four corners. An actual square thing necessarily follows that which makes a square square; it cannot avoid this. From this we know that the square is real. Since the square is real but not actual, it belongs to the realm of pure reality. . . .

When we say "There is a square," we are making a formal affirmation about reality. The statement "There is a square" does not imply an actual square thing. Much less does it imply a particular actual square thing. Therefore the statement does not affirm anything about actuality, but merely makes a formal affirmation about reality. From the point of view of our acquisition of knowledge, we must in our experience see an actual square thing before we can say that there is a square. But since we have said that there is a square, we see that even if in fact there is no actual square thing, we still can say there is a square.

Chu Hsi regards principle as that by which actual things necessarily are what they are and the specific principle according to which they should be. Our idea of principle is the same. A square thing must follow the principle of the square before it can be square, and it must completely follow the principle of the square before it can be perfectly square. Whether a square thing is perfectly square depends on whether or not it follows the principle of the square completely. According to this reasoning, the principle of the square is the standard of all square things; it is the specific principle according to which they should be. The *Book of Odes* says, "Heaven produces the teeming multitude. As there are things, there are their specific principles." This was often quoted by the Neo-Confucianists of the Sung period. Ch'eng I-ch'uan said, "As there are things, there must be their specific principles. One thing necessarily has one principle." The principle of a class of things is the same as the specific principle of that class of things. We often say, "This square thing is more square or less square than the other square thing." In saying so we are following this standard. Without this standard no criticism is possible. Those who do not accept the existence of principle have overlooked this point.

Sung Neo-Confucianists also have the theory that the "principle is one but its manifestations are many," which Chu Hsi also held. But when he talked about principle being one and its manifestations being many, the principle he talked about is already different from the principle when he discussed it [as such]. In commenting on the *Western Inscription* by Chang Heng-ch'ü (Chang Tsai, 1020–1077), Chu Hsi said, ". . . . There is nothing in the entire realm of creatures that does not regard Heaven as the father and Earth as the mother. This means that the principle is one. . . . Each regards his parents as his own parents and his son as his own son. This being the case, how can principle not be manifested as many? . . ." The principle referred to here concerns the realm of that which exists after physical form and is with it (*hsing-erh-hsia*). It makes an affirmation about actuality. According to this theory, among individual, actual things there are certain internal relations. But this is a question about actuality. To say that there must be relations [among them] is to make an affirmation about actuality.

In our system we can still say that "the principle is one but its manifestations are many." But when we say so, the principle we are talking about is still the principle when we discuss it as such. Let us first take things in a certain class. The things in this class all follow one principle. However, although they all follow the same principle, they each have their own individuality.

From the point of view of things of this class being related within the class, we can say that their principle is one but its manifestations are many. As we said before, the principle of a class implies the principle of a general class. From the point of view of specific classes within a general class, all specific classes belong to the general class but at the same time possess that which makes them specific classes. The relation among the specific classes within the general class can also be stated in terms that the principle is one but its manifestations are many. . . .

This is our theory that the principle is one but its manifestations are many. This theory is presented in its logical aspect. It only makes an affirmation about reality. It does not imply that there are internal relations among actual things, and therefore does not make any affirmation about actuality. . . .

2. Principle and Material Force

There are two aspects in every actually existing thing, namely, its "what" and that on which it depends for its existence or to become actually what it is. For example, every round thing has two aspects. One is that "it is round." The other is that on which it depends for existence, that is, to become actually round. This "what" is the thing's essential element in the class to which it belongs and the thing's nature. The reason that it exists is the foundation of the thing's existence. Its "what" depends on the principle it follows. That on which it depends for existence is the material which actualizes the principle. . . .

Material is either relative or absolute. Relative material has the two aspects just described. Absolute material, on the other hand, has only one of these aspects, namely, that it can be material simple and pure. Take a building, for example. . . . Bricks and tiles are material for the building, but they are relative and not absolute material. Earth is material for bricks and tiles, but it is still relative and not absolute material, for it still possesses the two aspects described above. . . .

When the nature of the building is removed, it will cease to be a building but only bricks and tiles. When the nature of bricks and tiles is removed, they will cease to be bricks and tiles but only earth. The nature of earth can also be removed, *ad infinitum.* At the end there is the absolute material. This material is called matter in the philosophies of Plato and Aristotle. . . . Matter itself has no nature. Because it has no nature whatsoever, it is indescribable, inexplicable in speech, and unrealizable in thought. . . .

We call this material *ch'i* (material force). . . . In our system material force is entirely a logical concept. It is neither a principle nor an actual thing. An actual thing is that which is produced by what we call material force in accordance with principle. Those who hold the theory of principle and material force should talk about material force in this way. But in the history of Chinese philosophy, those who held the theory of principle and material force in the past never had such a clear view of material force. In Chang Tsai's philosophy, material force is entirely a scientific concept. If there is the material force which he talked about, it is a kind of an actual thing. . . . Even what Ch'eng I and Chu Hsi called material force does not seem to be a completely logical concept. For instance, they often described material force as clear or turbid. The way we look at the matter, the material force that can be described as clear or turbid is no longer material force [as such] but material force in accordance with the principle of clearness or turbidity. When they talked about material force as clear or turbid, they did not make clear whether they were talking about material force itself or about material force achieving the principle of clearness or turbidity. . . .

We shall first discuss [Chu Hsi's statement], "There has never been any material force without principle." This can very easily be proved. When we said that [what Ch'eng I called] the material force of the true source has no nature whatsoever, we spoke entirely from the point of view of logic. From the point of view of fact, however, material force has at least the nature of existence. If not, it fundamentally does not exist. If material force does not exist, then there will not be any actual thing at all. If material force has the nature of existence, it means that it follows the principle of existence. Since it at least has to follow the principle of existence, therefore "There has never been any material force without principle."

(Chu Hsi also said), "There has never been any principle without material force." This saying cannot be interpreted to mean that all principles are with material force, for if so, it would mean that all principles are actually exemplified and that there would be no principle which is only real but not actual. This statement merely says, "There must be some principles with material force," or "There has never been the time when all principles are without material force." This has been proved above, for at least the principle of existence is always followed by material force.

3. Tao, Substance and Function, and Universal Operation

What we call the material force of the true source is the Non-ultimate, and the totality of all principles is the Great Ultimate. The process from the Non-ultimate to the Great Ultimate is our world of actuality. We call this process "The Non-ultimate and also the Great Ultimate." The Non-ultimate, the Great Ultimate, and the Non-ultimate-and-also-the-Great-Ultimate are, in other words, the material force of the true source, the totality of principle, and the entire process from material force to principle, respectively. Collectively speaking, they are called Tao (the Way). . . .

Why have Tao in addition to the Great Whole or the universe? Our answer is that when we talk about the Great Whole or the universe, we speak from the aspect of tranquillity of all things, whereas when we talk about Tao, we speak from the aspect of activity of all things. . . .

The principle followed by "fact" (which includes all facts) is the Great Ultimate in its totality, and the material force depended on by "fact" is the Non-ultimate in its totality. (Actually the Non-ultimate has no totality to speak of. We merely say so.) In the first chapter we said that according to the old theory (of Sung Neo-Confucianists), principle is substance while actual things that actualize principle are function. But according to the concept of "the Non-ultimate and also the Great Ultimate," the Great Ultimate is substance and the "and also" is function. As all functions are included in this function, it is therefore (what Chu Hsi called) the total substance and great functioning. . . .

All things (meaning both things and events) go through the four stages of formation, flourish, decline, and destruction. Old things go out of existence this way and new things come into existence this way. This successive coming-into-existence and going-out-of-existence is the universal operation of the great functioning. The universal operation of the great functioning is also called the process of creation and transformation. The formation and flourish of things are creation, while their decline and destruction are transformation. The creation and transformation of all things are collectively called the process of creation and transformation. At the same time each thing or event is a process of creation and transformation. Since all things are each a process of creation and transformation, they are collectively called ten thousand transformations (all things). The term "transformation" may also involve both meanings of creation and transformation. Therefore the process is also called great transformation. The universal operation of the great transformation is the same as the universal operation of the great functioning. Our actual world is a universal operation.

The *Lao Tzu* and the "Appended Remarks" of the *Book of Changes* have a common idea, that is, that when things reach their limit, they return to their origin. . . . According to the law of circular movement described above, things in the universe come into existence and go out of existence at all times. They are always in the process of change. This is the daily renewal of the substance of Tao.

The daily renewal of the substance of Tao can be seen from four points of view. . . . (1) We can, from the point of view of classes, see the production and extinction of their actual members. Looked at this way, the daily renewal of the substance of Tao is cyclical. (2) We can, from the point of view of principle, see whether its actual exemplification tends to be perfect or not. Looked at this way, the daily renewal of the substance of Tao is one of progress and retrogression. (3) We can, from the point of view of the universe, see the increase or decrease of classes which have members in the actual world. Looked at this way, the daily renewal of the substance of Tao is one of increase and decrease. (4) And we can, from the point of view of an individual entity, see the process of its movement from one class to another. Looked at this way, the daily renewal of the substance of Tao is one of transformation and penetration.

"One Bright Jewel," from *Shōbōgenzō*

Dogen

The great master Gensha had the religious name Shibi; his lay surname was Sha. In lay life he enjoyed fishing and used to ply his boat on the Nandai river, following the ways of the fishermen. He must have had, *without expectation,* the *golden fish* which *comes up by itself without being fished out.* At the beginning of the Kantsū era of the Tang dynasty (860–873), he suddenly wished to *leave the world;* he left his boat and went into the mountains. He was thirty years old at the time. Realizing the peril of the ephemeral world, he came to know the lofty value of the Buddha Way. Finally he climbed Snowy Peak Mountain, called on the great Zen master Seppō, and worked on the Way day and night.

One time, in order to make a thorough study of Zen as taught all over the country, he took his knapsack and headed out of the mountain, but on the way he stubbed his toe on a rock, and as it bled painfully, he suddenly had a powerful insight and said, *This body is not existent—where does pain come from?* So he then went back to Seppō. Seppō asked him, *Which one is the ascetic Shibi?* Gensha said, *I never dare fool people.* Seppō especially liked this saying, and said, "Who does not have this saying? Who can utter this saying?" Seppō asked further, "Ascetic Shibi, why don't you travel to study?" He replied, *Bodhidharma did not come to China, the second patriarch did not go to India.*[1] Seppō particularly praised him for this saying. Because he had up to then been a fisherman, he had never seen the various scriptures and treatises even in dreams, yet nevertheless because the depth of his aspiration was paramount, a determined spirit beyond others had appeared. Seppō thought him outstanding in the community and praised him as being a standard among his disciples. He dressed in plain muslin, and because he never replaced his one robe, it was all patched. He used paper for his underclothing, and also wore mugwort plants. He didn't call on any teacher except Seppō. Nevertheless, he had accomplished the power to inherit his teacher's way.

After he had finally attained the Way, he said to people, *The whole world in all ten directions is a single bright jewel.* Then a monk asked, *I hear you have a saying, that the whole world in all ten directions is one bright jewel—how can a student understand this?* The master said, *The whole world in all ten directions is one bright jewel—what does it have to do with understanding?* The next day the master

Reprinted from Thomas Cleary, trans., *Shōbōgenzō: Zen Essays by Dōgen.* Honolulu: University of Hawaii Press, 1986, pp. 58–63. Copyright 1986 by University of Hawaii Press; reprinted with permission.

asked that monk, *The whole world in all ten directions is one bright jewel—how do you understand?* The monk replied, *The whole world in all ten directions is one bright jewel—what does it have to do with understanding?* The master said, *I knew you were making a living in a ghost cave in the mountain of darkness.*[2]

This saying, the whole world in all ten directions is one bright jewel, began with Gensha. The essential message is that *the whole universe* is not *vast,* not *small,* not *round or square,* not *balanced and correct,* not *lively and active,* not *standing way out.* Because furthermore it is not *birth and death, coming and going,* it is *birth and death, coming and going.* Being thus, *having in the past gone from here,* it *now comes from here.* In making a thorough investigation someone must see through it as being weightless, someone must find out it is being single-minded.

All ten directions is the *nonceasing* of *pursuing things as oneself, pursuing oneself as things.* Expressing *when emotions arise wisdom is blocked* as blockage is *turning the head, changing the face,* it is *setting forth events, meeting the situation.* Because of *pursuing self as things,* it is the *all ten directions* which is *unceasing.* Because it is the principle of incipience, there is superabundance in the mastery of the pivot of function. *Is one bright jewel,* though not yet a name, is expression. This has come to be taken as a name. As for *one bright jewel,* it is *even ten thousand years;* as it *extends through antiquity, yet unfinished,* it *extends through the present, having arrived.* Though there is *the present of the body* and *the present of the mind,* it is *a bright jewel.* It is not the *plants and trees* of *here and there,* not the *mountains and rivers* of *heaven and earth*—it is *a bright jewel.*

How can a student understand? As for this saying, even if it seems that the monk was *sporting active consciousness,* it is *the great function manifesting being a great rule.* Going onward, one should cause *a foot of water, a foot of wave*[3] to stand out high. This is what is called *ten feet of jewel, ten feet of brightness.* To express what he meant to say, Gensha said, *The whole world in all ten directions is one bright jewel—what does it have to do with understanding?* This saying is an expression of Buddhas succeeding to Buddhas, Zen adepts succeeding to Zen adepts, Gensha succeeding to Gensha. In trying to escape succession, though it is not that there could be no place to escape, even if one clearly escapes for the time being, as long as there is the arising of expression, it is the covering of time by manifestation.

The next day Gensha asked that monk, "The whole world in all ten directions is one bright jewel—how do you understand?" This says, *yesterday I spoke a definite principle;* today, using a second layer, he *exudes energy*[4]—*today I speak the indefinite principle*—he is *pushing yesterday over, nodding and laughing.* The monk said, "The whole world in all ten directions is one bright jewel— what does understanding have to do with it?" We could call this *riding a thief's horse in pursuit of the thief.* In an ancient Buddha's explanation for you, it is *acting among different species.*[5] For a time you should *turn the light around and introspect*—how many levels of *what has it to do with understanding* are there? In trying to say, though one may say it is *seven milk pancakes, five vegetable pancakes,* this is the teaching and practice of *south of Shō, north of Tan.*[6]

Gensha said, "I knew you were making a living in a ghost cave in the mountain of darkness." Know that *sun face, moon face*[7] has never changed since remote antiquity. *Sun face* comes out together with *sun face,* and *moon face* comes out together with *moon face,* so therefore *if the sixth month you say is just the right time, you cannot say your nature is mature.*[8] Therefore the beginning or beginninglessness of this *bright jewel* has no point of reference—it is *the whole world in all ten directions is one bright jewel.* He doesn't say two or three—the *whole body* is one single *eye of truth,* the *whole body* is the *embodiment of reality,* the *whole body* is one phrase, the *whole body* is light, the *whole body* is the whole body. When being the *whole body,* the *whole body* has no obstruction—it is *perfectly round,* it *rolls smoothly.* Because the qualities of the *bright jewel* are thus manifest, there are the *Kannon and Miroku*[9] of the present *seeing form and hearing sound,* there are the *old Buddhas and new Buddhas* who *appear physically to expound the truth.* At *this precise time,* be it hung in the sky, or inside one's clothing, or under the jaw, or in the topknot, in each case it is *the whole world in all ten directions is one bright jewel.*

Hanging it inside the clothing is considered to be the way—don't say you'll hang it on the outside. Hanging it in the topknot or under the jaw is considered to be the way—don't try to sport it on the outside of the topknot or jaw. There is a close friend who gives the jewel to you while you're intoxicated with wine—to a close friend the jewel should be given. At the time when the jewel is hung, one is always intoxicated with wine. *Being thus* is the *one bright jewel* which is *the whole world in the ten directions.* This being so, then though it seems to go changing faces, turning or not turning, yet it is *a bright jewel.* It is precisely knowing that the jewel has all along been thus that is itself the *bright jewel.* The *bright jewel* has *sound and form* which sounds this way. In being *already at thusness,* as far as worrying that oneself is not the *bright jewel* is concerned, one should not suspect that that is not the jewel. Worrying and doubting, grasping and rejection, action and inaction are all but temporary views of small measure. What is more, it is merely causing resemblance to small measure. Isn't it lovely—such lusters and lights of the *bright jewel* are unlimited. Each flicker, each beam, of each luster, each light, is a quality of the whole world in all ten directions. Who can take them away? There is no one casting a tile in the marketplace.[10] Don't bother about *not falling into* or *not being blind to*[11] the cause and effect of mundane existences—the unclouded original bright jewel which is *true through and through* is the face; the *bright jewel* is the eyes.

However, for me and you both, the *thinking of everything, not thinking of anything* which doesn't know what is the *bright jewel* and what is not the *bright jewel* may have gathered fodder of clarity, but if we have, by way of Gensha's saying, also heard and known and understood what the body and mind which are the *bright jewel* are like, the mind is not oneself—as being who would we bother to grasp or reject becoming and extinction as being the *bright jewel* or not being the *bright jewel?* Even if we doubt and worry, that does not mean it is not that this is not the *bright jewel.* Since it is not the action or thought caused by something existing which is not the *bright jewel,* the simple fact is that *forward steps and backward steps* in the *ghost cave in the mountain of darkness* are just *one bright jewel.*

Notes

1. The implication of this is that reality is omnipresent.

2. "Ghost cave in the mountain of darkness" is usually used in Zen to refer to being sunk in quiescence, stillness, formless concentration, nonknowing. It is also called falling into one-sided emptiness or nihilistic emptiness. This is its usage in reference to meditation; it is also used to refer to clinging to stagnant, stereotyped concepts.

3. "Water" stands for essence, emptiness, noumenon; "waves" stands for characteristics, appearances, phenomena. "A foot of water, a foot of wave" refers to perfect realizational integration of emptiness and existence.

4. "Exude energy" or "show life" is used to refer to active function or flexibility, not being stuck in one position or cliche.

5. "Acting among different species" is a technical term in the Chinese parent school of Sōtō Zen and basically means acting in the world in whatever forms may be appropriate. Sōzan (Ts'ao shan), a progenitor of the school, wrote, "Bodhisattvas' assimilation to different species means first understanding oneself, then after that entering the different kinds in birth and death to save others; having already realized nirvana, they do not abandon creatures in birth and death—helping themselves and others, they vow that all sentient beings shall attain buddhahood." Sōzan discusses various types or aspects of "acting among different species," but in general "different species" means the world of differentiation, all kinds of different forms and states.

6. "Seven milk pancakes, five vegetable pancakes" means "everything," and "south of Shō, north of Tan," means "everywhere" (cf. *Blue Cliff Record,* case 18). Everything is "the bright jewel," everything everywhere is *thusness*—specific understandings or descriptions have their place and use, but are by nature fragmentary and do not capture the whole. Yet since this principle extends to all specifics, as the Kegon philosophy emphasizes, one is all and all are one. In Zen synecdoche, any particular object can be used to represent all being.

7. Cf. *Blue Cliff Record,* case 3.

8. An ancient teacher said, "Every day is a good day." Cf. *Blue Cliff Record,* case 6.

9. Kannon is Avalokiteśvara, the bodhisattva of compassion; Miroku is Maitreya, the bodhisattva of kindness.

10. "Casting a tile" to draw a piece of jade means to give a little to get more; someone once posted two lines of verse in a temple where a famous poet was expected to visit, provoking the poet to complete the verse. The lines added by the poet were superior, and the man who wrote the first two lines was said to have thrown a tile and drawn a piece of jade.

11. In a well-known Zen story, an old man told the Zen master Hyakujō that he had been a teacher in the past, but when a student asked if someone who is highly cultivated in meditation falls into the province of cause and effect, he denied it and became a "wild fox." Then the old man posed the same question to Hyakujō, who answered that someone who is highly cultivated "isn't blind to cause and effect."

"The Fundamental Mode of True Reality"

Nishida Kitaro

The facts we experience seem varied, but they are all the same reality and are all established by means of the same mode. Let us now discuss this fundamental mode of reality.

First we must recognize the functioning of a unifying factor behind all of reality. Some scholars think that certain simple, independent constituents—such as the atoms expounded by atomists—are the fundamental reality. Such constituents are abstract concepts formulated for the sake of explanation, and they cannot actually exist. Assume for the sake of argument that here is an atom. It must have some sort of qualities or activity, for that which is without qualities or activity is no different from nothingness. But the functioning of one thing is necessarily in opposition to another, so there must be a third thing to join the first two and enable each to function with respect to the other. For example, when the motion of material object A is transmitted to object B, there must be a force acting between them. And in the case of qualities, when one quality is established, it is established in opposition to another. For instance, if red were the only color, it would not appear to us as such, because for it to do so there must be colors that are not red. Moreover, for one quality to be compared with and distinguished from another, both qualities must be fundamentally identical; two things totally different with no point in common cannot be compared and distinguished. If all things are established through such opposition, then there must be a certain unifying reality concealed at their base.

In the case of material phenomena, this unifying reality is a physical power in the external world; in the case of mental phenomena, it is the unifying power of consciousness. As I stated before, since material phenomena and mental phenomena are identical in pure experience, these two types of unifying activity are fundamentally one: the unifying power at the base of our thinking and willing and the unifying power at the base of the phenomena of the universe are one and the same. The laws of logic and mathematics, for example, are the fundamental principles by which the phenomena of the universe come into being.

In the establishment of reality, then, both a unity at the base of reality and mutual opposition or contradiction are necessary. Heraclitus said that strife is the father of all things—reality is established by contradictions. Red things come into being in opposition to things that are not red, and things that function are established in opposition to things that function reciprocally. When these contradictions disappear, reality disappears as well. On a fundamental level, contradiction and unity are simply two views of one and the same thing. Because there is unity there is contradiction, and because there is contradiction there is unity. Like black and white, things that are the same in all respects except one are the most opposed; but things that have no clear opposition, such as virtue and a triangle, also lack clear unity. The most powerful reality is the one that most thoroughly harmonizes and unifies various contradictions.

The idea that the unifier and the unified are two separate things derives from abstract thinking—in concrete reality the two cannot be separated. A "tree" exists through the unification of the branches, leaves, roots, and trunk, parts that perform various functions. Yet a tree is not merely a collection of these parts, for without a power unifying the entire tree, the various parts are insignificant. A tree exists, then, upon the opposition and unity of its parts.

When the unifying power and that which is unified are split apart, the entity does not become a reality. For example, when a person piles stones, the stones and the person are separate things; the pile of stones is artificial and does not become an independent reality.

The fundamental mode of reality is such that reality is one while it is many and many while it is one; in the midst of equality it maintains distinctions, and in the midst of distinctions it maintains equality. Since these two dimensions cannot be separated, we can say that reality is the self-development of a single entity. Independent, self-sufficient true reality always exhibits this mode; things that do not exhibit this mode are abstract concepts formulated by us.

A reality is that which constitutes in itself a single system. This systematic character induces us to believe that it is an indisputable reality. In contrast, things that do not constitute a system—such as dreams—are believed to be unreal.

A reality that is both one and many must be self-moved and unceasing. A state of quiescence is a state of independent existence free from conflict with others; it is a state of a oneness that rejects plurality. In such a situation, reality cannot come into being.

When a certain state of affairs is established through unity, an opposing state of affairs is necessarily established at the same time. If a unity comes into being a disunity immediately arises and breaks it up. True reality emerges through such infinite opposition. Physicists, basing their argument on the law of the conservation of energy, talk as if there were a limit to reality, but their view is an assumption made for the sake of explanation. Like assertions about a possible limit to space, their view entails abstract consideration of one side of the matter and forgetfulness of the other.

A living thing contains unlimited oppositions and has the ability to give rise to unlimited variation. Spirit is called a living thing because it always includes infinite oppositions and never stops. When it is fixed in a single state and cannot switch to opposing states, it dies.

I have stated that reality is established by means of that which opposes it, but opposition here does not come from other things: it comes from within reality itself. Because there is a unity at the base of opposition, and because unlimited oppositions inevitably develop from the internal character of reality, true reality is the free development that emerges from the internal necessity of a single unifying factor. For example, various geometric forms are possible by virtue of spatial determinations, and while mutually opposing each other they maintain their particular characters. But they do not oppose each other separately, for they are linked by the necessary character of the single factor called space; geometric forms are the unlimited development of spatial qualities. In the same way, what we term natural phenomena do not consist apart from our phenomena of consciousness. They are established by one unifying activity, so they should be regarded as the development of nature as a single entity.

Hegel asserted that any rational thing is real and reality is necessarily rational. Although many thinkers have taken issue with his assertion, people with certain perspectives take it to be an irrefutable truth. No matter how minute, the phenomena of the universe do not occur accidentally with no relation to what precedes or follows them: they necessarily occur for a reason. Our viewing their occurrence as accidental comes from a lack of knowledge.

We usually hold that there is some agent of activity from which activity arises, but in terms of direct experience it is the activity that is real. A so-called agent is an abstract concept, and the idea that there is an agent of activity apart from the activity itself comes from thinking that the opposition between the unity and its content indicates two independent realities. . . .

It is usually thought that subject and object are realities that can exist independently of each other and that phenomena of consciousness arise through their activity, which leads to the idea that there are two realities: mind and matter. This is a total mistake. The notions of subject and object derive from two different ways of looking at a single fact, as does the distinction between mind and matter. But these dichotomies are not inherent in the fact itself. As a concrete fact, a flower is not at all like the purely material flower of scientists; it is pleasing, with a beauty of color, shape, and scent. Heine gazed at the stars in a quiet night sky and called them golden tacks in the azure. Though astronomers would laugh at his words as the folly of a poet, the true nature of stars may very well be expressed in his phrase.

In the independent, self-sufficient true reality prior to the separation of subject and object, our knowledge, feeling, and volition are one. Contrary to popular belief, true reality is not the subject matter of dispassionate knowledge; it is established through our feeling and willing. It is not simply an existence but something with meaning. If we were to remove our feelings and the will from this world of actuality, it would no longer be a concrete fact—it would become an abstract concept. The world described by physicists, like a line without width and a plane without thickness, is not something that actually exists. In this respect, it is the artist, not the scholar, who arrives at the true nature of reality. Each and every thing we see or hear contains our individuality. Though we might speak of identical consciousness, our consciousnesses are not truly the same. When viewing a cow, for example, farmers, zoologists, and artists have different mental images. Depending on one's feeling at the moment, the same scenery can appear resplendently beautiful or depressingly gloomy. Buddhist thought holds that according to one's mood the world becomes either heaven or hell. Thus our world is constructed upon our feeling and volition. However much we talk about the objective world as the subject matter of pure knowledge, it cannot escape its relation to our feelings.

People think that the world seen scientifically is most objective in that it exists independently of our feeling and volition. But it is in no way divorced from the demands of feelings and the will because scientific inquiry derives from actual demands in our struggle for survival. As especially Jerusalem has said, the idea that a power in the external world performs various activities—this idea being the fundamental principle of the scientific world view—is generated by analogical inference from one's will. Ancient explanations of things in the universe were anthropomorphic, and they are the springboard from which contemporary scientific explanations developed.

Taking the distinction between subject and object as fundamental, some think that objective elements are included only in knowledge and that idiosyncratic, subjective events constitute feeling and volition. This view is mistaken in its basic assumptions. If we argue that phenomena arise by means of the mutual activity of subject and object, then even such content of knowledge as color or form can be seen as subjective or individual. If we argue further that there is a quality in the external world that gives rise to feeling and volition, then they come to possess an objective base, and it is therefore an error to say they are totally individual. Our feeling and volition allow for communication and sympathy between individuals; they have a trans-individual element.

Because we think that such emotional and volitional entities as joy, anger, love, and desire arise in individual people, we also think that feeling and the will are purely individual. Yet it is not that the individual possesses feeling and the will, but rather that feeling and the will create the individual. Feeling and the will are facts of direct experience.

The anthropomorphic explanation of the myriad things in the universe is the way of explanation used by ancient people and naive children in all eras. Although scientists might laugh it away—indeed, it is infantile—from a certain perspective this is the true way of explaining reality. A scientist's way of explanation is slanted toward just one aspect of knowledge, whereas in a complete explanation of reality we must satisfy intellectual demands as well as the demands of feeling and the will.

To the Greeks, all of nature was alive. Thunder and lightning were the wrath of Zeus on Mount Olympus, the voice of the cuckoo was Philamela's lament of the past. To the natural eye of a Greek, the true meaning of the present appeared just as it was. Contemporary art, religion, and philosophy all strive to express this true meaning.

"The Standpoint of Śūnyatā"

Nishitani Keiji

That a thing actually *is* means that it is absolutely unique. No two things in the world can be completely the same. The absolute uniqueness of a thing means, in other words, that it is situated in the absolute center of all other things. It is situated, as it were, in the position of *master,* with all other things positioned relative to it as *servants.*

To our ordinary way of thinking, though, it is simply a contradiction to claim that this is how it is with everything that "is," and yet that the "world" is constituted through all such things being gathered into one. How is it possible that something in the position of master to other things can at the same time stand in the position of servant to all other things? If we grant that each and every thing, in its mode of being as what it is in itself, enjoys an absolute autonomy and occupies the rank of master seated at the center of everything, how are we to avoid thinking of such a situation as complete anarchy and utter chaos? Is this not diametrically opposed to conceiving of the world as an order of being?

This sort of objection arises because one is only thinking on the field of ordinary consciousness, which covers the expanse between sensation and reason and leaves the field of śūnyatā out of the picture. That beings one and all are gathered into one, while each one remains absolutely unique in its "being," points to a relationship in which, as we said above, all things are master and servant to one another. We may call this relationship, which is only possible on the field of śūnyatā, "circuminsessional."

To say that a certain thing is situated in a position of servant to every other thing means that it lies at the ground of all other things, that it is a constitutive element in the being of every other thing, making it to be what it is and thus to be situated in a position of autonomy as master of itself. It assumes a position at the home-ground of every other thing as that of a retainer upholding his lord. The fact that A is so related to B, C, D . . . amounts, then, to an absolute negation of the standpoint of A as master, along with its uniqueness and so, too, its "being." In other words, it means that A possesses no substantiality in the ordinary sense, that it is a *non*-self-nature. Its being is a being in unison with emptiness, a being possessed of the character of an illusion.

Seen from the other side, however, the same could be said respectively of B, C, D . . . and every other thing that is. That is to say, from that perspective, they all stand in a position of servant to A, supporting its position as master and functioning as a constitutive element of A, making it what it is. Thus, that a thing *is*—its absolute autonomy—comes about only in unison with a subordination *of* all other things. It comes about only on the field of śūnyatā, where the being of all other things, while remaining to the very end the being that it is, is emptied out. Moreover, this means that the autonomy of this one thing is only constituted through a subordination *to* all other things. Its autonomy comes about only on a standpoint from which it makes all other things to be what they are, and in so doing is emptied of its own being.

In short, it is only on a field where the being of all things is a being at one with emptiness that it is possible for all things to gather into one, even while each retains its reality as an absolutely unique being. Here the being of all things, as well as the world as a system of being, become possible. If we exclude the field of śūnyatā and try to conceive at the same time of the *reality* of things (the fact that things *are*), and the fact that all things gather into one, we find that the more deeply we think it over, the more we swing toward anarchy and chaos.

All things that are in the world are linked together, one way or the other. Not a single thing comes into being without some relationship to every other thing. Scientific intellect thinks here in terms of natural laws of necessary causality; mythico-poetic imagination perceives an organic, living connection; philosophic reason contemplates an absolute One. But on a more essential level, a system of circuminsession has to be seen here, according to which, on the field of śūnyatā, all things are in a process of becoming master and servant to one another. In this system, each thing is itself in not being itself, and is not itself in being itself. Its being is illusion in its truth and truth in its illusion. This may sound strange the first time one hears it, but in fact it enables us for the first time to conceive of a *force* by virtue of which all things are gathered together and brought into relationship with one another, a force which, since ancient times, has gone by the name of "nature" (*physis*).

To say *that a thing is not itself* means that, while continuing to be itself, it is in the home-ground of everything else. Figuratively speaking, its roots reach across into the ground of all other things and helps to hold them up and keep them standing. It serves as a constitutive element of their being so that they can be what they are, and thus provides an ingredient of their being. *That a thing is itself* means that all other things, while continuing to be themselves, are in the home-ground of that thing; that precisely when a thing is on its own home-ground, everything else is there too; that the roots of every other thing spread across into its home-ground. This way that everything has of being on the home-ground of everything else, without ceasing to be on its own home-ground, means that the being of each thing is held up, kept standing, and made to be what it is by means of the being of all other things; or, put the other way around, that each thing holds up the being of every other thing, keeps it standing, and makes it what it is. In a word, it means that all things "are" in the "world."

To imply that when a thing is on its own home-ground, it must at the same time be on the home-ground of all other things sounds absurd; but in fact it constitutes the "essence" of the existence of things. The being of things in themselves is essentially circuminsessional. This is what we mean by speaking of beings as "being that is in unison with emptiness," and "being on the field of emptiness." For this circuminsessional system is only possible on the field of emptiness of or śūnyatā.

As I have already noted, if the field of śūnyatā be excluded, for a thing to be on its own home-ground and to be "itself" would be for it not to be in the home-ground of all other things; and, conversely, for it to be on the home-ground of other things would be for it not to be itself. In that case, there would in truth be no way for us to explain the fact that all things "are" in the "world." Only on the field of śūnyatā, where being is seen as being-*sive*-nothingness, nothingness-*sive*-being, is it possible for each *to be itself* with every other, and so, too, for each *not to be itself* with every other.

The interpenetration of all things that comes about here is the most essential of all relationships, one that is closer to the ground of things than any relationship ever conceived on the fields of sensation and reason by science, myth, or philosophy.

Even the likes of Leibniz's system of monads reflecting one another like living mirrors of the universe, for example, can in the final analysis, be returned to this point.

Now the circuminsessional system itself, whereby each thing in its being enters into the home-ground of every other thing, is not itself and yet precisely as such (namely, as located on the field of śūnyatā) never ceases to be itself, is nothing other than the *force* that links all things together into one. It is the very force that makes the world and lets it be a world. The field of śūnyatā is a *field of force*. The force of the world makes itself manifest in the force of each and every thing in the world.

To return to a terminology adopted earlier on, the force of the world, or "nature," becomes manifest in the pine tree as the *virtus* of the pine, and in the bamboo as the *virtus* of the bamboo. Even the very tiniest thing, to the extent that it "is," displays in its act of being the whole web of circuminsessional interpenetration that links all things together. In its being, we might say, the world "worlds." Such a mode of being is the mode of being of things as they are in themselves, their non-objective, "middle" mode of being as the selfness that they are.

3

Self

Go into your own room and get the Upanishads out of your Self. You are the greatest book that ever was or ever will be, the infinite depositary of all that is. Until the inner teacher opens, all outside teaching is in vain. It must lead to the opening of the book of the heart to have any value. (Vivekananda)[1]

Indian Philosophies

Hindu Perspectives

The burning question throughout orthodox Indian thought concerns the nature of the self. What constitutes the true self? Who am "I" in essence? As we have seen with regard to reality, there are a variety of Hindu perspectives on the self.

Upanishads: Tat Tvam Asi

It is difficult to find a more imaginative depiction of the nature of the true self than what we find in the Upanishads. The true self, called *atman,* is eternal. And nearly every one of the principal Upanishads examines the nature of this *atman,* or personal essence, in a distinct way. For instance, in the *Chandogya Upanishad,* the father Uddalaka Aruni teaches his son Svetaketu that our real self is like the unseen essence of the seed of the Nyagrodha tree:

> "Bring hither a fruit of that *nyagrodha* tree." "Here it is, Venerable Sir."
> "Break it." "It is broken, Venerable Sir." "What do you see there?"
> "These extremely fine seeds, Venerable Sir." "Of these, please break

133

one." "It is broken, Venerable Sir." "What do you see there?" "Nothing at all, Venerable Sir."

Then he said to him, "My dear, that subtle essence which you do not perceive, verily, my dear, from that very essence this great *nyagrodha* tree exists. Believe me, my dear.

That which is the subtle essence, this whole world has for its self. That is the true. That is the self. That art thou Svetaketu."[2]

Uddalaka then directs his son to place salt into a cup filled with water. The next day, Svetaketu discovers that the salt is dissolved. Uddalaka now instructs him:

"Please take a sip of it from this end." He said, "How is it?" "Salt.". . . "Verily indeed, my dear, you do not perceive Pure Being here? Verily, indeed, it is here.

That which is the subtle essence this whole world has for its self. That is the true. That is the self. That art thou, Svetaketu."[3]

In this same work, the *atman* is described as that deepest part of us that sees, the seer in the eye. A selection from the *Chandogya Upanishad* is found at the end of this chapter. The reading illustrates the Hindu notion of *tat tvam asi*. We also find in the *Katha Upanishad* the comparison of *atman* to the root of a tree, whereas our senses and reason are the branches.

Indeed, as we saw in Chapter 2, the most important teaching in the Upanishads consists of the discovery that *atman* is, in essence, identical to *Brahman—tat tvam asi*. This identity is the essential teaching in the shortest of the principal Upanishads, the *Mandukya Upanishad:*

All this is, indeed, Brahman. This *Atman* is Brahman.[4]

Orthodox Schools

Samkhya   The fundamental aim in Samkhya is to enable us to differentiate that which is truly self from that which appears as self. In this regard, the two dominant ideas in Samkhya are *purusha* and *prakriti*. We must comprehend these ideas if we are to get some sense of how Samkhya views our true identity.

Purusha refers to spirit, or *atman*. In the Samkhya teaching, *purusha* is both being and consciousness. (Samkhya views *atman* as having these two attributes, whereas in the Vedanta system, *atman* consists of three: being, consciousness, and bliss, or what is known as *sat-cit-ananda*.) Because *purusha* is *atman,* it is my genuine self as pure consciousness, unblemished awareness.

Because there are an infinite number of *purushas,* there is an infinity of souls, or *atman*. *Purusha* is not bounded in shape or size but is infinite. It is the true self, and true self is eternal and infinite. It is not at all affected by what takes place due to the activity of *prakriti*. In this way, *purusha* is distinct from all things both mental and physical. It is important to note that *purusha* is not the same as mind, and it is definitely not ego. *Purusha* is a steady spectator that never changes while all else does.

Prakriti is often referred to as Nature, or original nature. *Prakriti* is not matter *per se,* but the pristine stuff of matter. Its basic trait is constant change. In fact, it is the primordial fabric of all that comes to exist, including mind. However, as opposed to *purusha,* it is totally unconscious. All that comes from *prakriti* becomes the object of disinterested observation by *purusha.* Also, in contrast to *purusha,* it is not manifold and infinite, but one, although its products—all objects in the world—certainly appear to be manifold.

As we stated, *purusha* is that which observes the objects that come from *prakriti.* And here lies one of our basic errors: We misconstrue the real observer to be our own ego. But, in reality, according to the Samkhya school, the ego is not the real observer, but rather a product of *prakriti.* And this in turn means that even the ego is an object for the true observer, *purusha,* who is the genuine self.

Let us put it another way. Pure observation requires a distance from the object of knowledge; without this distance, the knowledge is tainted with subjectivity. Pure knowledge demands noninvolvement. For Samkhya, only *purusha* is capable of this noninvolvement. Ego and mind are both products of *prakriti,* and they themselves are the objects of the knower, *purusha.*[5]

Before we look at the evolution of things from the union of *purusha* and *prakriti,* let us look more closely at *prakriti. Prakriti,* although unconscious, has three attributes, also called *gunas: sattva,* clarity; *rajas,* activity; and *tamas,* passivity. These *gunas* participate in the evolution from *prakriti. Sattva* refers to that which is clear, or light. It is the feature of clarity associated with intellect. *Rajas* is the active energy and is more assertive. It is expressed in the passions. *Tamas* is the passive force, as in inertia.

Before *purusha* "observes" *prakriti*—that is, in its pristine state—the three *gunas* are in a state of balance and are inert. Once *purusha* pays attention to *prakriti,* the stasis is upset. These three attributes then vie among themselves as to which will assume control over the other two. How the world unfolds is the result of this contention among these attributes.

No one of these forces exists in isolation from the other two. Yet, one or two will always be predominant. For example, the constant motion of a waterfall indicates that *rajas* (activity) governs the other two *gunas,* although both passivity and clarity are not totally eclipsed. A person who manifests apathy and lacks luster in his or her life-style may be more overcome by the *guna* of *tamas,* or passivity. In contrast, a person of sensitivity and intelligence seems to have more *sattva.*[6]

Let us be more specific concerning this evolution from *prakriti.* How does this occur in the first place? It results from the linking up of *purusha* with *prakriti,* which happens rather mysteriously. Essentially, the *purusha,* as pure consciousness, inspires the unconscious *prakriti* in such a way that the world is produced. Remember that the *prakriti* is one, whereas *purushas* are infinite. Thus, we have an infinity of "reflections" from this association.[7]

We also need to keep in mind that this "conjunction" between *purusha* and *prakriti* is an apparent bond, not a real one. Raju gives a good example: The sun that reflects itself in the ocean is still itself and distinct from the ocean. It is important to keep this in mind. The *purusha* always acts only as observer—no more, no less.

The first thing that comes from *prakriti* is what is called "reason." This is natural because *prakriti* is activated into production not on its own, but through the inspiration of *purusha*, which is pure consciousness. Remember that *prakriti* by itself is unconscious. Also, reason is the first to come about because *sattva* is initially superior to the other two *gunas*. The term for reason is *buddhi*. *Buddhi* is sometimes called *mahat*, or "great," because of the great role that reason occupies in this scheme. Furthermore, reason remains impersonal.

Not so with ego, which is intensely personal. The ego then comes from reason and is distinguished from reason because the ruling *guna* is less likely to be *sattva*. Instead, it is *rajas*. Ego is actively self-referential, assimilating all things within its own point of reference: my book, my body, my world. It seems as if the existence of ego is immediately present to us. We perceive our experiences in terms of self-reference: "I will play tennis this afternoon." "I am thirsty." This "I" is ego. Life seems to make better sense to us when there is this self-referential feature, for it enables self-reflection, evaluation, comparison, and judgment.

Therefore, ego is the result of *prakriti*, and all other objects evolve further from ego. As to these other objects, Samkhya explicitly mentions mind, five senses, five organs, five subtle elements, and five gross elements. Reason, ego, and mind are the three inner senses according to Samkhya. (The regular senses are the outer senses.) Mind is given a special status as a "connecting link between the inner senses and the outer senses and organs."[8]

Among the selections at the end of the chapter is one by a noted commentator of the school, Ishvarakrishna. His *Samkhya Karikas* are concise explications of the Samkhya teaching and are among the most important writings of the school. Ishvarakrishna described how, in this whole process, *purusha* recognizes the miseries and suffering associated with the production of the world. The union of *purusha* with *prakriti* is compared to that of a person who is lame with a person who is blind. Suffering ultimately originates from a wrong conception of genuine self. The aim in the Samkhya teachings is to personally differentiate between false self (ego, mind, and so on) and true self (*purusha*); that is, the goal is to distinguish between *purusha* and *prakriti*. The Yoga school, our next topic, then elaborates on techniques to achieve this state of discernment.

Yoga   The Yoga school adopts this Samkhya teaching to aid us in the path to self-realization through looking inward. Yoga is the psycho-physical practice of self-cultivation. We see this illustrated in its key text, the *Yoga Sutras* by Patanjali. (A commentary on this work is included at the end of this chapter.)

The most important discovery is that of the true self, the *atman* or *purusha*. Mental forces often act to obstruct our realization of *atman*. Yogic techniques attempt to bring about a fundamental harmony between the mental and the physical.[9]

The highest state that one can reach in yoga is called *samadhi*, which literally refers to a condition of pure, "untainted" knowledge, complete in itself. It is a step higher than that of *dhyana*. Whereas *dhyana* still assumes an object of meditation, *samadhi* is the state in which the subject and object are one. *Samadhi* is reached by ascending eight steps, which, in effect, constitute yogic practice:

1. self-discipline
2. good behavior
3. proper postures
4. proper breathing
5. subsiding of senses
6. proper concentration
7. meditation
8. *samadhi*

Again, what is most essential in both Samkhya and Yoga is that complete realization entails experiencing the essential difference between one's true self, *atman* or *purusha*, and that which is not self (although it appears as such), *prakriti*. Only then can there be liberation from *samsara*, the wheel of birth, death, and rebirth.

Advaita Vedanta   Remember that for the Nyaya-Vaishesika school, the true self possesses being but is not conscious. For the Samkhya and Yoga schools, the self is both being and consciousness. The Vedanta schools posit the self as being, consciousness, and bliss (*sat-cit-ananda*).[10]
    Advaita accepts the analysis of the human person in terms of five sheaths that cover the self, as found in the *Taittaraya Upanishad*. Starting from the outer layer, these sheaths are:

sheath of food
sheath of vitality
sheath of mind
sheath of intellect
sheath of bliss

These are then related to what are called the three bodies: the gross body, the subtle body, and the causal body. The gross body is immersed in physical things; the subtle body deals with the intellectual, emotional, and volitional aspects of the personality. The causal body is associated with the sheath of bliss and therefore with deep aspects of consciousness, or the unconscious. Moreover, the subtle body and the causal body survive the physical death of the gross body. While embodied, the Self is referred to as *jiva*, also called the "empirical self" in Advaita. The main idea here is that as long as the Self is embodied, it is not entirely free and suffers from *avidya*, ignorance of its true nature.
    Avidya, the source of bondage to *samsara*, consists in confusing one's real self with aspects that are external to self. It also lies in the confusion of one's self with personal aspects such as one's body or mind. In all these cases,

self is thought to be identical to the psycho-physical properties that in actuality constitute the sheaths overlaying the genuine Self. Enlightenment can occur only with realization of one's true self, *atman,* and therefore as *Brahman.*

Aurobindo and Divine Descent

Aurobindo's account of self occurs within the context of the evolution of the world from its divine source. The Divine descends to the human level and issues to each being a "spark of Divinity" called a "psyche," or soul. In this way, the soul is enclosed within matter. This divine descent is called "involution." On a mundane level, however, we are less conscious of our divine nature, or soul, and we identify more with matter and concentrate more on mind than on soul.

Therefore, the aim is to reunite with this divine source. This is the ascent, or "spirit's return to itself," and is termed "evolution" by Aurobindo. In this ascent, genuine knowledge of the Divine cannot be achieved through the mind, which tends to fragment knowledge. Intellect is subordinate to intuition, for intuition offers a moment of release from mental structures that by nature divide an experience. It is through Aurobindo's type of yoga that this integration with the Divine can occur. A selection from his *The Life Divine* is included at the end of this chapter.

Buddhist Perspectives

We need to examine carefully the Buddhist perspectives on the nature of self because they are radically different from the orthodox Indian teachings. To review, according to orthodox Brahmanic teachings, an independent entity, eternal and perfect, exists and is called *atman.* In the time that *atman* is embodied, it is viewed as *jiva,* as a separate soul, although in reality it is *atman.* For most orthodox schools, with the exception of those of Ramanuja and Madhva, *atman* is identical with *Brahman.* This seems to be the prevailing interpretation of *tat tvam asi.*

In contrast, Buddhists hold that there is no unique individual self. Their concept of self is therefore called "no-self," or *anatman.* (The Pali term is *anatta.*)

This is probably the most difficult teaching in Buddhism. It is especially challenging for us, raised in the Western tradition, because we often assume the existence of some personal entity, or self, an idea that must sound strange to many Buddhists. The idea of *anatman* conflicts with the deep-rooted need for a lasting primordial entity or substance. This particular Buddhist teaching may also explain why Buddhism eventually lost favor among Indians.[11] (A portion from the *Milindapanha,* or *Questions of King Milinda,* is included at the end of this chapter, along with some of the *Visuddhi-Magga.* These are early Buddhist texts, and the *Milindapanha* records dialogues between the Greek King Milinda and Nagasena, a Buddhist monk.)

Basic Themes

Can we be clearer about this no-self? Let us start with the Noble Truths. As we recall, according to the first Noble Truth, aging, illness, and death are the natural truths of existence, strong testimony to the universality of suffering. The Second Noble Truth is our concern here. According to the Buddha, the cause of suffering lies in the fundamental attitude we have toward these realities. Suffering results from *trsna,* or craving. It is ultimately a consequence of our tendency to cling to what is essentially impermanent. It is like standing in a stream of water, attempting to grab handfuls of the water as it flows by. Reality is this stream. The Buddha taught that all things are impermanent. Not even the self is permanent, for the self does not exist. Yet there is a strong human desire to cling to things, experiences, people, and ideas, especially the idea of self because of the desire for permanence.

The strong empirical basis of Buddhism is an important feature here. The Buddha was reluctant to assume an eternal entity called *atman* because there was no genuine empirical verification for such an entity.

Through an empirical analysis, the Buddha asserted that each individual "person" is composed essentially of a bundle of components: the five aggregates, known as *skandhas.* These five components, which always undergo change, are form, sensation, perception, mental constructs, and consciousness. Form is the body, the physical character of the "person." Form is known as *rupa.* The other four *skandhas* are made up of mental states. Sensations occur from contact of the body with the world surrounding it; they come about through sense-impressions. When these sensations are absorbed through the brain, they become perceptions. Mental formations such as ideas and desires then result from these perceptions. Consciousness is a sort of stream that links all this together and is at the same time inspired by mental phenomena. Consciousness is also the link to the next rebirth. It is often synonymous with "mind."

Therefore, these mental states, sensations, feelings, will, consciousness, and so on work together with the form. All these constitute the "person," referred to as *nama-rupa* (name-form).

Remember that all these skandhas undergo constant change. This sustains the belief in no-self. Yet, we now face a critically important question: If there is no self, then what is it that is reborn (Buddhists still adhere to a doctrine of rebirth)? Along the same lines, how can we explain karma? Remember that karma is essentially the principle of moral causality by which past actions and thoughts influence future states and events. (This concept will be examined in more detail in Chapter 6. Suffice it for now to say that Buddhists believe in rebirth, but not in the rebirth of an independent entity called soul. Nevertheless, what is reborn must contain the karma of previous lives. And it is this karma that determines the state of the next existence. Karma therefore plays a significant role in rebirth and is a crucial element in the whole issue of personal identity. Karma presupposes a continuity to my existence that enables me to look back at my life and view it as a succession of causally connected phenomena.

One of the most important Buddhist teachings surrounding this idea of no-self is that of dependent origination, called *pratityasamutpada*. Buddhists apply this teaching to the idea of "person" by describing the person in terms of twelve links, which act as prevailing conditions that bring about the coming-to-be and the falling-away of each other. These twelve links are ignorance, action-intentions, consciousness, name and body, the sixfold sphere of sense-contact, contact, sensation, craving, grasping, becoming, birth, and old age and death.

What dependent origination means is that everything, including "self," is essentially both the cause and effect of everything else. What we think of as "self" is actually a sequence of mental activities that brings about the illusion of an enduring entity. It is therefore quite natural for us to assign substantiality to this sequence. We presume that thinking occurs due to a thinker, and that acting occurs due to an actor.

We make the glaring assumption that behind mental activity there is an independent self. Within the spectrum of dependent origination, however, nothing can be independent. Dependent origination teaches us that everything is a stream of mental activity in constant flux. All that we can actually verify is this stream, but not an entity behind the scenes or some "ghost in the machine." Therefore, what we consider to be a controlling entity behind this bundle of mental activity is simply a process of mental activity—no more nor less.

For this reason, Buddhists place great emphasis on meditation. The aim in Buddhist meditation is to be aware of the mind as mind, as suchness (as opposed to a "thinker" behind the mind). The Buddhist term for this suchness is *tathata*. The Buddha is often referred to as Tathagata, "who is such as he is," because he apparently achieved this realization of *tathata*. This is not easy because the mind can be a wild elephant, carrying us off onto all varieties of detours. The idea is to be aware of things as they are without imposing conceptual webs, particularly that of self.

The materialists equated self with body. Because matter is real, it would be improper to assign another, higher reality to some nonmaterial factor. Buddhists do not go to this extreme of identifying the body as self. They merely assert that the notion of self entails metaphysical assumptions that have no empirical basis.

In other words, Buddhists attempt to steer a path between two extremes: between denying any personal self whatsoever and asserting an eternal substantial self. Because they believe in rebirth, there must be some sort of connecting link from death to the next birth. Therefore, they do not assume the materialist position. At the same time, they avoid the Brahmanic teaching of an eternal self. This outlook exemplifies the Middle Way of Buddhism.

Mahayana

Nagarjuna   As we said, Nagarjuna's key work is his *Madhyamika Karika,* the entire text of which is a refutation of the idea of substantiality. All reality consists in elements in various modes of associations with each other. For

Nagarjuna, there are no grounds to assume any self-subsistent entity underlying such elemental action.

Nagarjuna provided an incisive account of causality and change in view of nonsubstantiality. The pivotal teaching in all this is that of dependent origination. Nagarjuna set out to demonstrate in deft strokes that neither change nor causation assumes an entity independent of such activity, substantial in nature.

Let us look more closely at his essay "Examination of Self-Nature," which is included as a selection at the end of the chapter. The Sanskrit title for this essay is "*Svabhava pariksa.*" *Svabhava* means "self-nature," suggesting an entity that is self-sufficient, what we call substance. Nagarjuna argues that dependent origination does not allow for the existence of *svabhava*.

Recall that the central idea in Nagarjuna is *sunya,* or emptiness, which demands transcending even our conceptions of reality. Through the distinctions we often draw between the concepts of existence and nonexistence, permanence and disruption, identity and difference, one and the many, and unity and plurality, we actually reinforce the illusion of *svabhava*. (Nagarjuna then went on to argue against the idea of a permanent entity that transmigrates because the concept of transmigration implies movement and thus change, contradictory to permanence.)

This is why his emphasis on the fourfold negation is important as a useful conceptual tool. In it we see that *sunya* refers to what is not. *Sunya* is not: Being, non-Being, both Being and non-Being, or neither Being nor non-Being. In other words, the fourfold negation can be translated as: A is neither B, nor non-B, nor both, nor neither. All that can truly be said about reality is that nothing can truly be said; therefore, all is *sunya*. If there is anything we can say about reality, it is that reality is therefore Void, empty, or *sunya*.

Does this mean that Nagarjuna was essentially a nihilist? Even nihilism is a description that sets itself against the opposite standard of realism. Nagarjuna proposed a theory (or better, a nontheory) transcending nihilism. One can say that he tread a metaphysical middle way, *madhyamika,* between no-being and all-being. We see this in his discussion of "self-nature."[12]

Vasubandhu   In his *Vimsatika,* Vasubandhu set out to demonstrate that reality is pure consciousness, *vijnana,* and that all things exist only as objects of consciousness. He did this in the face of opponents who advanced arguments to the contrary: that objects do exist apart from mind or our consciousness of them. (Throughout the works, the terms *consciousness, thought,* and *mind* are used interchangeably.)

Vasubandhu discredited the two things we normally take for granted: the existence of objects apart from our consciousness of them, and the existence of a self as subject of our consciousness. He rejected objective existence based on the evidence of the senses. Objects in a dream are a case in point. In a similar way, we are as if we were in a dream state, mistaking what we perceive as being objectively real. The difference is that when we dream we have the good fortune of awakening from our dream state and recognizing it as such. This is generally not the case with regard to our existence because we are generally under the spell of *maya* and *avidya*.

Vijnana is a term that means consciousness. In fact, *vijnana* means "pure consciousness," and achieving this state is the paramount aim among the school's followers. *Vijnana* is also the ultimate reality, the ground for all conscious determinations. The only reality is this Supreme Consciousness, or *vijnana*. This being the case, then what is the relationship between this absolute and its expression in manifold consciousness? What accounts for its change from one pure consciousness to many consciousnesses?

Another selection at the end of this chapter is taken from Vasubandhu's philosophical-psychological treatise *Trimsika,* one of his most important works. It is noted for both its brevity—it is only thirty verses (*trimsika*)—and its profundity. It is an analysis of the evolution of consciousness, and is more of a philosophical examination of psychology. What Vasubandhu argued is that consciousness develops as part of the pattern of dependent origination. In other words, consciousness itself is not external to this process. Consciousness does not at all presuppose or intimate a conscious subject that we call self, external to this dynamic process. Therefore, there is no subject of consciousness, no entity outside of the process. Consciousness occurs as a stream or process.

The only reality is pure consciousness. Due to its own force or power (*sakti*), however, this pure consciousness undergoes three "transformations" in which the illusion or "metaphor" of an individual self and objective reality occurs. In other words, everything is actually the manifestation of consciousness. Let us briefly review these three transformations.

First, pure consciousness transforms itself into "seed-consciousness," or *alaya-vijnana.* The term *seed* is significant because it suggests that which naturally produces. *Alaya*-consciousness is the receptacle, also called "storehouse," that contains the seeds of all the dispositions that form one's character. That is, it contains the "seeds" of all phenomena or objects of perception, both physical and mental.

Second, our sense of a separate self comes from the *alaya-vijnana.* As the text indicates, this self is accompanied by four ailments (also referred to as "defilements"). These four ailments are "self-view, self-confusion, self-esteem, and self-love."[13] Only through the "cessation" of these ailments can realization of our true nature come about. And our true nature is reality, or pure consciousness.

It is important to note that the transformation from *vijnana* to a plurality of consciousnesses is only apparent; it does not really take place. The plurality we see is the result of *maya,* which causes the illusion of reality, including the reality of selves.

Third, this results in the perception of "sense-objects" along with accompanying mental states. The text provides an interesting simile concerning the relation between these mental states and the *alaya-vijnana* as "waves" to "water." In other words, waves appear to be separate from the ocean, but they are not separate. In the same way, external objects come about as seemingly separate phenomena. Yet, all this is essentially the transformation of pure consciousness. This store-consciousness "develops like the currents in a stream." It undergoes constant movement, only to cease when one awakens to the reality of pure consciousness.

In this way (working backward), all phenomena (including the "self") are transformations of store-consciousness. This is why we say that *alaya-vijnana* contains the seeds of all phenomena, mental and physical. At the same time, the store-consciousness is a self-manifestation of pure consciousness, *vijnana,* which is the only reality.

It is clear that the main thrust in Vasubandhu's *Trimsika* is that the self as a substantial entity is not real. In addition, the objects we think of as real are also not real. Two underlying errors pervade our lives: that the object world exists, and that the separate self exists. All other errors result from these two errors. Vasubandhu attempted to shatter these two beliefs in his work.

Realizing this pure consciousness cannot be the result of intellection, however, because intellect still lies within the sphere of finite determination—that is, conceptualizing with respect to an object of our intellect. Pure consciousness can only be realized by going beyond the subject-object split. The means to attain such a state necessitates Yoga practice. That is, Yoga can provide the therapeutic methodology needed to reach this "*Dharma*-body of the Sage."

Chinese Philosophies

What is our real self according to Chinese thought? The more typical Chinese approach seems to be less disposed toward abstract speculation. To be precise, for many Chinese philosophers the individual is not viewed simply as a knowing subject, but as a moral agent. The self encompasses both knowing and doing. These two aspects—knowing and acting—define the self. Therefore, a natural connection exists between Chinese notions of self and ethical action.

Let us pursue this line of thought further. In general, Chinese philosophy views the self in terms of the relationships that form and ultimately define each person. In Confucianism, for instance, within this relational context the importance of duties and obligations is highlighted. The continuance of such duties—for example, through ritual—reinforces group harmony. At the risk of generalization, we can thus claim that the self is viewed in terms of the multiple obligations inherent within specific relationships.

Thus, the idea of self can be seen on a number of levels, each reflective of the other: Confucians depict these levels as self and other, self and family, family as a microcosm of society, and society as a microcosm of humanity; Taoists view these levels as self and nature, and humanity as a microcosm of the cosmos.[14]

Chuang Tzu: "Forget the Self"

Chuang Tzu represented a unique position regarding matters of self, constantly urging us to "forget the self." By this he meant going beyond the conventional separation:

world ≠ self

This is also a forgetting of the world. In other words, once we let go of the sense of an individual, separate self, then we also let go of the world.

A device used by Chuang Tzu may help here. He sometimes compared the true mind to a mirror. The "perfect person's" mind is like a clear mirror: It passively yet clearly receives images. It accepts all which comes before it, and it does so without interpretation and judgment. In this respect, it is in its true state, without conceptualizing and without desiring:

> By Inaction, one can become the centre of thought, the focus of responsibility, the arbiter of wisdom. Full allowance must be made for others, while remaining unmoved oneself. There must be a thorough compliance with divine principles, without any manifestation thereof. All of which may be summed up in the word *passivity* [*wu-wei*]. For the perfect man employs his mind as a mirror. It grasps nothing: it refuses nothing. It receives, but does not keep. And thus he can triumph over matter, without injury to himself.[15]

This mirror-mind illustrates the idea of *wu-wei,* or nonaction, spontaneity. This mirror-mind is true mind because it is untainted by subjectivity; that is, it sees and accepts things as they are.

The source of this mirror-mind is the genuine self, which is not tied to an idea or image of reality, but instead reflects reality. In this way, it can forget itself. It enables the distorted notion of self as ego to be seen for what it is. That is, our genuine self is not that bundle of concepts and desires that forms our ego. If it is viewed as such, then a bifurcation between subject and object recurs. Self transcends this dichotomy between self and world. All is one in harmony.[16]

Therefore, the path to enlightenment for Chuang Tzu lay in an intuitive awareness that frees the power of the mind by freeing one from ordinary habits of conceptualization.

Confucius and Tung Chung-shu

A dominant trend in Chinese thought is the idea that both the individual and the social world exist together, and this idea is expressly taught in Confucianism. Important texts are the *Analects, Mencius, Doctrine of the Mean,* and *Commentaries on the I Ching.* For instance, the *Doctrine of the Mean* teaches the universal principle of Tao, or *ch'eng,* which is described as the unity of the individual self and the world.

In other words, what these key texts illustrate is not the "forgetting" of both self and world stressed by Chuang Tzu. Instead, we have the harmony of both self and world while still recognizing their unique aspects. Neither of them is submerged into a state of oneness. Harmony assumes distinction. This is the essential teaching in Confucianism. Confucians view harmony in a way that is different from Taoists.

With Neo-Confucians we have a more metaphysical interpretation of this relation between self and world. Universal principle is now engaged through individuals who are distinct. Nevertheless, this occurs within a stream of universal harmony.

The *Analects* lack an abstract discussion of the nature of self. In down-to-earth imagery and expression, Confucius instead stressed what is involved in the proper cultivation of self:

> The Master said, "Hold faithfulness and sincerity as first principles. Have no friends not equal to yourself. When you have faults, do not fear to abandon them."[17]
>
>   The master said, "The leaving virtue without proper cultivation; the not thoroughly discussing what is learned; not being able to move towards righteousness of which a knowledge is gained; and not being able to change what is not good—these are the things which occasion me solicitude."[18]

By cultivating one's self, one is on the way to becoming a superior person:

> Tsze-lu asked what constituted the superior man. The Master said, "The cultivation of himself in reverential carefulness." "And is this all?"said Tsze-lu. "He cultivates himself so as to give rest to others," was the reply. "And is this all?" again asked Tsze-lu. The Master said, "He cultivates himself so as to give rest to all the people."[19]

Concerning the self, a most interesting correlation was established by a Han Dynasty Confucianist, Tung Chung-shu. He asserted a link between the forces of yin and yang and human nature and feelings: Human nature (*hsing*) represents the force of yang, whereas human feelings (*ch'ing*) are associated with yin. He also assigned to yin a lesser metaphysical status than to yang. Therefore, human nature, because it reflects yang, is positive. Human feelings and emotions, on the other hand, particularly feelings centering around the self (such as jealousy), are negative because they reflect yin.

In view of this combination of both yang and yin forces in the human, Tung Chung-shu claimed that the whole of human nature is neither intrinsically good nor evil. Instead, it is a mixture of strength and weakness. Yet its nature is such that it has the potential for good, and the ideal is to cultivate the virtue of *jen*, which means human-heartedness.

Neo-Confucianists

Chu Hsi School

Ch'eng Yi stressed that the investigation of things would lead to an understanding of the principle of things, their *li*. In the same way, the investigation of our self would eventually lead to an understanding of the principle of self. This knowledge of the principle of self would, in turn, lead to the ultimate principle.

Consistent with what we have seen so far in Chinese thought, Chu Hsi's concern lay more with the proper cultivation of self, and less with an abstract investigation into the nature of self.

For Chu Hsi, true self awareness exists in realizing the oneness of one's self with everything else. Let us review how he arrived at this position. Along with Ch'eng Yi, Chu Hsi held that the first step to self-cultivation is learning— not learning for the sake of acquiring knowledge, but learning as a means of obtaining insight into our own self-principle. Chu Hsi referred to this act as "probing principle."[20] "Probing" is an appropriate word because it denotes the idea of persistent investigation. Genuine study means uncovering layer after layer until we realize principle.

Proper investigation of things leads to an understanding of their principle, or *li*, which in turn leads to an understanding of the principle, or *li*, of oneself. Therefore, this world is extremely important because it is the vehicle through which our self understanding can occur. And most importantly, this *li* is universally shared by all. It is the same principle in all things and all people.

Here we see an intimate relation between self and *li*. The principle of all things is *li*, and that holds for the individual person as well. His or her principle is genuine self, *li*. This *li* is, at the same time, universal, not disparate. In fact, it is *li* that makes us all in essence one with the world.

When we understand our principle, we are connected to our true nature. This is what Chu Hsi called *ch'eng*, which means "truthfulness." Once we understand our principle, we then realize universal principle.

Wang Yang-ming School: Intuitive Knowledge of Self

Along with Chu Hsi, Wang Yang-ming has had a profound influence on both Chinese and Japanese thought. He believed that each of us is capable of understanding our nature and principle, which means that we are also capable of knowing our self by studying our own mind. Each of us possesses the intuitive sense of what is good and real. Sincere study will therefore naturally lead to the development of our true nature. The result of study naturally expresses itself through acting in accordance with what we discover concerning our true nature. Action thereby completes genuine knowledge. This sustains Wang Yang-ming's belief that knowledge and action are interdependent.

This symbiotic relationship between knowledge and action has direct bearing on Wang Yang-ming's view of the self. As with other Chinese philosophers, his view of self dealt essentially with self-cultivation. The selection at the end of the chapter demonstrates this through his conversation with Hsiao Hui.

Hsiao Hui questions how it is possible to cultivate one's self. In response, Wang Yang-ming indicates that one cannot separate mind from bodily self. True self exists in the proper harmony between mind and body, and mind acts as regulator of bodily self. "The original character of the mind" is "your true self." Yet body is not separate from mind because "the true self is born from the body." Here, Wang Yang-ming provides us with the notion of the self as an acting together of mind and body through intuitive knowledge of what is right.

In another passage, Wang Yang-ming spoke of the self-poise of the superior person in that " . . . the mind is not embarrassed by desire and that the individual can find himself in no situation in which he is not himself."[21]

As we can see, Wang Yang-ming placed much importance on the role of intuitive knowledge. Through this intuition, an inner grasp of heavenly principle lies within us. This is why the superior person acts prudently and does not succumb to distracting desires. (This particular quality in the superior person is described more fully in Wang Yang-ming's Letter to Shu Kuo-yung at the end of this chapter.) The significant point here is that the intuitive knowledge of one's nature is also knowledge of one's true self.

Buddhists

Hsuan-tsang and Consciousness Only

Hsuan-tsang, the founder of the school of Consciousness Only, commented on Vasubandhu's *Trimsika* in the *Treatise on the Establishment of the Doctrine of Consciousness-Only*.[22] Part of this commentary is included at the end of this chapter. The culminating point in his entire analysis is that what we think of as "self" and external realities do not in themselves exist. They are the products of mental activities; reality is "mere ideation." He demonstrated this in his analysis of consciousness.

Hsuan-tsang classified consciousness into eight levels. The eighth level, *alaya,* is the primary consciousness, or store-consciousness, in which the seeds of all other aspects of mind are stored. The seeds in the *alaya* consciousness engender the seven other levels.

This *alaya-vijnana* goes through transformations that produce phenomena, which are also known as *dharmas,* composite elements of existence. What is important is that these transformations, in their various modifications, continue to inspire *alaya* in a sort of mutual relationship so that the actions of each type of consciousness affects all the others. One transformation brings about the view through which consciousness misconstrues its true being as that of intellect, desires, and emotions. These are essentially self-referential.

Hsuan-tsang did not claim that only consciousness exists. What he claimed is that nothing exists separately from consciousness. In a sense, external realities do exist as objects of this consciousness. Apart from consciousness, things do not exist. We can see from this that Hsuan-tsang inherited the teachings of the Yogacara school, or *Vijnanavada,* in Buddhism.

Ch'an Buddhism

The teaching that runs throughout Ch'an Buddhism is nonattachment. With respect to ideas concerning the self, this is all-important. In other words, one must be free from attachment to self; furthermore, one needs to be free from attachment to the ideas of both self and not-self. This is genuine freedom.

Recall Hui-neng's verse in the *gatha* contest (described in Chapter 1):

The *Bodhi* is not like a tree,
The clear mirror is nowhere standing.
Fundamentally not one thing exists;
Where, then, is a grain of dust to cling?

Here, Hui-neng rejects the dualistic view of mind. He taught that the mind is one and pure, unclouded by attachments. This is the state of no-thought, or no-mind (also "no-abiding.") What all this points to is detachment—living within the world without being attached to it, living as I am with my thoughts, feelings, and desires, without being overcome by them.

━━━━━━ Japanese Philosophies ━━━━━━

At this point, let us remind ourselves that we cannot properly separate questions of self from other questions, such as those concerning knowledge. Metaphysics, ontology, and epistemology are all related. The question of self concerns how we know the self.

Because Buddhists proposed the radical thesis of no-self, the issue of self is inherently important to them. From our discussion we can conclude that Buddhists generally agree that the usual view of self obtained through conceptualization is not the genuine self. Whatever this genuine self may be, it lies beyond our intellectual grasp.

However, we can still know the self. If so, then how can the self be known without making it an object of conceptualization? The Japanese Buddhist response is consistent with Buddhist teachings in that knowledge of the self is *prajna,* or wisdom in intuition. Japanese philosophy especially emphasizes the crucial role of a knowing intuition that goes beyond the conventional knowing involved in conceptualization.

Nishida reminds us that "To study oneself is to forget oneself. To forget oneself is to realize oneself as all things."[23] For much of Japanese philosophy, in order to know our true self we must let go of the subject-object dichotomy with which we have been conditioned. We must let go of the voice of intellect in our pursuit and let our intuition open us up and allow awakening. In this awakening, not only do we awaken to our self, but we awaken to all reality. Before we look more closely at some Japanese Buddhist teachings, let us review some ideas from the Neo-Confucian school.

Shushi, Chu Hsi Neo-Confucianism

The Japanese school of Shushi adopts much of Chu Hsi's perspectives on self, which are based on his ideas of *li* and *ch'i*. As we saw in Chapter 2, each human person is endowed with *li*, principle or original nature. At the same time, each person possesses varying degrees of *ch'i* that determine the individuality of that person. According to Masao Maruyama,

The Specific Ether of a sage is completely pure and clear, so his Original Nature appears in its entirety. But an ordinary person has a more or less turbid Specific Ether, giving rise to various human desires.[24]

The aim is to return to one's original nature, which is the goal of the ethics of Chu Hsi.

As we also stated, for Chu Hsi one cannot separate metaphysical principles from physical principles. The decree of Heaven already exists in nature. This is why the investigation of particular things leads us to their particular principles. Furthermore, it leads us to an understanding of the principle of self, which is one with the universal principle.

Japanese Buddhism

Zen

Ki of Unryuin monastery:
    Q. "What is my self?"
    A. "It is like you and me."
    Q. "In this case, there is no duality."
    A. "Eighteen thousand miles off!"
Tokuichi of Ryugeji monastery:
    Q. "What is my self?"
    A. "You are putting frost on top of snow."[25]

These series of questions and answers in Zen are known as *mondos,* and they illustrate the use of *prajna* as intuitive process in order to discover solutions to seemingly insurmountable problems such as self, Tao, and Buddha-nature. For instance, another *mondo* uses the mirror as a simile of the self. As an "old mirror" it is pure, undiscriminating self; as "polished" it is not discriminating. It is still the same self.

Mu-shin is an important idea here. It literally means "no-mind" and refers to the idea that mind or self cannot be grasped as if it were some object of ordinary knowledge. Just as there is no-mind, so also there is no-self. The two are synonymous.

Dogen: Zazen *and No-self*

What can we say about Dogen's views concerning the true self? First, recall that Dogen was deeply aware of the Buddha-nature permeating all things in existence. For him, this original enlightenment allows for the possibility of the practice of cultivation through *zazen,* or sitting meditation. Through *zazen* we can awaken to our true nature, the real Self, our Buddha-nature. Let us pursue this idea further.

Dharma refers to things in existence. (It can also mean the teachings of the Buddha.) One philosopher refers to *dharma* as the "Being of beings," or their essence. This being said, *zazen* is the practice whereby the "*dharma* moves the self," and not the other way around.[26] *Zazen* is a lack of deliberation, and this reveals the self. This is all-important, for it enables us to realize the inadequacies of intellectual effort in coming to a realization of true self. Remember that for Buddhists, true self is no-self.

As with much of Asian philosophy, the point of reference must be considered. If we try to know the self through ordinary intellectual means—which assume that subject-object and mind-body distinctions are real—that self which is known remains the object of one's knowledge. For Dogen and other Buddhists, this is not the true self because we are still in a subject-object framework.

A good illustration of this path to true self lies in Dogen's famous "Genjokoan" in his *Shobogenzo,* found at the end of this chapter. In it Dogen distinguishes between ordinary "sentient beings" and "Buddhas." Buddhas are those who have realized their true self. This takes place by "forgetting oneself":

> Studying the Buddha Way is studying oneself. Studying oneself is forgetting oneself. Forgetting oneself is being enlightened by all things. Being enlightened by all things is causing the body-mind of oneself and the body-mind of others to be shed.[27]

Knowing one's true nature also means knowing the nature of "all things." When this happens, we are in touch with our Buddha-nature. This genuine awakening to our Buddha-nature is called *satori,* the realization of self as no-self. By no-self, we mean that we have shed the body-mind and subject-object duality that is maintained in a self-oriented point of reference.

Kyoto School

Nishida Kitaro

Let us first state what can be construed as the extreme positions with regard to the nature of the self:

- Self is an object or some thing.
- Self is nothing.

Nishida Kitaro attempted to steer a path between these two extremes.

For Nishida, we cannot truly know the self if we take it to be either the subject or object of our knowing process. That is to say, the self is a place, or *basho,* that *gives rise to knowledge.* The self is neither the subject of an experience nor the object of knowing. The self *is* the experience. Nishitani described this rapport between experience and self, "of which it is said not that there is experience because there is a self, but rather that there is a self because there is experience."[28] This confirms the long-standing Buddhist teaching of no-self. The actual self is a process. To this process, Nishida assigned a term, *koiteki chokkan,* acting intuition.

Let us be clearer. In what way would self be *basho?*[29] *Basho* literally means "place" or "field" and suggests an all-embracing environment within which all activity occurs. Because it is all-embracing, this place or field is without boundaries and without a center of reference. Imagine an infinite circle without a circumference and without a center. As Yuasa stated:

> The *basho* is a fundamental restriction on beings' existence; without it, no beings can exist in the world."[30]

Even though *basho* is without boundaries, boundaries are in practice erected. They are constructed by our empirical self, or ego. Our empirical self, however, is not our true self, but instead the self as subject, a self-referential point of view whereby all else becomes the object for the empirical self. In other words, whereas *basho* is a primordial field of oneness, discrimination now results from the construction of boundaries. The discriminating self, as subject, is not the true self. The genuine self, for Nishida and in line with Buddhist teachings, is thus a "self that is not a self." This is why Nishida claimed that the self "lives by dying."[31]

This is also why Nishida emphasized the faculty of intuition, not in a passive but in an active sense. It is through this active intuition that self realizes itself. Discursive, analytical knowledge is insufficient.

For instance, consider the example of viewing a mountain. From one perspective, the "I" is imbedded in a world of subject-object, and the mountain is the object of my knowledge. From another perspective, I realize the essential unity of all things. In this case, there is no subject-object duality, and the mountain is no longer separate from me. This active intuition maintains both perspectives at the same time.[32] When this secret is mastered, living is dying and vice versa. Apparent contradictions are resolved.

For Nishida, the self constitutes a unity of contradictions. What are these contradictions? As we just noted, living is dying and dying is living. The opposition we normally pose between life and death is embraced in the *basho* of self. We die and live at each single moment. (This may help explain the Buddhist antipathy towards the Brahmanic teaching of *atman.*) This is the singular Buddhist truth of nonsubstantiality; it reflects the paradox of our existence.

When seen from our ordinary perspective, this paradox of life and death gives way to anxiety. When viewed from the perspective of the *basho* of self, the paradox is embraced:

> My very existence is, therefore, an absolute contradiction, and it is this very realization that enables me to become truly self conscious. My individuality is my mortality, and my true nothingness is my immortality. I am a contradictory self, and my awareness of this is the ground of my religious awareness."[33]

In his *Inquiry into the Good,* Nishida occasionally spoke of "forgetting the self." What does this mean? The everyday self with which we are able to objectify other things and experiences can in turn be objectified, and it is not our true self. This is not to infer that the true self cannot be known at all. The true self knows itself, and it is through the true self that we are able to discern the reality underlying all of existence. It is this true self that transcends the intellectual discriminatory stance that views existence in terms of subject-object. According to Nishida's renowned student, Nishitani Keiji,

> Our true self is a self able to perceive itself in the unifying self behind the whole of nature, in the self with which nature is provided. It is a self capable of grasping the life or unifying power of nature immediately and intuitively. It sees itself as the unifying power of the universe in every tree and flower.[34]

From this we see that there is no real tension between the self and the world. The realization of self brings about the discovery of the universal oneness of all things.

We can become aware of our true self only when we are free from the ordinary attitude of discrimination. This occurs when we personally realize that the world reflects our Self, and Self reflects the world. As Nishida tells us in his *Inquiry into the Good:*

> To say that we know reality does not mean that we know things outside the self but that we know the self itself.[35]

In all this, we see that Nishida reflected the Zen Buddhist teaching in which the goal is not to transcend our nature, but to see "directly into our nature." Seeing directly into our nature is called *kensho.*

Tanabe Hajime: Self Through Metanoesis

Tanabe's approach to self took place within the context of his emphasis on species; that is, the individual is defined within an historical and collective milieu.

Buddhist teachings distinguish between self-power (*jiriki*) and other-power (*tariki*). Self-power assumes that the realization of our true Buddha-nature can occur through our own effort. Other-power assumes the opposite. Whereas Nishida pointed to self-power, this was rejected by Tanabe.

To a limited degree, self-power does exist for Tanabe, in what Zen calls the Great Death. The Great Death is death to the self *as self.* For Tanabe, we bring about the Great Death when we are genuinely repentant of our fundamental condition and have faith in some Other-power. Yet, it is precisely this Other-power that brings about our metaphysical conversion, what he calls "metanoesis." Metanoesis assumes the absoluteness of some Other-power, even though it is initiated by the acting self.

Why should there be an attitude of repentance? This is where species comes in, which Tanabe described as an "irrational" force. On the other hand, he spoke of the "rational" individual. Furthermore, as "rational," I assert my freedom. Here we have a conflict between the "rational" freedom-seeking individual and the "irrational" forces of species. In this tension, the force of species usually wins out. In this elementary condition, irrationality generally dominates the individual.

Realizing this, remorse and repentance are necessary for our genuine conversion. This is more of a philosophical conversion, a metanoesis. Only through this metanoesis is the authentic self revealed. This explains why, as we said earlier, absolute nothingness, for Tanabe, is the ground of an external force acting on the self. For Tanabe, Other-power is the crucial element.

Watsuji Tetsuro: Self and Climate

Watsuji Tetsuro offered us a unique description of self. First of all, he was not addressing self as Self, as a metaphysical concept or ground of reality. He was focusing on the individual self. And his position reflects the general orientation of the Japanese toward this individual self. Moreover, it has far-reaching implications, particularly in ethics.

Although intrigued by Martin Heidegger's *Sein und Zeit (Being and Time)*, Watsuji perceived certain limitations in Heidegger's analysis. Heidegger defined our existence within the context of time, and Watsuji felt that the all-important dimension of space was not given fair attention. For Watsuji, time-consciousness is inherently linked to some consciousness of space. Indeed, human existence reveals a fundamental orientation in space. Most importantly, our human existence must be understood in terms of our primary outward orientation within our environment.

In one of his major works, *Fudo* (also entitled *Climate and Culture*), Watsuji claimed that our existence is shaped very much by climate. (A portion of *Fudo* is included at the end of this chapter.) Climate sets the conditions for the development of both culture and self. Watsuji essentially interpreted climate on two levels: the natural climate of weather and geography, and the human climate of relationships. These two views of climate affect his view of self.

The individual self is enmeshed within a network of relations that act on the self and vice versa. Therefore, he supported the idea that self cannot authentically be viewed as a separate subject. We all somehow partake in actualizing self. If there is any prominent message throughout Watsuji's work, it is that "I" is not an isolated entity. Instead, the "I" is a "we."

Let us now sketch his first level of climate as natural environment. (*Fudo* literally means "wind and earth.") This type of climate is existentially significant, for it has a bearing on how we both perceive and participate in this environment. In other words, climate acts to define us just as we act to interpret climate.

It is our spatiality that enables us to act first within and upon the world. We do not initially cogitate about it. There is thus an embodied character to my self. Watsuji used the example of feeling "cold" from the outside weather. His analysis revealed that coldness is not solely outside of me, but the weather, normally conceived as "outside," enters into me and affects my "intentionality."[36] He underscored the idea that climate does not possess an independent existence outside of subject. There is, in this way, an interdependency between self and climate. Thus far Watsuji has pointed out to us the external forces that form our self. A genuine realization of self opens up, according to Watsuji, when "we find ourselves—ourselves as an element in the 'mutual relationship'—in climate."[37] This "self-apprehension" is quite distinct from our ordinary view of the self:

> Such self-apprehension is not the recognition of the "I" as the subject that feels the cold and heat or as the subject that is gladdened by the cherry blossoms.[38]

Let us now more closely review Watsuji's second level of climate, human climate. We participate in a social web of connections: spouses, parents, children, siblings, friends, associates, colleagues, and so on. This web forms the web of self. This means that my involvement in a social climate (and vice versa) is not solely limited to my existence, but in turn affects the existence of others. My involvement in an environment is "our" involvement. And it is not "I" who experiences weather, but "we." To view the individual as an isolated subject is inappropriate. As we will see, this has a direct bearing on ethics—for example, in the sphere of individual rights. (Ethics in Japanese thought does not emphasize individual autonomy to the same degree expressed in Western thought.)

The Japanese word *ningen* is used to refer to "person." *Ningen* has two characters. The first character designates "person" as an individual; the second refers to the idea of "between." We therefore get the impression of the relation between one person and the other, or among people. This "betweenness," or what is called *aidagara,* is an essential point in the notion of self.[39]

Aidagara is this "in-betweenness" that permeates our existence and reveals the spatial quality of our existence. This is a lived space—in other words, a relationality—because we live in relationship. We are somehow linked with things in our environment, both the natural climate and human climate.

It is precisely this spatial quality of our lives that defines our lives. It also asserts that we are embodied beings who interact with others. Self and other, and self and climate, mutually interact.

Study Questions

India

1. Discuss the meaning and significance of *tat tvam asi* in the Upanishads.
2. Discuss the relationship between *purusha* and *prakriti,* and discuss how it relates to the issue of personal identity in Samkhya.
3. Discuss the process involved in the evolution that occurs from the joining of *purusha* with *prakriti.* How does "ego" come about?
4. What role does Yoga play in the teachings of Samkhya?
5. How are the five sheaths associated with the three bodies in Advaita Vedanta?
6. What is *jiva* in Advaita Vedanta?

7. Discuss Aurobindo's thesis of divine descent and ascent.
8. Discuss some of the major themes in Buddhism concerning the self and no-self.
9. Describe the Five Skandhas, and discuss their effect on the Buddhist teaching of no-self.
10. Explain how dependent origination relates to the Buddhist view of no-self.
11. Discuss the key ideas in Nagarjuna's "Examination of Self-Nature." How do they support his views on nonsubstantiality and *sunyata*?
12. Describe the major ideas in Vasubandhu's *Trimsika,* and explain how the illusion of "self" comes about through the transformations from the pure consciousness, or *vijnana*.

China

13. Discuss the natural link between personal identity and moral action in Chinese thought.
14. What does Chuang Tzu mean by "forgetting" the self?
15. Describe the cultivation of self found in the *Analects.*
16. How does Tung Chung-shu's correspondence theory relate to a view of the self?
17. Explain the relation between self and *li* in Chu Hsi. What is the purpose in his investigation of things?
18. How does the relation between knowledge and action in Wang Yang-ming relate to self-cultivation? What is the role of intuitive knowledge?
19. Describe Hsuan-tsang's theory of "mere ideation." How does it relate to the Buddhist view of no-self?
20. How is the Ch'an teaching of detachment relevant to the Buddhist view of no-self?

Japan

21. Explain how Japanese neo-Confucianism adapts the significance of the relation between *li* and *ch'i,* and how this affects views of self.
22. Explain the Zen teaching of *mu-shin,* or no-mind.
23. Describe the relation between *zazen* and no-self for Dogen. Illustrate with leading ideas from his "Genjokoan."
24. How did Nishida Kitaro attempt to avoid the extreme views of self?
25. In what way is self understood in terms of *basho,* according to Nishida Kitaro?
26. How does Nishida's discussion of self point to self as a "unity of contradictions"?
27. Explain how metanoesis plays a central role in Tanabe Hajime's view of self?
28. How does Tanabe's discussion of self differ from that of Nishida?
29. Discuss the relationship between self and climate for Watsuji Tetsuro. Illustrate this with leading ideas in his *Fudo.*

Notes

1. Brian Brown, ed., *The Wisdom of the Hindus: Philosophies and Wisdom from Their Ancient and Modern Literature,* foreword by Jagadish Chandra Chatterji (Garden City, N.Y.: Garden City Publishing Co., 1938), 242–43.

2. *Chandogya Upanishad* VI.12.1–3, in S. Radhakrishnan, ed. and trans., *The Principal Upanisads* (London: George Allen & Unwin Ltd., 1953), 462.

3. *Chandogya Upanishad* VI.13,2–3, in Radhakrishnan, *The Principal Upanisads,* 463.

4. *Mandukya Upanishad* 2, in Swami Nikhilananda, trans., *The Upanishads,* abridged ed. (New York: Harper & Row, 1964), 164.

5. P. T. Raju, *Structural Depths of Indian Thought* (Albany: State University of New York Press, 1985), 314.

6. Raju, *Structural Depths,* 161.

7. This idea is more fully discussed in Raju, *Structural Depths,* 309–11.

8. Raju, *Structural Depths,* 315.

9. Yoga was not the sole property of the Yoga and Samkhya schools. Despite their differences, many other schools used the methods of Yoga as taught by Patanjali. Even the Vedanta school used Patanjali's system, as is illustrated by the commentary on the Yoga Sutras by Vivekananda.

10. In contrast to Sankara, Ramanuja argued that the self is not pure consciousness because knowledge and the self are distinct.

11. David Kalupahana claims that the Buddha did not intend to deny the self, but to deny instead any possibility of our being able to discuss it, let alone reasonably think about it. See his *Buddhist Philosophy: A Historical Analysis* (Honolulu: University of Hawaii Press, 1976), 41.

12. See Raju, *Structural Depths,* 158–59.

13. Kalupahana, *A History of Buddhist Philosophy,* 192.

14. The Chinese scholar T'ang Chun-I deftly describes the rapport between individual self and world by pointing out the meanings of the Chinese terms for "subject" and "object." A variety of terms are used for each. For subject, we have *chu, jen,* and *chien. Chu* means "host," *jen* refers to "man," and *chien* means "seeing." The terms used for object are *pin, ching,* and *hsiang. Pin* means "guest," *ching* means "environment," and *hsiang* means "that which is seen." The pairs therefore mean "host-guest," "man-environment," and "seeing-seen." In all cases there is a shared affinity between subject and object. Ideally, symmetry must exist between host and guest, people and environment, and seeing and seen. See T'ang Chun-I, "The Individual and the World in Chinese Methodology," in Charles A. Moore, ed., *The Chinese Mind: Essentials of Chinese Philosophy and Culture* (Honolulu: University of Hawaii Press, 1967), 281.

15. Herbert A. Giles, trans., *Chuang Tzu: Mystic, Moralist, and Social Reformer,* 2nd ed., rev. (London: Bernard Quaritch, 1926), 97–98.

16. See Lee Yearley, "The Perfected Person in the Radical Chuang-tzu," in Victor H. Mair, ed., *Experimental Essays on Chuang-tzu,* Asian Studies at Hawaii, No. 29 (Hawaii: University of Hawaii Press, 1983), 132–34, for further discussion of this mirror metaphor.

17. *Analects* IX.24, in James Legge, trans., *Confucius: Confucian Analects, The Great Learning, and The Doctrine of the Mean* (New York: Dover, 1971), 224.

18. *Analects* VII.3, in Legge, 195.

19. *Analects* XIV.55, in Legge, 292.

20. Chu Hsi, *Learning to Be a Sage: Selections from the Conversations of Master Chu, Arranged Topically,* trans. Daniel K. Gardner (Berkeley: University of California Press, 1990), 117.

21. Wang Yang-ming, *The Philosophy of Wang Yang-ming,* Frederick Goodrich Henke, trans. (London: Open Court Publishing Co., 1916), 260.

22. Note that Hsuan-tsang's commentary is also an interpretation. The question is whether or not, and to what extent, Vasubandhu's ideas may have undergone modification through his eyes. This is important because it gives us some indication of the status of Indian Buddhist ideas in China.

23. Cited by Ueda Yoshifumi, "The Status of the Individual in Mahayana Buddhist Philosophy," in Charles A. Moore, ed., *The Japanese Mind: Essentials of Japanese Philosophy and Culture* (Honolulu: University of Hawaii Press, 1987), 170.

24. Maruyama Masao, *Studies in the Intellectual History of Tokugawa Japan,* trans. Mikiso Hane (Princeton, N.J.: Princeton University Press, 1974, 1989), 23.

25. These are from the *Records of the Transmission of the Lamp,* xxii, 45b and xxi, 41a, cited in Suzuki Daisetz Teitaro, "Reason and Intuition in Buddhist Philosophy," in Moore, 87.

26. Cited in Yuasa Yasuo, *The Body: Toward an Eastern Mind-Body Theory,* ed. Thomas P. Kasulis, trans. Nagatomo Shigenori and Thomas P. Kasulis, SUNY Series in Buddhist Studies (Albany: State University of New York Press, 1987), 115.

27. Thomas Cleary, trans., *Shōbōgenzō: Zen Essays by Dōgen* (Honolulu: University of Hawaii Press, 1986), 32.

28. Nishitani Keiji, *Nishida Kitarō,* trans. Yamamoto Seisaku and James W. Heisig, Nanzan Studies in Religion and Culture (Berkeley: University of California Press, 1991), 172.

29. Some of this discussion is adapted from the rendition of Nishida given by Yuasa Yasuo in *The Body,* 56–65.

30. Yuasa, 57. Yuasa compares Nishida with Heidegger. Just as Heidegger posited time as the fundamental ground for all existence, Nishida posited space or spatiality in his theory of *basho.*

31. Nishida Kitaro, *Intelligibility and the Philosophy of Nothingness: Three Philosophical Essays,* trans. Robert Schinzinger (Honolulu: East-West Center Press, 1958), 7.

32. Robert E. Carter, *The Nothingness Beyond God: An Introduction to the Philosophy of Nishida Kitaro* (New York: Paragon House, 1989), 54.

33. Carter, 95.

34. Nishitani, 119.

35. Cited in Nishitani, 124.

36. Watsuji Tetsuro, *Climate and Culture: A Philosophical Study,* trans. Geoffrey Bownas, Classics of Modern Japanese Thought and Culture (Westport, Conn: Greenwood Press, 1988), 2–5.

37. Watsuji, 5.

38. Watsuji, 5.

39. Yuasa, 37.

From the *Chandogya Upanishad*

Ninth [Section]

1. "As the bees, my son, make honey by collecting the juices of distant trees, and reduce the juice into form,

2. "And as these juices have no discrimination, so that they might say, I am the juice of this tree or that, in the same manner, my son, all these creatures, when they have become merged in the True (either in deep sleep or in death), know not that they are merged in the True.

3. "Whatever these creatures are here, whether a lion, or a wolf, or a boar, or a worm, or a midge, or a gnat, or a mosquito, that they become again and again.

4. "Now that which is that subtile essence, in it all that exists has its self. It is the True. It is the Self, and thou, O Svetaketu, art it."

"Please, Sir, inform me still more," said the son.

"Be it so, my child," the father replied.

Tenth [Section]

1. "These rivers, my son, run, the eastern (like the Gangâ) toward the east, the western (like the Sindhu) toward the west. They go from sea to sea (i.e. the clouds lift up the water from the sea to the sky, and send it back as rain to the sea). They become indeed sea. And as those rivers, when they are in the sea, do not know, I am this or that river,

2. "In the same manner, my son, all these creatures, when they have come back from the True, know not that they have come back from the True. Whatever these creatures are here, whether a lion, or a wolf, or a boar, or a worm, or a midge, or a gnat, or a mosquito, that they become again and again.

3. "That which is that subtile essence, in it all that exists has its self. It is the True. It is the Self, and thou, O Svetaketu, art it."

"Please sir, inform me still more," said the son.

"Be it so, my child," the father replied.

Eleventh [Section]

1. "If some one were to strike at the root of this large tree here, it would bleed, but live. If he were to strike at its stem, it would bleed, but live. If

Reprinted from F. Max Müller, trans., *The Upanishads,* Part I, New York: Dover, 1962 (originally published in *Sacred Books of the East,* Vol. I, 1879), pp. 101–108.

he were to strike at its top, it would bleed, but live. Pervaded by the living Self that tree stands firm, drinking in its nourishment and rejoicing;

2. "But if the life (the living Self) leaves one of its branches, that branch withers; if it leaves a second, that branch withers; if it leaves a third, that branch withers. If it leaves the whole tree, the whole tree withers. In exactly the same manner, my son, know this. Thus he spoke:

3. "This (body) indeed withers and dies when the living Self has left it; the living Self dies not.

"That which is that subtile essence, in it all that exists has its self. It is the True. It is the Self, and thou, *Svetaketu*, art it."

"Please, Sir, inform me still more," said the son.

"Be it so, my child," the father replied.

Twelfth [Section]

1. "Fetch me from thence a fruit of the Nyagrodha tree."

"Here is one, Sir."

"Break it."

"It is broken, Sir."

"What do you see there?"

"These seeds, almost infinitesimal."

"Break one of them."

"It is broken, Sir."

"What do you see there?"

"Not anything, Sir."

2. The father said: "My son, that subtile essence which you do not perceive there, of that very essence this great Nyagrodha tree exists.

3. "Believe it, my son. That which is the subtile essence, in it all that exists has its self. It is the True. It is the Self, and thou, O *Svetaketu*, art it."

"Please, Sir, inform me still more," said the son.

"Be it so, my child," the father replied.

Thirteenth [Section]

1. "Place this salt in water, and then wait on me in the morning."

The son did as he was commanded.

The father said to him: "Bring me the salt, which you placed in the water last night."

The son having looked for it, found it not, for, of course, it was melted.

2. The father said: "Taste it from the surface of the water. How is it?"

The son replied: "It is salt."

"Taste it from the middle. How is it?"

The son replied: "It is salt."

"Taste it from the bottom. How is it?"

The son replied: "It is salt."

The father said: "Throw it away and then wait on me."

He did so; but salt exists for ever.

Then the father said: "Here also, in this **body**, forsooth, you do not perceive the Truth (Sat), my son; but there **indeed it is.**

3. "That which is the subtile essence, **in it all that exists** has its self. It is the True. It is the Self, and thou, O *Svetaketu*, art it."

"Please, Sir, inform me still more," said the son.

"Be it so, my child," the father replied.

Fourteenth [Section]

1. "As one might lead a person with his eyes covered away from the Gandhâras, and leave him then in a place where there are no human beings; and as that person would turn towards the east, or the north, or the west, and shout, 'I have been brought here with my eyes covered, I have been left here with my eyes covered,'

2. "And as thereupon some one might loose his bandage and say to him, 'Go in that direction, it is Gandhâra, go in that direction'; and as thereupon, having been informed and being able to judge for himself, he would by asking his way from village to village arrive at last at Gandhâra,—in exactly the same manner does a man, who meets with a teacher to inform him, obtain the true knowledge. For him there is only delay so long as he is not delivered (from the body); then he will be perfect.

3. "That which is the subtile essence, in it all that exists has its self. It is the True. It is the Self, and thou, O *Svetaketu*, art it."

"Please, Sir, inform me still more," said the son.

"Be it so, my child," the father replied.

Fifteenth [Section]

1. "If a man is ill, his relatives assemble round him and ask: 'Dost thou know me? Dost thou know me?' Now as long as his speech is not merged in his mind, his mind in breath, breath in heat (fire), heat in the Highest Being (devatâ), he knows them.

2. "But when his speech is merged in his mind, his mind in breath, breath in heat (fire), heat in the Highest Being, then he knows them not.

"That which is the subtile essence, in it all that exists has its self. It is the True. It is the Self, and thou, O *Svetaketu*, art it."

"Please, Sir, inform me still more," said the son.

"Be it so, my child," the father replied.

From the *Sâmkhya Kârikâ*

Ishvarakrishna

I. From the disagreeable occurrence of the threefold pain, (proceeds) the enquiry into the means which can prevent it; nor is the enquiry superfluous because ordinary (means) exist, for they fail to accomplish certain and permanent prevention of pain.

ANNOTATION.

. . . The subject-matter of the Sâmkhya System comprises the well-known Twenty-five Tattvas or Principles, from the knowledge of which results the destruction of the three kinds of pain. Cf. Gaudpâda's *Bhâsyam.*

The Supreme Good is Moksa or Release which consists in the permanent impossibility of the incidence of pain in any form whatever, that is, in recovering that state of the pristine purity of the Self in which the occurrence of pain is impossible, in other words, in the realisation of the Self as Self pure and simple.

II. Like the ordinary, is the scriptural (means ineffectual), for it is attended with impurity, waste, and excess. (The means which is) the opposite of both is preferable, as it consists in a discriminative knowledge of the Manifest, the Unmanifest, and the Knower.

ANNOTATION.

"Scriptural" here refers to the rituals laid down in the Vedas, and not to their Jñâna-Kânda portion, for Discriminative Knowledge also is enjoined in them.

"Vijñâna" means knowledge of discrimination. Knowledge of the Manifest leads to the knowledge of its cause, the Unmanifest. And knowledge of both as existing for the sake of another, leads to the knowledge of the Self. The Manifest begins with Mahat and includes Ahamkâra, the five Tan-mîtras, the eleven Indriyas, and the five Great Elements. The Unmanifest is the Pradhâna, i.e., Prakriti. The Knower is Purusa. These are the Twenty-five Tattvas. . . .

III. The Root Evolvent is no evolute; Mahat, etc., are the seven evolvent-evolutes; the sixteen are mere evolutes; (that which is) neither evolvent nor evolute, is Purusa.

Reprinted from Nandalal Sinha, trans., *The Sâmkhya Philosophy,* Allababad: Sudhindra Nath Vasu, 1915, pp. 1–23.

ANNOTATION.

By "Prakṛiti" is meant that which procreates or evolves—the Pradhâna, that is, that in which all things are contained, and in its general significance, it denotes that which becomes the material cause of another Tattva.

The Root Evolvent is the state of equipoise of Sattva, Rajas, and Tamas. It has no root of its own and is the root of all things. Hence it is not a product. To imagine a root for the Root Evolvent would entail infinite regression.

Evolvent-Evolutes: Mahat springs from the Pradhâna and, in its turn, gives rise to Ahaṃkâra; Ahaṃkâra, in its turn, to the Tan-mâtras of Sound, Touch, Smell, Form, and Taste; and these, in their turn, respectively to the gross elements of Ether, Air, Earth, Fire, and Water.

It is next to be considered how the existence of the Tattvas described above can be rationally established. The causes of cognition and non-cognition are, therefore, expounded in the following four Kârikâs.

IV. Perception, Inference, and Testimony (are the Proofs; by these) all proofs being established, Proof is intended to be threefold. From Proof verily is the establishment of the Provables.

V. Perception is the ascertainment of each respective object (by the Senses). Inference has been declared to be threefold. It is preceded by the mark and it is preceded by the thing of which it is the mark. While Testimony is the statement of trustworthy persons and the Veda.

VI. (Intuition of sensible things is from perception). But the intuition of super-sensible things is from Sâmânyato Dṛiṣṭa and Seṣa-vat Inference. And super-sensible things not established from that even, are established from Testimony and Revelation.

ANNOTATION.

Prakṛiti and Puruṣa are not objects of perception and therefore they are unreal, argue our opponents; for a hare's horn or a castle in the air is not perceived, because it is unreal. It is, accordingly, next pointed out that perception cannot be the sole test of reality, because there are well-known causes from which even admittedly existent things are not perceived. These causes are declared in the next Kârikâ.

VII. (Apprehension of even existing things may not take place) through extreme remoteness, nearness, impairment of the senses, non-presence of the mind, extreme fineness, intervention, suppression by other matters, inter-mixture with likes, and other causes.

VIII. From extreme fineness is the non-apprehension of Prakṛiti, and not from her non-existence, because there is apprehension of her from the effect. And that effect is Mahat, etc., similar and dissimilar to Prakṛiti.

IX. The effect is ever existent, because that which is non-existent, can by no means be brought into existence; because effects take adequate material causes; because all things are not produced from all causes; because a competent cause can effect that only for which it is competent; and also because the effect possesses the nature of the cause.

X. The Manifest is producible, non-eternal, non-pervading, mobile, multiform, dependent, (serving as) the mark (of inference), a combination of parts, subordinate. The Unmanifest is the reverse (of this).

XI. The Manifest is constituted by the three Guṇas, is non-discriminative, objective, common, non-intelligent, prolific. So is also the Pradhâna. Puruṣa is the reverse of them both (in these respects), and yet is similar (to the Pradhâna and also to the Manifest in those other respects mentioned in the preceding Kârikâ.)

XII. The Guṇas possess the nature of pleasure, pain and dullness; serve the purpose of illumination, activity, and restraint; and perform the function of mutual domination, dependence, production, and consociation.

XIII. Sattva is considered to be light and illuminating, and Rajas, to be exciting and restless, and Tamas, to be indeed heavy and enveloping. Like a lamp (consisting of oil, wick, and fire), they co-operate for a (common) purpose (by union of contraries).

XIV. The proof of non-discriminativeness, and the rest (in the Manifest and the Unmanifest) is from their being constituted by the three Guṇas and from absence of their non-concomitance. From the effect possessing the attributes of the cause is proved the Unmanifest also.

XV–XVI. Of the particulars (*e.g.,* Mahat and all the rest down to the earth), there exists an Unmanifest cause: because the particulars are finite; because they are homogeneous; because production is through power; because there is differentiation of effect from cause or difference of cause and effect; and because there is reunion of the multiform effect with the cause.

It operates, in the form of the three Guṇas and by combination, undergoing transformation, (diversified) according to the differences severally of the other Guṇas depending on the principal Guṇa.

ANNOTATION.

Because they are homogeneous: Homogeneousness is the possession of a common form among a number of distinct individuals. The presence of a common form infers a common origin.

Because production is through power: Power inhering in the cause is nothing but the unmanifested state of the effect.

Differentiation and reunion: Discrete products of every sort of form from Mahat down to a jar, for instance, successively rise from their causes at the time of creation and disappear into them at the time of destruction and universal dissolution. The ultimate points in the process of evolution and involution are one and the same. It is the absolute unmanifested state of a single entity. It is called the Unmanifest, the Pradhâna and Prakṛiti.

XVII. Puruṣa exists: since the aggregate must be for the sake of the non-aggregate; since there must exist an entity in which the properties of being constituted by the three Guṇas and the rest do not appear; since there must be a superintendent; since there must be an experiencer; and since activity is for the sake of abstraction.

ANNOTATION.

Since there must exist an entity, etc.: Hereby is prevented the inference of an aggregate by the aggregate. For all aggregates possess the three Guṇas, whereas Puruṣa is free from them, as declared in Kârikâ XI. Therefore, the entity for which the aggregate is, must be a non-aggregate. And Puruṣa is a non-aggregate.

XVIII. From the individual allotment of birth, death and the Instruments, from non-simultaneous activity (towards the same end), and from the diverse modification of the three Guṇas, multitude of Puruṣas is verily established.

XIX. And from that contrast it is proved that this Puruṣa is witness, solitary, indifferent, spectator, and non-agent.

ANNOTATION.

That contrast: that is, Puruṣa is not constituted by the three Guṇas, is discriminative, is not objective but subjective, is not common, is intelligent, and is not prolific (see Kârikâ XIV).

Because he is intelligent and subjective, he is spectator and witness. A witness is one to whom objects are shown. Prakṛiti exhibits herself to Puruṣa.

From his not being constituted by the three Guṇas follow his solitariness and indifference. For solitariness consists in the absolute non-existence of the three sorts of pain, and indifference denotes absence of love for pleasure and hate for pain. But pleasure and pain are properties of the three Guṇas. And because Puruṣa is not constituted by the three Guṇas, he is absolutely free from pleasure, pain and bewilderment.

And since he is discriminative and non-prolific, he is not the agent.

But if Puruṣa is a non-agent, how does he make determination? as I will perform acts of merit, I will not perform acts of demerit: hence Puruṣa must be the agent; neither is Puruṣa the agent;—thus there is, may say our opponent, defect in both the theories. Accordingly, the seeming agency of Puruṣa is explained in the next Kârikâ.

XX. Therefore (the inference that intelligence and agency belong to one and the same subject is a mistake.) Through conjunction with Puruṣa, the non-intelligent Effect appears as if it were intelligent, and although agency is of the Guṇas, the indifferent (Puruṣa) appears, in the same way, as if he were the agent.

XXI. The conjunction of Puruṣa and the Pradhâna is, like that of the halt and the blind, for mutual benefit, that is, for the exhibition of the Pradhâna to Puruṣa and for the isolation of Puruṣa. From this conjunction proceeds Creation.

ANNOTATION.

The halt and the blind: "As a lame man and a blind man, deserted by their fellow-travellers, who, in making their way with difficulty through a forest, had been dispersed by robbers, happening to encounter each other, and entering into conversation so as to inspire mutual confidence, agreed to divide between them the duties of walking and of seeing; accordingly the lame man was mounted on the blind man's shoulders, and was thus carried on his journey, whilst the blind man was enabled to pursue his route by the directions of his companion. In the same manner, the faculty of seeing is in soul, not that of moving; it is like the lame man: the faculty of moving, but not of seeing, is in nature; which resembles, therefore, the blind man. Further, as a separation takes place between the lame man and the blind man, when their mutual object is accomplished, and they have reached their journey's end, so nature, having effected the liberation of soul, ceases to act; and soul, having contemplated nature, obtains abstractedness, and consequently, their respective purposes being effected, the connexion between them is dissolved."—Gauḍapâda's Bhâṣya, translated by Wilson.

XXII. From Prakṛiti (evolves) Mahat; thence, Ahaṃkâra; and from this, the sixteenfold set; from five, again, among the sixteenfold, the five Elements.

XXIII. Ascertainment is Buddhi. Virtue, knowledge, dispassion and power are its forms or manifestations or modifications, partaking of Sattva. Those partaking of Tamas, are the reverse of these.

XXIV. Self-assertion is Ahaṃkâra. From it proceeds a twofold evolution only: the elevenfold set and also the fivefold Tan-mâtra.

ANNOTATION.

Self-assertion: All that is considered and reasoned refers to me, in this I am competent, all these objects of sense are for my sake only, this does not concern any one else but me, hence I am,—such abhimâna, self-assertion or consciousness by reference to oneself, from its having an uncommon or unique operation of its own, is called Ahaṃkâra, by working upon which Buddhi determines that this is to be done by me.

Commentary on Patanjali's
Yoga Aphorisms

Swami Vivekananda

1. *Now concentration is explained.*
2. *Yoga is restraining the mind-stuff (Chitta) from taking various forms (Vrittis).*

A good deal of explanation is necessary here. We have to understand what *Chitta* is, and what are these *Vrittis*. I have this eye. Eyes do not see. Take away the brain centre which is in the head, the eyes will still be there, the retinae complete, and also the picture, and yet the eyes will not see. So the eyes are only a secondary instrument, not the organ of vision. The organ of vision is in the nerve centre of the brain. The two eyes will not be sufficient alone. Sometimes a man is asleep with his eyes open. The light is there and the picture is there, but a third thing is necessary; mind must be joined to the organ. The eye is the external instrument, we need also the brain centre and the agency of the mind. Carriages roll down a street and you do not hear them. Why? Because your mind has not attached itself to the organ of hearing. First, there is the instrument, then there is the organ, and third, the mind attachment to these two. The mind takes the impression farther in, and presents it to the determinative faculty—*Buddhi*—which reacts. Along with this reaction flashes the idea of egoism. Then this mixture of action and reaction is presented to the *Puruṣa,* the real Soul, who perceives an object in this mixture. The organs (*Indriyas*), together with the mind (*Manas*), the determinative faculty (*Buddhi*), and egoism (*Ahamkâra*), form the group called the *Antahkaraṇa* (the internal instrument). They are but various processes in the mind-stuff, called *Chitta*. The waves of thought in the *Chitta* are called *Vritti* ("the whirlpool" is the literal translation). What is thought? Thought is a force, as is gravitation or repulsion. It is absorbed from the infinite storehouse of force in nature; the instrument called *Chitta* takes hold of that force, and, when it passes out at the other end it is called thought. This force is supplied to us through food, and out of that food the body obtains the power of motion, etc. Others, the finer forces, it throws out in what we call thought. Naturally we see that the mind is not intelligent; yet it appears to be intelligent. Why? Because the intelligent soul is behind it. You are the only sentient being; mind is only the instrument through which you catch the external world. Take this book; as a book it does not exist outside, what exists outside is

Reprinted from Swami Vivekananda, *Vedanta Philosophy: Raja Yoga and Other Lectures*, New York: Weed–Parsons, 1897, pp. 104–19.

unknown and unknowable. It is the suggestion that gives a blow to the mind, and the mind gives out the reaction. If a stone is thrown into the water the water is thrown against it in the form of waves. The real universe is the occasion of the reaction of the mind. A book form, or an elephant form, or a man form, is not outside; all that we know is our mental reaction from the outer suggestion. Matter is the "permanent possibility of sensation," said John Stuart Mill. It is only the suggestion that is outside. Take an oyster for example. You know how pearls are made. A grain of sand or something gets inside and begins to irritate it, and the oyster throws a sort of enamelling around the sand, and this makes the pearl. This whole universe is our own enamel, so to say, and the real universe is the grain of sand. The ordinary man will never understand it, because, when he tries to, he throws out an enamel, and sees only his own enamel. Now we understand what is meant by these *Vrittis*. The real man is behind the mind, and the mind is the instrument in his hands, and it is his intelligence that is percolating through it. It is only when you stand behind it that it becomes intelligent. When man gives it up it falls to pieces, and is nothing. So you understand what is meant by *Chitta*. It is the mind-stuff, and *Vrittis* are the waves and ripples rising in it when external causes impinge on it. These *Vrittis* are our whole universe.

The bottom of the lake we cannot see, because its surface is covered with ripples. It is only possible when the ripples have subsided, and the water is calm, for us to catch a glimpse of the bottom. If the water is muddy, the bottom will not be seen; if the water is agitated all the time, the bottom will not be seen. If the water is clear, and there are no waves, we shall see the bottom. That bottom of the lake is our own true Self; the lake is the *Chitta*, and the waves the *Vrittis*. Again, this mind is in three states; one is darkness, which is called *Tamas*, just as in brutes and idiots; it only acts to injure others. No other idea comes into that state of mind. Then there is the active state of mind, *Rajas*, whose chief motives are power and enjoyment. "I will be powerful and rule others." Then, at last, when the waves cease, and the water of the lake becomes clear, there is the state called *Sattva*, serenity, calmness. It is not inactive, but rather intensely active. It is the greatest manifestation of power to be calm. It is easy to be active. Let the reins go, and the horses will drag you down. Any one can do that, but he who can stop the plunging horses is the strong man. Which requires the greater strength, letting go, or restraining? The calm man is not the man who is dull. You must not mistake *Sattva* for dullness, or laziness. The calm man is the one who has restraint of these waves. Activity is the manifestation of the lower strength, calmness of the superior strength.

This *Chitta* is always trying to get back to its natural pure state, but the organs draw it out. To restrain it, and to check this outward tendency, and to start it on the return journey to that essence of intelligence is the first step in *Yoga*, because only in this way can the *Chitta* get into its proper course.

Although this *Chitta* is in every animal, from the lowest to the highest, it is only in the human form that we find intellect, and until the mind-stuff can take the form of intellect it is not possible for it to return through all these steps, and liberate the soul. Immediate salvation is impossible for the cow and the dog, although they have mind, because their *Chitta* cannot as yet take that form which we call intellect.

Chitta manifests itself in all these different forms—scattering, darkening, weakening, and concentrating. These are the four states in which the mind-stuff manifests itself. First a scattered form, is activity. Its tendency is to manifest in the form of pleasure or of pain. Then the dull form is darkness, the only tendency of which is to injure others. The commentator says the first form is natural to the *Devas,* the angels, and the second is the demoniacal form. *Vikshipta* is when it struggles to centre itself. The *Ekâgra,* the concentrated form of the *Chitta,* is what brings us to *Samâdhi.*

> 3. *At that time (the time of concentration) the seer (the Puruṣa) rests in his own (unmodified) state.*

As soon as the waves have stopped, and the lake has become quiet, we see the ground below the lake. So with the mind; when it is calm, we see what our own nature is; we do not mix ourselves but remain our own selves.

> 4. *At other times (other than that of concentration) the seer is identified with the modifications.*

For instance, I am in a state of sorrow; some one blames me; this is a modification, *Vṛitti,* and I identify myself with it, and the result is misery.

> 5. *There are five classes of modifications, painful and not painful.*
> 6. *(These are) right knowledge, indiscrimination, verbal delusion, sleep, and memory.*
> 7. *Direct perception, inference, and competent evidence, are proofs. . . .*
> 8. *Indiscrimination is false knowledge not established in real nature.*

The next class of *Vṛittis* that arise is mistaking the one thing for another, as a piece of mother-of-pearl is taken for a piece of silver.

> 9. *Verbal delusion follows from words having no (corresponding) reality.*

There is another class of *Vṛittis* called *Vikalpa.* A word is uttered, and we do not wait to consider its meaning; we jump to a conclusion immediately. It is the sign of weakness of the *Chitta.* Now you can understand the theory of restraint. The weaker the man the less he has of restraint. Consider yourselves always in that way. When you are going to be angry or miserable, reason it out, how it is that some news that has come to you is throwing your mind into *Vṛittis.*

> 10. *Sleep is a Vṛitti which embraces the feeling of voidness.*

The next class of *Vṛittis* is called sleep and dream. When we awake we know that we have been sleeping; we can only have memory of perception. That which we do not perceive we never can have any memory of. Every reaction is a wave in the lake. Now, if, during sleep, the mind had no waves, it would have no perceptions, positive or negative, and, therefore, we would not remember them. The very reason of our remembering sleep is that during sleep there was a certain class of waves in the mind. Memory is another class of *Vrittis*, which is called *Smriti*.

> 11. *Memory is when the (Vrittis of) perceived subjects do not slip away (and through impressions come back to consciousness).*

Memory can be caused by the previous three. For instance, you hear a word. That word is like a stone thrown into the lake of the *Chitta;* it causes a ripple, and that ripple rouses a series of ripples; this is memory. So in sleep. When the peculiar kind of ripple called sleep throws the *Chitta* into a ripple of memory it is called a dream. Dream is another form of the ripple which in the waking state is called memory.

> 12. *Their control is by practice and non-attachment.*

The mind, to have this non-attachment, must be clear, good and rational. Why should we practise? Because each action is like the pulsations quivering over the surface of the lake. The vibration dies out, and what is left? The *Samskâras,* the impressions. When a large number of these impressions is left on the mind they coalesce, and become a habit. It is said "habit is second nature;" it is first nature also, and the whole nature of man; everything that we are is the result of habit. That gives us consolation, because, if it is only habit, we can make and unmake it at any time. This *Samskâra* is left by these vibrations passing out of our mind, each one of them leaving its result. Our character is the sum-total of these marks, and according as some particular wave prevails one takes that tone. If good prevail one becomes good, if wickedness one becomes wicked, if joyfulness one becomes happy. The only remedy for bad habits is counter habits; all the bad habits that have left their impressions are to be controlled by good habits. Go on doing good, thinking holy thoughts continuously; that is the only way to suppress base impressions. Never say any man is hopeless, because he only represents a character, a bundle of habits, and these can be checked by new and better ones. Character is repeated habits, and repeated habits alone can reform character.

> 13. *Continuous struggle to keep them (the Vrittis) perfectly restrained is practice.*

What is this practice? The attempt to restrain the mind in the *Chitta* form, to prevent its going out into waves.

> 14. *Its ground becomes firm by long, constant efforts with great love (for the end to be attained).*

Restraint does not come in one day, but by long continued practice.

> 15. *That effect which comes to those who have given up their thirst after objects either seen or heard, and which wills to control the objects, is non-attachment.*

Two motives of our actions are (1) What we see ourselves; (2) The experience of others. These two forces are throwing the mind, the lake, into various waves. Renunciation is the power of battling against these, and holding the mind in check. Renunciation of these two motives is what we want. I am passing through a street, and a man comes and takes my watch. That is my own experience. I see it myself, and it immediately throws my *Chitta* into a wave, taking the form of anger. Allow not that to come. If you cannot prevent that, you are nothing; if you can, you have *Vairâgyam*. Similarly, the experience of the worldly-minded teaches us that sense enjoyments are the highest ideal. These are tremendous temptations. To deny them, and not allow the mind to come into a wave form with regard to them, is renunciation; to control the twofold motive powers arising from my own experience, and from the experience of others, and thus prevent the *Chitta* from being governed by them, is *Vairâgyam*. These should be controlled by me, and not I by them. This sort of mental strength is called renunciation. This *Vairâgyam* is the only way to freedom.

16. *That extreme non-attachment, giving up even the qualities, shows (the real nature of) the Puruṣa.*
17. *The concentration called right knowledge is that which is followed by reasoning, discrimination, bliss, unqualified ego.*
18. *There is another Samâdhi which is attained by the constant practice of cessation of all mental activity, in which the Chitta retains only the unmanifested impressions. . . .*

"The Eternal and the Individual"

Sri Aurobindo

There is then a fundamental truth of existence, an Omnipresent Reality, omnipresent above the cosmic manifestation and in it and immanent in each individual. There is also a dynamic power of this Omnipresence, a creative or self-manifesting action of its infinite Consciousness-Force. There is as a phase or movement of the self-manifestation a descent into an apparent material inconscience, an awakening of the individual out of the Inconscience and an evolution of his being into the spiritual and supramental consciousness and power of the Reality, into his own universal and transcendent Self and source of existence. It is on this foundation that we have to base our conception of a truth in our terrestrial being and the possibility of a divine Life in material Nature. There our chief need is to discover the origin and nature of the Ignorance which we see emerging out of the inconscience of matter or disclosing itself within a body of matter and the nature of the Knowledge that has to replace it, to understand too the process of Nature's self-unfolding and the soul's recovery. For in fact the Knowledge is there concealed in the Ignorance itself; it has rather to be unveiled than acquired: it reveals itself rather than is learned, by an inward and upward self-unfolding. But first it will be convenient to meet and get out of the way one difficulty that inevitably arises, the difficulty of admitting that, even given the immanence of the Divine in us, even given our individual consciousness as a vehicle of progressive evolutionary manifestation, the individual is in any sense eternal or that there can be any persistence of individuality after liberation has been attained by unity and self-knowledge.

This is a difficulty of the logical reason and must be met by a larger and more catholic enlightening reason. . . .

The first difficulty for the reason is that it has always been accustomed to identify the individual self with the ego and to think of it as existing only by the limitations and exclusions of the ego. If that were so, then by the transcendence of the ego the individual would abolish his own existence; our end would be to disappear and dissolve into some universality of matter, life, mind or spirit or else some indeterminate from which our egoistic determinations of individuality have started. But what is this strongly separative self-experience that we call ego? It is nothing fundamentally real in itself but only a practical constitution of our consciousness devised to centralise the

Reprinted from Sri Aurobindo, *The Life Divine,* New York: Dutton, 1949, pp. 330–31, 332–35; reprinted with permission from Sri Aurobindo Ashram, Pondicherry, India.

activities of Nature in us. We perceive a formation of mental, physical, vital experience which distinguishes itself from the rest of being, and that is what we think of as ourselves in nature—this individualisation of being in becoming. We then proceed to conceive of ourselves as something which has thus individualised itself and only exists so long as it is individualised—a temporary or at least a temporal becoming; or else we conceive of ourselves as someone who supports or causes the individualisation, an immortal being perhaps but limited by its individuality. This perception and this conception constitute our ego-sense. Normally, we go no farther in our knowledge of our individual existence.

But in the end we have to see that our individualisation is only a superficial formation, a practical selection and limited conscious synthesis for the temporary utility of life in a particular body, or else it is a constantly changing and developing synthesis pursued through successive lives in successive bodies. Behind it there is a consciousness, a Purusha, who is not determined or limited by his individualisation or by this synthesis but on the contrary determines, supports and yet exceeds it. That which he selects from in order to construct this synthesis, is his total experience of the world-being. Therefore our individualisation exists by virtue of the world-being, but also by virtue of a consciousness which uses the world-being for experience of its possibilities of individuality. These two powers, Person and his world-material, are both necessary for our present experience of individuality. If the Purusha with his individualising syntheses of consciousness were to disappear, to merge, to annul himself in any way, our constructed individuality would cease because the Reality that supported it would no longer be in presence; if, on the other hand, the world-being were to dissolve, merge, disappear, then also our individualisation would cease, for the material of experience by which it effectuates itself would be wanting. We have then to recognise these two terms of our existence, a world-being and an individualising consciousness which is the cause of all our self-experience and world-experience.

But we see farther that in the end this Purusha, this cause and self of our individuality, comes to embrace the whole world and all other beings in a sort of conscious extension of itself and to perceive itself as one with the world-being. In its conscious extension of itself it exceeds the primary experience and abolishes the barriers of its active self-limitation and individualisation; by its perception of its own infinite universality it goes beyond all consciousness of separative individuality or limited soul-being. By that very fact the individual ceases to be the self-limiting ego; in other words, our false consciousness of existing only by self-limitation, by rigid distinction of ourselves from the rest of being and becoming is transcended; our identification of ourselves with our personal and temporal individualisation in a particular mind and body is abolished. But is all truth of individuality and individualisation abolished? does the Purusha cease to exist or does he become the world-Purusha and live intimately in innumerable minds and bodies? We do not find it to be so. He still individualises and it is still he who exists and embraces this wider consciousness while he individualises: but the mind no longer thinks of a limited temporary individualisation as all ourselves but only as a wave of becoming thrown up from the sea of its being or else as a form or centre of universality. The soul still makes the world-becoming the material for individual experience, but instead of regarding it as something outside and larger than itself on which it has to draw, by which it is affected, with which it has to make accommodations, it is aware of it subjectively as within itself; it embraces both its world-material and its individualised experience of spatial and temporal activities in a free and enlarged consciousness. In this new consciousness the spiritual individual perceives its true self to be one in being with the Transcendence and seated and dwelling within it, and no longer takes its constructed individuality as anything more than a formation for world-experience.

Our unity with the world-being is the consciousness of a Self which at one and the same time cosmicises in the world and individualises through the individual Purusha, and both in that world-being and in this individual being and in all individual beings it is aware of the same Self manifesting and experiencing its various manifestations. That then is a Self which must be one in its being,—otherwise we could not have this experience of unity,— and yet must be capable in its very unity of cosmic differentiation and multiple individuality. The unity is its being—yes, but the cosmic differentiation and the multiple individuality are the power of its being which it is constantly displaying and which it is its delight and the nature of its consciousness to display. If then we arrive at unity with that, if we even become entirely and in every way that being, why should the power of its being be excised and why at all should we desire or labour to excise it? We should then only diminish the scope of our unity with it by an exclusive concentration accepting the divine being but not accepting our part in the power and consciousness and infinite delight of the Divine. It would in fact be the individual seeking peace and rest of union in a motionless identity, but rejecting delight and various joy of union in the nature and act and power of the divine Existence. That is possible, but there is no necessity to uphold it as the ultimate aim of our being or as our ultimate perfection.

Or the one possible reason would be that in the power, the act of consciousness there is not real union and that only in the status of consciousness is there perfect undifferentiated unity. Now in what we may call the waking union of the individual with the Divine, as opposed to a falling asleep or a concentration of the individual consciousness in an absorbed identity, there is certainly and must be a differentiation of experience. For in this active unity the individual Purusha enlarges its active experience also as well as its static consciousness into a way of union with this Self of his being and of the world-being, and yet individualisation remains and therefore differentiation. The Purusha is aware of all other individuals as selves of himself; he may be a dynamic union become aware of their mental and practical action as occurring in his universal consciousness, just as he is aware of his own mental and practical action; he may help to determine their action by subjective union with them: but still there is a practical difference. The action of the Divine in himself is that with which he is particularly and directly concerned; the action of the Divine in his other selves is that with which he is universally concerned, not directly, but through and by his union with them and with the Divine. The individual therefore exists though he exceeds the little separative ego; the universal exists and is embraced by him but it does not absorb and abolish all individual differentiation, even though by his universalising himself the limitation which we call the ego is overcome.

"There Is No Ego," from the *Milindapañha* and the *Visuddhi-Magga*

Translated from the Milindapañha

Then drew near Milinda the king to where the venerable Nāgasena was; and having drawn near, he greeted the venerable Nāgasena; and having passed the compliments of friendship and civility, he sat down respectfully at one side. And the venerable Nāgasena returned the greeting; by which, verily, he won the heart of king Milinda.

And Milinda the king spoke to the venerable Nāgasena as follows:—
"How is your reverence called? Bhante, what is your name?"

"Your majesty, I am called Nāgasena; my fellow-priests, your majesty, address me as Nāgasena: but whether parents give one the name Nāgasena, or Sūrasena, or Virasena, or Sihasena, it is, nevertheless, your majesty, but a way of counting, a term, an appellation, a convenient designation, a mere name, this Nāgasena; for there is no Ego here to be found."

Then said Milinda the king,—
"Listen to me, my lords, ye five hundred Yonakas, and ye eighty thousand priests! Nāgasena here says thus: 'There is no Ego here to be found.' Is it possible, pray, for me to assent to what he says?"

And Milinda the king spoke to the venerable Nāgasena as follows:—
"Bhante Nāgasena, if there is no Ego to be found, who is it then furnishes you priests with the priestly requisites,—robes, food, bedding, and medicine, the reliance of the sick? who is it makes use of the same? who is it keeps the precepts? who is it applies himself to meditation? who is it realizes

Reprinted from Henry Clarke Warren, trans., *Buddhism in Translations,* Cambridge, Mass.: Harvard University Press, 1953, pp. 129–34.

the Paths, the Fruits, and Nirvana? who is it destroys life? who is it takes what is not given him? who is it commits immorality? who is it tells lies? who is it drinks intoxicating liquor? who is it commits the five crimes that constitute 'proximate karma'? In that case, there is no merit; there is no demerit; there is no one who does or causes to be done meritorious or demeritorious deeds; neither good nor evil deeds can have any fruit or result. Bhante Nāgasena, neither is he a murderer who kills a priest, nor can you priests, bhante Nāgasena, have any teacher, preceptor, or ordination. When you say, 'My fellow-priests, your majesty, address me as Nāgasena,' what then is this Nāgasena? Pray, bhante, is the hair of the head Nāgasena?"

"Nay, verily, your majesty."

"Is the hair of the body Nāgasena?"

"Nay, verily, your majesty."

"Are nails . . . teeth . . . skin . . . flesh . . . sinews . . . bones . . . marrow of the bones . . . kidneys . . . heart . . . liver . . . pleura . . . spleen . . . lungs . . . intestines . . . mesentery . . . stomach . . . faeces . . . bile . . . phlegm . . . pus . . . blood . . . sweat . . . fat . . . tears . . . lymph . . . saliva . . . snot . . . synovial fluid . . . urine . . . brain of the head Nāgasena?"

"Nay, verily, your majesty."

"Is now, bhante, form Nāgasena?"

"Nay, verily, your majesty."

"Is sensation Nāgasena?"

"Nay, verily, your majesty."

"Is perception Nāgasena?"

"Nay, verily, your majesty."

"Are the predispositions Nāgasena?"

"Nay, verily, your majesty."

"Is consciousness Nāgasena?"

"Nay, verily, your majesty."

"Are, then, bhante, form, sensation, perception, the predispositions, and consciousness unitedly Nāgasena?"

"Nay, verily, your majesty."

"Is it, then, bhante, something besides form, sensation, perception, the predispositions, and consciousness, which is Nāgasena?"

"Nay, verily, your majesty."

"Bhante, although I question you very closely, I fail to discover any Nāgasena. Verily, now, bhante, Nāgasena is a mere empty sound. What Nāgasena is there here? Bhante, you speak a falsehood, a lie: there is no Nāgasena."

Then the venerable Nāgasena spoke to Milinda the king as follows:—

"Your majesty, you are a delicate prince, an exceedingly delicate prince; and if, your majesty, you walk in the middle of the day on hot sandy ground, and you tread on rough grit, gravel, and sand, your feet become sore, your body tired, the mind is oppressed, and the body-consciousness suffers. Pray, did you come afoot, or riding?"

"Bhante, I do not go afoot: I came in a chariot."

"Your majesty, if you came in a chariot, declare to me the chariot. Pray, your majesty, is the pole the chariot?"

"Nay, verily, bhante."

"Is the axle the chariot?"

"Nay, verily, bhante."

"Are the wheels the chariot?"

"Nay, verily, bhante."

"Is the chariot-body the chariot?"

"Nay, verily, bhante."

"Is the banner-staff the chariot?"

"Nay, verily, bhante."

"Is the yoke the chariot?"

"Nay, verily, bhante."

"Are the reins the chariot?"

"Nay, verily, bhante."

"Is the goading-stick the chariot?"

"Nay, verily, bhante."

"Pray, your majesty, are pole, axle, wheels, chariot-body, banner-staff, yoke, reins, and goad unitedly the chariot?"

"Nay, verily, bhante."

"Is it, then, your majesty, something else besides pole, axle, wheels, chariot-body, banner-staff, yoke, reins, and goad which is the chariot?"

"Nay, verily, bhante."

"Your majesty, although I question you very closely, I fail to discover any chariot. Verily now, your majesty, the word chariot is a mere empty sound. What chariot is there here? Your majesty, you speak a falsehood, a lie: there is no chariot. Your majesty, you are the chief king in all the continent of India; of whom are you afraid that you speak a lie? Listen to me, my lords, ye five hundred Yonakas, and ye eighty thousand priests! Milinda the king here says thus: 'I came in a chariot'; and being requested, 'Your majesty, if you came in a chariot, declare to me the chariot,' he fails to produce any chariot. Is it possible, pray, for me to assent to what he says?"

When he had thus spoken, the five hundred Yonakas applauded the venerable Nāgasena and spoke to Milinda the king as follows:—

"Now, your majesty, answer, if you can."

Then Milinda the king spoke to the venerable Nāgasena as follows:—

"Bhante Nāgasena, I speak no lie: the word 'chariot' is but a way of counting, term, appellation, convenient designation, and name for pole, axle, wheels, chariot-body, and banner-staff."

"Thoroughly well, your majesty, do you understand a chariot. In exactly the same way, your majesty, in respect of me, Nāgasena is but a way of counting, term, appellation, convenient designation, mere name for the hair of my head, hair of my body . . . brain of the head, form, sensation, perception, the predispositions, and consciousness. But in the absolute sense there is no Ego here to be found. And the priestess Vajirā, your majesty, said as follows int he presence of The Blessed One:—

"'Even as the word of "chariot" means
That members join to frame a whole;
So when the Groups appear to view,
We use the phrase, "A living being.*" ' "

"It is wonderful, bhante Nāgasena! It is marvellous, bhante Nāgasena. Brilliant and prompt is the wit of your replies. If The Buddha were alive, he would applaud. Well done, well done, Nāgasena! Brilliant and prompt is the wit of your replies."

Translated from the Visuddhi-Magga

Just as the word "chariot" is but a mode of expression for axle, wheels, chariot-body, pole, and other constituent members, placed in a certain relation to each other, but when we come to examine the members one by one, we discover that in the absolute sense there is no chariot; and just as the word "house" is but a mode of expression for wood and other constituents of a house, surrounding space in a certain relation, but in the absolute sense there is no house; and just as the word "fist" is but a mode of expression for the fingers, the thumb, etc., in a certain relation; and the word "lute" for the body of the lute, strings, etc.; "army" for elephants, horses, etc.; "city" for fortifications, houses, gates, etc.; "tree" for trunk, branches, foliage, etc., in a certain relation, but when we come to examine the parts one by one, we discover that in the absolute sense there is no tree; in exactly the same way the words "living entity" and "Ego" are but a mode of expression for the presence of the five attachment groups, but when we come to examine the elements of being one by one, we discover that in the absolute sense there is no living entity there to form a basis for such figments as "I am," or "I"; in other words, that in the absolute sense there is only name and form. The insight of him who perceives this is called knowledge of the truth.

He, however, who abandons this knowledge of the truth and believes in a living entity must assume either that this living entity will perish or that it will not perish. If he assume that it will not perish, he falls into the heresy of the persistence of existences; or if he assume that it will perish, he falls into that of the annihilation of existences. And why do I say do? Because, just as sour cream has milk as its antecedent, so nothing here exists but what has its own antecedents. To say, "The living entity persists," is to fall short of the truth; to say, "It is annihilated," is to outrun the truth. Therefore has The Blessed One said:—

"There are two heresies, O priests, which possess both gods and men, by which some fall short of the truth, and some outrun the truth; but the intelligent know the truth.

"And how, O priests, do some fall short of the truth?

"O priests, gods and men delight in existence, take pleasure in existence, rejoice in existence, so that when the Doctrine for the cessation of existence

---

*That is, "a living entity."

is preached to them, their minds do not leap toward it, are not favorably disposed toward it, do not rest in it, do not adopt it.

"Thus, O priests, do some fall short of the truth.

"And how, O priests, do some outrun the truth?

"Some are distressed at, ashamed of, and loathe existence, and welcome the thought of non-existence, saying, 'See here! When they say that on the dissolution of the body this Ego is annihilated, perishes, and does not exist after death, that is good, that is excellent, that is as it should be.'

"Thus, O priests, do some outrun the truth.

"And how, O priests, do the intelligent know the truth?

"We may have, O priests, a priest who knows things as they really are, and knowing things as they really are, he is on the road to aversion for things, to absence of passion for them, and to cessation from them.

"Thus, O priests, do the intelligent know the truth."

"Examination of Self-Nature," from *Madhyamika Karika*

Nagarjuna

Verse 1

The rise of self-nature by relational and causal conditions is not justifiable. For, such a self-nature will have a character of being made or manipulated.

Verse 2

How is it possible for the self-nature to take on the character of being made? For, indeed, the self-nature refers to something which cannot be made and has no mutual correspondence with something else.

Verse 3

Where self-nature is non-existent, how could there be an extended nature? For, indeed, a self-nature which has the nature of being extended will be called an extended nature.

Reprinted from Kenneth Inada, trans., *Nagarjuna: A Translation of His Mulamadhyamakakarika*, Tokyo: Hokuseido Press, 1970, pp. 97–100; © 1970 Hokuseido Press; reprinted with permission.

Verse 4

Again, separated from self-nature and extended nature, how could existence be? For, indeed, existence establishes itself in virtue of either self-nature or extended nature.

Verse 5

If existence does not come to be (i.e., does not establish itself), then certainly non-existence does not also. For, indeed, people speak of existence in its varying nature as non-existence.

Verse 6

Those who see (i.e., try to understand) the concepts of self-nature, extended nature, existence, or non-existence do not perceive the real truth in the Buddha's teaching.

Verse 7

According to the Instructions to Kātyāyana, the two views of the world in terms of being and non-being were criticized by the Buddha for similarly admitting the bifurcation of entities into existence and non-existence.

Note: The Sanskrit, Kātyāyanāvavāda, either refers to the sūtra or to the instruction given to Kātyāyana by the Buddha.

Verse 8

If existence is in virtue of a primal nature, then its non-existence does not follow. For, indeed, a varying character of a primal nature is not possible at all.

Verse 9

If primal nature does not exist, what will possess the varying character? If, on the other hand, primal nature does exist, what then will possess the varying character?

Verse 10

Existence is the grasping of permanency (i.e., permanent characteristics) and non-existence the perception of disruption. (As these functions are not strictly possible), the wise should not rely upon (the concepts of) existence and non-existence.

Verse 11

It follows that permanency means that existence based on self-nature does not become a non-entity and disruption means that what formerly was existent is now non-existent.

Trimsika-Karika (Thirty Verses)

Vasubandhu

The metaphors of "self" and "events" which develop in so
    many different ways
take place in the transformation of consciousness: and this
    transformation is of three kinds:
Maturation, that called "always reflecting," and the percep-
    tion of sense-objects.
Among these, "maturation" is that called "the store-conscious-
    ness" which has all the seeds.

Its appropriations, states, and perceptions are not fully con-
    scious,
yet it is always endowed with contacts, mental attentions,
    feelings, cognitions, and volitions.

Its feelings are equaniminous: it is unobstructed and in-
    determinate.
The same for its contacts, etc. It develops like the currents
    in a stream.

Its de-volvement takes place in a saintly state: Dependent
    on it there develops
a consciousness called "manas," having it as its object-of-
    consciousness,
    and having the nature of always reflecting;

It is always conjoined with four afflictions, obstructed-but-
    indeterminate,
known as view of self, confusion of self, pride of self, and
    love of self.

Reprinted from Stefan Anacker, trans., *Seven Works of Vasubandhu,* Delhi: Motilal Banarsidaas, 1984, pp. 186–89; © Motilal Banarsidaas; reprinted with permission.

And wherever it arises, so do contact and the others. But
    it doesn't exist in a saintly state,
or in the attainment of cessation or even in a supermundane
    path.

This is the second transformation. The third is the apprehension of sense-objects of six kinds: it is either beneficial,
    or unbeneficial, or both.

It is always connected with *sarvatragas* and sometimes with
    factors that arise specifically,
with beneficial events associated with citta, afflictions, and
    secondary afflictions: its feelings are of three kinds.

The first are contact, etc.; those arising specifically are
zest, confidence, memory, concentration, and insight;

The beneficial are faith, inner shame, dread of blame.
the three starting with lack of greed, vigor, tranquility,
    carefulness, and non-harming;
the afflictions are attachment, aversion, and confusion,

pride, views, and doubts.
The secondary afflictions are anger, malice, hypocrisy,
    maliciousness, envy, selfishness, deceitfulness,

guile, mischievous exuberance, desire to harm, lack of shame,
lack of dread of blame, mental fogginess, excitedness,
    lack of faith, sloth, carelessness, loss of mindfulness,

distractedness, lack of recognition, regret, and torpor,
initial mental application, and subsequent discursive
    thought: the last two pairs are of two kinds

In the root-consciousness, the arising of the other five takes
    place according to conditions,
either all together or not, just like waves in water.

The co-arising of a mental consciousness takes place always
    except in a non-cognitional state,
or in the two attainments, or in torpor, or in fainting, or in a
    state without citta.

This transformation of consciousness is a discrimination, and
as it is discriminated, it does not exist, and so everything
    is perception-only.

Consciousness is only all the seeds, and transformation
    takes place in such and such a way,
according to a reciprocal influence, by which such and
    such a type of discrimination may arise.

The residual impressions of actions, along with the residual
    impressions of a "dual" apprehension,
cause another maturation (of seeds) to occur,
    where the former maturation has been
    exhausted.

Whatever range of events is discriminated by whatever dis-
    crimination

is just the constructed own-being, and it isn't really to
be found.—

The interdependent own-being, on the other hand, is the
discrimination which arises from conditions,
and the fulfilled is its★ state of being separated always
from the former.★★

So it is to be spoken of as neither exactly different nor non-
different from the interdependent,
just like impermanence, etc., for when one isn't seen, the
other is.

The absence of own-being in all events has been taught with
a view towards
the three different kinds of absence of own-being in the
three different kinds of own-being.

The first is without own-being through its character itself,
but the second
because of its non-independence, and the third *is*
absence of own-being.

It is the ultimate truth of all events, and so it is "Suchness,"
too,
since it is just so all the time, and it's just perception-only.

As long as consciousness is not situated within perception-
only,
the residues of a "dual" apprehension will not come to an end.

And so even with the consciousness: "All this is perception
only,"
because this also involves an apprehension,
For whatever makes something stop in front of it isn't
situated in "this-only."

When consciousness does not apprehend any object-of-con-
sciousness,
it's situated in "consciousness-only,"
for with the non-being of an object apprehended, there is
no apprehension of it.

It is without citta, without apprehension, and it is supermundane knowledge;
It is revolution at the basis, the ending of two kinds of
susceptibility to harm.

It is the inconceivable, beneficial, constant Ground, not liable
to affliction,
bliss, and the liberation-body called the Dharma-body of the
Sage.

★the interdependent's.
★★the constructed.

From *Instructions for Practical Life*

Wang Yang-ming

Hsiao Hui made inquiry saying: "One's own passion is hard to control. What remedy is there for this?"

The Teacher said, "You must take your own passion and control it for yourself." He further said. "The individual must have a mind which devotes itself to self, for then he can control himself. Being able to control himself, he can complete himself."

Hsiao Hui said, "I have a mind greatly devoted to myself, but I do not know why I am unable to control myself."

The Teacher said, "Tell me what sort of devotion to self your mind manifests."

After a long time Hui said, "With my whole mind I desire to be a good man. Therefore I say that I have a mind greatly devoted to self. As I think of it, I realize that this devotion is to the bodily self alone and that it has not been devotion to the true self."

The Teacher said: "Has it, then, been the case that your true self has been separated from your bodily self? I fear lest perhaps you have even failed to devote yourself to the bodily self. Tell me, is not what you call the bodily self to be identified with your ears, eyes, nose, hands, and feet?"

Hui said, "It is just as you say. The eyes desire beauty, the ears music, the mouth tasty morsels, and the four members idleness and pleasure. In consequence of this I am unable to control myself."

The Teacher said: "Lust causes one's eyes to become blind, licentious music causes his ears to become deaf, gluttony causes his taste to fail him, wild pursuit on the hunt causes him to become violent. All these things are harmful to your ears, eyes, mouth, nose, hands, and feet. How can this be construed as devotion to them? If you are truly devoted to them, you must reflect upon the manner in which the ears, eyes, mouth, and four members are to be used, and if the situation is not in accordance with propriety, you should not see, hear, speak, or act. Then first are you able fully to realize the true functions of ears, eyes, mouth, nose, and the four members, and can be said to have true devotion to ears, eyes, mouth, nose and the four members. At present you constantly strive wildly for external things, and devote yourself to fame and gain. These are all things external to the body itself. When you devote yourself to your ears, eyes, mouth, nose, and four members, so that

Reprinted from Frederick G. Henke, trans., *The Philosophy of Wang Yang-ming*, London: Open Court Publishing Co., 1916, pp. 130–32.

you do not see, hear, speak, or act that which is contrary to propriety, does this imply that your ears, eyes, mouth, nose, and four members have the ability in themselves not to see, or hear, or speak, or act? That ability must come from the mind. Seeing, hearing, speaking, and acting are to be identified with the mind. The sight of the mind manifests itself in the eyes; its hearing in the ears; its speech through the mouth; and its activity by means of the hands and feet. When your mind is absent there are no ears, eyes, mouth, or nose. The mind is not merely to be identified with flesh and blood. If it were, how does it come that though flesh and blood are still present the dead man cannot see, hear, speak, or act? It is the mind that is able to see, hear, speak, and act. It is nature, it is heaven-given principles. If one has this nature, he is able to develop the principle of the growth of nature—benevolence (the highest virtue). If the growth of the mind manifests itself in sight, one is able to see; if in audition, one is able to hear; if in speech, one is able to speak; if in the four members, one is able to act. All are a development of natural law. In the capacity of ruler of the person it is called mind. The original character of the mind thus is in complete harmony with natural law and in complete accord with propriety. This is your true self, and this true self is the master of the body. If there is no true self, there is also no body. The true self is born from the body; and without it, it is dead. If you devote yourself truly to the bodily self, you must protect and maintain the original nature of the true self. You must be cautious with reference to that which you have not seen, and apprehensive of that which you have not heard. You need only fear lest perchance you have injured the true self and are in danger of acting counter to the rules of propriety. It is as though one were being cut with a knife or stuck with a needle until one cannot endure it. The knife and the needle must be taken out of the wound, before one can have a mind devoted to self and be able to control one's self. Since you frankly admit that you have a thief as a son (admit your shame), why do you say that you have a mind devoted to self and yet cannot control yourself?"

One of the students had sore eyes, and was exceedingly melancholy about it. The Teacher said, "You evaluate your eyes too high and your mind too low."

From a Letter to Shu Kuo-yung

Wang Yang-ming

What the superior man means by being self-poised and careful is not what is meant by being under the influence of terror, sorrow, and distress, but by being cautious with reference to that which is not seen, and apprehensive with reference to that which is not heard. The saying of the superior man regarding freedom does not carry with it the connotation of the swaggering and dissipation implied in giving rein to the seven passions and in acting unscrupulously. It means that the mind is not embarrassed by desire and that the individual can find himself in no situation in which he is not himself. The mind is by very nature the embodiment of heaven-given principles; and the clear, intelligent realization of these principles is what is meant by intuitive knowledge. The cautiousness and apprehensiveness of the superior man is probably due to his clear, intelligent perception. If there is anything that obscures or tends toward dissipation, it degenerates into self-abandonment, moral deflection, depravity, and recklessness, so that the correctness of the original nature is lost. If the cautiousness and apprehensiveness of the superior man is never interrupted, heaven-given principles will be constantly cherished. Moreover, in him who clearly and intelligently perceives and realizes heaven-given principles, the original nature is free from defect or obscuration. No selfish desire intervenes to annoy and give trouble. There is nothing present because of which the mind is either in dread, or in sorrow and distress, or because of which it is under the influence of fond regard or of passion, or with reference to which it has foregone conclusions and arbitrary predeterminations, obstinacy and egoism, or because of which it is discontented or ashamed. But it (the original nature) is clear and bright. Filled and satiated, it manifests itself in such a way that all the movements, of the countenance and of every turn of the body, are exactly adjusted. They carry out the desires of the mind, but not to excess. This is what is meant by truly dropping one's dignity and being untrammelled and self-contained.

Such a condition is begotten out of a constant cherishing of heaven-given principles, and the constant cherishing of heaven-given principles is begotten when cautiousness and apprehension are uninterrupted. Who would say that an increase of self-poise and carefulness involves the embarrassment of losing one's freedom? Such an individual fails to know that freedom is original to the mind, and that self-poise and carefulness are manifestations

Reprinted from Frederick G. Henke, trans., *The Philosophy of Wang Yang-ming,* London: Open Court Publishing Co., 1916, pp. 260–62.

of freedom. To distinguish them as two things, and thus divided to use the mind, causes mutual opposition. As soon as there is much opposition, one drifts into a desire to assist the growth materially. Thus, what you designate as self-poise and carefulness is what the Great Learning means by terror, sorrow and distress, and not what the Doctrine of the Mean describes as being cautious and apprehensive. The philosopher Ch'eng always said that what people thought of as lacking purpose really could be said to connote the absence of a selfish mind and not the loss of mind. To be cautious regarding that which one has not seen, and apprehensive regarding that which one has not heard, shows that there must be purpose present. To be under the influence of dread, sorrow and distress implies that there must be selfish purpose present. The cautiousness and fearfulness of Yao and Shun, and the carefulness and respectfulness of Wen Wang signify self-poise and carefulness. They spontaneously arise out of the original nature of the mind, and are not manifested because of any special reason. Self-poise and carefulness make no distinction between activity (excitement) and rest (tranquility). Self-poise is for the purpose of rectifying the mind, and righteousness for the purpose of correcting the conduct. When both self-poise and righteousness have been fixed, the heaven-appointed way will be open, and there will be no doubt concerning the individual's conduct. In all that you have written, the underlying idea is correct. You may use this to encourage yourself, but certainly not to reprove others. The superior man does not seek the confidence of others; for if he has confidence in himself, that is enough. He does not seek notoriety or popularity: if he knows himself, that is enough. Because I have not completed my father's grave and am exceedingly occupied with affairs, and your messenger waits for the reply, I have written in a careless, incoherent manner.

"The Nonexistence of the Self," from *The Treatise on the Establishment of the Doctrine of Consciousness-Only*

Hsuan-tsang

1. Because the ideas of the self (*atman*) and dharmas are [constructions produced by causes and therefore] false,
   Their characters of all kinds arise.
   These characters are [constructions] based on the transformations of consciousness,
   Which are of three kinds.
2a. They are the consciousness (the eighth or storehouse consciousness) whose fruits (retribution) ripen at later times,

   The consciousness (the seventh or thought-center consciousness) that deliberates, and the consciousness (the sense-center consciousness and the five sense consciousness) that discriminates spheres of objects.

The Treatise says:

Both the world and sacred doctrines declare that the self and dharmas are merely constructions based on false ideas and have no reality of their own. . . . On what basis are [the self and dharmas] produced? Their characters are all constructions based on the evolution and transformation of consciousness. . . .

How do we know that there is really no sphere of objects but only inner consciousness which produces what seems to be the external spheres of objects? Because neither the real self nor the real dharma is possible.

Why is the real self impossible? Theories of the self held by the various schools may be reduced to three kinds. The first holds that the substance of the self is eternal, universal, and as extensive as empty space. It acts anywhere and as a consequence enjoys happiness or suffers sorrow. The second holds that although the substance of the self is eternal, its extension is indeterminate, because it expands or contracts according to the size of the body. The third holds that the substance of the self is eternal and infinitesimal like an atom, lying deeply and moving around within the body and thus acts.

The first theory is contrary to reason. Why? If it is held that the self is eternal, universal, and as extensive as empty space, it should not enjoy happiness or suffer sorrow along with the body. Furthermore, being eternal and universal, it should be motionless. How can it act along with the body? Again, is the self so conceived the same or different among all sentient beings? If it is the same, when one being acts, receives the fruits of actions, or achieves salvation, all beings should do the same. But this would of course be a great mistake. If it is different, then the selves of all sentient beings would universally penetrate one another and their substance would be mixed, and since the field of abode of all selves is the same, the acts of one being or the fruits of action received by him should be the act or fruits of all beings. If it is said that action and fruits belong to each being separately and there would not be the mistake just described, such a contention is also contrary to reason, because action, fruits, and body are identified with all selves and it is unreasonable for them to belong to one self but not to another. When one is saved, all should be saved, for the Dharma (truth) practiced and realized would be identical with all selves.

The second theory is also contrary to reason. Why? If in substance the self always remains in the same state, it should not expand or contract along with the body. If it expands or contracts like wind in a bag or a pipe, it is not always remaining in the same state. Furthermore, if the self follows the body, it would be divisible. How can it be held that the substance of the self is one? What this school says is like child's play.

The last theory is also contrary to reason. Why? Since the self is infinitesimal like an atom, how can it cause the whole big body [that extends throughout the world of form] to move? If it is said that although it is small it goes through the body like a whirling wheel of fire so that the whole body seems to move, then the self so conceived is neither one nor eternal, for what comes and goes is neither eternal nor one.

Furthermore, there are three additional theories of the self. The first holds that the self is identical with the aggregates (namely, matter, sensation, thought, disposition, and consciousness). The second holds that it is separated from the aggregates. And the third holds that it is neither identical with nor separated from the aggregates. The first theory is contrary to reason, for the self would be like the aggregates and are therefore neither eternal nor one. Furthermore, the internal matters (the five senses) are surely not the real self, for they are physically obstructed (or restricted) like external matters. The mind and mental qualities are not the real self either, for they are not always continuous and depend on various causes to be produced. Other conditioned things and matters are also not the real self, for like empty space they are without intelligence.

The second theory is also contrary to reason, for the self would then be like empty space, which neither acts nor receives fruits of action.

The last theory is also contrary to reason. This theory allows that the self is based on the aggregates but is neither identical with nor separated from them. The self would then be like a vase [which depends on clay] and has no reality of its own. Also, since it is impossible to say whether it is produced from causes or not produced from causes, it is also impossible to say whether it is a self or not. Therefore the real self conceived in the theory cannot be established.

Again, does the substance of the real self conceived by the various schools think or not? If it does, it would not be eternal, because it does not think all the time. If it does not, it would be like empty space, which neither acts nor receives fruits of action. Therefore on the basis of reason, the self conceived by the theory cannot be established.

Again, does this substance of the real self conceived by the various schools perform any function or not? If it does, it would be like hands and feet and would not be eternal. If it does not, it would be like [illusory] horns of a hare and not the real self. Therefore in either case, the self conceived by them cannot be established.

Again, is the substance of the real self conceived by the various schools an object of the view of the self or not? If it is not, how do advocates of the theory know that there is really a self? If it is, then there should be a view of the self that does not involve any perversion, for that would be knowledge of what really is. In that case, how is it that the perfectly true doctrines believed in by those holding the theory of the self all denounce the view of the self and praise the view of the non-self? [Advocates of the theory themselves] declare that the view of the non-self will lead to Nirvāna while clinging to the view of the self will lead to sinking in the sea of life and death (transmigration). Does an erroneous view ever lead to Nirvāna and a correct view, on the contrary, lead to transmigration?

Again, the various views of the self [actually] do not take the real self as an object, because it has objects [which are not itself] like the mind takes others [such as external matters] as objects. The object of the view of the self is certainly not the real self, because it [the view] is an object like other dharmas. Therefore the view of the self does not take the real self as an object. Only because the various aggregates are transformed and manifested by inner consciousness, all kinds of imagination and conjecture result in accordance with one's own erroneous opinions. . . .

"The Issue at Hand"
("Genjokōan") from *Shōbōgenzō*

Dogen

When all things are Buddha-teachings, then there is delusion and enlightenment, there is cultivation of practice, there is birth, there is death, there are Buddhas, there are sentient beings. When myriad things are all not self, there is no delusion, no enlightenment, no Buddhas, no sentient beings, no birth, no death. Because the Buddha Way originally sprang forth from abundance and paucity, there is birth and death, delusion and enlightenment, sentient beings and Buddhas. Moreover, though this is so, flowers fall when we cling to them, and weeds only grow when we dislike them.

Acting on and witnessing myriad things with the burden of oneself is "delusion." Acting on and witnessing oneself in the advent of myriad things is enlightenment. Great enlightenment about delusion is Buddhas; great delusion about enlightenment is sentient beings. There are also those who attain enlightenment on top of enlightenment, and there are those who are further deluded in the midst of delusion. When the Buddhas are indeed the Buddhas, there is no need to be self-conscious of being Buddhas; nevertheless, it is realizing buddhahood—Buddhas go on realizing.

In seeing forms with the whole body-mind, hearing sound with the whole body-mind, though one intimately understands, it isn't like reflecting images in a mirror, it's not like water and the moon—when you witness one side, one side is obscure.

Studying the Buddha Way is studying oneself. Studying oneself is forgetting oneself. Forgetting oneself is being enlightened by all things. Being enlightened by all things is causing the body-mind of oneself and the body-mind of others to be shed. There is ceasing the traces of enlightenment, which causes one to forever leave the traces of enlightenment which is cessation.

When people first seek the Teaching, they are far from the bounds of the Teaching. Once the Teaching is properly conveyed in oneself, already one is the original human being.

When someone rides in a boat, as he looks at the shore he has the illusion that the shore is moving. When he looks at the boat under him, he realizes the boat is moving. In the same way, when one takes things for granted with confused ideas of body-mind, one has the illusion that one's own mind and

Reprinted from Thomas Cleary, trans., *Shōbōgenzō: Zen Essays by Dōgen,* Honolulu: University of Hawaii Press, 1986, pp. 32–35. © 1986 by University of Hawaii Press; reprinted with permission.

own nature are permanent; but if one pays close attention to one's own actions, the truth that things are not self will be clear.

Kindling becomes ash, and cannot become kindling again. However, we should not see ash as after and the kindling as before. Know that kindling abides in the normative state of kindling, and though it has a before and after, the realms of before and after are disconnected. Ash, in the normative state of ash, has before and after. Just as that kindling, after having become ash, does not again become kindling, so after dying a person does not become alive again. This being the case, not saying that life becomes death is an established custom in Buddhism—therefore it is called *unborn*. That death does not become life is an established teaching of the Buddha; therefore we say *imperishable*. Life is an individual temporal state, death is an individual temporal state. It is like winter and spring—we don't think winter becomes spring, we don't say spring becomes summer.

People's attaining enlightenment is like the moon reflected in water. The moon does not get wet, the water isn't broken. Though it is a vast expansive light, it rests in a little bit of water—even the whole moon, the whole sky, rests in a dewdrop on the grass, rests in even a single droplet of water. That enlightenment does not shatter people is like the moon not piercing the water. People's not obstructing enlightenment is like the drop of dew not obstructing the moon in the sky. The depth is proportionate to the height. As for the length and brevity of time, examining the great and small bodies of water, you should discern the breadth and narrowness of the moon in the sky.

Before one has studied the Teaching fully in body and mind, one feels one is already sufficient in the Teaching. If the body and mind are replete with the Teaching, in one respect one senses insufficiency. For example, when one rides a boat out onto the ocean where there are no mountains and looks around, it only appears round, and one can see no other, different characteristics. However, this ocean is not round, nor is it square—the remaining qualities of the ocean are inexhaustible. It is like a palace, it is like ornaments, yet as far as our eyes can see, it only seems round. It is the same with all things—in the realms of matter, beyond conceptualization, they include many aspects, but we see and comprehend only what the power of our eye of contemplative study reaches. If we inquire into the "family ways" of myriad things, the qualities of seas and mountains, beyond seeming square or round, are endlessly numerous. We should realize there exists worlds everywhere. It's not only thus in out of the way places—know that even a single drop right before us is also thus.

As a fish travels through water, there is no bound to the water no matter how far it goes; as a bird flies through the sky, there's no bound to the sky no matter how far it flies. While this is so, the fish and birds have never been apart from the water and the sky—it's just that when the need is large the use is large, and when the requirement is small the use is small. In this way, though the bounds are unfailingly reached everywhere and tread upon in every single place, the bird would instantly die if it left the sky and the fish would instantly die if it left the water. Obviously, water is life; obviously the sky is life. There is bird being life. There is fish being life. There is life being bird, there is life being fish. There must be progress beyond this—there is cultivation and realization, the existence of the living one being like this. Under these circumstances, if there were birds or fish who attempted to traverse the waters or the sky after having found the limits of the water or sky, they wouldn't find a path in the water or the sky—they won't find any place. When one finds this place, this action accordingly manifests as the issue at hand; when one finds this path, this action accordingly manifests as the issue at hand. This path, this place, is not big or small, not self or other, not preexistent, not now appearing—therefore it exists in this way. In this way, if someone cultivates and realizes the Buddha Way, it is *attaining a principle, mastering the principle;* it is *encountering a practice, cultivating the practice.* In this there is a place where the path has been accomplished, hence the unknowability of the known boundary is born together and studies along with the thorough investigation of the Buddha Teaching of this knowing—therefore it is thus. Don't get the idea that the attainment necessarily becomes one's own knowledge and view, that it would be known by discursive knowledge. Though realizational comprehension already takes place, implicit being is not necessarily obvious—*why necessarily* is there obvious becoming?

Zen Master Hōtetsu of Mt. Mayoku was using a fan. A monk asked him about this: "The nature of wind is eternal and all-pervasive—why then do you use a fan?" The master said, "You only know the nature of wind is eternal, but do not yet know the principle of its omnipresence." The monk asked, "What is the principle of its omnipresence?" The master just fanned. The monk bowed.

The experience of the Buddha Teaching, the living road of right transmission, is like this. To say that since (the nature of wind) is permanent one should not use a fan, and that one should feel the breeze even when not using a fan, is not knowing permanence and not knowing the nature of the wind either. Because the nature of wind is eternal, the wind of Buddhism causes the manifestation of the earth's being gold and by participation develops the long river into butter.

The Phenomena of Climate

Watsuji Tetsuro

I use our word Fu-do, which means literally, "Wind and Earth," as a general term for the natural environment of a given land, its climate, its weather, the geological and productive nature of the soil, its topographic and scenic features. The ancient term for this concept was Sui-do, which might be literally translated as "Water and Earth." Behind these terms lies the ancient view of Nature as man's environment compounded of earth, water, fire, and wind. It is not without reason that I wish to treat this natural environment of man not as "nature" but as "climate" in the above sense. But in order to clarify my reason, I must, in the first place, deal with the phenomenon of climate.

All of us live on a given land and the natural environment of this land "environs" us whether we like it or not. People usually discern this natural environment in the form of natural phenomena of various kinds, and accordingly concern themselves with the influences which such a natural environment exercises upon "us"—in some cases upon "us" as biological and physiological objects and in other cases upon "us" as being engaged in practical activities such as the formation of a polity. Each of these influences is complicated enough to demand specialized study. However, what I am here concerned with is whether the climate we experience in daily life is to be regarded as a natural phenomenon. It is proper that natural science should treat climate as a natural phenomenon, but it is another question whether the phenomena of climate are in essence objects of natural science.

By way of clarifying this question, let me quote as an example the phenomenon of cold, which is merely one element within climate, and is something distinct and evident as far as our common sense is concerned. It is an undeniable fact that we feel cold. But what is this cold that we feel? Is it that air of a certain temperature, cold, that is, as a physical object, stimulates the sensory organs in our body so that we as psychological subjects experience it as a certain set mental state? If so, it follows that the "cold" and "we" exist as separate and independent entities in such a manner that only when the cold presses upon us from outside is there created an "intentional" or directional relationship by which "we feel the cold." If this is the case, it is natural that this should be conceived in terms of the influence of the cold upon us.

Reprinted from Watsuji Tetsuro, *Climate and Culture: A Philosophical Study (Fudo)*, Geoffrey Bownas, trans., Westport, Conn.: Greenwood Press and Yushodo Publishing, 1988, pp. 1–4. Copyright 1935 by Mrs. Masako Watsuji and Iwanami Shoten Publishing, Tokyo; reprinted with permission of Mrs. Watsuji and Iwanami Shoten Publishers.

But is this really so? How can we know the independent existence of the cold before we feel cold? It is impossible. It is by feeling cold, that we discover the cold. It is simply by mistaking the intentional relationship that we consider that the cold is pressing in on us from outside. It is not true that the intentional relationship is set up only when an object presses from outside. As far as individual consciousness is concerned, the subject possesses the intentional structure within itself and itself "directs itself towards something." The "feeling" of "feeling the cold" is not a "point" which establishes a relationship directed at the cold, but it is in itself a relationship in virtue of its "feeling" and it is in this relationship that we discover cold. The intentionality of such a relational structure is thus a structure of the subject in relation with the cold. The fact that "We feel the cold" is, first and foremost, an "intentional experience" of this kind.

But, it may be argued, if this is the case, is not the cold merely a moment of subjective experience? The cold thus discovered is cold limited to the sphere of the "I." But what we call the cold is a transcendental object outside the "I," and not a mere feeling of the "I." Now how can a subjective experience establish a relation with such a transcendental object? In other words, how can the feeling of cold relate itself to the coldness of the outside air? This question involves a misunderstanding with regard to the object of the intention in the intentional relationship. The object of intention is not a mental entity. It is not cold as an experience independent of objective cold that is the intentional object. When we feel the cold, it is not the "feeling" of cold that we feel, but the "coldness of the air" or the "cold." In other words, the cold felt in intentional experience is not subjective but objective. It may be said, therefore, that an intentional relation in which we feel the cold is itself related to the coldness of the air. The cold as a transcendental existence only exists in this intentionality. Therefore, there can be no problem of the relationship of the feeling of cold to the coldness of the air.

According to this view, the usual distinction between subject and object, or more particularly the distinction between "the cold" and the "I" independently of each other, involves a certain misunderstanding. When we feel cold, we ourselves are already in the coldness of the outside air. That we come into relation with the cold means that we are outside in the cold. In this sense, our state is characterized by "ex-sistere" as Heidegger emphasizes, or, in our term, by "intentionality."

This leads me to the contention that we ourselves face ourselves in the state of "ex-sistere." Even in cases where we do not face ourselves by means of reflection or looking into ourselves, our selves are exposed to ourselves. Reflection is merely a form of grasping ourselves. Furthermore, it is not a primary mode of self-revelation. (But if the word "reflect" is taken in its visual sense, i.e., if it is understood as to dash against something and rebound from it and to reveal oneself in this rebound or reflection, it can be argued that the word may well indicate the way in which our selves are exposed to ourselves.) We feel the cold, or we are out in the cold. Therefore, in feeling the cold, we discover ourselves in the cold itself. This does not mean that we transfer our selves into the cold and there discover the selves thus transferred.

The instant that the cold is discovered, we are already outside in the cold. Therefore, the basic essence of what is "present outside" is not a thing or object such as the cold, but we ourselves. "Ex-sistere" is the fundamental principle of the structure of our selves, and it is on this principle that intentionality depends. That we feel the cold is an intentional experience, in which we discover our selves in the state of "ex-sistere," or our selves already outside in the cold.

We have considered the problem in terms of individual consciousness in the experience of cold. But, as we have been able to use the expression "we feel cold," without any contradiction, it is "we," not "I" alone that experience the cold. We feel the same cold in common. It is precisely because of this that we can use terms describing the cold in our exchange of daily greetings. The fact that the feeling of cold differs between us is possible only on the basis of our feeling the cold in common. Without this basis it would be quite impossible to recognise that any other "I" experiences the cold. Thus, it is not "I" alone but "we," or more strictly, "I" as "we" and "we" as "I" that are outside in the cold. The structure of which "ex-sistere" is the fundamental principle is this "we," not the mere "I." Accordingly, "ex-sistere" is "to be out among other 'I's'" rather than "to be out in a thing such as the cold." This is not an intentional relation but a "mutual relationship" of existence. Thus it is primarily "we" in this "mutual relationship" that discover our selves in the cold.

4

Knowledge

Chuang Tzu and Hui Tzu were strolling along the dam of the Hao River when Chuang Tzu said, "See how the minnows come out and dart around where they please! That's what fish really enjoy!"

Hui Tzu said, "You're not a fish—how do you know what fish enjoy?"

Chuang Tzu said, "You're not I, so how do you know I don't know what fish enjoy?"

Hui Tzu said, "I'm not you, so certainly I don't know what you know. On the other hand, you're certainly not a fish—so that still proves you don't know what fish enjoy!"

Chuang Tzu said, "Let's go back to your original question, please. You asked me *how* I know what fish enjoy—so you already knew I knew it when you asked the question. I know it by standing here beside the Hao." (Chuang Tzu)[1]

Indian Philosophies

Hindu Perspectives

Epistemology in Indian thought has not received its fair share of attention. As we will see, quite a few Indian philosophers have constructed rather elaborate theories concerning the sources and the aims of knowledge.[2]

Generally, Indians' epistemological interests revolve around the following basic questions: (1) What are the sources of knowledge? That is, how is it that we generally know? (2) What are the grounds for valid knowledge? How do we attain correct knowledge? (3) What are the objects of our knowledge? (4) How is it that we know that we know? (5) What are the sources of error?

To begin with, we need to emphasize one crucial point: Knowledge is not a subject studied merely for its own sake. The study of knowledge is essential for learning the right path to liberation. It is a means to the end of spiritual awakening, to the realization of one's genuine self and the nature of reality.

Nyaya School

The Nyaya school has had a far-reaching effect on the development and understanding of Indian logic. *Nyaya,* which literally means "argumentation," is generally regarded as one of the most important analyses in Indian orthodox epistemology. In its emphasis on correct reasoning, it lays the groundwork for other systems.

The school was founded about two centuries after Buddhism and Jainism, allegedly by Gautama. Both Buddhism and Jainism utilized logical analysis in their critique of the Brahmanic, orthodox teachings. These circumstances forced Nyaya to develop ways to logically defend and criticize mainstream teachings. Both the Nyaya and Vaisheshika schools work together to undermine Buddhist skepticism concerning the validity and source of knowledge.

Nyaya was later divided into the Older Nyaya and New Nyaya, or the Older and New Logic schools, in about the thirteenth century. The most important proponents of the New Logic school were Gangesa and his brilliant student Raghunatha.

The primary text of the Nyaya school is Gautama's famous *Nyayasutra,* a portion of which is included at the end of this chapter. His technique is extremely methodical. The text points to sixteen categories or questions that must be addressed in any sound theory of knowledge. Some of these categories concern the sources of knowledge, the objects of knowledge, and the aim of knowledge. Although it is beyond the scope of this text to go into detail concerning each one of the categories, we will examine some of the more important features of valid knowledge.

Nyaya claims that there are four sources of valid knowledge: perception, inference, comparison, and verbal testimony. Let's consider each in turn.

Perception   Perception occurs when there is contact between our senses and an object. However, this perception is not immediate, for it involves six senses: the five usual senses of sight, hearing, touch, smell, and taste, and a sixth, internal sense called mind, or *manas.*

To illustrate, suppose my seeing comes into contact with a bird outside my window. Along with seeing the bird, my mind transmits this impression to the unconscious *atman,* my genuine self. Nyaya upholds that the *atman* is by nature unconscious. This signal from the mind stimulates consciousness in the *atman. Manas* is that feature of mind that connects with *atman* and thus arouses consciousness, or *buddhi.* This results in the perception, "There is a bird."

We see from this that my perception takes place in two stages. It is first indeterminate, without assigning any attributes. This is pure perception without any idea about the perception. It then becomes determinate, and the perception is characterized and defined. Note also that *atman* and mind are distinct. Even though *atman* is the true knower, once it is conscious it is not on that account identified with mind.

What is most important in this is that the object of my sense impression, a bird, must exist in order for such an impression to occur. In this aspect, the Nyaya school supports a realist epistemology. There is, in actuality, an object of my knowledge.

The theory is much more complex than this scant skeleton description. What is important for us to remember is that the collaboration of the externally oriented senses (sight, sound, smell, touch, and taste) and the internal sense of mind produces perception. Moreover, not only does this process produce the perception of outside objects such as birds, but also the perception of internal events such as feelings. Perception is thus a source of valid knowledge.

In the previous example it seems that perception can occur only through some sense medium. This is the usual type of perception. However, Nyaya teaches that knowledge is also possible through unusual, or extraordinary means of perception. Nyaya asserts three distinct kinds of this exceptional perception. The first kind occurs when I simultaneously perceive the universal as well as the particular. In other words, not only do I perceive an individual bird, but also the universal of "birdness" that is shared by all birds. In this way I can indirectly perceive all other birds, not only this one bird I perceive directly.

Second, we can make sensory associations through perception. When I see a bird, I may also see that it looks light in weight. But such lightness is a feature of the tactile sense, so in this case my visual sense also connects with the tactile sense. My mind identifies a visual object with lightness, and yet there is no direct tactile contact.

Yoga is a path to the third kind of exceptional perception. Yogis are said to possess extraordinary powers of perception, seeing objects and events at long distances without the medium of ordinary sensory contact. It is claimed that this phenomenon demonstrates the power of the infinite *atman*, unconfined within any psycho-physical parameters. It is precisely the confinement of the infinite self within my body that is a source of my ignorance and suffering.

In this regard, knowledge obtained through ordinary sensory contact is limited because it is still obtained through inherently imperfect bodily mechanisms. One purpose behind Patanjali's *Yoga Sutras* is to offer some techniques to free oneself from bodiliness through a concentration that assumes a mind-body unity.

Inference   The second source of valid knowledge is inference, a form of knowledge that already assumes some information from which a conclusion is made. Here is the classic example of inference in Indian philosophy:

There is fire somewhere on this mountain.
This is because there is smoke on this mountain.
If there is fire, there is smoke. For example, a kitchen filled with
    smoke is discovered to have fire.
This mountain has smoke in a similar manner.
Therefore, this mountain must have fire.[3]

Here we have a type of syllogism used to demonstrate inference. It is
a form of reasoning known as *tarka,* stated in five assertions:

1. The primary hypothesis: There is fire somewhere on this mountain.
   This is the *probandum,* or that which needs to be proven.
2. The principal reason(s) supporting this claim: There is smoke on the
   mountain.
3. The major theory behind the claim: Whenever there is smoke, there
   is also fire. There are also supporting examples (called middle terms).
   In this case, the example concerns smoke in the kitchen as an indication of fire in the kitchen. This need for example is very important in Nyaya logic, which demands a concrete, empirical basis for
   making claims.

       This major theory, or premise, is also crucial because it estab-
   lishes a relationship between fire and smoke (that is, between the
   major and the middle terms). Yet, it not only establishes a relationship between the individual things designated by the terms, but also
   with the entire class of things so designated. This entire class is
   known as the universal. In other words, the relationship in the
   premise is not only between a smoky mountain and a fiery kitchen,
   but between all things that have smoke and all things that are on fire.
4. This major premise and supporting examples are now applied to the
   case under consideration. Here we see that in a fashion similar to
   the kitchen, there is smoke on the mountain.
5. The conclusion is asserted: The claim made in the first assertion is
   reiterated, but this time with the weight of evidence.

In any case, the inference occurs because a particular sign (smoke) gives
rise to a particular explanation (the presence of fire). This five-step schema
is required in Nyaya for proper disciplined formulation in debates. The Nyaya
school addresses the various problems that arise because of insufficient attention to this process and puts forth an elaborate examination of various
fallacies or unsound reasoning. In addition, the initial claim is not to be construed as a definitive statement, but instead serves to invite further discussion and rebuttal. All hypotheses by their very nature are tentative.

What becomes evident in this is that causality—the relationship between
cause and effect—is an important ingredient in Nyaya logic. In this system,
there are three essential kinds of causes. The first is that cause that already
exists in a material way, out of which an effect is produced. The scholar P. T.
Raju calls this cause "inhering." The "inhering" cause of the great image
of Roshana Buddha (or the "Great Buddha") in the Todaiji Temple is the

material out of which it is made. Raju calls the second kind of cause "non-inhering," or "relational." It is the putting together of the material elements into that cohesive whole that we call the Great Buddha. The third type of cause is the "efficient" cause, or the builders themselves.[4]

The cause stands separately from the effect and is its antecedent. In addition, a specific cause will produce its specific effect. We need to be careful not to confuse an apparent cause with a real cause. For example, in applying Nyaya logic, we see that life and death cannot be viewed as a causal relationship, for life is not the cause of death. Even though there is a temporal sequence from life to death, the relation is not one of cause and effect. One very important point in Nyaya is that specific effects are definitely brought about by their specific causes, and none other.

Nyaya also teaches that the effect cannot exist until it exists as effect; that is, it does not already exist in some form within its cause. On this point Nyaya opposes the teaching in both the Samkhya-Yoga and the Vedanta schools, which declare that something cannot come from nothing; what exists must have already existed. Therefore, what exists as effect must somehow preexist in its cause, just as the cause is another effect, which preexists in another cause, and so on.

According to Nyaya, the effect does not exist in any way prior to its existence as effect. Before it exists as effect, it is nonbeing, or *a-sat*. This theory is called *asatkaryavada,* the theory of the "prior non-being of the effect."[5]

In its views on reality and particularly on the nature of this universe, the Nyaya school upholds Vaisheshika metaphysics. Therefore, the material, inhering cause of the universe are the indestructible atoms (of earth, air, fire, and water). The efficient cause of the universe is, of course, *Brahman,* or God. In this way we see that Nyaya's realist epistemology offers a logical support for the Vaisheshika atomist theory.

Comparison   Similarity or comparison is the next ground of valid knowledge for the Nyaya school. Here we note a thing's similarity to something with which we are familiar. (A comparison is implied in the example of smoke in the kitchen and smoke on the mountain.) This is particularly how we familiarize ourselves with new terminologies. The Sanskrit term for comparison is *upamana,* which is somewhat like analogy. (For Buddhists, *upamana* is essentially included under testimony and inference, whereas in the Samkhya school it is another label for inference.)

Verbal Testimony   Verbal testimony is the fourth ground for valid knowledge in the Nyaya school. The term for this is *agama.* Testimony comes from a person who is authoritative and reliable. In the case of the Vedas, the reliability of their teachings comes from the belief that they are the teachings of *Brahman,* or God. As we have said, the seers were convinced of the divine authority of these teachings through *sruti,* or being heard. The reliability of the Vedas, therefore, is different from that of humans; only humans who are trustworthy can convey dependable knowledge.

Right knowledge comes about through correspondence between an object known and the knowing. Absent this correspondence, there are no grounds for asserting truth.

As the sources of invalid, incorrect knowledge, the Nyaya school posits memory, doubt, error, and *tarka* (hypothesis).[6] As for the objects of knowledge, Gautama noted twelve, the most important being *atman,* or true self. Also included are the body, senses, sense-objects, consciousness, and mind.[7]

New Logic (Navya Nyaya) School

The New Logic school has been particularly influential since the thirteenth century. This school came about through the amalgamation of Nyaya and Vaisheshika teachings. Gangesa, regarded as the founder of the New Logic school, offers a brilliant defense of Nyaya teachings against the sharp criticism leveled by the Advaitin scholar Sriharsa.

The New Logic school became so convincing in its methodology that other schools adopted its analytic posture. For instance, even though Mimamsa and Vedanta refuted earlier ideas in the traditional Nyaya school, they later used the logic of *Navya-nyaya* (Neo-Nyaya). Indeed, the New Logic school offers a rich field of analytic investigation and illustrates all the more the critical mindedness of Indian philosophers. It also anticipates many ideas that only later became more current in Western linguistic philosophy and symbolic logic.

The chief thrust of this New Logic school appears to be the need to clearly define terms of logical analysis. It maintains the correlation between an object's real existence and the ability to produce a precise definition of it. In other words, what is real can be strictly defined.[8] One of its most important teachings is that negation itself can be perceived. The selections at the end of this chapter demonstrate aspects surrounding the defining of negation, or "absence."

The Hindu scholar B. K. Matilal prefers to use the term *absence* instead of negation for the Sanskrit *abhava*.[9] In our discussion of the Nyaya school's sources of valid knowledge, we saw that "absence," or *abhava,* is not one of them. Nevertheless, the Old Logic school maintained that it *is* an object of knowledge, for absence can be inferred. For example, a withering plant may infer the absence of proper soil. This is a difficult topic. Still, negation provides a basis for metaphysics and is an interesting paradigm for Nyaya logic. (The difficulty of the readings may perhaps challenge some students to explore Nyaya logic further.)

In the first reading at the end of this chapter, we have Gautama's propositions in his *Nyayasutra* along with Vatsyayana's famous commentary; they address the problem of whether or not absence can be an object of knowledge or cognition. Gautama argued against an imaginary opponent that it can. The next reading is Gangesa's further defense of this proposition, again refuting opposing arguments, from his famous *Tattvacintamani.* Notes included in this rendition are by Matilal and are included to provide some clarity. Then, a brief section from the beginning of Raghunatha's *Nan-vada* is also included at the end of this chapter; it depicts his defense of these propositions in more definitional terms. He introduced the semantic character of negative particles: no-, non-, un-, and so on. He therefore discussed negation in more linguistic categories, and his argument moved to an analysis of features inherent in the Sanskrit language.[10] Moreover, his discussion elaborated in great detail on the meanings contained within sentences.

Today there seems to be increasing interest in the classic Nyaya teachings. Many current thinkers are both defending some Nyaya ideas and applying them to areas such as ontology, epistemology, and logic.

Yoga School: Restraining Citta

Although the Yoga school does not offer a theory of knowledge as such, it declares that knowledge in itself is not enough. Its view of knowledge is therefore one of the actualization of knowledge.

The Yoga school is associated with Samkhya. As we recall, Samkhya teaches us that the first thing that comes from the association of *prakriti* with *purusha* is reason. This is called *citta* in Yoga. *Citta* brings about the evolution of all other things and continues to manifest itself in a multitude of ways. The essential aim in yoga, therefore, is to somehow contain the force of *citta.*

One way this can be done is to channel its manifestation into a single path or point, which enables the traffic of thoughts to be fixed and reduced. Therefore, the concentration of one's mind is essential. This demands a strict practice of yoga. The school teaches various methods of concentration in order to release the hold our intellect has on us. Yoga techniques help to establish a collaboration between the mental and the physical.

In doing this, the system of Yoga offers a rather sophisticated analysis of the human body, including the relationship between its constituent nervous centers, or *chakras,* and the body's energy source, or *kundalini.* Yoga uses proper posture, breathing, and concentration to arouse this energy source, so that harmony between the physical and the mental can occur.

Vedanta Schools

Sankara's View of Knowledge   In determining whether or not the world is an illusion, remember that Sankara avoided the extreme position of Gaudapada, who literally believed that the world does not exist. Although Sankara admitted the existence of the world, he also held that the world as ordinarily perceived is illusion, and that we are constantly under this spell of illusion, or *maya.* This has a direct bearing on Sankara's theory of knowledge.

Advaita Vedanta points to a distinction between mundane knowledge and higher knowledge. Mundane knowledge is superficial knowledge, knowledge of the world we normally experience. Higher knowledge is knowledge of a deeper, genuine Reality. This ultimate Reality is *Brahman,* which is one's Self.[11]

As ultimate Reality, *Brahman* cannot be known through ordinary intellectual means. The knowledge of *Brahman* is an intensely intimate and permeating experience that is intuitive and immediate. We normally cannot grasp this Reality because we are under the customary cloud of *maya* and are therefore ignorant of our natures.

This is not to denigrate the value of ordinary knowledge, which is necessary for us to function properly. Mundane knowledge does have its legitimate role: "The entire complex of phenomenal existence is considered as true as long as the knowledge of Brahman being the Self of all has not arisen; just as the phantoms of a dream are considered to be true until the sleeper wakes."[12] Therefore, within our ordinary existence in which we have not attained higher knowledge, lower knowledge is valuable and necessary.

All we need to know about the world we live in can be known through this lower knowledge. In contrast to the Nyaya school, Advaita Vedanta assumes six sources of valid knowledge, or *pramanas*. Sankara may have assumed only three sources of cognition: perception, inference, and verbal testimony; his students and later exponents apparently accepted the Mimamsa scheme of six grounds, which are the means to obtain knowledge about this phenomenal world.

Before we look at these six sources, note that Sankara proposed that there is already an inherent degree of validity in cognition due to the conditions for knowledge. If I see a moving object outside my window and believe that it is a rabbit, then there is an assumption on my part that my judgment is, at least temporarily, valid.[13] Only if my judgment can be contradicted can it be refuted. The determining standard rests on the principle of noncontradiction.

This original assumption of validity proposed by the Advaitins is rejected by the Nyaya school, in which the criterion for the validity of a belief is its correspondence with what is real. Recall the process involved in inference in the Nyaya position, which points to the need for empirical support and practical application as demonstrated in the five steps of inference. For the Advaitin, the major premise is a key element in the argument. Yet, if one uses the methodology of Nyaya, this major premise in turn needs further support and justification. In other words, the supposition "All times there is smoke are times there is fire" warrants further justification. Resorting to inferences in this manner can go on almost endlessly. Therefore, instead of emphasizing the role of inference, the Advaitin stresses the principle of noncontradiction as the decisive factor in whether or not a belief is valid.[14]

Now let us look at the six *pramanas* or sources of valid cognition: perception, inference, comparison, verbal testimony, postulation, and noncognition.[15] As with the Nyaya school, *perception* originates out of an initial contact between sense and sense-object. Perception can be either indeterminate or determinate. Indeterminate perception is that preconceptual encounter without any designation of the specific object. Once this designation occurs, the perception is determinate. Again, as in the Nyaya school, mind, or *manas*, collects this sensory data and then integrates the object within itself. However, it does not do this of its own power but through the power of self, the *atman*, which is conscious. In contrast to the Nyaya belief, Advaita Vedantins hold that *atman* is naturally conscious and thus already actively committed to empirical "realities." Perception, therefore, is not a distancing between self and object, but an involvement with the object on the part of the self.

Another means for valid cognition is *inference.* Inference, as with other schools, is derivative knowledge, or knowledge that results from some association with other information. In the Advaita school, inference is valued for its more pragmatic role; that is, as long as it cannot be contradicted, its propositions are tentatively asserted. Inference is helpful in obtaining knowledge on the mundane level of phenomenal reality because "if all reasoning were unfounded, the whole course of practical human life would have come to an end."[16]

Analogies, or *comparisons,* are the third source of cognition. They are quite useful in illuminating phenomenal reality. Analogies are often used in Indian literature. It is important that they not be viewed as rhetorical or dialectical devices, for they are not intended to demonstrate rigorously the truth or falsity of claims. Analogies are not intellective tools; instead, they are devices used to induce a more personal sense or experience of an idea or proposition.

Verbal testimony is sanctioned by most orthodox schools. This enables the Vedas to assume great authority in its teachings, in which both the words themselves and their utterance are important. This power of words is called their *sakti.* Throughout Indian thought in general, a special emphasis is placed on the sounds of words.[17]

Postulation, the fifth source of valid cognition, means asserting a specific fact or rule. This kind of assertion is usually enacted to resolve some dispute.

Finally, *noncognition* results in the knowledge of negation. The question here is, how does one know of absence? (As previously mentioned, this is the question addressed in the first three selections at the end of this chapter.[18])

Ramanuja's View of Knowledge   Sankara depicted the nature of Brahman as *nirguna,* or without attributes. Ramanuja criticized this position. For Ramanuja, there is a need for attributes. To claim that *Brahman* is without attributes is a misinterpretation of the Upanishadic statement "*neti neti*" (not this, not this). Ramanuja not only had a different view of reality from Sankara, but he also proposed a different theory of knowledge.

For Ramanuja, there exists three *pramanas,* or means of valid cognition: perception, inference, and verbal confirmation. This verbal confirmation is the testimony given in the Vedas concerning God. For Ramanuja, the earlier Vedas depicting rituals and ways to worship God are just as significant as the later Vedas discussing the nature of God. (This is not so with Sankara, who contended that the later Vedas intend a higher realization of Brahman, beyond ritual and intellect.) Therefore, verbal testimony is an equally important factor in knowing God, and the ritual expressions are necessary tokens on the path to knowledge.[19]

Radhakrishnan's Synthesis of Vedanta Schools

In his *Idealist View of Life,* Radhakrishnan attempted to integrate the positions of Sankara and Ramanuja. One way in which he undertook this was by emphasizing the foundational aspect of intuition. On a cognitive level, the qualified nondualism of Ramanuja makes sense, and there appears to be a distinction between the world and *Brahman*. On an intuitive level, however, ordinary distinctions are blurred and an integration between God and world becomes obvious through personal realization.

Radhakrishnan posited intuition as the **ground** for all other forms of thought, and he contrasted intuition and **intellect**. He claimed that it is precisely through intuitive knowledge that we know the self. In fact, this "self-knowledge . . . seems to be the only true and direct knowledge we have; all else is inferential."[20] A selection from Radhakrishnan's *Idealist View of Life* is found at the end of this chapter.

Buddhist Perspectives

The Buddhist aim in any inquiry is to achieve some modicum of truth. Truth, for orthodox Indians and Buddhists, is not the result of logical analysis, but instead comes from *prajna,* "wisdom," or better still, the "eye of wisdom." *Prajna* is a total personal realization.

Buddhists constantly remind us of the limitations of ordinary knowledge. This is why the Buddha often insisted upon silence as a response to metaphysical questions. This does not mean that as a teaching Buddhism is essentially skeptical with regard to knowledge. Rather, Buddhism emphasizes the need for critical thinking based on solid empirical evidence and for applying the test of experience. The target of Buddhist criticism is groundless speculation.

Let us first note that Buddhist epistemology is not at all homogenous. There are various positions on a number of questions. Nevertheless, Buddhists are of one voice in their rejection of the authority of the Vedas and in their acceptance of the Four Noble Truths.

The Buddhist critique of the infallibility of Vedic teaching finds support in an appeal to ordinary experience. In this regard, there is no concentrated effort to provide a theory of knowledge in the early development of Buddhism. Yet, due to more sophisticated analyses from opposing schools such as the Nyaya, explanations of knowledge were formed and became more elaborate.

Buddhist Sources of Knowledge

Most Buddhists accept only perception and inference as sources for valid knowledge. This demonstrates the more empirical thrust of their teachings. Verbal testimony is ruled out as a source of knowledge; instead, listening to testimony and accepting it can be reduced to both perception and inference.

Many Buddhists define perception as an indeterminate contact between sense and sense-object. This is perception of an object without the accompanying classification of the object. What is especially important is that the object of perception is always of something specific or particular, not of something universal. (Universals enter in with inference.) This is essential because, for Buddhists, the relationship between the particular and the universal is not a real one. The particular is simply given a name (bird or stone, for example) in order to distinguish it from all other things. It is not viewed as actually being a member of a larger class (the universal). Buddhists are nominalists in that they do not assign any real existence to the class of universals. Universals—for example, the class of stones or birds—are merely useful names.[21]

The criterion for valid knowledge is not the principle of noncontradiction, which is a purely formal principle. The criterion for validity lies in the functional value of knowledge itself. This is because Buddhists do not separate existing from acting. Being and acting mutually define each other. Therefore, it is the capacity to result in an anticipated action that is the test of validity.

Early Buddhism (Theravada)

Sarvastivada   Sarvastivadins believed in the real existence of constituent elements called *dharmas.* In order to account for the continuity among these *dharmas,* Sarvastivadins claimed further that there is some sort of underlying eternal nature. This view was enhanced by their belief that each *dharma* was momentarily fixed in time and space.

From this metaphysical position, their theory of knowledge and perception becomes clear. Due to the momentary, static quality in *dharmas,* our perception of the world can be direct; our sense organs can come into contact with things as they are. If everything is always changing, as we find in the later Sautrantika school, then our perceptions would be indirect and would capture only a fleeting representation or trace of each moment.

Sautrantika and Vaibhashika   The Sarvastivadin school was later split into two further schools, the Sautrantika and the Vaibhashika. The real differences between them center on their theories of knowledge. For both the Sautrantika and Vaibhashika schools, perception assumes a strong connection between consciousness and its object. The nature of this connection is a point of contention. Let us briefly look at each position.

For the Sautrantika school, nothing is actually "real" in an objective sense. This view refutes the notion of *svabhava,* an eternal nature underlying things. Only each present moment exists, but the nature of each moment is not to the slightest degree permanent.

This means that, for the Sautrantikas, the connection between consciousness and its object is one of similarity. Consciousness is similar to its object because it "coincides with . . . the form of the object," an idea referred to as a "representative theory of perception."[22] In this case, it is only through inference that we establish that there is an object, because it is not actually perceived. Therefore, for Sautrantika, only inference is a valid means for knowledge.

On the other hand, adherents of the Vaibhashika school are known as "substantival realists." This means that they believe that all phenomena are real and can be reduced to various kinds of substances, such as those that are physical and those that are mental. This also means that the connection between consciousness and its object is one of identity. Vaibhashika adherents believe that there is a direct perception of the object, an idea called the "presentative theory of perception."[23] Here there is an identity between the form of consciousness and the form of the object. Illusion comes about when we confuse a form for an object that is not of that object.

Mahayana Schools

Nagarjuna: Knowledge and **Sunya**   Nagarjuna's dialectic is a monument in Indian critical analysis and has considerable epistemological merit. He deftly applied the meaning of *sunya* to both knowledge and reality itself. In his great work, *Madhyamika Karikas,* he offered a deconstructive view in which nothing can actually be claimed about reality, whether positive, negative, both, or neither. Whereas the Vijnanavada school posed *vijnana* as ultimately real, Madhyamika goes further in asserting that what is real is void. All that can be said is that ultimate reality is *sunya,* void, emptiness. And *sunya* does not mean nothingness, but that which lies beyond anything positive or negative, neither Being nor non-Being.

Sunyata requires a way of knowing in which conceptualization is fundamentally bracketed. By this we mean that our ordinary way of knowing is, at least temporarily, suspended so that we can see and know a thing, person, or event in its pure state of being, as it is. Our conventional way of knowing is, for Nagarjuna, an entrapment in ignorance.

Therefore, perception and inference may be legitimate grounds for ordinary knowledge, but they are ineffective in attaining genuine knowledge of ultimate reality. Because reality lies beyond subject-object dualities, any cognition assuming these is, in the long run, false. Nevertheless, we live in a world that is our field of action. For this reason, knowledge, albeit on this ordinary level, can be said to be either valid or invalid.[24]

Yogacara (Vijnanavada)   The Yogacara school contributes more to a theory of knowledge than many of the other Buddhist schools. It accepts the theory of perception proposed by the Vaibhashika school. But, whereas Vaibhashika adherents believe in the separate existence of the object of perception, members of the Yogacara school reject any independent existence of the object.

For Yogacara, nothing exists outside of consciousness, and ultimate reality is absolute consciousness. Therefore, knowing this ultimate reality is a matter of intuition rather than intellection. This is the higher level of knowing, so that what we know through perception and inference is still not genuinely true because the objects of perception and inference do not in themselves exist.

Nevertheless, on a mundane or practical level, knowledge enables us to act appropriately in this world. Cognition is thus given a more functional role. Even though the world we experience is itself a projection of consciousness, we still need to be able to live within this world. In this regard, the only genuine grounds for mundane knowledge are perception and inference.

The criterion for valid cognition is whether or not the knowledge leads to effective action. If the object of my knowledge is a glove, then effective activity deals in some way with wearing the glove.

Inference enables me to relate knowledge and action. This can come about because, in contrast to the immediacy of perception, inference deals with universals. Recall that inference is especially illustrated by the *tarka* in Hindu thought. In this *tarka,* or syllogism, the Nyaya school posited five constructs. In contrast, the Buddhists maintain only two:

Wherever there is smoke, there is fire, as in the kitchen;
This mountain has smoke necessarily related to fire.[25]

Buddhist Logic

Dignaga's Teachings   The scholastic drive to engage in dialectic discussion and analyses evoked the need for an examination of the principles of logical inquiry. This was particularly urgent if Buddhists were to attain some degree of success in debating with Hindu scholars.

The real systematic exposition of Buddhist logic and epistemology comes from Dignaga, a pioneer in Indian logic. Although he was an adherent of the Yogacara school, Dignaga was also sympathetic to certain Sautrantika teachings. His epistemology is more difficult to describe and evaluate because few of his writings have survived.

Dignaga's most important concern was with the means of knowledge, or *pramana*. True knowledge must be based on proper grounds, and for Dignaga there were two grounds for cognition: perception and inference. The object of perception is the individual or the particular; the object of inference is the universal. This distinction later led him to question the reliability of the knowledge we obtain based on inference.

Dignaga described perception as a basic form of knowing without conceptualizing. What Dignaga meant by conceptualizing is a matter of interpretation. For some idea of his meaning we can resort to Kalupahana's analysis. Kalupahana contended that Dignaga sought to stay clear of the two extreme interpretations of realism and nominalism. The realist interpretation presumes a strict correspondence between the term and its object.[26] The nominalist interpretation merely views the term as a name and not as a designation of anything objective. In other words, the realist claims that terms are about real objects.

Because he sought to avoid both of these outlooks, Dignaga believed that perception is not totally devoid of conceptualizing, for it involves some concepts, or ideas of things. To an extent, perception involves the activity of mind, or *manas,* and the object of *manas* is an idea or concept.[27] Moreover, subjective biases are already present within perception; that is, any perception of an object is naturally tainted by internal as well as external conditions. For example, my own moods, state of health, and physical environment color my perception. Therefore, pure perception without any conceptualization does not occur.

Despite all this, perception does not entail metaphysical, or higher-level, concepts. As for the meaning of these higher-level concepts, Kalupahana cited Dignaga's example of the distinction between my perceiving "blue" and my knowing something "as blue."[28] My perceiving something blue involves knowing the concept of "blue." My knowing something "as blue" involves more: the recognition of blueness as universal, as an attribute of some object.[29]

Inference is the source of this higher level of cognition. It is the activity of mind that goes beyond direct perception. Evaluations also enter into this level of cognizing. We can therefore say that a higher level of conceptualizing comes about when consciousness becomes conscious of itself as being conscious. For example, it is one thing to directly perceive the newspaper; it is quite another to recognize myself as perceiving the newspaper. It is this latter that goes beyond direct perception and brings us into inference.

We know for a fact that not all of our knowing is a result of direct perception. Having never been in Wisconsin does not mean that Wisconsin does not exist. I can infer that it does exist from other objects of cognition, such as maps and testimonies of others who have been there. My knowledge of Wisconsin, however, remains indirect.

What is critically important in all of this is that the status of the objects that are known through inference does not reflect the status they occupied in direct perception. As we said earlier, the particular is the object of perception, whereas the universal is the object of inference. And this is why Dignaga refuted the actual existence (as well as nonexistence) of universals.

Dignaga's view of logic is especially important. He was critical of the supposition that a system of logic can reveal absolute truths. A good example of this is his theory of exclusion. Let us return again to the classic *tarka* of the smoke on the mountain. We see that the major premise is that wherever there is smoke, there is fire. Yet the truth of this premise is difficult to verify with absolute certainty. Furthermore, whether or not this premise is true affects the soundness of the entire argument. Because of this, Dignaga proposed a more inductive approach.

Logical analysis, although it seeks to reflect actual experience, is inherently separated from actualities. (For example, setting up dichotomies such as Being and Nothingness makes less sense than viewing the distinction as that between Being and non-Being.) Dignaga pointed out to us the limits of logic.

Dignaga trod the same path as the Buddha and Nagarjuna in warning us against the dangers of excessive abstraction. What we know through the two sources of cognition—perception and inference—is different from what is real. Both perception and inference have their limits; to assume that they provide absolute truths is a gross fallacy. Dignaga's teaching is an elaborate demonstration of the mechanisms involved in knowing and illustrates the inherent limits of logic and language.

Dharmakirti: Knowledge and Action   Even more significant, perhaps, is Dharmakirti, whose ideas became the basis for later formulations. His thought was especially influential in Tibet. A selection from his work is included at the end of this chapter.

Dharmakirti's special interest was not so much the nature of knowledge itself, but of knowledge as a basis for "successful action." For him, correct knowledge leads to appropriate action. The nexus between knowledge and action was stated by Dharmakirti at the very beginning of his famous work *Nyaya-bindu:*

> All successful human action is preceded by right knowledge. Therefore this (knowledge will be here) investigated.[30]

By grounding action in knowledge, Dharmakirti supplied his account with a strong empirical footing. His interest lay in knowledge as the basis for our everyday experience. In this respect, he emulated the Buddhist tradition and is in the company of the Buddha, Nagarjuna, and Dignaga in claiming that the test of reality or truth lies in experience.

Esoteric Buddhism

Esoteric forms of Buddhism illustrate the urge to transcend ordinary ways of knowing in order to reach a higher consciousness. The practice of rituals and techniques of concentration are means for the adept to reach deeper levels of awareness. True learning does not come about merely through reading scriptures or studying texts, but through the guidance of a spiritual mentor or guru. The goal in all this is union with the Absolute.

The Vajrayana school is an example. It embodies the metaphysics of the Yogacara-Madhyamika system. Its underlying premise is that the Buddha-nature within each one of us lies dormant; thus its goal is to awaken this aspect in us. How is this possible? Let us review some techniques.

Through discipline, the practitioner utilizes techniques of imaging transcendent Buddhas or *bodhisattvas,* our protectors and guides along our path to awareness. In essence, this image depicts our own Buddha-nature. With enough practice, we eventually identify with the image. And when this takes place, a sort of mystical union occurs. This union, sometimes represented in Buddhist art as the sexual union between male and female, links together the human and the divine aspects within each being.

Another important technique is the use of mantras, which are sacred utterances and syllables. Some of the more popular mantras address male and female deities. One of the most celebrated of mantras is the prayer to Avalokitesvara: *"Om Mani Padme Hum."*

Mudras—sacred gestures—are also utilized. They consist of ritualized movements of the hands and fingers that accompany the mantras. The ultimate result is a oneness among speech, mind, and body, as we see the interconnectedness between bodily and psychic states.

Chinese Philosophies

Chinese thought does not appear to have demonstrated the elaborate epistemology found in Indian systems. Yet, neither are epistemological concerns absent in Chinese philosophy. On the contrary, the unique linguistic character of Chinese eventually compelled Chinese thinkers to be more aware of the relationship between ways of knowing and thinking within the parameters of their language.[31] Yet, epistemological inquiry did not last for too long because there was greater interest in matters of practical and aesthetic concern.

Chuang Tzu

Chuang Tzu showed some degree of skepticism with regard to matters of knowledge. For instance, in his *Chuang-tzu* he illustrated how the validity of diverse viewpoints depends on various perspectives. When it comes to argumentation, determining the rightness or wrongness of each position most often depends on the acceptability of one's initial premises.

Chuang Tzu therefore stressed an underlying relativity in what we can and cannot know. (His famous chapter, "On Equality," supports this in describing the equality of all things.) In a sense, he represents many Chinese philosophers who do not accept a strict correspondence between our cognition and unchanging, enduring truths. And his skepticism is such that even he was skeptical of his own position.

Chuang Tzu did not claim that we cannot know anything at all. Rather, he countered what we think we know as absolute truth with his emphasis on relativity. What Chuang Tzu seems to suggest is that there is no universal discourse. And because we are discourse-dependent, Chuang Tzu points to the relativity of our positions.

The philosopher Fung Yu-lan described this aspect of Chuang Tzu by drawing a distinction between "having-no knowledge" and "having no-knowledge." For Fung, Chuang Tzu's position is that of "having no-knowledge," a state that comes about after we acquire knowledge and then transcend the boundaries of knowledge by recognizing its limits. On the other hand, "having-no knowledge" is the condition of original ignorance, a lack of knowledge.[32]

Confucianists

Confucius and Mencius

Confucius undoubtedly provided one of the best examples of the love for learning. Learning in itself cannot be divorced from the learner, for personal cultivation is the aim. All the disciplines in philosophy—logic, epistemology, metaphysics, and so on—have value only insofar as they can be applied to human conduct. They seek to improve the life of each human being, both internally and externally, in his or her relation with the world. This is called cultivating the "Inner Sage" and the "Outer King." Knowledge is not valued for its own sake; purely abstract discussions without any empirical value are generally disdained. Personal moral cultivation remains the test of truth. We see this view throughout Chinese philosophy.

A good example of this outlook lies in the philosophy of Mencius. For Mencius, it is precisely our ability to think that constitutes our human essence. (This is illustrated by Wang Ch'ung in his critique of superstitious beliefs in the selection at the end of this chapter.) We can know our own natures by exercising our mind, and this thinking must be done with the proper attitude of sincerity. Sincerity remains a principal virtue, and its Chinese term is *ch'eng*. Cultivating character requires sincere deliberation. According to Mencius,

> The difference between a man and an animal is slight. The common man disregards it altogether, but the True Gentleman guards the distinction most carefully. Sun understood all living things, but saw clearly the relationships that exist uniquely among human beings. These relationships proceed from Humanity and Justice. It is not because of these relationships that we proceed towards Humanity and Justice.[33]

Therefore, genuine learning, in Mencius's view, leads us to discover "Humanity and Justice." This is possible because latent within us lie the seeds of the four virtues: *jen, i, li,* and *chih*.

Hsun Tzu: Correspondence of Names

One topic of interest during the period of a Hundred Schools was the meaning of names. Just what is the relationship between actual life and the names we assign within our actual life? This issue is called the "rectification of names." Hsun Tzu was the first to tackle this question more logically. Confucius and Mencius were also interested in the rectification of names, and they treated this inquiry within the context of their ethical philosophy. We can say the same for Hsun Tzu. However, with Hsun Tzu, we see a more nearly complete attempt at purely logical analysis. The Chinese scholar Wing-tsit Chan described his approach as the "nearest approach to logic in ancient Chinese philosophy."[34]

For Hsun Tzu, the purpose of devising names is to point to realities so that, based on practice, there would be a natural correspondence between the name and the reality. In addition, the purpose for naming is to discriminate among things as well as to indicate resemblances. Different things have different names, and similar things have similar names.

Fallacies occur when there is a lack of correspondence between names and the realities they designate. For example, Hsun Tzu pointed to a fallacy in the Mohist's statement that "to kill a robber is not to kill a man." He claimed that this is a misuse of names because the designation "robber" still falls within the class of "man."[35]

For Hsun Tzu, three kinds of fallacies can occur due to the misappropriation of names:

1. "Using names as to confuse names." The Mohist's statement illustrates this. Here, we have a wrong application of both "robber" and "man."
2. "Using actualities as to confuse names." Hsun Tzu cited the example referred to in Chuang Tzu (Chapter 33): "The desires seek to be few." "Desires" are real experiences that are in the realm of the particular; they can be specific desires. The name "desires," however, can also designate the class of desires to which the particular belongs. If it is the case that there is a particular manifestation of desires that "seek to be few," it would be illogical to infer that this is the nature of desires as a universal. (In traditional Western logic, this is somewhat comparable to hasty generalization.)
3. "Using names to confuse actualities." Here, Hsun Tzu illustrated with "A [white] horse is not a horse." As we will see, this is the famous theme in Kung-sun Lung. Certainly, a particular white horse is not identical to the universal "horse," yet particular horses do belong to the class of horse. In this case, it appears that the interpretation of "is not" is skewed in Kung-sun Lung's example and does not correspond to reality. This correspondence is the chief reason for names, and their valid use depends on this criterion.

School of Names (Logicians)

The relationship between real life and names assigned in real life was of interest and concern to Chinese philosophers. Different philosophical schools treated this subject from different perspectives. Taoists approached this issue from a metaphysical view; Confucianists were interested in this issue from a moral perspective. Hsun Tzu's work was the first attempt at logical analysis, although his fundamental interest in the question grew out of his moral teaching.

The School of Names, or Logicians, was interested in this from a purely formal point of view. Yet, due to the Chinese temperament and practicality, their influence on Chinese thought remains minimal.

Hui Shih and Kung-sun Lung are representatives of this school. Hui Shih's celebrated paradoxes demonstrate that all concepts possess a relative nature. In contrast, Kung-sun Lung pointed to a permanency behind concepts, as seen in his discussion of the white horse.

In his classic essay on this subject, "The White Horse Discourse," Kung-sun Lung intended to demonstrate logically that "a white horse is not a horse." He does this through a series of arguments containing a unique and complex stream of reasoning. The complexity is all the more compounded by inherent difficulties in the Chinese language. His purpose was to distinguish between the abstract and the concrete, or between the universal and the particular, and the Chinese language makes this quite difficult.

In Chinese, the term that describes a specific horse can also be used to designate the abstract idea of horse; that is, the Chinese term can designate both the particular and the universal. *Ma,* the Chinese term for horse, can therefore mean "horse" as a universal, "a horse" as a particular, or "the horse" as specific.[36]

To be sure, Kung-sun Lung was quite aware of the insurmountable practical difficulties his thesis—"a white horse is not a horse"—presents in actual life. It would be difficult for a thief to persuade a farmer that the farmer's white horse is not really a horse. Let us briefly summarize his argument in his White Horse Discourse.

In the statement "A white horse is not a horse," the object-term "horse" refers to the universal aspect of horse. On the other hand, "a white horse" refers to a particular horse. This particular is not the same as the universal. Even the term "white horse" has the qualifier "white," which can also refer to the universal idea of white, even though in its use here it is designated to be this white horse. "White" here is specific with respect to the horse and does not designate the universal of whiteness.

Kung-sun Lung had a number of aims in this discourse. One was to describe the difference between the particular and the universal. This being the case, what is referred to by "white horse" is different from "horse." Therefore, "a white horse is not a horse."

Kung-sun Lung also attempted to be clear about the meaning of a universal by identifying the three features of universals. First, universals are not the same as actual things. *Chih,* the Chinese term for "universal," literally means "to point to," or "finger." As a "pointing to," the universal is a name. And this is the crucial point, for a name does two things: It points to an actual thing, and it points to a universal that encompasses the actual thing. Second, universals are both distinct and independent. The two universals in our example are "whiteness" and "horseness," each of which can exist independently of the other. He discussed this further in other essays. Thus, in his "Discourse on Hard and White," the subject is a hard, white stone. In perceiving a hard, white stone, Kung-sun Lung revealed that both hardness and whiteness are separate and independent universals. The visual perception of the stone captures its whiteness; the tactile perception takes in its hardness. Both are distinct. Third, universals remain "concealed." As universals, they cannot be perceived, but reveal themselves only in actual things, or particulars. The universal manifests itself within the particular, and the particular cannot be what it is unless the universal exists.[37]

Because universals are independent and separate, they continue to exist even though they cannot be perceived as such until they are manifested in the concrete.

Ch'an Buddhism: No-Mind

Any attempt to uncover any specific theory of knowledge in Ch'an Buddhism is perplexing, for the goal for the Ch'an Buddhist school is to reach a state of liberation beyond mind and knowledge. This is called the state of no-mind whereby one is identified with *wu,* which is interpreted as the original mind and not as literal nothingness. Experiencing this state is intensely personal. Although it is ineffable, it is still powerfully known by the one who experiences it.

Ch'an Buddhists claim that the state of no-mind, or no-thought, is genuine freedom—freedom from feelings and even freedom from thought. Freedom from feelings does not mean that there are no feelings, but rather that one is not attached to one's feelings. As long as we cling to feelings, we are not free from them.

In the same way, the state of no-thought means that we are free from thought. This does not mean the absence of thought, but freedom from attachment to our thoughts. For instance, the devoted student of Hui-neng, Shen-hui, criticized the Hinayana Buddhist:

> The śrāvaka (adherent of Hīnayāna), cultivating and abiding in emptiness (k'ung), is bound by that emptiness; cultivating and abiding in intent meditation (samādhi or ting), he is bound by that meditation; cultivating and abiding in quiescence (ching), is bound by that quiescence; cultivating and abiding in silence (chi), is bound by that silence.[38]

Ch'an Buddhism provides a disciplined method to free the mind from its attachment to ideas and feelings. Accordingly, it is hardly an escape from the world. In fact, it synthesizes a unique blend of transcendence and immanence. It means viewing the mountain and the river in a different way: Before awakening, the mountain is a mountain and the river is a river; upon awakening, the mountain and the river still remain what they are, but the experience of the mountain and the river is radically changed because the experiencer is changed. The experiencer is now awakened and is no longer attached to the ideas, concepts, or feelings concerning the mountain and the river. The experiencer is now a sage, and in this way the sage can truly act and be totally present:

> Simply void your entire mind: this is to have unpolluted wisdom. Daily go out, stay at home, sit, or sleep, but in every word you say, do not attach yourself to the things of purposeful activity. Then, whatever you say or wherever you look, all will be unpolluted.[39]

Wang Yang-ming: Intuitive Knowledge

Wang Yang-ming had no systematic theory of knowledge and posited the importance of intuition over intellection. He believed that the mind possesses an innate "intuitive knowledge" of things. Wang's emphasis on intuition was a response to Chu Hsi's rationalism. All things share in this intuitive knowledge, or Heavenly Principle; principle and mind are the same. But here he parted company with Chu Hsi on at least two counts. First, Chu Hsi assumed a distinction between mind and principle, and between li and ch'i, whereas Wang did not. Second, Chu Hsi stressed the intense investigation of things in order to arrive at an understanding of their principle. For Wang, since mind is principle, an understanding of principle lies in the understanding of mind and not through the investigation of external objects or things. Thus, rather than investigate the external to discover principle, Wang recommended that we become more aware of the internal, our mind and original nature, which necessitates an attitude of sincerity.

Chang Tung-sun: Culture and Knowledge

In the theory of knowledge, Chang Tung-sun stands out as one of the most influential of contemporary philosophers in China. He developed a cohesive system of epistemology, which he referred to as an "epistemological criticism."[40] Chang pointed out the synthetic character of knowledge; that is, knowledge is the integration of sensations, perceptions, and conceptions. A selection from his "A Chinese Philosopher's Theory of Knowledge" is included at the end of this chapter.

What Chang intended to demonstrate is that the ordering of our knowledge is not the sole prerogative of the mind. There already exists some order in the world that our mind integrates. In this respect, cultural factors are an indelible aspect in the knowing process. He underscores the interrelationship between culture and knowing.

With respect to knowledge and culture, Chang asserted that ideas and theories are the glue that holds a society together. Ideas are therefore valued because they essentially reflect social needs and truths. Therefore, cultural constructs play a leading role in the knowing process; there is an intimate relation between social dynamics and concepts.[41]

■■■■■ Japanese Philosophies ■■■■■

As in China, Japanese theories of knowing are to a great extent tempered by inherent features within the language. The Japanese language is quite rooted in Chinese, using Chinese characters along with its own syllabary systems of *katakana* and *hiragana*. The character, or ideograph, plays a dominant role in how ideas are conceived. In addition, a character can assume a variety of meanings, depending on its use and context.

The Japanese language therefore seems less conducive to abstract formal expression, which contributes to the absence of an abstract, formalized epistemology throughout Japanese thought. Perhaps the closest approximation to Western formalism is in the philosophy of Nishida Kitaro. Yet, even with Nishida, the substance of his logic is quite consistent with Japanese tradition. The language is filled with imagery and is more emotive than intellectual. And clearly, Japanese thought highlights intuitive thinking, as will be apparent when we review some attempts to form a theory of knowing.

Japanese Buddhism

Tendai School: Higher Knowledge as Samadhi

The Tendai Japanese school essentially adopted most of the teachings of its counterpart, T'ien-t'ai, in China. Tendai Buddhism was one of the two influential schools of Buddhism during the Heian period. (The other school was

Shingon.) Buddhism gained prominence during this time, especially under the patronage of the ruling Fujiwara clan.

Tendai teachings assume an important distinction between mundane knowledge and higher knowledge. According to its key text, the *Saddharma-pundarika-sutra (Lotus Sutra)*, those who realize the true nature of things experience higher knowledge and are the buddhas. Realizing the true nature of things means realizing their suchness, or *tathata,* the true state of things, whether or not we know them as such. Our empirical knowledge has no bearing on *tathata.*

In this realization, called *samadhi,* one is aware of *tathata,* the suchness of reality, and is one with suchness. This has also been called the highest state of wisdom, or perfect wisdom (*prajna-paramita*). The three paths to this higher knowledge—meditation, discipline, and insight—are referred to as the "three-fold learning."[42] What is most important to understand is that knowledge in this higher sense is not merely intellective; it permeates one's entire being. Wisdom pulsates through every fiber of a person, and the conventional dichotomies assumed in ordinary learning are transcended. These three paths underscore the faculty of intuition, which ultimately means the intuition concerning the essential oneness of all things.

Zen Buddhism

We can generally speak of two levels when discussing the question of knowledge: an ordinary level of subject and object, and a higher level of *prajna* or wisdom. The aim in Buddhism is to reach this higher level, and Japanese Buddhists follow in this long tradition. And for the more practically minded Chinese and Japanese, the pursuit of *prajna* meant less attention to formal epistemological questions.

The approaches to real knowledge in Buddhism are uniquely illustrated in various ways, ranging from the Buddhist sutras, especially the *Prajna-Paramita,* to Nagarjuna and Dogen. Probably the most extreme expression of Buddhist approaches to genuine knowing lies in the *mondos* and *koans* of Zen Buddhism.

A *koan* is a riddle or paradox (for example, entering the "gateless gate") used as a means to achieve enlightenment, or *satori.* At face value they defy all logical rules. The whole point of a *koan* is to exhaust the intellect in such a way that the mind is released to intuitive insight.

In other words, Buddhists recognize that we are involved not only in this world, but in its ways of thinking. The subject-object distinction is natural to us because we are naturally clouded by illusion, or *maya.* Our mind occupies many rooms, yet we are not aware of many rooms because intellect is the dominant way we think. And in this way we mistakenly conceive of knowing within subject/object, "I"/not-"I," self/world dualities. The *koan* exercise is a riddle that tests our reasoning to the limit, and we achieve insight only upon encountering this limit. Once we release ourselves from the tight grip of intellect, other ways of knowing, especially intuition, illuminate our thinking.

Therefore, the purpose of the *koan* is to remind us of the fallibility of our knowledge, to point to an underlying reality that cannot be grasped through ordinary ways of knowing. *Koans* are an important tool in Zen because they allow us to discover for ourselves the limits of intellect. If we maintain an open attitude, *koans* allow us to be shocked into awakening through intuition.

To illustrate, let's consider a classic *koan:*

What is the sound of one hand clapping?

There are at least three levels upon which we can perceive this koan.

At the first, most superficial level, the "sound of one hand clapping" is a contradiction. It defies our common understanding of what constitutes "clapping." It is contradictory because logic specifies what is illogical according to the principle of noncontradiction. This level of understanding assumes the ordinary subject-object dichotomy; accordingly, this *koan* makes no sense.

On a second level, the *koan* is obviously a riddle. Given what we know of and how we define "clapping," its question challenges logic. And, by meditating diligently upon this *koan,* we come to realize the limits of our reason in formulating a solution. Therefore, on this level of understanding, the *koan* reveals the limits of intellect.

The *koan* can be seen on yet another level. The *koan* itself is expressed through language, which is also used to point to reality. However, this reality can be properly understood only by transcending language. In other words, an essential ingredient in resolving the *koan* is to look beyond the language to its true meaning.

When this occurs, the experience is one of awakening, known as *satori.* It is an instant realization of the meaning *behind* the *koan,* not the meaning *of* the *koan.* Once we realize the meaning behind the *koan,* we experience its real truth, and it is no longer either a contradiction or a riddle.

Consider another famous *koan:*

A monk once asked master Joshu, "Has a dog the Buddha Nature or not?" Joshu said, "Mu."[43]

How can we grasp the meaning behind Joshu's response? Again, this *koan* can be viewed on different levels. On a superficial level, *mu* literally means "nonbeing," or nothingness, or even "no." But it does not really mean no as opposed to yes. Therefore, it appears as though Joshu could not give an answer one way or another.

On another level, *mu* means "nothingness," as that which transcends the ordinary distinction between yes and no. It means that ordinary distinctions are ultimately false, and that we therefore must transcend them in order to grasp the meaning of the *koan.* Put another way, on an ordinary level we differentiate between the dog and the human, and we also differentiate between ordinary nature and Buddha nature. Awakening to the real meaning behind the *koan* means realizing that ultimately there is no distinction.

Mu represents, in this sense, what has been called the "gateless barrier" (gateless gate) in Zen. How we approach *mu* will determine how we view the *koan*. On a purely logical level, the *koan* is treated superficially. Only when we dig deeper and discern the absence of differentiation do we discover the truth of the oneness of all things. The *koan* manifests the Zen belief that language is simply a pointer, a guidepost, to reality. To mistake the pointer for that to which it points is a common error from which the *koan* seeks to free us.

Dogen

Dogen, in Zen tradition, also pointed out the limits of intellect. In Dogen we again discover an unconventional epistemology. We see this, for example, in his *Genjokoan,* in which the path to Self does not lie in conceptual analysis.

Conceptual analysis remains self-referential, which means that our knowing assumes an individual self as the point of reference, as subject:

object—subject—object

Furthermore, it assumes an object of knowledge distinct from the subject. For Dogen, this "acting on and witnessing myriad things with the burden of oneself is 'delusion.' "[44]

The proper way to real Self-discovery is through practice, not through knowing. By practice, Dogen meant the practice of *zazen,* which leads to genuine knowing. Dogen therefore demanded that body-mind be let go.

Nishida Kitaro

Nishida respected the analytic tradition of the West by using Western categories to elucidate Eastern ideas, especially those of Zen Buddhism. This effort produced a unique logic. At the same time, from the start Nishida realized the inadequacies of language in understanding reality. For this reason, Nishida started with the particular individual in a world of lived experience; he then established that the defining aspect of the individual is its active involvement in this world. In turn, the world also acts upon the individual.

Acting Intuition

A crucial idea in Nishida's view of knowledge is his "acting intuition," a unique theory that has metaphysical as well as epistemological significance. Acting intuition essentially refers to action grounded upon intuition. And for Nishida, intuition is the basic way of knowing. Both acting and intuiting work together.

The term *intuition* is not very clear in Nishida. What is conspicuous is that, for Nishida, intuition is not viewed as a passive faculty. According to one commentator, to have intuition means that one must

> understand, as well as accept, the Being of the beings found in the world and to do so through the body's perceptual functions.[45]

This means that action and intuition are interdependent. In other words, the epistemological thrust we find in Nishida is tempered by the bodily character of our existence.

With Nishida's theory of acting intuition, the emphasis is placed on acting-within-the-world, rather than on reasoning-about-the-world, which reflects a more disembodied epistemology. This is very important. In this sense, intuition is regarded as an active force and is therefore not akin to the more passive sense-intuition.

This active aspect of acting intuition is like the pianist who has transcended the ordinary distinction between her and the music she plays. Moreover, there is no distinction between her and the piano. She is one with the piano, one with the keys, one with the music. Mental activity and physical activity are in harmony.

The same can be said for many artistic and athletic efforts. The martial artist is one with movement. No degree of intellection, no matter how slight, must interfere with the *kendo* master, or with the movement of a *kata* in karate. There is oneness with action. These are expressions of Nishida's acting intuition. Bodiliness no longer assumes the heaviness of objectivity, for objectivity is shattered. And the duality of subject-object is overcome through diligent practice and discipline. A selection concerning intuition from Nishida's *An Inquiry into the Good* is found at the end of this chapter.

Basho

This brings us to another key idea in Nishida's understanding of knowledge: his concept of *basho,* or place or field. Here we consider *basho* as it relates to Nishida's discussion of knowing. Nishida identified two kinds of *basho: yu no basho,* or the "basho of being," and *mu no basho,* or the "basho of nothingness."[46] The *basho* of being is the basis, or field, for all knowledge that still assumes a point of reference, the subject. We call this knowledge self-referential, and it is the cognitive standpoint we normally assume. Inquiry into the nature of reality often occurs on this self-referential level. This is demonstrated, for example, when we posit Being as ultimate reality. For Nishida, this level was not radical enough.

The *basho* of nothingness goes deeper. Whereas the *basho* of being continues to assume a self-referentiality, the *basho* of nothingness realizes that this perspective is incomplete. A genuine grounding goes deeper, and it is the ground of the *basho* of being. This deeper, more profound ground demands the negation of a self-reference—which is why it is the most challenging and difficult to comprehend.

Yet, how is it possible to negate self-reference? Consider the comments of the philosopher Yuasa Yasuo:

> Kant's consciousness in general is a logical abstraction from the empirical ego-consciousness. In contrast, Nishida's *basho* vis-a-vis nothing is the *basho* that can be reached by denying the fact that the self is such an ego-consciousness or, to be more precise, by letting it *disappear.* Stated differently, the ego-consciousness revealed in ordinary

experience has an invisible bottom layer. If we classify the ego-consciousness that relates itself to the everyday life-space as "the layer of bright consciousness," there is also the layer of the concealed, dark *cogito* at its base. "To immerse consciousness in the bottom of consciousness" is to look existentially into this layer of the dark *cogito* not apparent on the surface of consciousness.[47]

This means that there is a deeper level of knowing that forms the basis for our regular ways of knowing.

Pure Experience

We need to see all this in the wider context of Nishida's emphasis on pure experience, discussed in his *An Inquiry into the Good.* Pure experience is that immediate experience that occurs without the mediacy of reflection. It is prereflective, and the two modes of subject and object do not yet arise. This is our immediate contact with the world, and it is therefore pure and unblemished by ideas, concepts, evaluations, and judgments.[48]

Nishida and Aristotle

One way to understand Nishida's theory of knowledge is to contrast it with Aristotle's logic.[49] In Aristotle's formulation, predication of things involves some degree of classification. This means that the object is seen or implied as belonging to some category. In this way, the particular object is transcended by an implicit appeal to its category, or universal. Therefore, predication is essentially that of universals. And here is the problem: If, as Carter interpreted it, predication is of universals, then how is it even possible to know the particular?

Nishida felt that knowledge of the particular is both possible and necessary for knowledge of universals. And, most importantly, we "know" the particular precisely because of active intuition. This, for Carter, is Nishida's "Copernican revolution" in his logic.[50]

Nishida used the example of "red" and "color." To perceive red as a color, it would seem that one must first be in contact with all reds and then from this experience conclude that there is a color called red. Yet, in one's initial encounter with red, one is also already intuiting a sense of what color is.[51]

Therefore, both "red" and "color" are already united. Nishida integrated both the subject and the object through our intuition. To know red is to know color, and to know color is to know its particular manifestations (in this case, red). To know both red and color is to know, intuitively, that place from which all colors arise. As Carter put it, it is to know the "system of colors," just as to know the number "seven" and the concept "number" is to already know the "number-system." Knowing these "systems" means knowing the *basho,* or field, from which all else arises. And we know this field intuitively.

Double Aperture

The way to genuine understanding is to assume two postures simultaneously. Carter called this a "double aperture" whereby one focuses on the part, the individual, and even the elements of a judgement (subject and predicate) on the one hand, and on the "field" or place on the other. It is the stance of the recognition of the "contradictory self-identity" of things, using Nishida's phrase.[52]

This is genuine knowing, involving the integration and identity of particular and universal, of red and color or seven and number.

Despite the highly abstract quality of many of Nishida's writings, we must remember that he was quite critical of abstraction. Nishida intended a concrete logic based on reality. And reality lies deeper than the abstract ideal form we impose on it with formal logic. Thus Nishida referred to what is real as the "self-unification" of the polar opposites of subject and object.[53] What he meant is that Reality is a predicate; it is action. To live is to act. And his logic and epistemology was meant to impart this feature.

In all of this we see that epistemology in Japanese thought is generally less formalized. Instead, the Japanese appear to be more interested in knowledge that is more immediate and direct. There is an appeal to direct experience, without the mediation of formalized constructs. For this reason, sense impression and intuition appear to play a more prominent role in knowing.

In order to gain a better sense of what Buddhism is saying, we must emphasize again the important distinction between a conventional way of knowing and a higher way of knowing. The conventional way of knowing presumes a subject-object disparity. On this level, that which is said to be known is the object for the knower, who is the subject. Therefore, even if we know the self on this level, we know the self conceptually, as an object of knowing. This way of knowing the self remains incomplete.

Buddhism proposes and focuses on a higher level of knowing that goes beyond this conventional, reflective approach. It does not delve too much into formal analysis about the conventional ways of knowing, or those areas in epistemology with which we are ordinarily concerned.

We need to be especially careful here. We are not saying that Buddhism is a type of mysticism that seeks to leap beyond conventional ways of knowing. For Buddhists, transcending the conventional subject-object way of knowing is possible. Yet it is possible only by going through our ordinary knowing process. The path to this higher stage, *samadhi,* demands discipline and intense meditation and years of training.

Study Questions

India

1. How are perspectives on the nature of knowledge related to the goal of liberation in Indian thought?
2. Discuss the four sources of valid knowledge in Nyaya philosophy.
3. Describe the processes involved in perception according to Nyaya teachings.
4. Describe how knowledge is possible through so-called extra-ordinary means of perception in Nyaya.

5. Using a *tarka,* point out the processes involved in inference, according to the Nyaya school.

6. In Nyaya teachings, describe both the role of causality in inference and the three different kinds of causality. What is the significance of *asatkaryavada* in this?

7. From the teachings of the Navya Nyaya, discuss features surrounding the definition of "negation" or "absence."

8. Explain how Yoga seeks to control or restrain the force of *citta.* Why is this important?

9. What are the two kinds of knowledge according to Sankara?

10. How does Sankara assume an original kind of validity to knowledge? Why is this rejected by the Nyaya school?

11. Discuss the sources of knowledge according to Sankara. Compare and contrast these with the teachings in Nyaya.

12. What are the sources of knowledge according to Ramanuja? Point out the essential differences with Sankara.

13. How does Radhakrishnan, in his *Idealist View of Life,* seek to integrate the positions of Sankara and Ramanuja with respect to knowledge? From the reading, what is the role of intuition?

14. How do the Buddhist sources of knowledge demonstrate Buddhism's empirical emphasis? How does this relate to the knowledge of universals?

15. Compare and contrast the positions of the Sarvastivada, Sautrantika, and Vaibhashika Buddhist schools concerning their views of knowledge.

16. How does Nagarjuna apply the meaning of *sunya* to his view of knowledge? Illustrate through ideas from his *Madhyamika Karika.*

17. Explain the view of knowledge in the Yogacara school.

18. Discuss Dignaga's sources for cognition.

19. How do Dignaga's sources for knowledge affect his critique of logic?

20. Explain the relation between knowledge and action in Dharmakirti. Illustrate through ideas in his selection.

21. Discuss some of the means to higher knowledge in the Vajrayana form of esoteric Buddhism.

China

22. How does Chuang Tzu's more relativist position affect his view of the nature of knowledge?

23. What is the role of knowledge in the teachings of Confucius and Mencius?

24. Discuss Hsun Tzu's approach to the "rectification of names." According to Hsun Tzu, how do fallacies occur?

25. Discuss the relation between particulars and universals in Kung-sun Lung. Illustrate with ideas from his "White Horse Discourse." Why is it that "a white horse is not a horse"?

26. How does "no-mind" relate to knowledge in Ch'an Buddhism?

27. Discuss aspects of Wang Yang-ming's emphasis on intuition. In what ways does he differ from Chu Hsi?

28. Describe the relation between culture and knowledge in Chang Tung-sun. Illustrate with ideas from his selection.

Japan

29. How does the Japanese language manifest views of the nature of knowing?
30. In Tendai Buddhism, how is higher knowledge viewed as *samadhi*?
31. Describe the significance of *koans* in Zen Buddhism. What role do they play in attaining a higher knowledge? Illustrate with classic *koans.*
32. How does Dogen point out the limits of reason in Zen Buddhism?
33. What is the meaning of acting intuition in Nishida Kitaro?
34. What is the significance of *basho* in Nishida's view of knowledge?
35. What are the major features in Nishida Kitaro's view of knowledge? How is his view distinct from Aristotle?

Notes

1. Burton Watson, trans., *Chuang Tzu: Basic Writings* (New York: Columbia University Press, 1964), 110.
2. Along with the orthodox teachings, the epistemological contributions by the Jains need to be more fully recognized. Their teachings contain an elaborate epistemology that forms the basis for their strict moral code. For instance, the Jains' idea of "multiple modality" is especially important. It expresses itself in two ways: (a) Nothing can be established as absolutely true, and (b) there still exists a slight degree of veracity in all things. All things are relative with reference to various perspectives or standpoints. See more in P. T. Raju, *Structural Depths of Indian Thought* (Albany: State University of New York Press, 1985), 113–15.
3. P. T. Raju, *Philosophical Traditions of India* (London: George Allen & Unwin Ltd., 1971), 139.
4. See Raju, *Philosophical Traditions,* 142.
5. Raju, *Structural Depths,* 209.
6. Chandradhar Sharma, *A Critical Survey of Indian Philosophy* (Delhi: Motilal Banarsidass, 1976), 192.
7. Raju, *Philosophical Traditions,* 137.
8. Raju, *Structural Depths,* 262–63.
9. Bimal Krishna Matilal, trans., *The Navya-Nyāya Doctrine of Negation: The Semantics and Ontology of Negative Statements in Navya-nyāya Philosophy,* Harvard Oriental Series (Cambridge, Massachusetts: Harvard University Press, 1968), 104.
10. Discussion of this negation is adapted from Matilal, 104–49.
11. Eliot Deutsch, *Advaita Vedanta: A Philosophical Reconstruction* (Honolulu: University of Hawaii Press, 1990), 84.
12. George Thibaut, trans., *The Vedānta Sūtras of Bādarāyana with the Commentary by Śankara: Part I* (New York: Dover, 1962) II.I.14, 324.
13. Adapted from Deutsch's discussion, 86–88.
14. Deutsch, 88–89.
15. Raju, *Philosophical Traditions,* 68.
16. Thibaut, *Vedanta Sutras* II.1.11, 315.
17. This emphasis was particularly great in Mimamsa, which is why Mimamsa adherents paid great attention to the literal adherence to the Vedas.
18. One of Sankara's most noted followers, Sri Harsa, rejected all six of these grounds. For him, the only knowledge was high knowledge, or the intuition of *Brahman;* all

else is false knowledge. What about an object that is actually an illusion? (In other words, it is nonreal.) Advaitins do not claim that the object does not exist. They claim instead that the object cannot be explained. One cannot therefore describe the object as any of the four negations: It is neither real, unreal, nor both, nor neither. What is illusion simply cannot be explained away as either existing or not existing.

19. The scholar M. Hiriyanna described Ramanuja's interpretation of "*tat tvam asi*": "Here the word 'That' finally denotes God having the entire universe as his body; and 'thou,' God having the individual soul as his body." See M. Hiriyanna, *The Essentials of Indian Philosophy* (London: George Allen & Unwin Ltd., 1960), 184.

20. S. Radhakrishnan, *An Idealist View of Life* (London: George Allen & Unwin Ltd., 1932), 139. As we can see in his description of intuitive knowledge, Radhakrishnan demonstrated his comparative interests in addressing how this intuitive knowledge of self is found in Western thinkers as well.

21. Raju, *Structural Depths,* 163–64.

22. Raju, *Structural Depths,* 165.

23. Raju, *Structural Depths,* 165.

24. Keep in mind that for Buddhists, the concept of "person" is considered within a psycho-physical process. There is no static entity outside of this process. This may make more sense if we recall that for Buddhists, the mind (*citta*) is considered to be another sensory organ. Mind belongs to an internal sense, distinct from the five external senses.

25. Raju, *Structural Depths,* 167. See his analysis for further discussion.

26. David J. Kalupahana, *A History of Buddhist Philosophy: Continuities and Discontinuities* (Honolulu: University of Hawaii Press, 1992), 196.

27. Kalupahana, *A History of Buddhist Philosophy,* 198.

28. Cited in Kalupahana, *A History of Buddhist Philosophy,* 197.

29. Kalupahana, *A History of Buddhist Philosophy,* 197.

30. F. Th. Stcherbatsky, trans., *Buddhist Logic* (New York: Dover Publications, 1962) Vol. 2, 1.

31. For a good discussion of the style of debates in logic, see A. S. Cua, *Ethical Argumentation: A Study in Hsun Tzu's Moral Epistemology* (Honolulu: University of Hawaii Press, 1985).

32. Fung Yu-lan, *A Short History of Chinese Philosophy,* ed. Derk Bodde (New York: Free Press, 1966), 116.

33. W. A. C. H. Dobson, trans., *Mencius: A New Translation Arranged and Annotated for the General Reader* (University of Toronto Press, 1963), 6.19 (4B.19), 141.

34. Wing-tsit Chan, trans., *A Source Book In Chinese Philosophy* (Princeton, N.J.: Princeton University Press, 1963), 128. At the same time, Hsun Tzu advanced a theory of knowledge in which he addressed the relationship among sense impression, knowing, and the object of knowledge. He included the mind as part of our faculty for knowing and thus distinguished it from that which senses.

35. Chan, from Hsun Tzu, Ch. 22, in *Source Book,* 127.

36. Fung, *Short History,* 90.

37. Adapted from Fung Yu-lan, *A History of Chinese Philosophy,* Vol. 1, translated by Derk Bodde (Princeton: Princeton University Press, 1952), 205–09.

38. Cited in Fung, *History of Chinese Philosophy,* Vol. 2, 395.

39. Cited in Fung, *History of Chinese Philosophy,* Vol. 2, 403.

40. Chang was especially critical of Kant's separation of sense-data and form.

41. In this respect we see Chang's affinity to Marxism, and his work was a theoretical stepping stone to a cultural revolution.

42. Suzuki Daisetz Teitaro, "Reason and Intuition in Buddhist Philosophy," in Charles Moore, ed., *The Japanese Mind: Essentials of Japanese Philosophy and Culture* (Honolulu: University of Hawaii Press, 1987), 98.

43. Zenkei Shibayama, *Zen Comments on the Mumonkan,* trans. Sumiko Kudo (New York: Mentor Book, New American Library, 1974), 19.

44. Thomas Cleary, trans., *Shōbōgenzō: Zen Essays by Dōgen* (Honolulu: University of Hawaii Press, 1986), 32.
45. Yuasa Yasuo, *The Body: Toward an Eastern Mind-Body Theory,* ed. Thomas P. Kasulis, trans. Shigenori Nagatomo and Thomas P. Kasulis, SUNY Series in Buddhist Studies (Albany: State University of New York Press, 1987), 67.
46. This and some of the following is adapted from Yuasa's analysis, 61–63.
47. Yuasa, 61.
48. There are similarities here with Husserl's phenomenology. Yuasa contended that one difference between Nishida and Husserl in this regard lies in this: Husserl demanded a theoretical "bracketing" to attain this experience, whereas Nishida required a non-theoretical, "practical activity" to attain such pure experience. See Yuasa, 64–65. We can understand why critics accuse Nishida of mysticism, though unjustly.
49. This discussion is condensed from Robert E. Carter, *The Nothingness Beyond God: An Introduction to the Philosophy of Nishida Kitaro* (New York: Paragon House, 1989), 25–31.
50. Carter, 27.
51. Carter, 27–29.
52. Carter, 32.
53. Nishida Kitaro, *Intelligibility and the Philosophy of Nothingness: Three Philosophical Essays,* trans. Robert Schinzinger (Honolulu: East-West Center Press, 1958), 51.

From the *Nyayasutra,* with Commentary by Vatsyayana

Gautama

Nyāyasūtra 2.2.7:

Abhāva is not a means of true cognition, because there is no such object of true cognition as an *absence.*

Vātsyāyana: Since absence is found to be an object in many cases of true cognition, the argument that *abhāva* is not a means of true cognition because there is no such object of true cognition as absence is rather high-handed.

[Vātsyāyana introduces *sūtra* 2.2.8 as follows:] Many examples could be adduced, of which our author now furnishes a simple one.

Nyāyasūtra 2.2.8:

For, where several [cloths] are marked, since there are those unmarked which are marked [out] by the absence of marks, it is proved that this [viz., absence] is an object of valid cognition.

Vātsyāyana: This absence [which is under discussion] is proved to be a *prameya.* How? Because, when cloths which are marked are not to be taken, those cloths which are not marked and are to be taken are marked [out to us] by the [very] absence of marks on them. A man in the presence of both sorts may be told, "Bring the unmarked cloths," and by means of absence of marks he will cognize those cloths on which no mark appears, and, having cognized them, he will bring them. Here [the cognition of] absence of marks is the cause of his true cognition [that is, it is a *pramāṇa*], which proves that the absence [is a *prameya,* an object of a true cognition].

Nyāyasūtra 2.2.9:

If you say, "[There can be] no absence without the thing's [first] being present," [we say] no, because the mark can be [present] on something else.

Vātsyāyana: [Opponent.] Where a thing has been and ceases to be, there we can speak of absence. But it is not the case that the marks were once on the unmarked cloths and have now ceased to be there. Therefore we cannot speak of absence of marks on them. [The answer to this is] no, because the marks can occur on other things. Just as a man sees the presence of marks on other cloths, just so does he not see marks on the unmarked cloths. By seeing the absence of marks the man cognizes the object [viz., the unmarked cloths] by absence. . . .

"A Discourse on Absence," from *Tattvacintamani*

Gangesa

1. Now, [one may object that] an absence (e.g., of a pot on a ground) is surely identical with a presence (e.g., of a ground which lacks a pot). Hence direct contacts (e.g., of sight and ground) are the means of our apprehending [what is called absence], and hence the relation qualifier-ness does not serve as the apprehensional connection.

NOTES: The apprehensional connections are the various systems of linkage between sense and object which render apprehension (i.e., perceptual

Reprinted from Bimal Krishna Matilal, trans., *The Navya-Nyaya Doctrine of Negation: The Semantics and Ontology of Negative Statements in Navya-nyaya Philosophy.* Cambridge, Mass.: Harvard University Press, 1968, pp. 109–11. Copyright 1968 by the President and Fellows of Harvard College; reprinted with permission.

cognition) possible. They are of six types (listed by Uddyotakara on *NS* I.I.4), the first being contact of sense with object; the second, inherence (of a quality) in an object with which the sense is in contact; and so on. The sixth type of apprehensional connection, according to the Nyāya theory, is the relation qualifier-ness, i.e., the relation by which an absence of x qualifies an entity y with which the sense is connected. The objector here holds that there is no cognized object called 'absence' over and above the objects that are present and are directly perceived through the ordinary and well-known sense-object connections. There is no such thing as absence, and hence the relation qualifier-ness is unnecessary.

2. On this matter the Old Nyāya argued as follows. We do have such unrefuted cognitions as "There is no pot here on (the) ground," and such a cognition does not refer to a ground as its objective content because in that case the same cognition might refer to a ground with a pot on it. Neither does the cognition refer to *mere* ground, for we have not yet accepted a [separate entity] *mereness*. Further, if you say that *mereness* is merely the ground, you are guilty of tautology. Furthermore, if there were no difference [between absence of pot and the ground on which it occurs], the relation of superstratum-substratum [that holds between them] would be impossible. . . .

3. Now [the objector may reply as follows]. An absence must be described as having a substratum even by those who accept absence as an additional entity, because one can only speak of an absence in connection with some place etc. So there must be [according to you] in the ground [which lacks a pot] some special property (*viśeṣa*) which is the substratum of the absence. This special property cannot be the mere ground, for it might occur in a ground that has a pot on it. It cannot be identical with a ground that has an absence, because such an explanation would suffer from circularity. Nor can it be identical with a ground that has a pot, for that would be self-contradictory.

NOTES: The opponent tries to bring against the Naiyāyika the very dilemma that the Naiyāyika has used against him. The *ON*, he says, must admit that there is some special property in the ground when the ground lacks a pot. How else would that ground be distinguishable from the ground which possesses a pot? Now, what can be the identity condition of that special property? The same difficulties present themselves as were presented to the objector in finding an identity condition for the mere ground.

4. To this [the Old Nyāya] said: No, because [each] such special property would be nothing more than the substratum of [each] absence, and there would be no consecutive character (*anugama*) [to give such special properties an independent existence]. As for their serving as substrata to a unitary superstratum (viz., absence of pot), that is possible despite their lack of a consecutive character, just as there are substrata of [presence of] pot.

NOTES: The Nyāya reply points out that 'the property of having no pot' has no special character over and above that of its *dharmin* (property-possessor). It is not like cow-ness, which the Naiyāyikas claim to be unitary, to carry over from one cow to the next while being distinct from those cow-individuals in which it resides. Hence one may not establish an L-relation between an absence and the said special property, but one must establish it between the absence and the independently existing locus of the absence, e.g., the ground.

5. Again, [if one asks] where an absence occurs, the answer is, where it is cognized to occur. Where is it so cognized? The answer is, where it does occur. On any other principle one would not even accept [universals like] cow-ness etc., for it would be possible to speak [of something as a cow] simply because of some special property of the locus [of the universal, cow-ness].

NOTES: The objector's difficulty has been in accepting a "nothing" as a "something." Hence he tried to find some positive entity to serve as the object or the reference of our negative cognitions. When his suggestions have been rejected, he says in effect, "Very well, suppose my suggestion will not work, still, your theory is unrealistic. Where could these absences ('absence' being a negative expression) you talk about occur ('occur' being a positive expression)?" Apparently the objector's mind does not balk at universals. So the ON answers him by saying that absences are no more unrealistic than cow-ness, etc.

The Nyāya argument for universals is basically epistemological. It may be briefly put as follows:

(a) We cognize some individuals as cows and apply the word 'cow' to them and not to anything else.
(b) Therefore, there is something present in those individuals which differentiates them from other things, and that something we call 'cow-ness.'
(c) Therefore, there is cow-ness. . . .

"A Discourse on the Significance of Negative Particles," from *Nañ-vāda*

Raghunatha

1. [Each of the particles referred to by the symbol] '*nañ*' may mean either a relational absence or a mutual absence.

NOTES: The symbol '*nañ*' stands, in general, for all the negative particles in Sanskrit. Thus the free particles '*na*', '*no*', etc., and the bound particles '*a-*' and '*an-*' in compounds are included under this general name. Such a particle, by virtue of its denotative function (*śakti*, as opposed to *lakṣaṇā*, indicative function), designates two types of absence—relational absence and mutual absence. These two types of absence are generally distinguished in the following way. In the first, it is denied that the counterpositive occurs by some relation other than the relation of identity in some other entity called the subjunct; in the second, it is denied that the counterpositive is in a relation of identity, i.e., is identical, with the subjunct. . . .

(a) There is a radical difference between the concept of relational absence and that of difference or mutual absence. Relational absence is illustrated by the cognition "There is no pot on the ground," mutual absence by "This cloth is not a pot." Raghunātha perhaps claims here that the meaning of 'no' in the first example differs fundamentally from that of 'not' in the second, and hence we must accept this necessary heaviness (*gaurava*), viz., two different denotative functions of the negative particle. . . .

2. In either case the property of being the counterpositive must be taken to be delimited by the property that also delimits the relational property *anvayitā-to-nañ* (i.e., the intensional property of being syntactically connected to *nañ*. This rule derives from the conventional manner of interpreting sentences. Thus one does not say, "A pot is not on a place which has a blue pot" or "A blue pot is not a pot," whereas one does say, "A yellow pot is not on this place which has a blue pot," or "A yellow pot is not [a] blue [pot]," etc.

NOTES: Where '*ghaṭa* (a pot)' is syntactically connected with '*nañ*', '*ghaṭa* (a pot)' is said to be an *anvayin* (syntactical correlate) to '*nañ*'. There will then come to reside in '*ghaṭa*' a relational abstract *anvayitā* to '*nañ*', which one might translate as the relational property of being that which is syntactically connected to '*nañ*'.

Reprinted from Bimal Krishna Matilal, trans., *The Navya-Nyaya Doctrine of Negation: The Semantics and Ontology of Negative Statements in Navya-nyaya Philosophy.* Cambridge, Mass.: Harvard University Press, 1968, pp. 148–49. Copyright 1968 by the President and Fellows of Harvard College; reprinted with permission.

The text anticipates the following difficulty. When an absence of pot is referred to in Sanskrit, whether it is the absence of a definite pot or an indefinite pot or all pots in general is not usually specified. As much as this is left ambiguous, it may be argued that since another pot is absent from a place where a particular pot is present, why shouldn't we say that there is absence of pot there also? And similarly, why not say about a particular pot (which is certainly not identical with a second pot) that it is also not [a] pot? The text seeks to avoid such confusion by specifying the delimitor of the property of being the counterpositive, i.e., the counterpositive-ness involved in each instance of absence. . . .

Ways of Knowing

Radhakrishnan

Different Ways of Knowing

While all varieties of cognitive experience result in a knowledge of the real, it is produced in three ways which are sense experience, discursive reasoning and intuitive apprehension. Sense experience helps us to know the outer characters of the external world. By means of it we obtain an acquaintance with the sensible qualities of the objects. Its data are the subject-matter of natural science which builds up a conceptual structure to describe them.

Logical knowledge is obtained by the processes of analysis and synthesis. The data supplied to us by perception are analysed and the results of the analysis yield a more systematic knowledge of the object perceived. This logical or conceptual knowledge is indirect and symbolic in its character. It helps us to handle and control the object and its workings. Conceptual explanations alter with the growth of experience and analysis. They are dependent on our perceptions, our interests, and our capacities. Both sense knowledge and logical knowledge are the means by which we acquire for practical purposes a control over our environment.

Both these kinds of knowledge are recognised as inadequate to the real which they attempt to apprehend. Plato contrasts the world of eternal forms with the transitory forms of sense impressions. The former is real, and the

Reprinted from S. Radhakrishnan, *An Idealist View of Life*. London: George Allen & Unwin, 1932, pp. 134–36, 138–42; reprinted with permission of HarperCollins Publishers Limited.

latter unreal. Knowledge is of the former, while the latter belongs to the realm of opinion. It is clear, however, that the objects revealed by logical knowledge are not those which we perceive. From the same position, it is sometimes argued that the perceived object is more real than the conceived one. The immediacy of the objects we perceive in sense experience is lost when the intellectual activities supervene. No amount of conceptual synthesis can restore the original integrity of the perceived object. Bradley and Bergson insist on the symbolic character of logical knowledge. Whatever be the object, physical or non-physical, intellect goes about it and about, but does not take us to the heart of it. He who speaks about sleep and discusses its nature and conditions knows all about sleep except sleep itself. All intellectual analysis is, for Bradley, a falsification of the real, in that it breaks up its unity into a system of separate terms and relations. Thought lives in the distinction between the reality of *that* and the abstract character of *what*. However wide the "what" may extend, it can never embrace the whole of existing reality. Intellectual symbols are no substitutes for perceived realities. Besides, the whole life of feeling and emotion, "the delights and pains of the flesh, the agonies and raptures of the soul" remain outside of thought. If thought is to be equal to the comprehension of these sides of life, then it is "different from thought, discursive and relational. It must have been absorbed in a fuller experience." Bradley's insistence on the separation in judgment of existence from character, as well as the assertion of the unity which is the basis of its separation, brings out the reality of a higher mode of apprehension than discursive reason. The unified structure of reality is revealed more in feeling than in thought, in what Bradley calls the higher unity, in which "thought, feeling and volition are blended into a whole." It is the creative effort of the whole man as distinct from mere intellectual effort that can comprehend the nature of reality. Bradley says: "We can form the general idea of an absolute experience in which phenomenal distinctions are merged, a whole become immediate at a higher stage without losing any richness." . . .

Intuitive Knowing

There is a knowledge which is different from the conceptual, a knowledge by which we see things as they are, as unique individuals and not as members of a class or units in a crowd. It is non-sensuous, immediate knowledge. Sense knowledge is not the only kind of immediate knowledge. As distinct from sense knowledge or pratyakṣa (literally presented to a sense), the Hindu thinkers use the term aparokṣa for the non-sensuous immediate knowledge. This intuitive knowledge arises from an intimate fusion of mind with reality. It is knowledge by being and not by senses or by symbols. It is awareness of the truth of things by identity. We become one with the truth, one with the object of knowledge. The object known is seen not as an object outside the self, but as a part of the self. What intuition reveals is not so much a doctrine as a consciousness; it is a state of mind and not a definition of the object. Logic and language are a lower form, a diminution of this kind of knowledge. Thought is a means of partially manifesting and presenting what is concealed in this greater self-existent knowledge. Knowledge is an intense and close communion between the knower and the known. In knowing the knower is establishing an identity with the known. In logical knowledge there is always the duality, the distinction between the knowledge of a thing and its being. Thought is able to reveal reality, because they are one in essence; but they are different in existence at the empirical level. Knowing a thing and being it are different. So thought needs verification.

There are aspects of reality where only this kind of knowledge is efficient. Take, e.g., the emotion of anger. Sense knowledge of it is not possible except in regard to its superficial manifestations. Intellectual knowledge is not possible until the data are supplied from somewhere else, and sense cannot supply them. Before the intellect can analyse the mood of anger, it must get at it, and it cannot get at it by itself. We know what it is to be angry by being angry. No one can understand fully the force of human love or parental affection who has not himself been through them. Imagined emotions are quite different from felt ones.

The great illustration of intuitive knowledge given by Hindu thinkers is the knowledge of self. We become aware of our own self, as we become aware of love or anger, directly by a sort of identity with it. Self-knowledge is inseparable from self-existence. It seems to be the only true and direct knowledge we have: all else is inferential. Śaṃkara says that self-knowledge which is neither logical nor sensuous is the presupposition of every other kind of knowledge. It alone is beyond doubt, for "it is of the essential nature of him who denies it." It is the object of the notion of self (*asmatpratyayaviṣaya*), and it is known to exist on account of its immediate presentation. It cannot be proved, since it is the basis of all proof. It is the light which is not nature, which is not man, but which made them both. All experience—cognition, affection, or conation—is always an experience to an "I." An "I" is implicit in all awareness. This "I" is not the body, however intimate the connection of the body with the "I" may be. The body is something which can be perceived by the senses. We do not say "I am the body," but only "I have a body." As part of the empirical consciousness, the reality of the body is that of the empirical world. We say "I see or hear," and not the eye sees or the ear hears. The "I" implicit in all knowledge is not something inferred from experience, but something immediately lived and known by experience. It is experienced as a fundamentally simple existent, and is not to be confused with the self as conceived. What is immediately apprehended is different from what is conceptually constructed. The self immediately known in experience is known as a "that" and not a "what." We have in this immediate apprehension a knowledge of acquaintance with being, and not knowledge about its essence or nature. What is immediately apprehended is known as unique, as subject of all experience while everything else is object. There is no real but only a logical distinction between subject and object in the immediate intuitive awareness of the self as real being. "That which knows and that which is known (reason and the world of reason) are really the same thing."

Many Western thinkers confirm this view of Saṁkara. The scepticism of Descartes reaches its limits and breaks against the intuitive certainty of self-consciousness: *Cogito ergo sum.* Unfortunately, Descartes' expression is misleading. Self-knowledge is far too primitive and simple to admit of an *ergo.* If the "I am" depends on an "I think," the "I think" must also depend on another "*ergo,*" and so on, and it will land us in infinite regress. "The man who calls this syllogism," says Hegel, "must know little more about a syllogism, save that the word '*ergo*' occurs in it. Where shall we look for the middle term? It was as a self-evident or immediate truth that the *cogito ergo sum,* the maxim on which the whole history of modern philosophy was built, was started by its author." It is not an inference, but the expression of a unique fact. In self-consciousness, thought and existence are indissolubly united. The self is the first absolute certainty, the foundation of all logical proofs. Descartes' "I am" is akin to the "I am" with which the ancient seer sought to convey to his people the ultimate authoritativeness of his Yahweh. Even Locke, who waged a vigorous polemic against innate ideas, concedes the reality of intuitions. "As for our own existence," says he, "we perceive it so plainly and so certainly that it neither needs nor is capable of proof." In Kant, the "I think" accompanies all representations. It is the vehicle of all concepts in general. All knowledge and logic start with this first principle of self-certainty. For Fichte, the knowledge of self is due to intuition. Schopenhauer contends that we become aware of something that is more than phenomenal in our inner experience. It is will, and all phenomena are its manifestations. Not through intellect, but through the immediate consciousness we have of our own volition, we attain to awareness of reality. Bergson holds a somewhat similar view. For him the true self is not the growing self which goes on gathering its past experience through memory and pressing forward to its future ends. It is to be defined by reference to pure duration which knows not past history or future progress. It is the undivided present to which the categories of time are irrelevant. We are or get near to pure duration only in those rare moments of real freedom. We cannot intuit pure duration if we do not get rid of our tendency to misinterpret what we see by applying to it the categories of the intellect. In other words, we can intuit pure duration only if we make ourselves into it. Ordinarily our life is not pure duration, for it is partly mechanised. This is Bergson's way of expressing the truth that intellect working with distinctions of the knower, the knowledge and the known cannot attain to self-knowledge where these three are not different. Intellect ignores the fundamental oneness of the movement which is indivisible and not distributed in its forms. Intuitive self-knowledge knows itself as a single indivisible act of knowledge, an act which is one with its self-existence. It is through intuitive understanding or sympathetic interpretation that we know other minds.

From *Nyaya-bindu (A Short Treatise of Logic)*, with Commentary by Dharmottara

Dharmakirti

1. Subject Matter and Purpose of This Work.

1. All successful human action is preceded by right knowledge. Therefore this (knowledge will be here) investigated.

But by making such a statement the subject-matter (of the work), its aim and its fitness (for that aim) are (indirectly) indicated. Indeed when it is being stated that right knowledge, the source of all (successful) human action, will be analysed in the present work, it is also implied that right knowledge is the subject-matter of this literary composition, its aim is an analysis of (the phenomenon) of knowledge, and the work itself represents the means through which the analysis (is achieved). . . .

2. Right Knowledge Defined.

Right knowledge is knowledge not contradicted (by experience). In common life we likewise say that (a man) has spoken truth when he makes us reach the object he has first pointed out. Similarly (we can also say) that knowledge is right when it makes us reach an object it did point to. But by "making us reach an object" nothing else is meant than the fact of turning (our attention) straight to the object. Indeed knowledge does not create an object and does not offer it to us, but in turning (our attention) straight to the object it (*eo ipso*) makes us reach it. Again "to turn a man straight to the object" is nothing else than to point it out as an aim of a (possible) purposive action. Indeed, (one should not imagine) that knowledge has the power forcibly to incite a man (against his will). . . .

For this very reason (as will be stated later on) the only ultimate result of an act of cognizing is (simply) a distinct cognition. When an object has been cognized, man has been (*eo ipso*) turned towards it and the object reached. The (proper) function of cognition is thus at an end just after the object has been cognized. For this very reason cognition is concerned with an object not yet cognized. But when it has been first cognized, the same act of cognition has also drawn (the attention) of man and has made him reach the object,

Reprinted from F. Th. Stcherbatsky, *Buddhist Logic.* New York: Dover, 1962, pp. 1, 2, 4–9, 12–17. © Dover Publications, Inc.; reprinted with permission.

(i.e., reach it by his cognition). Any further act concerning that very object cannot be regarded as its cognition. Consequently (a purposive action directed towards) an object already cognized will not be an act of cognizing it.

(Turning now to the different modes of cognition we see that) when an object has been apprehended by direct experience, it has been converted into an object of (possible) purposive action through sense-perception. Because (we say) that sense-perception has pointed out an object, when the function of that knowledge which consists in making us feel its presence in our ken is followed by a construction (of its image). Therefore (we say) that an object has been pointed out by sense-perception, when it is cognized as something directly perceived. Inference (or indirect cognition, differs) in that it points out the mark of the object, and by thus (indirectly) making sure (its existence) submits it as an object of possible purposive action. Thus it is that sense-perception points out a definite object, (i.e., an object localized in time and space) which appears before us directly, and inference likewise points out a definite object by way of the mark it is connected with. These two (methods of cognizing) point out definite objects, therefore they are right knowledge. What differs from them is not (right) knowledge. Knowledge is right when it makes us reach the object, and it makes us reach it when it has pointed to an attainable object. But an object pointed out in some different way, not according to the above mentioned two (methods of right knowledge), is either absolutely unreal as, e.g., water seen as a vision in a desert—it does not exist, it cannot be reached—or it is uncertain as to whether it exists or not as, e.g., every problematic object. Since there is no such object in the world, which at the same time would be existent and non-existent, therefore such (a problematic object) can never be attained. And all imagination which is not produced by the (real) mark of the object, which operates (freely) without taking notice of limitation (by reality) can but refer to a problematic fact (about which we neither know) that it exists nor that it does not exist. Such an object can never be reached. Therefore every cognition other (than perception or inference) is not a source of right knowledge, since it presents an object which cannot be reached, an object which is (either) absolutely unreal (or) uncertain as to whether it exists or not.

(Sentient beings) strive for desired ends. They want that knowledge which leads them to the attainment of objects fitted for successful action. The knowledge that is investigated by the theory (of cognition) is just the knowledge they want. Therefore right knowledge is knowledge which points to reality, (a reality which) is capable of experiencing purposive action. And that object alone which has been pointed out by such right knowledge can be "reached" (i.e., clearly and distinctly cognized), because, as we have stated above, we understand by "reaching" an object its definite cognition. Now, if there is a divergence between what is pointed out (by our cognition) and the real object, the latter has either a different quality or a different place or a different time. Indeed every variation in its characteristics (makes the characterized object) "another" object. (When we say that) the real object is "other" (we mean) that it either has another quality or another place or another time (than what is contained in our cognition). Thus cognition representing one form of the object, is not to be considered as a right cognition when the real object has a different form, e.g., the yellow conch-shell seen (by the daltonist) is not a right cognition of this conch-shell, since it is really white. Neither is cognition right when it wrongly represents the place of the object, e.g., the radiance of a jewel seen through the chink in a door, when mistaken for the jewel itself which is in the room (behind the door), is not a right cognition of this jewel. Nor is our cognition right when it represents the object as existing at a time when we really do not perceive it. E.g., seeing in a dream at midnight an object which we really have seen at noon cannot be considered as a right cognition of an object really present at midnight. . . .

3. Varieties of Right Knowledge.

In order to reject misconception regarding the number of its varieties, it is said,—

> 2. Right knowledge is twofold. . . .
> 3. Direct and indirect (perceptive and inferential).

The word for direct knowledge (or perception) means knowledge dependent upon the senses. (This meaning) of a knowledge dependent upon the senses is suggested by the etymological analysis of the word, not by its actual use (in philosophy). The idea of being dependent upon the senses contains, as its implication, the idea of direct knowledge which is thus being suggested. This alone is the real meaning of the term perception. Therefore any knowledge that makes the object (appear) before us directly is called perceptive. If the proper use of the word involved nothing but dependence upon the senses, then sense-knowledge (or sensation) alone could be called direct knowledge, but not (the three remaining varieties of it), mental sensation etc. Thus it is, e. g., that the (sanscrit) word *go* "cow," although it is etymologically derived from the root *gam* "to move," is actually used to express the idea of a cow. This idea is incidentally suggested by the fact of motion when it is inherent in the same object. But then it comes to be generally accepted to denote a cow, whether she moves or not.

(The word for inference means etymologically "subsequent measure"). The word "measure" suggests an instrument (by which an object is measured, i.e., cognized). A source of knowledge is thereby indicated, whose characteristic essence is coordination. It is called "subsequent measure," because it appears after the logical mark (or middle term) has been apprehended, and its concomitance (or major premise) has been brought to memory. When the presence of the mark upon the subject (i.e., the minor premise) has been apprehended, and the concomitance between the minor and the major term, (i.e., the major premise) brought to memory, the inference (or conclusion) follows. Therefore it is called "subsequent." . . .

The word "and" (connecting direct and indirect knowledge) coordinates perception and inference as having equal force. Just as perception is a source of right knowledge, because being always connected with some (real) object it leads to successful purposive action, just the same is the case of inference. It likewise is a source of right knowledge always connected with some (real) object, in as much as it leads to the attainment of an object circumscribed by its mark.

4. Perception Defined.

4. Direct knowledge means here neither construction (judgment) nor illusion.

The word "here" indicates localization, but it is (moreover) used to indicate a selection. Thus the meaning of the sentence is the following one. "Here," i.e., among direct and indirect knowledge—this is a reference to the inclusive whole, "direct knowledge"—this refers to one part of it. A part is thus separated or selected from the whole, because the latter is the general term (with reference to the former). Direct knowledge is here taken as subject and the characteristics of non-constructive and non-illusive (cognition) are predicated. (It is not a definition of its essence. What its essence is) you and I very well know (in general). It is a kind of cognition which makes us (feel) that the objects are present to us directly. It is (now intimated) that it should be viewed as (something) non-constructive and (something) containing no illusion. (It may be objected, that since we do not very well know what these characteristics mean, we neither can know what direct knowledge is. But this is not so!) We must not imagine that if (the notions of) non-constructive and non-illusive are not familiar to us, we must refer them to some different special kind of direct knowledge which has been given this name and is here spoken of. The term "direct knowledge" (or perception) is familiar to everybody from its application (to that variety of direct cognition) which makes the object present to our sense-faculties and which is invariably connected with them.

This (perception) is referred to, and the characteristics of being neither a construction nor an illusion are predicated. Not to be a construction means to be foreign to construction, not to have the nature of an arrangement (or judgment). "Not an illusion" means not contradicted by that (underlying) essence of reality which possesses efficiency. This essence consists of patches of colour which are the substratum underlying the arrangement (of parts in an object). Non-illusive means knowledge which is not at variance with this (direct reality).

(However, as they stand) these two characteristics are intended to clear away wrong conceptions, not (alone) to distinguish (direct from) indirect cognition. The characteristic of "not being a construction" would have been alone quite sufficient for that. But if (the second characteristic) of "not being an illusion" were not added, (the following misconception would not have been guarded against. (There are some who maintain that) the vision of a moving tree (by an observer travelling by ship) and similar perceptions are right perceptions, because (there is in this case an underlying reality which) is not a construction. Indeed a man acting upon such a perception reaches something which is a tree, hence (it is supposed) that experience supports his perception. It would thus be consistent knowledge and so far would be direct, as not being a (mere) construction. In order to guard against this view the characteristic of "not being an illusion" has been inserted. It is an illusion. It is not a (right) perception. Neither is it an inference, since it is not derived from some mark in its threefold aspect. No other way of cognition is possible. We maintain therefore that the vision of a moving tree is error. If it is error, how are we to explain that a tree is nevertheless reached (when acting upon such erroneous perception)? The tree is not (really) reached upon it, since a tree changing its position in space is the definite image (corresponding to the visual sensation), and a tree fixed on one place is actually reached. Therefore the object which has produced the sensation of a moving tree is not actually reached, and (*vice versa*) the tree actually reached is not (the object which) has produced the visual sensation. Nothing at all is reached on the basis of this (wrong cognition). If a tree is actually reached, it depends upon an altogether different cognitive act. Thus it is that the characteristic of "non-illusion" has been introduced in order to clear away the theory (that illusion may lead to success). . . .

"The Real Nature of Knowledge," from *Lun-Heng*

Wang Ch'ung

The Literati, discoursing on Sages, are of opinion that they know thousands of years of the past, and ten thousand future generations. Merely by the keenness of their sight, and the subtlety of their hearing, they are able to give the proper names to new things. They know spontaneously, without learning, and understand of themselves, without inquiring, wherefore the term Sage is equivalent with supernatural. They are like milfoil and the tortoise, which know lucky and unlucky auguries, whence the milfoil plant is regarded as supernatural, and the tortoise as a divine creature.

The talents of Worthies do not reach this standard; their intelligence is weaker and not so comprehensive, whence they are called Worthies. This

Reprinted from Alfred Forke, trans., *Lun-Hêng, Part II: Miscellaneous Essays of Wang Ch'ung.* New York: Paragon Book Gallery, 1962, pp. 114–17.

difference of name implies a difference of nature, for the substance being the same, the name uses to be equal. As for the name Sage, it is known that Sages are something extraordinary and different from Worthies.

When *Confucius* was about to die, he left behind a book of prophecies wherein he says, "I know not what sort of fellow, styling himself the First Emperor of *Ch'in*, comes to my hall, squats on my bed, and turns my clothes topsy-turvy. After arriving at *Sha-ch'iu* he will die." In course of time the king of *Ch'in*, having swallowed the empire, assumed the title of First Emperor. On a tour of inspection, he came to *Lu* and visited the home of *Confucius*. Then he proceeded to *Sha-ch'iu*, but on the road he was taken ill and expired.

Another entry is this, "*Tung Chung Shu* carries confusion into my book." Subsequently, the minister of *Chiang-tu*, *Tung Chung Shu* made special researches into the *Ch'un-ch'iu* and wrote comments and notes on it. The book of prophecies further says, "*Ch'in* will be ruined by *Hu*." Later on, the Second Emperor *Hu Hai* in fact lost the empire.

These three instances are used to bear out the statement that Sages foreknow ten thousand future generations.

Confucius ignored his descent, his father and mother having concealed it from him. He blew the flute and then of himself knew that he was a scion of *Tse*, a great officer of *Sung* of *Yin*. He did not consult books or ask anybody, his playing the flute and his genius alone revealed to him his generation. This would appear to be a proof of the faculty of Sages to know thousands of years of the past.

I say that all this is fallacy. Such miraculous stories are recorded in prophecy books and all in the style of *Hu* destroying the *Ch'in*, told in many books, or of the text of the Plan of the River. The plain illustrations of *Confucius* have been magnified with a view to prove wonders and miracles, or the stories were fabricated in later times to furnish evidence.

Kao Tsu having enfeoffed the king of *Wu*, and seeing him off, patted him on his shoulder saying, "Within fifty years hereafter, some one will revolt from the *Han* in the south-east. Will that not be you?" In the time of *Ching Ti*, *Pi* along with seven other States plotted a rebellion against the *Han*. Those who first made this statement had perhaps noticed the dispositions and the signs of the time, whence they surmised that a rebellion would come, but they ignored the name of the leader. *Kao Tsu* having observed the valour of *Pi*, then correctly hinted at him.

If from this point of view we consider *Confucius'* cognisance of *Ch'in Shih Huang Ti* and of *Tung Chung Shu*, it may be that at the time he merely spoke of somebody visiting his home and deranging his book, and, later on, people, remarking that *Ch'in Shih Huang Ti* entered his house, and that *Tung Chung Shu* studied his work, exaggerated the dicta of *Confucius* and wrote down the names of the principal persons.

If *Confucius* was endowed with supernatural powers, so that he could see the First Emperor and *Tung Chung Shu* ere they existed, then he ought to have at once been aware of his being a descendant of the *Yin* and a scion of *Tse* likewise, and have no need of blowing the flute to determine it. *Confucius* was unable to ascertain his family name without playing the flute, but his seeing the First Emperor and beholding *Tung Chung Shu* is like blowing the flute.

According to the narrative of *Shih Huang Ti*, he did not go to *Lu*; how then should he have entered the hall of *Confucius*, squatted down on his bed, and turned his clothes topsy-turvy? In the thirty-seventh year of his reign, on the *kuei-ch'ou* day of the tenth month, *Ch'in Shih Huang Ti* started on a journey to *Yün-mêng*. From afar he sacrificed to *Shun* in *Chiu-yi*. Floating down the *Yangtse*, he visited *Chieh-ko*, crossed the stream of *Mei-chu*, went over to *Tan-yang*, arrived at *Ch'ien-t'ang*, and approached the *Chê* river. The waves being very boisterous, he went 120 Li westward, crossed the stream at a narrow passage, and went up to *Kuei-chi*, where he made an oblation to Great *Yü*, and erected a stone with an encomiastic inscription. Then turning to the southern Sea, he went back. Passing *Chiang-ch'êng*, he sailed along the seashore northward as far as *Lang-yeh*, whence still further north he arrived at the *Lao* and *Ch'eng* Mountains. Then he proceeded to *Chefoo*, and always keeping near the sea-shore, reached to *P'ing-yuan* Ford, where he fell sick. He passed away on the *P'ing* Terrace in *Sha-ch'iu*.

Since he did not go to *Lu*, wherefrom does the Book of Prophecies derive its knowledge that *Shih Huang Ti* came to *Lu* as it says? This journey to *Lu* not being a fact that might be known, the words ascribed to *Confucius* "I know not what sort of a fellow," &c. are not trustworthy either, and this utterance being unreliable, the remark about *Tung Chung Shu* deranging his book becomes doubtful also.

In case records of famous deeds seem rather queer, they are the work of common people. All books, unless they be directly written by Heaven and Earth, go back on former events, there being reliable evidence. Those without experience, of course, cannot utilise these sources. All Sages foreseeing happiness and misfortune, meditate and reason by analogies. Reverting to the beginning, they know the end; from their villages they argue on the palace, and shed their light into the darkest corners. Prophecy books and other mystic writings see from afar what has not yet come to pass; they are aware of what is going to happen in future, which, for the time being, is still a void and wrapt in darkness. Their knowledge is instantaneous, supernatural, and passing all understanding.

Although ineloquent persons may not be qualified for it, still it is possible to predict calamities by observing analogies, or to predetermine future events by going back to their sources and examining the past. Worthies have this faculty as well, and Sages are not alone fit to do it.

When *Chou Kung* was governing *Lu*, *T'ai Kung* knew that his descendants would be reduced to impotence, and when *T'ai Kung* was ruling in *Ch'i*, *Chou Kung* saw that his scions would fall victims to robbery and murder. By their methods they foreknew the ultimate end, and perceived the signs of adversity and rebellion.

Chou having ivory chop-sticks made, *Chi Tse* administered reproof, and *Confucius* sighed because dummies were buried in *Lu*. From the ivory chop-sticks the one inferred the misery attending the search for dragon-liver, whereas the other saw in the dummies the danger that living persons might be interred along with the dead.

T'ai Kung and *Chou Kung* were both cognisant of what had not yet come to pass, as *Chi Tse* and *Confucius* were aware of what had not yet taken place. As regards the source from which they drew the knowledge of the future, there is no diversity between *Sages* and *Worthies*.

"A Chinese Philosopher's Theory of Knowledge"

Chang Tung-sun

Generally speaking, there are two kinds of knowledge, the perceptual and the conceptual. Take a table or a chair for instance. It can be touched and perceived directly. This is perceptual knowledge. The uniformity of nature and the idea of a **Supreme Being**, on the other hand, cannot be verified by the senses, and **causality, teleology**, and the like are also conceptual in nature. It may be noted that perceptual knowledge cannot be outside the conceptual, nor can conceptual knowledge be separated from the perceptual. As a matter of fact, any conceptual knowledge contains perceptual elements and vice versa. The differentiation between the two is always for the mere convenience of discussion. They do not exist separately.

The kind of knowledge treated in this essay, it will be seen, is not perceptual but conceptual knowledge. Insofar as the conceptual guides the perceptual, the importance of the former surpasses that of the latter. This point is often neglected by the empiricists, but from the standpoint of cultural history it is desirable to have it emphasized.

Conceptual knowledge is also interpretative in nature. By interpretation we understand the manipulation of concepts and the employment of categories. For instance the apprehension of a flower is a perception, but it is an interpretation to say that flowers are derived from leaves, or that the formation of the flower is for the purpose of reproduction. In an interpretation of this kind at least the following concepts are being used: any event must have its antecedent; each change must have its cause; and, the final

Reprinted from S. I. Hayakawa, *Our Language and Our World.* New York: Harper, 1959, pp. 299–300, 303–308. Copyright 1952 by the International Society for General Semantics; reprinted with permission.

result in a concept of evolution is so much the more derived from interpretation. Therefore, interpretative knowledge, because it contains concepts and results in concepts, is conceptual knowledge. The manipulation of concepts is for the purpose of interpreting perceived facts. Thus, it is evident that conceptual knowledge is interpretative knowledge, and interpretative knowledge is theoretical knowledge. . . .

. . . Almost all the philosophers, from remote times to our own, have been aware of the limitations imposed by language, with the implication that real thinking cannot be clothed in language. The ordinary view is something like this: thought is primary, and with new terms thought has a better chance for expression. But this argument does not necessarily reveal the nature of the development of human thought. As a matter of fact, it is better to say that language has been a contributing factor rather than an obstacle to the development of thought. Viewing human history as a whole, any new creation in language, e.g., new terminology, represents a development of thought along a new line. Language and thought are fundamentally indivisible. Any thought can only be articulated through language or symbol. That which cannot be thus articulated most likely will not be counted as thought. Although language and thought cannot be absolutely identified with each other, they cannot be separated. It is not that language limits thought or hinders it, but rather that language creates thought and develops it. Should we consider the two points together, namely, that thought develops with language and that language is a form of social behavior, it will be clear that apart from the experimental elements all knowledge is social.

With the cognizance of the determination of thought by social conditions, there develops the sociology of knowledge. But the sociology of knowledge has shown only that human thought is determined by socially visible or invisible forces without realizing that apart from all these immediate concrete forces there are underlying social forces of a remote nature. We may identify these remote forces with cultural relations. All thought, in addition to being influenced by our immediate social environment, is also molded by our remote cultural heritage. The immediate forces determine the trend of our thought, while the remote cultural heritage determines the forms in which thought is made possible. All these forces help to determine interpretative knowledge. With different interpretations come different cultures. And, being born into different cultures people learn to interpret differently. Thus we may use culture to explain categories, and categories to explain mental differences, e.g., those between the West and the East.

With regard to types of language, a distinction may be observed between "emotive language" and "referential language." The first is used to arouse, with necessary gestures and appropriate sounds, the corresponding gestures or mental attitudes in the person to whom they are addressed. The latter is used to refer to things and ideas about things, largely in terms of organized symbols or articulate language. According to Darwin, the animal expressions in the form of singing and roaring may be taken as the precursors of human language. Thus emotive language is nearer to elemental expressions and more concerned with mental attitudes while referential language, being nearer to abstract thinking, is more concerned with grammatical constructions than mere changes in sounds.

With grammar and sentence structure comes logic, and in this connection we have to deal for a moment with the nature of logic. Western logicians take it for granted that the object of logic is rules of human reasoning. This assumption, however, is not quite justified. Take Aristotelian logic, for example, which is evidently based on Greek grammar. The differences between Latin, French, English, and German grammatical forms do not result in any difference between Aristotelian logic and their respective rules of reasoning, because they belong to the same Indo-European linguistic family. Should this logic be applied to Chinese thought, it will prove inappropriate. This fact shows that Aristotelian logic is based on the structure of the Western system of language. Therefore, we should not follow Western logicians in taking for granted that their logic is the universal rule of human reasoning.

In so far as the object of logic lies in the rules of reasoning implied in language, the expression of reasoning must be implicitly influenced by language structure, and different languages will have more or less different forms of logic. Hence the difference between Chinese logic and Aristotelian logic. The traditional type of subject-predicate proposition is absent in Chinese logic. According to the usage of Western logic, in such a sentence as "A relates to B" the form is not a subject-predicate proposition but a relational proposition. Another sentence like "A is related to B" is in the form in question, because there is the distinction between the subject and predicate. For both forms, however, there is in literary Chinese only one, that is, *chia lien yi.* Although we may say colloquially *chia shih lien yi,* the function of the *shih* is that of the so-called "empty words," which are used only for emphasis or intonation, without any grammatical function. Both of these Chinese propositions mean the same thing, without grammatical distinction except that the latter is more emphatic. Neither is a subject-predicate proposition. *Lien* relates the two terms *chia* and *yi* but it is not a copula.

Regarding the "empty words" such as *che, yeh, hu, tsai, yi, wei,* and so forth, they were not primarily so, their original meaning having been lost. Their function is based on their sounds. As such sounds do not have proper characters, they are represented by characters of similar sounds, which are called "borrowed" words. Such a "borrowed" use denotes only the sound without any implications as to meaning. The original characters had their own meaning. For example, the *wei* mentioned a moment ago originally meant *hou* or "apes." It is the sound, not the meaning of the original, which is borrowed. In the formula ". . . *che . . . yeh*," *che* serves the function of a comma and *yeh* that of a full stop. According to the types of language mentioned above, the referential and the emotive, the Chinese "empty words" are emotive words. These empty-emotive words are closely related to the ideographic nature of Chinese characters, on which we will have more to say later. Now it suffices to say that Aristotelian logic is based on the sentence structure characterized by the subject-predicate form. Should we alter the sentence structure, the validity of the traditional Aristotelian logic may be questioned. With these preliminary remarks we may proceed to a discussion of the differences between the Western linguistic family and the Chinese language, and their respective influences on logic.

Western thought is in the last analysis confined to Aristotelian logic although later developments in logic have gone beyond the Aristotelian type. Modern mathematical logic, for example, is only an extension of formal logic. In no way can it unify all the forms of logic. The reason why Bertrand Russell is opposed to the idea of substance lies entirely in the fact that he has discovered a new logic not based upon the form of subject-predicate proposition. As a matter of fact, however, this new system of logic applies, apart from mathematics, only to the physical sciences. It is not applicable to the social sciences. Therefore, traditional logic is still the "living logic" in the mind of Western thinkers. Now it can be shown that the "ten categories" and the later modified "five predicables" in Aristotelian logic are based on Greek grammar. And so long as definition and division are derived from the "ten categories" and the "five predicables" they in their turn are limited by Greek grammar. The "fallacies" pointed out by Aristotle are essentially those found in the Greek language.

Apart from the obvious examples mentioned above, the basis of Aristotelian logic may be seen definitely to lie in the subject-predicate form of language structure. It is seen in the English sentence "it is," which means "it exists." The verb "to be" has the meaning of existence, and Western logic is closely related to the verb "to be" in Western languages. It must have occurred to the readers of Plato that the verb "to be" is quite rich in meaning. Many philosophical problems come from it. Because the verb "to be" has the meaning of existence, the "law of identity" is inherent in Western logic; without it there can be no logical inference. Western logic, therefore, may be called "identity logic."

The law of identity does not merely control logical operations such as deductions and inferences but also influences concepts of thought. As we know, Aristotle's philosophy was made possible entirely by the use of "identity logic." For him the substance is merely derived from the subject and the verb "to be." From the latter, because its implication of existence leads naturally to the idea of "being," and from the former because in a subject-predicate proposition the subject cannot be eliminated. From the indispensability of the subject in a sentence, only a short step leads to the necessity for a "substratum" in thought. For example, when we say, "This is yellow and hard," yellowness and hardness are the so-called "attributes" which are attributed to something, the something in this case being "this." The "something" in general is the substratum. With a substratum emerges the idea of "substance." The idea of substance is indeed a foundation or fountainhead for all other philosophical developments. If there is any description, it becomes an attribute. An attribute must be attributed to a substance, thus the idea of substance is absolutely necessary in thought in the same way as the subject is absolutely necessary in language. This is the reason why in the history of Western philosophy, no matter how different the arguments may be, pro or con, about the idea of substance, it is the idea of substance which itself constitutes the central problem.

The English word "it" also has its own peculiarities. It is a non-definitive. It denotes *something*, but not what. Once the *what* is stated there develop the subject and predicate, or in other words, the substance is characterized by its attributes and the attributes are attributed to the substance. Thus, the separation between existence and whatness was the fundamental condition under which the concept of the substance was born. And this condition is expressed only in Western language structure. It may be agreed then, after considering the peculiarities of the verb "to be" and the word "it," that many philosophical problems are merely problems of language.

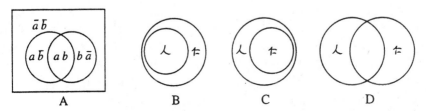

The Chinese language has its own peculiarities. First, it is not essential for a Chinese sentence to have a subject. It is often understood. In a sentence like *hsueh erh shih hsi chih pu yi yueh hu* ("When we study and constantly review it, is it not pleasant?"), *or kou chih yu jen yi wu o yeh* ("If there is devotion to benevolence, there is no evil"), the subject is eliminated. Examples of this kind are too numerous to mention. The above two are random examples from the *Analects*. Secondly, in Chinese there is no verb "to be" comparable to the English form. The colloquial *shih* does not convey the idea of existence. The literary *wei* on the other hand conveys an idea of *ch'eng* which means "to become." But in English "becoming" is exactly opposite to "being." Such a formula as ". . . *che* . . . *yeh*" does not mean anything identical, and consequently does not constitute a logical proposition in the Western sense. If we say "*jen che jen yeh*" ("To be a man is to be human"), we cannot say the first *jen* is the subject and the second *jen* (written with a different ideograph) the predicate. In such a sentence the idea cannot be expressed diagrammatically, as is often used in Figure A in the case of Western logic.

The other figures B, C, D cannot convey the exact idea of the sentence. It may be either of the three, or it may be in between the three. This is the best proof of the absence of the word "to be" in Chinese.

We have seen above that Western logic is essentially based upon the law of identity. Division, definition, syllogism, and even conversion and opposition are based upon it. All these are correlated and constitute a system. The basic structure of Chinese thought is different from this system. *The Chinese system of logic, if we may call it a system, is not based upon the law of identity.*

Let us begin with Western logical division. As it is based on the law of identity, it must be dichotomous in such forms as "A and not-A," "literary books and nonliterary books." Cases like "A and B" or "Good and Evil" are not dichotomous in form because besides A and B there may be C and besides Good and Evil there may be Not-Good and Not-Evil. Thus, there is the need in classification for the rule of exclusiveness. But Chinese thought puts no emphasis on exclusiveness, rather it emphasizes the relational quality between above and below, good and evil, something and nothing. All these relatives are supposed to be interdependent. In a sentence like *yu wu hsiang sheng, nan i hsiang ch'eng, ch'ng tuan hsiang chiao, ch'ien hou hsiang sui* ("Something and nothing are mutually generative; the difficult and the easy are mutually complementary; the long and short are mutually relative; the front and the rear are mutually accompanying"), we have a logic of a quite different nature. . . .

"Intellectual Intuition"

Nishida Kitaro

Intellectual intuition (*intellektuelle Anschauung*) is an intuition of ideal, usually trans-experiential things. It intuits that which can be known dialectically. Examples of this are found in the intuition of artists and people of religion. With respect to the process of intuiting, intellectual intuition is identical to ordinary perception, but with respect to content, intellectual intuition is far richer and more profound.

Some think of intellectual intuition as a kind of special mystical ability. Others think of it as an idle fancy cut off from experiential facts. I believe, however, that it is the same as ordinary perception and that the two cannot be clearly demarcated. Ordinary perception is never purely simple, for it contains ideal elements and is compositional. Though I am presently looking at something, I do not see it just as it is in the present; I see it as mediated in an explanatory manner through the force of past experience.

The ideal elements in perception are not associated ideas added from the outside—they are elements that structure a perception and a perception is transformed by them. The ideal elements hidden at the base of a perception can become extremely rich and profound, and they vary according to the talents or degrees of experiential development in people. With the advance of experience, both that which at first could not be experienced and that which could be only gradually known dialectically come to appear as intuitional facts. One cannot determine the scope of intuition by taking one's own present experience as the yardstick. Though there are things that I cannot intuit now, this does not mean that nobody can. It is said that when Mozart composed music, including his long pieces, he could discern the whole

Reprinted from Nishida Kitaro, *An Inquiry into the Good,* Masao Abe and Christopher Ives, trans. New Haven, Conn.: Yale University Press, 1990, pp. 30–34. Copyright 1990 by Yale University Press; reprinted with permission.

at once, like a picture or a statue. The ideal elements are not simply built in increments quantitatively, but become qualitatively profound. The culmination of this profundity is found in the intuition possessed by a person of religion who, through human love, can intuit the oneness of self and other. Whether a person's extraordinary intuition is simply an idle fancy or truly an objectively real intuition hinges on its relation to other things, on its effects. In terms of direct experience, an idle fancy and a genuine intuition have the same essential quality; there is only a quantitative difference in the scope of their unities.

Some people think that an intellectual intuition differs from ordinary perception in that it transcends space, time, and the individual person and directly penetrates the true nature of reality. But from the standpoint of pure experience in the strict sense, experience is not bound to such forms as time, space, and individual persons; rather, these discriminations derive from an intuition that transcends them. Furthermore, with respect to seeing reality directly, there is no distinction between subject and object in any state of direct experience—one encounters reality face to face. This is not limited to an individual intellectual intuition; Schelling's "identity" (*Identität*) is a state of direct experience. The distinction between subject and object is a relative form that arises when one has lost the unity of experience, and to regard subject and object as mutually independent realities is an arbitrary view.

Schopenhauer's pure intuition without will is not a special ability of a genius, but rather our most natural, unified state of consciousness. An innocent baby's intuitions fall into this category. Intellectual intuition is just that which deepens and enlarges our state of pure experience; it is the manifestation of a great unity in the systematic development of consciousness. When a scholar achieves a new idea, the moral person a new motive, the artist a new ideal, the religious person a new awakening, such a unity is manifesting itself. (These achievements are all rooted in mystical intuition.) If our consciousness were simply sensory, it would go no farther than being a state of ordinary perceptual intuition. But an idealistic spirit seeks an unlimited unity, which is provided in the form of intellectual intuition. Intellectual intuition, like perception, is the most unified state of consciousness.

Just as ordinary perception is considered merely passive, so is intellectual intuition considered a state of passive contemplation; however, a true intellectual intuition is the unifying activity in pure experience. It is a grasp of life, like having the knack of an art or, more profoundly, the aesthetic spirit. For example, when inspiration arises in a painter and the brush moves spontaneously, a unifying reality is operating behind this complex activity. Its transitions are not unconscious, for they are the development and completion of a single thing.

Intellectual intuition, the discernment of this single reality, can be found not only in the fine arts but in all of our disciplined behavior; it is an extremely ordinary phenomenon. Mainstream psychologists may argue that it is only a habit or an organic activity, but from the standpoint of pure experience it is actually the state of oneness of subject and object, a fusion of knowing and willing. In the mutual forgetting of the self and the object, the object does not move the self and the self does not move the object. There is simply one world, one scene. Intellectual intuition sounds like a subjective activity, but actually it is a state that has transcended subject and object. In fact, the opposition of subject and object comes into being by means of this unity, and things like artistic inspiration attain to it.

Intellectual intuition is not an intuition of an abstract universality apart from facts. Though the spirit of a painting may differ from the individual things depicted, it is not divorced from them. True universality and individuality are not opposed to each other. We can express the true universal through the determination of individuality. Each of the artist's exquisite brush strokes expresses the true meaning of the whole.

Intellectual intuition thus underlies thinking. Thinking is a type of system, and at its base there must be an intuition of unity. As James said in "The Stream of Thought" regarding the consciousness that "the pack of cards is on the table," when we become conscious of the subject, the predicate is implied, and when we become conscious of the predicate, the subject is implied. At the base of that consciousness, a single intuition is essentially identical to having the knack of an art. Stated broadly, a vast intuition functions behind such profound thought as the philosophies of Plato and Spinoza. In thought, a genius's intuition differs not in quality but in degree from ordinary thinking, and it is simply a new, profound intuition of unity.

Intuition lies at the base of all relations, and relations are established by means of it. However far and wide we extend our thought, we cannot go beyond basic intuition, for thought is established upon it. Thought cannot be explained exhaustively, for at its base exists an unexplainable intuiting upon which all proof is constructed. A certain mystical reality is always hidden at the base of thought, and this pertains even to the axioms of geometry. It is often said that thought can be explained but intuition cannot. The word "explanation" simply indicates the ability to return to the fundamental intuition. The intuiting that lies at the foundation of thought becomes the basis of explanation and is at the same time the power of thinking, not simply a static form of thought.

Intellectual intuition functions not only at the base of thinking but also at the base of the will. The will is established through this intuition because to will something is to intuit the oneness of subject and object. The advance of the will is the development and completion of this intuitional unity. From beginning to end, intuition functions at the base of the will, and the completion of intuitional unity constitutes the fulfillment of the will. Because this intuition is operative, we feel that the self functions in the will. The self does not exist apart from this intuition, for the true self is this unifying intuition. From this perspective, what the ancients spoke of as acting from morning to night without acting we might call a stillness in motion, a doing of nondoing. In this way we transcend both knowledge and the will, and in the intuition at their base we can discover their oneness.

True religious awakening is neither an abstract knowledge based in thinking nor a blind feeling. In this awakening we realize with our whole being the profound unity at the base of knowledge and the will. It is a kind of intellectual intuition, a deep grasp of life. The sword of logic cannot penetrate it and desire cannot move it. This awakening is the basis of all truth and contentment. Though their forms vary, all religions necessarily contain this fundamental intuition at their bases. And religion must exist at the base of learning and morality, which comes into being because of religion.

5

Ethics

Things have their root and their branches. Affairs have their end and their beginning. To know what is first and what is last will lead near to what is taught *in the Great Learning.*

The ancients who wished to illustrate illustrious virtue throughout the kingdom, first order well their own States. Wishing to order well their States, they first regulated their families. Wishing to regulate their families, they first cultivated their persons. Wishing to cultivate their persons, they first rectified their hearts. Wishing to rectify their hearts, they first sought to be sincere in their thoughts. Wishing to be sincere in their thoughts, they first extended to the utmost their knowledge. Such extension of knowledge lay in the investigation of things.

Things being investigated, knowledge became complete. Their knowledge being complete, their thoughts were sincere. Their thoughts being sincere, their hearts were then rectified. Their hearts being rectified, their persons were cultivated. Their persons being cultivated, their families were regulated. Their families being regulated, their States were rightly governed. Their States being rightly governed, the whole kingdom was made tranquil and happy.

. . . [A]ll must consider the cultivation of the person the root of *everything besides.*

It cannot be, when the root is neglected, that what should spring forth from it will be well-ordered. (*The Great Learning*)[1]

Indian Philosophies

Hindu Perspectives on Ethics

The essential aim of Indian philosophy is liberation from suffering. This compels its various schools to inquire about what constitutes the good life. And two aspects of the good life are significantly compatible: the highest good for the individual, and the highest social good.

Let us review some fundamental themes in the Indian quest for this good life.

Basic Themes in Hindu Ethics

Life's Four Goals   In Indian thought, there are four basic aims in life:

- To acquire some degree of material well-being
- To experience pleasure
- To live virtuously
- To attain spiritual awakening

These goals are not equally important. The highest goal is spiritual awakening. By itself, material well-being will not bring about immortality or liberation from suffering. Nevertheless, Hindus acknowledge the human need for some material security. What is crucial is our attitude toward this need. As for pleasure, there is an important distinction between that which is good and that which is pleasing. We all seek pleasure and to avoid pain. Yet pleasure in itself is not a good, but rather an instrumental good that enables other goods to come about, the highest being the spiritual pleasure attained through self-realization.

Life's Four Stages   Orthodox Indians believe that there are four stages in life. These stages—called *asramas,* meaning "rest-stops"—are student, householder, forest dweller, and hermit (*sannyasa*). The four stages are viewed as successive steps to spiritual awakening and perfection. This perfection is possible because our very nature is itself divine, or *atman.* Though not legally required, they are held up as ideals to strive for.

The *student* stage is a period of disciplined learning that is totally committed to proper study, especially of the teachings of the Vedas. There is a special relationship between the instructor and the student, for the teacher is viewed as a spiritual mentor.

The *householder* stage commences with marriage and the establishment of a family. A stable family life is essential to the cohesiveness of a society. During this time, the attainment of material security (*artha*) is important for the well-being of the family. Moreover, devotion to family life is a means of transcending one's own self interests.

The third stage is that of the *forest dweller.* At this point, individuals, having fulfilled familial responsibilities, are now ready for retreat from the family in order to nourish their spiritual nature and genuine selves. Again, this is a means to that spiritual realization that is the ultimate aim in orthodox Indian thought.

Finally, the *hermit,* in the stage of *sannyasa,* is the person who has disconnected himself from the world. This person is known as the *sannyasin,* whose highest goal is to achieve *moksha,* or spiritual awakening. The *sannyasin* embarks upon a solitary venture, no longer connected to family and society.

Dharma *Dharma,* an important idea in Indian ethics, comes from the root *dhr,* meaning "to nourish." Its meaning is traced back to the Rig Veda's use of *rita,* or order of the universe. The principle of *rita* is not confined to the physical realm, but is applied even more crucially to the moral level. This means that the universal moral order necessitates the priority of virtue.

Generally, *dharma* means that which is morally correct. *Dharma* also demands fulfillment of one's duties in accordance with one's role. Here is the advice given by a teacher to his student in the *Taittiriya Upanishad:*

> "Speak the truth. Do your duty [dharma]. Study the Wedas [Vedas]. Give what is fitting to the teacher; marry, continue the family. Neither neglect your spiritual nor your worldly welfare. Always learn and teach. Forget neither God nor ancestor. Your mother your goddess, your father your God, your guest your God, your teacher your God; copy our good deeds along, so escape blame.
>
> "Look for men greater than us, welcome them, give them hospitality."[2]

Dharma therefore means right action, and it includes viewing others as we view ourselves. In this way, we would be less inclined to harm another, just as we do not want to be harmed. *Dharma* must be an essential quality within us, for realizing our nature entails realizing our moral character as well.

Moksha *Moksha,* the supreme goal in orthodox Indian thought, refers to genuine spiritual awakening. (For Buddhists, the highest state is called *nirvana.*[3]) Yet, *moksha* has acquired a variety of meanings. For instance, in the Samkhya and Nyaya-Vaisheshika schools, *moksha* is negatively defined as liberation from suffering and misery. The Vedanta schools describe *moksha* positively as the highest bliss. In any case, *moksha* means liberation from *samsara,* the wheel of birth, death, and rebirth.

The many ways to achieve this highest goal of spiritual awakening can be reduced to three major paths, referred to as yogas: karma yoga, bhakti yoga, and jnana yoga. Yoga means "yoke" in the sense of joining together. It can mean the joining together of body and mind, or the joining together of oneself with Reality, *atman* and *Brahman,* realized as one in essence.

Karma yoga is a popular path to enlightenment. This is the way of action, or the way of work, and the path by which our labor and occupation bring us closer to personal realization. The Hindus stress the importance of fulfilling our duties in line with our class.

What is necessary, however, is that we fulfill our duties without being attached to them. In other words, we should work without concern for the consequences of our work. This means that we should not perform our responsibilities *in order* to be recognized or praised. As we will see, a highly important teaching in the *Bhagavad Gita* is to not be attached to the fruits of one's efforts. As long as we are attached to what we do, we work from a self-interested reference point, still enmeshed by desires. The ultimate goal is *moksha,* and not recognition, praise, fame, or reward. The way of action is particularly emphasized, for example, in the Mimamsa school.

Bhakti yoga, which appeals to our more interiorized needs, is the path of devotion and of prayer. This is the path of love of *Brahman* or God. This path satisfies our emotional needs to express devotion through prayer and sacrifice. The notion of *Brahman* as *nirguna* (without qualities or attributes) does not satisfy our need for some positive, more concrete image with which we can more readily identify. Even the attributes of *sat-cit-ananda* (being-consciousness-bliss) can be less satisfying.

Bhakti yoga can lead to union with the divine in the most intimate way. Bhakti yoga is expressed in the religious sects of Saivism and Vaisnavism. (Saivism is a sect that emphasizes devotion to God as Shiva; Vaisnavism is a branch that emphasizes devotion to Vishnu.) The philosophical schools that especially underscore the way of devotion are the Vedanta teachings of Ramanuja and Madhva:

> Lead me from the unreal to the real!
> Lead me from darkness to light!
> Lead me from death to immortality![4]

Jnana yoga addresses another need in us—the need to know. It is the way to *moksha* through knowledge. Proper knowledge is necessary if we are to root out our natural ignorance of our real nature. Our most fundamental error lies in mistaking our ego for our true self. Awakening to the truth of *tat tvam asi* can occur through cultivation of knowledge.

This knowledge is not purely cerebral, but instead a knowledge that involves the total person from the depths of his or her being. It is a knowing that is immediate and total. Yet, in order to gain this intuitive insight, both the cultivation of intellect and the proper state of mind are important. Jnana yoga is quite involved, entailing personal, moral cultivation and intensive study and meditation. The way of knowledge is the focus in Advaita Vedanta, in Jainism, and in Buddhism.

Karma   Any discussion of ethics in Indian philosophy must take into account the belief that our particular quality of existence is to some extent the result of our ethical conduct in former lives. In past existences we have accumulated karma that determines our next rebirth. This will be examined more closely in Chapter 6. However, a review of the meaning of karma is crucial to an understanding of Indian ethics.

Literally, karma refers to an "act" or deed. It is a law pertaining to the moral sphere; it is the principle of moral causality. This means that each deed and thought brings about its specific effect, if not in this life, then in another. This effect is at least twofold: (1) An act or thought produces its particular negative or positive effect, and (2) It contributes to the formation of that person's moral character. A habit of good deeds results in good character, whereas a habit of bad deeds produces bad character. Each action and thought either enhances or detracts from our moral personality.

What is especially important in karma is that we are the sole determiners of what we become. Indians generally believe that we are the ultimate managers of our destiny. Therefore, even though, due to past karma, we are born into a particular class, we still possess the freedom to affect our destinies. Although we are often constrained by our circumstances and conditions, as humans we still possess the free will to determine how we respond to those conditions. The law of karma is not a rigid determinism that rules out freedom; rather, it places a premium on individual responsibility for one's actions. It remains one of the most profound and far-reaching teachings in Indian thought.

Our human existence has a special status with respect to karma: We are chained to the wheel of *samsara,* of birth, death, and rebirth. Yet, this does not guarantee constant rebirth in a human form. Rebirths usually occur in other realms (as animals or insects, for example) and on different planes. Let us be clearer.

As we live, we accumulate karma. Just think of the remarkable amount of karma we accrue in one day, let alone in one lifetime. When we die, we have karma that has not been actualized or effected. We can call this our karmic residue. In other words, not all karma exhausts itself right away, and instead it becomes a latent force in later rebirths. Much of this residue is spent in our rebirths in other forms; only occasionally are we reborn in human form.

However, only humans can bring about karma. In other words, our rebirths in other psycho-physical forms are the result of the products of our karma, even though as humans we can also experience the product of our karma. But we can produce karma only as humans because only as humans do we possess the reason and free will that constitutes moral and immoral behavior.

Therefore, only humans can experience *moksha,* the spiritual awakening that liberates us from the cycle of *samsara.* Remember that the goal in Indian thought is not longevity, but breaking out of *samsara* and realizing total freedom.

Hindus believe that being born into a particular social caste is the result of one's karma. Therefore, this caste system reinforced the teaching of karma. The complex caste system in India had many divisions comprising four main classes that constituted the society: *brahmanas,* or priest-teachers; *kshatriyas,* or warriors; *vaisyas,* or traders and merchants; and *shudras,* or laborers. Those outside society were considered outcasts, referred to as "untouchables."

Brahmanas were the spiritual guides of the community. They were the educators and teachers of the Vedas and were sought out for spiritual advice. *Ksatriyas* were the protectors of the community. Many were soldiers and enforcers of the laws, responsible for protecting society from invasion. *Vaisyas* were the merchants and professionals responsible for maintaining the economic state of the community, including farmers, cattle raisers, and traders. *Shudras* were the laborers. It is important to realize that the status of the laborer was not at first viewed as inferior to that of other classes, for the laborer played a valuable part in the functioning of society.

Within this division of labor, Indian society was able to maintain harmony and complementarity among the different classes. The purpose behind this allotment of responsibilities was the collective well-being.

The Sanskrit word for class is *varna,* which literally means "color." Throughout its history, India managed to assimilate a variety of racial groups, including the indigenous Dravidians, the conquering Aryans, Persians, Greeks, and Huns. Although *varna* may have originally referred to the pigmentation of the skin, color later referred to one's character.[5]

In connection with this, recall the Samkhya theory of the three *gunas:* clarity, activity, and passivity. Each individual possesses these *gunas* in varying degrees. Personal growth consisted of progressing through the predominant *gunas* from passivity to activity to clarity. (These same three *gunas* were also represented by black, red, and white, respectively.) Furthermore, it was believed that just as individuals had certain predominant *gunas,* the same could be said for certain classes. For example, the *brahmanas* possessed more clarity, or *sattva,* which is why they were the accepted teachers and spiritual leaders. The warriors possessed more activity, or *rajas;* the traders and merchants possessed more passivity, or *tamas.* The laborers had little development of any of these *gunas.* So we see that class membership was originally intended to be determined by character, not by birth.[6]

The social rules among the classes were not always hard-and-fast duties, for occasionally they were amenable to varying circumstances. There are abundant examples of individuals infringing upon social rules and justifying their actions through an appeal to personal conscience. In other words, the class system did not obliterate the importance of personal conscience. However, it is crucial that one be able to properly discriminate between personal conscience and personal desires. Within this class system, the freedom of the individual to pursue his or her own moral path is not absolutely prohibited. There are examples of *brahmanas* who became warriors in the *kshatriya* class.[7] Switching castes, however, was generally discouraged as a social practice, and it was important that members of various castes adhere to the prescribed rules of their caste. Such rules were set up as ideal, social, ethical codes.

Bhagavad Gita: The Meaning of Dharma

The *Bhagavad Gita* is one of the most influential works in Indian thought. The action takes place just before the Pandavas battle their cousins, the Kauravas. Arjuna becomes despondent and experiences a moral conflict: He is reluctant to fight against his cousins, for it is clear that the outcome of the battle will mean death for many of them and for his own family and friends as well. In a heartrending scene, just as Arjuna is about to cast his weapons down, Krishna consoles him and engages him in a discussion about the nature of action and duty, or *dharma.* Consequently, Krishna reveals his true, divine nature to Arjuna, and Arjuna achieves an understanding that transcends the ordinary human level of knowledge. The work is a powerful account of the meaning of action and *dharma* in the context of this moral conflict.

It is clear that Arjuna comes to this battle with designs for victory. After all, he and his Pandava brothers are the rightful inheritors of the kingdom, which was unjustly taken from them by the Kaurava clan. Even on the eve of battle, Arjuna reassures his elder brother that their cause is just.

Arjuna's feelings change, however, when he actually confronts the enemy. Faced with imminent bloodshed, pangs of distress wrack him. He does not suddenly transform into a pacifist opposed to all forms of violence; such a view is inconsistent with his lifestyle as a warrior. Arjuna realizes that war will not only destroy family and friends, but will lead to the decline of social order, with its emphasis on clan authority. Many elders will be killed, further eroding the social order.[8]

Despondent, Arjuna presents all sorts of reasons for throwing down his weapons to Krishna, who listens patiently. In many respects Arjuna is not simply surrendering to waves of emotion, for he presents some moral grounds for not fighting. His reasoning is essentially utilitarian, perceiving the long-range devastating results of war for all the parties involved. And these considerations come into sharp conflict with what he intellectually knows to be his duty.

Krishna's response to Arjuna's personal quandary can be interpreted on a number of levels. On the same basic, human level, Krishna provides Arjuna reasons why he should fight. He chastises Arjuna's emotional attachment to the body, arguing that death does not truly occur because the soul is immortal. Krishna speaks of the immortal self:

> Never is he born nor dies;
> Never did he come to be, nor will he ever come to be again:
> Unborn, eternal, everlasting he—primeval:
> He is not slain when the body is slain.
>
> If a man knows him as indestructible,
> Eternal, unborn, never to pass away,
> How and whom can he cause to be slain
> Or slay?[9]

Furthermore, Krishna points out to Arjuna some undesirable consequences that would result if Arjuna refuses to fight:

> But if thou wilt not wage this war
> Prescribed by thy (caste-) duty,
> Then, by casting off both honour and (caste-) duty,
> Thou wilt bring evil on thyself.
>
> Yes, this thy dishonour will become a byword
> In the mouths of men in ages yet to come;
> And dishonour in a man well-trained to honour
> [Is an ill] surpassing death.[10]

Now Krishna raises the most crucial argument: A moral act can only be such if there is no personal attachment to the results (gains or otherwise) of the act. Motives of personal benefit and profit have no part in ethical action:

> Work alone is thy proper business,
> Never the fruits [it may produce];

Let not your motive be the fruit of work,
Nor your attachment to [mere] worklessness (*akarma*).[11]

Krishna's rebuttals are presented on the human plane that Arjuna well understands. However, Krishna is a god in disguise, and his most overpowering attempt to move Arjuna from his lethargy comes when he shares with Arjuna a perspective that goes beyond the limited human plane. Arjuna is thus compelled to view his dilemma in a different light, and from Krishna's cosmic and divine view the dilemma disappears.

This vision is transformative. From his limited human perspective, Arjuna was attached to his actions; from his new perspective, he is freed from such attachment. In this all-embracing cosmic vision, all of his former concerns are essentially irrelevant. Arjuna is now spiritually enlightened, and in his enlightened state the ethical conflict disappears. From this perspective, he realizes he must do what he had intellectually known all along—his duty.

Dharma, or action without attachment to its results, does not mean purposeless action, for action is only meaningful if there is some purpose behind it. Nor is *dharma* that which is without desire. Desireless action is again meaningless action. *Dharma,* or right action, derives from the essential attitude one takes toward purpose and desire.

As long as action occurs within a self-referential context, it is wrong action and not *dharma.* One cannot escape action, for living is acting. Yet the goal is to act properly; the aim is right action or *dharma.* Therefore, the primary yoga emphasized in the *Bhagavad Gita* is that of action, or karma yoga.

Mimamsa School: Metaphysical Status of Dharma

The primary teaching in this school concerns the meaning and significance of *dharma,* or "right action." Basically, right action is that which follows the Vedic prescriptions. Sometimes the term *dharma* is translated as "duty" (as it often is in the *Bhagavad Gita*). Jaimini, the founder of the Mimamsa school, refers to *dharma* as a command to action. And the prescribed actions in the Veda concern rituals, prayers, sacrifices, and other social duties.

An important idea in this school is that the effects of these acts will take place—if not in this life, then in another. Therefore, an act's effect lies in a state of latent actualization. The renowned philosopher in the school, Kumarila, assigned the term *apurva* to this latent state.

What we have in the Mimamsa school is a metaphysical status bestowed upon *dharma. Dharma* is the foundational force behind all things and is that which keeps all things together. Due to its unseen energy, results often occur much later than the performance of the actual cause. In other words, in this dynamic idea of activity, causation itself is dynamic. The action we perform continues beyond the activity itself to eventually bring about an effect.

Advaita Vedanta and Ethics

A moral sensitivity permeates Advaita Vedanta's epistemological and metaphysical considerations. Its raison d'être centers around the oneness of *atman* and *Brahman* and its concomitant nonduality. Therefore, the major moral standard in Advaita teachings is whether our acts or thoughts pull us away from or bring us closer to the realization of this oneness. The actions and thoughts of those who are pulled away from the path to *moksha* are, to various degrees, mired in ego-consciousness. Actions and thoughts leading to the supreme goal of self-discovery are morally appropriate.

In Advaitin ethics, a most crucial factor in awakening lies with jnana yoga, the path of knowledge. *Jnana,* or proper knowledge, is the means to the practice of virtue. And this practice, along with the practice of raja yoga, or meditation, brings us closer to our ultimate goal.

Gandhi: Ahimsa and Satyagraha

In his life and teachings, Gandhi brought together the teachings of Christ, the Buddha, and Mahavira in his interpretation of the *Bhagavad Gita's* karma yoga, or philosophy of action. Even with this eclectic basis, he considers himself first and foremost a Hindu. Nevertheless, he emphasized a universalism among religions that lies in the ideas of nonviolence, *ahimsa,* and compassion. Compassion is meaningless unless actualized in practice; nonviolence and love are the keys to genuine self-determination and governance of others. All this demands strict self-discipline.[12]

Gandhi centered his teaching on the idea of *satyagraha,* which literally means "commitment to truth." For Gandhi, God is Truth, and the Truth of existence lies in compassion. Within a political and social context, *satyagraha* expresses itself in nonviolent resistance to manifestations of nontruth as found, for example, in unjust laws. *Satyagraha* is an expression of Gandhi's belief that truth will eventually prevail over injustice.

Buddhist Perspectives on Ethics

The Four Noble Truths

A fitting introduction to Buddhist ethics is found in the Four Noble Truths. Similar to a medical diagnosis, the Buddha first states what is wrong. The First Truth declares that all existence is permeated with suffering; the Second Truth leads us more into ethics. What is the cause of suffering? If we can determine its cause, or etiology, then we may be able to eradicate it. We are told that the cause of suffering lies in *trsna,* our craving.

The elimination of craving lies at the heart of Buddhist ethics, and it can come about only through detachment. By detachment, Buddhists do not mean the suppression of desire, but rather not attaching ourselves to desires. Therefore, an integral standard for right action is whether or not it leads to detachment. This standard must be viewed in terms of the aim of detachment, which is nirvana, or the liberation from ego. (See the Fire-Sermon at the end of this chapter.)

Buddhist teachings have sometimes been viewed as pessimistic. However, the Buddha's message avoids pessimism because in the Third Truth he teaches that there is a way to be liberated from this suffering.

The Fourth Truth cites more specifically how this path to freedom can be achieved: Liberation can take place by diligently practicing the Eightfold Path to salvation, which consists of:

- right views
- right thought
- right speech
- right conduct
- right livelihood
- right effort
- right mindfulness
- right concentration

Let us briefly review the Eightfold Path, which is included in the selections at the end of the chapter.

Right views consist of knowing the Four Truths. This also means knowing the proper goal of spiritual enlightenment. *Right thought* means acquiring purity of heart and sincerity in our lives. Both right view and right thought emphasize proper knowledge as essential on the way to enlightenment.

Right speech means getting rid of bad habits such as lying and gossip. Buddhists believe that our speech reflects our character: What is within us naturally manifests itself in how we express ourselves in speech. Therefore slander, cursing, and other forms of negative speech are proscribed. *Right conduct* prohibits, for example, murder, theft, and living unchastely. *Right livelihood* entails pursuing a profession that does not bring about unnecessary suffering to others. It warns against professions engaging in violence, such as warfare and hunting. It also prohibits the drinking of liquor. Right speech, right conduct, and right livelihood emphasize proper behavior on the path toward enlightenment.

Right effort is training the mind to guard against unhealthy thoughts, for it can easily be distracted so that we can lose sight of the goal of enlightenment. We have the potential to control our mental activity. *Right mindfulness* means being fully attentive to one's state of mind and body, especially when they are agitated. *Right concentration* is knowing and practicing the proper techniques of meditation. Right effort, right mindfulness, and right concentration emphasize the importance of mental focus and meditation, the harmony of body and mind. For Buddhists, meditation is a crucial step toward enlightenment.

The Middle Way

According to legendary accounts, Siddhartha personally experienced the need for a middle way just before attaining his awakening. It is said that a maiden visited the Bodhi tree to offer gifts of food to the spirit of the tree. She believed that the emaciated man, Siddhartha, exhausted in sleep under the tree, was the spirit incarnated, so she set the food before him. Upon his awakening, and after eating the small portions placed near him, he intuitively sensed that the true way was a middle path between asceticism and physical indulgence.

This Middle Way became the cornerstone of Buddhist teachings and Buddhist ethics.

Siddhartha's previous ascetic practices had been too extreme. Through these practices he was still held captive to the desire for liberation, even at the price of sacrificing his personal health. He also knew that the other extreme of self-indulgence was certainly not the way to enlightenment. The Middle Way steers a balanced path between these two extremes of defect and excess.

Sangha

The famous historical example of the ethical teaching of detachment lies with the Sangha, or order of monks. The Sangha upheld the importance of discipline and detachment expressed in over 220 rules in its *Vinaya,* or teachings regarding discipline. These rules were essentially prohibitions—for example, against killing, theft, lying, malice, slander, and gossip. There were also strict rules regarding sexual abstinence and owning private property, the violation of which could lead to expulsion from the Sangha or other less severe punishments.

What is most important about these rules, however, is the attitude one takes toward them. The spirit in which the rule is considered counts more than strict adherence. Rules are intended to cultivate in the monk a genuine spirit of detachment and discipline, with nirvana as the supreme aim.

The Sangha was not absolutely cloistered. During the rainy season, monks spent most of their time in quiet meditation. Otherwise, monks often traveled to surrounding communities, begging and acting as spiritual examples to the community. Begging was a common practice, and it was looked upon positively as an opportunity for the layperson to be charitable. In begging, the potential giver can practice virtue and so effect positive karma.

Karma

As it is in the orthodox tradition, karma is a crucial teaching underlying Buddhist ethics. Karma, the law of moral causation, is caused by both the intent and the act. Karma's effects reflect whether the weight of intentions and actions is negative or positive.

For Buddhists, karma also comes about as a response to external factors such as environment and other specific conditions. Moreover, it comes from unconscious motives and drives, such as the unconscious desire for immortality. When we consider these factors, we get away from a mechanistic notion of karma (as we find in Jainist teachings) and see a variety of mitigating circumstances and variables that effect karmic action.[13]

Virtues

Cultivating good character demands the practice of virtue, or *paramita.* The four basic virtues are: love, compassion, sympathetic joy, and impartiality.

Metta is the term for love. In the spirit of love, all people are seen as equal. Metta also means charity, which is performed without self-reference, without any thought of personal gain. This can occur if the giver gives without making any distinctions among creatures.

Karuna is the term for compassion, which involves direct empathy with the suffering of another.

Sympathetic joy is the other side of compassion. In it one shares in another's happiness or joy. One is able to do this because there is no jealousy or envy.

Impartiality has also been called equanimity, or steady-mindedness. This attitude is an important contrast to feelings of intense emotion or desires, which can easily overwhelm a person. A person with equanimity cannot be so easily overcome.

Dependent Origination

We can see that the practice of virtue requires that we detach ourselves from considerations of "I." This is especially enhanced in the Buddhist teaching of *pratityasamutpada*, or dependent origination, which reinforces the belief that we are not isolated, independent entities. Thus the idea that we are solely responsible for our own salvation is foreign to Buddhist ethics. Compassion for other creatures is quite natural and broadens the sphere of responsibility to include all other things.

This is an important point. The notion of individual interests and rights is not a primary consideration. Buddhist ontology repudiates the primacy of the individual. A strong sense of individualism is absent in a Buddhist climate that teaches nonsubstantiality. In this respect, *pratityasamutpada* sustains the Buddhist teaching of *karuna*.

Bodhisattva: *Compassion*

Our discussion leads us now to one of the most contentious issues since the Fourth Buddhist Council: the status of the *arhats*, those who have attained the state of liberation. Many have challenged the transcendent status of these *arhats* and have felt that the emphasis on personal salvation as an *arhat* detracted from the real Buddhist message of compassion for others.

This contention was one of the dividing lines between the early, conservative Theravada school and the later Mahayana. For the Theravada, the only *bodhisattva* was the Buddha; no others could reach this same spiritual height. Therefore, one must strive to become an *arhat*. Because the *arhat* reaches enlightenment only after acquiring wisdom, or *prajna*, the emphasis is therefore on insight. Moreover, once the *arhat* attains enlightenment, the *arhat* is free from *samsara* and is not reborn.

In contrast, the Mahayana school rejected this notion and claimed that we are all equally capable of attaining Buddhahood. Therefore, our ideal is the *bodhisattva*. The *arhat*, for Mahayana, is inferior to the *bodhisattva*. For the *arhat*, salvation is an individual enterprise, and the *arhat* enters his vessel by himself to cross from the shore of ignorance to enlightenment.

This is not the case with the *bodhisattva*, who willingly returns to the cycle of *samsara* in order to guide others to enlightenment and freedom from suffering. The motivation for this is the genuine compassion, called *karuna*, which the *bodhisattva* possesses in addition to wisdom, or *prajna*. The *bodhisattva* incorporates both wisdom and compassion.

By eventually idealizing the *bodhisattva* and claiming it to be the proper goal for enlightenment, Mahayana teachings gave a subordinate role to the goal of nirvana. Instead, the state of *bodhi,* or awakening, acquired prominence, as did the belief in multiple *bodhisattvas* existing in various realms, all seeking to aid in the enlightenment of humans. For example, one of the more popular celestial *bodhisattvas* is Avalokitesvara, who is the exemplar of compassion, or *karuna*. His name combines the words *ishvara* (lord) and *avalokita,* meaning "he who watches with compassion." He bestows comfort and safety on all.

We see from all this that compassion is perhaps the most indispensable virtue. Buddhists have devised specific practices to cultivate compassion, focusing particularly on detachment from self-interests and material goods. Compassion and detachment work together: We are able to empathize more readily with others to the extent that we are detached from self-interests.

In all this we must foster a proper state of mind and must always guard our thoughts. All suffering ultimately originates in the mind, which can be like a raging elephant. (The selection from the *Dhammapada* at the end of the chapter tells us of the influence of the mind.) So, Buddhists constantly speak of maintaining vigilance over one's thoughts.

Buddhist Critique of Castes

How do these ethical precepts affect the Buddhist view of society? Do Buddhists teach a social ethic? To begin with, Buddhists oppose what, in their view, is a static depiction of the social order in orthodox teachings, which appear to bestow a divine sanction for the social caste structure.

The prevailing belief that one is born into classes that genuinely represent our spiritual status is rejected by Buddhists. Buddhists believe that castes are formed to classify the various occupations, and that they are not divinely ordained. They are against any view that treats castes hierarchically and in which the fourth class, the *shudras,* are looked down upon. Buddhists also criticize those *brahmanas* who sometimes abused their privileges. Buddhists are opposed to the spiritual elitism the class structure provoked.

The Buddha insisted on the fundamental equality of all people. (Membership in his Sangha could come from any of the classes.) Each person has the potential to achieve enlightenment. Later Mahayana teachings broadened this idea even further, declaring that all psycho-physical beings—all sentient creatures, not just humans—possess Buddha-nature.

Keep in mind that Buddhists are not advocating a Marxist notion of a classless society; some class structure is necessary. We see this within the Sangha, in which there is a strict hierarchy and structure. Hierarchy need not mean a spiritual elitism. What the Buddha pointed to is the need for fair interaction among the classes, a mutual give-and-take with reciprocal rights and bligations. An example of this lies in the relationship between parents and children:

> In five ways a child should minister to his parents as the Eastern quarter: Once supported by them I will now be their support; I will

perform duties incumbent upon them; I will keep up the lineage and tradition of my family; I will make myself worthy of my heritage.

In five ways, parents thus ministered to as the Eastern quarter by their child, show their love for him: they restrain him from vice, they exhort him to virtue, they train him to a profession, they contract a suitable marriage for him, and in due time they hand over his inheritance.[14]

Without this system of mutual obligations and rights, society breaks down.

Buddhists place great emphasis on familial relations. After all, family stability enhances social cohesion. The Buddha speaks of the duties toward one's parents, particularly when they get old:

"He who being rich does not support mother or father who are old or past their youth—that is a cause of loss."[15]

To conclude, the freedom from suffering that the Buddhist sets as the supreme goal occurs gradually in stages. This is a very important idea. The novice cannot attain this freedom right away; it can come about only after a long and ordered process involving training, discipline, meditation, and practice of virtue. The gradualness of the process reflects its difficulty, but it also gives hope to all people in various stages in their lives. The image often used is that of a lotus growing in mud. We are all lotuses in mud; we habitually allow the mud to taint our nature. Buddhism teaches that we are also capable of rising above the mud.

■■■■ Chinese Philosophies ■■■■

In Chinese thought, a teaching is valued primarily in terms of how it may lead to personal moral cultivation. The moral law is the foundation for all others. There is a rich connection between truth and experience. Truth is both discovered and expressed in action. Let us review some recurrent traits throughout Chinese philosophy.[16]

Ethical teachings in China center around the need for harmony between self and society. Recall that the Chinese term for humanity is *jen,* a twofold character meaning both an individual person and more than one. The collective welfare usually overrides individual interests, and the family is the most vital group within the collective. Confucius pointed out repeatedly that the dynamics within the family are the source of ethical values, a notion especially reinforced in the ideas of Mencius. Family harmony is given highest consideration.

Ancient Schools and Ethics

The period of the Hundred Schools is known for its intense debates. For instance, Confucianists were offended by what they perceived was an escapist morality of Taoists. Mo Tzu and the Mohists challenged Confucian teachings with their strong utilitarianism. Han Fei Tzu challenged both Confucian and Mohist ideas by elevating the status of laws to produce social order. One of the most burning issues concerned human nature: Is it essentially good, evil, or neutral?

Confucianists

Confucius The most significant moral question Confucius addressed concerns the relationship between social harmony and personal integrity. For Confucius, the two must be maintained in proper balance by living a virtuous life. The most important virtues are *jen,* or human-heartedness; *li,* or propriety, etiquette; and *chih,* righteousness.

Jen is indispensable in attaining harmony, especially within the five, crucial human relationships:

- between ruler and minister
- between father and son
- between elder brother and younger brother
- between husband and wife
- between friend and friend

Jen is referred to in many passages of the *Analects* as "goodness," "human-heartedness," "compassion," and "benevolence." *Jen* more broadly means a condition of virtue and of moral excellence:

> The Master said, "The determined scholar and the man of virtue will not seek to live at the expense of injuring their virtue. They will even sacrifice their lives to preserve their virtue complete."[17]

This general meaning of *jen* is defined more specifically as filial piety, propriety, and generosity; a person possesses compassion for all. When Confucius was asked by Fan Ch'ih about the meaning of *jen,* he replied, "It is to love *all* men."[18] *Jen* is illustrated further in Confucius's famous Golden Rule:

> Tsze-kung asked, saying, "Is there one word which may serve as a rule of practice for all one's life?" The Master said, "Is not RECI-PROCITY such a word? What you do not want done to yourself, do not do to others."[19]

This rule requires sincerity and commitment to others. *Jen* is the main thread that runs throughout the teachings in the *Analects.*

As with *jen, li* can be defined in both a narrow and a broad sense. In its narrow sense, *li* means specific social rules such as codes of etiquette and manners; in its broad sense, *li* refers to ritual. It appears that Confucius was more concerned with this general meaning of *li.* For Confucius, ritual was essential for two basic reasons: Ritual maintains social harmony, and ritual is necessary for personal moral cultivation.

As proper conduct, *li* is an appropriate expression of *jen.* For instance, filial piety, crucial to social harmony, must be expressed consistently with rules of propriety. Yet, *li* cannot be mechanically enacted:

> The Master said, "If a man be without the virtues proper to humanity, what has he to do with the rites of propriety? If a man be

without the virtues proper to humanity, what has he to do with
music?"[20]

Li must be conducted in the proper spirit of sincerity and respect.

According to Confucius, there must be rules of propriety. This gives
special value to human behavior. Moral excellence requires a cultivation of
both proper attitude and right expression. One without the other is empty
and directionless. The Chinese scholar Anthony Cua describes this twofold
aspect in ethics:

> A moral action, on this view, can be *completely* described only in terms
> of the satisfaction of both the internal *jen* criterion and external *li*
> criterion. What is thus a single description of moral action is, to the
> Western eye, a duality of logically independent descriptions: a descrip-
> tion of an action as conforming to a moral standard or rule, and a
> description of the *style* or manner of performance.[21]

The *Analects* often allude to this ideal integration of both *jen* and *li* embodied
in the perfect person, or *chun-tzu*.

Chih, or righteousness, demands individual integrity, which means living according to sound moral principles. *Chih* blends all the virtues together
and demands authenticity in thought and in action.

Mencius and the Four Beginnings

Mencius's ethical teachings center around
his view of human nature. He believed that we are all born with a capacity
for goodness in four connected ways, known as the "Four Beginnings." We
come into existence with the inborn virtues of *jen* (humanity), *i* (righteousness), *li* (propriety), and *chih* (wisdom).

Jen is human-heartedness and shows itself in compassion. *I*, righteousness, arises when there is the sense of guilt and disaffection. *Li* is propriety
and comes about with an awareness of what is appropriate and what is not.
Chih, wisdom, originates through the discernment of what one ought to do
and ought not to do. These Four Beginnings are innate and constitute our
inner sovereignty.

The goal is to cultivate these four seeds in oneself, which also requires
us to recognize these four seeds in all others as well. Each of us possesses
the potential for "sageliness within and kingliness without."

Let us now consider how Mencius applied *jen,* for instance, to governing. In governing, *jen* can be manifested through equitable distribution of
land for the people. This idea challenges the long-held feudal system in which
ordinary people worked as serfs on parcels of land owned by nobles and feudal
lords. At the same time, there must be clear divisions of labor within the state.
(This is one of the reasons why the rectification of names is important for
Confucius. The name must be appropriate to specific roles, for in this way
pertinent duties are clear.) For example, the duties of the nobility were to
ensure economic security and education for their people. Mencius felt that
the ruler must also possess the greatest virtue, must be a Sage-king who acts
in accord with the will of Heaven.

Mencius is especially known for his emphasis on filial devotion and family relationships. Not only is the family bond the basis of all human relationships, but it can be the fullest and most concrete demonstration of moral excellence.

Hsun Tzu   Hsun Tzu radically disagreed with Mencius concerning human nature. As is apparent in the selection at the end of this chapter, Hsun Tzu argued that we are more naturally inclined towards evil, and that we actualize our evil natures by allowing our desires to overrule our reason.

There are two prominent features within the human psyche: emotions and intellect. For Hsun Tzu, it is precisely through our reason that we can regain some control over our desires; it is through intellect that we are able to reasonably assess the benefits and harms of certain courses of action and to choose that which will produce the most benefits. Whereas there is a strong utilitarian thrust in Hsun Tzu's philosophy, it is nevertheless a utilitarianism aimed at achieving the proper Confucian goal of harmony.

For Hsun Tzu, virtue requires that we also act in the spirit of authentic sincerity. In this way, through repeated practice of virtue, we are able to go beyond our original natures. This is quite different from Mencius, who claimed that by living virtuously we are living in accord with our real natures.

Hsun Tzu agreed with Mencius that the ruler must also be a sage. However, not only must the Sage-king be wise, he must also be able to exert power if necessary. This is an important ingredient for Hsun Tzu because of what he perceived to be the fundamental weakness in human nature. As different as some of Hsun Tzu's ideas may be from some Confucian ideals, he is still essentially a Confucianist due to his strong **humanism**.

Tao Te Ching

The ethical teachings in the *Tao Te Ching* emanate from the poem's strong naturalism, which differs from the strong humanist emphasis in Confucius. The *Tao Te Ching* teaches that each person must follow her or his *te*, or natural power, which is a principle of spontaneity and sustains us. Through it we remain in harmony with *Tao* and with Nature. Living according to *te* means living a life of simplicity and natural harmony. Being ruled by intellect dampens the power of *te*; being ruled by desires also weakens *te*:

> Therefore Tao gives them birth,
> Teh [Te] fosters them,
> Makes them grow, develops them,
> Gives them a harbor, a place to dwell in peace,
> Feeds them and shelters them.[22]

One of the influential themes running throughout the *Tao Te Ching* is *wu-wei*, which literally means "nonaction." It is a letting-be, a yielding to the natural flow of things that is opposed to any type of aggression. This is the lesson we can assimilate from Nature. For instance, a waterfall is a fitting symbol of *wu-wei* in that the water, mountain, and rocks yield to each other; in doing so, they fulfill their nature.

A person in the ideal state lives in harmony with nature. The ideal ruler rules according to *wu-wei,* not imposing an artificial regime of unnecessary laws. (Again, we see the contrast with Confucius, for whom laws are necessary.)

Mohists and Legalists

Mo Tzu and Universal Love   Mo Tzu's ethics are convincing indicators of his utilitarian outlook. For instance, he criticized the elaborate funeral rituals of the Confucians because they were a waste of resources. He was also opposed to warfare and unnecessary conflict because they did not produce overall benefit for the people.

Perhaps Mo Tzu's most important ethical teaching is his "universal love," which urges us to love everyone equally, without partiality. Mo Tzu encouraged universal love because, if practiced, it leads to good results for most people. War violates universal love and is the severest expression of partiality. A selection from Mo Tzu describing universal love is found at the end of this chapter.

How does universal love fit into Mo Tzu's ideas of human nature? Our natures are decidedly weak, but they are not necessarily evil. (Here he disagreed with Hsun Tzu.) Mo Tzu compared our natures to "pure silk," which acquires whatever color it is stained in.[23] Mo Tzu is less concerned with our original nature than with what we can become.

Mo Tzu's utilitarianism inspired his political philosophy in which he believed in a strong yet benevolent ruler who can maintain order. This ruler is one who knows the will of Heaven.[24] The final aim is to sustain an orderly society, one with the greatest benefits, prosperity, and progress for all people.

Han Fei Tzu and the Legalists   For Han Fei Tzu and the Legalists, our natures are inherently corrupt and we are less capable of living virtuously. Social order, therefore, can only result from strict adherence to law.

How can law be enforced, particularly if our natures are corrupt? *Shu* refers to a particular manner of governing that requires a strong and strict ruler. Moreover, this ruler need not be a sage within. After all, Han Fei Tzu downplayed the possibility of virtue, even for the ruler. Instead, the ruler must rule with a heavy hand, continually and consistently rewarding those who obey and punishing those who violate the laws.

The ruler conducts *shu* in at least three ways. First, he properly delegates authority. Second, he prohibits the spread of independent teachings. (Historically, this was the time of the infamous Burning of the Books.) Finally, the ruler exercises his power through a system of reward and punishment. The most important ingredient in all this is the critical significance of laws; the state can maintain order only through its laws.

Chinese Buddhism and Fa-tsang

Fa-tsang represents the Hua Yen school, which stresses the interdependency of all things. An analogy lies in a building and its rafters. Even though the building's roof is supported by its rafters, the meaning of the rafter does not exist in and of itself; it exists in its function for the building. Seen separately, it possesses no force or meaning. The whole must be considered to define the power of the particular, so that "the perfect building is inherent in the one rafter."[25]

What are the ethical implications of this? Just as the individual rafter contributes to the existence of the whole building, the whole building contributes to the meaning of the rafter. In like manner, there is mutual responsibility toward all things assumed by my being involved in the universe.[26]

Recognizing this is realizing *sunyata* and is the attainment of "Great Wisdom." However, lingering in Great Wisdom is insufficient because Mahayana teachings require universal compassion. Fa-tsang therefore advocated going beyond Great Wisdom to Great Compassion, or *Mahakaruna*.

Neo-Confucianism and Ethics

Neo-Confucianists point to an intrinsic goodness in human nature and the potential for virtue. Desires are part of the natural order and do not constitute anything evil. It is the attitude and attachment to these desires that brings about immorality. Furthermore, the criterion for ascertaining the goodness or badness of an action lies in whether or not the action is performed from a point of self-centeredness.

The Ch'eng Brothers, Chu Hsi, and the School of Principle

Ch'eng Yi held that we essentially manifest principle, or *li*. This principle is our nature, and principle is intrinsically good. Moral cultivation is therefore the cultivation of our true nature and comes about in a number of ways. The most important way is to know *li*. Through an understanding of *li* we can obtain moral growth.

According to Ch'eng Yi, we study principle through the study of things. He encouraged the investigation of a single thing, for in this process we learn about its *li*. By learning of the *li* of a single thing, we gain insight into the *li* behind all things. And the learning of *li* naturally leads to moral conduct.

Like his brother Ch'eng Yi, Ch'eng Hao emphasized awareness of the oneness of all being and taught that each act should be inspired by this awareness. An understanding of *li* demands freedom from ego and self-interest. This freedom from self is compared to a brilliant mirror in that we must have our minds as clean as a polished mirror.

As is apparent from the selection at the end of this chapter, Chu Hsi gave a renewed thrust to Confucian ethics. His ethics was based on his metaphysical synthesis of *T'ai-chi, li,* and *ch'i. T'ai-chi,* the Supreme Ultimate, exists within each of us like a pearl in mud. We need to purify the mud in order for the pearl to shine forth.[27]

However, *ch'i* acts as an impediment that keeps our original nature from shining forth. Chu Hsi affirmed Ch'eng Yi's belief that diminution of the effect of *ch'i* results only from understanding our own nature, or *li*. This also means understanding the nature of all things. Herein lies moral cultivation.

Moral cultivation therefore starts with the investigation of all things. This must be a concentrated effort, earnest and serious. So much investigation is necessary because through this we come to understand the nature of things, *li*. Because all principles are ultimately one, by understanding the principle of external things we come to know our own principle as well, which in turn leads to the liberating knowledge of the Supreme Reality within all things. In this fashion we can cultivate our moral natures.

Wang Yang-ming and the School of Mind

It is important to place Wang Yang-ming's ethical teaching in its proper context. The Neo-Confucianism of Chu Hsi, dominant as it was for centuries, succumbed to misinterpretations and abuses. Its emphasis on the investigation of things in order to discover their *li*, or principle, eventually transformed into overly specialized analyses. With Chu Hsi and Ch'eng Yi's interpretation of the classics as the official basis for civil service examinations, a rigid type of learning eventually set in, requiring fragmented, specialized, rote knowledge.

Wang, who was raised in a culture that became increasingly dissatisfied with the rationalist Neo-Confucian thought, opposed Chu Hsi on a number of points. First, Wang disagreed with Chu Hsi's differentiation between mind and principle, and he considered the investigation of all things to be futile. Wang also believed that because the will precedes knowledge of things, any investigation must be based on a sincere will.

Perhaps Wang Yang-ming's most original idea is the oneness of knowledge and action. Action is the completion of knowledge, and knowledge necessarily compels action. This idea is grounded in his belief that mind and principle are identical.

The unity of knowledge and action is discussed throughout Wang Yang-ming's works. This is the topic in his Letter to Ku Tung-ch'iao found at the end of this chapter. In it he criticized current trends of superficial learning, claiming that the prestige of the state has eroded because of ignorance of the teachings of past sages. He upheld the sages of the past who harmonized knowledge and action. This unity is also emphasized in his *Instructions for Practical Life*, conversations recorded by his student, Ts'u Ai. In it the alleged solidarity of knowledge and action was challenged through the example of filial piety. People know of the principle of filial piety, but it is a fact that not all people fulfill it. Wang's response is that selfishness has worked to corrupt the "original character" of this unity of "knowledge and practice." Wang then goes on to provide some analogies from aesthetics and psychology.[28] Our perception of an object as beautiful is already a response to that object.

At the same time, this response comes from an intuitive knowledge of the object as beautiful. Such knowledge is therefore prereflective. In the same way, already intuiting the idea of filial piety entails responding to it in some way.

Knowledge is intuitive knowledge. Because the mind is principle, and principle is good, we intuitively know what is good. Intuitive knowledge is further motivated through will and is completed in action. Therefore, not only do we intuitively know what is good, but we innately have the capacity to do what is good.

Wang compared intuitive knowledge to the sun and desires to clouds that block out the sun. He spoke of seven feelings—joy, grief, anger, fear, hate, love, and desire—that form a natural part of the mind and are not in themselves good or evil. Evil comes about when attachment to these feelings occurs, for this taints the natural state of mind and intuitive knowledge.

The "ethics of engagement" is a fitting description of Wang's ethics. Once there is sincere will and innate knowledge, action is spontaneous. In this way, not only is moral balance restored socially, but inwardly one realizes the essential oneness with all things.

Rather than investigate external things to discover their principle, Wang recommended that we become aware of mind and our original nature, which means we must cultivate a sincerity of will. Proper investigation of mind can occur only with this sincerity.

The sage's mind is a clear mirror that allows intuitive knowledge to express itself while cultivating sincerity of will. In this way, we act naturally and know the good, and we express our feelings without any attachment. This is a unity of activity and quiescence that comes close to the Ch'an teaching of the tranquility of mind.

What is most important in Wang Yang-ming is that genuine moral understanding necessitates an active response; it is not simply a cognitive knowing without some embodiment in action. Wang presented moral understanding as a dynamic undertaking, as a corrective to an abstract approach to ethics.

Empirical School

Tai Chen sought to restore a balance he felt somehow went astray in the Neo-Confucian positions. In doing so, he revived the practical ethics of Confucius and Mencius. His teaching seeks to return to down-to-earth, concrete, and practical concerns. In this way, it is less abstract and somewhat empirical. For him, *li* is immanent in *ch'i;* they both comprise *Tao*. As a result, feelings and desires are immanent in human nature. Knowledge is also a natural faculty through which feelings and desires can be kept in balance and properly cultivated. This results in virtuous behavior, especially *jen*.

Desires and feelings, kept in balance by knowledge, allow for a more complete expression of our natures. Harmony is the aim in human life. Without this balance we can be pulled into either extreme of excess or defect, disrupting our natural harmony. It is precisely due to knowledge that virtue is possible.

K'ang Yu-wei offered an interesting philosophy of history that supports his teaching concerning social ethics and practical reform. For K'ang, history is the progressive maturing of *jen*. According to K'ang, Confucius taught of three ages: the Age of Disorder, the Age of Approaching Peace, and the Age of Universal Peace. The Age of Disorder had already appeared. The Age of Approaching Peace still exists, for conflict still exists due to discriminations. Eventually it will lead to the Age of Universal Peace,[29] with its elimination of all boundaries (racial, class, political, and so on).

This elimination of boundaries can occur only through the cultivation of *jen*. For K'ang, *jen* thus becomes the ground for political reform, for it constitutes our true spiritual nature and especially means compassion and empathy for the sufferings of others.

■ Japanese Philosophies ■

It appears that Japanese philosophy has not fully developed the notion of a separate, personal individuality. This has far-reaching repercussions in ethics. Naturally, the most important features are other-oriented, stressing duties, obligations, loyalty, faith, and compassion. (More extensive considerations of individuality are now entering the scene in contemporary Japanese thought.[30])

Japanese Buddhism

Karma

Even though early Buddhism's main hold was upon the nobility, it had a far-reaching effect on almost all facets of Japanese life, especially morality. Probably one of the most significant ideas was its teaching of karma, which we recall, establishes a vital causal link among past, present, and future lives. Even though the notion of the transmigration of souls does not seem to be an indigenous doctrine, the belief in karma gradually acquired more recognition so that by the tenth century the literature is filled with references to *sukuse*, or destiny. This belief in destiny, or *inga* ("cause and effect"), strikes deep chords in the Japanese temperament. According to the historian George Sansom,

> there can be no doubt that the adoption of this one idea, which is
> entirely foreign and has no indigenous counterpart, brought about
> a truly revolutionary change in the moral outlook of the Japanese
> people.[31]

In much of Japanese literature there is a pervading sense of near resignation to the power of karma. This virtual resignation produces a melancholic disposition known as *mono no aware*, a realization of karma, or destiny, and the transience of reality, as in a "floating world."

In this context, the Japanese were attracted to the idea of retreat into monastic or convent living. We see this toward the end of the *Tale of Genji*, when Ukifune desires to become a nun. Despite protestations from Ukifune's sister, the priest that administers vows encourages her:

"For you . . . there remains only one thing—to pursue your devotions. Whether we are young or old, this is a world in which we can depend on nothing. You are quite right to regard it as an empty, fleeting place."[32]

Liberation is thus sought by retreating from worldly desires, in accordance with Buddhist teachings.[33]

Nichiren: Hokke School and the Lotus Sutra

Remember that these were extreme times: constant earthquakes, epidemics, typhoons, administrative intrigues, monastic corruption, and an unsettled warrior class. And Nichiren's approach demanded extreme measures. His methodology was more militant in expression, and he boldly assaulted the teachings of Jodo and Zen as being quietistic and passive and therefore less concerned with social reform. Actually, his teachings appealed to many samurai, who became his followers.

Nichiren's work was a reform effort within the Tendai school. He both simplified and universalized the complex teaching in the *Lotus Sutra* so that even ordinary people could grasp its message. The utterance of the formula "*Namu Myoho-Renge-Kyo*" (Homage to the Scripture of the Lotus of the Good Law) in the spirit of sincerity and total faith is enough to warrant salvation.

Dogen and the Shikan Taza School

Recall that for Dogen, the Buddha-nature permeates all things, and in this sense we are already enlightened. For Dogen, the expression of this primal enlightenment is manifested through the practice of *zazen*, in this context the essence of Buddhism. His school is sometimes referred to as *Shikan Taza*, meaning "just sitting" or "*zazen* only."

Zazen entails the proper bodily posture, the practice of breathing techniques, and so forth in an attempt to unify the physical and the spiritual. There are also mental prerequisites: One must cultivate the proper attitude, that of selflessness.

This is a crucial point, for it means that *striving* to achieve enlightenment is actually counterproductive. This is a difficult teaching in Zen, yet it is the secret behind *zazen*. Because *zazen* itself is enlightenment, its goal does not lie outside of its practice. Dogen warned us against perceiving *zazen* as separate from its goal. In this respect, the genuine meaning of *zazen* has definite ethical implications for ordinary and monastic life alike. It is a necessary basis for inculcating proper attitude and behavior.

Japanese Neo-Confucianism

Chu Hsi School (Shushi)

Throughout his practical ethics, Chu Hsi provided a basis for underscoring the importance of relationships, for stressing the virtues of benevolence and righteousness. For the Japanese, the attraction of Confucianism lies precisely in its emphasis on human relationships. Chu Hsi's ethics and emphasis on relationships can be seen within the context of his teaching of *li*, or principle. In Chu Hsi's thought, *li* is both a moral and a natural law. In other words, because all things manifest Heaven's *li*, humanity participates in the creative power of heaven. Therefore, by obeying the will of Heaven, humanity sustains Heaven's creative power. This entails, for example, the reciprocity of affection and duties in human relationships, such as the father's affection and the son's devotion. By performing our duties we act according to *li*, and we participate in Heaven's design.

In this regard, the two virtues of benevolence and righteousness (*jin* and *gi*) are the ethical cornerstones in Chu Hsi's thought. They point to the dignity of both humanity and the social order. For Chu Hsi, maintaining the social order is the most important feature.

How does Chu Hsi's ethics relate to the political sphere? Chu Hsi scholars teach that the ruler acts as "Heaven's representative" and aids in "actualizing Heaven's Law in all phases of social life."[34] This idea found ready acceptance among rulers, for it was an ethic that was duty-centered. Principles—that is, *li*—governed all behavior, and humanity is to be obedient to these principles. The "ideal ruler" is thus referred to as a "benevolent autocrat."[35]

Fujiwara Seika   Fujiwara Seika represents Chu Hsi's brand of Neo-Confucianism. He deftly combined the idea of the Way of Heaven with the Chu Hsi concept of principle, or *li*. This means that, because principle is innate, virtue is innate as well. An analogy again involves a clear mirror. Our natures are like that mirror, which needs to be constantly polished because the film of desires often clouds it. For Fujiwara, virtue and desires stand in opposition. With sincerity and right conduct we can steadfastly polish the mirror of our true and original nature.

Another important idea in Fujiwara is his distinction between the gentleman and the small man. The gentleman works on behalf of the collective well-being, whereas the small man is driven purely by self-interest. For the gentleman, there is no real distinction between government of oneself and of others.

Kaibara Ekken and Jin   For Kaibara Ekken there is a natural link between metaphysics and ethics. Just as the cosmic generative processes continually nourish and sustain, humanity should similarly act as sustainer and nourisher through *jin*, the Japanese equivalent of *jen*. *Jin* is the most important of the virtues, which include sincerity, faithfulness, and honesty.

Heaven and earth are our cosmic "parents." In reciprocity we have a constant obligation toward heaven and earth, just as we do in our ordinary human family. Serving our human family is an expression of service to our cosmic parents. Filiality is a necessary debt to ensure the natural order. Thus, Kaibara shows us his utmost respect for all living things.[36]

The aim in Kaibara's ethics is to realize our essential harmony with all existence, which demands the extension of one's heart to all things. His ethics is a cultivation of mind and heart, and it is especially seen in his essay "*Yamato Zokkun*," a portion of which is included at the end of this chapter.

Ogyu Sorai and Kogakuha

In Chu Hsi's school, personal morality and public values are compatible. According to Ogyu, the two remain distinct; personal motives (*kokoro*) may clash with what is in the public interest. The celebrated example is the vendetta carried out by the forty-seven *ronin* to avenge the insult to their lord. Ogyu argued that even though their act was "righteous," this matter was primarily a private one. From a public viewpoint, their private issue conflicted with what was in the best public interests. In this case, public interests assume priority. For this reason, he urged that they be allowed to commit *seppuku*, or ritual disembowelment. And this became the official verdict.

Ogyu's view of human nature did not contain the optimism of Ito Jinsai. He contended that essentially we are not capable of becoming sages. Therefore, he looked to the state and its ruler to bestow peace and order. In this light, he suggested some innovative proposals for social and political reform. For instance, he sought to improve the samurai's life-style and economic status.

Bushido

It is often said that the spirit of Japanese ethics is typified in the code of Bushido, or the Way of the Warrior. One exponent is Yamago Soko, a scholar of the Kogakuha school who constructed a rather stern Bushido code in which the welfare of the group supersedes individual concerns. Bushido exacts self-discipline and loyalty to one's lord, which are to be instilled through diligent training, both physical and mental. Let us look at some features of Bushido.

Preparing to Die: Two Kinds of Death

A classic manifesto of this code is the *Hagakure,* attributed to Yamamoto Tsunetomo (c. 1716), in which we find the famous expression:

> "Bushido consists in dying—that is my conclusion."

What does this mean? "Dying" means a number of things for the samurai. First, it refers to that physical death for which the samurai must always be prepared. The true samurai is ready to die at any moment, which allows the freedom to be fully present to the moment.

In order to be successful in a life-and-death encounter, the samurai must be absolutely present in both mind and body. He cannot be distracted by thoughts that pull him away from the moment. The art of swordsmanship demands complete awareness and a molding together of mind and body:

> When one eternally repeats his vow to die at any moment at the call
> of his duty every morning and every evening, one can act freely in

Bushido at a moment's notice, thus fulfilling his duties as a feudal vassal without a flaw, even to the last moment of his life.[37]

In this terse statement we see the meaning of Bushido. The ever-present thought of death actually frees one from clinging to life.

Fear of dying comes from clinging to this life and from the desire to live. It is this clinging to life that the samurai must die to. This is the second meaning of "dying." Dying is a letting-go or detachment from one's desires. This is why the samurai trains himself to die by constantly absorbing himself with the thought of death. The samurai must overcome any denial of death. By training himself to be ready to die, ironically enough, the warrior allows himself the freedom to be fully present in confrontation.

Giri

The alpha and omega of a samurai's life is service, service, service— nothing but service.[38]

One of the most important virtues in Bushido is loyalty, which is done out of duty, called *giri*, whether to one's liege lord, or shogun, or family. This is foremost in the mind of the samurai, so much so that he is willing to die for his lord.

We must be careful not to confuse this loyalty with blind loyalty. A samurai may question the actions or motives of his lord, even though this could mean the risk of death. A true samurai is not a passive follower, but one who thinks independently while remaining loyal to his lord. For example, in a recent film by Akira Kurosawa, *Ran,* there is an incident in which a retainer refuses to honor the request of his lord's wife to go out and bring back the head of the lord's sister. Instead, he returns with the head of a stone fox, insinuating that the cunning wife was herself a fox.

It is not purely out of duty that a samurai is loyal, but rather from a commitment to service. Service was often considered the proper response to the protection and care the lord has provided for his retainers, and it is to be performed in the spirit of gratitude. A relatively recent example of this was the service performed by young fighter pilots who volunteered to die for their country during the kamikaze attacks toward the end of World War II. Just before their mission, many of them wrote letters of gratitude for both their country and their families.

Pure Heart

In addition to these two requirements of preparedness for death and service, the Bushido code also requires an immediate response that is "pure." The samurai must be pure in heart, for then he can respond immediately to a situation.

Self-interested motives, whether conscious or unconscious, can obstruct a pure heart. Furthermore, a warrior may deliberate on factors such as the consequences of his actions. In order to be pure in heart, one must act immediately without attachment to any thought of the possible rewards of one's actions. (As we saw in the *Bhagavad Gita,* this is one of the core teachings of Krishna.) In this way, the samurai trains himself to act without self-reference.

So, we see a strong Stoic emphasis in Bushido, a strict control over one's emotions and desires. At the same time, there is the strict cultivation of such other-directed virtues as compassion and fortitude. The four "vows" mentioned in the *Hagakure* are:

> Never to be outdone in the Way of the Samurai.
> To be of good use to the master.
> To be filial to my parents.
> To manifest great compassion, and to act for the sake of Man.[39]

In view of these features—dying at each moment, unending service, and purity of heart—the spirit of Bushido reflects basic values expressed throughout Japan's history. In other words, what the notions of dying, service, and sincerity have in common is the absence of self-interest. As we have seen, this is an important and constant element in Japanese ethics. Bushido ultimately means the dying of the self. It means not having private interests at the center of one's morality.

Nishida Kitaro and the Unifying Power of Consciousness

Nishida's approach to ethics cannot be separated from his analysis of reality. The two go together, so that the "good" that is to be sought after is the reality that transcends our ordinary subject-object duality. The good can be attained in true Buddhist fashion only by a letting go, or by forgetting of self.

In his *An Inquiry into the Good,* Nishida criticized a number of philosophical positions that focus on only a part of the human psyche. For Nishida, the good can be attained only when all faculties are balanced in a healthy synthesis. He called this the "unifying power of consciousness."

This "unifying power of consciousness" is the true "personality" existing deep within each of us. Realizing this personality is realizing the good. Yet even though we tend to break consciousness down into disparate elements, such as intellect, will, and feeling,

> [t]he true unity of consciousness is a pure and simple activity that comes forth of itself, unhindered by oneself; it is the original state of independent, self-sufficient consciousness, with no distinction among knowledge, feeling, and volition, and no separation of subject and object.[40]

Nishida admitted that properly knowing what is good and what is not good is a fundamental problem. Let us briefly review his critique of some traditional ethical theories.[41]

First, the class of theories he called "intuitive" were found to be unsatisfactory. *Intuition* is a term that lacks clarity. Further, he chastised the "authority theory," which posits morality in absolute terms of what is and is not good. The authority rests upon some external figure or text. Nishida ruled out any morality based on fear and power.

Next, Nishida examined the rationalist theories (what he called "dianoetic ethics") in which knowledge and reason play major roles. These theories assume a link between what is good and what is true. Proponents therefore appeal to our rational natures as human beings. The problem with this approach is that while it extols reason, it also downplays other aspects of our human psyche such as will and desire:

> Even Confucius' maxim, "Do not do unto others what you would not have others do unto you," is nearly meaningless without the motivation of sympathy. If abstract logic were the motivation of the will, then those who are most adept at reasoning would be the best people. No one can deny, however, that ignorant people are sometimes actually better than those who have knowledge.[42]

Grounding morality solely on reason does not satisfactorily value the complexity of the personality, with its feelings and volition.

Nishida then went on to criticize hedonist theories that state that the good is personal pleasure. Hedonism is built on the edifice of self.

Nishida viewed utilitarianism as hedonism on a wider scale. In utilitarianism, pleasure is broadened to mean collective well-being in terms of what is publicly pleasing. He found fault with this because, first of all, not all pleasures are the same, and second, the self-interested viewpoint is not the only perspective. Nishida claimed that "Humans have an innate instinct of altruism."[43] Furthermore, it would be wrong to presume that pleasures are the only goals that humans seek.

Nishida then proceeded to claim that the good is attained when one discovers the self, and that is reality. "Thus, to seek the good and to return to it is to know the true reality of the self."[44] At the same time, in true Zen fashion, the good can be reached only by emptying the self.

Watsuji Tetsuro and *Aidagara*

Whereas Nishida is known primarily for his attempt to inscribe a metaphysical system as well as a new logic, Watsuji is prominent in the area of ethics. He was both a historian of Japanese ethics, and a formulator of a unique ethical position.[45]

An intriguing work is his *Fudo (Climate and Culture)*, written in 1928–29. As we saw earlier, Watsuji was so impressed with Heidegger's *Being and Time* that he wrote *Fudo* to complement Heidegger's emphasis on time modality. *Fudo* addresses the familiar (though taken-for-granted) realm of spatiality. Watsuji sought to account for the role of space and geography in the formation of cultural attitudes. In other words, just as Heidegger argued that we are by nature future-oriented beings, Watsuji contended that we are by nature outward-bound.

The final selection at the end of this chapter is taken from *Fudo,* which literally means "wind and earth" and generally means "climate"; it indicates the geography and environment that act to effect a culture's outlook and character. The term *fudo* suggests a reciprocity between climate and cultural disposition. For Watsuji, "climate" is a broad notion, and it encompasses not only the environmental, but also interpersonal features—our social geography.

Watsuji studied three kinds of climate—monsoon, desert, and pastoral—and contended that each endows inhabitants with a unique temperament. The monsoon climate, to which both Japan and India belong, is a strong factor in producing a culture that emphasizes compliance, cooperation, and (sometimes) submission. Desert climates, such as we find in African and Arab countries, tend to evoke a more aggressive, almost warlike temperament. Greece and most of Europe typify a pastoral, grassy climate, which tends to produce a more rational disposition.

Watsuji claimed that the more compliant temperament in Japan has a bearing on its moral demeanor. For instance, its monsoon climate naturally manifests itself sporadically and in extremes. Such is the case with the Japanese, who sometimes react in extreme and unpredictable ways.

For Watsuji, *aidagara,* "in-betweenness," remains an underlying element in ethics. Ethics must be grounded on the relationality of our existence. In other words, I am defined by my relationship within my various relevant groupings: marriage, family, community, society, culture, world, and universe. *Aidagara* gives a more Japanese stamp to morality.

To illustrate, the Japanese term for ethics is *rinri,* consisting of two characters. The first, *rin,* points to the communal bond or relationship with others. The second, *ri,* means reason, or the principle of relationality of self and other. In addition, as we stated earlier, the character for "man" represents a "being-involved-in-the-world."

Study Questions

India

1. Describe the four goals and the four aims in Hindu thought.
2. Explain the meaning of *dharma* in Hindu philosophy.
3. What is the highest goal in Hindu philosophy, and what are the various paths, or yogas, to achieve this?
4. Discuss the meaning of karma in Hindu philosophy and its significance in ethical action. How is this related to the traditional caste structure?
5. Discuss the meaning of *dharma* in the *Bhagavad Gita* in view of Arjuna's moral dilemma.
6. Explain the response of Krishna to Arjuna's conflict in the *Bhagavad Gita.*
7. How does the Mimamsa teaching raise *dharma* to a metaphysical status?
8. Explain the central moral standard in Advaita Vedanta.
9. Describe the significance of *ahimsa* and *satyagraha* in the teachings of Gandhi.

10. Describe the ethical components in the Buddhist Four Noble Truths, particularly in the Eightfold Path.
11. In what way does the Buddhist Middle Way provide a basis for Buddhist ethics?
12. Illustrate some Buddhist ethical teachings as manifested in the early Sangha.
13. What is the Buddhist view of karma? What aspects are distinct from the orthodox view?
14. Describe the most important Buddhist virtues.
15. What is the significance of dependent origination in Buddhist ethics?
16. Describe the Mahayana Buddhist ideal of *bodhisattva*. How is this distinct from the Theravada Buddhist ideal of *arhat*?
17. What are some Buddhist views concerning the class structure, or castes?

China

18. Describe the centrality of ethics in Chinese thought. What is the significance of *jen*?
19. How did Confucius address the relationship between social order and personal integrity? What are the most important virtues in this regard?
20. Discuss the "Four Beginnings" according to Mencius.
21. Contrast Hsun Tzu's view of human nature with that of Mencius. How does Hsun Tzu's position reflect his utilitarianism?
22. What is the significance of *wu-wei* in the *Tao Te Ching*?
23. Describe Mo Tzu's theory of universal love, and explain how it relates to his view of human nature.
24. What is Han Fei Tzu's view of human nature, and how does this affect the role of the ruler and of the government?
25. According to Ch'eng Yi, how does moral cultivation come about? How is this elaborated further by Chu Hsi?
26. What were some of Wang Yang-ming's points of contention with Chu Hsi's thought? Explain their relevance for Wang Yang-ming's ethical theory.
27. Highlight essential features in Wang Yang-ming's "ethics of engagement."
28. Describe Tai Chen's and K'ang Yu-wei's responses to rationalist neo-Confucian teachings and their relevance for ethics.

Japan

29. Explain how the teaching of karma plays a vital role in Japanese Buddhist views of morality.
30. How did Nichiren seek to reform Tendai teachings?
31. What is the significance of the "*zazen* only" teaching of Dogen?
32. Explain the meaning of *jin* and *gi* in the Japanese neo-Confucian school of *Shushi*.
33. Describe some of the main ethical teachings of Fujiwara Seika.
34. Describe some ethical teachings in Kaibara Ekken, especially his centrality of *jin*. Illustrate through ideas in his "*Yamato Zokkun.*"

35. How did Ogyu Sorai view the conflict between public values and individual morality? Illustrate this through the story of the forty-seven *ronin*.
36. Describe some of the main aspects of Bushido. How do these express certain Japanese ethical views?
37. What does "pure heart" mean in Bushido?
38. Explain how the good can be attained only through the "unifying power of consciousness" in Nishida Kitaro.
39. Examine Nishida's critique of some traditional ethical positions.
40. Discuss the significance of *aidagara* in the ethical teachings of Watsuji Tetsuro. Illustrate this with ideas from his *Fudo*.

Notes

1. *The Great Learning,* 3–7, in James Legge, trans., *Confucius: Confucian Analects, The Great Learning, and The Doctrine of the Mean* (New York: Dover, 1971), 357–59.
2. *Taittiriya Upanishad* I.xi.1, in Shree Purohit Swami and W. B. Yeats, trans., *The Ten Principal Upanishads* (New York: Macmillan, 1975), 68.
3. Nirvana has been given different meanings by Buddhists. Some claim it to be a negative state of extinction of desire; others describe it in more positive terms. For an excellent analysis, see Guy Richard Welbon, *The Buddhist Nirvāna and Its Western Interpreters* (Chicago: University of Chicago Press, 1968).
4. *Brihadaranyaka Upanishad* I, in Swami and Yeats, 119.
5. T. M. P. Mahadevan, "Social, Ethical, and Spiritual Values in Indian Philosophy," in *The Indian Mind: Essentials of Indian Philosophy and Culture,* ed., Charles A. Moore (Honolulu: East-West Center Press, University of Hawaii Press, 1967), 161–62.
6. Mahadevan, 162–63.
7. P. T. Raju, *The Philosophical Traditions of India* (London: George Allen & Unwin Ltd., 1971), 205.
8. See M. M. Agrawal's "Arjuna's Moral Predicament" in Bimal Krishna Matilal, ed., *Moral Dilemmas in the Mahābhārata* (Delhi: Motilal Banarsidass, 1989), 129–42.
9. *Bhagavad Gita* II.20,21, in R. C. Zaehner, trans., *Hindu Scriptures* (London: Everyman's Library, J. M. Dent & Sons Ltd., 1966), 256.
10. *Bhagavad Gita* II.33.34, in Zaehner, 257.
11. *Bhagavad Gita* II.47, in Zaehner, 259.
12. Along these lines, the Jains believe in an infinite number of souls and hold that all these souls are equal. This metaphysical outlook supports their strict moral temperament and explains why their most important ethical principle is noninjury, or *ahimsa,* which extends to all forms of life. Jains also hold that one must ultimately be free from the burden of matter. For this reason, they go to extremes in ascetic practices, believing in the complete renunciation of all material concerns.
13. See the discussion in David J. Kalupahana, *Buddhist Philosophy: A Historical Analysis* (Honolulu: University of Hawaii Press, 1976), 48–49.
14. *Digha Nikaya* III, cited in Gunapala Dharmasiri, *Fundamentals of Buddhist Ethics* (Antioch, Calif.: Golden Leaves Publishing Co., 1989), 67.
15. *Sutta Nipata,* cited in Dharmasiri, 69.
16. Robert Allinson has described how the natural affinity the Chinese feel with nature has resulted in less concern for pondering deeper metaphysical questions. See Robert E. Allinson, "An Overview of the Chinese Mind," in Robert E. Allinson, ed., *Understanding the Chinese Mind* (Hong Kong: Oxford University Press, 1989), 14–16.
17. *Analects* XV.8, in Legge, 297.
18. *Analects* XII.22, in Legge, 260. This is not to be taken in the sense of Mo Tzu's universal love, however. And here is where the expression of *jen* in matters of *li,* or propriety, is significant. Confucius was well aware of the different contexts in which

action occurs, that the familial context is the most urgent and, usually, the most important and foundational.

19. *Analects* XV.23, in Legge, 301.
20. *Analects* III.3, in Legge, 155.
21. A. S. Cua, "An Excursion to Confucian Ethics," in *Dimensions of Moral Creativity: Paradigms, Principles, and Ideals* (University Park: Pennsylvania State University Press, 1978), 59.
22. Lin Yutang, trans. and ed., *The Wisdom of Laotse* (New York: Random House, 1948), 242.
23. Fung Yu-lan, *A History of Chinese Philosophy*, Vol. 1, trans. Derk Bodde (Princeton, N.J.: Princeton University Press, 1952), 96.
24. In Mo Tzu's political philosophy we see traces of the ethical code of obedience and discipline of the *hsieh*, or "knight-errant."
25. Quoted from the *Hua-yen Treatise* and cited in Dharmasiri, 17.
26. Dharmasiri, 19.
27. See this simile in Fung, *History of Chinese Philosophy*, Vol. 2, 559–60.
28. Anthony Cua has provided a probing analysis of Wang's position in his *The Unity of Knowledge and Action: A Study in Wang Yang-Ming's Moral Psychology* (Honolulu: University Press of Hawaii, 1982), 9ff.
29. Fung, *History of Chinese Philosophy*, Vol. 2, 681.
30. To illustrate, traditional Japanese language had no specific word for "right" in an ethical sense. Eventually, the term *kenri* came to signify "right." It combines two syllables: *ken*, meaning "power," and *ri*, meaning "interest."
31. George Sansom, *A History of Japan to 1334* (Stanford, Calif: Stanford University Press, 1958), 220.
32. Cited in Ivan Morris, *The World of the Shining Prince: Court Life in Ancient Japan* (Middlesex, England: Peregrine Books, 1985), 131.
33. In practice, the appeal of this type of Buddhism may have been less convincing for many Japanese because it teaches absolute detachment as the path to salvation. This meant a total renunciation, including family and friends. It was this extreme Buddhist renunciation of family that provided grounds for strong opposition from Chinese Confucianists.
34. Ishida Ichiro, "Tokugawa Feudal Society and Neo-Confucian Thought," compiled by Japanese National Commission for Unesco, *Philosophical Studies of Japan* V (1964), 11.
35. Ishida, 14.
36. Mary Evelyn Tucker, *Moral and Spiritual Cultivation in Japanese Neo-Confucianism: The Life and Thought of Kaibara Ekken, 1630–1714*, SUNY Series in Philosophy (Albany: State University of New York Press, 1989), 55.
37. *Hagakure*, Chap. 1, cited by Furukawa Tesshi, "The Individual in Japanese Ethics," in *The Japanese Mind: Essentials of Japanese Philosophy and Culture*, ed. Charles A. Moore (Honolulu: University of Hawaii Press, 1987), 230.
38. *Hagakure*, Chap. 1, cited in Furukawa, 233.
39. Yamamoto Tsunetomo, *Hagakure: The Book of the Samurai*, trans. by William Scott Wilson (Tokyo: Kodansha International Ltd., 1979), 169.
40. Nishida Kitaro, *An Inquiry into the Good*, trans. Masao Abe and Christopher Ives (New Haven: Yale University Press, 1990), 130–31.
41. See Nishida, 104–06.
42. Nishida, 113.
43. Nishida, 120.
44. Nishida, 126.
45. One of Watsuji's more popular works remains his *Sakoku*. In it he discusses the isolation policy, or seclusion (*sakoku*), of Japan from the rest of the world during the Tokugawa period. He finds this seclusion to be the major reason for Japan's defeat in World War II. Because of this *sakoku*, Japan has suffered from a lack of the rational, scientific Western spirit. We see that this theme is consistent with Watsuji's emphasis on intersubjectivity.

"The Fire-Sermon," from the *Maha-Vagga*

The Buddha

Then the Blessed One, having dwelt in Uruvelā as long as he wished, proceeded on his wanderings in the direction of Gayā Head, accompanied by a great congregation of priests, a thousand in number, who had all of them aforetime been monks with matted hair. And there in Gayā, on Gayā Head, The Blessed One dwelt, together with the thousand priests.

And there The Blessed One addressed the priests:—

"All things, O priests, are on fire. And what, O priests, are all these things which are on fire?

"The eye, O priests, is on fire; forms are on fire; eye-consciousness is on fire; impressions received by the eye are on fire; and whatever sensation, pleasant, unpleasant, or indifferent, originates in dependence on impressions received by the eye, that also is on fire.

"And with what are these on fire?

"With the fire of passion, say I, with the fire of hatred, with the fire of infatuation; with birth, old age, death, sorrow, lamentation, misery, grief, and despair are they on fire.

"The ear is on fire; sounds are on fire; . . . the nose is on fire; odors are on fire; . . . the tongue is on fire; tastes are on fire; . . . the body is on fire; things tangible are on fire; . . . the mind is on fire; ideas are on fire; . . . mind-consciousness is on fire; impressions received by the mind are on fire; and whatever sensation, pleasant, unpleasant, or indifferent, originates in dependence on impressions received by the mind, that also is on fire.

"And with what are these on fire?

"With the fire of passion, say I, with the fire of hatred, with the fire of infatuation; with birth, old age, death, sorrow, lamentation, misery, grief, and despair are they on fire.

"Perceiving this, O priests, the learned and noble disciple conceives an aversion for the eye, conceives an aversion for forms, conceives an aversion for eye-consciousness, conceives an aversion for the impressions received by the eye; and whatever sensation, pleasant, unpleasant, or indifferent, originates in dependence on impressions received by the eye, for that also he conceives an aversion. Conceives an aversion for the ear, conceives an aversion for sounds, . . . conceives an aversion for the nose, conceives an aversion for odors, . . . conceives an aversion for the tongue, conceives an aversion for tastes, . . . conceives an aversion for the body, conceives an aversion

Reprinted from Henry Clarke Warren, trans., *Buddhism in Translations,* Cambridge, Mass.: Harvard University Press, 1953, pp. 351–53.

for things tangible, . . . conceives an aversion for the mind, conceives an aversion for ideas, conceives an aversion for mind-consciousness, conceives an aversion for the impressions received by the mind; and whatever sensation, pleasant, unpleasant, or indifferent, originates in dependence on impressions received by the mind, for this also he conceives an aversion. And in conceiving this aversion, he becomes divested of passion, and by the absence of passion he becomes free, and when he is free he becomes aware that he is free; and he knows that rebirth is exhausted, that he has lived the holy life, that he has done what it behooved him to do, and that he is no more for this world."

Now while this exposition was being delivered, the minds of the thousand priests became free from attachment and delivered from the depravities.

"The Eightfold Path," from the *Digha-Nikaya*

The Buddha

And what, O priests, is the noble truth of the path leading to the cessation of misery?

It is this noble eightfold path, to wit, right belief, right resolve, right speech, right behavior, right occupation, right effort, right contemplation, right concentration.

And what, O priests, is right belief?

The knowledge of misery, O priests, the knowledge of the origin of misery, the knowledge of the cessation of misery, and the knowledge of the path leading to the cessation of misery, this, O priests, is called "right belief."

And what, O priests, is right resolve?

The resolve to renounce sensual pleasures, the resolve to have malice towards none, and the resolve to harm no living creature, this, O priests, is called "right resolve."

And what, O priests, is right speech?

To abstain from falsehood, to abstain from backbiting, to abstain from harsh language, and to abstain from frivolous talk, this, O priests, is called "right speech."

And what, O priests, is right behavior?

Reprinted from Henry Clarke Warren, trans., *Buddhism in Translations*, Cambridge, Mass.: Harvard University Press, 1953, pp. 372–74.

To abstain from destroying life, to abstain from taking that which is not given one, and to abstain from immorality, this, O priests, is called "right behavior."

And what, O priests, is right occupation?

Whenever, O priests, a noble disciple, quitting a wrong occupation, gets his livelihood by a right occupation, this, O priests, is called "right occupation."

And what, O priests, is right effort?

Whenever, O priests, a priest purposes, makes an effort, heroically endeavors, applies his mind, and exerts himself that evil and demeritorious qualities not yet arisen may not arise; purposes, makes an effort, heroically endeavors, applies his mind, and exerts himself that evil and demeritorious qualities already arisen may be abandoned; purposes, makes an effort, heroically endeavors, applies his mind, and exerts himself that meritorious qualities not yet arisen may arise; purposes, makes an effort, heroically endeavors, applies his mind, and exerts himself for the preservation, retention, growth, increase, development, and perfection of meritorious qualities already arisen, this, O priest, is called "right effort."

And what, O priests, is right contemplation?

Whenever, O priests, a priest lives, as respects the body, observant of the body, strenuous, conscious, contemplative, and has rid himself of lust and grief; as respects sensations, observant of sensations, strenuous, conscious, contemplative, and has rid himself of lust and grief; as respects the mind, observant of the mind, strenuous, conscious, contemplative, and has rid himself of lust and grief; as respects the elements of being, observant of the elements of being, strenuous, conscious, contemplative, and has rid himself of lust and grief, this, O priests, is called "right contemplation."

And what, O priests, is right concentration?

Whenever, O priests, a priest, having isolated himself from sensual pleasures, having isolated himself from demeritorious traits, and still exercising reasoning, still exercising reflection, enters upon the first trance which is produced by isolation and characterized by joy and happiness; when, through the subsidence of reasoning and reflection, and still retaining joy and happiness, he enters upon the second trance, which is an interior tranquilization and intentness of the thoughts, and is produced by concentration; when, through the paling of joy, indifferent, contemplative, conscious, and in the experience of bodily happiness—that state which eminent men describe when they say, "Indifferent, contemplative, and living happily"— he enters upon the third trance; when, through the abandonment of happiness, through the abandonment of misery, through the disappearance of all antecedent gladness and grief, he enters upon the fourth trance, which has neither misery nor happiness, but is contemplation as refined by indifference, this, O priests, is called "right concentration."

This, O priests, is called the noble truth of the path leading to the cessation of misery.

From *The Dhammapada*

The Twin-Verses.

1. All that we are is the result of what we have thought: it is founded on our thoughts, it is made up of our thoughts. If a man speaks or acts with an evil thought, pain follows him, as the wheel follows the foot of the ox that draws the carriage.

2. All that we are is the result of what we have thought: it is founded on our thoughts, it is made up of our thoughts. If a man speaks or acts with a pure thought, happiness follows him, like a shadow that never leaves him.

3. "He abused me, he beat me, he defeated me, he robbed me,"—in those who harbour such thoughts hatred will never cease.

4. "He abused me, he beat me, he defeated me, he robbed me,"—in those who do not harbour such thoughts hatred will cease.

5. For hatred does not cease by hatred at any time: hatred ceases by love, this is an old rule.

6. The world does not know that we must all come to an end here;—but those who know it, their quarrels cease at once.

7. He who lives looking for pleasures only, his senses uncontrolled, immoderate in his food, idle, and weak, Mâra (the tempter) will certainly overthrow him, as the wind throws down a weak tree.

8. He who lives without looking for pleasures, his senses well controlled, moderate in his food, faithful and strong, him Mâra will certainly not overthrow, any more than the wind throws down a rocky mountain.

9. He who wishes to put on the yellow dress without having cleansed himself from sin, who disregards also temperance and truth, is unworthy of the yellow dress.

10. But he who has cleansed himself from sin, is well grounded in all virtues, and endowed also with temperance and truth, he is indeed worthy of the yellow dress.

11. They who imagine truth in untruth, and see untruth in truth, never arrive at truth, but follow vain desires.

12. They who know truth in truth, and untruth in untruth, arrive at truth, and follow true desires.

13. As rain breaks through an ill-thatched house, passion will break through an unreflecting mind.

14. As rain does not break through a well-thatched house, passion will not break through a well-reflecting mind.

Reprinted from F. Max Müller, trans., *The Dhammapada,* London: The Sacred Books of the East, Oxford University Press, 1924, Vol. X, Pt. I, pp. 3–15, 20–26, 78–80.

15. The evil-doer mourns in this world, and he mourns in the next; he mourns in both. He mourns and suffers when he sees the evil (result) of his own work.

16. The virtuous man delights in this world, and he delights in the next; he delights in both. He delights and rejoices, when he sees the purity of his own work.

17. The evil-doer suffers in this world, and he suffers in the next; he suffers in both. He suffers when he thinks of the evil he has done; he suffers more when going on the evil path.

18. The virtuous man is happy in this world, and he is happy in the next; he is happy in both. He is happy when he thinks of the good he has done; he is still more happy when going on the good path.

19. The thoughtless man, even if he can recite a large portion (of the law), but is not a doer of it, has no share in the priesthood, but is like a cowherd counting the cows of others.

20. The follower of the law, even if he can recite only a small portion (of the law), but, having forsaken passion and hatred and foolishness, possesses true knowledge and serenity of mind, he, caring for nothing in this world or that to come, has indeed a share in the priesthood.

On Earnestness.

21. Earnestness is the path of immortality (Nirvâna), thoughtlessness the path of death. Those who are in earnest do not die, those who are thoughtless are as if dead already.

22. Having understood this clearly, those who are advanced in earnestness delight in earnestness, and rejoice in the knowledge of the Ariyas (the elect).

23. These wise people, meditative, steady, always possessed of strong powers, attain to Nirvâna, the highest happiness.

24. If an earnest person has roused himself, if he is not forgetful, if his deeds are pure, if he acts with consideration, if he restrains himself, and lives according to law,—then his glory will increase.

25. By rousing himself, by earnestness, by restraint and control, the wise man may make for himself an island which no flood can overwhelm.

26. Fools follow after vanity, men of evil wisdom. The wise man keeps earnestness as his best jewel.

27. Follow not after vanity, nor after the enjoyment of love and lust! He who is earnest and meditative, obtains ample joy.

28. When the learned man drives away vanity by earnestness, he, the wise, climbing the terraced heights of wisdom, looks down upon the fools, free from sorrow he looks upon the sorrowing crowd, as one that stands on a mountain looks down upon them that stand upon the plain.

29. Earnest among the thoughtless, awake among the sleepers, the wise man advances like a racer, leaving behind the hack.

30. By earnestness did Maghavan (Indra) rise to the lordship of the gods. People praise earnestness; thoughtlessness is always blamed.

31. A Bhikshu (mendicant) who delights in earnestness, who looks with fear on thoughtlessness, moves about like fire, burning all his fetters, small or large.

32. A Bhikshu (mendicant) who delights in reflection, who looks with fear on thoughtlessness, cannot fall away (from his perfect state)—he is close upon Nirvâna.

Thought.

33. As a fletcher makes straight his arrow, a wise man makes straight his trembling and unsteady thought, which is difficult to guard, difficult to hold back.

34. As a fish taken from his watery home and thrown on the dry ground, our thought trembles all over in order to escape the dominion of Mâra (the tempter).

35. It is good to tame the mind, which is difficult to hold in and flighty, rushing wherever it listeth; a tamed mind brings happiness.

36. Let the wise man guard his thoughts, for they are difficult to perceive, very artful, and they rush wherever they list: thoughts well guarded bring happiness.

37. Those who bridle their mind which travels far, moves about alone, is without a body, and hides in the chamber (of the heart), will be free from the bonds of Mâra (the tempter).

38. If a man's faith is unsteady, if he does not know the true law, if his peace of mind is troubled, his knowledge will never be perfect.

39. If a man's thoughts are not dissipated, if his mind is not perplexed, if he has ceased to think of good or evil, then there is no fear for him while he is watchful.

40. Knowing that this body is (fragile) like a jar, and making his thought firm like a fortress, one should attack Mâra (the tempter) with the weapon of knowledge, one should watch him when conquered, and should never rest.

41. Before long, alas! this body will lie on the earth, despised, without understanding, like a useless log.

42. Whatever a hater may do to a hater, or an enemy to an enemy, a wrongly-directed mind will do him greater mischief.

43. Not a mother, not a father will do so much, nor any other relatives; a well-directed mind will do us greater service.

The Fool.

60. Long is the night to him who is awake; long is a mile to him who is tired; long is life to the foolish who do not know the true law.

61. If a traveller does not meet with one who is his better, or his equal, let him firmly keep to his solitary journey; there is no companionship with a fool.

62. "These sons belong to me, and this wealth belongs to me," with such thoughts a fool is tormented. He himself does not belong to himself; how much less sons and wealth?

63. The fool who knows his foolishness, is wise at least so far. But a fool who thinks himself wise, he is called a fool indeed.

64. If a fool be associated with a wise man even all his life, he will perceive the truth as little as a spoon perceives the taste of soup.

65. If an intelligent man be associated for one minute only with a wise man, he will soon perceive the truth, as the tongue perceives the taste of soup.

66. Fools of poor understanding have themselves for their greatest enemies, for they do evil deeds which bear bitter fruits.

67. That deed is not well done of which a man must repent, and the reward of which he receives crying and with a tearful face.

68. No, that deed is well done of which a man does not repent, and the reward of which he receives gladly and cheerfully.

69. As long as the evil deed done does not bear fruit, the fool thinks it is like honey; but when it ripens, then the fool suffers grief.

70. Let a fool month after month eat his food (like an ascetic) with the tip of a blade of Kusa grass, yet is he not worth the sixteenth particle of those who have well weighed the law.

71. An evil deed, like newly-drawn milk, does not turn (suddenly); smouldering, like fire covered by ashes, it follows the fool.

72. And when the evil deed, after it has become known, turns to sorrow for the fool, then it destroys his bright lot, nay, it cleaves his head.

73. Let the fool wish for a false reputation, for precedence among the Bhikshus, for lordship in the convents, for worship among other people!

74. "May both the laymen and he who has left the world think that this is done by me; may they be subject to me in everything which is to be done or is not to be done," thus is the mind of the fool, and his desire and pride increase.

75. "One is the road that leads to wealth, another the road that leads to Nirvâna"; if the Bhikshu, the disciple of Buddha, has learnt this, he will not yearn for honour, he will strive after separation from the world.

The Wise Man (*Pandita*).

76. If you see a man who shows you what is to be avoided, who administers reproofs, and is intelligent, follow that wise man as you would one who tells of hidden treasures; it will be better, not worse, for him who follows him.

77. Let him admonish, let him teach, let him forbid what is improper!— he will be beloved of the good, by the bad he will be hated.

78. Do not have evil-doers for friends, do not have low people for friends: have virtuous people for friends, have for friends the best of men.

79. He who drinks in the law lives happily with a serene mind: the sage rejoices always in the law, as preached by the elect (Ariyas).

80. Well-makers lead the water (wherever they like); fletchers bend the arrow; carpenters bend a log of wood; wise people fashion themselves.

81. As a solid rock is not shaken by the wind, wise people falter not amidst blame and praise.

82. Wise people, after they have listened to the laws, become serene, like a deep, smooth, and still lake.

83. Good men indeed walk (warily) under all circumstances; good men speak not out of a desire for sensual gratification; whether touched by happiness or sorrow wise people never appear elated or depressed.

84. If, whether for his own sake, or for the sake of others, a man wishes neither for a son, nor for wealth, nor for lordship, and if he does not wish for his own success by unfair means, then he is good, wise, and virtuous.

85. Few are there among men who arrive at the other shore (become Arhats); the other people here run up and down the shore.

86. But those who, when the law has been well preached to them, follow the law, will pass over the dominion of death, however difficult to cross.

87, 88. A wise man should leave the dark state (or ordinary life), and follow the bright state (of the Bhikshu). After going from his home to a homeless state, he should in his retirement look for enjoyment where enjoyment seemed difficult. Leaving all pleasures behind, and calling nothing his own, the wise man should purge himself from all the troubles of the mind.

89. Those whose mind is well grounded in the (seven) elements of knowledge, who without clinging to anything, rejoice in freedom from attachment, whose appetites have-been conquered, and who are full of light, they are free (even) in this world. . . .

The Elephant.

320. Silently I endured abuse as the elephant in battle endures the arrow sent from the bow: for the world is ill-natured.

321. They lead a tamed elephant to battle, the king mounts a tamed elephant; the tamed is the best among men, he who silently endures abuse.

322. Mules are good, if tamed, and noble Sindhu horses, and elephants with large tusks; but he who tames himself is better still.

323. For with these animals does no man reach the untrodden country (Nirvâna), where a tamed man goes on a tamed animal, viz. on his own well-tamed self.

324. The elephant called Dhanapâlaka, his temples running with pungent sap, and who is difficult to hold, does not eat a morsel when bound; the elephant longs for the elephant grove.

325. If a man becomes fat and a great eater, if he is sleepy and rolls himself about, that fool, like a hog fed on grains, is born again and again.

326. This mind of mine went formerly wandering about as it liked, as it listed, as it pleased; but I shall now hold it in thoroughly, as the rider who holds the hook holds in the furious elephant.

327. Be not thoughtless, watch your thoughts! Draw yourself out of the evil way, like an elephant sunk in mud.

328. If a man find a prudent companion who walks with him, is wise, and lives soberly, he may walk with him, overcoming all dangers, happy, but considerate.

329. If a man find no prudent companion who walks with him, is wise, and lives soberly, let him walk alone, like a king who has left his conquered country behind,—like an elephant in the forest.

330. It is better to live alone, there is no companionship with a fool; let a man walk alone, let him commit no sin, with few wishes, like an elephant in the forest.

331. If the occasion arises, friends are pleasant; enjoyment is pleasant, whatever be the cause; a good work is pleasant in the hour of death; the giving up of all grief is pleasant.

332. Pleasant in the world is the state of a mother, pleasant the state of a father, pleasant the state of a Samana, pleasant the state of a Brâhmana.

333. Pleasant is virtue lasting to old age, pleasant is a faith firmly rooted; pleasant is attainment of intelligence, pleasant is avoiding of sins.

"That the Nature Is Evil"

Hsun Tzu

The nature of man is evil; the good which it shows is factitious. There belongs to it, even at his birth, the love of gain, and as actions are in accordance with this, contentions and robberies grow up, and self-denial and yielding to others are not to be found; there belong to it envy and dislike, and as actions are in accordance with these, violence and injuries spring up, and self-devotedness and faith are not to be found; there belong to it the desires of the ears and the eyes, leading to the love of sounds and beauty, and as the actions are in accordance with these, lewdness and disorder spring up, and righteousness and propriety, with their various orderly displays, are not to be found. It thus appears, that to follow man's nature and yield obedience to its feelings will assuredly conduct to contentions and robberies, to the violation of the duties belonging to every one's lot, and the confounding of all distinctions, till the issue will be in a state of savagism; and that there must be the influence of teachers and laws, and the guidance of propriety and righteousness, from which will spring self-denial, yielding to others, and an observance of the well-ordered regulations of conduct, till the issue will be a state of good government.—From all this it is plain that the nature of man is evil; the good which it shows is factitious.

To illustrate.—A crooked stick must be submitted to the pressing-frame to soften and bend it, and then it becomes straight; a blunt knife must be submitted to the grindstone and whetstone, and then it becomes sharp: so,

Reprinted from James Legge, trans., *The Chinese Classics,* Vol. II, rev. 2nd ed., Oxford: The Clarendon Press, 1895, pp. 81–88.

the nature of man, being evil, must be submitted to teachers and laws, and then it becomes correct; it must be submitted to propriety and righteousness, and then it comes under government. If men were without teachers and laws, their condition would be one of deflection and insecurity, entirely incorrect; if they were without propriety and righteousness, their condition would be one of rebellious disorder, rejecting all government. The sage kings of antiquity, understanding that the nature of man was thus evil, in a state of hazardous deflection, and incorrect, rebellious and disorderly, and refusing to be governed, set up the principles of righteousness and propriety, and framed laws and regulations to straighten and ornament the feelings of that nature and correct them, to tame and change those same feelings and guide them, so that they might all go forth in the way of moral government and in agreement with reason. Now, the man who is transformed by teachers and laws, gathers on himself the ornament of learning, and proceeds in the path of propriety and righteousness is a superior man; and he who gives the reins to his nature and its feelings, indulges its resentments, and walks contrary to propriety and righteousness is a mean man. Looking at the subject in this way, we see clearly that the nature of man is evil; the good which it shows is factitious.

Mencius said, "Man has only to learn, and his nature appears to be good"; but I reply,—It is not so. To say so shows that he had not attained to the knowledge of man's nature, nor examined into the difference between what is natural in man and what is factitious. The natural is what the constitution spontaneously moves to:—it needs not to be learned, it needs not to be followed hard after; propriety and righteousness are what the sages have given birth to:—it is by learning that men become capable of them, it is by hard practice that they achieve them. That which is in man, not needing to be learned and striven after, is what I call natural; that in man which is attained to by learning, and achieved by hard striving, is what I call factitious. This is the distinction between those two. By the nature of man, the eyes are capable of seeing, and the ears are capable of hearing. But the power of seeing is inseparable from the eyes, and the power of hearing is inseparable from the ears;—it is plain that the faculties of seeing and hearing do not need to be learned. Mencius says, "The nature of man is good, but all lose and ruin their nature, and therefore it becomes bad"; but I say that this representation is erroneous. Man being born with his nature, when he thereafter departs from its simple constituent elements, he must lose it. From this consideration we may see clearly that man's nature is evil. What might be called the nature's being good, would be if there were no departing from its simplicity to beautify it, no departing from its elementary dispositions to sharpen it. Suppose that those simple elements no more needed beautifying, and the mind's thoughts no more needed to be turned to good, than the power of vision which is inseparable from the eyes, and the power of hearing which is inseparable from the ears, need to be learned, *then we might say that the nature is good, just as* we say that the eyes see and the ears hear. It is the nature of man, when hungry, to desire to be filled; when cold, to desire to be warmed; when tired, to desire rest:—these are the feelings and nature of man. But now, a man is hungry, and in the presence of an elder he does not dare to eat before him:—he is yielding to that elder; he is tired with labour, and he does not dare to ask for rest:—he is working for some one. A son's yielding to his father and a younger brother to his elder, a son's labouring for his father and a younger brother for his elder:—these two instances of conduct are contrary to the nature and against the feelings; but they are according to the course laid down for a filial son, and to the refined distinctions of propriety and righteousness. It appears that if there were an accordance with the feelings and the nature, there would be no self-denial and yielding to others. Self-denial and yielding to others are contrary to the feelings and the nature. In this way we come to see how clear it is that the nature of man is evil; the good which it shows is factitious.

An inquirer will ask, "If man's nature be evil, whence do propriety and righteousness arise?" I reply:—All propriety and righteousness are the artificial production of the sages, and are not to be considered as growing out of the nature of man. It is just as when a potter makes a vessel from the clay;—the vessel is the product of the workman's art, and is not to be considered as growing out of his nature. Or it is as when another workman cuts and hews a vessel out of wood;—it is the product of his art, and is not to be considered as growing out of his nature. The sages pondered long in thought and gave themselves to practice, and so they succeeded in producing propriety and righteousness, and setting up laws and regulations. Thus it is that propriety and righteousness, laws and regulations, are the artificial product of the sages, and are not to be considered as growing properly from the nature of man.

If we speak of the fondness of the eyes for beauty, or of the mouth for *pleasant* flavours, or of the mind for gain, or of the bones and skin for the enjoyment of ease;—all these grow out of the natural feelings of man. The object is presented and the desire is felt; there needs no effort to produce it. But when the object is presented, and the affection does not move till after hard effort, I say that this effect is factitious. Those cases prove the difference between what is produced by nature and what is produced by art.

Thus the sages transformed their nature, and commenced their artificial work. Having commenced this work with their nature, they produced propriety and righteousness. When propriety and righteousness were produced, they proceeded to frame laws and regulations. It appears, therefore, that propriety and righteousness, laws and regulations, are given birth to by the sages. Wherein they agree with all other men and do not differ from them, is their nature; wherein they differ from and exceed other men, is this artificial work.

Now to love gain and desire to get;—this is the natural feeling of men. Suppose the case that there is an amount of property or money to be divided among brothers, and let this natural feeling to love gain and to desire to get come into play;—why, then the brothers will be opposing, and snatching from, one another. But where the changing influence of propriety and righteousness, with their refined distinctions, has taken effect, a man will give up to any other man. Thus it is that if they act in accordance with their natural feelings, brothers will quarrel together; and if they have come under the transforming influence of propriety and righteousness, men will give up to other men, to say nothing of brothers. *Again,* the fact that men WISH to do what is good, is because their nature is bad. The thin wishes to be thick; the ugly wish to be beautiful; the narrow wishes to be wide; the poor wish to be rich; the mean wish to be noble:—when anything is not possessed in one's self, he seeks for it outside himself. But the rich do not wish for wealth; the noble do not wish for position:—when anything is possessed by one's self, he does not need to go beyond himself for it. When we look at things in this way, we perceive that the fact of men's WISHING to do what is good is because their nature is evil. It is the case indeed, that man's nature is without propriety and benevolence:—he therefore studies them with vigorous effort and seeks to have them. It is the case that by nature he does not now propriety and righteousness:—he therefore thinks and reflects and seeks to know them. Speaking of man, therefore, as he is by birth simply, he is without propriety and righteousness, without the knowledge of propriety and righteousness. Without propriety and righteousness, man must be all confusion and disorder; without the knowledge of propriety and righteousness, man must be all confusion and disorder; without the knowledge of propriety and righteousness, there must ensue all the manifestations of disorder. Man, as he is born, therefore, has in him nothing but the elements of disorder, passive and active. It is plain from this view of the subject that the nature of man is evil; the good which it shows is factitious.

When Mencius says that "Man's nature is good," I affirm that it is not so. In ancient times and now, throughout the kingdom, what is meant by good is a condition of correctness, regulation, and happy government; and what is meant by evil, is a condition of deflection, insecurity, and refusing to be under government:—in this lies the distinction between being good and being evil. And now, if man's nature be really so correct, regulated, and happily governed in itself, where would be the use for sage kings? where would be the use for propriety and righteousness? Although there were the sage kings, propriety, and righteousness, what could they add to the nature so correct, regulated, and happily ruled in itself? But it is not so; the nature of man is bad. It was on this account, that anciently the sage kings, understanding that man's nature was bad, in a state of deflection and insecurity, instead of being correct; in a state of rebellious disorder, instead of one of happy rule, set up therefore the majesty of princes and governors to awe it; and set forth propriety and righteousness to change it; and framed laws and statutes of correctness to rule it; and devised severe punishments to restrain it: so that its outgoings might be under the dominion of rule, and in accordance with what is good. This is *the true account of* the governance of the sage kings, and the transforming power of propriety and righteousness. Let us suppose a state of things in which there shall be no majesty of rulers and governors, no influence of propriety and righteousness, no rule of laws and statutes, no restraints of punishment:—what would be the relations of men with one another, all under heaven? The strong would be injuring the weak, and spoiling them; the many would be tyrannizing over the few, and hooting them; a universal disorder and mutual destruction would speedily ensue. When we look at the subject in this way, we see clearly that the nature of man is evil; the good which it shows is factitious.

He who would speak well of ancient times must have undoubted references in the present; he who would speak well of Heaven must substantiate what he says from *the state of* man. In discourse and argument it is an excellent quality when the divisions which are made can be brought together like the halves of a token. When it is so, the arguer may sit down, and discourse of his principles; and he has only to rise up, and they may be set forth and displayed and carried into action. When Mencius says that the nature of man is good, there is no bringing together in the above manner of his divisions. He sits down and talks, but there is no getting up to display and set forth his principles, and put them in operation:—is not his error very gross? To say that the nature is good does away with the sage kings, and makes an end of propriety and righteousness; to say that the nature is bad exalts the sage kings, and dignifies propriety and righteousness. As the origin of the pressing-boards is to be found in the crooked wood, and the origin of the carpenter's marking-line is to be found in things not being straight; so the rise of princes and governors, and the illustration of propriety and righteousness, are to be traced to the badness of the nature. It is clear from this view of the subject that the nature of man is bad; the good which it shows is factitious.

A straight piece of wood does not need the pressing-boards to make it straight;—it is so by its nature. A crooked piece of wood must be submitted to the pressing-boards to soften and straighten it, and then it is straight; it is not straight by its nature. So it is that the nature of man, being evil, must be submitted to the rule of the sage kings, and to the transforming influence of propriety and righteousness, and then its outgoings are under the dominion of rule, and in accordance with what is good. This shows clearly that the nature of man is bad; the good which it shows is factitious.

An inquirer may say *again*, "Propriety and righteousness, though seen in an accumulation of factitious deeds, do yet belong to the nature of man; and thus it was that the sages were able to produce them." I reply:—It is not so. A potter takes a piece of clay, and produces an earthen dish from it; but are that dish and clay the nature of the potter? A carpenter plies his tools upon a piece of wood, and produces a vessel; but are that vessel and wood the nature of the carpenter? So it is with the sages and propriety and righteousness; they produced them, just as the potter works with the clay. It is plain that there is no reason for saying that propriety and righteousness, and the accumulation of their factitious actions, belong to the proper nature of man. Speaking of the nature of man, it is the same in all,—the same in Yâo and Shun and in Chieh and the robber Chih, the same in the superior man and in the mean man. If you say that propriety and righteousness, with the factitious actions accumulated from them, are the nature of man, on what ground do you proceed to ennoble Yâo and Yü, to ennoble *generally* the superior man? The ground on which we ennoble Yâo, Yü, and the superior man, is their ability to change the nature, and to produce factitious conduct. That factitious conduct being produced, out of it there are brought propriety and righteousness. The sages stand indeed in the same relation to propriety and righteousness, and the factitious conduct resulting from them, as the potter does to his clay:—we have a product in either case. This representation makes it clear that propriety and righteousness, with their factitious results, do not properly belong to the nature of man. *On the other hand,* that which we consider mean in Chieh, the robber Chih, and the mean man generally, is that they follow their nature, act in accordance with its feelings, and indulge its resentments, till all its outgoings are a greed of gain, contentions, and rapine.—It is plain that the nature of man is bad; the good which it shows is factitious.

Heaven did not make favourites of Tsǎng *Shǎn, Min* Tsze-ch'ien, and Hsiâo-chi, and deal unkindly with the rest of men. How then was it that they alone were distinguished by the greatness of their filial deeds, that all which the name of filial piety implies was complete in them? The reason was that they were entirely subject to the restraints of propriety and righteousness.

Heaven did not make favourites of the people of Ch'i and Lû, and deal unkindly with the people of Ch'in. How then was it that the latter were not equal to the former in the rich manifestation of the filial piety belonging to the righteousness of the relation between father and son, and the respectful observance of the proprieties belonging to the separate functions of husband and wife? The reason was that the people of Ch'in followed the feelings of their nature, indulged its resentments, and condemned propriety and righteousness. We are not to suppose that they were different in their nature.

What is the meaning of the saying, that "Any traveller on the road may become like Yü?" I answer:—All that made Yü what he was, was his practice of benevolence, righteousness, and his observance of laws and rectitude. But benevolence, righteousness, laws, and rectitude are all capable of being known and being practised. Moreover, any traveller on the road has the capacity of knowing these, and the ability to practise them:—it is plain that he may become like Yü. If you say that benevolence, righteousness, laws, and rectitude are not capable of being known and practised, then Yü himself could not have known, could not have practised them. If you will have it that any traveller on the road is really without the capacity of knowing these things, and the ability to practise them, then, in his home, it will not be competent for him to know the righteousness that should rule between father and son, and, abroad, it will not be competent for him to know the rectitude that should rule between sovereign and minister. But it is not so. There is no one who travels along the road, but may know both that righteousness and that rectitude:—it is plain that the capacity to know and the ability to practise belong to every traveller on the way. Let him, therefore, with his capacity of knowing and ability to practise, take his ground on the knowableness and practicableness of benevolence and righteousness;—and it is clear that he may become like Yü. Yea, let any traveller on the way addict himself to the art of learning with all his heart and the entire bent of his will, thinking, searching, and closely examining;—let him do this day after day, through a long space of time, accumulating what is good, and he will penetrate as far as a spiritual Intelligence, he will become a ternion with

Heaven and Earth. It follows that *the characters of* the sages were what any man may reach by accumulation.

It may be said:—"To be sage may thus be reached by accumulation;—why is it that all men cannot accumulate *to this extent?*" I reply:—They may do so, but they cannot be made to do so. The mean man might become a superior man, but he is not willing to be a superior man. The superior man might become a mean man, but he is not willing to be a mean man. It is not that the mean man and the superior man may not become the one the other; their not becoming the one the other is because it is a thing which may be, but cannot be made to be. Any traveller on the road may become like Yü:—the case is so; that any traveller on the road can really become like Yü:—this is not a necessary conclusion. Though any one, however, cannot really become like Yü, that is not contrary at all to the truth that he may become so. One's feet might travel all over the world, but there never was one who was really able to travel all over the world. There is nothing to prevent the mechanic, the farmer, and the merchant from practising each the business of the others, but there has never been a case when it has really been done. Looking at the subject in this way, we see that what may be need not really be; and although is shall not really be, that is not contrary to the truth that it might be. It thus appears that the difference is wide between what is really done or not really done, and what may be or may not be. It is plain that these two cases may not become the one the other.

Yâo asked Shun what was the character of the feelings proper to man. Shun replied, "The feelings proper to man are very unlovely; why need you ask about them? When a man has got a wife and children, his filial piety withers away; under the influence of lust and gratified desires, his good faith to his friends withers away; when he is full of dignities and emoluments, his loyalty to his sovereign withers away. The natural feelings of man! The natural feelings of man! They are very unlovely. Why need you ask about them? It is only in the case of men of the highest worth that it is not so."

There is a knowledge characteristic of the sage; a knowledge characteristic of the scholar and superior man; a knowledge characteristic of the mean man; and a knowledge characteristic of the mere servant. In much speech to show his cultivation and maintain consistency, and though he may discuss for a whole day the reasons of a subject, to have a unity pervading the ten thousand changes of discourse:—this is the knowledge of the sage. To speak seldom, and in a brief and sparing manner, and to be orderly in his reasoning, as if its parts were connected with a string:—this is the knowledge of the scholar and superior man. Flattering words and disorderly conduct, with undertakings often followed by regrets:—these mark the knowledge of the mean man. Hasty, officious, smart, and swift, but without consistency; versatile, able, of extensive capabilities, but without use; decisive in discourse, rapid, exact, but the subject unimportant; regardless of right and wrong, taking no account of crooked and straight, to get the victory over others the guiding object:—this is the knowledge of the mere servant.

There is bravery of the highest order; bravery of the middle order; bravery of the lowest order. Boldly to take up his position in the place of the universally acknowledged Mean; boldly to carry into practice his views of the doctrines of the ancient kings; in a high situation, not to defer to a bad sovereign, and in a low situation not to follow the current of a bad people; to consider that there is no poverty where there is virtue, and no wealth or honour where virtue is not; when appreciated by the world, to desire to share in all men's joys and sorrows; when unknown by the world, to stand up grandly alone between heaven and earth, and have no fears:—this is the bravery of the highest order. To be reverently observant of propriety, and sober-minded; to attach importance to adherence to fidelity, and set little store by material wealth; to have the boldness to push forward men of worth and exalt them, to hold back undeserving men, and get them deposed:—this is the bravery of the middle order. To be devoid of self-respect and set a great value on wealth; to feel complacent in calamity, and always have plenty to say for himself; saving himself in any way, without regard to right and wrong; whatever be the real state of a case, making it his object to get the victory over others:—this is the bravery of the lowest order.

The *fan-zâo* and the *chü-shû* were the best bows of antiquity; but without their regulators, they could not adjust themselves. The *tsung* of duke Hwan, the *chûeh* of Tâi-kung, the *lû* of king Wăn, the *hû* of prince Chwang, the *kan-tsiang, mŏ-yê, chü-chüeh* and *p'i-lü* of Ho-lü—these were the best swords of antiquity; but without the grindstone and whetstone they would not have been sharp; without the strength of the arms that wielded them they would not have cut anything.

The *hwâ-liû*, the *li-ch'i*, the *hsien-li*, and the *lü-r*—these were the best horses of antiquity; but there were still necessary for them the restraints in front of bit and bridle, the stimulants behind of whip and cane, and the skillful driving of a Tsâo-fû, and then they could accomplish a thousand *li* in one day.

So it is with man:—granted to him an excellent capacity of nature and the faculty of intellect, he must still seek for good teachers under whom to place himself, and make choice of friends with whom he may be intimate. Having got good masters and placed himself under them, what he will hear will be the doctrines of Yâo, Shun, Yü, and T'ang; having got good friends and become intimate with them, what he will see will be deeds of self-consecration, fidelity, reverence, and complaisance:—he will go on from day to day to benevolence and righteousness, without being conscious of it: a natural following of them will make him do so. On the other hand, if he live with bad men, what he will hear will be the language of deceit, calumny, imposture, and hypocrisy; what he will see will be conduct of filthiness, insolence, lewdness, corruptness, and greed:—he will be going on from day to day to punishment and disgrace, without being conscious of it; a natural following of them will make him do so.

The Record says, "If you do not know your son, look at his friends; if you do not know your prince, look at his confidants." All is the influence of association! All is the influence of association!

"Universal Love"

Mo Tzu

Universal Love. Part I.

It is the business of the sages to effect the good government of the world. They must know, therefore, whence disorder and confusion arise, for without this knowledge their object cannot be effected. We may compare them to a physician who undertakes to cure men's diseases:—he must ascertain whence a disease has arisen, and then he can assail it with effect, while, without such knowledge, his endeavours will be in vain. Why should we except the case of those who have to regulate disorder from this rule? They must know whence it has arisen, and then they can regulate it.

It is the business of the sages to effect the good government of the world. They must examine therefore into the cause of disorder; and when they do so they will find that it arises from the want of mutual love. When a minister and a son are not filial to their sovereign and their father, this is what is called disorder. A son loves himself, and does not love his father;—he therefore wrongs his father, and seeks his own advantage: a younger brother loves himself, and does not love his elder brother;—he therefore wrongs his elder brother, and seeks his own advantage: a minister loves himself, and does not love his sovereign;—he therefore wrongs his sovereign, and seeks his own advantage:—all these are cases of what is called disorder. Though it be the father who is not kind to his son, or the elder brother who is not kind to his younger brother, or the sovereign who is not gracious to his minister:— the case comes equally under the general name of disorder. The father loves himself, and does not love his son;—he therefore wrongs his son, and seeks his own advantage: the elder brother loves himself, and does not love his younger brother;—he therefore wrongs his younger brother, and seeks his own advantage: the sovereign loves himself, and does not love his minister;— he therefore wrongs his minister, and seeks his own advantage. How do these things come to pass? They all arise from the want of mutual love. Take the case of any thief or robber:—it is just the same with him. The thief loves his own house, and does not love his neighbour's house;—he therefore steals from his neighbour's house to benefit his own: the robber loves his own person, and does not love his neighbour;—he therefore does violence to his neighbor to benefit himself. How is this? It all arises from the want of mutual

Reprinted from James Legge, trans., *The Chinese Classics,* Vol. II, rev. 2nd. ed., Oxford: The Clarendon Press, 1895, pp. 101–05.

love. Come to the case of great officers throwing each other's Families into confusion, and of princes attacking one another's States:—it is just the same with them. The great officer loves his own Family, and does not love his neighbour's;—he therefore throws his neighbour's Family into disorder to benefit his own: the prince loves his own State, and does not love his neighbour's;—he therefore attacks his neighbour's State to benefit his own. All disorder in the kingdom has the same explanation. When we examine into the cause of it, it is found to be the want of mutual love.

Suppose that universal, mutual love prevailed throughout the kingdom;—if men loved others as they love themselves, disliking to exhibit what was unfilial. . . . And moreover would there be those who were unkind? Looking on their sons, younger brothers, and ministers as themselves, and disliking to exhibit what was unkind. . . . the want of filial duty would disappear. And would there be thieves and robbers? When every man regarded his neighbour's house as his own, who would be found to steal? When every one regarded his neighbour's person as his own, who would be found to rob? Thieves and robbers would disappear. And would there be great officers throwing one another's Families into confusion, and princes attacking one another's States? When officers regarded the Families of others as their own, what one would make confusion? When princes regarded other States as their own, what one would begin an attack? Great officers throwing one another's Families into confusion, and princes attacking one another's States, would disappear.

If, indeed, universal, mutual love prevailed throughout the kingdom; one State not attacking another, and one Family not throwing another into confusion; thieves and robbers nowhere existing; rulers and ministers, fathers and sons, all being filial and kind:—in such a condition the nation would be well governed. On this account, how may sages, whose business it is to effect the good government of the kingdom, do but prohibit hatred and advise to love? On this account it is affirmed that universal mutual love throughout the country will lead to its happy order, and that mutual hatred leads to confusion. This was what our master, the philosopher Mo, meant, when he said, "We must above all inculcate the love of others."

Universal Love. Part II.

Our Master, the philosopher Mo, said, "That which benevolent men consider to be incumbent on them as their business, is to stimulate and promote all that will be advantageous to the nation, and to take away all that is injurious to it. This is what they consider to be their business."

And what are the things advantageous to the nation, and the things injurious to it? Our master said, "The mutual attacks of State on State; the mutual usurpations of Family on Family; the mutual robberies of man on man; the want of kindness on the part of the ruler and of loyalty on the part of the minister; the want of tenderness and filial duty between father and son and of harmony between brothers:—these, and such as these, are the things injurious to the kingdom."

And from what do we find, on examination, that these injurious things are produced? Is it not from the want of mutual love?

Our Master said, "Yes, they are produced by the want of mutual love. Here is a prince who only knows to love his own State, and does not love his neighbour's;—he therefore does not shrink from raising all the power of his State to attack his neighbour. Here is the chief of a Family who only knows to love it, and does not love his neighbour's;—he therefore does not shrink from raising all his powers to seize on that other Family. Here is a man who only knows to love his own person, and does not love his neighbour's;—he therefore does not shrink from using all his resources to rob his neighbour. Thus it happens, that the princes, not loving one another, have their battle-fields; and the chiefs of Families, not loving one another, have their mutual usurpations; and men, not loving one another, have their mutual robberies; and rulers and ministers, not loving one another, become unkind and disloyal; and fathers and sons, not loving one another, lose their affection and filial duty; and brothers, not loving one another, contract irreconcilable enmities. Yea, men in general not loving one another, the strong make prey of the weak; the rich do despite to the poor; the noble are insolent to the mean; and the deceitful impose upon the stupid. All the miseries, usurpations, enmities, and hatreds in the world, when traced to their origin, will be found to arise from the want of mutual love. On this account, the benevolent condemn it."

They may condemn it; but how shall they change it?

Our Master said, "They may change it by the law of universal mutual love and by the interchange of mutual benefits."

"How will this law of universal mutual love and the interchange of mutual benefits accomplish this?

Our Master said, "*It would lead* to the regarding another's kingdom as one's own: another's family as one's own: another's person as one's own. That being the case, the princes, loving one another, would have no battle-fields; the chiefs of families, loving one another, would attempt no usurpations; men, loving one another, would commit no robberies; rulers and ministers, loving one another, would be gracious and loyal; fathers and sons, loving one another, would be kind and filial; brothers, loving one another, would be harmonious and easily reconciled. Yea, men in general loving one another, the strong would not make prey of the weak; the many would not plunder the few; the rich would not insult the poor; the noble would not be insolent to the mean; and the deceitful would not impose upon the simple. The way in which all the miseries, usurpations, enmities, and hatreds in the world, may be made not to arise, is universal mutual love. On this account, the benevolent value and praise it."

Yes; but the scholars of the kingdom and superior men say, "True; if there were this universal love, it would be good. It is, however, the most difficult thing in the world."

Our Master said, "This is because the scholars and superior men simply do not understand the advantageousness *of the law,* and to conduct their reasonings upon that. Take the case of assaulting a city, or of a battle-field, or of the sacrificing one's life for the sake of fame:—this is felt by the people everywhere to be a difficult thing. Yet, if the ruler be pleased with it, both officers and people are able to do it:—how much more might they attain to universal mutual love, and the interchange of mutual benefits, which is different from this! When a man loves others, they respond to and love him; when a man benefits others, they respond to and benefit him; when a man injures others, they respond to and injure him; when a man hates others, they respond to and hate him:—what difficulty is there in the matter? It is only that rulers will not carry on the government on this principle, and so officers do not carry it out in their practice."

"Moral Cultivation," from
The Complete Works of Chu Hsi

Chu Hsi

How to Study

1. *Question:* Does what is called the fundamental task consist only in preserving the mind, nourishing the nature, and cultivating and controlling them?

Answer: Both the effort of preserving and nourishing and that of the investigation of principle to the utmost must be thorough. However, the effort of investigating principle to the utmost is already found within that of preserving and nourishing, and the effort of preserving and nourishing is already found within that of the investigation of principle to the utmost. To investigate principle to the utmost is the same as investigating to the utmost what is preserved, and to preserve and nourish is the same as nourishing what has been investigated.

2. Now there is nothing for the student to do except to examine all principles within his mind. Principle is what is possessed by the mind. Always preserve this mind to examine all principles. These are the only things to do.

3. Although literature cannot be abolished, nevertheless the cultivation of the essential and the examination of the difference between the Principle of Nature (*T'ien-li,* Principle of Heaven) and human selfish desires are things that must not be interrupted for a single movement in the course of our daily

Reprinted from Wing-tsit Chan, *A Sourcebook in Chinese Philosophy,* Princeton, N.J.: Princeton University Press, 1963, pp. 605–09. Copyright 1963 by Princeton University Press; renewed 1991. Reprinted with permission of Princeton University Press.

activities and movement and rest. If one understands this point clearly, he will naturally not get to the point where he will drift into the popular ways of success and profit and expedient schemes. I myself did not really see the point until recently. Although my past defect of emphasizing fragmentary and isolated details showed different symptoms from these ways of life, yet the faults of forgetting the self, chasing after material things, leaving the internal empty, and greedily desiring the external remain the same. Master Ch'eng said, "One must not allow the myriad things in the world to disturb him. When the self is established, one will naturally understand the myriad things in the world." When one does not even know where to anchor his body and mind, he talks about the kingly way and the despotic way, and discusses and studies the task of putting the world in order as if it were a trick. Is that not mistaken?

4. I have heard the sayings of Master Ch'eng I, "Self-cultivation requires seriousness. The pursuit of learning depends on the extension of knowledge." These two sayings are really the essentials for the student to advance in establishing himself in life. And the two efforts have never failed to develop each other. However, when Master Ch'eng taught people to hold fast to seriousness, he meant nothing more than the primary importance of being orderly in clothing and appearance, and by the extension of knowledge he meant no more than to find out, in reading books and history and in dealing with things, where their principles are. The teachings are nothing like the absurd, wild, and unreasonable theories of recent times.

Preserving the Mind and Nourishing the Nature

5. If one can in his daily life and at leisurely moments decidedly collect his mind right here, that is the equilibrium before the feelings of pleasure, anger, sorrow, and joy are aroused, and is the undifferentiated Principle of Nature. As things and affairs approach, the mind can clearly see which is right and which is wrong accordingly. What is right is the Principle of Nature, and what is wrong is in violation of the Principle of Nature. If one can always collect the mind like this, it would be as if he holds the scale and balance to measure things.

6. The mind embraces all principles and all principles are complete in this single entity, the mind. If one is not able to preserve the mind, he will be unable to investigate the principle to the utmost. If he is unable to investigate principle to the utmost, he will be unable to exert his mind to the utmost.

7. *Someone asked*: How about guarding against depravity and concentrating on one thing? *Answer*: Concentrating on one thing is similar to "holding the will firm," and guarding against depravity is similar to "never doing violence to the vital force." To guard against depravity merely means to prevent depraved forces from entering [the mind], whereas in concentrating on one thing one protects it from the inside. Neither should be unbalanced in any way. This is the way the internal and the external mutually cultivate each other.

Holding Fast to Seriousness (Ching)

8. The task of seriousness is the first principle of the Confucian School. From the beginning to the end, it must not be interrupted for a single moment.

9. Seriousness merely means the mind being its own master.

10. If one succeeds in preserving seriousness, his mind will be tranquil and the Principle of Nature will be perfectly clear to him. At no point is the slightest effort exerted, and at no point is the slightest effort not exerted.

11. To be serious does not mean to sit still like a blockhead, with the ear hearing nothing, the eye seeing nothing, and the mind thinking of nothing, and only then it can be called seriousness. It is merely to be apprehensive and careful and dare not give free rein to oneself. In this way both body and mind will be collected and concentrated as if one is apprehensive of something. If one can always be like this, his dispositions will naturally be changed. Only when one has succeeded in preserving this mind can he engage in study.

12. It is not necessary to talk much about the doctrine of holding fast to seriousness. One has only to brood over thoroughly these sayings [of Ch'eng I], "Be orderly and dignified," "Be grave and austere," "Be correct in movement and appearance and be orderly in thoughts and deliberations," and "Be correct in your dress and dignified in your gaze," and make real effort. Then what [Ch'eng] called straightening the internal life and concentrating on one thing will naturally need no manipulation, one's body and mind will be serious, and the internal and external will be unified.

> *Comment.* Like Ch'eng I, Chu Hsi struck the balance between seriousness and the investigation of things in moral cultivation. He said that seriousness is the one important word transmitted in the Confucian School, that it is the foundation in Ch'eng I's teachings, and that it is Ch'eng's greatest contribution to later students. His own contribution in this regard is to have steered the doctrine away from the subjective emphasis evident in Ch'eng Hao toward a unity of internal and external life.

Tranquillity

13. In the human body there is only a [combination of] activity and tranquillity. Tranquillity nourishes the root of activity and activity is to put tranquillity into action. There is tranquillity in activity. For example, when the feelings are aroused and all attain due measure and degree, that is tranquillity in activity.

14. About response to things. Things and the principle [inherent] in my mind are fundamentally one. Neither is deficient in any degree. What is necessary is for me to respond to things. Things and the mind share the same principle. To be calm is to be tranquil. To respond is to be active.

15. Ch'eng I sometimes also taught people sitting in meditation. But from Confucius and Mencius upward, there was no such doctrine. We must

search and investigate on a higher plane and see that sitting in meditation and the examination of principle do not interfere with each other, and then it will be correct.

The Examination of the Self and Things

16. There is dead seriousness and there is living seriousness. If one merely adheres to seriousness in concentrating on one thing and, when things happen, does not support it with righteousness to distinguish between right and wrong, it will not be living seriousness. When one becomes at home with it, then wherever there is seriousness, there is righteousness, and wherever there is righteousness, there is seriousness. When tranquil, one examines himself as to whether one is serious or not, and when active, one examines himself as to whether he is righteous or not. Take, for example, the cases of "going abroad and behaving to everyone as if you were receiving a guest and employing the people as if you were assisting at a great sacrifice." What would happen if you were not serious? Or the cases of "sitting as if one is impersonating an ancestor, and standing as if one is sacrificing." What would happen if you were not serious? Righteousness and seriousness must support each other, one following the other without beginning or end, and then both internal and external life will be thoroughly penetrated by them.

17. If the Principle of Nature exists in the human mind, human selfish desires will not, but if human selfish desires win, the Principle of Nature will be destroyed. There has never been a case where both the Principle of Nature and human selfish desires are interwoven and mixed. This is where the student must realize and examine for himself.

18. "Thinking alone can check passionate desires." What do you think of the saying? *Answer*: Thinking is the same as examining. It means that when one is angry, if one can directly forget his anger and examine the right and wrong according to principle, then right and wrong will be clearly seen and desires will naturally be unable to persist.

19. To say that one must examine at the point where the feelings are about to be aroused means to be careful when thoughts and deliberations are just beginning, and to say that one must examine after the feelings have been aroused means that one must examine one's words and actions after they have taken place. One must of course be careful about thoughts and deliberations when they begin, but one must not fail to examine his words and action after they have taken place.

Letter to Ku Tung-ch'iao

Wang Yang-ming

The Knowledge of the Sage

Moreover, in explaining the Analects, you say that being born with knowledge includes both righteousness and natural law, but that with regard to the constant changing of the rites of propriety, music, renowned men, and things, one must wait until one has learned before one can get at the truth connected therewith. These things certainly have a relation to carrying out the tasks of the sage. If the sage is not able to know these before he has learned them, then it cannot be said of him that he is born with knowledge (of them). To say that the sage is born with knowledge refers to righteousness and knowledge, but it does not refer to ceremonies, music, renowned names, and things, for these things have no vital relation to the task of the sage. If the saying that the sage is born with knowledge refers only to righteousness and natural law, and not to ceremonies, music, renowned names, and things, then, he who knows after study need only learn to know righteousness and natural law; and he who knows after a painful feeling of ignorance also need know only righteousness and natural law.

Present-day Students are Mistaken

At present students who are trying to learn to become sages are not able to learn to know that which the sage is able to know, and yet with unremitting energy they devote themselves to seeking that which the sage is unable to know, as though it were learning. Has the student not thereby lost the means by which he hopes to become a sage? All that I have said corresponds to the points regarding which you are in doubt, and to a small extent explains them; but it does not constitute an exhaustive discussion, and without this there is no clear understanding in the Empire. The more there are who are learning in this way to become sages, the more difficult they are to manage. They enter the class of animals and barbarians, and yet seem to think that they have the learning of the sage. Though my sayings may be temporarily understood, the situation will ultimately be like the ice which while melting in the west freezes in the east, or the fog which is dissipated in front but rises in clouds in the rear. Thought I discuss vociferously until I am distressed unto death, I shall eventually not be able to save anything at all in the Empire.

Reprinted from Frederick Henke, trans., *The Philosophy of Wang Yang-ming*, London: Open Court, 1916, pp. 326–27, 330–34.

The Mind of the Sage Described

The mind of the sage considers heaven, earth, and all things as one substance. He makes no distinctions between the people of the Empire. Whosoever has blood and life is his brother and child. There is no one whom he does not wish to see perfectly at peace, and whom he does not wish to nourish. This is in accordance with his idea that all things are one substance. The mind of everybody is at first not different from that of the sage. If there is any selfishness in it, which divides it through the obscuration of passion and covetousness, then that which is great is considered small and that which is clear and open as unintelligible and closed. Whoever has this mind gets to the place where he views his father or son or elder and younger brothers as enemies. The sage, distressed because of this, uses the occasion to extend his virtuous attitude, which considers heaven, earth, and all things as one substance, by instructing the people and causing them to subdue their selfishness, remove the obscuration, and revert to the original nature of their minds. . . .

Later Decay of State Was Due to Heterodoxy and Sham

. . . The decay of the Three Dynasties was due to the extinction of rule by right, and increase of rule by might. After Confucius and Mencius had died, the learning of the sages became obscure and strange, and heterodox teachings unreasonable. The teachers did not consider the learning of the sages as instruction, nor did the students consider it as learning. The followers of those that ruled by might secretly appropriated things that seemed to be like those of the first king. Externally they made use of his doctrines, but it was done in order to assist their own selfish desires. There was no one in the Empire who did not respect and cherish this point of view. The doctrine of the sages was obstructed with a luxuriant growth of weeds. The people imitated one another and daily sought knowledge through which they might become wealthy and powerful—plans directed toward deception, and schemes for rebellion, things that impose upon heaven and injure mankind. Temporary success was utilized in the earnest pursuit of honor and gain. Of men such as Kuan, Shang, Su, Chang, and their class, there were an indefinite number.

The Learning of the Sages Was Entirely Neglected

After a long time of quarreling, plundering, sorrow, and affliction without ceasing, these men sank into the condition of animals and savages, and even their violent schemes could not all be carried out. All scholars were extremely distressed in their noblemindedness. They sought to find the sage emperor's laws and regulations, and arrange and renovate what was distressing them. Their purpose was to restore the path of the former kings. As the learning of the sages was left in the distance, the transmitted precepts of violent practices became more numerous, intense, and pervasive. Even those who had the knowledge of the virtuous man could not avoid being tainted by the practices then prevalent. That they explained and renovated their doctrines in order to spread enlightenment over the world, only extended the boundary of force. The gate and wall of the learning of the sage could not be seen. Under such circumstances expository learning prevailed and was transmitted for the sake of making reputation. Learning that consisted in remembering and reciting was considered extensive; and formal learning was viewed as elegant. Men of this type confusedly and noisily came up in great numbers and disputed among themselves in order to establish their point of view in the Empire. I do not know how many groups there were. They came from ten thousand by-paths and a thousand different ways, but I do not know what they attained.

Wang Describes the Worldly Students

The students of the world may be compared to a theatre where a hundred different acts are presented. The players cheer, jest, hop, and skip. They emulate one another in cleverness and ingenuity; they laugh in the play and strive for the palm of beauty. On all sides the people emulate one another in striving to see. They look toward the front and gaze toward the rear, but cannot see it all. Their ears and their eyes are confused; their mental and physical energy is disturbed and confounded. Day and night they spend in amusement until they are steeped in it and rest in it, as though they were insane. They do not know what has become of their family property. Under the influence of the sayings of such scholars, princes and kings are confused and devote their lives to vain, useless literary style. They do not themselves know what they say. Some among them realize the empty distance between their doctrines and those of the sages, and their errors and perversity. They realize that they have branched off and have impeded the doctrine of the sages, and even rouse themselves to extraordinary effort, because they desire to see the truth and reality underlying all action. But the highest standpoint these views may in time reach, pertains merely to getting wealth, honor, or gain—the occupation of the five tyrants (of the sixth century B.C.). The learning of the sages is left farther and farther in the distance and is more and more obscured, while practices are directed toward acquiring honor and gain. The farther they go, the more they fall into error. Though some among them have been deceived by Buddhism and Taoism, yet even the sayings of Buddha and Lao-tzu, in last analysis, are unable to overcome the mind that is devoted to honor and gain. Though they have weighed the opinions of the mass of scholars, the discussions of these also are unable to break into their point of view—that of devoting themselves to honor and gain. When we consider present conditions, we find that the poison of honor and gain has penetrated the innermost recesses of the mind, and the practice thereof has become second nature.

For several thousand years people have mutually boasted of their knowledge; they have crushed one another because of power, and wrangled with one another for gain. They have mutually sought for superiority in cleverness, and each has sought for reputation. When they come into prominence and are appointed to official position, those who should be in control of the taxes also desire to serve as military officials, and those who are in charge of the laws, ceremonies, and music, also wish positions on the Board of Civil Office. He who holds the position of a prefect or a magistrate thinks of being the treasurer of a province or a provincial judge; he who is censor hopes to become a prime minister. As a matter of fact, he who is unable to carry out the particular task of his position cannot hold other official positions at the same time, and he who does not understand these sayings (of the sages) cannot expect the praise that attaches to them. Where memory and ability to recite are extensive, they tend to increase pride; and extensive knowledge tends toward doing evil. Much hearing and seeing tends toward disorderly behavior in discussion, and wealth in literary style tends to patch up and brighten one's hypocrisy. It was because of this that Kao, K'uei, Chi, and Hsieh were unable to unite two things in one office. But present-day young students who are just beginning to learn, all desire to understand their sayings and investigate their methods and mysteries. Under false pretenses, they have said that they wish to reform the affairs of the Empire, but this is not the real idea of their minds. They are looking for something to help their selfishness and fulfill their desires.

Alas! because of these abuses, and because of this purpose and these devices of study, they naturally should hear the instruction of the sages. But they view it as an excrescence, a tumor, a handle-hole, and thus they consider their intuitive faculty as insufficient. They are certain to reach the point where they say that the learning of the sages is of no value. Alas! how can the scholars living on earth still seek the learning of the sages, or how can they still discuss it? Who is there among the scholars of this generation who, desiring to devote himself to study, is not in toilsome labor and great difficulty, is not also bigoted, does not stick to literary style, and is not in great danger? Alas, one can but feel sympathy for them! It is fortunate that heaven-given principles are in the mind of man; that in last analysis there is something which cannot be destroyed; and that the clearness of the intuitive faculty is the same as in the most ancient times. Thus, when they hear my exhaustive discussion they must surely commiserate their own condition and be in distress because of it. They must be sorry to a degree that is painful. They must rise up with renewed effort, as water flows into a river in spite of every hindrance. Only the superior scholar can promote this. To whom shall I look for it?

"The Art of the Mind-and-Heart," from *Yamato Zokkun*

Kaibara Ekken

It is said that the mind-and-heart is the heavenly lord and the master of the body. Therefore, it is by thinking that we fulfill our function [as human beings]. The five senses are called the five organs of control. An organ directs or performs a role. The ears are in charge of hearing, the eyes are in charge of seeing, the mouth is in charge of eating and talking, the nose is in charge of smelling, the hands and feet are in charge of moving. These five controlling organs have their respective roles; they have nothing to do with anything else but that. Since the mind is the heavenly lord, it is the master that governs and controls the five senses. There will be no regrets and no mistakes in the operations of the five senses if we act by carefully considering whether or not a thing is correct or if we reflect thoroughly about the actions of the five senses. If the mind fails in its function, if without forethought we yield to the desires of the five senses, and if we do not consider the moral propriety of what we do, then human desires will do as they please and heavenly principles will be destroyed. This is because the mind loses control and cannot think clearly. . . .

We should act solely with a humane mind-and-heart by exerting ourselves in planning for the people, or recommending their talents to the lord or to councillors, sparing people harm, being compassionate and helpful toward those who are poor and distressed, and treating people with kindness. We must not expect that other people will gladly repay us, nor should we act with a view to gaining a [good] reputation. This is hidden virtue. If we do good for our own sake or if we give to people and then expect repayment, our heart's humaneness will be empty. If we act like this, even if we exert ourselves to do good, our actions may be right but all in vain, because our heart is wrong. This is because it is not the Way of sincerity. . . .

. . . The heavenly Way implies that in spring there is birth, in summer there is growth, in autumn there is harvest. The three seasons all have their activities. In winter, however, the life-force is simply hidden and quiet and there is no activity. Just as during the night when people are sleeping they rest without doing anything, so during the winter the life-force is closed up and stored, yet it is the root of the coming spring and the genesis of life. During the winter when the cold is severe, the vital spirit is controlled and

Reprinted from Mary Evelyn Tucker, *Moral and Spiritual Cultivation in Japanese Neo-Confucianism*, Albany: State University of New York Press, 1989, pp. 202, 204, 207, 214–15. Copyright 1989 by State University of New York Press; reprinted with permission.

thus it will flourish in the following season. Therefore, in a mild winter when there is lightning and the vital force moves and dissipates, the growth of the following spring is weak and in autumn the five kinds of grain do not ripen well. When people do not sleep through the night, their blood is not quiet and the next day their energy is weak. By nourishing the human mind in times of quiet, we should make it the basis of movement. When the mind is not quiet but is restless, there will be no energy to be diligent in our work and we will vacillate and make many mistakes. . . . In the *Book of Ritual* it says, "The Noble Person is content to obtain the Way; the petty person is content to obtain the things he desires." If we control desires by means of the Way, we will have contentment and will not be led astray; if we lose the Way on account of desires, we will not have contentment and will be confused. The true person passes his days in contentment; the petty person passes his days in anxiety. I am a foolish old man, and since my remaining days are few, I should have a method of making a day into a month, and making a month into a year. It is foolish to waste time carelessly and not enjoy even one day or one hour.

The capacity for joyful contentment is implanted by the workings of heaven in the human heart and thus we possess it originally. However, when we have selfish desires we are harmed by the cravings of the senses, we are overtaken by feelings of joy and anger, pity and fear, and we lose contentment. The Noble Person is not destroyed by emotions and desires and never loses contentment. No matter what calamities he may encounter, they do not alter the natural happiness which is his. Moreover, when we are in contact with the wind and the flowers, the snow and the moon, the original contentment of the heart is deepened through harmony with these external things. This does not mean that enjoyment comes for the first time through contact with external things. Rather, external things only augment our original joyful contentment. The Way of heaven and earth, the transformations of yin and yang, the cycle of the four seasons are always harmonious. This is the joyful contentment of heaven and earth. This joy, however, is not only for humans; birds fly, fish leap, birds chirp, animals cry out, vegetation flourishes, flowers bloom, fruit is produced—these are expressions of the will of heaven and the natural delight of all things. Through these expressions, we should realize that there is joyful contentment from the beginning in the human heart. To be led astray by desires and lose this contentment is contrary to the Way of heaven and earth. . . .

From *Fudo (Climate and Culture)*

Watsuji Tetsuro

I have defined climate as a means for man to discover himself. But what is this "man"? If one is to interpret climate as one of the forms of limitation on human existence, one should attempt to state, in broad terms, the place this limitation has in the general structure of human existence.

By "man" I mean not the individual (anthrōpos, homo, homme, etc.) but man both in this individual sense and at the same time man in society, the combination or the association of man. This duality is the essential nature of man. So neither anthropology, which treats man the individual, nor sociology, which takes up the other aspect, can grasp the real or full substance of man. For a true and full understanding, one must treat man both as individual and as whole; it is only when the analysis of human existence is made from this viewpoint that it becomes evident that this existence is completely and absolutely negative activity. And human existence is precisely the realisation of this negative activity.

Human existence, through fragmentation into countless individual entities, is the activity which brings into being all forms of combination and community. Such fragmentation and union are essentially of a self-active and practical nature and cannot come about in the absence of self-active entities. Hence, space and time in this self-active sense, form the fundamental structure of these activities. It is at this point that space and time are grasped in their essential form and their inseparability becomes distinct. An attempt to treat the structure of human existence as one of time only would fall into the error of trying to discover human existence on the level only of individual consciousness. But if the dual character of human existence is taken as the essential nature of man, then it is immediately clear that space must be regarded as linked with time.

With the elucidation of the space-and time-nature of human existence, the structure of human association also appears in its true light. The several unions and combinations that man fashions evolve intrinsically according to a certain order. They are to be regarded as not static social structures but as active and evolving systems. They are the realisation of negative activity. This is how history took shape.

Here the space-and time-structure of human existence is revealed as climate and history: the inseparability of time and space is the basis of the inseparability of history and climate. No social formation could exist if it lacked all foundation in the space-structure of man, nor does time become history unless it is founded in such social being, for history is the structure of existence in society. Here also we see clearly the duality of human existence—the finite and the infinite. Men die; their world changes; but through this unending death and change, man lives and his world continues. It continues incessantly through ending incessantly. In the individual's eyes, it is a case of an "existence for death," but from the standpoint of society it is an "existence for life." Thus human existence is both individual and social. But it is not only history that is the structure of social existence, for climate is also a part of this structure and, at that, a part quite inseparable from history. For it is from the union of climate with history that the latter gets its flesh and bones. In terms of the contrast between spirit and matter, history can never be merely spiritual self-development. For it is only when, as self-active being, the spirit objectivises itself, in other words, only when it includes such self-active physical principle that it becomes history, as self-development. This "self-active physical principle," as we might term it, is climate. The human duality, of the finite and the infinite, is most plainly revealed as the historical and climatic structure.

It is here that climate is revealed; for mankind is saddled not simply with a general past but with a specific climatic past; a general formal historical structure is substantiated by a specific content. It is only in this way that the historical being of mankind can become the being of man in a given country at a given age. Again, climate as this specific content does not exist alone and in isolation from history, entering and becoming a part of the content of history at a later juncture. From the very first, climate is historical climate. In the dual structure of man—the historical and the climatic—history is climatic history and climate is historical climate. History and climate in isolation from each other are mere abstractions; climate as I shall consider it is the essential climate that has not undergone this abstraction.

. . . Climate, then, is the agent by which human life is objectivised, and it is here that man comprehends himself; there is self-discovery in climate. We discover ourselves in all manner of significances every day; it may be in a pleasant or a sad mood, but such feelings or tempers are to be regarded not merely as mental states but as our way of life. These, moreover, are not feelings that we are free to choose of ourselves, but are imposed on us as pre-determined states. Nor is it climate only that prescribes such pre-determined feelings, for our individual and social existence controls the way of life of the individual, which is dependent on it in the form of pre-existent relationships, and imparts to him determined moods; it may sometimes impart to society a determined mood in the form of an existent historical situation. But the imposition of climate, united and involved with these, is the most conspicuous. . . .

. . . So even the awakening of the Japanese people which blazed at the time of the foreign wars of the Meiji period was not a topic of theory in and for itself but was rather interpreted in terms of the analogy of the old traditional family unity. The Japanese, it was said, were one great family which regarded the Imperial House as the home of its deity. The people as a whole are nothing but one great and unified house, all stemming from an identical ancestor. Thus the entire state is "the house within the household" and the fence that surrounds the latter is broadened in concept to become the boundaries of the state. Within the borders of this state as a whole, there should be the same unreserved and inseparable union that is achieved within the household. The virtue that is called filial piety from the aspect of the household becomes loyalty from the standpoint of the state. So filial piety and loyalty are essentially identical, the virtue prescribing the individual in accordance with the interests of the whole.

The claims of this loyalty and filial piety, viewed as a single virtue, include a fair degree of patent irrationalities, whether regarded theoretically or historically. The family is the *alpha* of all human communities, as being a unit of personal, physical, community life; the state is the *omega* of all human communities, as being a unit of spiritual community life. The family is the smallest, the state the largest unit of union. The building up of the connection is different in each. So to regard family and state in the same light as human structures is mistaken. Further, speaking now historically, the filial piety that was stressed so heavily in the Tokugawa period does not by any means exhaust the sum total of the prescriptions laid on the individual in virtue of his membership of the house as a whole. In China, the relationship between father and son was denominated by a separate term but "filial piety" in the Tokugawa period signified only the son's relationship of service to his parents. In the same way, loyalty was understood in the narrow sense of the personal relationship between retainer and feudal lord, and had no connection with the state as a whole. Hence the reverence for the Emperor which symbolised the reversion to the state as a whole was essentially different from loyalty as it was understood in the Tokugawa period. Thus, the fact of the correspondence of the relationship of service to a parent with that of service to one's feudal lord is no proof of the correspondence of loyalty i[n] the sense of reverence for the Emperor (loyalty that is, in the significance not of an individual relationship but of a reversion of the individual to the whole) with filial piety understood as the prescriptions laid on the individual by the family as a whole.

Even so, there is a deal of historical sense in the assertion of identity between loyalty and filial piety, both of them directed towards an understanding of the nation as a whole in terms of the analogy of the house. This is the familiar trait of the Japanese; the attempt to interpret the nation as a whole in terms of the distinctive Japanese way of life. And the simple fact that this particular and unique way of life was feasible hints that while the distinctiveness of the Japanese was best exemplified in the way of life of the household, at the same time in the way of life of the nation as a whole a similar distinctiveness was reflected. . . .

6

Death

In the *Mahabharata* there is a beautiful story of the wise princess Savitri and her encounter with Yama, the Lord of Death. She chooses to marry the prince Satyavan, despite his humble surroundings where he cares for his mother and blind father, whose kingdom has been wrongfully taken. She also knows (from a soothsayer) that Satyavan will die in a year, although Satyavan is not aware of this. Nevertheless, her love is strong:

> "To Satyavan alone is my heart given, and though Death will take
> him in a year, yet him only will I wed."

The fateful day arrives, and she accompanies him as he goes out to cut wood. Wielding his axe, he suddenly collapses with pain and becomes lifeless. Savitri sees Yama, the Lord of Death, drawing Satyavan's soul to him with his chord. We read on:

> Strong was Death.
> But the woman was brave.
> She rose up and followed in the steps of Death. . . .
> "I must go," she replied, "where my husband goes. . . . The wise
> men say that to walk seven steps with another makes them friends.
> So let me walk more than seven steps with you. And the wise men
> also say that the best road to walk is that of right [virtue]."
> "Well have you convinced me," said the Lord of Death, "and in
> return for the good words, I promise that, except the soul of Satyavan,
> I will give you what you will." . . .

Savitri asks for the restoration of her father-in-law's health and eyesight. And Yama grants her wish. She continues:

"I shall never be weary of the way that my husband goes. There is no sweeter fruit on earth than the company of those we love."

Yama, approving of these words and her faith, grants her another wish. Savitri requests that the family's kingdom be restored. She continues:

"Master of Death, hear me once more. What is the goodness of the good man? Is it kindness to all things in earth, air or sea? It is indeed, and even if the enemy seeks help, the good man will be ready to grant him aid."

"Fair is your saying, princess; and for these blessed words I will promise yet another boon. Speak."

"O Death, I would be mother to noble children, and teach them to walk in the steps of their dear father, Satyavan. Give me my prince."

Then Yama, King of Death, shook the chord that he held in his hand.

"Lady, your husband shall reign long years with you, and your sons shall reign after you."

Savitri quickly ran to where the body of her husband lay and watched him come back to life. Satyavan spoke:

"I have slept a long time. Just as I was falling into slumber, I seemed to see a vision of a shadow that seized my very life in a magic noose, and bore it away I know not where."

"It was Yama, Lord of Death. But he is not here. Rise, Satyavan, for it is night, and we must go home."[1]

Indian Philosophies

Hindu Perspectives on Death

"It is not always a fact that the pain of death is greater for men than the pain of living. It is we ourselves who have made death a fearful thing." (Gandhi, *The Diary of Mahadev Desai*)

One of the most plaguing questions in philosophy concerns death. It is the culmination of all the previous questions. What is the ultimate design of my existence? And is death my final chapter?

Throughout Indian thought there seems to be a general consensus that physical death does not bring about the end of personal existence. Of all subjects we've treated, there appears to be more agreement on this most difficult and challenging of topics. Almost all Indian philosophical systems, orthodox and heterodox, construct an edifice of survival and immortality. Almost all schools of thought propose that a genuinely sound attitude toward death necessitates an awareness of, preparation for, and acceptance of death.

Upanishads

Katha Upanishad: *Yama's Lesson*   The *Katha Upanishad* relates a famous story that concisely conveys the Hindu perspective on death. While in a bad mood, Auddalaki Aruni offers his son, Nachiketas, to Yama, the ruler of the dead, and Yama allows three wishes, or "boons," to his son. Nachiketas's first wish is to be reconciled with his father; his second is to know more about fire; his last wish is to know the secret of death. Yama is reluctant to grant him this last wish, offering all else instead, including women and wealth. Yet Nachiketas is insistent. (A selection from this story is presented at the end of this chapter.)

The most important message is the need to maintain a proper attitude toward death. As long as one is attached to the ways of the world and to material things and pleasures, one is also attached to life and will be punished through rebirth. Being reborn is not a blessing for the Hindus, for it represents a second death.

The genuine self is the *atman* and not the physical body. Although the physical body dissolves, the self survives because it is eternal. This self is accompanied by the karma of the individual, and the orientation of this karma essentially determines the next existence.

For an analogy, think of a chariot. The soul, *atman*, is a passenger in the chariot, which is driven by *buddhi*, or consciousness, the charioteer. The horses represent the senses, whereas the reins represent *manas*, or mind. The aim is to achieve a state of control over the chariot, especially over the horses. The inability to reach this state commits one to rebirth into *samsara*.

It is only through personal realization of one's *atman*, and of the truth that *atman* is *Brahman*, can one be liberated from this cycle of *samsara*, or wheel of birth, death, and rebirth. Yama reveals to Nachiketas the eternal nature of the self, unvanquished by death. This is the secret of life, revealed through death.

Chandogya Upanishad: Tat Tvam Asi   The *Chandogya Upanishad* contains the famous equation, *tat tvam asi*. Svetaketu is taught that once we realize this truth, at death the self is incorporated into *Brahman*:

> "My dearest child, all these creatures [here] have Being as their root, Being as their resting place, Being as their foundation. . . .
> "My dear boy, when a man dies, his voice is absorbed into the mind, his mind into breath, breath into light-and-heat and light-and-heat into the highest substance.
> "This finest essence,—the whole universe has it as its Self: That is the Real: That is the Self: That *you* are, Svetaketu!"[2]

In contrast, rebirth is inevitable for the person suffering under the cloud of *maya* and *avidya*.

Brihadaranyaka Upanishad   In the *Brihadaranyaka Upanishad* we find the sage Uddalaka and his son Svetaketu, who is asked many questions by the *kshatriya*

Jaivali. Many of these questions he cannot answer, particularly those concerning death. Jaivali then offers to teach the young man, who refuses because it would be condescending for him to learn from someone of a lower class. Svetaketu recounts this to his father, who then goes to learn from Jaivali. From Jaivali, Uddalaka discovers the secret of death: Realizing the truth of one's genuine nature leads one out of the cycle of *samsara*. (The full account is in the *Brihadaranyaka Upanishad* VI.2.)

In the same Upanishad, the soul is compared to a caterpillar passing from the tip of one blade of grass to another:

> Now as a caterpillar, when it has come to the end of a blade of grass, in taking the next step draws itself together towards it, just so this soul in taking the next step strikes down this body, dispels its ignorance, and draws itself together.[3]

Transmigration,* Samsara, *and Karma   There does not seem to be sufficient evidence to indicate that belief in transmigration of souls was endemic before the Aryan invasion. Furthermore, the Vedic literature also lacks concrete references to transmigration as such. Yet, as we have seen, there are direct references within some of the major Upanishads. By the time of the Buddha, transmigration was fairly well established.[4]

The earliest mention of transmigration may be in the *Brihadaranyaka Upanishad* (3.2), in which Yajnavalkya is questioned about the whereabouts of people when they die. In response, Yajnavalkya conveys the notion of karma, but does so in secret.[5] It did not take long for this secret to be made public, and it became accepted by almost all Indians as an essential orthodox teaching.

The idea of transmigration was so powerful that even heterodox Buddhists believed in some form of rebirth, although Buddhists still had to reconcile their belief in some form of rebirth with their teaching of *anatman*, or no-soul. That is, if there is rebirth, just what is it that is reborn?

For Hindus, this was less of a problem. They asserted an eternal, incorruptible *atman* that embarked on a countless series of rebirths in psycho-physical forms. This idea remains an integral element in Hindu thought.

From all this, it is clear that the belief in the transmigration of souls is associated with the teachings of karma and *samsara,* the endless cycle of birth, death, and rebirth that includes all living psycho-physical forms within its scheme: gods, humans, animals, insects, and demons. (This scheme excludes plants. But remember that for the heterodox Jains, plants—and also water, rocks, and air—harbor souls.)

As we saw in Chapter 5, karma literally means "action" or "deed." Karma is such a powerful force that it regulates future states of existing for the soul and thus governs what psycho-physical form it re-enters. It is the principle of moral causality; that is, all actions, whether positive or negative, will have their effect at some future time. Much of what we are is the result of past karma.

Karma offers for the Hindu, and for the Buddhist as well, a principle of universal justice. What karma means is that we are the ultimate arbiters of our fate. We become what we decide. If we live virtuously, then we will be rewarded, if not in this life, then in future lives. On the other hand, if we are of questionable character and deed, we will be punished. Most Indians believe that justice will eventually prevail, and that our just rewards or penalties will occur.

We must be clear that karma does not simply refer to physical deeds; moral causation includes desires and intentions as well. This is clear in one of the earliest references to karma in Indian literature, in the *Brihadaranyaka Upanishad*:

> According as one acts, according as one conducts himself, so does he become. The doer of good becomes good. The doer of evil becomes evil. One becomes virtuous by virtuous action, bad by bad action.
>
> But people say: "A person is made [not of acts, but] of desires only."
>
> [In reply to this I say:] As is his desire, such is his resolve; as is his resolve, such the action he performs; what action (*karma*) he performs, that he procures for himself.[6]

Here, the sage Yajnavalkya links desire, will, and actions and asserts that karma is a matter of mind, character, and works.

In any case, even though the burning out of our karmic residue seems to be an inexorable, natural law, not all Hindus view this in exactly the same way. Some assign a more active role to God, or Ishvara, in the transmigration process, coming close to a Christian notion of grace. That is, some Hindus believe that Ishvara acts upon us to affect our karma. Though gratuitous, it is often in response to devotional practices. This belief seems to be more popular among the Saivite Hindus.

Bhagavad Gita

> What is night for all beings is the time of waking for the disciplined soul; and what is the time of waking for all beings is night for the sage who sees.[7]

The *Bhagavad Gita* centers around the conversation between Krishna and Arjuna on the eve of battle, when Arjuna is acutely despondent over having to lead his forces against his cousins, knowing the terrible bloodshed and misery that will result. Krishna reminds Arjuna that the genuine self cannot perish. Viewing the self as physical is an ordinary perspective, and clinging to this mistaken view warrants continual rebirth.

Krishna instructs Arjuna that that which exists can never cease to exist, just as that which does not exist cannot come into existence. In this way, the *Atman* always was and is, and always will be. It can never suffer destruction. Krishna thereby attempts to open Arjuna's eyes, mind, and heart to a more inclusive, divine perspective. For Krishna, those who truly know *Brahman,* and thus know their true natures, will return to *Brahman,*— ". . . knowers of *Brahman* go to *Brahman.*" Krishna instructs Arjuna:

"Never was there a time when I was not, not thou, nor these lords of men, nor will there ever be a time hereafter when we all shall cease to be.

"As the soul passes in this body through childhood, youth and age, even so is its taking on of another body. The sage is not perplexed by this."[8]

Krishna then reassures Arjuna that, knowing this, there is no reason for sadness:

"For to the one that is born death is certain and certain is birth for the one that has died. Therefore for what is unavoidable, thou shouldst not grieve.

"Beings are unmanifest in their beginnings, manifest in the middles and unmanifest again in their ends, O Bharata (Arjuna). What is there in this for lamentation?"[9]

Krishna also tells Arjuna that each person must be vigilant of their final thoughts at death. The power of karma reaches new depths in Krishna's enlightened instruction. Our last thought before death will have a direct effect on our future state: Only by having one's mind focused on *Brahman* can one return to *Brahman*.

This takes special training and practice, or yoga, and a lifetime of vigilance. And it is through this yoga that we can achieve liberation from *samsara*. The way to liberation lies especially in bhakti yoga. Here, constant devotion to God is necessary.

Advaita Vedanta

As we have seen, Sankara's Advaita system teaches the absolute oneness of *atman* and *Brahman*. While *atman* is embodied, it is referred to as *jiva* (also called *jivatman*). Both terms refer to soul or self—namely, that which is the essence of the individual, without which that individual no longer is. And as long as one remains in a state of ignorance concerning one's genuine identity— *tat tvam asi*—self continues to be reborn into *samsara,* and *atman* continues to be embodied as *jiva. Moksha* is that experience of liberation from *samsara* that results from the shattering of *avidya,* or ignorance.

What is especially interesting in this is that Hindus contend that the *jiva* is without origin. It preexists and thus has no real beginning. After all, it is *Brahman,* and *Brahman* is eternal. Attempting to untangle the beginnings of transmigration is difficult. Instead, Hindu texts invest much of their energies exploring, repeatedly, the reasons why *samsara* and transmigration continue eternally. The message in the *Brihadaranyaka Upanishad* clearly suggests that human ignorance is the cause of transmigration.

Although it preexisted, *jiva* is not necessarily eternal. It is hoped that at some point in the future it will realize its oneness with *Brahman* and will thus free itself from the illusion of separateness.

In order to fathom more clearly this Indian notion of transmigration, let us look at the different kinds of bodies that are postulated.[10] Three bodies make up the individual: gross, subtle, and causal. The gross body is the physical body as we commonly know it, the one that will decompose upon physical death.

For our purposes, we can combine the subtle and causal bodies and refer to them collectively as the subtle body, *linga sharira*. Whereas the gross body actually dies, the subtle body continues to live. Moreover, it acts as a crucial link to the next incarnation. This subtle body consists of the mental or psychic components of an individual.[11]

We must keep in mind that this subtle body is not solely intellective or perceptive; it is the mental composite that also comprises the inner dispositions of that individual person. These dispositions are the result of many lifetimes and consist of spiritual and moral sensibilities. And according to the principle of karma, habits acquired throughout our existences continue to enhance these dispositions, called *samskaras,* which are always in dynamic interaction with karma, both past and current. These dispositions are contained in one's subtle body, which to a large extent determines the future direction one takes in one's new psycho-physical organism.

This makes little sense if we are not able to reify somehow the contents of our mental life; that is, we need to view our every thought, desire, and emotion as a sort of "thing" that exists apart from our consciousness once it is experienced. This psychic bundle survives the death of the gross body and the extinguishing of that consciousness. The mental life of the individual, accrued over countless lifetimes, continues to live as a force that links each of us to our next rebirth in a specific psycho-physical form. This new existence takes place in a new gross body in some embryonic existence, which inherits a bundle of predominant dispositions and karma accumulated over past lifetimes.

All this leads us to the Advaitin distinction between true Self and nonself. The genuine Self is ultimately real, and all else is illusion because what is real is that which does not undergo change. When we view the three bodies (gross, subtle, and causal) as acting as a manifestation of Self, we see that they are all subject to change; they are not immortal. For this reason, they do not constitute the real Self. Sankara thereby believed that the Self, which does not undergo any change, remains immortal and is therefore real. Personal realization of one's own Self-nature leads to genuine immortality because one is no longer tied to the cycle of *samsara*.

Hindu theistic groups claim that *moksha* leads to immortality, freedom from rebirth, only after this life. In addition, the orthodox schools of Nyaya-Vaisheshika and Samkhya claim that the liberation attained while embodied in this life is not total. Absolute freedom comes after death.

The Advaitin position is quite different. It claims that the freedom attained by the *jivanmukta,* or one who has been liberated during one's life, is total. The very nature of the Self supports this position, for the Self is eternal. Nothing material can affect it in any way. Even though the state of enslavement or bondage is a fact on the ordinary level of our experience, it does not possess the status of reality because bondage is not eternal. Only what is real can be eternal. (Remember that the body's existence is not in itself bondage, but the identification with the body is bondage.) In any case, for Sankara and the Advaita school, immortality is not a state to be attained only after death; it can be attained in this life upon the realization of one's self.

To conclude, in answer to the question, What survives death? We see that a nearly endless journey within *samsara* is produced by desire. The mechanism through which this journey occurs lies within the subtle body, which is the storehouse for a person's desires and thoughts. The subtle body, upon the death of the gross body, carries within itself the impressions that have become the karmic residue of the previous lives. This subtle body then links itself with a new body carrying these lasting impressions—not just any new body, however, but one that reflects the dominant dispositions acquired.

Hindus believe that rebirth can occur on any number of levels of existence. They presume various planes of existence comparable to hells, purgatories, and heavens not on this earthly plane. These levels are encountered either to suffer punishment or gain reward. The same can be said for rebirths into animal and insect forms.

Nevertheless, only on this earthly plane can there be insight into one's genuine nature. *Moksha,* or freedom from rebirth, can come about only on the human level; that is, only as a human can the *jiva* achieve positive karma and gain self-realization.

Buddhist Perspectives on Death

A legendary account of Siddhartha's meditation under the Bodhi tree describes how he encountered three watches, or three stages, during his enlightenment or spiritual awakening. In his first watch he gained insight into all of his previous lives and experiences. In the second watch he witnessed the rebirths of all other beings and discerned the indelible law of karma as the principle that determines the quality of rebirths. During the third watch he realized another enduring principle—that of dependent origination, or *pratityasamutpada,* the interrelationship and interdependency of all things with each other.

This experience produced a total and irrevocable awakening in Siddhartha, a realization that the key to liberation from suffering lies in being free from all attachments. Guiding others to this understanding was his life's work, and he set out to preach his message, or *dharma.*

When the Buddha preached his *dharma,* one of the most contentious issues among his listeners was the subject of death, especially the question of whether or not there was an afterlife, or whether or not the soul was immortal. Many of his listeners seemed genuinely puzzled over the Buddha's teachings. As we know, when they approached him with these metaphysical questions, he was reluctant to provide a definite answer.[12] (Selections from the *Majjhima-Nikaya,* the *Milindapanha,* and the *Visuddhi-Magga* are included at the end of this chapter.)

Major Themes in the Buddhist View of Death

The Three Signs of Existence   The Buddha often pointed to what are called the three characteristics, or signs, of existence: *dukkha,* suffering; *anicca,* impermanence; and *anatta,* no-self. Together these three signs are a clue to Buddhist teachings concerning death and survival.

Dukkha does not mean only "pain" or "suffering"; it also means a "dislocation," and even "dissatisfaction" or "discontent." *Dukkha* does not mean that we suffer pain at every moment of our lives, even though at all times there is someone, somewhere, experiencing suffering. Pleasure is accompanied by pain, youth by age, health by illness, life by death. This is a universal truth.

Buddhists admit that our most universal desire is for happiness. Yet, we live in an existence imbued with *anicca,* or impermanence, which means that the content we experience in this changing world is temporary. The realization of this can produce a deep-rooted dissatisfaction, which is why Buddhists consider the genuine cause of suffering or dissatisfaction to be *trsna.* It is not the reality of change, *anicca,* that brings about our discontent and suffering; it is our attachment to this reality and our desire for permanence that causes frustration.

Therefore, the cause of our natural condition of suffering lies within ourselves. We crave to own that which we cannot own. More precisely, craving comes from desire, and desire itself reflects some degree of dissatisfaction with our current state. Such discontent is not only over what we have, but especially with who we are.

One of the most poignant depictions of the universal reality of suffering is in the story of Kisagotami. Upon the death of her young son, Kisagotami went to the Buddha, imploring him to bring the child back to life. Gautama asked her to collect a mustard seed from each household that had not experienced death. Of course, she found none. Instead she discovered the truth of the ubiquity of death, how it has touched all of us in some way.[13]

This story reflects the first three Noble Truths: Suffering is universal; craving permanence causes suffering; yet, we can still be liberated. Siddhartha learned of this early in his life as he ventured out of the protected castle and encountered the facts of aging, labor, illness, and death. The central focus of the Four Noble Truths, mentioned in Chapter 2, lies around the centrality of suffering as a universal, existential truth.

As we also saw, this does not leave us in a sea of pessimism. The Third Noble Truth tells us that we can liberate ourselves from suffering, and the Fourth Noble Truth describes how. The source of freedom comes from within, not from some external power. And the Eightfold Path is the course of action one must take in order to attain this final freedom from suffering, which will in turn lead us to total awakening, or what the Buddhists call nirvana.

Anicca means "impermanence" or "process." For Buddhists, all things are in constant process. Flux is a universal law, and nothing is exempt from change. That which changes is thereby nonsubstantial.

The doctrine of *anicca* is reached through a strict empirical analysis. As things appear, all things arise and fall at the same time. Nothing stays the same. Birth results in death.

For Buddhists, the most powerful illusion under which we suffer is that of a separate entity called self, or "I." This is the point at which Buddhists come into direct conflict with the Hindu teaching of *atman*.

For the man wounded by the arrow, the reality is the wound itself, and not some transcendent cause behind it. Seeking that which is extrinsic to experience undermines the experience. In this way, Buddhists are radically empirical. For them, reality is sought within the experience itself. In this fashion they deny the existence of a transcendent, personal self. Presuming the existence of a substantial self illustrates our tendency to cling to some semblance of permanence. The belief in a self reflects *trsna*, desire, and ignorance.

Yet, a plaguing problem now enters the Buddhist scheme. If there is no soul or self, and if Buddhists still insist on rebirth, then just what is it that is reborn? In other words, there must be some type of continuity. Without some continuity, memory of one's previous lives makes little sense. The Buddha himself remembered his previous lives, and they were remembered by him as *his* life, no one else's. How do we reconcile no-self with karma? If the state of rebirth is due to karma, then how can the personal ownership attributed to karma occur without an idea of self?

Karma   In response to the question of continuity, as far as the facts reveal our personhood consists of five *skandhas*, or aggregates, also called "heaps." And it is precisely karma that is the causal nexus among varying sets or bundles of *skandhas*. Even though no set of *skandhas* is identical to another, a continuity is established precisely because of the karmic process.

In short, the notions of karma and rebirth are intimately linked. Reconciling both of these with the idea of no-self, called *anatta* or *anatman*, is not only a daunting task for the Western interpreter, but for Indian scholars as well. These ideas were controversial even for followers and contemporaries of the Buddha.

In order to understand all this, we need to look at other crucial Buddhist teachings surrounding death: *samsara*, *pratityasamutpada*, and nirvana.

Samsara *and* Pratityasamutpada   Even though the concepts of *samsara* and dependent origination mutually reinforce one another, they still present rather challenging positions for the Western student.

Dependent origination expresses itself in what Buddhists call the twelve preconditions, which clearly illustrate for them the causal nexus underlying all things. The twelve preconditions are often depicted as a wheel—thus the wheel of birth, death, and rebirth, or *samsara*. The preconditions seem to start from desire and end with death, only to start again with desire. Much of Buddhist philosophy has been an attempt to analyze more precisely the nature of the relationships existing among these twelve preconditions.

The essential point behind this wheel is that all things are caused; moreover, each condition is both cause and effect, and each is thereby dependent on each of the others, none being excluded. What is especially important in *samsara* is that it exists in and of itself, not dependent on some outside force or transcendent power. There is no transcendent creator God in Buddhism.

Because each condition is causally related to all the others, no one condition exists permanently by itself. And here we have a radical teaching: Nothing exists substantially, even the knower of this theory.

When we realize this truth, we attain *prajna*, the wisdom that constitutes understanding of this wheel of causation. *Prajna* shatters our natural state of ignorance, *avidya*.

Nirvana   Literally, the term *nirvana* means "to extinguish," as in a flame. What is nirvana, and just what is it that is extinguished? What is extinguished is not the physical body (as some interpreters have it), but our attachment to all things, especially to our sense of "I," "mine," or a subsistent self. Furthermore, it is the extinction of desire, of *trsna*, of craving. Buddhists do not desire to die, but they seek to cease to desire.

This is a state of utter peacefulness in which a person is free from the pangs of desire. There is no longer attachment to objects and thoughts. In a sense, there is a cessation of thoughts, for the person is unmoved by desires or thoughts.[14] The person who has attained nirvana is totally free and unaffected by phenomena because she or he has reached that realization of the nature of things whereby there is no substantiality nor permanence, and thus no self or ego.

This detachment extends itself to all things, and thus death is seen for what it is, not as the greatest evil, but as an expression of being's pulse:

> As Sariputta asks, how can a person be interested in the afterlife, if he is not in any way attached to the present life?[15]

In early Buddhism, the person who reaches nirvana is called an *arhat*. What can be said for the *arhat* who has died after having experienced nirvana? Not much. The Buddha was asked this question, and he responded with silence. What the Buddha perhaps meant to indicate is that any explanation or analysis of this state of the *arhat* after death cannot be made because it is beyond logical analysis. Again, we see the conspicuous empiricism of early Buddhism. The Buddha avoided empty speculation on metaphysical issues such as the state of the *arhat* after death.

In Theravada Buddhism, the Buddha's followers offered various interpretations of his response. One is that the *arhat* is totally extinguished. Another is that the *arhat* exists forever in some other realm, as pure *citta* (mind) along with other pure *cittas*. Both views were criticized by other Buddhists, who claimed, first of all, that nothing can be totally extinguished, and second, that the survival of the *arhat* as *citta* seems contrary to the absence of ego.

Rebirth   With the foregoing discussion in mind, we are now ready to clarify the Buddhist view of rebirth. As we stated, the "person," or psycho-physical organism, essentially consists of five *skandhas*, or five aggregates: "matter, sensations, perceptions, mental formations, and consciousness."[16] This constitutes the "I." At death, these *skandhas* dissolve. So, again we are back to our initial question: If rebirth occurs, then what is it that survives?

All this is quite difficult to summarize because there seems to be various Buddhist interpretations of this continuity. We can say this: What survives is a stream of karmic residue from previous lives, or *skandhas*. This karmic residue is driven forward by craving and eventually associates with a new psycho-physical form in an embryonic state.

This is not identical to the Vedantist teaching of the *linga sharira*, or subtle body, for this karmic residue is not self-aware. It is more like the unconscious energies that propel us. Let us look at this more closely.

How Does Rebirth Occur?   Buddhists tell us that the final conscious moments at death leave an imprint on our karmic residue and have a special effect on rebirth. To illustrate, if my final moments are an expression of *trsna*, or clinging, then it most likely signifies an habitual orientation of *trsna* throughout my life. We are creatures of habit, and perhaps we even die in a way that is consistent with the way we live. Thus, this final conscious thought brings about an orientation, or impulse, in the new form. Nevertheless, there is an unbroken current of mental activity.

We see that a stream of mental dispositions in a karmic residue passes from one form to the next. Simply stated, this is what accounts for the continuity from one life to the next. Just how this is enacted is rather mysterious, and there is little analysis of this that is appealing and logically sufficient. In the *Milindapanha* (71.16), continuity is analogous to a lamp whose light is transmitted to another lamp. Just as there is no substantial flame per se for the lamp, there is no substantive self or soul in the body.

When Does Rebirth Occur?   In order for rebirth to occur, the timing must be right. Coitus must take place between a couple, and the female must be in the proper time to conceive. If the timing is appropriate, the traces of desire, in varying degrees, in this surviving consciousness enable its rebirth in a new form. The absence of desire, if nirvana occurred in the previous life, frees consciousness from rebirth.

In early Buddhism there was no belief in a disembodied survival, of a consciousness surviving for some time without entering a psycho-physical form. Later schools did develop teachings about an intermediate state. For instance, we find teachings of the *bardo*, or intermediate state, in Tibetan Buddhism. Prayers from the *Bardo Thodol*, or the *Tibetan Book of the Dead*, are read to the deceased, intending to aid the stream of consciousness of the deceased in its intermediate state. How this stream of consciousness endures this state determines its next rebirth.

Where Does Rebirth Take Place?   Most rebirths do not transpire on the human plane. Instead, rebirths usually take place on other levels of existence, such as the purgatorial or the *deva* world of angels, or else on the higher Brahma levels.[17] Nevertheless, as in the orthodox teachings, rebirth on the human level is necessary to produce positive karma and to attain nirvana.

The most crucial idea in this entire discussion is the distinction between identity and continuity; that is, for Buddhists, the absence of personal identity does not necessarily mean the absence of continuity. Nevertheless, the Buddhist notion of survival, combined with the teaching of *anatta,* remains for many students a constant stumbling block for understanding.

Early Buddhist View of Death: A Review

It is perhaps helpful to briefly review these early Buddhist teachings. At death, we have the disintegration of the five aggregates. Still, some invisible mental energy exists and carries its karmic residue to a new form. It is a sort of psychic bundle of energy that somehow interacts with its milieu to effect the birth of a new physical being. In this new form, even while in gestation, senses become more developed, as do the mental activities of feeling and perception. At the same time, desires also develop so that the process continues. Death, therefore, is merely the ephemeral end of a particular phase within the stream of existence.

Liberation from this wheel of birth, death, and rebirth requires the discovery that *dukkha, trsna,* and rebirth are connected. With a proper mental and physical attitude, one must practice the Eightfold Path. For instance, right mindfulness demands proper meditation, and this in turn requires proper physical rapport so that mind and body can work in symmetry. This necessitates relaxing the mind, so that there is an active passivity. In this way, intuition is developed.

Through insight, the three aspects of existence—*dukkha, anicca,* and *anatta*—are genuinely understood. Only in this way can we attain wisdom. This leads to nirvana and to the state of the *arhat,* literally a "worthy one." As to the fate of this *arhat* upon death, the Buddha remains essentially silent.

Nagarjuna: Death as Sunya

Hindus often construe Buddhist teachings as being nihilistic, especially the ideas of *anatman* (or *anatta*) and nirvana. In the face of this criticism, Nagarjuna founded his influential school called the Madhyamika, or "Middle Way." Using the same analytic spirit of Hindu critics, he defended Buddhism as teaching neither a system of Being nor one of non-Being. In doing so he constructed a sophisticated justification of Buddhism as a teaching of the Middle Way between total affirmation and negation.

For Nagarjuna, all things are empty, *sunya,* and therefore devoid of self-subsistence. To be *sunya* does not mean to be nonexistent; it means that things are simply what they are. This has a decidedly profound effect on how we view death. If we look at death from our ordinary perspective, we naturally fear it and become anxious because we view it in relation to life. We see it as the loss of life and all that life means to us. If we view death as *sunya,* we see that death is simply that which is, as suchness. This is enormously difficult for us. But, if we can view things as *sunya,* then we have attained *prajna,* or wisdom. *Prajna,* therefore, is a state of genuine freedom from attachment to thought.

■ Chinese Philosophies ■

The sun at noon is the sun declining; the creature born is the creature dying. (Hui Shih's fourth paradox)

There is no consensus about immortality among the Chinese. Whereas many simply deny the soul's survival, many others believe in immortality, though often in more cosmic terms, such as a revived participation in the universe.

Sharp debates concerning immortality took place between Buddhists and Taoists, particularly during the fifth and sixth centuries C.E.[18] These debates centered around the existence of the Chinese notion of soul, called *shen-ming*. This soul is defined in the *Book of Rites (Li-chi)*:

> All creatures must die; dying they return to earth. (The part returning to earth) is called their *kuei* (or *po*). Bones and flesh are buried below; they disappear and become jungle and fields. The Breath (*ch'i*) of the creatures rises and shows; it shines above, (therefore it is called) *ming*. A smelling vapor (appears) sickening (the mourners) at heart. This is the essence of the (dead) creature. In it *shen* (or *hun*) manifests itself."[19]

In this we see that *shen-ming* acts as the essence that gives the body life.

Taoism

Tao Te Ching

The *Tao Te Ching* describes the essence of Tao as constant and regenerative. Tao is the absolute way that produces the universal forces of yin and yang:

> Out of Tao, One is born;
> Out of One, Two; Out of Two, Three;
> Out of Three, the created universe.
> The created universe carries the *yin* at its back and the *yang* in front;
> Through the union of the pervading principles it reaches harmony.[20]

Yin and yang interpenetrate each other; in the same way, life and death mutually define each other:

> Out of life, death enters.
> The companions (organs) of life are thirteen;
> The companions (organs) of death are (also) thirteen.
> What send man to death in this life are also (these) thirteen.
> How is it so?
> Because of the intense activity of multiplying life.[21]

Wisdom lies in accepting what is natural. In this way, we become a sage. Nature is the fullest expression of the interaction of yin and yang. Just as death exists in life, so also life exists in death. Death, therefore, is not the finale. Nature shows continual rebirths in various ways.

Chuang Tzu's View of Death

Chuang Tzu is one of the best examples of this view. For Chuang Tzu, life and death occupy the same reality. When death was imminent for Chuang Tzu and his followers were discussing arrangements for a lavish funeral, Chuang Tzu insisted on a simple burial.

In the second chapter of the work entitled *Chuang Tzu*, "The Identity of Contraries," we read that all things are of equal value, including death:

> A vast mountain is a small thing. Neither is there any age greater than that of a child cut off in infancy. . . . The universe and I came into being together; and I, and everything therein, are ONE.[22]

Death is not a radically different state from life, but merely a transition from one manifestation of being to the next. Tao by its very nature does not change. Life and death are equal manifestations of Tao.

Understanding this may enable us to look at life and death differently. To illustrate, after the death of his wife, Chuang Tzu, naturally saddened at first, was later discovered beating a drum, acting inappropriately and not according to the Confucian mourning ritual. When asked to explain himself, Chuang Tzu compared his wife's death to the change among the four seasons:

> For not nature only but man's being has its seasons, its sequence of spring and autumn, summer and winter. If some one is tired and has gone to lie down, we do not pursue him with shouting and bawling. She whom I have lost has lain down to sleep for a while in the Great Inner Room. To break in upon her rest with the noise of lamentation would but show that I knew nothing of nature's Sovereign Law.[23]

According to Chuang Tzu, there is no essential difference between ourselves and all that surrounds us. We are one with the universe, and the universe, as revealed through the seasonal cycles, is permanent. Living in harmony with Nature ensures one's immortality in oneness with Nature. One lives in harmony with Nature by avoiding conflicts that arise from self-centeredness. Nature simply flows according to its principle.

Religious Taoism: Seeking Longevity

Some practices among religious Taoists even focused on seeking some type of physical immortality. They sought an elixir, or secret concoction, that would guarantee longevity. (Chuang Tzu was opposed to this interest in longevity, which continued into the Han period.) To illustrate, a certain Yang Chu proclaimed:

> "As moldering bones, all men are equal; who can differentiate here? Let us therefore seize the moment of life—why concern ourselves with the time after death?"[24]

This materialist sentiment sustained a preoccupation in prolonging this life. Many ordinary people believed in the "immortal" (*hsien*), one who is capable of immortality by transforming his body into elementary parts. Approaches to human physiology involved specific practices with the aim of extending physical longevity indefinitely. Breathing exercises, gymnastics, and sexual techniques were all used to achieve this goal.[25]

Confucianism

Confucius on Death

> Chi Lu asked about serving the spirits *of the dead.*
> The Master said, "While you are not able to serve men, how can you serve *their spirits?" Chi Lu added,* "I venture to ask about death?" He was answered, "While you do not know life, how can you know about death?"[26]

In response to Chi Lu's questions about death, Confucius made it clear that the most important concerns should first deal with the living. He refused to speculate about the afterlife, the soul, and immortality. His paramount interest was in proper relations, *li,* in sustaining proper relations through propriety, or ritual, and in correct behavior.

Confucius's emphasis on relationality is not limited to the living. Filiality also expresses itself in the veneration bestowed to deceased ancestors. (Ancestor "reverence" is a more fitting term than ancestor "worship.") Proper observances include funeral rites, mourning, and constant offerings and prayers. Thus there is a strong link between the living and the dead.

Later texts ascribed more explicit ideas in these matters. For instance, the *Hsun Tzu* reveals how the mourning ritual offers a legitimate framework for the expression of grief and for enhancing filiality among the living. It is the major demonstration of respect for the deceased. To illustrate, in a text called the "Scripture on Filiality" we have a description of specific details surrounding mourning, such as the three-year period of grieving and making offerings:

> When parents are alive, to serve them with love and reverence; when deceased, to cherish their memory with deep grief—this is the sum total of man's fundamental duty, the fulfillment of mutual relations between the living and the dead, the accomplishment of the filial son's service of his parents.[27]

Wang Ch'ung: Melting the Ice

During the time of Wang Ch'ung, the popular belief was that when people die, they become ghosts that can affect and harm the living. Wang Ch'ung was strongly opposed to such beliefs. For him, personal experiences and perceptions are not necessarily valid grounds for the existence of ghosts; visual perceptions can easily fool us. The appeal must be to intellect over perception and must be based on fact. For him, reason must be the cornerstone of argument, as can be seen in his selection at the end of the chapter.

In addition, Wang Ch'ung found no sound evidence to support the claim that we are immortal. We perceive that we are similar to other creatures in that our consciousness becomes extinct at death. Upon bodily death, our essence, or *shen* (also known as "breath"), no longer exists in the same state and therefore dissipates. Wang Ch'ung used the image of a flame being extinguished to signify death:

> "For what is the difference between a sick man about to die and a light about to go out? When a flame is extinguished, its radiation is dispersed and only its candle remains, and when a man dies, his vital essence is gone and the body alone remains. To assert that a man after death is still conscious is like saying that an extinguished flame may again have light."[28]

Wang Ch'ung stated that "man's life within the universe is like ice," and the warmth of the other seasons works to melt the ice, just as death brings about the dissolution of the individual. For him, winter is the time of life, solidifying the water into ice: "Since the water of spring cannot become ice again, how can the soul of a dead man become a body again?"[29]

In the same spirit, he criticized the popular belief in determinism. Wang strongly felt that events occur due to chance, or luck, and not in some preordained pattern. In other words, he emphasized fate, or *ming*. He cited the early death of Yen Hui, a favorite student of Confucius. Death is not predetermined by some external force; it is solely a matter of misfortune, whereas long life is a matter of good luck:

> If a short life be spoken of as unlucky, then longevity must be a matter of luck, and a short life, something unlucky.[30]

Mo Tzu on Death

Mo Tzu's views on death were based on his utilitarianism. As we know, he criticized the elaborate funeral rituals of the Confucians as a waste of time and resources. For Mo Tzu, mourning rituals must be shortened and simplified in order to produce the greatest practical benefit for everyone involved.

He was also critical of an extended mourning period because he felt it was not conducive to the well-being of the family. Among Confucians, it was the tradition to mourn the death of a parent for three years. During this time, sexual relations were prohibited. Mo Tzu must have felt that this detracted from enhancing the relationship between husband and wife, and that it would have a negative effect on the entire family.

Chinese Buddhism

Seng Chao on Time and Change

One of Seng Chao's most interesting ideas concerns time and change. He discussed this idea in a chapter of his *Chao Lun,* entitled "On Time." (Selections from this work are included at the end of the chapter.) In it he discusses the problem of change with respect to aging. There is a monk, a Brahmacarin, who returns to his home when he is an old man. Despite the neighbors' declarations upon seeing a person from the past, he remarks, "I look like the man of the past, but I am not he." Seng Chao sought to demonstrate that each moment is new. The past moment is not the same moment in the present. The Brahmacarin of the past is not the Brahmacarin of the present.

However, even though this principle of flux points to the reality of change, it also points to the truth of immutability. That is, the past moment is permanent in the past, and each moment remains in its own moment. Therefore, each moment possesses its own permanence and stability. Furthermore, even though the past moment is past, the past continues to have an effect on the present and future, and this effect is possible only because the past remains permanent.

Ch'an Buddhism

Hui-neng is one of the greatest teachers in the Ch'an school. His interpretation of Ch'an closely approximates the Madhyamika teachings and reveals a keen personal sense of the meaning of *sunya,* or emptiness. For this is the goal of Ch'an meditation: to concentrate to such an extent that one is able to view things in their original being as *sunya* and *tathata,* emptiness and suchness. (Hui-neng's teachings have profoundly influenced Eisai and Dogen in Japan.)

Recall his famous verse that earned for him the title of Sixth Patriarch:

The Bodhi is not like a tree,
The clear mirror is nowhere standing.
Fundamentally not one thing exists;
Where, then, is a grain of dust to cling?

The meaning behind this verse is essentially that nothing is permanent. All is void, including the Bodhi tree and the mirror, the knower, and the self. This void is certainly germane in our discussion of death.

The notion of void, emptiness, or *sunya,* is illustrated in both China and Japan through a series of famous drawings accompanied by verses, known as the "Ox-Herding" pictures. The pictures consist of scenes of an ox-herder and his ox framed within circles called *enso.* The circles are highly symbolic of both completion and void. Throughout all of this, the ox represents the individual's Buddha-nature. In the *Six Oxherding Pictures* by Jitoku, the first three circles show the herdsman's efforts to seek, catch, and tame his ox. In the fourth circle, tamer and ox rest together by a stream.[31]

The fifth circle is especially important because it is empty. In a sense, this is a surrender to a kind of death whereby there is no longer the seeker and his nature. This death leads to *sunyata,* emptiness. Here, there is total liberation from self, which means that there is freedom from the search and from the discrimination between the self and the ox that has been the dominant attitude throughout the search. The experience of this freedom is known in Zen as the Great Death—the shattering of discriminatory consciousness that considers all things within the parameters of the distinction between "I" and "not-I."[32]

This Great Death does not result in oblivion, however. The sixth and final *enso* reveals the individual herdsman, this time playing and facing the Buddha. In a sense, nothing has changed because everything is what it was. However, in the most radical way the herdsman's understanding of all things has changed because he has lived the Great Death and now knows his Buddha-nature.

Social Immortality

In many respects the real merit in immortality for the Chinese is social, not individual, for great value is placed on immortality in the sense of being remembered for one's virtuous character, one's impressive deeds, and one's teachings.

1. Awakening of Faith*

An instruction is given for the first time by a good teacher, and faith
    is awakened;
A thought of faith once awakened is the basis of the way forever.
A spot of white is therefore observed on the ox head.

---

*These renditions of Jitoku's *Six Oxherding Pictures* were drawn by Sherry Monarko. The titles above each picture and the remarks below them are taken from the original work by Jitoku Eki (*The Six Oxherding Pictures*), cited in Abbot Zenkei Shibayama, *A Flower Does Not Talk: Zen Essays*, trans. Sumiko Kudo (Rutland, VT: Charles E. Tuttle Company, 1970), 169–99.

2. First Entering

Faith, already awakened, is refined at every moment.
Suddenly come to an insight, joy springs up in the mind.
First it starts from the top; therefore the head is now completely white.

3. Not Thoroughly Genuine Yet

An insight has already been attained and is gradually refined.
The wisdom is bright and clear, but is not still quite genuine yet.
Half of the body is now white.

4. True Mind

Delusions no longer prevail; just one true mind.
Pure, immaculate, serene; the whole body is thoroughly white.

5. Both Forgotten

Both the man and the Dharma are forgotten and the boy and
   the ox are asleep.
Forever transcending all the forms, there is only the great Void.
This is called the Great Emancipation, and the Life of the
   Buddhas and Patriarchs.

6. Playing

The source of life is extinguished, and from the death he revives;
Assuming any shape according to the conditions and playing around in
    whatever places he finds himself in.
His personality has been changed, but what he does is not different.

Let us explain. Not all Confucians believe in the soul's immortality;
neither is the idea of total extinction appealing. One's life extends beyond
one's body. For example, children of the deceased possess a part of the
deceased's life. For the Chinese, there is no individual per se apart from the
relations that define that individual: father to son, husband to wife, son to
father, employer to employee, teacher to student, and so on. There is, in this
way, an extension of life beyond the individual. If life is viewed in this interconnected way, then life continues beyond death in the same fashion. Immortality reaches into the spheres of our family, workplace, ideas, and friends.

Japanese Philosophies

The cherry blossom, or *sakura,* blooms for less than one week out of the year.
Of all the flowers, the Japanese can truly relate to the *sakura* for its beauty,
all the more intensified by the fact that it is so transient. It dies away just
after reaching its peak of color and life. Its delicate blossoms are easily scattered by the wind or rain. The *sakura* reveals at least two immeasurable human
truths for the Japanese: First, life is like the *sakura,* in that what is of beauty
does not last; second, the beauty of reality lies precisely in its impermanence.
The *sakura* inspires the Japanese attitude of *mono no aware,* the "sadness of
things," in which existence bears a "sad beauty." This is the way of being.

Basic Japanese Themes Concerning Death

Transience

The Japanese have long been acutely aware of the transitoriness of all things. Reality is both intrinsically fleeting and brimming with suffering. Yet suffering is momentary. Ivan Morris tells us of a poem based on the *Nirvana Sutra* and used by children to aid in memorizing the Japanese alphabet of forty-seven phonetic syllables:

> Brightly colored though the blossoms be,
> All are doomed to scatter.
> So, in this world of ours,
> Who will last forever?
> Today, having crossed the mountain recesses of Samskrita,
> I shall be free of fleeting dreams,
> Nor shall I be fuddled [by the pleasures of this world].[33]

In what is perhaps the world's first psychological novel, Murasaki's *The Tale of Genji,* many of the characters grow weary of life's impermanence. In the final book of this work, called "The Floating Bridge of Dreams," we see a strong Buddhist flavor. Life is likened to a bridge that is a mirage, linking us from one state of being to the next. This reminds us of the popular image among the Japanese of the "floating world."[34]

The revered Zen monk Ikkyu reminded us of this floating, transient world when he described himself as the "son of an errant cloud." It is said that, on New Year's Day, he once paraded through the streets carrying a skull and his poem called "Skeleton," which teaches an "indifference toward life and death" and openly disputes the belief in an afterlife.[35]

Continuity Through Ancestors

Despite the truth of life's transience, a continuity is still established through ancestral ties. Many Japanese believe in the persistence of life's stream through generations, linking past and future. It is thought that the spirit of a deceased relative lingers around his or her earthly abode for a period of thirty-three years. The spirit returns to the family once a year during the festival of O-Bon and certifies the intimate link between the living and the dead.

Dying Properly

Death is viewed as an essential part of existence. In fact, the most crucial concern for many Japanese is not the fact of death, but how to approach death with dignity and equanimity. It is not unusual for elderly Japanese to go to Buddhist temples in order to pray for a quick and painless death.

In his 1952 classic *Ikiru (To Live),* the great filmmaker Akira Kurosawa revealed the story of a small-time bureaucrat who confronts the truth of his impending death from cancer. He can come to terms with this truth only by facing his absolute solitariness. He then devotes himself totally to building parks for children, a task that is not easy because he must overcome official obstacles. In this way he not only faces death with equanimity, but immortalizes himself through his actions while alive.

All this requires mental preparation, termed *shugyo,* an idea expressed in many forms, from religion to art. An extreme example is ritual suicide or *seppuku,* which eventually became antiquated with the end of feudalism and the rise of modernism. The most recently publicized example of *seppuku* was the suicide in 1970 of the accomplished literary figure Mishima Yukio. His ritual suicide occurred after a failed attempt to take over army headquarters with his own right-wing band called the Shield Society.

After the twelfth century, *seppuku* came to be ritualized in precise fashion. There was often an appropriate place to perform *seppuku,* such as a Buddhist temple or garden, both places of purity. (Shinto beliefs contend that death and anything associated with death is a form of defilement. Therefore, Shinto shrines were out of bounds because the death would desecrate the shrine's purity.) There were special types of clothing, usually white, for the occasion. One of the most important aspects of *seppuku* was appointing a trusted friend or guardian to act as a "second" or assistant. This trusted person would behead the individual immediately after the disembowelment.[36]

The main intent behind *seppuku* was to regain honor after defeat or shame, often in the context of battle, or a failed mission, or if held captive by an enemy. Such honor, or "face-saving," could be restored by a controlled act of effecting one's own death. Needless to say, self-disembowelment demands the utmost self-control. Suicide committed in composure was viewed with great respect.

Of course, this attitude is not shared by all. American servicemen often called the Japanese suicide planes near the end of World War II *baku* planes, or "idiot" planes; the Japanese called them *kamikaze,* which means "divine wind." Divine Wind was the name of the first flight that embarked upon its suicidal mission; the name also refers to the times when foreigners attempted to invade Japan's shores. On both occasions the foreign fleets were destroyed by violent storms at sea. The Japanese believed they received divine protection, and hence the term.

Though perhaps it is difficult for us to comprehend, we must remember that from early on, the samurai was accustomed to this consciousness of death, and this consciousness came to reflect a general Japanese attitude toward death and self-control.

Bushido

The most conspicuous example of this resoluteness toward death and the importance attached to dying properly lies in the code of *Bushido,* or Way of the Warrior, which requires that the samurai always be ready to die. It also commands strict loyalty to one's *daimyo,* or feudal lord. In an early work called *Manyoshu* we read:

> He who dies for the sake of his Lord does not die in vain, whether
> he goes to the sea and his corpse is left in a watery grave, or whether

he goes to the mountain and the only shroud for his lifeless body is
the mountain grass.[37]

Bushido demands that death be approached with resoluteness and acceptance. Before putting on a helmet, the samurai often girded themselves
with a headband, or *hachimaki,* which signified individual resolve and determination. It meant not only facing the enemy, but facing death with courage.
This same practice continued into World War II, when kamikaze pilots also
wore *hachimaki* to show that they were prepared to meet death. To further
demonstrate their resolve, kamikaze pilots wrote farewell letters and poems
to their family, especially to their parents. There is a long tradition behind
this final testament.

This resoluteness toward death demanded the utmost training in self-
discipline, both physically and mentally. And this was a vital reason why Zen
was appealing to samurai. Zen training demands the same uncompromising
self-restraint.

This spirit of *Bushido* can be found in a work called the *Hagakure,* which
provides some theoretical basis for the Way of the Warrior. It states:

> The Way of the Samurai is found in death. When it comes to either/or,
> there is only the quick choice of death. It is not particularly difficult.
> Be determined and advance. . . .
>   We all want to live. And in large part we make our logic according
> to what we like. . . . To die without gaining one's aim *is* a dog's death
> and fanaticism. But there is no shame in this. This is the substance
> of the Way of the Samurai. If by setting one's heart right every morn-
> ing and evening, one is able to live as though his body were already
> dead, he gains freedom in the Way. His whole life will be without
> blame, and he will succeed in his calling.[38]

In this way, the samurai seeks a state of mind that transcends any distinction
between life and death. Speculations concerning the afterlife were generally
scorned by samurai. If immortality was to be attained at all, it came about
through the manner in which one dies.[39]

Japanese Buddhism and Death

Jodo: Tariki

Pure Land Buddhism, or the Jodo school, gained popularity in Japan with
its teaching that, after death, one enters the "Pure Land" paradise where all
other *bodhisattvas* live. Bear in mind, however, that the ultimate goal is not
merely to attain this paradise. Once one enters the "Pure Land," the realm
where all other *bodhisattvas* are, one then must work for the liberation of all
of humanity. It is the saving power of Amida Buddha that enables this. It
is thereby an other-directed power, or *tariki,* coming from the grace of Amida.
The special school of Jodo that emphasizes this *tariki* power of Amida is the
Shinran.

Zen Buddhism

Both the monk and the warrior were attracted to the teachings of Zen because of its strict self-discipline. Zen training was particularly appealing for the samurai due to its emphasis on preparedness for death in order to overcome death. The samurai needed to "practice dying" in full awareness and preparation for impending death. A great thinker in this regard was Suzuki Shosan (1579–1655), who trained as a samurai and later practiced Zen. The secret in the practice of dying is to realize that death is *sunya,* just as the self is *sunya.* Let us look at some of the Zen practices that help to inculcate this realization.

The practice of *zazen* requires that each moment be accepted in its suchness. Thoughts are not clung to, but are simply allowed to come and go. The "stream of life and death" is likened to the stream of thoughts during *zazen,* without having to impose or force thoughts.

Even the regulated breathing techniques during *zazen* reflect this. After practice, they become second-nature for the adept. At the same time, the practitioner is able to allow breathing to uninterruptedly take its course. All existence is this rhythm of breath.

In the same way, the *koan* is designed to stir up an exhaustive intellectual effort to find an "answer." In this pursuit of an answer, the student seeks stability. In enervating one's intellect, however, one eventually realizes that there is no "answer," and that stability as such does not exist. The *koan* reveals the futility of intellect. In this way, genuine enlightenment comes about, called *satori.*

In a sense, death is the ultimate *koan.* Before *satori,* we wonder how we would deal with this "enemy." And realization occurs when we realize that death is not the enemy; craving is the enemy. Even more radically, there is no enemy.

Dogen: Life Is Death Is Sunya

Dogen was two years old when his father died, and seven when his mother died. It is said that he was struck by life's impermanence when he viewed the smoke rising from the incense burning during his mother's funeral.[40] The awareness of life's impermanence stayed with him all through his life. For Dogen, how we view death affects how we view existence.

His essay in the *Shobogenzo,* called "Shoji" ("Birth and Death"), is a remarkably concise statement of his position on death. (It is included at the end of this chapter.) He contended that our ordinary attitude toward life and death is wrong:

It is a mistake to assume that one moves from birth to death.[41]

Moving from birth to death is an attitude that assumes that birth is separated from death. For Dogen, we need to realize that life and death occur together at the same time. In other words, Dogen tells us that we are always dying. Death exists at each moment, just as life also fills each moment. A genuine awareness of life and death as occurring always and everywhere enables one to transcend the distinction between the two. It also points to the essential *sunyata,* or emptiness, of being.

Genuine awakening comes about when life and death are no longer discriminated; this entails a nondualist perspective. As the Japanese philosopher Abe Masao remarked:

> Accordingly, from life's point of view each thing—death included—is life's total presencing; while from death's point of view each thing—life included—is death's total presencing.[42]

When we realize this equality of life and death, we realize that neither in itself exists. This is the realization of *sunyata,* or emptiness.

This leads us to an important idea in Dogen. Nirvana, the experience of awakening, is not a state reached beyond the life-death stream, but is attained ultimately within it:

> Simply understanding that birth and death is itself nirvana, there is nothing to reject as birth and death, nothing to seek as nirvana. Only then will one have some measure of detachment from birth and death.[43]

Dogen basically tells us that either rejecting this life-death stream or attaching oneself to it results in continued ignorance and enslavement to the stream. Awakening can occur only when one is totally free of attachment to this stream, and this includes attachment to the desire to be detached.

Awakening exists precisely in the practice of *zazen.* The reality of our original Buddha-nature needs to be awakened, and this realization comes about through what he called the "casting off of body-mind." Practice is necessary. This is the critical discovery of the founder of Soto Zen, who attributed to *zazen* a vital role in liberation from the life-death stream.[44]

Abe Masao described Dogen's teachings in terms of an important Buddhist distinction between existence as "something that undergoes birth-and-death" and as "something that must die."[45] This latter viewpoint—"something that must die"—is inaccurate for a number of reasons. First, it assumes a strictly linear conception of time and history. Such a linear representation is foreign to Buddhism, and especially foreign to the Japanese. Next, it views life and death as a static progression, which takes us to the third weakness: It assumes a fundamental difference between life and death. As we have said, the Japanese tend to view life and death as one inseparable flowing stream.

The description of existence as "something which undergoes birth-and-death" comes closer to the Buddhist teaching for the Japanese. In this view, life and death are not mutually exclusive, but rather mutually defining.

This brings us to a profound idea: The ultimate aim in Buddhism is not physical immortality. The aim is to free oneself from *shoji,* birth and death. And this occurs *through* birth and death, not apart from it:

> Its [Buddhism's] aim is not immortality and eternal life through a resurrection that conquers death, but the unborn and undying (*fusho-*

fumetsu) state of nirvana realized directly in and through birth-and-death by liberation from birth-and-death itself.[46]

Let us look at some differences between the positions of Dogen and the Shinran school. For Dogen, the Buddha-nature is found in all being. In contrast, according to Shinran our human natures are essentially corrupt as we suffer the sins of karma. Human existence suffers from the peculiar inheritance of sin. For Shinran, there is thus a unique problem associated with being human, as distinct from nonhumans.

Because of their differences, their ways to liberation are also unlike. For Dogen, liberation occurs through genuine self-awakening to one's true nature and to the nature of all things. This is full realization of true *Dharma*. This is what he meant by the casting off of body-mind. In doing so, the Self is awakened, and one is free from birth-and-death through embracing a perspective that transcends distinctions among beings.[47]

For Shinran, because of our naturally corrupt natures we cannot embrace the dimension of all beings; the ego is deeply rooted in the human soil. Liberation for humans is not possible without the external guidance and support of Amida Buddha, in response to our prayers and faith. Amida's grace acts upon those who realize fully both the nature of existence and the corrupt nature of the human.

Some Japanese Customs Concerning Death

The notion of an eternal soul, or *tama,* originated around the fourth century. *Tama* has some association with "breath" or "wind" and refers to a vital force or soul. However, the Japanese generally seem to be more interested in this life than in some afterlife. For example, an early practice was *tamayobi,* literally meaning "calling the soul." This was calling the soul back into this life, so that death would not result, and was performed by calling the person's name.

The Buddha supposedly died with his head facing north. It is still customary to place corpses in this same direction. (This is why it is considered bad luck to sleep with one's head to the north.) The body is also dressed in clothes and sandals appropriate for its "journey." Even money is sometimes included to pay to cross the river Sanzu. Cremation still occurs, which suggests that the journey will continue after death, not by the body but by the soul. There is often a family vigil that continues into the night and the following day. During this vigil a Buddhist priest chants a sutra to ease the soul's journey.[48]

The soul journeys into the paradise of "Pure Land," a place of purity. On the other hand, survivors remain in defilement until they are purified by participating in the mourning ritual, which then qualifies mourners to enter through the holy gate (*tori*) of the Shinto shrine.[49] This view of the freshly dead and the belief concerning defilement and purification has stayed with the Japanese since ancient times.

Through the rituals that purify the dead, the soul is able to join the ranks of other ancestor-spirits. Purification rituals therefore enable the connection between the living and the dead to be sustained.

The observation or remembrance of the day of death is called *meinichi*. The beliefs surrounding this commemoration are derived from Buddhism and the Chinese notion of ancestor veneration. It is thought that the spirit of the deceased continues to live and will be appeased by these memorials. The link between the living and the dead is maintained through this ritual as well.

The ideograph *meinichi* consists of two characters, denoting "life" and "day." In this regard, the commemoration of one's death is not merely a "deathday," but also a "lifeday," an occasion for all relatives to come together and to participate. Therefore, this observance celebrates the solidarity of the survivors and reaffirms family unity. Because of this, an immortality is sustained; the memory of the deceased serves to validate the continued existence of the family as a cohesive unit.

Study Questions

India

1. Describe teachings concerning death found in the *Katha Upanishad*.
2. Describe the relevance of *tat tvam asi* with respect to the meaning of death, as found in the *Chandogya Upanishad*.
3. Discuss the meaning of transmigration in Hindu philosophy in the context of both *samsara* and karma.
4. Discuss Krishna's message related to the meaning of death in the *Bhagavad Gita*. In what way does it attempt to address Arjuna's personal conflict?
5. Discuss the essential aspects in Vedanta's teachings concerning death and survival: *atman* and *jiva*, gross body and subtle body, and the distinction between true self and false self.
6. Discuss the three signs of existence, or three marks, in Buddhism, and explain how these have a bearing on the Buddhist teachings concerning death and survival?
7. What role does karma play in the Buddhist teachings concerning death and survival?
8. Discuss the significance of both *samsara* and *pratityasamutpada* in Buddhism. How do they reinforce each other with respect to teachings concerning death and survival?
9. What is the meaning of nirvana in Buddhism?
10. Buddhists believe in rebirth, but they do not believe in an independent entity called *atman*. Explain the Buddhist notion of rebirth in this regard. How does rebirth occur? When? Where?
11. In what way did Nagarjuna's teaching of *sunya* influence his view of death?

China

12. What are some of the views of the Chinese toward death and survival?
13. Explain how some ideas in the *Tao Te Ching* relate to death. How were these ideas expressed by Chuang Tzu?

14. Describe the religious Taoist quest for longevity.
15. What was Confucius's attitude toward issues surrounding death and survival, and what was his most important concern?
16. Describe Wang Ch'ung's opposition to prevailing superstitions surrounding death. What were his views of death and chance?
17. Describe Mo Tzu's critique of elaborate funerals in light of his utilitarianism.
18. Discuss Seng Chao's views of time and change. How do these relate to Chinese Buddhists' views of death? Illustrate with ideas from the selection.
19. Explain views of death in Ch'an Buddhism with reference to both Hui-neng and the Great Death.
20. What is the meaning of social immortality in Chinese teachings?

Japan

21. Examine the basic themes in Japanese thought that have a direct bearing on their views toward death.
22. Describe how the notion of transience occupies an important position in Japanese thought.
23. Discuss the significance of dying properly in Japanese thought and culture.
24. Discuss how the code of Bushido represents some Japanese attitudes toward death. Give examples. What is the importance of the text *Hagakure*?
25. What are the Jodo teachings concerning the after-death state, or the "Pure Land"?
26. How do the Zen practices of *zazen* and the *koan* relate to Zen attitudes toward life and death?
27. According to Dogen, what is the relationship between life-and-death and *sunya*? Illustrate with his selection, "*Shoji*."
28. In his commentary on Dogen's philosophy, what did Abe Masao mean by the distinction between "something that must die" and "something that undergoes birth-and-death"?
29. Explain some differences between Dogen and Shinran.
30. Describe some Japanese customs surrounding death.

Notes

1. From the *Mahabharata,* in Brian Brown, ed., *The Wisdom of the Hindus: Philosophies and Wisdom from Their Ancient and Modern Literature* (Garden City, N.J. and New York: Garden City Publishing Co., 1938), 35–42.
2. *Chandogya Upanishad* VI.viii.6–7, in R. C. Zaehner, trans., *Hindu Scriptures* (London: Everyman's Library, J. M. Dent & Sons Ltd., 1966), 109.
3. *Brihadaranyaka Upanishad* IV.4.3, in Robert Ernest Hume, trans., *The Thirteen Principal Upanishads,* 2nd rev. ed. (London: Oxford University Press, 1971), 140.
4. Transmigration was not universally accepted, however. A small band of materialists lead by Ajita Kesakambalin refuted the idea. This led a heterodox group with a larger following, called the Carvakan school (also known as Lokayata), to reject the idea

of survival. The Materialist school did not survive for long in India; by medieval times it had essentially dissipated and its influence became minimal.

5. This led the Indian scholar A. L. Basham to propose that the idea of transmigration came about as a secret teaching among some of the sages, who only later made this teaching more public. Basham, in opposition to other scholars, feels that the transmigration theory actually originated in secret among elite brahmans. See A. L. Basham, *The Origins and Development of Classical Hinduism,* annotated by K. Zysk, ed. Kenneth G. Zysk (Boston: Beacon Press, 1989), 43–45. See also the excellent discussion in Wendy D. O'Flaherty, ed., *Karma and Rebirth in Classical Indian Traditions* (Berkeley: University of California Press, 1980). She describes karma more in terms of sacrificial actions.

6. *Brihadaranyaka Upanishad* IV.4.5, in Hume, 140.

7. S. Radhakrishnan, trans., *The Bhagavadgītā* (London: George Allen & Unwin Ltd., 1971), 127–28.

8. Radhakrishnan, *The Bhagavadgītā* II. 12–3, 103–04.

9. Radhakrishnan, *The Bhagavadgītā* II. 27–28, 110–11.

10. The kinds of bodies are described in an interesting analysis by John Hick. Much of the following is adapted from Hick's discussion in *Death and Eternal Life* (San Francisco: Harper & Row, 1980), 311–20.

11. Hick, 315–16.

12. According to another account, while the Buddha was dying from eating bad food, he conveyed to his beloved disciple Ananda the wish that subsequent pilgrims should visit four places: where he was born, where he attained awakening, where he preached his first sermon, and where he died. But more importantly, he gave Ananda this instruction: "Do not honor my remains." See Kenneth Paul Kramer, *The Sacred Art of Dying: How World Religions Understand Death* (New York: Paulist Press, 1988), 49.

13. C. A. F. Rhys Davies, trans., *Psalms of the Early Buddhists* (London: Luzac, 1964), 213–23; taken from Dhammapala's commentary on the Therigatha.

14. It is said that Ananda reported the Buddha to be dead, but he was corrected by Anuruddha because the Buddha was in this state of absolute peacefulness, which appears to be a death state. See David J. Kalupahana, *Buddhist Philosophy: A Historical Analysis,* (Honolulu: University of Hawaii Press, 1976), 71.

15. Kalupahana, *Buddhist Philosophy,* 74.

16. Kenneth Paul Kramer, *The Sacred Art of Dying: How World Religions Understand Death* (New York: Paulist Press, 1988), 51.

17. See Hick, 346.

18. Walter Liebenthal, "The Immortality of the Soul in Chinese Thought," *Monumenta Nipponica* 8, 1952, 329.

19. Cited in Liebenthal, 333. Chinese characters for the Chinese terms, found in the original citation, are not included here.

20. *Tao Te Ching* 42, in Lin Yutang, trans., *The Wisdom of Laotse* (New York: Modern Library, Random House, Inc., 1948), 214.

21. *Tao Te Ching,* 50, in Lin Yutang, 233.

22. Herbert A. Giles, trans., *Chuang Tzu: Mystic, Moralist, and Social Reformer,* 2nd ed., rev. (London: Bernard Quaritch, Limited, 1926), 23.

23. Arthur Waley, *Three Ways of Thought in Ancient China* (London: George Allen & Unwin Ltd., 1939), 21–22.

24. Cited in Paul U. Unschuld, *Medicine in China: A History of Ideas* (Berkeley: University of California Press, 1985), 109.

25. It was also believed that the essence of the individual consisted in water. In this regard, semen production was incorporated in sexual therapeutic techniques. See Unschuld, 111.

26. *Analects* XI.11, in James Legge, trans., *Confucius: Confucian Analects, The Great Learning, and The Doctrine of the Mean,* (New York: Dover, 1971), 240–241.

27. Cited in Kramer, 89.

28. Cited in Fung Yu-Lan, *A History of Chinese Philosophy* Vol. 2, trans. Derk Bodde (Princeton, N.J.: Princeton University Press, 1953), 157.

29. In Fung, *History of Chinese Philosophy*, Vol. 2, 157–158.
30. Alfred Forke, trans., *Lun-Hêng: Philosophical Essays of Wang Ch'ung, Part 1*, 2nd ed., (New York: Paragon Book Gallery, 1962), 151.
31. There are a number of different versions of the ox-herding pictures. Often, they are depicted in ten scenes. Jitoku Eki's twelfth-century representation is most succinct. His pictures are described in Abbot Zenkei Shibayama, *A Flower Does Not Talk: Zen Essays*, trans. Sumiko Kudo (Rutland, Vt.: Charles E. Tuttle Company, 1970), 152–203.
32. Kramer, 63.
33. Quoted in Ivan Morris, *The World of the Shining Prince: Court Life in Ancient Japan* (Middlesex, England: Peregrine Books, 1985), 122–23.
34. Morris, *World of the Shining Prince*, 127; see also note 39.
35. Heinrich Dumoulin, S. J., *A History of Zen Buddhism*, trans. Paul Peachey (Boston: Beacon Press, 1969), 185.
36. Disembowelment occurred when the individual thrust his short sword into his abdomen, going from right to left through what was considered the vital center of the body, thereby achieving ultimate victory over the body. Yet, through all of this, the most important feature in *seppuku* was not the technique, but the mental poise or composure assumed during the entire ritual. In this way, death was transcended.
37. Cited in Robert J. Lifton, *The Broken Connection: On Death and the Continuity of Life*, 1979 (New York: Basic Books, 1983), 396.
38. Yamamoto Tsunetomo, *Hagakure: The Book of the Samurai*, trans. William Scott Wilson (Tokyo: Kodansha International Ltd., 1979), 17–18.
39. This Bushido spirit is exhibited in other facets of life. To some degree it survives in the business world of today's Japan. Though things appear to be slightly changing, companies traditionally offer lifetime employment to workers, enabling lifelong stability for individuals and families in exchange for loyalty and total dedication to one's work. There is an intense work ethic in Japan, and private interests are subordinate to the well-being of the company, which represents a kind of family.
40. Abe Masao, *A Study of Dogen: His Philosophy and Religion*, ed. Steven Heine (Albany: State University of New York Press, 1992), 111.
41. Thomas Cleary, trans., *Shōbōgenzō: Zen Essays by Dōgen* (Honolulu: University of Hawaii Press, 1986), 122.
42. Abe, 114.
43. Cleary, 122.
44. Abe, 157.
45. Abe, 145.
46. Abe, 145.
47. See the discussion in Abe, 147–54.
48. See Robert J. Lifton, *The Broken Connection: On Death and the Continuity of Life* (New York: Basic Books, 1983), 95–96.
49. The indigenous belief system in Japan is Shinto, and it has always considered death to be a defilement. Shinto rituals are often performed to purify one's contact with death. Later, due to Buddhist influences combined with the Shinto purification concerns, cremation became more widespread.

From the *Katha Upanishad*

First [Section]

. . . 20. Nachiketas[1] said: "There is that doubt, when a man is dead,—some saying, he is; others, he is not. This I should like to know, taught by thee; this is the third of my boons."

21. Death said: "On this point even the gods have doubted formerly; it is not easy to understand. That subject is subtle. Choose another boon, O Nachiketas, do not press me, and let me off that boon."

22. Nachiketas said: "On this point even the gods have doubted indeed, and thou, Death, has declared it to be not easy to understand, and another teacher like thee is not to be found:—surely no other boon is like unto this."

23. Death said: "Choose sons and grandsons who shall live a hundred years, herds of cattle, elephants, gold, and horses. Choose the wide abode of the earth, and live thyself as many harvests as thou desirest."

24. "If you can think of any boon equal to that, choose wealth, and long life. Be (king), Nachiketas, on the wide earth. I make thee the enjoyer of all desires."

25. "Whatever desires are difficult to attain among mortals, ask for them according to thy wish;—these fair maidens with their chariots and musical instruments,—such are indeed not to be obtained by men,—be waited on by them whom I give to thee, but do not ask me about dying."

26. Nachiketas said: "These things last till tomorrow, O Death, for they wear out this vigour of all the senses. Even the whole of life is short. Keep thou thy horses, keep dance and song for thyself."

27. "No man can be made happy by wealth. Shall we possess wealth, when we see thee? Shall we live, as long as thou rulest? Only that boon (which I have chosen) is to be chosen by me."

28. "What mortal, slowly decaying here below, and knowing, after having approached them, the freedom from decay enjoyed by the immortals, would delight in a long life, after he has pondered on the pleasures which arise from beauty and love?"

29. "No, that on which there is this doubt, O Death, tell us what there is in that great Hereafter. Nachiketas does not choose another boon but that which enters into the hidden world."

Reprinted from F. Max Müller, trans., *The Upanishads,* Pt. II, New York: Dover, 1962, pp. 5–14.

Second [Section]

1. Death said: "The good is one thing, the pleasant another; these two, having different objects, chain a man. It is well with him who clings to the good; he who chooses the pleasant, misses his end."

2. "The good and the pleasant approach man: the wise goes round about them and distinguishes them. Yea, the wise prefers the good to the pleasant, but the fool chooses the pleasant through greed and avarice."

3. "Thou, O Nachiketas, after pondering all pleasures that are or seem delightful, hast dismissed them all. Thou hast not gone into the road that leadeth to wealth, in which many men perish."

4. "Wide apart and leading to differing points are these two, ignorance, and what is known as wisdom. I believe Nachiketas to be one who desires knowledge, for even many pleasures did not tear thee away."

5. "Fools dwelling in darkness, wise in their own conceit, and puffed up with vain knowledge, go round and round, staggering to and fro, like blind men led by the blind."

6. "The Hereafter never rises before the eyes of the careless child, deluded by the delusion of wealth. 'This is the world,' he thinks, 'there is no other';—thus he falls again and again under my sway."

7. "He (the Self) of whom many are not even able to hear, whom many, even when they hear of him, do not comprehend; wonderful is a man, when found, who is able to teach him (the Self); wonderful is he who comprehends him, when taught by an able teacher."

8. "That (Self), when taught by an inferior man, is not easy to be known, even though often thought upon; unless it be taught by another, there is no way to it, for it is inconceivably smaller than what is small."

9. "That doctrine is not to be obtained by argument, but when it is declared by another, then, O dearest, it is easy to understand. Thou has obtained it now; thou art truly a man of true resolve. May we have always an inquirer like thee!"

10. Nachiketas said: "I know that what is called a treasure is transient, for that eternal is not obtained by things which are not eternal. Hence the Nachiketa fire(-sacrifice) has been laid by me (first); then, by means of transient things, I have obtained what is not transient (the teaching of Yama)."

11. Yama said: "Though thou hadst seen the fulfillment of all desires, the foundation of the world, the endless rewards of good deeds, the shore where there is no fear, that which is magnified by praise, the wide abode, the rest, yet being wise thou hast with firm resolve dismissed it all."

12. "The wise who, by means of meditation on his Self, recognises the Ancient, who is difficult to be seen, who has entered into the dark, who is hidden in the cave, who dwells in the abyss, as God, he indeed leaves joy and sorrow far behind."

13. "A mortal who has heard this and embraced it, who has separated from it all qualities, and has thus reached the subtle Being, rejoices, because he has obtained what is a cause for rejoicing. The house (of Brahman) is open, I believe, O Nachiketas."

14. Nachiketas said: "That which thou seest as neither this nor that, as neither effect nor cause, as neither past nor future, tell me that."

15. Yama said: "That word (or place) which all the Vedas record, which all penances proclaim, which men desire when they live as religious students, that word I tell thee briefly, it is Om."

16. "That (imperishable) syllable means Brahman, that syllable means the highest (Brahman); he who knows that syllable, whatever he desires, is his."

17. "This is the best support, this is the highest support; he who knows that support is magnified in the world of Brahmâ."

18. "The knowing (Self) is not born, it dies not; it sprang from nothing, nothing sprang from it. The ancient is unborn, eternal, everlasting; he is not killed, though the body is killed."

19. "If the killer thinks that he kills, if the killed thinks that he is killed, they do not understand; for this one does not kill, nor is that one killed."

20. "The Self, smaller than small, greater than great, is hidden in the heart of that creature. A man who is free from desires and free from grief, sees the majesty of the Self by the grace of the Creator."

21. "Though sitting still, he walks far; though lying down, he goes everywhere. Who, save myself, is able to know that God who rejoices and rejoices not?"

22. "The wise who knows the Self as bodiless within the bodies, as unchanging among changing things, as great and omnipresent, does never grieve."

23. "That Self cannot be gained by the Veda, nor by understanding, nor by much learning. He whom the Self chooses, by him the Self can be gained. The Self chooses him (his body) as his own."

24. "But he who has not first turned away from his wickedness, who is not tranquil, and subdued, or whose mind is not at rest, he can never obtain the Self (even) by knowledge."

25. "Who then knows where He is, He to whom the Brahmans and Kshatriyas are (as it were) but food, and death itself a condiment?"

Third [Section]

1. "There are the two, drinking their reward in the world of their own works, entered into the cave (of the heart), dwelling on the highest summit (the ether in the heart). Those who know Brahman call them shade and light; likewise, those householders who perform the Trinâkiketa sacrifice."

2. "May we be able to master that Nachiketa rite which is a bridge for sacrificers; also that which is the highest, imperishable Brahman for those who wish to cross over to the fearless shore."

3. "Know the Self to be sitting in the chariot, the body to be the chariot, the intellect (buddhi) the charioteer, and the mind the reins."

4. "The senses they call the horses, the objects of the senses their roads. When he (the Highest Self) is in union with the body, the senses, and the mind, then wise people call him the Enjoyer."

5. "He who has no understanding and whose mind (the reins) is never firmly held, his senses (horses) are unmanageable, like vicious horses of a charioteer."

6. "But he who has understanding and whose mind is always firmly held, his senses are under control, like good horses of a charioteer."

7. "He who has no understanding, who is unmindful and always impure, never reaches that place, but enters into the round of births."

8. "But he who has understanding, who is mindful and always pure, reaches indeed that place, from whence he is not born again."

9. "But he who has understanding for his charioteer, and who holds the reins of the mind, he reaches the end of his journey, and that is the highest place of Vishnu."

10. "Beyond the senses there are the objects, beyond the objects there is the mind, beyond the mind there is the intellect, the Great Self is beyond the intellect."

11. "Beyond the Great there is the Undeveloped, beyond the Undeveloped there is the Person (purusha). Beyond the Person there is nothing—this is the goal, the highest road."

12. "That Self is hidden in all beings and does not shine forth, but it is seen by subtle seers through their sharp and subtle intellect."

13. "A wise man should keep down speech and mind; he should keep them within the Self which is knowledge; he should keep knowledge within the Self which is the Great; and he should keep that (the Great) within the Self which is the Quiet."

14. "Rise, awake! having obtained your boons, understand them! The sharp edge of a razor is difficult to pass over; thus the wise say the path (to the Self) is hard."

15. "He who has perceived that which is without sound, without touch, without form, without decay, without taste, eternal, without smell, without beginning, without end, beyond the Great, and unchangeable, is freed from the jaws of death."

16. "A wise man who has repeated or heard the ancient story of Nachiketas told by Death, is magnified in the world of Brahman."

17. "And he who repeats this greatest mystery in an assembly of Brâhmans, or full of devotion at the time of the Srâddha sacrifice, obtains thereby infinite rewards."

---

[1]The spelling of Nachiketas has been changed here from the original "Nakiketas" to be consistent with the main text.

"Questions Which Tend Not to Edification," from the *Majjhima-Nikaya*

Thus have I heard.

On a certain occasion The Blessed One was dwelling at Sāvatthi in Jetavana monastery in Anāthapiṇḍika's Park. Then drew near Vaccha, the wandering ascetic, to where The Blessed One was; and having drawn near, he greeted The Blessed One; and having passed the compliments of friendship and civility, he sat down respectfully at one side. And seated respectfully at one side, Vaccha, the wandering ascetic, spoke to The Blessed One as follows:—

"How is it, Gotama? Does Gotama hold that the world is eternal, and that this view alone is true, and every other false?"

"Nay, Vaccha. I do not hold that the world is eternal, and that this view alone is true, and every other false."

"But how is it, Gotama? Does Gotama hold that the world is not eternal, and that this view alone is true, and every other false?"

"Nay, Vaccha. I do not hold that the world is not eternal, and that this view alone is true, and every other false."

"How is it, Gotama? Does Gotama hold that the world is finite, . . ."

"How is it, Gotama? Does Gotama hold that the soul and the body are identical, . . ."

"How is it Gotama? Does Gotama hold that the saint exists after death, . . ."

"How is it, Gotama? Does Gotama hold that the saint both exists and does not exist after death, and that this view alone is true and every other false?"

"Nay, Vaccha. I do not hold that the saint both exists and does not exist after death, and that this view alone is true, and every other false."

"But how is it, Gotama? Does Gotama hold that the saint neither exists nor does not exist after death, and that this view alone is true, and every other false?"

"Nay, Vaccha. I do not hold that the saint neither exists nor does not exist after death, and that this view alone is true, and every other false."

"How is it, Gotama, that when you are asked, 'Does the monk Gotama hold that the world is eternal, and that this view alone is true, and every other false?' you reply, 'Nay, Vaccha. I do not hold that the world is eternal, and that this view alone is true, and every other false'?

Reprinted from Henry Clarke Warren, trans., *Buddhism in Translations*, Cambridge, Mass.: Harvard University Press, 1953, 123–28.

"But how is it, Gotama, that when you are asked, 'Does the monk Gotama hold that the world is not eternal, and that this view alone is true, and every other false?' you reply, 'Nay, Vaccha. I do not hold that the world is not eternal, and that this view alone is true, and every other false'?

"How is it, Gotama, that when you are asked, 'Does Gotama hold that the world is finite, . . .'?

"How is it, Gotama, that when you are asked, 'Does Gotama hold that the soul and the body are identical, . . .'?

"How is it, Gotama, that when you are asked, 'Does Gotama hold that the saint exists after death, . . .'?

"How is it, Gotama, that when you are asked, 'Does the monk Gotama hold that the saint both exists and does not exist after death and that this view alone is true, and every other false?' you reply, 'Nay, Vaccha. I do not hold that the saint both exists and does not exist after death, and that this view alone is true, and every other false'?

"But how is it, Gotama, that when you are asked, 'Does the monk Gotama hold that the saint neither exists nor does not exist after death, and that this view alone is true, and every other false?' you reply, 'Nay, Vaccha. I do not hold that the saint neither exists nor does not exist after death, and that this view alone is true, and every other false'? What objection does Gotama perceive to these theories that he has not adopted any one of them?"

"Vaccha, the theory that the world is eternal, is a jungle, a wilderness, a puppet-show, a writhing, and a fetter, and is coupled with misery, ruin, despair, and agony, and does not tend to aversion, absence of passion, cessation, quiesence, knowledge, supreme wisdom, and Nirvana.

"Vaccha, the theory that the saint neither exists nor does not exist after death, is a jungle, a wilderness, a puppet-show, a writhing, and a fetter, and is coupled with misery, ruin, despair, and agony, and does not tend to aversion, absence of passion, cessation, quiesence, knowledge, supreme wisdom, and Nirvana.

"This is the objection I perceive to these theories, so that I have not adopted any one of them."

"But has Gotama any theory of his own?"

"The Tathāgata, O Vaccha, is free from all theories; but this, Vaccha, does The Tathāgata know,—the nature of form, and how form arises, and how form perishes; the nature of sensation, and how sensation arises, and how sensation perishes; the nature of perception, and how perception arises, and how perception perishes; the nature of the predispositions, and how the predispositions arise, and how the predispositions perish; the nature of consciousness, and how consciousness arises, and how consciousness perishes. Therefore say I that The Tathāgata has attained deliverance and is free from attachment, inasmuch as all imaginings, or agitations, or false notions concerning an Ego or anything pertaining to an Ego, have perished, have faded away, have ceased, have been given up and relinquished."

"But, Gotama, where is the priest reborn who has attained to this deliverance for his mind?"

"Vaccha, to say that he is reborn would not fit the case."

"Then, Gotama, he is not reborn."

"Vaccha, to say that he is not reborn would not fit the case."

"Then, Gotama, he is both reborn and is not reborn."

"Vaccha, to say that he is both reborn and not reborn would not fit the case."

"Then, Gotama, he is neither reborn nor not reborn."

"Vaccha, to say that he is neither reborn nor not reborn would not fit the case."

"When I say to you, 'But, Gotama, where is the priest reborn who has attained to this deliverance for his mind?' you reply, 'Vaccha, to say that he is reborn would not fit the case.' And when I say to you, 'Then, Gotama, he is not reborn,' you reply, 'Vaccha, to say that he is not reborn would not fit the case.' And when I say to you, 'Then, Gotama, he is both reborn and not reborn,' you reply, 'Vaccha, to say that he is both reborn and not reborn would not fit the case.' And when I say to you, 'Then, Gotama, he is neither reborn nor not reborn,' you reply, 'Vaccha, to say that he is neither reborn nor not reborn would not fit the case.' Gotama, I am at a loss what to think in this matter, and I have become greatly confused, and the faith in Gotama inspired by a former conversation has now disappeared."

"Enough, O Vaccha! Be not at a loss what to think in this matter, and be not greatly confused. Profound, O Vaccha, is this doctrine, recondite, and difficult of comprehension, good, excellent, and not to be reached by mere reasoning, subtle, and intelligible only to the wise; and it is a hard doctrine for you to learn, who belong to another sect, to another faith, to another persuasion, to another discipline, and sit at the feet of another teacher. Therefore, Vaccha, I will now question you, and do you make answer as may seem to you good. What think you, Vaccha? Suppose a fire were to burn in front of you, would you be aware that the fire was burning in front of you?"

"Gotama, if a fire were to burn in front of me, I should be aware that a fire was burning in front of me."

"But suppose, Vaccha, some one were to ask you, 'On what does this fire that is burning in front of you depend?' what would you answer, Vaccha?"

"Gotama, if some one were to ask me, 'On what does this fire that is burning in front of you depend?' I would answer, Gotama, 'It is on fuel of grass and wood that this fire that is burning in front of me depends.'"

"But, Vaccha, if the fire in front of you were to become extinct, would you be aware that the fire in front of you had become extinct?"

"Gotama, if the fire in front of me were to become extinct, I should be aware that the fire in front of me had become extinct."

"But, Vaccha, if some one were to ask you, 'In which direction has that fire gone,—east, or west, or north, or south?' what would you say, O Vaccha?"

"The question would not fit the case, Gotama. For the fire which depended on fuel of grass and wood, when that fuel has all gone, and it can get no other, being thus without nutriment, is said to be extinct."

"In exactly the same way, Vaccha, all form by which one could predicate the existence of the saint, all that form has been abandoned, uprooted, pulled out of the ground like a palmyra-tree, and become non-existent and not liable to spring up again in the future. The saint, O Vaccha, who has been released from what is styled form, is deep, immeasurable, unfathomable, like the mighty ocean. To say that he is reborn would not fit the case. To say that he is not reborn would not fit the case. To say that he is both reborn and not reborn would not fit the case. To say that he is neither reborn nor not reborn would not fit the case.

"All sensation . . .

"All perception . . .

"All the predispositions . . .

"All consciousness by which one could predicate the existence of the saint, all that consciousness has been abandoned, uprooted, pulled out of the ground like a palmyra-tree, and become non-existent and not liable to spring up again in the future. The saint, O Vaccha, who has been released from what is styled consciousness, is deep, immeasurable, unfathomable, like the mighty ocean. To say that he is reborn would not fit the case. To say that he is not reborn would not fit the case. To say that he is both reborn and not reborn would not fit the case. To say that he is neither reborn nor not reborn would not fit the case."

When The Blessed One had thus spoken, Vaccha, the wandering ascetic, spoke to him as follows:

"It is as if, O Gotama, there were a mighty sal-tree near to some village or town, and it were to lose its dead branches and twigs, and its loose shreds of bark, and its unsound wood, so that afterwards, free from those branches and twigs, and the loose shreds of bark, and the unsound wood, it were to stand neat and clean in its strength. In exactly the same way doth the word of Gotama, free from branches and twigs, and from loose shreds of bark, and from unsound wood, stand neat and clean in its strength. O wonderful is it, Gotama! O wonderful is it, Gotama! It is as if, O Gotama, one were to set up that which was overturned; or were to disclose that which was hidden; or were to point out the way to a lost traveller; or were to carry a lamp into a dark place, that they who had eyes might see forms. Even so has Gotama expounded the Doctrine in many different ways. I betake myself to Gotama for refuge, to the Doctrine, and to the Congregation of the priests. Let Gotama receive me who have betaken myself to him for refuge, and accept me as a disciple from this day forth as long as life shall last."

"No Continuous Personal Identity," from the *Milindapanha* and the *Visuddhi-Magga*

From the Milindapañha

"Bhante Nāgasena," said the king, "is a person when just born that person himself, or is he some one else?"

"He is neither that person," said the elder, "nor is he some one else."

"Give an illustration."

"What do you say to this, your majesty? When you were a young, tender, weakly infant lying on your back, was that your present grown-up self?"

"Nay, verily, bhante. The young, tender, weakly infant lying on its back was one person, and my present grown-up self is another person."

"If that is the case, your majesty, there can be no such thing as a mother, or a father, or a teacher, or an educated man, or a righteous man, or a wise man. Pray, your majesty, is the mother of the *kalala*[1] one person, the mother of the *abbuda*[1] another person, the mother of the *pesī*[1] another person, the mother of the *ghana*[1] another person, the mother of the little child another person, and the mother of the grown-up man another person? Is it one person who is a student, and another person who has finished his education? Is it one person who commits a crime, and another person whose hands and feet are cut off?"

"Nay, verily, bhante. But what, bhante, would you reply to these questions?"

Said the elder, "It was I, your majesty, who was a young, tender, weakly infant lying on my back, and it is I who am now grown up. It is through their connection with the embryonic body that all these different periods are unified."

"Give an illustration."

"It is as if, your majesty, a man were to light a light;—would it shine all night?"

"Assuredly, bhante, it would shine all night."

"Pray, your majesty, is the flame of the first watch the same as the flame of the middle watch?"

Reprinted from Henry Clarke Warren, trans., *Buddhism in Translations*, Cambridge, Mass.: Harvard University Press, 1953, pp. 148–50.

"Nay, verily, bhante."

"Is the flame of the middle watch the same as the flame of the last watch?"

"Nay, verily, bhante."

"Pray, then, your majesty, was there one light in the first watch, another light in the middle watch, and a third light in the last watch?"

"Nay, verily, bhante. Through connection with that first light there was light all night."

"In exactly the same way, your majesty, do the elements of being join one another in serial succession: one element perishes, another arises, succeeding each other as it were instantaneously. Therefore neither as the same nor as a different person do you arrive at your latest aggregation of consciousnesses."

"Give another illustration."

"It is as if, your majesty, new milk were to change in process of time into sour cream, and from sour cream into fresh butter, and from fresh butter into clarified butter. And if any one, your majesty, were to say that the sour cream, the fresh butter, and the clarified butter were each of them the very milk itself—now would he say well, if he were to say so?"

"Nay, verily, bhante. They came into being through connection with that milk."

"In exactly the same way, your majesty, do the elements of being join one another in serial succession: one element perishes, another arises, succeeding each other as it were instantaneously. Therefore neither as the same nor as a different person do you arrive at your latest aggregation of consciousnesses."

"You are an able man, bhante Nāgasena."

—From the Visuddhi-Magga

Strictly speaking, the duration of the life of a living being is exceedingly brief, lasting only while a thought lasts. Just as a chariot-wheel in rolling rolls only at one point of the tire, and in resting rests only at one point; in exactly the same way, the life of a living being lasts only for the period of one thought. As soon as that thought has ceased the being is said to have ceased. As it has been said:—

"The being of a past moment of thought has lived, but does not live, nor will it live.

"The being of a future moment of thought will live, but has not lived, nor does it live.

"The being of the present moment of thought does live, but has not lived, nor will it live."

---

1. Various stages of the embryo.

"Simplicity of Funerals," from *Lun Heng*

Wang Ch'ung

Sages and Worthies all are agreed in advocating simplicity of funerals and economy of expenses, but the world sets high store on expensive funerals, and there are many that do amiss by their extravagance and lavishness. The reason is that the discussions of *Confucianists* on this subject are not clear, and that the arguments put forward by the *Mêhists* are wrong. As to the latter, the *Mêhists* contend that men, after their death become ghosts and spirits, possess knowledge, can assume a shape, and injure people. As instances they adduce Earl *Tu* and others. The *Confucianists* do not agree with them, maintaining that the dead are unconscious, and cannot be changed into ghosts. If they contribute to the sacrifices and prepare the other funeral requisites nevertheless, they desire to intimate that they are not ungrateful to the deceased, and therefore treat them as though they were alive.

Lu Chia speaks like the *Confucianists* and, whatever he says, avoids giving a distinct answer. *Liu Tse Chêng* wrote a memorial on the simplicity of funerals, pleading for economy, but he did not exhaust the subject.

Thus ordinary people, on the one side, have these very doubtful arguments, and, on the other, they hear of Earl *Tu* and the like, and note that the dead in their tombs arise and have intercourse with sick people whose end is near. They, then, believe in this, and imagine that the dead are like the living. They commiserate them that in their graves they are so lonely, that their souls are so solitary and without companions, that their tombs and mounds are closed and devoid of grain and other things.

Therefore they make dummies to serve the corpses in their coffins, and fill the latter with eatables, to gratify the spirits. This custom has become so inveterate, and has gone to such lengths, that very often people will ruin their families and use up all their property for the coffins of the dead. They even kill people to follow the deceased into their graves, and all this out of regard for the prejudices of the living. They ignore that in reality it is of no use, but their extravagance is eagerly imitated by others. In their belief, the dead are conscious and do not distinguish themselves from the living.

Confucius condemned these practices, but could not establish the truth, and *Lu Chia*, in his essay, does not adopt either alternative. The memorial of *Liu Tse Chêng* does not do much to elucidate the assertion of the *Confucianists* that the dead are unconscious, or the arguments of the *Mêhists* to

Reprinted from the 1911 ed. of Alfred Forke, trans., *Lun-Hêng: Miscellaneous Essays of Wang Ch'ung, Part II,* 2nd ed., New York: Paragon Book Gallery, 1962, pp. 369–74.

the effect that they are conscious. The subject not being borne out by proofs, and the question not being settled by evidence, there is nothing but empty words and futile talk, and even the views of the most honest people do not find credence. Therefore, the public remains wavering and ignorant, and those who believe in a lucky and unlucky destiny, dread the dead, but do not fear justice; make much of the departed, and do not care for the living. They clear their house of everything for the sake of a funeral procession.

Provided that the disputants and men of letters have proofs such as Earl *Tu* adduced by the *Mêhists,* then the truth that the dead are unconscious can be borne out, and the advice to be economical and not to squander too much money on burials, be substantiated. Now the *Mêhists* say that the *Confucianists* are wrong, and the *Confucianists* think the same of the *Mêhists*. Since they both have their different tenets, there is such a discrepancy of opinions, and a consensus so difficult to be attained.

In this dispute of the two schools, the problem of life and death has not yet been solved, nobody having ever been resuscitated by sacrifices. As a matter of fact, the dead are hidden from our view, being dissolved and belonging to another sphere than the living, and it is almost impossible to have a clear conception of them. Unless, however, their state of consciousness or unconsciousness be ascertained, the true nature of ghosts cannot be determined. Even men of great learning and able scholars may be unfit to discover the truth, though they avail themselves of all the old and modern literature, plunging into the works of the various schools of thought, and perusing them page after page and paragraph after paragraph.

To attain this aim there must first be a holy heart and a sage mind, and then experience and analogies are to be resorted to. If anybody in his reasoning does not use the greatest care and discernment, taking his evidence indiscriminately from without, and thus establishing right and wrong, he believes in what he has heard or seen from others, and does not test it in his mind. That would be reasoning with ears and eyes, and not with the heart and intellect. This reasoning with ears and eyes conduces to empty semblances, and if empty semblances be used as proofs, then real things pass for fictions. Ergo, right and wrong are independent of eyes and ears, and require the use of the intellect.

The *Mêhists,* in their investigations, do not inquire into things with their mind, but thoughtlessly believe the reports of others. Consequently, they fail to find the truth in spite of the plainness of their proofs. An opinion incompatible with truth, however, is not apt to be imparted to others, for though they may have the sympathies of illiterate people, they do not find favour with the learned. It is owing to this that the maxim of the *Mêhists* that all expenses for the various things employed at funerals are unprofitable does not gain ground.

A man of *Lu* was going to put cat's-eyes into a coffin. *Confucius,* upon hearing of it, went across the court-yard, passed over the steps (of the hall), and remonstrated; this was a breach of *etiquette*. The intention of *Confucius* was to avert a calamity. Calamities very often originate from covetousness. Cat's-eyes are precious stones; when the man of *Lu* put them into the coffin, wicked people spied it out, and their greed was roused. The desires of wicked people having been excited, they do not fear laws or penalties, and break tombs open. *Confucius,* from some insignificant indications, foresaw this result, therefore he crossed the court, ascended the steps (of the hall), and, in order to avert this calamity, straightforth made his remonstrance. But since he did not show that the dead are deprived of consciousness, barely limiting himself to a remonstrance, on the ground that the grave might be violated, people would not have listened to him, even though he had possessed the same influence on mankind as *Pi Kan.* Why? Because the wealth of the feudatory lords was so great, that they were not apprehensive of poverty, and their power so strong, that they did not fear a desecration of their graves.

Thus, the doubts concerning the dead were not solved, and for a dutiful son the best plan was to follow the advice imposing upon him the heaviest obligations. Had it been plainly shown that the dead have no knowledge, and that sumptuous burials are of no advantage, the discussion would have been closed, and the question settled, and after it had been made public, the custom of using cat's-eyes would have been abandoned, and there would have been no occasion for crossing the court-yard and remonstrating. Now, the problem was not solved, and barely a strong protest made. That is the reason why *Confucius* could not carry through his doctrine.

Confucius perfectly well understood the true condition of life and death, and his motive in not making a clear distinction is the same which appears from *Lu Chia's* words. If he had said that the dead are unconscious, sons and subjects might perhaps have violated their duties to their father and sovereign. Therefore they say that the ceremony of funeral sacrifices being abolished, the love of sons and subjects would decrease; if they had decreased, these persons would slight the dead and forget the deceased, and, under these circumstances, the cases of undutiful sons would multiply. Being afraid that he might open such a source of impiety, the Sage was reluctant to speak the truth about the unconsciousness of the dead.

However, different spheres must not be confounded. The care taken in abundantly providing for the wants of the living leads to moral perfection, but how does carelessness about the dead interfere with it? If the dead possess knowledge, then a disregard might have evil consequences, but if they are unconscious, a neglect cannot cause any injury. The conviction of their unconsciousness does not necessarily lead to an ill-treatment of the dead, whereas the ignorance of this fact involves the living in ruinous expense.

A dutiful son nursing a sick parent before his death, calls in the diviners and requests the services of physicians with the hope that the malady may be expelled, and the medicines prove efficacious. But, after the death of his parent, nobody—be he as wise as *Wu Hsien,* or as clever as *Pien Ch'io*—can bring him back to life again, well knowing that, when, by death, the vital fluid is destroyed, there is absolutely no help, and no treatment whatever would be of any benefit to the dead. Is there any great difference in an expensive funeral? By supineness with regard to the deceased, people fear to violate the moral laws, but would it not likewise be an impiety to dismiss the diviners and keep the physicians from the dead?

As long as a parent is alive, he takes an elevated seat in the hall, but, after death, when buried, stays under the yellow springs. No human being lives under the yellow springs, yet those burying the dead have not the slightest scruples about it, because the dead inhabit quite a different region, and cannot live together with the living. If they were to be taken care of like living people, and supposed to take offence, they ought to be buried in their house and be close to the living. Those ignorant of the unconsciousness of the dead, are afraid that people might offend against their parents. They only know that, having been buried, they live under the yellow springs, but do not think of the separation from their ancestors.

When a parent is in jail, and his case still pending, a dutiful son hurries about, to rescue him from this danger, but after the case has been tried, and a penalty has been fixed, there is no escape left, and even a *Tsêng Tse* or a *Min Tse Ch'ien* could do nothing but sit down and weep. All schemes would be in vain and lead to useless trouble. Now, the souls of deceased parents decidedly have no consciousness, and are in a similar position to imprisoned parents who cannot be rescued from their punishment. Those who ignore the unconsciousness, apprehend lest people should show a disregard for their ancestors, but do not take exception that, when punishment is settled, parents are abandoned.

When a sage has established a law furthering progress, even if it be of no great consequence, it should not be neglected; but if something is not beneficial to the administration, it should not be made use of in spite of its grandeur. Now, how does all the care bestowed on the dead benefit mutual good feeling, and how could any disregard or neglect violate any law?

Confucius further said that "spirit vessels" are not substantial, but merely symbolical and imaginary. Therefore puppets are made to resemble men, and effigies like living persons. In *Lu* they used dummies for burials. *Confucius* sighed, seeing in this custom an indication that living men would be interred together with the dead. This sigh was an expression of grief, and if (at funerals) things had to be used as if for the living, he warned against an overstraining of this principle. Dummies being buried, it was to be feared that later on, living men might be forced to accompany the dead, but why did *Confucius* not consider the possibility that for "spirit vessels," real vessels might be placed in the graves in future? He obviated human sacrifices, but did nothing to prohibit the use of funeral gifts. He valued human life so much, that he was afraid of wasting it, and he felt pity for the individual but no sympathy for the State. In this his reasoning was wrong.

In order to prevent the water from leaking out, one must stop all the holes, then the leakage ceases. Unless all the holes be stopped, the water finds an outlet, and having an outlet, it causes damage. Unless the discussion on death be exhaustive, these extravagant customs are not stopped, and while they are going on, all sorts of things are required for burials. These expenses impoverish the people, who by their lavishness bring themselves into the greatest straits.

When *Su Ch'in* was envoy of *Yen*, the people of *Ch'i* were in the habit of erecting enormous sepulchres, filled with heaps of valuables. *Su Ch'in* personally did nothing to incite them. When all their wealth was gone, and the people greedy for money, the exchequer empty, and the army good for nothing, the troops of *Yen* suddenly arrived. *Ch'i* was unable to stand its ground:—the State was ruined, the cities fell, the sovereign left his country, and his subjects dispersed. Now, as long as people are in the dark, regarding the unconsciousness of the dead, they will spend all their money for the sumptuous burial of a parent, and be ruined in the same manner as *Ch'i* was by the cunning of *Su Ch'in*.

The device of the *Mêhists* is self-contradictory:—on the one side, they advocate a simple burial, and on the other, they honour ghosts. To justify this veneration, they refer to Earl *Tu*, who was a dead man. If Earl *Tu* be deemed a ghost, then all the dead really possess knowledge, and if they do, they would be incensed at the shabbiness of their burials.

There is a general craving for luxuriance and a strong aversion to paucity. What advantage, therefore, would the veneration of ghosts bring to those guilty of mean burials? Provided that ghosts be not dead men, then the belief in Earl *Tu* is preposterous, if, however, ghosts be dead men, then a mean burial would not be proper. Thus theory and practice of the *Mêhists* are inconsistent, head and tail do not agree, and it cannot but be wrong. But right and wrong not being understood, cannot be practised. Therefore the public should carefully consider what has been written, and having done so, they may bury their dead in a simple style.

"On Time," from *Chao Lun*

Seng Chao

I. 1

That birth and death alternate, that winter and summer succeed each other, that all things glide along and move is a generally accepted proposition. But to me this is not so.

I. 2

The *Fang-kuang* says: "There is no dharma that goes and comes; there is none that alters its position (in the temporal order)." On investigating this quotation we find that "non-moving" here does not mean that motion must cease in order to produce rest but that there is rest with motion going on.

There is rest with motion going on; therefore, though (things) move they are forever at rest.

Motion need not cease in order to produce rest; therefore, though (things) are at rest they do not cease moving.

It follows that motion and rest are not two separate states though those who are mistaken (about the nature of things) believe that they are. Hence the true language (of the sūtras) is discredited by conflicting interpretations and its sense is misrepresented by those who insist upon the separation (of these states). It is, therefore, no easy matter to speak about the coincidence of rest and motion.

For when one uses the true language, he gives offence to the public, but when he complies with the public he distorts the true meaning. Distorting the true meaning he misses the nature (of things) and has no chance of finding it (later), while giving offence to the public he hears his words called "tasteless and without flavour." Thus it happens that the average man is unable to decide whether he should accept or reject (the fact of coincidence) while the inferior person claps his hands (in glee) and pays no attention. Being near and yet unrecognized such is the nature of things.

I, however, cannot let it alone. I must concentrate upon the relation between motion and rest. Realizing that what I say is not final, I shall try to discuss it. . . .

Reprinted from Walter Liebenthal, trans., *Chao Lun: The Treatises of Seng-chao*. Hong Kong: Hong Kong University Press, 1968, pp. 45–52. Copyright 1968 by Hong Kong University Press; reprinted with permission.

II. 3

. . . How sad that the notions of people are always erroneous, that in the very presence of the truth they do not awake to it! They know that what (has gone to) the past cannot come (back to the present) and infer that what is now can pass (over to the past). (I answer:) If what is in the past cannot come (back to the present leaving its position unoccupied), where should what is now go to (supposed that it could pass over to the past)?

Demonstration

Looking for what has been "once" in the time where once it has been, one notices it has never failed to be "once." Looking for what has been once in the time which is now, he notices that it has never been "now." That it has never been "now" proves that it cannot come (up to and mix with "things present"). That it has always been "once" makes it certain that it cannot leave ("things past").

The same reasoning, applied to what is now, would prove that what is now cannot leave "now," and so on.

It follows that whatever is past is "past" by its very nature. For, it could not have started from "present" and passed over to "past." (It proves further that) what is present is "present" by its very nature and could not have come over from "past" to "present."

Therefore Chung-ni says: "(Yen-) hui, seeing you (I feel that) you are a new (person who has not been here before), but a moment later you are (already) no more (the same person I have seen)." Thereby it becomes clear that no intercourse is possible between things belonging to different time-periods.

Thus, if this intercourse is absolutely impossible, nothing at all can change. That is to say, the raging storm (at the end of a world) which uproots mountains in fact is calm; the two streams of China rush along and yet do not flow; the hot air which can be seen in spring time dancing on the surface of a lake is not moving; sun and moon, revolving in their orbits, do not turn round. There is no need to wonder at this after (what I have said above).

II. 4

(Objection:) There is a saying of the Sage. "The life of men passes away, quicker than streams flow." Therefore by realizing the impermanence (of things), the Śrāvaka attains Enlightenment; by awakening to the fact that life is conditional the Pratyekabuddha is induced to leave (the world) and to join the Real. If no changes are produced by these efforts, why strive for change and climb the steps to Enlightenment?

(Answer:) Let us look again at the saying of the Sage. Hidden is its meaning, difficult to grasp. (Things) seem to move but he says they are at rest, they seem to leave (their position in time) but he says they remain there. A

Sage-like intelligence is needed to understand what is not warranted by the simple facts.

Therefore, when (the sūtras) say that (things) pass they say so with a mental reservation. For they wish to contradict people's belief in permanence. When they say that things last, they say so with a mental reservation, in order to express disapproval of what people understand by "passing." Neither do they want to say things (bound as they are to their respective position in the sequence of time periods) may advance beyond that position nor that they may stay behind.

Therefore the *Ch'eng-chu* says: "The Bodhisattva taking his stand among those who believe in the permanence (of dharma) preaches the doctrine of impermanence." The *Mahāyāna śāstra* says: "Dharma do not move, there is no place to which they go or from which they come." (The disparity between these quotations is for the benefit of an ordinary audience, whose ability to understand must be taken into consideration.) They purport the same idea. Their wording may be contradictory but not their aim. It follows that with the sages: "Permanence" has not the meaning of staying behind (while the Wheel of Time, or Karma, moves on). "Impermanence" has not the meaning of outpacing (the Wheel).

Therefore, we might as well say that things, though passing (along with the Wheel), preserve their (temporal or karmic) identity as (say that things), though preserving their (temporal or karmic) identity, pass along (with the Wheel). They pass along but cannot jump positions; they retain their (temporal or karmic) identity but do not preserve their (physical) identity.

What Chuang Sheng called (the impossibility of) "hiding a mountain in a swamp," and what K'ung Tzu spoke about as he stood by a river, refers to the lack of permanence in the general flux which both these men's words deplore. They do not say that one can be rid of to-day and pass on (to to-morrow). It is evident that the thoughts of the Sages cannot be compared with what is thought by human beings.

People who say that the body as possessed by an individual in youth and in age is the same and that (human) substance lasts through a life of a hundred years, only know that years pass, but are not conscious of the fact that the body does likewise. This is explained in a story. A Brahmacārin left his family. White-haired, he came home. Neighbours recognizing him said: "Is the man who once left us still living?" The Brahmacārin answered: "I look like him but am not the same man." The neighbours were startled and not convinced by his words. That is what Chuang Tzu meant by saying: "A strong man takes the mountain on his back and goes away. Stupid men do not comprehend." Doesn't this apply to our problem?

Considering the sort of mental barrier, different in each case (which must be broken down) the Tathāgata preaches in order to remove existing doubts. Aware of the fact that neither positive nor negative assertions can be true, he yet intentionally makes one-sided statements. Paradoxical, though unambiguous, such is the language of the Sages alone.

Therefore, when he has in mind the final truth (*paramārtha satya*), he says that (things) do not move; when he teaches conventional truth (*laukika satya*), he says that everything flows. Though there are a thousand different ways of expressing (the truth), when understood they all convey the same meaning. . . .

II. 5

. . . Therefore, what people call permanence I call impermanence and vice versa. But then impermanence and permanence, though seemingly different, are ultimately the same. That is why it is said in a Classic: "True words seem contradictory. Who dares to trust them?" These words are fraught with meaning.

People who seek (in vain) ancient (events) in our time conclude that (things) are impermanent; I, who seek (in vain) present (events) in ancient times, know that (things) are permanent.

If (what occurs) to-day could have occurred in ancient times, there (would be no reason to) distinguish ancient times from our time; if (what has occurred in) ancient times could occur again to-day, there (would be no reason to) distinguish our time from ancient times.

Because our time is free from ancient (events) we know that nothing returns; because ancient times are free from present (events) we know that nothing leaves (the historical *milieu* to which it belongs).

(Conclusion:) As (what has occurred in) ancient times cannot occur (again) in our time, and (what occurs) to-day cannot have occurred in ancient times, (or else) as each individual is stationed (permanently) in (his period), who, then, is able to move freely to and fro (among the historical periods)?

Then the four seasons, fleet as the wind, and the Great Bear, revolving with lightning speed; if you understand the least of what I have said, (you should realize) that these, rapid as they are, do not move.

"Shoji" ("Birth and Death"), from *Shōbōgenzō*

Dogen

"Because there is Buddha in birth and death, there is no birth and death."
Also, "because there is no Buddha in birth and death, one is not deluded
by birth and death." These are the words of two Zen teachers called Kassan
and Jōsan. Being the words of enlightened people, they were surely not
uttered without reason. People who want to get out of birth and death should
understand what they mean.

If people seek Buddha outside of birth and death, that is like heading
north to go south, like facing south to try to see the north star: accumulating
causes of birth and death all the more, they have lost the way to liberation.
Simply understanding that birth and death is itself nirvana, there is nothing
to reject as birth and death, nothing to seek as nirvana. Only then will one
have some measure of detachment from birth and death.

It is a mistake to assume that one moves from birth to death. Birth,
being one point in time, has a before and after; therefore in Buddhism birth
is called unborn. Extinction too, being one point in time, also has before and
after, so it is said that extinction is nonextinction. When we say "birth" there
is nothing but birth, and when we say "extinction" there is nothing but extinction. Therefore when birth comes it is just birth, and when extinction comes
it is just extinction. In facing birth and extinction, don't reject, don't long.

This birth and death is the life of Buddha. If we try to reject or get
rid of this, we would lose the life of the Buddha. If we linger in this and cling
to birth and death, this too is losing the life of the Buddha; it is stopping
the Buddha's manner of being. When we have no aversion or longing, only
then do we reach the heart of the Buddha.

However, don't figure it in your mind, don't say it in words. Just letting go of and forgetting body and mind, casting them into the house of
Buddha, being activated by the Buddha—when we go along in accord with
this, then without applying effort or expending the mind we part from birth
and death and become Buddhas. Who would linger in the mind?

There is a very easy way to become a Buddha: not doing any evil, having no attachment to birth and death, sympathizing deeply with all beings,
respecting those above, sympathizing with those below, not feeling aversion
or longing for anything, not thinking or worrying—this is called Buddha.
Don't seek it anywhere else.

Reprinted from Thomas Cleary, trans., *Shōbōgenzō: Zen Essays by Dōgen*. Honolulu: University
of Hawaii Press, 1986, pp. 122–23. Copyright 1986 by University of Hawaii Press; reprinted
with permission.

Glossary

Words appear here, as they do in the text, in a more simplified Romanization. Usually, these same terms are presented in their transliteral form along with diacritical marks. The author has chosen to avoid presenting terms in this way in order to ease the reader's introduction into Asian thought. This more simplified version can facilitate proper pronunciation.

abhava   Negation or absence; a term especially scrutinized by the Navya Nyaya, or New Logic, school.

Abhidharma   Buddhist literature that constitutes the analytic part of the Buddhist canon; commentaries on the early teachings of Buddha, or *dharma*.

Abhidharma Kosa   A synopsis of the Abhidharma writings by the Buddhist Vasubandhu, who wrote from a Sarvastivadin perspective.

Advaita   Meaning "nondual," the school of Vedanta established by Sankara; Advaita Vedanta is the most influential of Vedanta schools.

agama   Texts venerated because of their traditional importance.

Agni   The Vedic god of fire.

ahimsa   Noninjury; emphasized especially in Jainism and in the teachings of Gandhi.

aidagara   Meaning "in-betweenness," a key idea in the philosophy of Watsuji Tetsuro.

Aitareya Upanishad   One of the principal Upanishads.

alaya-vijnana   Meaning "store-consciousness," a major idea in the Vijnanavada, or Yogacara, school of Buddhism.

Amida   Also known as Amitabha, the God of Endless Light, and object of reverence in the Japanese Jodo school.

Analects   A Chinese classic and exposition of the sayings of Confucius compiled by his students.

ananda   Meaning "bliss," one of three attributes of Brahman: *sat-cit-ananda,* or being-consciousness-bliss.

anatman   Meaning "no-soul," referring to Buddhist idea of no-self; that is, no enduring, individual entity called self; the Pali term is *anatta;* one of the three marks
of existence, the other two being *dukkha* and *anicca.*

anicca   Meaning "no-permanence," one of the three marks of existence in Buddhism,
the other two being *dukkha* and *anatman.*

Aranyaka   Part of the Veda dealing with sacrifice.

arhat   The ideal state to achieve in early Buddhism, Theravada; the *arhat* is one who
has reached enlightenment and has attained complete wisdom, or *prajna.*

Arjuna   The leading character in the beloved *Bhagavad Gita* and leader of the Pandavas.

artha   The purpose of life, or the means to a secure life, such as material comfort
or wealth.

Artha Shastra   A work on society and governance written by Kautilya.

Aryadeva   Nagarjuna's student who helped spread his teachings on *Madhyamika,* or
the "middle way."

asat   Meaning "nonbeing" or nonexistence.

asatkaryavada   Theory that the effect does not preexist its cause in any way; the cause
therefore produces something new; its opposite is *satkaryavada.*

ashrama   One of the stages in life in India, such as student, householder, or hermit.

Ashvaghosa   Buddhist philosopher who provided the earliest orderly treatise of
Mahayana teachings. He taught that all reality is *tathata,* or suchness.

Asoka   Emperor who was an influential patron of Buddhism. Due to his efforts, Buddhism spread throughout parts of India.

astika   A believer in the orthodox Indian teachings, as opposed to the unbeliever, or
nastika.

Atharva Veda   Fourth collection of Vedas.

atman   A key orthodox Indian teaching; the individual soul or true self; the Upanishads
teach that the individual self is identical to the universal soul, *Brahman*; *atman*
is eternal.

Aurobindo Ghose   Contemporary philosopher in India.

Avatamsaka Sutras   Major Mahayana texts that stress Buddha-nature in all sentient
beings. These works formed the basis for the Chinese Hua-yen and the Japanese
Kegon schools.

Avatamsaka Sutras   Major Mahayana texts that emphasize the Buddhahood of all sentient beings; a key text in the Japanese Kegon school.

avidya   A condition of ignorance, of not knowing our genuine natures.

Badarayana   Author who synopsized ideas from the Upanishads in his *Brahma Sutra*
(also known as *Vedanta Sutra*); the *Brahma Sutra* is one of three major texts of
the Vedanta school, the other two being the Upanishads and the *Bhagavad Gita.*

bakufu   The government of the shogun, or military leader, in Japan during feudal
times.

bardo   Intermediate state between death and rebirth; *Tibetan Book of the Dead,* or *Bardo
Thodol,* describes this.

Bardo Thodol   Name for the *Tibetan Book of the Dead,* from which prayers are recited
to the soul of the deceased in order to guide it on its journey through the intermediate states before rebirth.

basho   Meaning "place" or "field," a major concept in the philosophy of Nishida
Kitaro.

Bhagavad Gita   Beloved poem, "Sung by the Lord," describing Krishna's teaching to
Arjuna on the eve of battle between the Pandavas and the Kauravas; popular
section in the *Mahabharata.*

bhakti   Meaning "devotion," a path, or yoga, to enlightenment; *bhakti yoga* is the way of prayer and sacrifice.

Bhaskara   Philosopher of Vedanta (tenth century) who was a significant influence on Ramanuja.

bhikku   A Buddhist monk and mendicant.

Bhutatathata   A name for the ultimate reality, or pure suchness, in Mahayana Buddhism; a leading idea in Ashvaghosa.

bodhi   Meaning "understanding" or "wisdom."

bodhicitta   "Heart of wisdom," or that Buddha-nature within each sentient creature.

Bodhidharma   Indian Buddhist who introduced the teachings of *dhyana,* which later became Ch'an (Zen in Japan) to China, c. sixth century.

bodhisattva   The ideal in Mahayana Buddhism; a *bodhisattva* is one who is both enlightened and seeks to guide others to awakening on account of genuine compassion; the *bodhisattva* ideal incorporates both wisdom, *prajna,* and compassion, *karuna.*

Brahman   The Absolute Reality, without limits; the condition for all reality.

brahmana   Part of the Vedic text; also the highest class, called priestly in India.

Brihadaranyaka Upanishad   One of the principal Upanishads.

Buddha   Meaning "one who is awakened," historically referring to Siddhartha Gautama after having achieved enlightenment.

Buddhaghosa   Theravadin Buddhist philosopher who wrote commentaries on the Buddhist canon; especially known for his *Visuddhimagga,* c. fourth century.

buddhi   Referring to mind, reason, or intellect in orthodox Indian schools.

Bushido   The Way of the Warrior; a code of morality during feudal times in Japan.

Carvaka   Materialist school in India; reduces all things to matter.

Ch'an   Chinese Buddhist school of meditation or *dhyana,* transmitted to Japan and known there as Zen Buddhism.

ch'eng   Chinese term for the virtue of sincerity.

Ch'eng Yi   Chinese philosopher who along with Chu Hsi helped form the school of Principle in Neo-Confucianism.

ch'i   Material energy or principle of matter; a major idea in neo-Confucianism along with *li;* sometimes referred to as ether.

Chandogya Upanishad   One of the principal Upanishads.

Chang Tung-sun   Contemporary philosopher known for his analysis of culture and knowledge.

chih   Practical moral knowledge; also, a Chinese term for wisdom, for practical ethical knowledge; one of the "four beginnings" in Mencius.

Chu Hsi   The great twelfth-century Chinese philosopher who synthesized major ideas in Neo-Confucianism.

Chuang Tzu   Influential early Taoist thinker. His teachings are in his *Chuang-tzu.*

citta   Reasoning faculty, that which integrates perception and conception; sometimes used along with *buddhi* in Samkhya-Yoga; power of the mind.

daimyo   Japanese feudal lord with enough land to produce a certain large output of rice.

darshana   Meaning "point of view" or vision, a term that comes close to "philosophy."

devas   Deities that bestow light or provide for the senses.

Dhammapada   "Words of the Teaching," an early text and collection of sayings attributed to the Buddha; expresses the substance of much of Buddhist morality.

dharma   Referring to proper action, especially ethical action, or virtue, duty; can also mean the principle of existence and also material elements; also refers to the Buddha's teachings, as *Dharma.*

Dharma Shastras   Early Indian works dealing with the interpretation of *dharma,* or moral duty.

Dharmakirti   Celebrated sixth-century Buddhist philosopher who elaborated further on ideas in the Logical School of Dignaga.

dhyana   "Meditation," and the basis for later schools of Chinese Ch'an and Japanese Zen Buddhism.

Dignaga   Pioneer Buddhist philosopher who founded the School of Logic; was a student of Vasubandhu; authored the *Pramana-Samuch-chaya.*

Dogen   Celebrated thirteenth-century Zen master and founder of Soto Zen Buddhism; composed *Shobogenzo.*

Dravidians   The indigenous people who inhabited the Indus Valley before the invasion of the Aryan tribes.

dukkha   Meaning "suffering and pain"; the first Noble Truth of Buddhism is that all reality consists of *dukkha;* one of the three marks of existence in Buddhism, the other two being *anatman* and *anicca.*

Dvaita   Meaning "dualist," refers to the school of Vedanta founded by Madhva, thirteenth century.

Eisai   Alleged to be the father of Zen Buddhism in Japan, c. thirteenth century; he founded the Rinzai sect of Zen.

enso   Circle; for example, the Ten Oxherding *Enso.*

Fudo   Major text, translated as *Climate,* written by contemporary Japanese philosopher Watsuji Tetsuro.

Fujiwara   Famous ruling clan in Japan for close to two centuries, from the ninth to the twelfth centuries.

Fujiwara Seika   Sixteenth- and seventeenth-century philosopher who helped spread the thought of Chu Hsi in Japan.

Fung Yu-lan   Contemporary Chinese philosopher and historian of philosophy.

Gangesa   Founder of the Navya-Nyaya, or Neo-Nyaya (New Logic) school, and author of *Tattvacintamani,* c. thirteenth century.

gatha   Stanza or verse.

Gaudapada   First systematic treatment of Advaita Vedanta, later elaborated on by Sankara.

Gautama Siddhartha   Family name for the Buddha.

"Genjokoan"   Meaning "The Issue at Hand," one of the essays in *Shobogenzo,* written by Dogen.

giri   Japanese term for "duty" or "obligation."

guna   Meaning "attribute" or "characteristic," referring to material elements; an important teaching in Samkhya in which things can assume a combination of one to three *gunas: sattva, rajas,* and *tamas.*

hachimaki   Japanese headband symbolizing commitment and resolve; often worn by samurai under helmets; represents mental discipline.

Hagakure   Eighteenth-century Japanese text expressing the teachings of Bushido; also known as *Nabeshima rongo,* or "Teachings of the Nabeshima Clan."

Han Fei Tzu   Early Chinese legalist philosopher.

Han   Famous dynasty in Chinese history that saw the dominance of Confucianism and the rivalry between the Old Text and the New Text schools.

Harivarman   Third-century Buddhist thinker who formed a school emphasizing *asat* (nonbeing) as opposed to Vaibhashika realism's stress on *sat* (being).

Hatano Seiichi   Contemporary Japanese philosopher, especially noted for his philosophy of religion; authored *Time and Eternity.*

Hayashi Razan   A leading representative of the Chu Hsi school (*Shushi*) adopted in Japan during the Tokugawa period.

Heian   Celebrated period in Japan, eighth to twelfth centuries, which saw the growth of Japanese Buddhism in the form of the Tendai and Shingon schools.

Hinayana   Derogatory term given by Mahayana Buddhists to the older, more conservative Buddhism, known as Theravada. Literally means "lesser vehicle," whereas Mahayana means "greater vehicle."

Hokke   Japanese term for the Lotus school founded by Nichiren, thirteenth century; Hokke was a subdivision of the Jodo school.

Honen   Together with Shinran, the founder of the Amida school in Japan, twelfth to thirteenth century.

hsieh   Chinese term for equivalent of a "knight-errant."

hsing   Chinese Taoist term for a thing's own nature; also human nature.

Hsiung Shih-li   Contemporary Chinese philosopher.

Hsun Tzu   Confucian, c. third century B.C.E.

Hua-yen   Chinese Buddhist school whose major text is the *Avatamsaka Sutra.*

Hui Shih   Representative of the Chinese School of Names, and famous for his Ten Paradoxes.

I Ching   Famous Chinese *Book of Changes,* originally used for divination and expressing ideas of yin and yang and Chinese cosmology.

Indra   Vedic god of war.

Indus   Name of the fertile valley populated by indigenous Dravidians and later by conquering Aryans. Also name of a river, after which the term "Hindu" was adopted.

Ishvara   *Brahman* as the personal God or Lord.

Ishvarakrishna   Wrote the *Samkhya Karika,* a major text in the Samkhya school, fifth century.

Ito Jinsai   One of the first philosophical opponents of Chu Hsi thought, he advocated a return to early Japanese texts.

Jain   Heterodox Indian belief system, practicing strict forms of asceticism and believing in *ahimsa,* noninjury.

jen   Chinese term for the most important virtue of humaneness; can also mean virtue.

jin   Japanese equivalent of Chinese *jen,* meaning human-heartedness or kindness.

jiriki   Meaning "self-power."

jiva   *Atman* as embodied in human form; source of moral action in the human.

jivanmukta   One who is liberated while in the body.

jivatman   Ego or soul that is considered to be an independent entity; Buddhists generally believe that such an entity does not exist.

Kaibara Ekken   Japanese Confucianist, seventeenth to eighteenth centuries; author of *Yamato Zokkun.*

kalpa   Measurement for an extremely long period of time.

kama   Meaning "enjoyment," "pleasure," or "love."

Kama Sutra   A discourse on sensual pleasures and love written by Vatsyayana.

kami   Divine beings or spirits in Japanese thought.

Kanada   Founder of the orthodox Hindu school of Vaisheshika.

kanji   Chinese ideograms or characters that form the basis for Japanese.

karma   Means activity or the product of moral or immoral action; the principle of moral causation in Indian thought.

karuna   Compassion.

Katha Upanishad   One of the principal Upanishads.

Katthavatthu   A portion of the *Abhidharmapitaka,* the third part of the Buddhist canon or *Tripitaka*; it addresses the various schools of thought at that time in Buddhism.

Kegon   Japanese Buddhist school during the Nara period, introduced into Japan c. eighth century; centers around teachings of *Avatamsaka Sutras.*

Kena Upanishad   One of the principal Upanishads.

kendo   The Japanese martial art of fencing.

kenri   Japanese term for "right," as in moral right.

ki   Japanese equivalent of Chinese *ch'i,* or principle of matter.

koan   Riddle used in Zen practice to show the limits of reason.

Kogakuha   Japanese "Ancient School of Learning," seeking to revive early teachings of Confucius and Mencius, in reaction against Chu Hsi (*Shushi*) teachings.

Kojiki   "Record of Ancient Things," it is the oldest official account of early Japanese history, c. 712. Another old record is *Nihon-shoki,* c. 720.

kokoro   Japanese term for "heart" or "self."

Krishna   Manifestation of *Brahman*; incarnated in the *Bhagavad Gita* as the charioteer for Arjuna.

kshatriya   Warrior class, the protectors, in Indian society.

Kukai   Legendary eighth- to ninth-century founder of Shingon, alleged to be originator of Cha-no-yu in Japan.

Kumarajiva   Pilgrim to China and translator of many Buddhist works into Chinese.

Kumazawa Banzan   Seventeenth-century Japanese neo-Confucian and representative of the O-Yomei, or Wang Yang-ming, school.

Kung-sun Lung   Chinese philosopher of the school of Names, known for his theory of universals and his "Discourse on a White Horse."

Kuo Hsiang   Third-century neo-Taoist, known especially for his commentary on *Chuang-tzu.*

Lankavatara Sutra   Early Mahayana sutra that has a significant effect on Zen teachings.

Lao Tzu   Legendary composer of the *Tao Te Ching,* c. fifth century.

li   First refers to the early Confucian virtue of proper conduct and propriety; it also refers to the neo-Confucian theory of the principle or essence of all things that come into existence; in neo-Confucianism, it is a major teaching along with *ch'i.*

Li Chi   Classic Chinese text, *Book of Rites.*

Li Ao   Precursor to neo-Confucianism.

lila   The "play" of the divine or *Brahman*; the universe is a self-expression of this play.

linga sharira   Subtle body, that which survives physical death and is associated with new psycho-physical form.

Lokayata   Another term for the school of materialism, also referred to more specifically as Carvaka.

Lumbini   Alleged to be the birthplace of Buddha, near the border of India and Nepal; site of pilgrimages.

Madhva   Thirteenth-century founder of Dvaita Vedanta, or dualist Vedanta.

Madhyamika Karika   Nagarjuna's most significant text, fully titled as *Mulamadhyama-kakarika,* or *Verses on the Basics of the Middle Way*; its teaching of *sunyata* occupies a central role.

Madhyamika   Meaning Middle Way, refers to Buddhist teachings as represented by Nagarjuna.

Mahabharata   Classic Indian epic tale of the conflict between the two clans of Kauravas and Pandavas.

mahakaruna   Great compassion.

Mahasanghika Name of the Buddhist contingent that broke off from the traditional Theravada group, c. third century B.C.E.

Mahavairocana The supreme Buddha.

Mahavira The leading exponent and organizer of Jainism, c. sixth century.

Mahayana Meaning "great vehicle," referring to one of two major Buddhist schools; more liberal than the earlier Theravada (Hinayana, "lesser vehicle").

Maitreya Name for the Buddha-to-be, or the Buddha who will appear in the future.

manas Mental basis for sensory awareness and perception.

mandala Sacred circle; special insight symbolized in circular fashion; inner state depicted in form of circle.

Mandukya Upanishad One of the principal Upanishads.

Manu Fourth-century composer of India's early treatise on law and society, *Code of Manu.*

Manyoshu Japanese Nara text of verses, meaning "Many Leaves," consisting of early and native Japanese poems.

Mao Tse-tung Major twentieth-century Chinese political leader integrating ideas from Marx, Lenin, and traditional philosophies.

Mappo Meaning the "latter end of the Law," referring to a future time of degeneracy, and a popular Buddhist belief in eleventh-century Japan; helped to instill later Jodo school.

Meiji Restoration Marked the end of Tokugawa rule and the opening up of Japan to Western influence, starting in 1868.

meinichi "Deathday," or commemoration day of a death; an illustration of ancestor reverence and an occasion for family to be reunited in Japan.

Mencius Early (fourth-century) Confucian philosopher noted for his positive view of human nature.

Milindapanha "Questions of King Milinda," a record of conversations between the Greek king Milinda and the learned Buddhist Nagasena.

Mimamsa One of the six orthodox Hindu schools of philosophy.

Mishima Yukio Contemporary literary figure whose failed coup attempt by his small band called the "Shield Society" led to his suicide by *seppuku.*

Mito Seventeenth-century school of historians that sought to revive interest in Japanese literature and early history; later supported the ascendancy of the emperor in place of the shogun.

Miura Baien Eighteenth-century Japanese neo-Confucian deeply influenced by Western science and rationalism.

Mo Tzu Early Chinese philosopher who expressed strong utilitarianism.

Moggaliputta Alleged to preside over the Third Buddhist Council, and, as a result, composed his *Katthavatthu,* as official summary of Buddhist teachings.

Mohandas Gandhi Celebrated supporter of Indian independence; known especially for his teachings on *ahimsa* and *satyagraha.* Assassinated by Indian nationalist in 1948.

Mohist School based on utilitarian teachings of Mo Tzu.

moksha The goal in Hindu philosophy; the state of enlightenment or liberation whereby one realizes one's genuine nature.

mondo Zen practice of question and answer.

Motoori Norinaga A leading eighteenth-century representative of the School of National Learning (Kokugaku), which arose in Japan in opposition to the Chu Hsi school (or *Shushi*).

mudras Sacred gestures, often practiced along with mantras (sacred expressions or chants) in Esoteric Buddhism, such as Tantra.

Mundaka Upanishad   One of the principal Upanishads.

Nagarjuna   Second-century Buddhist philosopher, representing the Madhyamika school and author of *Madhyamika Karika.*

Nakae Toju   Established the O-Yomei school in Japan and led philosophical opposition to Chu Hsi, or *Shushi,* seventeenth century.

nama-rupa   Name-form aggregate, or the composite of both psyche and physical body in Indian thought.

Nara   Early period during which initial Buddhist schools were formed in Japan.

Nasadiya Hymn   Famous hymn in Rig Veda (10.129) that introduces some philosophic speculation in Vedic literature; Hymn of Creation.

nastika   A disbeliever, or one who belongs to the heterodox teachings in Indian philosophy; *astika* is a believer.

Navya Nyaya   New Logic, or Neo-Logic, school represented by Gangesa, twelfth century, and Ragunatha, sixteenth century.

nembutsu   Constant repetition of the name of the Buddha in order to gain entrance into the Pure Land; practiced especially in the Jodo school in Japan.

Nichiren   Thirteenth-century Japanese reformer who appealed to national spirit; founded Hokke school; stressed the necessity of the *Lotus Sutra,* or *Saddharmapundarika Sutra.*

Nimbarka   Fourteenth-century Vedantist who was strongly influenced by Ramanuja, though taught his own form of Vedanta.

nirguna   Meaning "without attributes," referring to the aspect of *Brahman* as unnameable or indescribable.

nirvana   The goal in Buddhism; this is the state of enlightenment, or extinction from desires.

Nishida Kitaro   Renowned modern Japanese philosopher; founder of the Kyoto school of philosophy. Authored the famous *Inquiry into the Good.*

Nishitani Keiji   Contemporary Japanese philosopher; third celebrated representative of the Kyoto school of philosophy, the first two being Nishida Kitaro and Tanabe Hajime.

Nyaya   One of six major orthodox Hindu schools in philosophy; the Hindu school of logic.

O-Yomei   Japanese school and rendition of the philosophy of Wang Yang-ming.

Oda Nobunaga   One of three great unifiers in Japan leading to the Tokugawa period.

Ogyu Sorai   Defender of Confucian thought in seventeenth- to eighteenth-century Japan, especially in the realm of morality; also supported the strong rule of the bakufu.

Oshio Heihachiro   Exponent of O-Yomei philosophy and leader of small rebellion that failed; afterward committed suicide.

Pali   Original language in which the earliest Buddhist documents were written. Texts of the Theravada schools were written in Pali, whereas the texts of the Mahayana schools were written in Sanskrit.

parinirvana   The highest state of nirvana in which one who experiences nirvana leaves the impermanent world, as the *arhat.*

Patanjali   Traditionally ascribed as the composer of the *Yoga Sutras*; his system of yoga is also known as Raja Yoga.

pitaka   Meaning "basket," portions of the Buddhist canon, officially known as Tripitaka, or Three Baskets.

prajna   Meaning "wisdom" and "knowledge."

Prajnaparamita Sutras   Meaning the *Transcendental Wisdom Sutras*; they are the foundational sutras of Mahayana Buddhism.

prakriti   The principle of physical existence in the Samkhya school.

pramana   Source of knowledge or cognition.

pratityasamutpada   Theory of dependent origination, a major theme throughout Buddhist teachings.

pudgala   Personal entity in Buddhism, consisting of mind and body.

purusha   Meaning "spirit," referring to the principle of spiritual existence in the Samkhya school.

Purva Mimamsa   One of the six orthodox Hindu schools in philosophy.

Radhakrishnan   Contemporary Indian philosopher, historian of Indian philosophy, and statesman.

Raghunatha   Sixteenth-century logician of Navya Nyaya school and author of *Padarthanirupana* and *Didhiti.*

Rahula   Name of the Buddha's son, meaning "chain."

rajas   One group of *gunas,* or constituent elements, of activity or passion.

Rama   Principal figure in the epic *Ramayana.*

Ramakrishna   Nineteenth-century Hindu who emphasized realization of inner spiritual and divine nature; the ultimate center of conflict is spiritual; his mission was carried further by Swami Vivekananda.

Ramanuja   Eleventh-century philosopher who is the founder of Visistadvaita Vedanta (qualified nondualism).

Ramayana   A beloved and popular major epic of India, authored by Valmiki.

Rangaku   Meaning "Dutch Learning," and referring to the influence of Western ideas, especially through the Dutch, at the start of the Meiji Restoration.

ri   Japanese equivalent of Chinese *li,* meaning principle of existence; used in the Japanese neo-Confucian schools.

Rig Veda   A significant and more speculative portion of the Vedic literature.

Rinzai   School of Zen Buddhism in Japan adapting the Chinese Lin-chi Ch'an sect and known for its use of *koans* and emphasis on instantaneous awakening.

rishi   Meaning "seers," referring to transmitters of sacred teachings in India.

rita   Principle of order in the Vedas.

ronin   Wandering, or masterless, samurai.

Ryoanji   Temple site of the famous Zen garden in Kyoto.

Saddharmapundarika Sutra   Translated as the *Discourse on the Lotus of the True Dharma,* or *Lotus Sutra*; a major work in Mahayana Buddhism, with far-reaching influence in Japanese Buddhism.

saguna   Meaning "with attributes," referring to *Brahman* as being described, with characteristics, and nameable.

Saicho   Originally named Dengyo Daishi, who established Tendai school in eighth-to ninth-century Japan.

sakoku   Meaning "isolation," referring to the long period of isolation before the Meiji Restoration in Japan; also the title of a book by Watsuji Tetsuro.

sakura   Japanese cherry blossom, in bloom for only one week of the year, symbolizing life's transience.

Sama Veda   Portion of Vedic literature.

samadhi   State of deep concentration; the goal to reach in Yoga meditation.

sambhogakaya   Body of Bliss, one of three Buddha-bodies, the heavenly expression of the Buddha; the other two bodies are *dharmakaya* (absolute body) and *nirmanakaya* (earthly body).

samhita   Portions of the Vedic literature, or collection.

Samkhya   One of six orthodox Hindu schools, stressing the distinction between *purusha* and *prakriti.*

Samkhya Karika   Classic text on Samkhya philosophy written by Ishvarakrishna.

Sammitiya   Theravadin Buddhist school, advocating a *pudgala.*

samsara   Wheel or cycle of birth, death, and rebirth in Indian thought.

samskara   Natural tendencies or impressions; potentialities.

Sangha   The early Buddhist order.

Sankara   Celebrated eighth-century Indian philosopher who championed the school of Advaita Vedanta (nondualism), the most influential of the six orthodox Hindu schools.

sannyasin   One who withdraws from society in order to reach higher spiritual realization; a stage in life in Indian thought.

Sanron   One of the Buddhist schools during Japanese Nara period.

Sarvastivada   Older Buddhist school, often referred to as realists.

sat   Meaning "being," or "existence."

satkaryavada   The theory that holds that the effect preexists in some way in its cause. This is in contrast to the theory of *asatkaryavada.*

satori   The experience of awakening, or enlightenment, in Zen Buddhism.

sattva   Meaning "transparence," one of the three *gunas*; generally refers to the *guna* of intellect.

satyagraha   Meaning "total commitment to truth," the major principle in the teachings of Mohandas Gandhi.

Sautrantika   Early Buddhist school known for its realism.

seppuku   Suicide by disembowelment, at times accompanied by decapitation.

shastra   Treatise, for example, *Dharma Shastras, Treatises on Law and Society.*

shen   Chinese term originally meaning spirit; aspect of mind.

Shingon   Influential Buddhist school founded by Kukai during the Heian period in Japan.

Shinran   Helped establish the Amida school in thirteenth-century Japan, along with Honen.

Shobogenzo   Well-known collection of essays written by Dogen, the Zen Buddhist philosopher.

shudra   Laboring class in traditional Indian society.

Shushi   Japanese equivalent of the Chinese neo-Confucian Chu Hsi school of Principle.

Sita   Wife of Rama and a major character in the epic *Ramayana.*

skandhas   Also known as aggregates, or constituent parts of the individual in Buddhism.

smrti   Meaning "that which is remembered," referring to major texts such as the epics and *shastras.*

sruti   Meaning "that which is listened to," referring to key sacred texts believed to be divinely inspired, such as the Vedas and Upanishads, constituting authoritative teachings.

Sthaviravada   An early school in Buddhism, referring to the "Elders."

sukuse   Japanese term for "destiny," somewhat resembling karma.

sunya   Meaning "empty," pertaining to theory of emptiness, or *sunyata.*

sunyata   Meaning "emptiness," referring to major idea of void in Mahayana Buddhism; it means that all things are essentially void of self-subsistence or self-nature or permanence.

sutra   Short saying or aphorism; *sutras* were popular devices because they were easier to remember.

svabhava   Self-nature, or that which exists independently.

svetambara   Meaning "clothed in white," referring to a group of Jains; they were less strict than the other group, called *digambara,* or "clothed with the sky" (that is, naked).

T'ai-chi   The Supreme Ultimate, the absolute principle, in Confucianism. The Supreme Ultimate in Chinese philosophy.

T'ien   Chinese term for heaven.

T'ien-t'ai   Chinese school of Buddhism.

Tai Chen   Eighteenth-century Chinese philosopher who represents the empirical response to neo-Confucianism.

Taittiriya Upanishad   One of the principal Upanishads.

tamas   One of *gunas* of *prakriti,* meaning the "dark," or passive, inert aspects.

Tanabe Hajime   Contemporary Japanese philosopher; second major representative of the Kyoto School of philosophy; the other two are Nishida Kitaro and Nishitani Keiji.

Tantra   An esoteric school in Indian philosophy practicing sacred chants, gestures, and mysteries.

Tao   The Way, or ultimate principle of reality in Taoism. Principle of harmony.

Tao Te Ching   Classic and foundational Taoist text, allegedly written by Lao Tzu.

tariki   Meaning "other-power."

tarka   Argument in logic; popular in Nyaya and in Buddhist logic.

tat tvam asi   Meaning "that you are," a major teaching in the Upanishads; "that" refers to *Brahman,* and "you" refers to *atman*; therefore *atman* is identical in essence to *Brahman.*

Tathagata   "One who has reached complete thusness," the title of tribute given to the Buddha.

tathata   Meaning "suchness," the state of reality.

Tattvacintamani   Text of the Navya Nyaya school, written by Gangesa in the twelfth century.

te   Meaning "power" or "virtue" in Taoist thought; that principle by which a thing is naturally and spontaneously itself.

Tendai   A major Buddhist school during the Heian period in ninth-century Japan, established by Saicho (Dengyo Daishi); the equivalent of the Chinese T'ien-t'ai school.

tetsugaku   Meaning the "science of questing wisdom," an equivalent for "philosophy" in Japan, introduced by the modern philosopher Nishi Amane.

Theravada   Early and more traditional school of Buddhism; generally more conservative in practice and doctrine.

Todaiji   Famous temple that was the center of Nara Buddhism, built in the eighth-century and housing the great statue of Roshana Buddha; also known as *Dai-Kegonji,* or Great Temple of Kegon.

Tokugawa   Famous period in Japanese history led by Tokugawa clan and shogunate.

Trimsika   "Thirty Verses"; noted text written by Vasubandhu, representing Yogacara teachings in Buddhism.

Tripitaka   Meaning the "Three Baskets," the official Buddhist texts, or canon.

trsna   Refers to desire or clinging, especially clinging to permanence; this is, for Buddhists, the ultimate source of individual suffering and is the Second Noble Truth.

Tung Chung-shu   Second-century Chinese Confucian philosopher who helped establish Confucian thought as the official teaching; known for his theory of correspondence.

upamana   Comparison; sometimes cited as a source of cognition, or *pramana.*

Upanishads   Writings at the end of the Vedas, more speculative in content.

Vaibhashika   Early school in Buddhism known for its realism.

Vairocana   The Lord of the demons, mentioned in the Upanishads.

Vaisheshika   One of the six orthodox Hindu schools in philosophy, known for its theory of atomism; generally coupled with Nyaya as both share many ideas.

vaishnavite   Follower in the theistic school of Vaishnavism, viewing *Brahman* as personal Lord, with significant difference between human and divine.

Vardhamana   The name for Mahavira, the leading representative and organizer of Jainism, c. sixth century.

varna   Meaning "color," referring to class and caste.

Varuna   A principal god in the *Rig Veda*, ruler of the heavens.

Vasubandhu   Philosopher first affiliated with the earlier Sautrantika school of Buddhism, and later the leading representative of Yogacara Buddhism, or Vijnanavada; younger brother of Asangha; wrote *Trimsika* and *Vimsatika*.

Vatsyayana   Author of the text on sensual pleasure and love, the *Kama Sutra*.

Vedanta   Most influential of six orthodox Hindu schools, essentially based on teachings in the Upanishads. Three subdivisions are Advaita (nondualist), Visistadvaita (qualified nondualist), and Dvaita (dualist).

Vedas   Earliest works in Indian thought.

vijnana   Referring to consciousness; sometimes used with *buddhi*; a key teaching in the Vijnanavada school of Buddhism.

Vijnanavada   Also called Yogacara; a major school in Buddhism.

Vimsatika   A major text written by Vasubandhu, a leading representative of the Yogacara Buddhist school.

vinaya   Meaning "discipline"; a portion of Buddhist *Tripitaka*, or Buddhist canon, constitutes texts on Buddhist *vinaya*.

Visistadvaita   Meaning "qualified nondualism," refers to the school of Vedanta represented by Ramanuja.

Visuddhimagga   Meaning "Path of Purification," a leading fifth-century text written by Buddhaghosa and a summary of the early Buddhist teachings.

Vivekananda   Modern philosopher in India, representing Vedanta.

Wang Yang-ming   Chinese Neo-Confucian who represents the school of Mind, or idealist school, in opposition to Chu Hsi's rationalist school.

Watsuji Tetsuro   Contemporary Japanese philosopher known for his philosophical anthropology, and author of *Fudo (Climate and Culture)*.

wu   Chinese term for "nonbeing."

wu wei   A major idea in Chinese philosophy, especially in Taoism, meaning "nonaction" and referring to nonassertion, a way of acting by not acting.

Yajnavalkya   Well-known sage described in the *Brihadaranyaka Upanishad*.

Yajur Veda   One of four Vedic groups of texts.

yama   Japanese term for "mountain."

Yamago Soko   Japanese philosopher of the Kogakuha School (Ancient Learning) and leading representative of the teaching of Bushido, or Way of the Warrior.

Yamato Zokkun   Work written by Kaibara Ekken, neo-Confucian Japanese philosopher.

yang   One of the two universal forces, being the active principle; paired with yin.

yi   Confucian virtue of righteousness and moral obligation.

yin   One of the two universal forces, and is the receptive principle; major idea in Chinese thought; paired with yang, the active principle.

Yin-Yang   Early Chinese school based on the mutual interdependency of universal forces of yin and yang.

yoga   Path to achieve enlightenment; refers to a union of mind and body.

Yogacara   Also called the Buddhist school of Vijnanavada; the name Yogacara comes from its emphasis on Yoga as a means to realize one's nature.

Yomei-gaku   Also known as O-Yomei, the Japanese equivalent of the Wang Yang-ming school of Neo-Confucianism.

yu   Chinese term for "being."

zazen   Sitting meditation in Zen Buddhism.

Zen   Japanese style of Buddhist practice, based on Chinese Ch'an teachings and *dhyana* practice.

Bibliography

General Studies

*Bonevac, Daniel, and Stephen Phillips, eds. *Understanding Non-Western Philosophy: Introductory Readings*. Mountain View, California: Mayfield Publishing Company, 1993.

Carmody, Denise Lardner, and John Tully Carmody. *Ways to the Center*. 3rd ed. Belmont, California: Wadsworth Publishing Company, 1989.

de Bary, Wm. Theodore. *East Asian Civilizations: A Dialogue in Five Stages*. Cambridge, Massachusetts: Harvard University Press, 1988.

de Bary, Wm. Theodore, and Irene Bloom, eds. *Approaches to the Asian Classics*. New York: Columbia University Press, 1990.

Hackett, Stuart C. *Oriental Philosophy: A Westerner's Guide to Eastern Thought*. Madison: University of Wisconsin Press, 1979.

Koller, John M. *Oriental Philosophies*. 2nd ed. New York: Charles Scribner's Sons, 1985.

Riepe, Dale, ed. *Asian Philosophy Today*. New York: Gordon and Breach Science Publishers, Inc., 1981.

Smart, Ninian. *The World's Religions*. Englewood Cliffs, New Jersey: Prentice Hall, Inc., 1989.

*Solomon, Robert C., and Kathleen M. Higgins, eds. *From Africa to Zen: An Invitation to World Philosophy*. Lanham, Maryland: Rowman & Littlefield Publishers, Inc., 1993.

General Studies In Indian Philosophies

*Anacker, Stefan, trans. *Seven Works of Vasubandhu: The Buddhist Psychological Doctor*. Religions of Asia Series. Delhi: Motilal Banarsidass, 1984.

*Asterisks indicate works that are essentially primary sources or readings.

*Aurobindo, Sri. *The Life Divine*. New York: E. P. Dutton & Co., Inc., 1949.

*Brown, Brian, ed. and intro. *The Wisdom of the Hindus: Philosophies and Wisdom from Their Ancient and Modern Literature*. Foreword by Jagadish Chandra Chatterji. Garden City, New York: Garden City Publishing Co., Inc., 1938.

*Carter, John Ross, and Mahinda Palihawadana, trans., notes, and commentary. *The Dhammapada*. New York: Oxford University Press, 1987.

*Conze, Edward, ed. *Buddhist Texts Through the Ages*. In collaboration with I. B. Horner, D. Snellgrove, and A. Waley. New York: Harper & Row, Harper Torchbooks, 1964.

*_____ . *Buddhism: Its Essence and Development*. Preface by Arthur Waley. 1951. New York: Harper Torchbooks, Harper & Row, 1975.

Dasgupta, Surendranath. *A History of Indian Philosophy*. 5 vols. Cambridge: Cambridge University Press, 1922–1955.

*de Bary, Wm. Theodore, ed. *The Buddhist Tradition in India, China and Japan*. Collaborated with Yoshito Hakeda and Philip Yampolsky. New York: Vintage Books, Random House, 1972.

*Edgerton, Franklin, trans. *The Beginnings of Indian Philosophy*. Cambridge, Massachusetts: Harvard University Press, 1965.

*Evans-Wentz, W. Y., compiler and ed. *The Tibetan Book of the Dead*. Psychological commentary by C. G. Jung; forewords by Lama Anagarika Govinda and Sir John Woodroffe. 3rd ed. London: Oxford University Press, 1960.

*Hakeda, Yoshito S., trans. and commentary. *The Awakening of Faith, Attributed to Aśvaghosa*. New York: Columbia University Press, 1967.

Hiriyanna, M. *The Essentials of Indian Philosophy*. London: George Allen & Unwin Ltd., 1960.

*Hume, Robert Ernest, trans. *The Thirteen Principal Upanishads*. Outline by Hume. 1921, 2nd rev. ed. London: Oxford University Press, 1971.

*Inada, Kenneth K., trans. and introductory essay. *Nāgārjuna: A Translation of His Mūlamadhyamakakārikā with an Introductory Essay*. Tokyo: The Hokuseido Press, 1970.

Koller, John M. *The Indian Way*. New York: Macmillan Publishing Co., 1982.

*Lamotte, Étienne. *Karmasiddhiprakarana: The Treatise on Action by Vasubandhu*. Translated into English by Leo M. Pruden. Berkeley, California: Asian Humanities Press, 1988.

*Le Mée, Jean, trans. *Hymns from the Rig Veda*. New York: Alfred A. Knopf, 1975.

*Lopez, Donald S., Jr. *The Heart Sutra Explained: Indian and Tibetan Commentaries*. SUNY Series in Buddhist Studies. Albany: State University of New York Press, 1988.

*Matilal, Bimal Krishna, trans. and notes. *The Navya-Nyāya Doctrine of Negation: The Semantics and Ontology of Negative Statements in Navya-nyāya Philosophy*. Harvard Oriental Series. Cambridge, Massachusetts: Harvard University Press, 1968.

Moore, Charles A., ed. *The Indian Mind: Essentials of Indian Philosophy and Culture*. Honolulu: East-West Center Press, University of Hawaii Press, 1967.

*Müller, F. Max, trans. *The Dhammapada: A Collection of Verses*. 2nd. rev. ed., 1881. The Sacred Books of the East, Vol. X, Part I. London: Oxford University Press, 1924.

*Nikhilananda, Swami, trans. *The Upanishads,* abridged ed. New York: Harper Torchbooks, Harper & Row, 1964.

*O'Flaherty, Wendy Doniger, trans. and annotated. *The Rig Veda: An Anthology*. London: Penguin Books, Ltd., 1981.

*Panikkar, Raimundo, trans. *The Vedic Experience: Mantramanjari*. Los Angeles: University of California Press, 1977.

Radhakrishnan, S. *Indian Philosophy*. 2 vols. London: George Allen & Unwin Ltd., 1923.

*_____ , ed., trans., intro., and notes. *The Principal Upanisads.* London: George Allen & Unwin Ltd., 1953.

*_____ , trans. and notes. *The Bhagavadgita.* London: George Allen & Unwin Ltd., 1971.

*_____ . *An Idealist View of Life.* London: George Allen & Unwin Ltd., 1932.

*Radhakrishnan, Sarvepalli, and Charles A. Moore, eds. *A Sourcebook in Indian Philosophy.* Princeton, New Jersey: Princeton University Press, 1957.

*Radhakrishnan, S., and J. H. Muirhead, eds. *Contemporary Indian Philosophy,* 2nd rev. ed. London: George Allen & Unwin Ltd., 1952.

Raju, P. T. *The Philosophical Traditions of India.* London: George Allen & Unwin Ltd., 1971.

_____ . *Structural Depths of Indian Thought.* Albany: State University of New York Press, 1985.

*Rhys Davids, C. A. F., trans. *Psalms of the Early Buddhists.* London: Luzac, 1964.

Sharma, Chandradhar. *A Critical Survey of Indian Philosophy.* Delhi: Motilal Banarsidass, 1976.

*Sinha, Nandalal, trans. *The Samkhya Philosophy.* Edited by Major B. D. Basu. Allahabad, Sudhindra Nath Vasu, 1915. The Sacred Books of the Hindus, Vol. XI. New York: AMS Press, Inc., 1974.

Smart, Ninian. *Doctrine and Argument in Indian Philosophy.* London: George Allen & Unwin Ltd., 1964.

Stcherbatsky, F. Th., trans. *Buddhist Logic.* 2 vols. New York: Dover Publications, Inc., 1962.

Stryk, Lucien, ed. *World of the Buddha: A Reader.* Commentaries by L. Stryk. Garden City, New York: Anchor Books, Doubleday & Company, Inc., 1969.

Swami, Shree Purohit, and W. B. Yeats, trans. *The Ten Principal Upanishads.* New York: Collier Books, Macmillan Publishing Co., Inc., 1975.

Thibaut, George, trans. *The Vedānta Sūtras of Bādarāyana with the Commentary by Śankara: Part I.* Oxford, Clarendon Press, 1890. The Sacred Books of the East, Vol. XXXIV. New York: Dover Publications, Inc., 1962.

Vivekananda, Swami. *Vedanta Philosophy: Raja Yoga and Other Lectures.* Albany, New York: Weed–Parsons, 1897.

Warren, Henry Clarke, trans. *Buddhism in Translations: Passages Selected from the Buddhist Sacred Books and Translated from the Original Pali into English.* Student's edition, 1896. Cambridge, Massachusetts: Harvard University Press, 1953.

Zaehner, R. C., trans. *Hindu Scriptures.* London: Everyman's Library, J. M. Dent & Sons Ltd., 1966.

General Studies in Chinese Philosophies

Allinson, Robert E., ed. *Understanding the Chinese Mind.* Hong Kong: Oxford University Press, 1989.

*Bloom, Irene, trans., ed., and intro. *Knowledge Painfully Acquired: The K'un-chih chi by Lo Ch'in-shun.* New York: Columbia University Press, 1987.

*Chan, Wing-Tsit, trans. and compiler. *A Source Book in Chinese Philosophy.* Princeton, New Jersey: Princeton University Press, 1963.

*_____ , trans. and notes. *Reflections on Things at Hand: The Neo-Confucian Anthology compiled by Chu Hsi and Lü Tsu-Ch'ien.* Records of Civilization: Sources and Studies, LXXV. New York: Columbia University Press, 1967.

*_____ , trans. and notes. *Instructions for Practical Living and Other Neo-Confucian Writings by Wang Yang-Ming.* Records of Civilization: Sources and Studies. New York: Columbia University Press, 1963.

*Chang Tung-sun. "A Chinese Philosopher's Theory of Knowledge." Trans. by Li An-che. In *Our Language and Our World: Selections from ETC.: A Review of General Semantics 1953–1958,* edited by S. I. Hayakawa, 299–323. New York: Harper & Brothers, Publishers, 1959.

*Chen, Ellen M., trans. and commentary. *The Tao Tè Ching: A New Translation with Commentary.* New York: Paragon House, 1989.

*Ching, Julia, trans. and annotation. *The Philosophical Letters of Wang Yang-ming.* Columbia, South Carolina: University of South Carolina Press, 1973.

*_____ . *To Acquire Wisdom: The Way of Wang Yang-ming.* Trans. by Ching. New York: Columbia University Press, 1976.

*Chu Hsi. *Learning to Be a Sage: Selections from the Conversations of Master Chu, Arranged Topically.* Commentary and translation by Daniel K. Gardner. Berkeley: University of California Press, 1990.

*Confucius. *Confucius: Confucian Analects, The Great Learning, and The Doctrine of the Mean.* Translated by James Legge. Clarendon Press, Oxford, 1893. New York: Dover Publications, Inc., 1971.

*Dobson, W. A. C. H., trans. and annotation. *Mencius: A New Translation Arranged and Annotated for the General Reader.* Toronto: University of Toronto Press, 1963.

*Forke, Alfred, trans. and annotated. *Lun-Hêng: Philosophical Essays of Wang Ch'ung, Part 1.* New York: Paragon Book Gallery, 1962.

*_____ , trans. and annotated. *Lun-Hêng: Miscellaneous Essays of Wang Ch'ung, Part II.* New York: Paragon Book Gallery, 1962.

Fung Yu-lan. *A Short History of Chinese Philosophy.* 1948. Edited by Derk Bodde. New York: Free Press, 1966.

_____ . *A History of Chinese Philosophy.* Translated by Derk Bodde. 2 vols. Princeton, New Jersey: Princeton University Press, 1952, 1953.

_____ . *The Spirit of Chinese Philosophy.* 1947. Translated by E. R. Hughes. London: Routledge & Kegan Paul Ltd, 1962.

*Giles, Herbert A., trans. *Chuang Tzu: Mystic, Moralist, and Social Reformer,* rev. 2nd ed., London: Bernard Quaritch, Limited, 1926.

*Giles, Lionel, trans. *The Book of Mencius* (abridged). London: John Murray, 1942.

*Henricks, Robert G., trans., intro., and commentary. *Lao-Tzu, Tè-Tao Ching: A New Translation Based on the Recently Discovered Ma-Wang-Tui Texts.* New York: Ballantine Books, Random House, Inc., 1989.

The I Ching or Book of Changes. Foreword by C. G. Jung; preface by Hellmut Wilhelm. Translated by Cary F. Richard, Wilhelm translation rendered into English by Baynes. Bollingen Series XIX. Princeton, New Jersey: Princeton University Press, 1967.

*Legge, James, trans., notes, and indexes. *The Chinese Classics: Vol II., The Works of Mencius.* 2nd. rev. ed. Oxford: Clarendon Press, 1895.

*Liebenthal, Walter, trans., intro., notes, and appendices. *Chao Lun: The Treatises of Seng-chao,* 2nd rev. ed. Hong Kong: Hong Kong University Press, 1968.

*Lin Yutang, trans., ed. *The Wisdom of Laotse.* New York: Modern Library, Random House, Inc., 1948.

Moore, Charles A., ed. *The Chinese Mind: Essentials of Chinese Philosophy and Culture.* Honolulu: University of Hawaii Press, 1967.

*Sun Tzu. *The Art of War.* Intro. by Samuel B. Griffith; foreword by B. H. Liddell Hart, translated by Griffith. London: Oxford University Press, 1963.

*Waley, Arthur. *Three Ways of Thought in Ancient China.* London: George Allen & Unwin Ltd., 1939.

*_____ , trans. *The Way and Its Power: A Study of the Tao Tê Ching and Its Place in Chinese Thought.* New York: Grove Press, Inc., 1958.

★Wang Yang-ming. *Instructions for Practical Living and Other Neo-Confucian Writings.* Translated by Wing-tsit Chan. New York: Columbia University Press, 1963.

★_____ . *The Philosophy of Wang Yang-ming.* Introduction by James H. Tufts, translated by Frederick Goodrich Henke. London: Open Court Publishing Co., 1916.

★Ware, James R., trans. *The Sayings of Chuang Chou.* New York: Mentor Classics, New American Library, 1963.

★Watson, Burton, trans. *Chuang Tzu: Basic Writings.* New York: Columbia University Press, 1964.

★_____ , trans. *Mo Tzu: Basic Writings.* New York: Columbia University Press, 1963.

★Wittenborn, Allen, trans. and commentary. *Further Reflections on Things at Hand: A Reader, Chu Hsi.* Lanham, Maryland: University Press of America, 1991.

★Yampolsky, Philip B., trans., intro. and notes. *The Platform Sutra of the Sixth Patriarch: The Text of the Tun-Huang Manuscript.* Records of Civilization, Sources and Studies. New York: Columbia University Press, 1967.

General Studies in Japanese Philosophies

★Blofeld, John, trans. *The Zen Teaching of Huang Po: On the Transmission of Mind.* New York: Grove Press, Inc., 1958.

★Cleary, Thomas, trans. *Shōbōgenzō: Zen Essays by Dōgen.* Honolulu: University of Hawaii Press, 1986.

★Hatano, Seiichi. *Time and Eternity.* Translated by Ichiro Suzuki. Japan: Printing Bureau, Japanese Government, 1963.

Moore, Charles A., ed. *The Japanese Mind: Essentials of Japanese Philosophy and Culture.* Honolulu: University of Hawaii Press, 1987.

Nakamura, Hajime. *A History of the Development of Japanese Thought from A.D. 592 to 1868.* 2nd ed. Tokyo: Kokusai Bunka Shinkokai, 1969.

★Nishida, Kitaro. *An Inquiry into the Good.* Intro. by Masao Abe, 1921; translated by Masao Abe and Christopher Ives. New Haven, Connecticut: Yale University Press, 1990.

★_____ . *Intelligibility and the Philosophy of Nothingness: Three Philosophical Essays.* Introduction by Robert Schinzinger, translated by Robert Schinzinger, Honolulu: East-West Center Press, 1958.

★_____ . *Intuition and Reflection in Self-Consciousness.* Translated by Valdo H. Viglielmo, Takeuchi Yoshinori, and Joseph S. O'Leary. SUNY Series in Philosophy; Nanzan Studies in Religion and Culture. Albany: State University of New York Press, 1987.

★_____ . *Last Writings: Nothingness and the Religious Worldview.* Translated by David Dilworth. Honolulu: University of Hawaii Press, 1987.

★Nishitani, Keiji. *Religion and Nothingness.* Foreword by Winston L. King, translated by Jan Van Bragt. Nanzan Studies in Religion and Culture. Berkeley: University of California Press, 1982.

★_____ . *The Self-Overcoming of Nihilism.* Translated by Graham Parkes and Setsuko Aihara. SUNY Series in Modern Japanese Philosophy. Albany: State University of New York Press, 1990.

Piovesana, Gino K., S. J. *Recent Japanese Philosophical Thought, 1862–1962: A Survey.* Tokyo: Enderle, Sophia University, 1968.

_____ . "Contemporary Japanese Philosophy." In *Asian Philosophy Today,* edited by Dale Riepe, pp. 223–291. New York: Gordon and Breach, Science Publishers, Inc., 1981.

Sansom, George. *A History of Japan to 1334.* Stanford, California: Stanford University Press, 1958.

_____ . *Japan: A Short Cultural History.* Stanford, California: Stanford University Press, 1978.

*Shibayama, Zenkei. *Zen Comments on the Mumonkan.* Translated by Sumiko Kudo. New York: Mentor Book, New American Library, 1974.

*_____ . *A Flower Does Not Talk: Zen Essays.* Translated by Sumiko Kudo. Rutland, Vermont: Charles E. Tuttle Company, 1970.

*Soho, Takuan. *The Unfettered Mind: Writings of the Zen Master to the Sword Master.* Translated by William Scott Wilson. Tokyo: Kodansha International Ltd., 1986.

*Tanabe, Hajime. *Philosophy as Metanoetics.* Trans. by Takeuchi Yoshinori, and Valdo Viglielmo and James Heisig. Nanzan Studies in Religion and Culture. Berkeley: University of California Press, 1986.

*Tsunoda, Ryusaku, Wm. Theodore de Bary, and Donald Keene, comps. *Sources of the Japanese Tradition.* Introduction to Oriental Civilizations. New York: Columbia University Press, 1958.

*Tucker, Mary Evelyn. *Moral and Spiritual Cultivation in Japanese Neo-Confucianism: The Life and Thought of Kaibara Ekken, 1630–1714.* Trans. by Tucker. SUNY Series in Philosophy. Albany: State University of New York Press, 1989.

*Watsuji, Tetsuro. *Climate and Culture: A Philosophical Study.* 1961. Translated by Geoffrey Bownas. Classics of Modern Japanese Thought and Culture. Westport, Connecticut: Greenwood Press, 1988.

*Yampolsky, Philip B., ed. and introduction. *Selected Writings of Nichiren.* Translated by Burton Watson and others. New York: Columbia University Press, 1990.

Special Topics in Indian Philosophies

Basham, A. L. *The Origins and Development of Classical Hinduism.* Annotated and edited by Kenneth G. Zysk. Boston: Beacon Press, 1989.

Chatterjee, Satischandra. *The Nyaya Theory of Knowledge,* 2nd ed. Calcutta: University of Calcutta Press, 1950.

Conze, Edward. *Buddhist Thought in India: Three Phases of Buddhist Philosophy.* Ann Arbor: University of Michigan Press, 1967.

Coomaraswamy, Ananda K. *Buddha and the Gospel of Buddhism.* Revised by Dona Luisa Coomaraswamy. 1916, Harper & Company, London. New York: Harper Torchbooks, Harper & Row, 1964.

Crawford, S. Cromwell. *The Evolution of Hindu Ethical Ideals.* Honolulu: University of Hawaii Press, 1982.

Datta, Dhirendra Mohan. *The Philosophy of Mahatma Gandhi.* Madison: University of Wisconsin Press, 1953.

Deutsch, Eliot. *Advaita Vedanta: A Philosophical Reconstruction.* Honolulu: University of Hawaii Press, 1990.

Dharmasiri, Gunapala. *Fundamentals of Buddhist Ethics.* Antioch, California: Golden Leaves Publishing Co., 1989.

Eliade, Mircea. *Yoga: Immortality and Freedom,* 2nd ed. Trans. by W. R. Trask. Princeton, New Jersey: Princeton University Press, 1969.

Gyatso, Tenzin. *The Buddhism of Tibet and the Key to the Middle Way.* London: George Allen & Unwin, 1975.

Hawley, John Stratton, ed. *Saints and Virtues.* Berkeley: University of California Press, 1987.

Herman, A. L. *An Introduction to Buddhist Thought: A Philosophic History of Indian Buddhism.* Lanham, Maryland: University Press of America, 1983.

Hirakawa, Akira. *A History of Indian Buddhism: From Śākyamuni to Early Mahāyāna.* Translated and edited by Paul Groner. Asian Studies at Hawaii. Honolulu: University of Hawaii Press, 1990.

Kalupahana, David J. *A History of Buddhist Philosophy: Continuities and Discontinuities.* Honolulu: University of Hawaii Press, 1992.

_____, trans. and annotation. *Nagarjuna: The Philosophy of the Middle Way.* SUNY Series in Buddhist Studies. Albany: State University of New York Press, 1986.

_____. *Buddhist Philosophy: A Historical Analysis.* Foreword by G. P. Malalasekera. Honolulu: University of Hawaii Press, 1976.

_____. *Causality: The Central Philosophy of Buddhism.* Honolulu: University of Hawaii Press, 1975.

Lamotte, Étienne. *History of Indian Buddhism: From the Origins to the Śaka Era.* Translated by Sara Webb–Boin and supervised by Jean Dantinne. Louvain-La-Neuve: Publications de L'Institut Orientaliste de Louvain, Peters Press, 1988.

Marlow, A. N., ed. *Radhakrishnan: An Anthology.* London: George Allen & Unwin Ltd., 1952.

Matilal, Bimal Krishna, ed. *Moral Dilemmas in the Mahābhārata.* Delhi: Motilal Banarsidass, 1989.

Potter, Karl H., ed. *Advaita Vedānta Up to Śankara and His Pupils.* Princeton, New Jersey: Princeton University Press, 1981.

_____, ed. *Indian Metaphysics and Epistemology: The Tradition of Nyāya-Vaiseṣika up to Gangesa.* Princeton, New Jersey: Princeton University Press, 1977.

Radhakrishnan, S., trans. and notes. *The Bhagavadgītā.* London: George Allen & Unwin Ltd., 1971.

Rahula, Walpola. *What the Buddha Taught,* 2nd ed. New York: Grove Press, 1978.

Ramanan, K. Venkata. *Nagarjuna's Philosophy.* New York: Samuel Weiser, 1979.

Sen, K. M. *Hinduism.* Middlesex, England: Penguin Books Ltd., 1961.

Senzaki, Nyogen, and Ruth Strout McCandless, comp., ed., and trans. *Buddhism and Zen.* Foreword by Robert Aitken. San Francisco: North Point Press, 1987.

Suzuki, Daisetz Teitaro. *Outlines of Mahayana Buddhism.* Prefatory essay by Alan Watts. New York: Schocken Books, 1963.

Welbon, Guy Richard. *The Buddhist Nirvāna and Its Western Interpreters.* Chicago: University of Chicago Press, 1968.

Special Topics in Chinese Philosophies

Bodde, Derk. "The Chinese View of Immortality: Its Expression by Chu Hsi and Its Relationship to Buddhist Thought." *Review of Religion* 6 (1942): 369–383.

Chan, Wing-tsit. *Chu Hsi: New Studies.* Honolulu: University of Hawaii Press, 1989.

_____, ed. *Chu Hsi and Neo-Confucianism.* Honolulu: University of Hawaii Press, 1986.

Ch'eng, Chung-ying. *New Dimensions of Confucian and Neo-Confucian Philosophy.* Albany: State University of New York Press, 1991.

Creel, H. G. *Confucius and the Chinese Way.* New York: Harper & Row, 1960.

Cua, A. S. *Ethical Argumentation: A Study in Hsun Tzu's Moral Epistemology.* Honolulu: University of Hawaii Press, 1985.

_____ . "An Excursion to Confucian Ethics." In *Dimensions of Moral Creativity: Paradigms, Principles, and Ideals,* 50–65. University Park: Pennsylvania State University Press, 1978.

_____ . *The Unity of Knowledge and Action: A Study in Wang Yang–Ming's Moral Psychology.* Honolulu: University Press of Hawaii, 1982.

de Bary, Wm. Theodore. *Learning for One's Self: Essays on the Individual in Neo-Confucian Thought.* New York: Columbia University Press, 1991.

_____ . *Neo-Confucian Orthodoxy and the Learning of Mind-and-Heart.* New York: Columbia University Press, 1981.

de Bary, Wm. Theodore, and Irene Bloom, eds. *Principle and Practicality: Essays in Neo-Confucianism and Practical Learning.* New York: Columbia University Press, 1979.

Gasster, Michael. *China's Struggle to Modernize,* 2nd ed. New York: Alfred A. Knopf, 1982.

Graham, A. C. *Disputers of the Tao.* La Salle, Illinois: Open Court Press, 1989.

_____ . *Later Mohist Logic, Ethics and Science.* Hong Kong: Chinese University Press, 1978.

Liebenthal, Walter. "The Immortality of the Soul in Chinese Thought." *Monumenta Nipponica* VIII. 1952.

Lowe, Scott. *Mo Tzu's Religious Blueprint for a Chinese Utopia: The Will and the Way.* Lewiston, New York: Edwin Mellin Press, 1992.

Mair, Victor H., ed. *Experimental Essays on Chuang-tzu.* Asian Studies at Hawaii, No. 29. Honolulu: University of Hawaii Press, 1983.

Unschuld, Paul U. *Medicine in China: A History of Ideas.* Comparative Studies of Health Systems and Medical Care. Berkeley: University of California Press, 1985.

Waley, Arthur, trans. *The Way and Its Power: A Study of the Tao Tê Ching and Its Place in Chinese Thought.* New York: Grove Press, Inc., 1958.

Special Topics in Japanese Philosophies

Abe, Masao. *A Study of Dogen: His Philosophy and Religion.* Edited by Steven Heine. Albany: State University of New York Press, 1992.

Carter, Robert E. *The Nothingness Beyond God: An Introduction to the Philosophy of Nishida Kitaro.* New York: Paragon House, 1989.

Doi, Takeo. *The Anatomy of Self: The Individual Versus Society.* Foreword by Edward Hall, translated by Mark A. Harbison. Tokyo: Kodansha International Ltd., 1986.

Dumoulin, Heinrich, S. J. *Zen Enlightenment: Origins and Meanings.* New York: John Weatherhill, 1979.

_____ . *A History of Zen Buddhism.* Translated by Paul Peachey. Boston: Beacon Press, 1969.

Franck, Frederick, ed. *The Buddha Eye: An Anthology of the Kyoto School.* Nanzan Studies in Religion and Culture. New York: Crossroad Publishing Company, 1982.

Furuta, Shokin. "The Development of Zen Thought in Japan." Compiled by the Japanese National Commission for Unesco. *Philosophical Studies of Japan* III (1961): 33–55.

Havens, Thomas R. H. *Nishi Amane and Modern Japanese Thought.* Princeton, New Jersey: Princeton University Press, 1970.

Herrigel, Eugen. *The Method of Zen.* Edited by Hermann Tausend, translated by R. F. C. Hull. New York: Pantheon Books, Inc., 1960.

Kapleau, Philip, ed. *The Three Pillars of Zen.* New York: Harper & Row, 1969.

Kasulis, Thomas P. *Zen Action, Zen Person.* Honolulu: University of Hawaii Press, 1981.

Maruyama, Masao. *Studies in the Intellectual History of Tokugawa Japan.* 1974. Translated by Mikiso Hane. Princeton, New Jersey: Princeton University Press, 1989.

Megume, Sakabe. "Watsuji Tetsuro—A Case of Philosophical Thinking in Modern Japan." In *Traditional Thought and Ideological Change,* edited by S. Cho and N. Runeby, pp. 155–169. Japanological Studies 8. Stockholm: University of Stockholm, 1988.

Morris, Ivan. *The World of the Shining Prince: Court Life in Ancient Japan.* Middlesex, England: Peregrine Books, 1985.

———. *The Nobility of Failure: Tragic Heroes in the History of Japan.* New York: Meridian, New American Library, 1975.

Nagatomo, Shigenori. *Attunement through the Body.* SUNY Series on the Body. Albany: State University of New York Press, 1992.

Nishitani, Keiji. *Nishida Kitaro.* Introduction by D. S. Clarke, Jr., translated by Seisaku Yamamoto and James W. Heisig. Nanzan Studies in Religion and Culture. Berkeley: University of California Press, 1991.

Nosco, Peter, ed. *Confucianism and Tokugawa Culture.* Princeton, New Jersey: Princeton University Press, 1984.

Ooms, Herman. *Tokugawa Ideology: Early Constructs, 1570–1680.* Princeton, New Jersey: Princeton University Press, 1989.

Shuntaroo, Itoo. "Nishi Amane (1829–1897) and the Modernisation of Japan: The Japanisation of Scientific Terminology." In *Traditional Thought and Ideological Change,* edited by S. Cho and N. Runeby, pp. 127–133. Japanological Studies 8. Stockholm: University of Stockholm, 1988.

Suzuki, Daisetz Teitaro. *What Is Zen?* New York: Perennial Library, Harper & Row, 1971.

———. *Zen and Japanese Culture.* Bollingen Series LXIV. Princeton, New Jersey: Princeton University Press, 1959.

Watts, Alan. *The Way of Zen.* New York: Random House, Inc., Vintage Books, 1957.

Yamamoto, Tsunetomo. *Hagakure: The Book of the Samurai.* Translated by William Scott Wilson, Tokyo: Kodansha International Ltd., 1979.

Comparative Studies

Abe, Masao. *Zen and Western Thought.* Foreword by John Hick, edited by William R. LaFleur. Honolulu: University of Hawaii Press, 1989.

Dilworth, David. "The Initial Formation of 'Pure Experience,' in Nishida Kitaro and William James." *Monumenta Nipponica* XXIV, no. 1–2. 1969.

Hawley, John Stratton, ed. *Saints and Virtues.* Berkeley: University of California Press, 1987.

Loy, David. *Nonduality: A Study in Comparative Philosophy.* New Haven, Connecticut: Yale University Press, 1988.

Parkes, Graham, ed. *Heidegger and Asian Thought.* Honolulu: University of Hawaii Press, 1987.

Parrinder, Geoffrey. *Avatar and Incarnation: A Comparison of Indian and Christian Beliefs.* New York: Oxford University Press, 1982.

Radhakrishnan, S. *Eastern Religions and Western Thought.* London: Oxford University Press, 1939.

Waldenfels, Hans. *Absolute Nothingness: Foundations for a Buddhist-Christian Dialogue.* Translated by J. W. Heisig. New York: Paulist Press, 1980.

Yuasa, Yasuo. *The Body: Toward an Eastern Mind-Body Theory.* Edited by Thomas P. Kasulis, translated by Shigenori Nagatomo and Thomas P. Kasulis. SUNY Series in Buddhist Studies. Albany: State University of New York Press, 1987.

Studies on Death

Badham, Paul, and Linda Badham, eds. *Death and Immortality in the Religions of the World.* The Contemporary Discussion Series. New York: Paragon House Publishers, 1987.

Carse, James P. *Death and Existence: A Conceptual History of Human Mortality.* Contemporary Religious Movements. New York: John Wiley & Sons, Inc., 1980.

Hick, John. *Death and Eternal Life.* San Francisco: Harper & Row, Publishers, 1980.

Kramer, Kenneth Paul. *The Sacred Art of Dying: How World Religions Understand Death.* New York: Paulist Press, 1988.

Lifton, Robert J. *The Broken Connection: On Death and the Continuity of Life.* 1979. New York: Basic Books, Inc., 1983.

Index

Abe Masao, 343
Absence, 15, 202–203, 227–232
Advaita Vedanta, 17, 61–64
  on death, 322–324
  ethics of, 260–261
  on self, 137–138
  sources of knowledge in, 203–205
Ahimsa, 14, 18, 261
Aidagara, 281
Analects, 145, 267, 268
Arhats, 264
Aristotle, and Nishida, 222
Arjuna, 12, 59, 258–260, 321–322
Asangha, 26, 71
Asatkaryavada, 61, 201
Atman, 11, 12
  Hindu versus Indian Buddhism on, 22
  and *jiva*, 322
  Krishna on, 59–60
  Samkhya on, 134
  Upanishads on, 58, 133, 134
  Vedanta school on, 61, 63, 64
  Yoga on, 136, 137
Atomist theory, 60–61
Aurobindo Ghose, Sri, 19, 138, 171–174
Avidya, 63–64

Badarayana, 61–62
Basho, 150–151
  Nishida Kitaro on, 221–222

Bhagavad Gita, 12, 14, 16
  on death, 321–322
  on *dharma*, 258–260
  on reality, 59–60
Bhagavan Das, 18
Bhakti yoga, 256
Bodhidharma, 34, 35
Bodhisattva, 3, 25, 211, 264–265
Brahman, 11, 12
  aspects of, 60
  Bhagavad Gita on, 59–60
  Ramanuja on, 17, 64–65
  Sankara on, 17, 61–64
  Upanishads on, 58–59, 134
Buddha
  dharma of, 21–22
  on ethics, 285–287
  as First Jewel of Buddhism, 20–21
  "silence" of, 65–66
  See also Gautama Siddhartha
Buddhism, 13
  Chinese, 33–36
    on death, 333–335
    on ethics, 271
    on reality, 77–81
    schools of, 34–36
    on self, 147–148
  Indian, 9, 19
    on death, 324–329, 353–358
    early, 20–22, 68, 207–208

Buddhism, Indian (*continued*)
  on ethics, 261–266, 285–293
  fate of, 27
  on knowledge, 206–211
  Mahayana, 13, 24–27, 34, 68–71,
    140–143, 208–209, 264–265
  on reality, 65–71
  sectarian, 22–24
  on self, 138–143
  Three Jewels of, 20–22
  Japanese
    on death, 341–344
    early, 40–42, 84–85
    ethics of, 274–275
    on knowledge, 217–220
    medieval, 43–46, 85–87
    on reality, 84–87
    on self, 149–150
Bushido (Way of the Warrior), 277–279,
  340–341

Carter, Robert, 90, 222–223
Carvaka, 9, 13
Caste system
  Hinduism on, 257–258
  Indian Buddhism on, 265–266
Ch'an Buddhism, 34, 35–36
  on death, 334–335
  on knowledge, 215–216
  on reality, 81
  on self, 147–148
Chang Tung-sun, 40
  on knowledge, 217, 243–248
Chatterji, Gadadhar (Ramakrishna), 18
Chen, Ellen M., 104–107
Ch'eng Hao, 37, 271
Ch'eng Yi, 37, 82
  on ethics, 271
Ch'i, 72
  Chu Hsi on, 113–116
  Kaibara on, 88
  and *li*, 82–83
Chih, 268
Chinese philosophies, 4
  ancient period of, 27–32, 73–75
  aspects of, 4–6
  on death, 330–338
  on ethics, 266–274
  on knowledge, 212–217
  middle period of, 32–36
  modern period of, 39–40
  Neo-Confucianist, phase of, 36–39,
    81–83, 145–147, 271–274
  on reality, 71–83
  on self, 5–6, 143–148
Chi-tsang, 34–35, 78

Chuang Tzu, 29–30, 57, 197
  on death, 331
  on knowledge, 212
  on self, 143–144
  on Tao, 73–74
Chu Hsi, 37, 82–83, 113–116
  on ethics, 271–272, 304–307
  on knowledge, 216
Chu Hsi school, 46–47, 87–88
  on ethics, 275–277
  on self, 145–146, 148–149
Citta, 203
Comparison, as source of knowledge, 201,
  205
Confucianism, 32–34
  on death, 332–333
  early Japanese, 42–43
  on ethics, 267–269
  on knowledge, 212–214
  on reality, 75–77
  and Taoism, 4–5
  Tokugawa, 46–49, 87–88
  See also Neo-Confucianism
Confucian school, 28–30
Confucius, 28
  on death, 332
  on knowledge, 212–213
  on self, 144–145
  on virtues, 267–268
Correspondence
  of names, 213–214
  Tung Chung-shu on, 75–76
Cua, Anthony, 268

Das, Bhagavan, 18
Datta, Narendranath, 18
Death
  Chinese philosophies on, 330–338
  Hinduism on, 318–324
  Indian Buddhism on, 324–329, 353–358
  Japanese philosophies on, 338–345
Dependent origination, 21–22, 84, 140, 264,
  324
  and *samsara*, 326–327
Dharma
  Bhagavad Gita on, 12, 59, 60, 258–260
  Dogen on, 149–150
  in Hindu ethics, 255
  Mimamsa school on, 260
  as teachings of Buddha, 21–22, 324
  Theravada schools on, 68
Dharmakirti, on knowledge, 211, 236–240
Dharma Shastras, 13
Dignaga, 26, 209–210
Dogen, 45, 86–87, 121–124
  on death, 342–344, 368

Dogen (*continued*)
on ethics, 275
on knowledge, 220
on self, 149–150, 190–192
Dualism, of Madhva, 17, 65
Dumoulin, Heinrich, 87

Eightfold Path, 67–68, 262, 286–287, 325
Eisai, 44, 45
Empirical school, 37, 38–39
on ethics, 273–274
on reality, 83
Ethics
Chinese philosophies on, 266–274
Hinduism on, 253–261
Indian Buddhism on, 261–266, 285–293
Japanese philosophies on, 274–281

Fa-tsang, 35, 80–81, 271
Five Cardinal Relationships, 5–6
Four Noble Truths, 21, 67, 139, 325
ethics of, 261–262
Fudo (Climate and Culture)
(Watsuji), 51, 153–154, 193–195, 280–281,
314–316
Fujiwara Seika, 46, 47, 276
Fung Yu-lan, 39, 116–120, 212

Gandhi, Mohandas Karamchand, 14, 18,
261, 318
Gangesa, 15, 202, 228–230
Gaudapada, 17, 61–62
Gautama, 198, 202
on absence, 202, 227–228
Gautama, Siddhartha, 13, 20, 262–263 *See
also* Buddha
Gi, 276
Giri, 278
Great Death, 334–335

Hagakure, 277, 279, 341
Han Fei Tzu, 31, 270
Harmony, Chinese philosophies on, 4–5, 73
Hatano Seiichi, 50
Hayashi Razan, 46, 47
Heian schools, 41–42
Hinduism
in age of Sutras, 14–16
on death, 318–324
from 1800 to present, 17–19
in Epic Age, 12–14
on ethics, 253–261
on knowledge, 197–206
on reality, 57–65
in Scholastic Age, 16–17
schools of, 15–16

Hinduism (*continued*)
on self, 133–138
in Vedic Age, 10–12
Hokke (Lotus) school, 43–44. *See also*
Nichiren
Hōnen Shōnin, 43
Hosso school, 41
Hsiung Shih-li, 40
Hsuan-tsang, 34, 35, 78–79
on self, 147, 187–189
Hsun Tzu, 332
correspondence of names of, 213–214
on ethics, 29, 269, 293–300
Hua-yen school, 35, 80–81. *See also* Fa-
tsang
Hui-neng, 334
Hui Shih, 30, 214
paradoxes of, 74–75, 330

I Ching, 31
on *T'ai-chi*, 72
yin and yang in, 75
Indian philosophies, 1, 9
on death, 318–329
on ethics, 253–266
on knowledge, 197–211
on self, 133–143
traits of, 1–3
See also Buddhism, Indian; Hinduism
Inference, as source of knowledge, 199–201,
205
Inoue Enryo, 50
Intuition
Nishida Kitaro on, 220–221, 248–251, 279
Radhakrishnan on, 233–235
Wang Yang-ming on, 146–147, 216–217
Ishida Baigan, 49
Ishvarakrishna, 161–165
Ito Jinsai, 48, 88, 277

Jainism, 9, 14
Japanese philosophies, 6
on death, 338–345
on ethics, 274–281
and Japanese language, 6–8
on knowledge, 217–223
of medieval Buddhism, 43–46
of modern period, 49–51
of period of antiquity, 40–43
on self, 148–154
of Tokugawa Confucianism, 46–49,
87–88
Jen, 5, 267–268, 273, 274
Ji, 84
Jin, 276
Jiriki, 85, 86

Jiva, 63
    in Advaita Vedanta, 137, 322, 324
Jnana yoga, 256, 261
Jodo (Pure Land) school, 43
    on death, 341
    on reality, 85
Jojitsu school, 41
Ju-ching, 45

Kaibara Ekken, 47
    on ethics, 276–277, 312–313
    on li and ch'i, 88
Kalacakra school, 27
Kalupahana, 209
Kama Shastra, 13
Kamo Mabuchi, 49
K'ang Yu-wei, 39, 274
Karma, 139, 320–321
    Hinduism on, 256–258
    Indian Buddhism on, 263, 326
    Japanese Buddhism on, 274–275
Karma yoga, 255
Kato Hiroyuki, 50
Kawakami Hajime, 50
Kegon School, 41, 84–85
Knowledge
    Chinese philosophies on, 212–217
    Hinduism on, 197–206
    Indian Buddhism on, 206–211
    Japanese philosophies on, 217–223
Koan, 218–220, 342
Kokugaku, 46, 49
Krishna, 12, 59–60, 258–260, 321–322
Kumarajiva, 34
Kumazawa Banzan, 47, 48
Kung-sun Lung, 30, 214–215
Kuo Hsiang, 33, 77
Kurosawa, Akira, 278, 339
Kusha school, 41
Kyoto school, 50, 51
    on reality, 80–92
    on self, 150–153

Lao Tzu, 29, 73
Legalist school, 31–32. See also Han Fei Tzu
Li, 72
    Ch'eng Yi on, 271
    and ch'i, 82–83
    Chu Hsi on, 113–116, 276
    and jen, 267–268
    Kaibara on, 88
    and self in Chu Hsi school, 145–146
Liao P'ing, 39
Logic school, 26
Lokayata, 13
Longevity, Taoism on, 331–332

Lotus school. See Hokke (Lotus) school
Loy, David, 87
Lu Hsiang-shan, 38, 83

Madhva, 16, 17, 65
Madhyamika. See Middle Way
Mahabharata, 12, 59, 317–318
Mahayana school, 13, 24–27, 34
    on bodhisattva, 264–265
    on knowledge, 208–209
    on reality, 68–71
    on self, 140–143
Mandalas, 10, 26
Mantras, 211
Mantra school, 27
Mao Tse-tung, 39
Maruyama, Masao, 148–149
Matilal, B. K. 202
Maya, 63–64
Meinichi, 345
Mencius, 28–29
    on ethics, 268–269
    on knowledge, 213
Middle Way
    of Buddha, 21, 262–263
    in China, 34
    Nagarjuna on, 26, 69–71, 329
Miki Kiyoshi, 50–51
Mimamsa school, 9, 15, 16, 260
Mishima Yukio, 340
Miura Baien, 49
Mohist school, 30. See also Mo Tzu
Moksha, 1, 12, 22
    paths to, 255–256
Morris, Ivan, 339
Motoori Norinaga, 49
Mo Tzu, 30
    on death, 333
    on universal love, 270, 301–304
Mudras, 211
Müller, F. Max, 158–160, 288–293, 349–352

Nagarjuna, 26, 41
    on death, 329
    on knowledge, 208
    on reality, 69–71, 102–104
    on self, 140–141, 178–180
Nakae Toju, 47–48
Names, correspondence of, 213–214. See
    also School of Names
Nara schools, 41
Nasadiya (Creation Hymn), 10, 14, 58, 97
Navya Nyaya. See New Logic school
Negation. See Absence
Neo-Confucianism
    Chinese, 36–39

Neo-Confusianism, Chinese (*continued*)
Empirical school of, 37, 38–39, 83, 273–274
on ethics, 271–274
on reality, 81–83
School of Mind of, 37, 38, 83, 272–273
School of Principle of, 37–38, 82–83, 271–272
on self, 145–147
Japanese, 46
Chu Hsi school of, 46–47, 87–88, 145–146, 148–149, 275–277
on ethics, 275–277
School of Ancient Learning of, 47, 48–49
on self, 148–149
Wang Yang-ming school of, 47–48, 146–147, 183–186
Neo-Taoism, 33, 77
New Logic School, on knowledge, 202–203, 227–232
Nichiren, 43–44
on ethics, 275
Nihility, 91–92
Nirguna, 62
Nirvana, 22, 71
Dogen on, 343
and Indian Buddhist view of death, 327
Nishi Amane, 50
Nishida Kitaro, 50, 51, 217
on ethics, 279–280
on knowledge, 220–223, 248–251
on reality, 89–90, 125–129
on self, 148, 150–152
Nishitani Keiji, 50, 51
on reality and *sunyata*, 91–92, 129–131
No-mind, 34, 149, 215–216
Noncognition, as source of knowledge, 205
Nondualism
of Ramanuja, 17, 64–65
of Sankara, 17, 61–64
No-self
Dogen on, 149–150, 190–192
Indian Buddhism on, 22, 138–140
Nyaya school, 3, 9, 15, 60
sources of knowlede in, 198–202

O'Flaherty, Wendy Doniger, 97
Ogyu Sorai, 48–49, 277
Onishi Hajime, 50
Oshio Heihachiro, 47, 48

Patanjali, 136, 166–170, 199
Perception
Dharmakirti on, 236–240
Ramanuja on, 205

Perception (*continued*)
as source of knowledge, 198–199, 204
Postulation, as source of knowledge, 205
Prakriti, 61, 134–136
Pratityasamutpada. See Dependent origination
Pure Land school. *See* Jodo (Pure Land) school
Purusha, 61
Samkhya on, 134–136
Yoga on, 136, 137

Radhakrishnan, Sarvepalli, 19
on knowledge, 205–206, 232–235
Raghunatha, on absence, 202–203, 231–232
Ramakrishna, 18
Ramanuja, 16, 17
on knowledge, 205
on reality, 64–65
Ramayana, 12–13
Rangaku (Dutch studies), 49
Reality
Chinese philosophies on, 71–83
Hinduism on, 57–65
Indian Buddhism on, 65–71
Japanese philosophies on, 84–92
Rebirth, 12, 22, 327–329. *See also* Transmigration
Ri, 84
Rig Veda, 10–11, 14
Nasadiya (Creation Hymn) of, 10, 14, 58, 97
Ritsu school, 41
Roy, Ram Mohan, 18

Saguna, 62–63
Samadhi, 136–137, 218
Samkhya school, 9, 15, 16
on reality, 61
on self, 134–136, 161–165
Samsara, 255, 257, 264, 320, 322, 323, 324
Hinduism on, 12, 22
and Indian Buddhist view of death, 326–327
Nagarjuna on, 71
Sangha, 22, 263
Sankara, 2–3, 16, 17, 98–101
on knowledge, 203–205
on reality, 61–64
Sanron school, 41, 84
Sarasvati, Dayananda, 18
Sarvastivadin school
on knowledge, 207
on reality, 68
Satkarya-vada, 61
Satyagraha, 18, 261

Sautrantika school
  on knowledge, 207
  on reality, 68
School of Ancient Learning, 47, 48-49
School of Mind, 37, 38
  on ethics, 272-273
  on reality, 83
School of Names, 30, 214-215
School of Principle, 37-38
  on ethics, 271-272
  on reality, 82-83
Self
  Chinese philosophies on, 143-148
  Hinduism on, 133-138
  Indian Buddhism on, 138-143
  Japanese philosophies on, 148-154
Seng Chao, 34, 77-78, 110-112
  on time and change, 333-334, 364-367
Seppuku, 340
Shastras, 13
Shingon school, 42, 85
Shinran, 43, 344
Shinto, 40
Shobogenzo (Dogen), 45, 121-124, 150,
    190-192, 342, 368
Shushi, 87, 148-149. *See also* Chu Hsi
    school
Six Oxherding Pictures (Jitoku), 334-338
Skandhas, 139, 326, 327-328
Smrti, 10
Social immortality, Chinese teachings on,
    335, 338
Sruti, 10
Sunya, 68-69, 70-71
  Nagarjuna on, 84, 141, 208, 329
  in ox-herding pictures, 334-335
Sunyata, 25, 26, 68-69, 84
  Nishitani on, 91-92, 129-131
  in ox-herding pictures, 334-335
  Seng Chao on, 110-112
Sutras, 14-16
Suzuki Shosan, 342

Tagore, Rabindranath, 18
Tai Chen, 39, 83
  on ethics, 273
T'ai-chi, 37-38
  Chu Hsi on, 271-272
  School of Principle on, 82, 83
Tama, 344
Tanabe Hajime, 50, 51
  on reality, 90-91
  on self, 152-153
T'an Ssu-t'ung, 39
Tantric Buddhism, 26-27

Tao, 29
  Chuang Tzu on, 73-74
  Lao Tzu on, 73
  Neo-Taoism on, 77
Taoism, 29-30
  and Confucianism, 4-5
  on death, 330-332
  on reality, 73-74.
  See also Neo-Taoism
Tao-sheng, 34
Tao Te Ching, 29, 73, 104-107
  on death, 330
  on ethics, 269-270
Tariki, 85, 86
Tarka, 200, 202
Tathagata, 26
Tat tvam asi, 12, 58
  Upanishads on, 134, 319
  Vedanta schools on, 17
Te, 29
  Lao Tzu on, 73
Tendai school, 41-42, 43, 44
  on knowledge, 217-218
  on reality, 85
Theravada school, 13, 23-24, 68
  on knowledge, 207-208
Three Jewels of Buddhism, 20-22
Three Signs of Existence, 68, 325-326
T'ien-T'ai school, 35, 79
Transience, Japanese philosophy
  on, 339
Transmigration, 12, 320-321, 322-324. *See
    also* Rebirth
Tung Chung-shu, 32-33
  on correspondence, 75-76
  on self, 145

Upanishads, 11-12, 16
  on death, 319-321, 349-352
  on reality, 58-59
  on self, 133-134, 158-160

Vaibhashika
  on knowledge, 207-208
  on school, 9, 15
  atomist theory of, 60-61
Vajrayana school, on knowledge, 211
Vardhamana, 14
Vasubandhu, 26, 71
  on self, 141-143, 180-182
Vedanta school, 9, 15, 16
  on knowledge, 203-205
  on reality, 61-65
Vedanta Sutra, 16
  Sankara's commentary on, 98-101

Vedas, 9, 10–11
  on reality, 58
Verbal confirmation, Ramanuja on, 205
Verbal testimony, as source of knowledge,
    201–202, 205
Vijnanavadin school, 26, 71
Virtues, Indian Buddhism on, 263–264
Vivekananda, Swami, 18, 133, 166–170

Wang Ch'ung, 33, 107–110
  on death, 332–333, 359–363
  on knowledge, 240–243
  on spontaneity, 76–77
Wang Pi, 33, 77
Wang Yang-ming, 38, 83
  on ethics, 272–273, 308–311
  on knowledge, 216–217
Wang Yang-ming school, 47–48
  on self, 146–147, 183–186
Warren, Henry Clarke, 174–178, 285–287,
    353–358
Watsuji Tetsuro, 51
  on ethics, 280–281, 314–316
  on self, 153–154, 193–195
Westernization, and Japanese philosophies,
    49–50
"White Horse Discourse" (Kung-sun
    Lung), 214–215
Wing-tsit Chan, 213
Wu, 72
  Chi-tsang on, 78
  Fa-tsang on, 81

Wu (*continued*)
  Seng Chao on, 77–78
  Tao as, 77
  T'ien-t'ai school on, 79
Wu-Wei, 29, 34, 269–270

Yamago Soko, 48, 277
Yamamoto Tsunetomo, 277
Yamazaki Ansai, 46–47
Yang, 31, 75
Yin, 31, 75
Yin-Yang school, 31
  on reality, 75
Yoga, types of, 255–256
Yogacara school, 26, 208–209
Yoga school, 9, 15, 16
  on knowledge, 203
  on reality, 61
  on self, 136–137, 166–170
Yu, 72, 77
  Chi-tsang on, 78
  Fa-tsang on, 81
  Seng Chao on, 77–78
  T'ien-t'ai school on, 79

Zazen, 149–150, 275, 343
Zen Buddhism, 44–46
  on death, 342
  experience emphasis of, 7
  on knowledge, 218–220
  on reality, 86–87
  on self, 149